Aileen
with best
regards.
Ken. 7. Feb. 76

D1356492

*Vision Critical Studies*

*General Editor: Anne Smith*

# Carlyle Past and Present

# CARLYLE
# PAST AND PRESENT

A Collection of New Essays

edited by
# K. J. Fielding and Rodger L. Tarr

VISION

Vision Press Limited
11-14 Stanhope Mews West
London SW7 5RD


ISBN 0 85478 373 3

**For Beth and Jean**

Printed in Great Britain
by Clarke, Doble & Brendon Ltd., Plymouth
MCMLXXVI

# Contents

# Editorial Note

To study Carlyle is to anatomize the nineteenth century, for all the issues that stirred the age are present in his work, and his is now what he himself once called 'the articulate audible voice of the past'. But more than that, his influence on his contemporaries—poets, novelists, and historians alike—is evident everywhere in the literature of his time, and continued, long after his death, to have its effect on writers with a social conscience on both sides of the Atlantic. An appreciation of Carlyle, therefore, sends us back to Victorian literature with a new and critical awareness.

A.S.

# Abbreviations

CL:           *Collected Letters of Thomas and Jane Welsh Carlyle*, Duke-Edinburgh edition, vols 1–4, 1812–28, edited C. R. Sanders, with K. J. Fielding, I. Campbell, J. Clubbe and Janetta Taylor (Durham, N.C. 1970).

Dyer:       I. W. Dyer, *A Bibliography of Thomas Carlyle's Writings and Ana* (Portland, Maine, 1928).

Froude, *Life*:       J. A. Froude, *Thomas Carlyle, A History of the First Forty Years of His Life, 1795–1835*, and *Thomas Carlyle, A History of His Life in London, 1834–1881* (London, 1882 and 1884), 4 vols.

Harrold, *Sartor*:     ed. C. F. Harrold, *Sartor Resartus* (New York, 1937).

LDP:       *Latter-Day Pamphlets*

NLS:       National Library of Scotland.

*Reminiscences* (Froude):     ed. J. A. Froude, *Reminiscences of Thomas Carlyle*, 2 vols (London, 1881).

*Reminiscences* (Norton):     ed. C. E. Norton, *Reminiscences of Thomas Carlyle*, 2 vols (London, 1887).

TC:       Thomas Carlyle: for personal references and for titles given in the notes.

Wilson, *Carlyle*:     The biography of Carlyle by D. A. Wilson, in six variously entitled volumes (London, 1923–34).

*Works*:       Carlyle, *Works*, Centenary edition, 30 vols (London, 1896–9).

Some accepted abbreviations for periodicals have also been used.

# Chronology

11

| | |
|---|---|
| 1839 | First English edition of *Essays, Chartism* |
| 1841 | *Heroes and Hero-Worship* |
| 1843 | *Past and Present* |
| 1845 | *Oliver Cromwell's Letters and Speeches* |
| 1848 | Articles for *Examiner* on Ireland |
| 1849 | First meets Froude; tour in Ireland; "Occasional Discourse on the Negro Question" |
| 1850 | *Latter-Day Pamphlets* |
| 1851 | *Life of John Sterling* |
| 1858–65 | *History of Frederick the Great*, vols 1 and 2 (1858), vol. 3 (1863), vol. 4 (1864), vols 5 and 6 (1865) |
| 1866 | Inaugural Address as Rector of University of Edinburgh; death of Jane Carlyle |
| 1867 | "Shooting Niagara: and After?" |
| 1869 | Audience with Queen Victoria |
| 1875 | *Early Kings of Norway* and *The Portraits of John Knox* |
| 1881 | Dies 5 February. *Reminiscences* published |

# A Preface by Carlyle

## AND BY THE EDITORS

Carlyle remains one of the most enigmatic Victorians. Looming over his contemporaries, he has been worshipped, distrusted and decried, but is still imperfectly understood. The magnetism of Carlyle seems even stranger because of his relationships with his fellow artists, whose various and often contradictory impressions have led to our own uncertainty. How is it, for example, that Ruskin can refer to him as "Master", Meredith as a "heaver of rocks, not a shaper", and Arnold finally as "dangerous", when each at some time came directly under his sway? Yet the proof of his importance still lies in his relation with his contemporaries, and modern students of Carlyle still have to come at the essence of the man.

No doubt the nemesis of Carlyle is the result of his writings. The transcendental *Sartor Resartus*, the apocalyptic *The French Revolution*, the elitist *Heroes and Hero-Worship*, the polemic *Past and Present*, and the historical and prophetic *Oliver Cromwell*, together with his earlier critical and historical essays, have brought him even more than the usual favour and disfavour that surround a controversial writer. But with "The Nigger Question" and *Latter-Day Pamphlets* he invited the stoning of a prophet. A result has been that it is still extremely difficult to approach Carlyle dispassionately, especially with the added offences of *Frederick* and "Shooting Niagara: and After?"

The present volume, therefore, is a survey; it is a series of fresh attempts to examine his work; they are *new essays* in that none has been published before, yet they chiefly return us to his own period; and we hope that they are part of a now widely re-

13

newed reconsideration of Carlyle. It may be too soon to assess
how far this has gone. Some of it has taken the form of re-editing, as in the on-going *Collected Letters of Thomas and Jane
Welsh Carlyle* which will give us at least a view of almost the
whole Victorian age by two of its keenest observers. Yet many of
the problems of revaluation remain to be resolved: stones are
being moved, but many are not yet overturned. These studies are
contributions to a work which must essentially be a co-operative
one.

Future study of Carlyle lies in seeing his relation to the past.
As Swinburne wrote of him and Newman in "Two Leaders"
(1876):

> Honour not hate we give you, love not fear,
> Last prophets of past kind, who fill the dome
> Of great dead Gods with wrath and wail, nor hear
> Time's word and man's: "Go honoured hence, go home,
> Night's childless children; here your hour is done;
> Pass with the stars, and leave us with the sun."[1]

It is because of this that his relations with men and movements
of his time are important for understanding the period. Whatever
he wrote, he was concerned with its effect on his own age; and
he was caught then, as now, between past and present. If we are
to show this dispassionately, therefore, we should like to argue
that the best preface to any review of his work may lie in his own
words, and that this is a good reason for taking advantage of a
happy accident that there are newly-discovered and unpublished
*disjecta membra* of Carlyle's which recall us to what he sought
to express.

First, a brief word as to their nature. They come from some
papers which have long been in the Forster Collection of the
Victoria and Albert Museum Library, which are among the earliest
drafts of his attempts to write the life of Cromwell during
1841–2.[2] There is a more detailed study to be made of them,
which will bring out even more clearly than we have always
known how impossibly difficult Carlyle found the work to write.[3]
In fact it was never written as he intended: the form of *Oliver
Cromwell's Letters and Speeches* was partly an evasion as well as
a solution of the problems of a considered *Life*. Over the years

spent in arriving at his method (as we have always known) Carlyle even broke off in the midst of his struggle to give three or four months to writing *Past and Present*, a historical study in which he more squarely faced the challenge of addressing his own times.[4] But before and after this, day after day, he sat at his desk and drove his pen across paper trying to discover what he wanted to say by the familiar process of writing it down first and then seeing what it meant.

As art this is dubious; as a means of understanding how Carlyle worked it deserves more thought; as an entry into his mind, especially at a time when he was re-examining his opinions, it has considerable interest.

Sometimes he goes back over past routines, rehearses ideas for *Past and Present* and *Cromwell*, agonises over the condition of England, and returns to his belief in *Heroes* as he had lectured on them in May 1840.[5] His "radicalism" of the thirties may be thought to have begun to change and fade, and it seems that his determination in spite of all difficulties to write about Cromwell came from his faith that his ideal hero should be a Puritan, inspired by a deity recognizably like the God of his fathers. His whole effort to find a fit form for his shifting beliefs helps to reveal the preconceptions underlying Carlylism of the early eighteen-forties. It may leave us with Swinburne, praising the thunderous art of Carlyle though believing it to belong to the past: yet not so much because what he says is only indirectly applicable to the present, but because his whole message is that we must continually try to discover the truth for ourselves.

Yet for our prefatory purposes we may take up three of his themes. First Carlyle's concern for the condition of England. Secondly, his problem in reconciling this with the study of History. Thirdly, the way in which these are related to an urgent insistence on sincerity, or even inspiration. Familiar such ideas may be; but they return us, in his own voice, to the fundamentals of *Carlylism*.

That *Cromwell* was written out of a concern with his own age is not new, but the insistence with which it comes through and the trouble it caused is one of the more striking features of the Forster manuscript. So tightly is it interwoven with all he writes in draft, that it is often inseparable; yet, as Carlyle's patience

15

breaks at the inaccessibility of the past, he bizarrely invokes Cromwell himself:

> *Enter the Ghost of Oliver Cromwell* (by way of Prologue, *loquitur*) on another Stage than that of Dr Laud. Who art thou of friendly mortal voices that hast awoke me from the iron sleep? . . . Who art thou? What meanest thou?—Ye people and populace of this Amphitheatre, aye there you are, new English faces, male and female, beautiful, young and old, foolish and not so foolish, even as our own were! The same and yet so different. Not Christ's Gospel now, and a Godly Ministry; but the People's Charter and Free Trade in Corn. My Poor beloved countrymen,—alas, Priests have become chimerical, and your Lords (Law-wards) do stick the stubble ground with dry bushes in preservation of their partridges. . . . My Children, my kindred, it is a comfort to me that I am dead, that I have not again to fight, and in such a cause as yours has grown.—And say, good unchristian people, why have you summoned me into the daylight? . . .

Then follows Carlyle's own comment: "What an amazing piece of work is this. Where *will* all this end; anywhere?—Ach." (f. 54v.)

Carlyle is convinced that "the epic of the Present is the thing always to write; the epic of the Present not of the past and dead" (f. 95v.); yet he has "funded" such toil in his study of the seventeenth century (f. 105v.) that he cannot give up. He thinks (at one moment) that a straight history, like *The French Revolution*, is not wanted: "Probably no one will ever make much of endeavouring to resuscitate (as in F.R.) the whole business—rather try to bring up the *soul* of it" (f. 103v.),—which may be found in Cromwell:

> —*Oliver Cromwell* (27 Septr 1841; Monday 1½ p.m.)!—

> O Oliver my hero . . . what is the use of man's writing; of man's understanding, which should be the basis of writing? That man may *see* the great things which are, which have been, which probably will be, in God's world here below.—If an Oliver Cromwell stood close by us, in the vesture and dialect of this our own time, he were of all men the worthiest to be written about. Two centuries lying heaped over him obscure the man; have abolished much that was transitory in the man. . . . He existed, he exists; can we not discern him, decipher him, present his lineaments to men?—[not likely I think!] (f. 107.).

16

It is likely that Carlyle's asides show that he had begun to recognize that though a history may aim to bring out the *soul* of a past period, it is hard to reconcile this with the set purpose of reflecting on the present. The problems of ordering a faithful interpretation are difficult enough without confusing the two ages. In August 1842 he confesses to Emerson, "One of my grand difficulties I suspect to be that I cannot write two Books at once; cannot be in the seventeenth century and in the nineteenth at one and the same moment."[6] For Carlyle's draft comments on the Long Parliament, for example, drift into topicalities, which were eventually to be no part of his terse introductory remarks on the same subject in the final text of *Cromwell*:[7]

> The English Parl*t* still exists; the last of our traditions in which some men still hope. I have looked upon it myself, not without astonishment, not without some earnestness of curiosity. There it still sits and simmers, passing thousands of acts yearly, delivering acres of printed talk yearly, at present in what they call the Reformed State. . . . Young men and old in frock [coats] and trousers with their legs folded . . . or sitting in ranged benches with their hats on, free and easy, mutually conversing humming Manifold; unfortunate dull orator entirely inaudible amid the din. . . . It is one of those 1001 private-bills about canals, highways, harbour-duties, turnpike rates, which pass here yearly, which have all to come hither that they may pass. It is the best way, sayst thou? Well, who knows! . . . But bills that wanted persons to pass them, surely at first thought one would fancy they might as well look out for somebody who *would* listen to them first of all! These are mysteries of State (f. 55v.).

It is much the same with his comments on the Church of his own day, which are implicit in *Cromwell* but not as direct as even in the surviving fragments of manuscript.[8]

Much of the Forster Manuscript was to be condensed into the opening chapter of *Cromwell*, "Anti-Dryasdust", expressing Carlyle's hope that History has something to teach, his exasperation with records, his contempt for historians and his aim to resuscitate "a Heroism from Past Time". Clearly he sees the paradoxes in History. He sets the highest value on "truth", which means that he must depend on documents, facts and firsthand authorities; but his real concern is with what is true in principle, which may be very loosely related to any one of these. Then, any historian must trace a path for us through a limitless past universe of action, for "Narrative is *linear*, Action is *solid*". Yet it is he who makes this path, "tracking it out with the eye not, as is more common, with the *nose*,"—that is, using "insight" not just laborious "research". Carlyle's half-simulated impatience is a way of dramatising his problems:

> For indeed the History of the Past is the real Bible. So did the god's which made this Universe manifest itself to us . . . even so if thou wilt think of it. That is the true series of incarnations and avatars. The splendour of God shone thro' the huge incondite chaos of *our* being, so and then so; and by heroism after heroism, we have come to what you see. The Bible of the Past, rich are they that have it written as some old Greeks, old Hebrews and others have it. But looking in Collins's Peerage and the illegible torpedo rubbish mounds I am struck dumb. English *Literature* (is a thing yet to be born) if Literature mean *speaking* in fit words what the gods were pleased to *act*. . . .
>
> "God is great," say the Moslems: yes, but Dryasdust and Human Stupidity are not small. It too is wide as Immensity, it too is deep as Hell; has a strength of slumberous torpor in it, the subduing of *which* will mean that the History of this Universe is complete. . . . [Yet] the gods will never conquer it, sings Schiller and say I (f. 4v.).

> Wilt thou look, O reader; shall we two endeavour to look earnestly together. Vain is Whitelocke, vain are Knebworth, Hardwick State Papers, Somers' Tracts Harl [eaian] Miscelly, and that fatal rubbish mound of "original documents", documentary of little, except of the stupidity of mankind. . . . Read no more there: believe me I have read till my soul is near extinction, and much I have read which no following son of Adam will ever more read; and in all this there is nothing visible but an undecipherable universe filled as with dirty undecipherable London fog (f. 111v.).

> He is a conservative (one of the truest) who brings back the Past vitally visible into the Present living Time. . . . Your dreary constitutional Hallams, your (who's?) are the true revolutionists, that would cut us off sheer asunder from whatsoever went before; representing all that went before as lifeless ashes, as a thing one blesses God one has no further trade with (f. 100).

18

The past belongs to Hela the Death Goddess . . . overspread with pale horror, with dim brown oblivion. And who are these, evidently kinsmen of the death goddess, that stand as Janitors admit[t]ing you, under heavy fees, to some view of the matter here and there? They are the Historians, bless their singular countenances,—on the whole as strange a people as I have ever seen. What an indistinct mouldy Whiteness overspreads their faces, so that no human feature can be clear, discovered; the features all gone, as in long-buried men, into a mealy damp-powdery, blank. . . . See with what amazing amorphous wrappages, like huge Irish watchcoats, quilted out of all the rags of Nature, they have indistinctly wrapt themselves; and stand, all winged, undecipherable, without form . . . By Heaven, the inner anatomy of one of these necromantic watchmen is a thing Science longs for; such a one I would go some miles to see dissected, and know what it was that he had within him, if aught (ff. 54–54v.).

It was not long after this that he came on the Camden Society's *Chronica Jocelini De Brakelonda*, and turned from Oliver to the Abbot Samson. At one moment he is writing about Cromwell's first letter, addressed to "Mr. Storie, at the sign of the Dog." Then, on the same page, he launches into a long continuous passage on "Jocelin of St. Edmundsbury. . . . One of those vanished Existences, utterly grown dark, whose works or footprints are still clear to our eyes" (f. 56v.).[9] What is common to both books and men is that, in Carlyle's sense, they are heroes, and such heroism means the ability to grasp what is true. As he says in *Past and Present*, it means " 'Hero-worship', if you will,—yes, friends; but, first of all, by being ourselves of heroic mind."[10]

This may not be a new light; but, again, what the draft shows is what came to Carlyle when he set himself to write *something* even though clear that it was not the subject of his new book. He is too bitter at his failure for it to be called almost automatic writing, but he is trying to draw on the well of his own belief. As he says: "We have written lately often of *Silence*: but how deeply at present do we feel that Speech too were glorious and blessed. Forms unutterable struggle like spirits in prison within us. . . . Thought, like the gods, is born of chaos; like lightning out of the black vague-rolling tempest: all chaos is the mother of thought, as Venus (Urania?) sprang from the foam of the sea" (f. 95). The basis of his thought is his belief in morality. As he was to restate it in *Past and Present*: "All religion" reminds us "of the quite *infinite* difference there is between a Good man and a Bad".[11]

But is there not, human at the heart of all, strangely hidden, sunk, overwhelmed yet not extinct, a light-element and fire-element, which if you but awaken it shall irradiate and illuminate the whole, and make life a glorious fixed landscape, rock-borne, sure, the home and conquest of the brave, no longer a shoreless, skyless wavering chaos wherein cowards weep and die. It is infinitely respectable this fact that poor man's convictions are primarily moral; that his life-theory, never so stupid logically, has ever a moral truth in it whereby it first became credible to him. Wild Odin with his red-bearded Thunder*god*, with his hoary *Jotun* Frost the glance of whose devil-eye splits rocks, found credence and apotheosis among the Northmen not for these things which are become foolish false, but for another thing which remains for ever wise and true. Ye Northmen, ye shall not fear death; a Supreme Power presides over that and all things, and has appointed *Valkyrs* Choosers. Death's appointers, unerring inexorable: them ye shall follow unreluctantly, nay joyfully; and know that He on high takes only the valiant to his bosom, tramples all cowards down to Hela and the realms of Night! Not a well-conditioned Norse heard that but answered, Yes. To the great-hearted melancholic Norsemen, sitting sulky, vacant there, . . . the whole universe a shimmering mask of vague unintelligibility to them, such news was as a spark of lightning, awakening their own inner light,—which then blazed and burnt! I myself to this hour have respect for it, and hope always to have. Neither do we find that Christianism, this faith of Oliver's, propagated itself much by publication of "Evidences," Bridgewater Treatises and such like in these early times. No: curiously enough it was by other ways. Infinite pity and admiration, infinite assent to a new form of nobleness again kindled all hearts nigh sunk unto death. . . . If you will have a man believe, convince his heart; let the poor man see face to face a truth, palpable veritable, of which there is no doubting: it is strange to what extent his logicalities on all sides will accommodate themselves to that (f. 106).

What seekest thou for new Gospels, religions of the Future? In the heroic hearts born into every generation, lo *there* is a new Gospel and religion, not of the Future only but of the Present, direct and indisputable revealed once more by the Almighty Highest! What wouldst thou, fool? Did not the Highest God make —thee. The small still voices that speak, if thou wilt listen, in thy own heart of hearts, are not these His voice withal,—monitions from the unfathomable ever-sacred heart of things? Thunders from Sinai &c; these may be needed for rude boyhood; a grown man can understand what is said to him without these! The heroes of any age are the true Gospel of that age. . . . ["intellect and virtue inseparable, nay identical": how very gently this began with me; and it goes swelling and deepening, so as to look really like a most important thing! The thought, all diluted into irrecognisability in the above, is nevertheless a true one: "Honour the able-man; and for this end (first of all) know him, know where to seek for him."] [Last night, 7 jany 1842, at H[enry] Taylor's talked of this].—(pen spoiled!) (f. 95v.).

*Aber es kam Nichts auf das Blatt!*—Worship of Heroes the only kind of Worship that remains to us? The only one, intrinsically, that man ever had? The "religion of the future" is even *this*;—and those wearisome confused adjustings of Church to State and controversies between High Church and the Voluntary Principle will, for one thing, abolish themselves and trouble us no more. Church and State being all one . . . and indeed all manner of true free universal principles, coalescing into Catholicism very difft from the poor old Pope's, as the seven coloured rays into floods of pure light. It will be a blessed time.—"O Jerusalem, Jerusalem, thou that killest the Prophets and stonest them that are sent unto thee!" O England, England, thou that doest even the like,—thou that misknowest the Heroes, hangest their dead bodies on gibbets, who rejoicest over the Quacks, saying, Be *ye* king over me;—and art now arrived at the gates of ruin and inanition by the leading of these same! Open thy heavy eyes, foolish country, look and see. Quacks lead thee, even hitherward; to no other goal, but to ruin and destruction only, could or can these leave thee: gravitation tends not more surely to the centre than Quackery does to the Devil. . . . (f. 154).

Even apart from the merely historical notes there is much more than this in the manuscript, which is not only of editorial interest. For part of its value lies in the sense it gives of bringing one closer to Carlyle in piecing the scraps together. It is even a reflection on his own technique in his published works: we ourselves play Editor to Teufelsdröckh and Sauerteig, seeking for inspiration in these fragments of Manuscript. Nor is this just a forced coincidence. Carlyle's mode of thought and expression depend on his breaking down accepted forms and recreating them according to his inner convictions, and here they wait to be re-assembled. In a somewhat similar way this meant that as a historian he had to master his subject so that he could identify himself with figures of the past, and make a forced use of their concerns to focus and express his own convictions about the present.

Other contributors to this volume have noticed how this is an essential part of Carlyle's method, and so it needs less comment here. It is certainly part of his *process* and a means of allowing the mere narrator to participate in, or to re-create the past, by playing roles.[12] He is still fascinated by the fancy he had indulged in *Sartor* (p. 261) of the "Time-annihilating Hat" which will bring periods together telescoping Time, though even that would not be enough:

> Every Historian should be provided with a *Time-Hat*: what . . . an amazing implement/. Fancy him entering one of those supper-parties where Edward Hyde sits listening . . . where Shakespeare etc sits incountering of wits with Benjn Jonson! But he would be a melancholy *foreigner* withal; the people's thoughts as strange to him as their costumes: we belong to our own century as to our own parish, and have to gaze with blank sad wonderment. . . . The vocables men utter with their tongues are hardly more diverse, than the thoughts they cherish in their hearts: what we can say is that one alphabet spells them all (f. 53v.).

The historian must be able to become one with his subject, as Carlyle is drawn to be with Abbot Samson, Cromwell or Frederick.

This is curiously revealed in the Forster manuscript, which has two striking passages which Carlyle did not publish; for it is not only fancy which sees in them his self-identification with Cromwell. Their interest lies both in this and in their being another newly-caught echo of that voice of his, like so "few other voices". The first passage comes in an account of his action at Cambridge, on 15 August 1842, to prevent the University Plate's being despatched to the royalists:

> Peace, ye Heads of Houses; go into your Lexicons again; suffi-cient for *this* day be the evil thereof. Mr. C in this work of his has authority which *he* is willing to venture on. The man wishes to be civil too; but urge him not. In those grey troublous eyes of his,

in that unbeautiful rough countenance of his, there is something dangerous. Ye hear how his common bass voice rises easily into harsh querulous tenor; and argumentative speech—like a prophetic chaunt becomes austere canto-fermo. His face will suddenly flush red, and again it will suddenly flush blackish bluish, and become of slate colour: I judge that his temper is none of the blessedest. He has an unpleasant breadth of jaw. Besides he preaches, plays, and has warts on his face. A man probably not without madness in him (f. 55).

Then, again, as he composes the letter "To Mr *Storie* at the Dog":

In some small chamber, warmed with wood faggots in a house on the South outskirts of St Ives, sits a robust middle-aged man, penning this epistle. . . . By intense inspection something of this man can be discerned. A man of simple farmer aspect; very far from beautiful, sorrowful rather, [*word uncertain*] cloudy-browed, what the common run of men call ugly. In those deep anxious eyes, plays for the present no smile;—yet have I seen them beam with honest laughter, and their sternness melt in the softest tears, for he is a living man this angry farmer. Between the brows what an ugly wart. The jaw too has dangerous squareness, under each ear, a dangerous angularity: dangerous if strong mean dangerous, as to the common run of man it does, the man's voice too is none of the musicalest: strong nor can you call it flatly dissonant, yet I think there is something of the metallic gong in it, oppressively impressive; and then alas it so easily rises into alt! and belches you forth a bellow withering men's very heart like few other voices of which you never heard, or speaks in a kind of inspired recitation or glowing canto-fermo, much too impressive on the auditor (f. 56).

History, said Carlyle, is "a looking both before and after",[13] and may even mean trying to look at one's own image. And if History is "the essence of innumerable Biographies"[14] it will remain unintelligible to the reader who cannot understand himself. Thus to read Carlyle's works is also to try to understand Carlyle.

## NOTES

1. *The Athenaeum* (8 Jan. 1876), p. 54, after the tributes to Carlyle on his eightieth birthday, 4 December 1875: "Night's childless children" is a phrase applied to the Furies by Aeschylus.

23

2. The Forster manuscript (F. 48.E36) was part of the original bequest of the Forster Collection, in 1876, to what is now the Victoria and Albert Museum, London; and soon after its receipt it was rather approximately put in order and bound. Since it was then even more approximately catalogued under John Forster's name, as " 'Statesmen of the Commonwealth' [1840] MS. and proofs, letters etc. . . . Also notes &c. by Mr. Carlyle", it has eluded notice, and I came to examine it only after it was kindly drawn to my attention by Mr Anthony Burton, Assistant Keeper. The present account is intended to be no more than a summary. The manuscript consists of 180 miscellaneous sheets, mostly on paper of the same size as used for *Past and Present* (8 by 13 inches), but with some odd letters and scraps. It is incomplete even as a draft: some of it having gone the way of all manuscript, and some apparently parcelled off separately and used as the basis of the *Historical Sketches* (London, 1902, uniform with the Centenary *Works*), edited by Alexander Carlyle. Much of it is made up of notes from Carlyle's reading. It is really *not* in chronological order, so that one of the first problems for future study will be to see what this was. Actual dated comments range, in the main sequence, from 20 December 1841 to 27 Nov. 1843, but it also includes some letters of 1844 and one of 1846 (KJF).

3. The difficulties were fairly well brought out by Froude through quotations from letters and the *Journal*, and he correctly inferred that "many pages were covered with writing of a sort". But he never saw this writing, and seems to have accepted that Carlyle burnt it. There has been a natural tendency to accept TC's self-reproaches, and some failure to see how thoroughly the ground was being laid for his book. (*Life*, III, 332–5.)

4. See especially Grace E. Calder, *The Writing of Past and Present, A Study of Carlyle's Manuscripts* (New Haven, 1949), Yale Studies in English 112. This is the authoritative work, based on the manuscript of the first draft (British Museum) and the printer's copy (Yale University Library). In spite of being written without reference to the miscatalogued Forster manuscript its authority remains, although a few conclusions might be questioned. We still do not know exactly when Carlyle started *Past and Present*, any more than we can give a precise date for the beginning of *Cromwell*.

5. "Heroes", of course, recur in *Past and Present* and *Cromwell*, but the drift of the manuscript sometimes appears to be back towards the lectures, and even the Clothes-Philosophy is revived (f. 111v.), and dropped only after an "Ach Himmel! O *where shall* I begin?"

6. *The Correspondence of Emerson and Carlyle*, ed. J. Slater (New York and London, 1964), p. 328.

7. *Works*, VI, 107.

8. The visit to the House of Commons was paid on 15 June 1842, and is described in similar terms in a letter from TC to his mother, 17 June,

NLS, MS, 521.5. He went to hear Charles Buller, since Mrs Buller wanted Carlyle to hear her son speak on the Church Patronage (Scotland) Bill. Evidently Carlyle barely exaggerates: on a "technical objection" the hearing was put off until 5 July, and it was then postponed for a further six months, to be followed by the Disruption of the Scottish Church. For "comments on the Church of his own day", see Forster manuscript, f. 52.

9. Cf. *Works*, X, 40.
10. *Works*, X, 35.
11. *Works*, X, 227.
12. See pp. 98 and 207 for method, and pp. 98, 178–80, and 208–9 for identification. Carlyle undeniably uses it from *Sartor* onwards, the parallels between *Frederick* and *Cromwell* being particularly clear. It is conceivable that the re-writing of part of the *French Revolution*, without "foul papers", made it less obvious there, though still a fundamental principle.
13. "On History," *Works*, XXVII, 83.
14. *Works*, XXVII, 86.


I expect to undertake a further study of the Forster manuscript in an attempt at least to solve unanswered questions about Carlyle's progress with Cromwell, just when he turned to *Past and Present*, and the relationship of the more important passages to the *Works*. (KJF).

# 1

# Carlyle Today

## by G. B. TENNYSON

In the National Portrait Gallery in London there is close to an entire floor devoted to portraits of figures from the nineteenth century. At the end of a long corridor, off which are situated various rooms for artists, literary figures, actors, and anti-slavery agitators, one enters at last a large octagonal room. In the centre of this room stands a pedestal topped by a rectangular glass case; inside the case stands a bust of Thomas Carlyle by Joseph Edgar Boehm. Behind the bust on the opposite wall hangs the very large, unfinished but superb portrait of Carlyle by John Everett Millais. On the left hand of the father, as the viewer sees it, hang portraits of John Stuart Mill, John Ruskin, and William Morris. All of these portraits are disposed around large relief letters which read—PROPHETS. As one enters the room Carlyle appears not only larger than life, but in a kind of double focus; his eminence in the portrait, higher and to the right of the bust, seems to be shimmering through the glass which enshrines his brooding countenance in three dimensions; and through the same glass gleams the legend of his role. Mill, Ruskin, and Morris recede as accent marks or satellites; the rest of the room scarcely has any existence: stray figures of explorers and scientists adorn the walls, but the room is unquestionably dominated by the image, one might almost say the presence, of Thomas Carlyle.

To a student of Carlyle the display is both awesome and gratifying. Awesome because Carlyle always appears to be sitting in judgment (a quality of the living Carlyle admirably captured by the more successful portraitists and sculptors), and, perhaps because he is shown twice, he seems to be following one with his eyes through the room. Gratifying because the arrangement also seems to be a judgment of posterity itself on Carlyle's place in Victorian life; gratifying, moreover, in a way that the fine statue on the Embankment, or the splendid Herdman portrait in Edinburgh can never be. The Embankment statue, after all, cannot be moved, fixed as it was by public subscription shortly after Carlyle's death. The Scottish National Portrait Gallery, for its part, can well be expected to have a display of one of Scotland's most illustrious sons. But the selection in the National Portrait Gallery seems one determined less by accident and more by choice than these other two, to be in fact the judgment of Britain on Carlyle. Never mind the fact that the National Portrait Gallery happens to have a treasure trove of Carlyle portraits, more perhaps than that of any single figure outside of recent monarchs. It has much else besides[1] and it could have arranged its Victorian display in ways that would have placed quite a different emphasis, or none at all, on Carlyle. So one must acknowledge that this display represents something quite intentional and something quite contemporary in terms of the present view of Thomas Carlyle.

Now, in one sense the display could not be more obvious. To students of the nineteenth century the presentation of Carlyle as an eminent Victorian and one whom it pleases critics to call a "prophet" must seem almost a cliché. But this is academic habit, and the National Portrait Gallery in following that habit in a contemporary exhibition for the average museum-goer serves to raise questions about the habit itself, questions which it is the academic obligation to answer.

The first question, it seems to me, is: how has Carlyle come to the eminence ascribed to him by the display in the Portrait Gallery? Has he always enjoyed it? What was his position in, say, July 1914 when the Millais portrait was slashed through the forehead and left eye by a suffragette, presumably on the grounds that Carlyle's well-known opposition to democracy and the ballot box was a contributory factor in the denial of the vote to women.[2] What in general has been the course of thought on Carlyle that has brought him to the present position of such prominence in the eyes of the keepers of the National Portrait Gallery? In short, what has been the history of Carlyle's reputation?

Another question raised by the display in the National Portrait

Gallery is suggested more specifically by the *mode* in which Carlyle is presented. Unlike Newman, who is to be found in company not only with Dr Pusey and the saintly John Keble, as is fitting, but cheek by jowl with a bust of Thomas De Quincey, stared at ruminantly by George Eliot, and on the very same wall with James Anthony Froude (all an illustration no doubt of T. S. Eliot's contention that old combatants are in death folded in a single party); unlike Macaulay, who looks prosperous among a category called "Men of Learning"; unlike the rather haunting Darwin portrait properly displayed next to his "Ape", T. H. Huxley, on a wall labelled "Scientists"; unlike all these, Carlyle and his satellites are labelled "Prophets". As I have said, this is a critical commonplace. But if we stop to think on the matter a moment it is a rather astonishing commonplace. In what other country and in what other age could we expect to find a category of writers publicly labelled "Prophets"? Indeed, outside of the Bible can we think of any *assemblage* of prophets? In the National Portrait Gallery itself no other age has a group of portraits so designated. The Victorian presentation is unique. The question that is thus raised is, what in fact *is* a prophet? And further, why is Carlyle one?

The question of Carlyle's prophetism and the question of Carlyle's reputation raised by the display in the gallery are curiously intertwined. They may almost be said to be one question. It is to this double-pronged question that this paper is addressed.

The raw material that one uses as the basis for generalizations about a writer's reputation is exceedingly difficult to itemize. It is, of course, not only those written treatments of the author's reputation (in Carlyle's case these are relatively few[3]), it is also the mass of material written about an author in general (in Carlyle's case the mass is relatively large), and beyond that it is the body of references and reflections in other works, in biographies, in contemporary accounts, in critical studies primarily devoted to matters other than reputation, and so on. Above all, it is the "feel" one acquires in going through scholarly and critical and historical material; and this cannot be pinned down to single works. My own recent massive encounter with Carlyle-related critical material has exposed me both to the specific treatments of Carlyle and his reputation and to the general feel of intellectual and critical response to Carlyle for the past one hundred and fifty years.[4] It is largely on the basis of this encounter that I shall endeavour to outline the state of Carlyle's reputation.

For purposes of seeing Carlyle's reputation in perspective, it is easiest to view it in three main stages. They are in the first instance chronological:

      I. Carlyle's lifetime (to 1881)
     II. From Carlyle's Death to about 1930
    III. From 1930 to the Present

But each period has its own character too and can be designated by an appropriate adjective as follows: The Popular, the Reactionary, and the Scholarly-Critical. And each period has its own book, or books, that sum up the dominant tone of the period. These works in turn were undertaken by characteristic types of Carlyle scholars for the period in question. Finally, each period and its dominant attitude cast some light on the idea of the prophet as exemplified in Carlyle.

Before looking at each period in greater detail it may be useful to summarize the general trend of Carlyle's reputation throughout the three periods. If it is a commonplace that Carlyle was an eminent Victorian and another commonplace that he is often viewed as a prophet, it is the greatest commonplace of all in Carlyle scholarship that his reputation, along with that of most of his fellow prophets and even most of the men of learning and the writers of the Victorian age in general, suffered an almost total eclipse after his death. Perhaps no one other than Ruskin plummeted more precipitously in public esteem and in general reader devotion. Of course this observation indicates that Carlyle had reached a rather high eminence, else his fall would not have appeared so dramatic. If we were plotting the whole course of Carlyle's reputation through the three periods on a graph, we would note a generally rising curve in Period I up to a very high peak towards the end of his life, a drastic plunge in Period II to a valley almost as deep as the peak was high, and a cautious rise in Period III to a modest eminence but with perhaps a further rise in prospect.

Let us trace this curious pattern in somewhat greater detail through the three main periods of Carlyle's reputation, with special stress on The Popular Period since it offers within itself a paradigm of what happened later.

The Popular Period. This runs from the late eighteen-twenties to Carlyle's death in 1881, for it is not until the late twenties that Carlyle can be said to have a reputation at all, following what has been described as the longest literary apprenticeship in English letters. While the graph described above pictures an upward swing throughout the Popular Period, a closer look reveals that only the main thrust is upward; there are some downturns as well. Or one could say that, while Carlyle's reputation increased consistently in his lifetime, the esteem in which he was held by knowledgeable people varied a good deal. From the point of view of simple notoriety, of course, Carlyle began in total obscurity and ended in total celebrity. But from the point of view of esteem the path was rockier and in some ways anticipated the period since his death.

Carlyle began by baffling readers, came to have an enormous hold on them and to be revered by them, and then he startled and disappointed his readers by his social intransigence, and finally more or less redeemed himself towards the end by another great work and died in honour. The illustrative documents in this phase are in fact Carlyle's own works, or at least the response to them. The early literary essays and *Sartor Resartus* (1833–34) represent the first stage, that of bafflement, though of course these works came to have an almost biblical force with later generations. Even from the start the bafflement was mixed with admiration and respect, but initially Carlyle seems to have enjoyed a reputation as a kind of brilliant eccentric. The second stage, that of adulation, is best represented by *The French Revolution* (1837) and *Past and Present* (1843). It was Carlyle's triumph with the twice-written *French Revolution* that rehabilitated his earlier writings and secured him a future reading public that would devour any word he chose to publish. Some of that public, though continuing to read him, felt considerable dismay with the publication of such works as *Latter-Day Pamphlets* (1850), and for some years while Carlyle traversed the vale of tears of research on *Frederick the Great* there were many who felt towards him primarily disenchantment. But at last, with *Frederick the Great* (1858–65),

31

Carlyle entered the fourth and last stage of his reputation in his lifetime, that of honour and reverence, and, though there were dissenters, it was essentially in a state of honour and reverence that Carlyle died.

This overview of the state of Carlyle's reputation in his lifetime lends itself fairly readily to documentation from his contemporaries. John Sterling, for example, on *Sartor Resartus* has rightly been much reprinted. His admiration for many of the sentiments mixed with his dismay at, and even distaste for, many of the modes of utterance in the work well captures what proved to be the contemporary reaction:

> The sense of strangeness is also awakened by the marvellous combinations, in which the work abounds to a degree that the common reader must find perfectly bewildering. This can hardly, however, be treated as a consequence of the *style*; for the style in this respect coheres with, and springs from, the whole turn and tendency of thought. The noblest images are objects of a humorous smile, in a mind which sees itself above all Nature and throned in the arms of an Almighty Necessity; while the meanest have a dignity, inasmuch as they are trivial symbols of the same one life to which the great whole belongs. And hence, as I divine, the startling whirl of incongruous juxtaposition, which of a truth must to many readers seem as amazing as if the Pythia on the tripod should have struck-up a drinking-song, or Thersites had caught the prophetic strain of Cassandra.[5]

Emerson's enthusiasm for the early Carlyle is also well-known, as is Mill's. Indeed, the three early enthusiasts, Sterling, Emerson, Mill, were heralds of the second phase of the Popular period, the phase of adulation, and they figured representatively in that phase. Mill, for example, was moved to a warm review of *The French Revolution* in his own Journal, *The London and Westminster Review*, which began:

> This is not so much a history, as an epic poem; and notwithstanding, or even in consequence of this, the truest of histories. It is the history of the French Revolution, and the poetry of it, both in one; and on the whole no work of greater genius, either historical or poetical, has been produced in this country for many years.[6]

John Sterling took extensive space in the same publication two years later to write an encomiastic account of Carlyle's works in which, significantly, he devotes considerable attention to the question of prophetism and of Carlyle's "teaching".[7] Indeed, Sterling in his review very largely captures what would come to be the dominant tone of the Victorian response to Carlyle, the tone that characterizes all of the Popular period.

Other adulators could be cited, not least among them Dickens who paid Carlyle the compliment of using *The French Revolution* as part of the raw material for a novel. But the point should be sufficiently clear: as a result of his triumph with *The French Revolution* Carlyle established himself as one of the great writers of the age. Even the setbacks of the period of disenchantment during the eighteen-fifties and the semi-reclusiveness of Carlyle's life after the death of Jane Welsh Carlyle in 1866 and after the publication of *Frederick the Great* never entirely dimmed the lustre of the reputation that stormed all before it in the eighteen-forties. Matthew Arnold, writing in the eighties, recalls some of that glory as it appeared to the Oxford undergraduate Arnold had been when Carlyle came fully into his own:

> Forty years ago, when I was an undergraduate at Oxford, voices were in the air there which haunt my memory still. Happy the man who in that susceptible season of youth hears such voices!
> There was the puissant voice of Carlyle; so sorely strained, overused, and mis-used since, but then fresh, comparatively sound, and reaching our hearts with true, pathetic eloquence.[8]

Arnold was obviously writing with full awareness of the years that had elapsed since Carlyle's puissant voice had stirred Oxford. He would have known that Carlyle's social views in "Occasional Discourse on the Negro Question" (1849), and especially the *Latter-Day Pamphlets* (1850), had quite turned much enlightened opinion against him. Mill and Carlyle ceased to be personal friends and Mill retorted to Carlyle's views with "The Negro Question" (1850). Emerson and the New England intellectuals were alarmed. Many agreed with Trollope, who said: "I look upon him as a man who was always in danger of going mad in literature and who has now done so."[9] Ruskin remained a notable exception to the prevailing view of the fifties, the period of disenchantment with Carlyle, and almost alone of prominent persons he congratulated Carlyle on the blistering *Latter-Day Pamphlets*. Arnold, however, sided with such as Mill and Emerson and Trollope and it was the Carlyle of this phase that Arnold dubbed a "moral desperado".

But the publication of *Frederick the Great* (1858–65) went far towards redeeming Carlyle in public esteem (though perhaps not in Arnold's esteem). The upturn in the sixties was also signalled by the election of Carlyle as Rector of Edinburgh University in 1866 in competition with none other than Benjamin Disraeli. By 1875 Carlyle was the reigning grand old man of English letters: a distinguished roster of literary figures presented him with a testimonial in that year affirming that Carlyle had in his own life comported himself as the Hero as Man of Letters. He had earlier declined a decoration and pension offered by Her Majesty's government through Disraeli, though he had been willing to accept in 1874 the Prussian Order of Merit proffered by Bismarck. When Carlyle died and by his own request was *not* buried in Westminster Abbey, the Dean of that foundation nevertheless preached a moving funeral sermon which contained the following observations characteristic of the Victorian estimate of Carlyle:

> It was customary for those who honoured him to speak of him as a 'prophet'. And if we take the word in its largest sense he truly deserved the name. He was a prophet, and felt himself to be a prophet, in the midst of an untoward generation; his prophet's mantle was his rough Scotch dialect, and his own peculiar diction, and his own secluded manner of life. He was a prophet most of all in the emphatic utterance of truths which no one else, or hardly any one else, ventured to deliver, and which he felt to be a message of good to a world sorely in need of them.[10]

Dean Stanley's remarks are a fitting terminus for considering the estimate of Carlyle in the Popular Period, for things would not be the same afterwards. But before moving to the next phase it is appropriate to look back and in looking back on the pattern of more than fifty years of Carlyle's reputation we are struck first of all by the enormous success of it. Carlyle succeeded against every odd; he simply imposed himself on his contemporaries. He would be heard; and he was heard. It is improbable, but it is true.

Carlyle's contemporaries viewed him with admiration bordering on reverence; even his enemies treated him with respect. If one had to settle upon a single word to characterize the general Victorian view of Carlyle, that word should be—Teacher. Victorians did not think of Carlyle primarily in literary terms; that is, they were not overly concerned about the proper literary category to place him in—essayist, historian or social critic. Nor did they preoccupy themselves unduly with analysis of Carlyle's style. Not that they were indifferent to it, not that they did not occasionally satirize it, and even from time to time, as in a Sterling or an Emerson, make valuable contributions towards understanding it. But they kept their eyes on Carlyle the Teacher.

Nor do I think the Victorian reaction to Carlyle was misplaced. It was the response he sought from his readers and in the main they made that response intelligently and thoughtfully. We should not let ourselves be misled because Victorian zeal for Carlyle the Teacher occasionally led to Victorian excesses of discipleship. To be sure, many Victorian readers made an easy transition from Teacher to Philosopher to Theologian and endeavoured to extract from Carlyle's writing the "system" that they felt sure must lie buried there. Something of this impulse must lie behind the Victorian equivalents of "The Thoughts of Chairman Thomas" that one still meets with in second-hand book-shops. These, of course, have fallen into great disrepute today; but I would suggest that the disdain aroused today is provoked really more by the idea of such compilations than by Carlyle himself. I have recently, for example, been working in an area where it is natural to come across such volumes as *The Christian Year Birthday Book* and *Heavenly Promises*, these being extracts from John Keble's *The Christian Year* arranged in special sequence for Victorian instruction and delight. They must seem a little superfluous to the twentieth century, considering how many copies of *The Christian Year* itself were (and are) available. But no matter: the twentieth century has found all of Keble superfluous. The volumes in question, though, do testify to the Victorian propensity for such collections and for making any favoured author into a teacher. They can be duplicated for most serious Victorian writers. There may be, for all I know, such a volume culled from the less incendiary passages in Swinburne. Carlyle, of course, was better suited than Swinburne for such treatments; he seems at times to have written with an eye towards them.

At all events, the key Victorian word for Carlyle was Teacher. And by that they meant not only the obvious, the didactic, the hortatory, the reproving, but even something of what we would understand by prophet. In fact, there is almost a formula in typical Victorian commentary on Carlyle, and it runs something like this: "Carlyle says so-and-so, or Carlyle does so-and-so, it is true, but the fact is that Carlyle is not a —— [here fill in "novelist", or "historian", or even "philosopher"], but a Prophet, and it is as a prophet that he is to be understood." Usually this sense of prophet equates with teacher and sage. Sometimes the analysis of prophetism is deeper, of course, but I think the Victorian emphasis always falls on the prophet as teacher. It is, in my judgment, far from the worst emphasis.

In great part the monument of the whole Victorian estimate of Carlyle is James Anthony Froude's four-volume *Thomas Carlyle* (1882, 1884), which appeared with almost indecent speed upon the death of Carlyle and which has been held ever since to be the "standard" biography. It is in a curious way both the shining example of the Victorian view of Carlyle as Teacher and the herald of a new and not very auspicious period in Carlyle's reputation— the Reactionary Period. As the capstone of the Victorian view of Carlyle as Teacher, Froude's *Life* really has no equal in breadth and in detail. Froude's view of Carlyle is in many ways entirely consistent with the widespread nineteenth-century view of him— Carlyle the rugged peasant's son emerging from the wilderness with his "Message" and his Teaching—indeed, these are among Froude's favourite words in connection with Carlyle. Froude sums up much of the Victorian attitude of sometimes uncomfortable reverence toward an acknowledged moral leader. Froude even seeks to justify the more debatable aspects of what he likes to call Carlyle's "creed", thus showing himself loyal to the end.

But Froude's *Life* is something other than a pious biography. Almost upon its appearance, coupled with that of the hastily-edited (by Froude) *Reminiscences* (1881), there was an outcry. The Oscar Wilde quip that every great man has his disciples and it is always Judas who writes the biography seemed to many the proper description of Froude's attitude toward Carlyle. Certainly today, it seems to me, the more interesting aspects of Froude's biography are not those having to do with Carlyle's emotional state but those having to do with Froude's. There is some reason to suspect that, when he came to write Carlyle's biography, Froude

felt toward Carlyle not unlike the way he felt toward the Tractarians when he came to write *The Nemesis of Faith*. Is it any
wonder that Froude's enemies sensed the same and titled one of
their anti-Froude works, *The Nemesis of Froude*?[11]

Thus at the very moment that Froude's *Life* stands as a sum-
mation of Victorian reverence towards a great teacher, it also
ushers in a new and rather untidy phase of Carlyle's reputation
that was to last for many years. It is the era I have dubbed the
Reactionary.

If the key word for the Popular period of Carlyle criticism is
Teacher, the key word for the Reactionary period is—Denouncer.
Now this phase, lasting for about fifty years following Carlyle's
death, is in many ways confused and at first seems not to lend
itself to easy categorization. It saw the appearance, for example,
of some notable works of scholarship—editions of letters and
occasional unpublished Carlyle works, for much of which we stand
indebted to the industry of Carlyle's nephew, Alexander Carlyle.
It was also the age of Traill's "Centenary Edition" of Carlyle's
works (1896–99) which for lack of a better still qualifies as the
standard edition. It saw, however, also a great quantity of biographical and quasi-biographical writing, especially that which
swirled around the Froude-Carlyle controversy, as it came to be
called, though I prefer to call it simply the Froude Controversy.
It saw too some specialist works of scholarship, editions of such
works as *The French Revolution* (by C. R. L. Fletcher, 1902, and
J. H. Rose, 1902), *Heroes* (by A. MacMechan, 1902), *Past and
Present* (by A. M. D. Hughes, 1918), and *Sartor Resartus* (by
MacMechan, 1896, and 1905) that continue to be of scholarly and
critical importance. It saw also many of those droning German
dissertations lauding the Sage. But still it had a dominant tone,
and that tone was set by what seemed to be Froude's undermining
of Carlyle's reputation as man and thinker. It was the negative in
Carlyle that came to dominate all consideration of him. Even
documents not directly involved in the Froude Controversy were
still animated by their stance one way or another on the Froude
issue.

It has been the fashion for many years now for scholars to say
as little as possible about the Froude Controversy, to pass over it
with a few discreet words as one of the displays of especially bad

temper on the part of our ancestors. Space prevents me from departing radically from this procedure, but I will say that I do not entirely endorse it. The effects of the Froude Controversy linger on today among undergraduates who ask confidently: "It's true, isn't it, that Carlyle was impotent?" or in glancing sneers at Carlyle from rather less innocent intellectuals. There is supposed to be a kind of gentleman's agreement among scholars that Waldo Hilary Dunn, after a lifetime of exculpating Froude, has conclusively proved (in *Froude and Carlyle*, 1930) that Froude was more sinned against than sinning. Personally, I find this absolution rather too generously given and in need of re-examination, but here I only want to cite the Froude Controversy to illustrate the temper of Carlyle criticism over a long period and not to reopen the controversy itself.

That temper, I have suggested, tended to turn Carlyle criticism into a battlefield over the negative aspects of Carlyle's life and thought. To write in denunciation of the great Denouncer was an act of courage, so it was thought; to write in defence of the great Denouncer was equally so, and an act of loyalty as well. Though I personally delight in this phase of Carlyle criticism as offering byways of such quaint interest as even the Victorian chrestomathies do not provide, I recognize that this is a personal and quixotic taste. Most readers do not care to know that Carlyle wore a truss, or that Jane Welsh was thought by Geraldine Jewsbury to have died *virgo intacta*. It is not squeamishness, I don't think: it is on the contrary a case of modern taste being too jaded for all this. The Froude controversy is simply no longer salacious *enough!* But what it did to Carlyle criticism cannot be so easily overlooked.

For fifty years Carlyle scholars and critics debated the negatives of Thomas Carlyle. We can divide most writers on the subject into two camps—the Loyalists and the Revisionists. The Loyalists were composed at first largely of those who had known and admired Carlyle, such men as his nephew Alexander, or the medical man, James Crichton-Browne, who became embroiled in the matter on Alexander's side. They were joined later by those who came under Carlyle's spell in the usual way, through his writings. Among these we may number most of the German academics whose tribe extended up to the second World War. For the most part they simply muddied already turbid waters by dragging Carlyle in to stand Godfather to whatever policy they wanted to defend at the moment on other grounds, the two most notable ones being Prussianism and Naziism. In a sense these men actually belong among the revisionists since they revised Carlyle to suit their own needs, but they felt themselves rather to be Loyalists, preserving in Germany even when it had been cast aside in Britain the true faith and the memory of a true Hero. There were, of course, also second generation Loyalists in Britain as well, and I will speak of two of these shortly. But Loyalists of whatever generation or country had this in common —they were defending a beleaguered holy place against the infidels and they fought with all of the zeal of a persecuted minority.

The Revisionists, for their part, looked to the Froude portrait as their standard, and also the subsequent Froude publications, not only Carlyle's own *Reminiscences*, which splendid book one can consider a casualty of the Reactionary phase since it was so rarely seen in its own right—not only, then, the *Reminiscences* and Froude's *Life*, but the posthumously published *My Relations with Carlyle* (1903), wherein Froude sought to justify the imputations he had made about the domestic relations of the two Carlyles, but only succeeded in making more explicit what was seen as treason to Carlyle and in provoking even more frenzied denials from the Loyalists. Even the valuable *Love Letters* (1909), which only now are being superseded by the *Collected Letters* (of Duke University and Edinburgh University) were provoked by the Froude "revelations" rather than by their inherent interest. Thus the Revisionists succeeded one way or another in dominating Carlyle scholarship for many years and in seizing at least most of the headlines during the Reactionary Period.

Revisionist documents of enduring value, apart from Froude's *Life* seen in its revisionist aspect, are actually very few. Certainly revisionism coloured everything said about Carlyle during these years, and thus the biographies and hence the received view of Carlyle may be said to have been deeply affected by the reactionary-revisionist ethos. Moreover, it continues today, and in contemporary scholarship on Carlyle's social and political views, revisionism may still be said to be dominant. One is still obliged to denounce the Denouncer on such matters as democracy, the vote, heroism, and discipline. I read in a book published in 1969 that only an occasional campus Carlylean still seeks to exonerate Carlyle of the darker charges hinting at Naziism that are levelled against him, these being taken simply as proven facts.[12] So, like the 1914 suffragette, we are still slashing Carlyle from forehead to eye on certain topics. One ought to add that, though this is Froude's legacy, it is doubtful that it was ever Froude's intention; for on these social matters Froude always sought to support Carlyle's views. Still it is the fruit of the revisionist spirit that has made Carlyle's name a dirty word in certain sacred modern precincts and Froude is its godfather. Despite all this, there is no outstanding purely revisionist document, as distinguished from the reactionary-revisionist *spirit*, that has survived the passage of the years. W. H. Dunn's Froude studies come as close as any to qualifying. The genteel mockery of a Lytton Strachey, while still entertaining, is not substantial enough to qualify. If one wanted to find a pure example of anti-Carlyle revisionism, one could go to Norwood Young's *Carlyle: His Rise and Fall* (London, n.d. [1927]), a late reactionary-revisionist document of a thoroughly vilifying nature, but it survives rather as a curiosity than anything else.

On the Loyalist side, there are more enduring documents. I have referred to some editions and volumes of letters. These are still of great value. There are also two works which stand, like Norwood Young, at the end of the period and, like Froude, both close it and open a new era. The first is David Alec Wilson's six-volume biography of Carlyle; the second is Isaac Watson Dyer's *Bibliography of Thomas Carlyle's Writings and Ana*. Wilson published his volumes over a ten-year period from 1923–34 (the last volume being completed after Wilson's death by D. W. MacArthur). Dyer's *Bibliography* appeared in 1928. Now Wilson's is the more backward-looking of the two works. His *Life* is clearly oriented towards the Reactionary period. It is an effort at total and documented vindication of Carlyle. It is not a wholly successful effort, although its industry is enormous. Wilson was the last of a dying race, that race of those who had known or almost known Carlyle in person and who felt it a personal duty to clear his name of the evil associations that had grown up around it. One would with reluctance send any but the most

40

specialist readers to Wilson today, but his volumes do mark a new era in their commitment to a thoroughly documentary approach to Carlyle and in their assumption that Carlyle is to be taken seriously again as a writer, though in Wilson's view the operative word would be "still".

Dyer's *Bibliography* reinforces the Wilson approach and subjects it to even greater rigour. It, too, enshrines the past in that it lists any and everything by and about Carlyle, which means a great deal of fugitive material from the Reactionary phase. But it also means much Victorian material and above all it means the fixing of the canon of Carlyle's writing and even such useful extras as a supplement on portraits of Carlyle. That Dyer too is a Carlyle disciple is evident time and again in his *Bibliography* in his frank pro-Wilson and anti-Froude sentiments. But what is uppermost is the accurate listing of works by Carlyle and works about him. There have been from time to time minor additions to Dyer, but no major overhaul. His book still stands as the definitive bibliography up to its time and as a continuing reproach to scholarship that there has been no successor to cover the forty-odd years of Carlyle scholarship that have succeeded upon Dyer.[13]

If the tone of open partisanship in Wilson and Dyer marks them as the last gasp of the Reactionary period with its personal animosities and its aura of denunciations and defences of Carlyle the man, the emphasis on scholarship, on accuracy, on amassing a wealth of detailed information that also characterizes these two works marks them as the beginning of a new era altogether. It is, of course, the Scholarly, or perhaps more precisely the Scholarly-Critical era in which we still find ourselves. The Popular period was dominated by the image of Carlyle as Teacher; the Reactionary period was dominated by the image of Carlyle as Denouncer, often as not turned back upon the Sage himself as Carlyle the Denounced. The Scholarly or Scholarly-Critical period is dominated by the image of Carlyle as Influence.

Perhaps the contentiousness of the Reactionary phase had been too bitter, perhaps it was just that the passage of years and the departure of persons who knew the period and the principals from first-hand experience had softened tempers, perhaps it was simply that Victorianism and those who made it were now phenomena of historical interest and could be placed along with mediaevalism, or Elizabethanism, or the attitudes of any era now definitely over and closed. However it was, in the thirties the scholars began to move in. Tentatively at first and not without setbacks over the next decades. The Second World War, for example, threatened to revive the hard feelings toward Carlyle generated by the First. And even more recently, the preoccupation, one might almost say the obsession, of modern times with race and racism has provoked ritual denunciations of Carlyle reminiscent of the Reactionary phase. But the main drift of the past forty years has been upward, and it has in Carlyle studies been directed toward seeing the man the Victorians venerated as a Professor-of-Things-in-General and the late Victorians and Edwardians alternately venerated and deplored as a Denouncer-of-Things-in-General, rather more as an Influence-on-Things-in-General.

The Influence approach is both safer and more in keeping with the supposed objectivity of scholarship than either of the previous approaches. One can, for instance, explore an influence without having to support it. One can for that matter lament it while still chronicling carefully how it was manifested. Thus it has been possible in the Scholarly period of Carlyle studies to write about Carlyle without necessarily appearing either as his sycophant or his grim-eyed detractor. Not that persons interested in Carlyle do not even today meet with charges of being at least crypto-Fascists merely because they are interested in Carlyle, but I am happy to say that that attitude is gradually being tempered and is restricted primarily to the academic groves in America and Britain that can always be relied upon to express in loftier language the sentiments of the popular press of thirty years ago. Still, to give credit where it is due, I should point out that the Scholarly revival itself stemmed from the Academy, once Wilson and Dyer and others had pointed the way.

It will not be surprising to learn that in the modern scholarly revival Americans have been in the forefront, although in its full extent the scholarly revival is very much an Anglo-American endeavour. But American graduate education was not modelled on German to no purpose, nor did American scholarship forget that Emerson set an example of American pioneering in Carlyle studies when he saw to it that *Sartor Resartus* appeared as a book in Boston before it did in Britain. In the early years of the modern scholarly revival we must look to such scholars as Emery Neff and Charles Frederick Harrold in the thirties and later to Hill Shine, Carlisle Moore, and Charles Richard Sanders for the most substantial work in Carlyle studies. I shall not itemize their achievements but simply say that they ranged from studies of influences on Carlyle to studies of his thought and to occasional editions of his work, though these have not in the main been the chief work of the scholarly period. Much else has been generated by the revival of interest in Carlyle. There is even a scholarly article on Carlyle's poetry, of all things. Of course it is American. British Carlyle scholarship was somewhat slower, although today there are notable Carlyle scholars in Britain too.

Doubtless the crowning achievement of the scholarly phase of the Scholarly-Critical Period will be the Duke-Edinburgh edition of the letters of the two Carlyles under the general editorship of C. R. Sanders. The project, which has already borne its first fruits in the first four volumes of Carlyle's letters (1971), is almost certain to stand as the greatest single monument to Carlyle produced by the Scholarly period, unless, wonder of wonders, a really scholarly edition of his works is undertaken in our time. The *Letters* edition is not only a work in the tradition of careful and accurate scholarship which has been the byword of the Scholarly period, it is also testimonial to Carlyle's pervasive Influence; for the publication of so many letters over such a long span of time is posited on the assumption that Carlyle's correspondence (and Jane's as well) not only tells us a great deal about a remarkable man, but that it casts light on the whole Victorian world, that it reveals the ideas and attitudes of an age, through one who both shared and shaped those ideas. I think that the scholarly labours of the past forty years, as well as what survives of the previous hundred years, amply confirm that the assumption on which the *Letters* edition has been undertaken is a very sound one, and the undertaking of the *Letters* edition is proof that the scholarship of the previous forty years has not been in vain.

There remains, then, in the survey of Carlyle's reputation only to say a word about the Critical phase of the Scholarly-Critical period. A critical dimension is, of course, evident in almost all that has been done on Carlyle and cannot be said to be a wholly new interest. But the way in which it has been pursued in recent years does represent a kind of new emphasis. For one thing the critical interest in Carlyle has become much more literary and technical than it used to be. There are in all periods valuable literary analyses, but the attention to nonfictional prose, Carlyle's chief medium after all, as a vehicle deserving the same kind of literary-critical analysis and consideration as, say, poetry or the novel is a growth of quite recent date. In Carlyle studies the chief spark for what is now a healthy and growing fire of critical studies was John Holloway's *Victorian Sage* of 1953. Here British criticism gave something to American and subsequent studies of Carlyle the literary artist are certainly indebted, for pioneering the topic if for nothing else, to Holloway's study. I have myself contributed in a modest way to the critical (and I hope also to the scholarly) phase of contemporary Carlyle studies, and I find in Holloway something fresh and exciting in approaches to Carlyle. Such scholar-critics as George Levine or Albert LaValley, show too that they too have been receptive to a more literary and aesthetic approach to Carlyle than has been common in Carlyle studies of earlier periods or even of the early part of the present Scholarly period. And to come very much up to date there are now booklength studies of Carlyle's impact on Dickens and countless other Carlyle studies underway. Most of the current work shares the twin interests of the Scholarly-Critical period—Carlyle as Influence and Carlyle as literary genius. Thus from the modern academy has come a kind of Scholarly-Critical palingenesis to Carlyle studies which can only serve to confirm, as perhaps it has helped to shape, the judgment of Carlyle as pre-eminent among Victorians.

Such a survey as the foregoing serves to confirm that the National Portrait Gallery display that began my reflections is right insofar as it is a judgment of Carlyle's *importance*. After all, any man who can generate more than 1,200 books and articles on his life and work cannot be entirely without interest. But there still remains the second question, the *mode* of Carlyle's appearance in the Gallery, that deserves a brief comment or two. It might seem that the three periods I have outlined do not tell us too much one way or the other about Carlyle as a Prophet, but

44

in fact I think they tell us a great deal, even, as we shall see, the Scholarly-Critical with its striving toward objectivity and merely establishing the facts.

The things that the three periods tells us are suggested by the secondary terms that I applied to each phase. These are: Teacher, Denouncer, Influence. I think it would be hard to find three terms more essential in delineating what a prophet is. I know that in vulgar use the word *prophet* is often synonymous with fortune-teller or predictor, and of course that *is* an aspect of prophetism. Recently I came across (in *The Times*!) the rather awkward word *futurologist*, which appears to be a man who specializes in extrapolating what life will be like 25 or 50 or 100 years hence based largely on statistical circumstances today. Well, perhaps a prophet is a kind of futurologist. But not, I think, quite the same kind as is domesticated in the Rand Corporation. A prophet may see into the future sometimes because he has seen so well into the past. A prophet is thus not merely someone who can predict the growth rate of the steel industry, but some-one who can predict the growth rate of human industry, if I may Carlylize for a moment. Nor may a prophet be content merely to pass on his statistics to the next office, for his statistics are always alarming and must be communicated to the world at large for its own benefit. The world must be instructed, it must be taught. The Victorians were very much on the right track in seeing Carlyle as a teacher, for that is what a prophet by the nature of the case must be.

But a prophet must be more than a teacher. It is not just a case of passing on the received word, which, I might add, comes to the prophet in a variety of ways, not the least important of which is the ancient wisdom which has fallen into desuetude. No, a prophet must do more than say what is right; or perhaps the way to put it is that a prophet often says what is right by pointing out what is wrong. Denunciation is as essential to prophetism as teaching. We might even venture a definition of prophetism as "teaching by denunciation". Now Carlyle was a great denouncer, one of the best we have ever had. It is not surprising that his denunciations got under the skin: they were so often right and so often tellingly put: they were *supposed* to get under the skin. But it is not surprising either that there was retaliation. The later years of Carlyle's life, as one reads the biographies, seem to be a series of encounters by Carlyle with impertinent visitors to the Chelsea House. And the encounters always seem to be occasions of irritation. The inevitable Americans, following Emerson, come and get their come-uppance. It must have been terribly exasperating. Something of the same feeling must have gnawed at many readers who never had the opportunity, or misfortune, to meet Carlyle in person. And when a man has spent fifty or sixty years infuriating people, it is no wonder they grow weary, however right many of his pronouncements may be. I am not suggesting, as has often been done, that Carlyle would be better off if he had died twenty or thirty years before. I am one of that small company that enjoy even the later Carlyle, even *Latter-Day Pamphlets* and even the insulting and testy old man who frightened off American pilgrims with roars of scorn. Not that I should have enjoyed receiving any of it personally and not that I personally agree with Carlyle's every utterance, but it is all a kind of sport that one can admire at spectator distance—bear or bull-baiting in which the bear or bull always wins.

Still, all this has its perils. And one of them is in sowing discontent and in provoking people to ideas of vengeance. I mean this now not only in a personal way but even from readers. And since Carlyle was, like all of us, only human, even if a prophet, he had the same clay feet that Froude had, or that Froude's elder brother had been shown to have as early as the eighteen-thirties. Besides, what better way to avoid the implications of a prophet's denunciations than to denounce the prophet himself? Hence the dominant tone of the second period of Carlyle studies. But it serves to remind us that Carlyle was not, could not be—no prophet can—a gentle teacher, sweetly leading his lamblike disciples down the flower-strewn path to the temple of Lady Wisdom. Carlyle was not cut out to be a John Keble or even a John Henry Newman, who could insinuate his criticisms with that subtlety that is at once his glory and the cause of most of his troubles. I hesitate to speculate on such matters, but perhaps if we were more aware of the genuine fire that was in Keble, we would have been less likely to relegate him to such quasi-oblivion as he now endures; and perhaps Newman survives so undefiled as he does because even his sweetest utterances have a sinewy

46

toughness that doesn't let go. Carlyle in any case had plenty of fire and toughness. Maybe too much. But that too is essential to prophetism. If the prophet singes the consciences, he has done a good part of his work. So the Denunciatory phase of Carlyle criticism is a phase that had to come and that should continue to serve as a reminder of just how much of a prophet Carlyle was. Nobody ever called Jeremiah soft.

As for Influence, it too is essential, unless one is going to remain a closet-prophet. A prophet worthy of the name must somehow affect people; he must strike that chord. And Carlyle did. He changed England in ways more profound than the railway. That story has still not been fully told. Perhaps it will be by future Carlyle studies. Robert Sencourt in his memoir of T. S. Eliot offers the kind of suggestion that scholars in the modern period have been exploring and will surely explore more extensively in the future. He writes:

> While still an undergraduate at Harvard, Tom Eliot had read *The Symbolist Movement in Literature*, by Arthur Symons, and found a gate opening into a new world. Symons began by taking up the conclusion of *Sartor Resartus* that the path to the supernatural ran along the external world. "It is in and through *Symbols*", Carlyle had written, "that man, consciously or unconsciously, lives, works and has his being." A symbol is a representation, but does not aim to be a reproduction: it denotes an idea or form; the seen points to the unseen. "In a Symbol," said Carlyle (or rather, his spokesman Teufelsdröckh), "there is concealment and yet revelation: hence therefore, by Silence and by Speech acting together, comes a double significance . . . In the Symbol proper, what we can call a Symbol, there is ever, more or less distinctly and directly, some embodiment and revelation of the Infinite."
>
> In the mid-nineteenth century this metaphysical vision had swept consciously into French literature, at first through Baudelaire and later through the poets Verlaine and Mallarmé. Now, in the elegant precision of Arthur Symons' book, Eliot became familiar with Rimbaud, Verlaine, Mallarmé, Maeterlinck and Huysmans.[14]

T. S. Eliot as a Carlyle epigone? Carlyle as a precursor of the Symbolist Movement? These are not fantastic notions at that. For the time is ripe, or soon will be, for another period in Carlyle studies that will correspond to the last stages of his own career. It is certainly true that few who have taken up the cross of Carlyle scholarship in modern times have been hostile to the man who taught Britain how to see herself in the modern world. But few also have yet been ready to take on and defend Carlyle steadily and whole to a new age that has not known him. These will be those who usher in a fourth stage.

Yet Carlyle is sometimes painted as a lonely and disillusioned old man who never suceeded in saving England. Well, it is of the nature of a prophet not to succeed too much; otherwise we should all be saved and the Jews would never have known the destruction of the Temple or the Babylonian captivity. Total success would deliver us not merely from present danger but from future peril as well. Not even Carlyle can do that. For the Oxford English Dictionary tells us that prophet comes from the Greek for "speaking forth". It defines prophet as:

> One who speaks for God . . . as the inspired revealer of his will; one who is held or (more loosely) claims to have this function; an inspired or quasi-inspired teacher.

It does not say a prophet must be successful, only that he be inspired with the will of God and speak it forth. Of course Carlyle says it better when he defines for us the special role of a prophet and offers proleptically, or prophetically, the justification for the mode of his own presentation in the National Portrait Gallery and for the attitude that modern criticism is again coming to hold towards him:

> Poet and Prophet differ greatly in our loose modern notions of them. In some old languages, again, the titles are synonymous; *Vates* means both Prophet and Poet; and indeed at all times, Prophet and Poet, well understood, have much kindred of meaning. Fundamentally indeed they are still the same; . . . .
>
> . . . the *Vates*, whether Prophet or Poet, . . . is a man sent hither to make [the divine mystery] more impressively known to us. That always is his message; he is to reveal that to us,—that sacred mystery which he more than others lives ever present with. While others forget it, he knows it;—I might say, he has been driven to know it; without consent asked of *him*, he finds himself living in it, bound to live in it. Once more, here is no Hearsay, but a direct Insight and Belief; this man too could not help being a sincere

48

man. . . . He is a *Vates*, first of all, in virtue of being sincere. So far Poet and Prophet, participators in the 'open secret,' are one.

With respect to their distinction again. The *Vates* Prophet, we might say, has seized that sacred mystery rather on the moral side, as Good and Evil, Duty and Prohibition; the *Vates* Poet on what the Germans call the aesthetic side, as Beautiful, and the like. The one we may call a revealer of what we are to do, the other of what we are to love. But indeed these two provinces run into one another, and cannot be disjoined. The Prophet too has his eye on what we are to love: how else shall he know what it is we are to do? (*On Heroes and Hero-Worship*, Lect. 3)

And in this way Carlyle delineates for us his own role and anticipates the modes in which subsequent criticism will approach him. Vates-Prophet, certainly; but with much of the Vates-Poet about him as well, as has become increasingly clear in our own time. Thus the matter of Carlyle Today leads inevitably to the matter of Carlyle Tomorrow. That is when I hope we will move to a new stage in our understanding of Carlyle and see that the prophet and the poet are one.

## NOTES

1. At any given time the National Portrait Gallery displays only a third of the more than 5,000 portraits in its collection.
2. The record of this event, including a photograph of the damaged portrait, is in the files of the National Portrait Gallery. The attack was presumably unaffected by the fact that TC himself had been a trustee of the Gallery, 1875–68; see also pp. 225–6.
3. The most notable reputation studies are: H. L. Stewart, "Carlyle and His Critics", *Nineteenth Century*, 86 (1919), 505–14, and his "Declining Fame of TC", *Transactions of the Royal Society of Canada*, Series 3, 14 (1920), 11–29; Frank Luther Mott, "Carlyle's American Public", *PQ*, 4 (1925), 245–64; Alan Carey Taylor, *Carlyle: sa première fortune littéraire en France (1825–1865)* (Paris, 1929), and his *Carlyle et la pensée latine* (Paris, 1937); Howard D. Widger, " TC in America: His Reputation and Influence", unpublished dissertation, Univ. of Illinois, 1945; and *TC, The Critical Heritage*, ed. Jules P. Seigel (London, 1971). See also "Carlyle's Reputation", in my chapter on Carlyle in *Victorian Prose, A Guide to Research*, ed. David J. DeLaura (New York, 1973).
4. The encounter in question was for the chapter in *Victorian Prose*. I

examined more than 1,200 separate items. This did not include all of the treatments of Carlyle in his own lifetime, though it included a good many of them, nor did it include all dissertations on Carlyle, though it included a large number of them also. As it happens, Carlyle is the single most frequent topic of doctoral dissertations in the field of Victorian literature, in part because of the considerable number of German dissertations on him. (See R. D. Altick and W. R. Matthews, *Guide to Doctoral Dissertations in Victorian Literature 1886–1958* [Urbana: Univ. of Illinois Press, 1960]).

The purpose of my examination was not to consider Carlyle's reputation *per se*, but to evaluate the existing body of scholarship and criticism on Carlyle. However, it is largely on the basis of the examination of this material that it has been possible to generalize in this paper about Carlyle's reputation.

5. John Sterling, letter to TC, 29 May 1835, quoted in Carlyle's *Life of John Sterling* (1851), and Harrold, *Sartor*, pp. 307–16.

6. *London and Westminster Review*, 27 (1838), 17.

7. *London and Westminster Review*, 33 (1839), 1–68.

8. "Emerson", *Discourses in America* in *The Works of Matthew Arnold*, 15 vols. (London, 1903), IV, 351.

9. *The Letters of Anthony Trollope*, ed. Bradford A. Booth (London, 1951), p. 15.

10. Arthur Penrhyn Stanley, funeral sermon on TC (1881) in *Sermons on Special Occasions*, reprinted in *TC, The Critical Heritage*, p. 516.

11. A. Carlyle and James Crichton-Browne, *The Nemesis of Froude* (London, 1903).

12. This unfortunate statement appears in that otherwise entertaining study by John Gross, *The Rise and Fall of the Man of Letters* (London, 1969), p. 30.

13. For a discussion of most of the post-Dyer works up to 1965, see Carlisle Moore, "TC" in *The English Romantic Poets and Essayists*, ed. C. W. and L. H. Houtchens (rev. ed.; New York, 1966), pp. 333–78, and up to 1971 the Carlyle chapter in *Victorian Prose*, ed. D. J. DeLaura, and the annual survey of scholarship in the autumn number of *Victorian Poetry*. See also R. L. Tarr (assisted R. E. Dana), *A Bibliography of English Language Articles on TC: 1900–1965*, Univ. of S. Carolina, Dept. of English, Bibliographical Series, 7 (1972).

14. Robert Sencourt, *T. S. Eliot, A Memoir* (New York, 1971), pp. 27–8.

# 2

# Carlyle on *Sartor Resartus*

## by JOHN CLUBBE

Several of Carlyle's major statements on his most enduring work, *Sartor Resartus*, have lately come to light. Until recently they have either remained unpublished or are known chiefly through the inaccurate transcriptions given in the first volume of Froude's biography. Froude refers to these and other statements by Carlyle on his life and works only as "a series of brief notes upon his early life".[1] At one point he cites "a German biography in which he was said to have learnt Hebrew" (I, 17), but otherwise he fails to indicate his source. The "German biography" is Friedrich Althaus's *Thomas Carlyle: Eine biographisch-literarische Charakteristik*. It appeared in the German periodical *Unsere Zeit* in July 1866,[2] and, in English translation, in 1974.[3] Althaus's work came upon the scene shortly after Carlyle had enjoyed one of his greatest triumphs delivering his inaugural address on 2 April as Rector of the University of Edinburgh. Three weeks after the address, Jane Welsh Carlyle, his wife for nearly forty years, died, and he plunged into a profound gloom and remorse that ended only with his life in 1881.

Sometime in July 1866 Carlyle received, probably from the author himself, Althaus's biography. Recognizing its importance, he thought "of having the poor Piece *interleaved* . . . and of perhaps correcting one or two blunders here & there" (*TR*, p. 23). Beginning on 29 August and continuing through the first ten days of September, he wrote his comments—some a few words, others the length of several paragraphs—on the inserted sheets or in the margins. Despite his referring to Althaus's work as a "poor Piece", he viewed it with unusual regard: "this," he said, "on the whole,

51

is considerably the best Sketch I have yet seen on the subject" (*ibid.*). No greater praise could come from one who had long advocated firm and demanding standards for the art of literary biography and who had despaired that anyone would "ever know my poor 'Biography' " (*ibid.*). That he fully intended his notes to Althaus to be used by subsequent biographers his preface makes clear. "The *fewer* errors they set afloat . . . on this subject, the better it will be" (*ibid.*), he writes there, and concludes in the afterword: "Here and there a bit of certainty may have its advantages" (p. 122). Some of the notes served as trial runs for incidents more fully narrated in the other reminiscences, in particular "Edward Irving", which he began soon after he completed the Althaus. Stimulated by the biography to look inward, he wrote the notes as a first thinking-through of much that he found painful to recall.

Carlyle's notes to Althaus range from the extensive and highly significant comments on *Sartor Resartus* to various autobiographical reminiscences: of his schooling and university career, of his plans for the ministry, of Professor John Leslie and of his relationship with Edward Irving, of the gradual working out at Hoddam Hill in 1825–1826 of his 1822 conversion, of his possible emigration to America in the 1830's, and of his father and mother and brother Alexander. He leaves valuable statements on the extent of his acquaintance with classical literatures and on his first knowledge of German, on other works beside *Sartor* (especially the *Life of Schiller, German Romance,* and *Frederick the Great*), on his intellectual debts to Goethe and to Jean Paul, on the development of his singular literary style, and on the "might is right" maxim popularly attributed to him. His clarifying comments on a host of other points, biographical and critical, will require significant modifications in subsequent accounts of his achievement. Althaus's biography, which owes much to statements obtained from Carlyle himself by their mutual friend Joseph Neuberg, has in itself new and authentic information. Althaus gave Neuberg questions to pose to Carlyle; and Neuberg, in turn, transmitted the answers to Althaus, "the greater part in Carlyle's very words".[4]

In the 1870's, along with Carlyle's other personal papers, the interleaved copy of Althaus's biography came into the hands of

Froude, whom Carlyle had entrusted with the task of writing his life. Froude made selective use of Carlyle's notes, published a few of them inaccurately and incompletely, and based statements in his narrative on others. Upon completion in 1884 of his four-volume biography, he returned Carlyle's papers to Mary Aitken Carlyle, Carlyle's niece. A family friend, Charles Eliot Norton used the notes to Althaus sparingly in preparing his edition of the Goethe-Carlyle correspondence,[5] and twenty years later Mary's husband, Alexander Carlyle, used them to support his thesis that much in *Sartor* was autobiographical.[6] The interleaved Althaus remained in his possession until his death in 1931. On 14 June 1932 the manuscript was sold as part of lot 203 at the great Sotheby sale of Carlyle's books, letters and manuscripts. It brought £23, a fraction of what it would bring today. Lot 203 also included a typed translation of Althaus's biography, two typed copies of Carlyle's notes, two letters from Althaus to Carlyle, and other biographical material by Carlyle or relating to him. In April 1934 the National Library of Scotland purchased the interleaved Althaus from Messrs Maggs, along with a typed copy by Alexander Carlyle of most of Carlyle's notes. The Library did not purchase the other items in lot 203, and I am unaware of their present whereabouts. The interleaved Althaus and Alexander Carlyle's typed copy are now catalogued as MS 1799 and MS 1800.

No other biographer or critic of Carlyle besides Froude, Norton, and Alexander Carlyle has, to my knowledge, made use of Carlyle's comments in the interleaved Althaus. Even David Alec Wilson, a close friend of Alexander Carlyle, did not have access to the Althaus manuscript in preparing his monumental six-volume biography of Carlyle (1923–1934).[7] Yet Carlyle himself intended the notes to complement his more extended biographical recollections in the other reminiscences. Not only, then, do they constitute a document of major significance in understanding Carlyle's life, but they also provide one of the few instances in literary biography in which the subject of the biography had the opportunity to comment extensively on his biographer's account. And when that person is Carlyle, whose writings on the art of literary biography have been influential and controversial and who denied that a true biography of himself could be written, the comments should prove of interest to the historian of literary biography.

The Althaus biography remains the closest we have—with the conjectural exception of Froude—to an authorized or approved biography. That Carlyle included a preface and an afterword to it indicates that he judged it in some degree valid as an interpretation of his life. Although he felt that Althaus had done a creditable job, there remained a great deal he did not know and could hardly be expected to know. Perhaps it was while writing the commentary to Althaus that Carlyle realized it had to be supplemented still more. It is even possible, though unlikely, that he might not have written his other autobiographical writings if the Althaus biography had not crossed his path when it did. In any event, Carlyle came to realize the necessity of clarifying many points about his life and his works that would be obscure to the inevitable biographers of the future. No other explanation begins to account for his protracted labours in the years following his wife's death when he wrote the reminiscences and edited her correspondence. Only through this work could he put his own life into perspective and attempt to come to terms with it. The concern that his biography be accurate explains his careful correction of dates and statements in Althaus's account; the concern that it be true explains his clarifying and interpretative comments. His desire both for accuracy and for truth is nowhere more evident than in the pains he took in preparing his observations on *Sartor*.

Since Carlyle had little to say about *Sartor* in the other reminiscences, unquestionably he meant his comments in Althaus to constitute his major statement. Despite his later professed depreciation of *Sartor*, he may have unconsciously divined that it was to be his most enduring work. While he explains in several letters what he is attempting to do in *Sartor*, only in the interleaved Althaus does he discuss its autobiographical significance. In a long appendix to the *Love Letters*, Alexander Carlyle affirmed *Sartor*'s value "as an autobiography of Carlyle in his early years" (II, 361) and on several occasions quoted in support of his views Carlyle's notes to Althaus. Critics since then have often ignored or denied the autobiographical elements in *Sartor*. Yet it is not necessary that *Sartor* be interpreted as literal autobiography for us to realize that Alexander Carlyle hardly exaggerates when he contends that chapters 5 through 9 of Book II are "founded on incidents and experiences in Carlyle's own history" and are "in fact

54

a sort of autobiography for the period mentioned, delineated poetically, spiritually and figuratively, yet true to life as regards the chief incidents and events, and not far from the truth even in the details" (II, 366). Indeed, his contention derives its chief support from Carlyle's own carefully considered observations. Their publication here, set within the context of the Althaus biography, should help to clarify the extent to which *Sartor* is autobiography.

Eight separate comments by Carlyle have to do with *Sartor*. They are printed below as Carlyle wrote them, except that his abbreviations (written in the crabbed shorthand of his later years) have been expanded. The method of presentation is ordinarily as follows: (*a*) a brief summary of the context in Althaus in which Carlyle's note appears; (*b*) the note itself; (*c*) indication of publication in Froude and, if published there, the importance of any major differences from his text; and (*d*) briefly, the note's significance for the interpretation of *Sartor*.[8]

1. Althaus quotes two paragraphs depicting the idyllic youth enjoyed by Diogenes Teufelsdröckh (*Sartor*, pp. 97–98). Carlyle comments: "*Sartor* is quite unsafe for details! Fiction *founded* perhaps on fact—a long way off" (*TR*, p. 28). Froude refers to, but does not quote, this comment (I, 15 and 26).

2. Althaus quotes or paraphrases several short passages describing Teufelsdröckh's early schooling (*Sartor*, pp. 104–105) and concludes: "Who does not already recognize in these traits the prototype of the sensitive soul, the stern, dissatisfied, idealistic, resigned 'weeping philosopher' of later years? Even if his discontented spirit sought refuge from the routine of school existence in tasks that he picked out for himself in the workshops of the real world, still the solid learning acquired in his school years did not serve him badly." Carlyle comments:

*Sartor* here, in good part; not to be trusted in details! "Greek", for example, consisted of the *Alphabet* mainly; "Hebrew" is quite a *German* entity,—nobody in that region, except my reverend old Mr Johnstone, could have read one sentence of it to save his life. I did get to read Latin & French with fluency (Latin *quantity* was left a frightful chaos, and I had to learn it afterwards); some geometry, algebra (*arithmetic* thoroughly well), vague outlines of geography &c I did learn;—all the Books I could get were also devoured; but my "Hang" [*the "bent toward abstract reflection"* *mentioned below by Althaus*] there is a myth. Mythically *true* is what Sartor says of his Schoolfellows, and not half of the truth. Unspeakable is the damage & defilement I got out of those coarse unguided tyrannous cubs,— especially till I revolted against them, and gave stroke for stroke; as my pious Mother, in her great love of peace and of my best interests, spiritual chiefly, had imprudently forbidden me to do. One way and another I had never been so wretched as here in that School, and the first 2 years of my time in it still count among the miserable of my life. "Academies", "High Schools", "Instructors of Youth"—Oh ye unspeakable!—(*TR*, pp. 31–32).

Althaus goes on to write that Carlyle's "memory was as retentive as his diligence and ability to learn were great" and that "he had in equal measure the gift of being able to cope with a mass of details and the bent toward abstract reflection". Froude publishes the passage inaccurately and with omissions (I, 17–18) and Alexander Carlyle a part of it accurately (*Love Letters*, II, 365). Froude's chief omission—leaving out at the beginning after "*Sartor*" the words "here, in good part"—alters the emphasis to imply that *Sartor* is nowhere "to be trusted in details", when clearly Carlyle intends to affirm that he based many details not only in the account of Teufelsdröckh's education but elsewhere on actual experiences. The second omission—"but my 'Hang' [*the "bent toward abstract reflection"*] there is a myth"— strongly suggests that the young Carlyle was more firmly rooted in the everyday world than Althaus (and later biographers) realized.

3. Althaus describes the grimness of Carlyle's life between the period of his abandoning schoolteaching in Kirkcaldy in November 1818, and of his agreeing to tutor Charles and Arthur Buller in January 1822. Carlyle, in a long passage containing three references to *Sartor*, indicates that in these years he "was entirely unknown in 'Edinburgh circles'; solitary, 'eating my own heart', fast losing my health, too; a prey, in fact, to nameless struggles and miseries, which have yet a kind of horror in them to my thought. Three weeks without *any* Sleep (from *im*possibility to be free of noise), &c &c." Further, he continues:

I had spent the winters [*of 1818–1822*] in Edinburgh, 'looking out for employment' on those dismal terms; the summers (had it only been for cheapness' sake) at my Father's. Nothing in *"Sartor"* thereabouts is *fact* (symbolical *myth* all) except that of the *"incident* in the Rue St Thomas de l'Enfer",—which occurred quite literally to myself in Lieth [*Leith*] Walk, during those 3 weeks of total sleeplessness, in which almost my one solace was that of a daily bathe on the sands between Lieth and Portobello. Incident was as I went *down* (coming *up* I generally felt a little refreshed for the hour); I remember it well, & could go yet to about the place.— (*TR*, pp. 48–9).

This passage is published inaccurately by Froude (I, 101), with two words—"thereabouts" after " '*Sartor*' " and "those" before "3 weeks"—omitted, and accurately by Alexander Carlyle (*Love Letters*, II, 380). Carlyle's note refers to the climactic moment of Teufelsdröckh's despair in "The Everlasting No" (*Sartor*, pp. 166–168), and Froude's omission of "thereabouts" significantly alters the sense of the passage. "It does not follow", Alexander Carlyle observes perceptively, "that because the work is mythical 'here' or 'thereabouts' (i.e. in one or two specified passages) it is mythical throughout."[9] He convincingly places Carlyle's conversion, set by Froude in June 1821, in July or early August 1821 or, more likely, 1822. The latter date is generally accepted today. That the conversion was not as abrupt as implied in *Sartor* and that his recovery extended over many years is the contention of two important articles by Carlisle Moore.[10] Several of Carlyle's notes to Althaus not given here corroborate that the recovery was not sudden, but imply that the idyllic year at Hoddam Hill in 1825–1826 marked the termination of the recuperative process.

4. In the long passage covering the years 1818–1822 Carlyle writes:

Try Scots Law [*1819–1820*]; write (pitifully enough) 'Articles' (as said was) for Brewster's *Encyclopedia* [*Feb. 1820–Jan. 1823*]; fight with the dismallest Lernean Hydra of problems, spiritual, temporal, eternal;—"eat my own heart"; but authentically take the Devil by the nose withal (see 'incident in Rue St Thomas'), and fling *him* behind me, 1820, '21, '22; till *Legendre* [*Dec. 1821; April–July 1822*] &c with *rather* improving prospect of wages; and finally on Irving's call to London, Charles Buller arrives, summer of 1823 [*Jan. 1822*], and pressure ["tightness" *crossed out*] of finance as good as disappears for the time. (*TR*, pp. 50–51).

This note again refers to Teufelsdröckh's conversion (*Sartor*, pp. 166–168). Though Froude alludes to the passage (I, 64, 78), he does not publish it, nor, to my knowledge, is it published elsewhere.

5. The third excerpt from Carlyle's long comment follows:

> In Edinburgh from my fellow creatures little or nothing but *vinegar* was my reception—cup [*i.e., a slight bow*] when we happened to meet or pass near each other;—my own blame mainly, so proud, shy, poor, at once so insignificant-looking and so grim and sorrowful. That in *Sartor*, of the '*worm* trodden & proving a *torpedo,* and sending you ceiling-high to be borne home on shutters' is not wholly a fable; but did actually befal once or twice, as I still (with a kind of small not ungenial malice) can remember. (*TR*, pp. 51–52).

Froude publishes this passage inaccurately (I, 57), omitting "—cup" and the clause "and sending you . . . on shutters". Carlyle's language in 1866 echoes the passage referred to in *Sartor Resartus*: "An ironic man, with his sly stillness, and ambuscading ways, more especially an ironic young man, from whom it is least expected, may be viewed as a pest to society. Have we not seen persons of weight and name coming forward, with gentlest indifference, to tread such a one out of sight, as an insignificancy and worm, start ceiling-high (*balkenhoch*), and thence fall shattered and supine, to be borne home on shutters, not without indignation, when he proved electric and a torpedo!" (*Sartor*, p. 129).

6. Carlyle's final three (unpublished) comments on *Sartor* have to do with his efforts to find a publisher for his manuscript and its reception by the public. When Althaus incorrectly states that in 1832 he settled permanently in London, Carlyle comments:

> no; went up [*from Craigenputtoch*] August 1831, with *Sartor* in my pocket, intending to be back in a month; could not get *Sartor* published (Reform-Bill agitation &c &c); . . . returned [*to Craigenputtoch*] (still with *Sartor* in my pocket), March 1832. . . . [*There*] I wrote *Diamond Necklace, Cagliostro,* and various things (*translation* a good part of them, *Mährchen* &c); was publishing *Sartor,* slit in Pieces (but rigorously *unaltered* otherwise) in *Fraser's Magazine* . . . (*TR*, p. 69).

7. Althaus later observes that "further attempts to publish *Sartor Resartus* as a book also proved unsuccessful", opposite which Carlyle notes: "there were none made" (*TR*, p. 74).

8. Althaus goes on to say that *Sartor* was "apparently much revised" in the interval between Carlyle's stay in London and its serial publication in *Fraser's* (Nov.–Dec. 1833; Feb.–April, June–Aug. 1834). Carlyle, denying this, writes:

> Not a letter of it altered; except in the *last* and the *first* page, a word or two! — — Nothing whatever of *"spätere Versuche"* [*further attempts*] either (as already marked): Fraser's Public liked the *Johnson* so much (which I had left with him, written there that winter) that he was willing to accept *Sartor* in the slit condition; had it so (probably on cheaper terms), went on with it obstinately till done,—tho', from his Public, he had a sore time with it: "What wretched unintelligible nonsense!" "Sir, if you publish any more of that d——d [*stuff?*], I shall be obliged to give up my Magazine!" and so forth,—in the whole world (so far as could be learned) only two persons dissentient, 1° a certain man called *Emerson,* in Concord Massachusetts, and 2° a certain Irish Catholic Priest, Father O'Shea of Cork (whom I have seen since, & who yet lives)[11] writing to him, each for himself, "So long as any thing by that man appears in your Magazine, punctually send it me."[12] So that Fraser conceived a certain terror, if also a certain respect, of my writings & me; and knew not what to do,—beyond standing by his bargain, with an effort. (*TR*, pp. 74–75).

Carlyle makes here the important disclosure that he did not alter significantly the manuscript of *Sartor* (completed late in July 1831) between its several rejections by London publishers in the autumn of 1831 and its serial publication in *Fraser's* in 1833–1834. Contrary to general opinion,[13] he did not submit it to Edinburgh publishers after the attempts in London had failed. Elsewhere in the notes to Althaus Carlyle stresses that, in changing nothing in *Sartor* except on the first and last pages, he bent neither to public opinion nor to pressure from the magazine's publisher, James Fraser. That he made no significant alterations in *Sartor* became a point of honour with him. G. B. Tennyson correctly notes, however, that in February 1833 Carlyle emended the name "Teufelsdreck" to the more subtle "Teufelsdröckh".[14]

Carlyle's comments on *Sartor Resartus* given here indicate that even in his old age he looked back with interest upon a literary work of whose ultimate value he was never altogether certain. Still, he wished to leave behind a record that would aid others in understanding this complex book and its relationship to his own life. Taken together, the comments to Althaus provide a valuable statement of his attitude toward the work by which he is most likely to be remembered.

## NOTES

1. Froude, *Life*, I, 16. Carlyle's notes on *Sartor* should be read in conjunction with two other important statements on the work: (1) in a letter to his publisher William Fraser of 27 May 1833, in *Letters of TC 1826–36*, ed. C. E. Norton (London, 1889), pp. 364–7; and (2) in a letter to John Sterling of 4 June 1835 in *Letters of TC to John Stuart Mill, John Sterling and Robert Browning*, ed. A. Carlyle (London, 1923), pp. 191–4.

2. (Leipzig), II, 1–41. Reprinted with minor revisions in Althaus's *Englische Charakterbilder* (Berlin, Verlag der Königlichen Geheimen Ober-Hofbuchdruckerei [R. v Decker], 1869), I, 237–322.

3. As part of *Two Reminiscences of TC*, ed. John Clubbe (Durham, N.C., 1974). I have thought it useful to bring together in this essay Carlyle's various pronouncements on *Sartor* scattered through the Althaus biography, in that they constitute, in effect, his only sustained commentary on *Sartor*. Further references to my edition (abbreviated *TR*) will be inserted parenthetically within the body of the essay.

4. Althaus, "Erinnerungen an Thomas Carlyle", *Unsere Zeit*, I [n.s.] (June 1881), 826. My translation.

5. *Correspondence between Goethe and Carlyle*, ed. C. E. Norton (London, 1887), pp. ix–x, 156.

6. *The Love Letters of TC and Jane Welsh*, ed. A. Carlyle (London, 1909), II, Appendix B, 365–81 *passim*.

7. See his *Carlyle*, IV, 124, 194.

8. I have placed editorial comments and conjectures within brackets in the text.

9. NLS, MS, 1800. Cf. *Love Letters*, II, 365–6.

10. "*Sartor Resartus* and the Problem of Carlyle's 'Conversion' ", *PMLA*, 70 (1955), 662–81, and "The Persistence of Carlyle's 'Everlasting Yea' ", *MP*, 54 (1957), 187–96.

11. Carlyle eventually met Father O'Shea in Cork and described his encounter in *Reminiscences of My Irish Journey in 1849* (London, 1882).

12. Cf. *The Correspondence of Emerson and Carlyle*, ed. Joseph Slater (New York and London, 1964), pp. 16, 98, 103.

13. E.g., Harrold, *Sartor*, p. xxvi, based on Wilson, *Carlyle*, II, 322.

14. *Sartor Called Resartus* (Princeton, 1965), p. 152.

# 3

# Carlyle, Mathematics and "Mathesis"

by CARLISLE MOORE

> On Poetry and geometric Truth,
> The knowledge that endures, upon these two,
> And their high privilege of lasting life,
> Exempt from all internal injury,
> He mused. . . .
>
> Wordsworth, *The Prelude*, V, 56–60

> When *will* there arise a man who shall do for the science of mind
> —what Newton did for that of matter—establish its fundamental
> laws on the firm basis of induction . . . a foolish question—for
> its answer is—never.
>
> Carlyle, *Collected Letters*, I, 84

Biographers of Thomas Carlyle who have noted his early interest in mathematics when he was a student and struggling writer in Edinburgh have accepted his own statement that the subject ceased to interest him about 1820 or 1821.[1] When at about the same time he discovered Goethe and the German philosophers, and began to make his way towards the Clothes Philosophy, it seemed clear that mathematics faded quickly from his thoughts leaving hardly a trace. It was indeed a transfer of allegiance, as if he had written "Close thy Newton, open thy Goethe". By 1831, in *Sartor Resartus*, he was soaring on such poetic and near-mystical heights that one might well grow sceptical of his earlier "mathematical prowess" and doubtful of its importance in his mature thought. More than most men of letters Carlyle appeared to be unlogical and un-

61

scientific. His manner of reasoning and arguing alienated many scientists of his day and prompted Darwin to remark of him, "I never met a man with a mind so ill adapted for scientific research",[2] and Herbert Spencer to call him a sloppy thinker, of little or no consequence in the history of English thought.[3] Darwin's judgement, if not Spencer's, seems true enough. Carlyle on the *Beagle* or in a Cambridge laboratory is hard to imagine without amusement. But research is one thing and comprehension is another. A fair rejoinder to Darwin may be found in the testimony of John Tyndall: "I do not know what Carlyle's aptitudes in the natural history sciences might have been," he wrote, "but in . . . physical subjects I never encountered a mind of stronger grasp and deeper penetration than his. . . . During my expositions, when they were clear, he was always in advance of me, anticipating and enunciating what I was about to say."[4] Lyell too respected him, and even Herbert Spencer felt his influence.[5] The Cambridge mathematician Augustus De Morgan praised his early mathematical work, particularly an original essay Carlyle wrote on Proportion, which was "as good a substitute for the fifth book of Euclid as could be given in the space", and showed that Carlyle "would have been a distinguished teacher and thinker in first principles".[6]

Such views are speculative at best. Carlyle did not become a mathematician or scientist. His struggles to find a career and his impulse to preach led him into the "other culture". During his early Edinburgh days, however, this course was hardly visible to him, anyway not practicable, and he spent a considerable part of his time and energies from 1809 to 1822 in learning, teaching, or writing mathematics. It has been suggested that under only slightly different circumstances he might have made it his career.[7] That he did not is perhaps most simply explained by his admiration for Goethe and by Jane's urging him to write a novel; but there are deeper causes, and it is just as obvious that he had literary ambitions from a very early age. His surprising talent in mathematics, his prolonged serious interest in it, and his eventual shift to literature, invite closer examination. It is proposed here to trace the course of that serious interest, through his reaction against mathematics, to his postulation of an ideal science as he groped towards a formulation of the Clothes Philosophy.[8]

The talent cannot really be explained; it was no doubt part of the intelligence he was born with. As for the serious interest, Carlyle himself attributed it, but only partly, to the inspiration and encouragement of his distinguished mathematics teacher at Edinburgh, Professor John Leslie, whose genius "awoke a certain enthusiasm in me". Froude laid it to Carlyle's temperament being "impatient of uncertainties" so that he "threw himself with delight into a form of knowledge in which the conclusions were indisputable".[9] For another dozen years, however, he was not only able to tolerate but even espouse uncertainties, if these could be balanced against one another. Only in the middle 1830's did impatience begin to harden his opinions, and even then uncertainties remained to humble him.[10]

"For several years," wrote Carlyle, "geometry shone before me as the noblest of all sciences, and I prosecuted it in all my best hours and moods."[11] Two conditions account for this. One was his cultural inheritance. In early nineteenth century England Isaac Newton was revered as the founder of new Truth—a Truth which was needed to strengthen the weakening faiths of orthodox religion. He was the genius who had geometrized space, who had brought mathematics into the arena of intellectual discourse, and had "explained" the phenomena of the heavens and the earth by a single mathematical law. His discoveries were taken as having re-established the idea of design and were regarded as counters to eighteenth century scepticism, for they were implicitly neither anti-Christian nor anti-Trinitarian, but brought mathematics, physics and astronomy together in a triumphant demonstration of cosmic order which pointed to God as creator of all things: "God said, Let Newton be! and all was light". At Cambridge, Wordsworth saw from his window the Roubiliac statue of Newton "with his prism and silent Face" which he would later describe as "the marble index of a mind for ever / Voyaging through strange seas of Thought alone."[12] And Carlyle, reading the *Principia* in 1817, observed that with Newton science enabled man to see past, present and future in a single view, to predict the future, and to ascertain permanent truths: "Assuredly the human species never performed a more honourable achievement" (*CL*, I, 103). In this he was only reflecting the general opinion.

Back of Newton was Euclid with his *Geometry*, even more than Newton the symbol of imperishable truth. Although a non-

Euclidean Geometry was then evolving in the work of such continental mathematicians as Gauss, Bolyai, and Lobachevski, it was
hardly known in England where geometry remained basically and
ultimately Euclidean, resting firmly on demonstrable proof
derived from self-evident assumptions.[13] Euclid was still alone in
looking on beauty bare. The Book of his *Elements* stood like a
rock against the flux of changing forms and ideas. To Wordsworth
it was the "Stone of abstract Geometry" which, as Auden puts
it, offered one of the two routes of salvation from the anxiety
of the dreamer—the other being the "Shell" of imagination and
instinct—and which represented "the transcendental stable reality
desired as a haven for the storm-tossed mariner".[14] For Carlyle
too the appeal of geometry lay in its clarity and precision, its
sure road to truth: "Where shall we find her in her native purity,"
he wrote his friend Robert Mitchell, "if not in the science of
quantity and number" (*CL*, I, 120, 16 Feb. 1818). There is a
special significance in his having been educated at Edinburgh
where mathematical thought was still dominated by synthetic
geometry at the expense of the analytic algebra which flourished
on the continent. While the Bernoullis, Euler, Laplace, and Lagrange were employing the more modern methods of algebraic
analysis, Scottish mathematicians like John Playfair and John
Leslie, though they were not unfamiliar with these methods and
on occasion admitted their superiority over the ancient geometry,
continued to teach geometry "to the almost total exclusion of
modern analysis".[15] Despite Newton's pioneer contributions,
British and Scottish mathematical thought and practice fell
behind. Scotland had particularly strong reasons for maintaining
this attitude. One of these was epistemological. Philosophers of
the Common Sense School like Thomas Reid and Dugald Stewart,
reacting against the earlier, Platonic conception of mathematics
as not needing empirical verification (an attitude shared by James
Beattie and John Playfair), insisted that mathematics must not
lose sight of its basis in sensory data.[16] The danger of analytic
algebra was that it threatened to lead mathematics away
from the very basis upon which its claims to authoritative truth
rested.

For this reason Leslie, who shared most of the views of the
Common Sense School, objected to the use of "imaginary" or

"impossible" numbers like the square root of minus one, since they could not be related to external objects. He also deplored the algebraists' concepts of "quantities less than nothing", or negative numbers, as well as complex numbers. The scope of mathematical inquiry had to be deliberately limited in order to protect its epistemological claim to truth.[17] This claim was important also to the Scottish moral philosophers; both James Beattie, and Dugald Stewart who gave the compulsory two- or three-year sequence of courses in Moral Philosophy at Edinburgh, brought mathematics to bear against Hume's attack on the bases of human morality. Nearly every University student learned in his moral philosophy class that the surest means of obtaining certain knowledge was to be found in the study of the foundations and principles of mathematics.[18] Both moral and intellectual training resulted from the process of mastering the axioms, theorems, and corollaries of Euclid and of solving original geometrical problems. Such training was seen as a prerequisite for all other studies, and for this purpose geometry was regarded as superior to analytic algebra. For John Robison, algebra with its symbolic methods was "little better than a *mechanical knack*, in which we proceed without ideas of any kind, and obtain a result without meaning and *without being conscious of any process of reasoning . . .*".[19] Geometrical methods might be slower but they exercised and disciplined the mind as algebra did not. Dugald Stewart recommended "the study of Greek geometry to strengthen the power of steady and concatenated thinking", and Leslie, also recommending "the geometry of the ancients", wrote in his *Elements of Geometry* (1809) that "While it traces the beautiful relations of figure and quantity, it likewise accustoms the mind to the invaluable exercise of patient attention and accurate reasoning. Of these distinct objects, the last is perhaps the most important in a course of liberal education." For Leslie, therefore, geometry belonged to the general culture by virtue of its intellectual, moral and aesthetic nature.[20]

Professor Leslie's influence on Carlyle is undeniable. Carlyle attended his classes for three years and received his personal advice and assistance on many occasions. If he and the Common Sense philosophers were right in thinking that geometry trained the intellect we may well ask how it trained Carlyle's. The question has importance because the early influences on Carlyle's thinking and writing are usually traced to his Calvinistic upbringing, and quite properly. But it should be noted that his interest in mathematics appeared earlier and was from the first stronger than his interest in entering the ministry, which had been his and his parents' expectation when they sent him to the University. His letters are filled with comments and reflections on his mathematical studies. Clearly he reveres geometry for its power both to establish truth and to train the intellect, and it appears that he followed Leslie in preferring synthetic geometry to analytic algebra. One of his real achievements was his solution for the third edition of Leslie's *Elements of Geometry* (1817) of the real roots of any quadratic equation by purely geometrical means, for which Leslie praised him in the text as "an ingenious young mathematician".[21] It is clear too that he sees no antagonism between mathematics and religion or between science and literature.[22] Nor is he yet attracted to idealism. Scottish philosophy and psychology seem barren (he criticizes Dugald Stewart for being "transcendental", Hartley's associational psychology for being "descendental"). Not even history has, by 1818, acquired its appeal for him: reading Gibbon he asks "I wonder what benefit is derived from reading all this stuff: . . . It is vain to tell us that our knowledge of human nature is encreased [by mere historical facts] . . . *Useful* knowledge of that sort is acquired not by reading but by experience" (*CL*, I, 121).

With all his talent and interest in mathematics, however, we must not forget that its attraction for him was practical—he knew it could be useful, could lead to jobs and perhaps to a career. At the same time, he began as early as 1817 to feel some discontentment with problem-solving, which "depends very much upon a certain slight of hand. . . I am not so sure as I used to be that it is the best way of employing one's self—Without doubt it concentrates our Mathematical ideas—and exercises the head; but little knowledge is gained by the process" (*CL*, I, 113). His literary activities gave him more pleasure but offered less support. He read novels, wrote poetry, wrote "literary" letters to his friends; in 1818 he made his first literary attempt with a "flowery sentimental" description of the Yarrow country and sent it to an Edinburgh magazine editor, who did not accept it.[23] He read

Mme. de Staël's *Germany* (CL, I, 109) with its introduction to the German philosophers. This book, though it left him cold at first (CL, I, 109, 265), may have started to reawaken in his mind some of the earlier, Platonic views of mathematicians which were current in Scotland when he was a student at Edinburgh. John Playfair and, before him, James Beattie, had believed that "the process of abstraction somehow frees mathematical reasoning from the necessity of empirical verification and inductive reasoning". They denied that sensory evidence was needed to justify the basic axioms of mathematics, not only because sensory evidence was untrustworthy but because mathematical evidence was either intuitive or demonstrable by logic.[24] Leslie, though he opposed this Platonizing of mathematical ideas, also opposed the empiricist approach, with his objection to the use of models in teaching geometry, which he called "quackish".

Signs of Carlyle's later attitude towards mathematics are thus already visible. He pressed forward with it, despite a few qualms, as much because it still fascinated him as because it offered a means of support. What he was later to write about Wotton Reinfred (1827) shows that he would not forget the fascination:

> Mathematics and the kindred sciences, at once occupying and satisfying his logical faculty, took much deeper hold of him; nay, by degrees, as he felt his own independent progress, almost alienated him for a long season from all other studies. 'Is not truth', said he, 'the pearl of great price, and where shall we find it but here?' He gloried to track the footsteps of the mighty Newton, and in the thought that he could say to himself: Thou, even thou, are privileged to look from his high eminence, and to behold with thy own eyes the order of that stupendous fabric; thou seest it in light and mystic harmony, which, though all living men denied, thou wouldst not even doubt![25]

This, defictionized, refers to the years between 1816 and 1820 when he was reading Newton and his mathematical and scientific interests were strongest. From the largely mythic accounts we have of his childhood (including his own accounts) we learn that it was his special talent in "figures" that induced his parents to send him to Annan Academy and eventually on to the University. Though he was not really a prodigy, his talent was recognized and encouraged, first by his father, then by relatives (Uncle Frank

Carlyle) and teachers (Mr Morley), until Professor Leslie singled him out for praise in 1810, and again in 1812 with a written certification stating that "Mr. Thomas Carlisle" possessed "talents peculiarly fitted for mathematical investigation".[26] According to a fellow student of Carlyle's he took the *dux* prize at that time "without much effort". (Wilson, *Carlyle*, I, 82.) Indeed he could not fail to recognize his own talents. As a boy he had enjoyed working out for himself mathematical puzzles in the *Belfast and County Almanack*. (Wilson, *Carlyle*, I, 69.) His early letters to Robert Mitchell, and to Hill and Murray, were filled with geometrical discourse. He and Mitchell were particularly fond of sending problems and solutions to one another, both of them reflecting Leslie's notion of mathematics as a discipline of the mind, yet also considering it a kind of diversion. When Mitchell asks Carlyle how it is possible to divide a circle into 360 degrees Carlyle quotes Gauss and Delambre in his demonstration that it cannot be done by plane geometry. (CL, I, 82–3.) They debate the perennial question whether an angle can be trisected with a ruler and compass. (CL, 1, 7–8, 27–28.) In another letter, out of sheer fun, Carlyle sends Mitchell a theorem and his elaborate demonstration of it done into Latin: "My dialect of that language is, I doubt not, somewhat peculiar—and you may chance to find some difficulty in interpreting it." And he goes on to "rate" his friend:

> Your Theorem about the heptagon does not answer exactly; it is only a very good approximation, as I perceive, and as you may perceive also, by consulting a table of sines and tangents.—I have forgot West's theorem about the circle and curves of the second order.—It is no great matter surely, since I should not be able to demonstrate it tho' I had it. I wish you would send it me notwithstanding.— I hope you have sustained no injury from your excursion to Edinr—I hope too that you spake to Mr. Leslie concerning the books. If you have not procured [me] one, I must request you to lend me yours immediately for a short time, if you can do without it: for one of the boys has begun conics & I have lent him my book—and should like to have another copy of it by me, to consult at home.—You must send me the theorem & book by Mr. Johnson of Hitchill—who I understand is to be at Ruthwell today and who can easily bring them to Annan.—A letter I am expecting with impatience—(CL, I, 73–6, 19 April 1816).

The playful manner here does not conceal Carlyle's serious concern with the subject of his ambition to improve his knowledge and skill. Thus he presses Mitchell for a prompt reply, and asks for books and more theorems to try his wits on. At this stage of his life mathematics is more avocation than vocation; it is a game.

The practice of exchanging original problems for solution led in 1814 to what seems to have been his first entry into print, in the small but lively newspaper, the *Dumfries and Galloway Courier*. Since Carlyle plunged *in medias res* it will be necessary to give some of the background. The 7 November 1813 issue of the *Courier* printed a letter addressed to The Editor, signed "ARITHMUS", in which it was proposed to establish a new section in the paper, a sort of Mathematician's Corner, which should complement its already popular "Poet's Corner." Readers were to be invited to send in mathematical or geometrical problems for solution by other readers who, it was hoped, would send in problems of their own and thus create a lively correspondence. The proposal was recommended as "productive of advantage" and likely "to improve the minds of your readers". "ARITHMUS" submitted four problems, and solutions began to appear in the issue of 14 December, from "A Constant Reader" and from "PHILO-MATHES", and in the issue of 21 December from "J.H.", and in the issue of 4 January 1814, from "A.B." "A.B." submitted fresh problems. The practice of anonymity thus begun was broken without warning in the 18 January issue by Messrs W. C. Walsh and W. C. Donald, of Mr White's Academy in Dumfries, who sent in more solutions, and by ALEX. GOLDIE, of Castle-Douglas, a week later. These exchanges were carried on in a vigorous if somewhat humourless way, with little or no comment on either the problems or the solutions and no discussion of the mathematical principles involved. In the 15 February issue some more solutions appeared and two new problems were submitted by "N". At this point Carlyle made his entrance, and the correspondence immediately changed character.

Writing to Carlyle a week later, his college friend, J. E. Hill, asked him "Whom do you intend to take care of the poor fellow's garden until he returns from the destination you appointed him lately—the centre of the earth?" and thus directs us to Carlyle's solutions of "N's" problems in the issue of 22 February.[27] "N's" problems read as follows:

(1) Let AB and BC be the given sides of a rectangle DB; it is possible to divide it into four equal areas, by means of curve lines running from A to C: What is the nature of the curve to be employed for the purpose? No answer to this question has yet been published.

(2) I have in my garden four trees, the third stands in a point equidistant from the first two—the fourth in a point equidistant from the other three—and the first is 20 yards distant from the second, and the third 30 yards from the fourth—to find the distance of all the trees from each other, and likewise the distance from the trees of a point in the garden, where, if I stand, I am equidistant from all the trees?[28]

Reading these in Edinburgh Carlyle at once sat down and dashed off a spirited reply which appeared in the next issue, that of February 22; but it appeared with a fatal misprint which, if it had no larger portent, was at least to stir up a tea-pot tempest. His reply:

To the Editor of the *Dumfries and Galloway Courier.*

Sir—The following are answers to the questions in your last number:

I    The rectangle is capable of being divided into 4 equal parts, by any of the common geometrical curves; though to divide it, we have only to find (by the rules of fluxions) the equation of the curve, whose area is $\frac{3}{4}$ that of the rectangle; to describe two such curves, on the opposite sides, and bisect the space included between them.

Note—The parabola will divide it into three equal parts.

II    Three of the trees are evidently in the circumference of a circle, whose centre is the fourth, and radius 30 yards. The third has one on each side, distant from each other 20 yards; and to find their distance from it, (they are both equal) is the problem—that is: the radius of a circle being 30, to find the chord of half the arc whose chord is 20. By the common rules of plane trigonometry, the result is 10.14 yards. Since, however, only *one* circle can pass through three points, it is evident that, *till the circumference of a circle is made to pass through its centre*, the fourth tree can never be in the circumference of one which passes through the other three; in other words, there can be no point in the garden which is equidistant from all the four.

70

If Mr N. is determined to be equidistant from all his trees, he must go to —— the centre of the earth.

I am, Sir, your &c.

THOMAS CARLYLE

Edinburgh, 18th Feb. 1814.

In the next number (1 March 1814), there appeared the answer to a question submitted earlier by Messrs W. C. Walsh and Donald, and appended to this a sarcastic reply to Carlyle by a reader who for reasons of his own resumed the practice of anonymity. With broad scorn he referred to "the method of Master Thomas Carlyle, of Edinburgh, ((see your last number); viz. the question 'is capable of being' solved 'by any of the common' methods; 'though to' do it 'we have only to find', by 'the rule of fluxions', or by the rule of three, or by the rule of *Thumb*, 'the equation' necessary, and the thing is done."

Irritated by Carlyle's lofty humour this country Jack intended to slay the giant of Edinburgh. His failure to perceive the obvious misprint of "capable" for "incapable", delivered him into Carlyle's unmerciful but still immature hands. The following reply, Carlyle's second contribution, appeared in the March 8 issue:

Sir—Respecting an extremely *acute* 'remark', which dropt from the pen of the right *ingenious*, and (I may say) right *Rule-of-Thumb-ic* 'mathematical' solver, to the question in your last, I think it necessary (since your correspondent, with *laudable modesty*, declines the honour of *fathering* his *jeu d'esprit*, though, haply, the only-begotten of his brain) merely to 'remark' in my turn, that I did not consider a provincial newspaper the proper vehicle for fluxionary investigations, and that 'capable', in my solution, was, by mistake, either in printing or transcribing, inserted instead of '*incapable*', as was evident to any person not blinded by conceit, and whose knowledge of his mother tongue amounts to an acquaintance with *The Adventures of THOMAS HICKATHRIFT*, or *The History of Jack the Giant-Killer*.

Having thus solved your question, and, 'lest he' might have been 'wise in his own conceit', answered 'a fool according to his folly', I beg leave to add, that, should any further *anonymous* attempts at wit appear in your paper against me, I shall regard them 'as the wind that bloweth', and suffer them quietly to 'fleer back' into the '*limbo of vanity*' whence they came—I have the honour to be, &c.

THOMAS CARLYLE

Edinburgh, 4th March, 1814.

Despite the threat, or perhaps because of it, this did not end the matter. Granted, he had sufficient reason to take offence, even allowing for the unperceived misprint, but this torrent of parody and abuse suggests that he took more offence than was given. On the other hand, his prevailing temper is not so much rancour as a boisterous humour that seems to burst exultantly through all bonds of restraint, as if now at last able to engage with someone in words, he gleefully joined combat, using the full battery of eighteenth-century invective and expecting his opponent to reply in kind. This was different from writing letters in private to his friends: he was answering an unknown assailant, and in full view of a small but definite public.

Even if he meant to silence his opponent, however, he should not have left himself vulnerable to counter-attack by referring to that opponent as "blinded by conceit", or to the *Courier* as a "provincial newspaper". The next issue of the *Courier* (March 15) carried another jibe from the same anonymous, and unabashed, critic.

> . . . We are strongly tempted to give another solution of the question by the *new method* (not Carlyleian till sanctioned by the public) first communicated to your scientific readers in your No. for the 22d ult. The method is certainly unrivalled for brevity, simplicity, and universality; rare and precious advantages! But they are unfortunately combined with a serious disadvantage, viz. the result is, at the bottom, universally the same as the question which ought to be answered. At a future opportunity we may, perhaps, give as great publicity to this new method as can be expected by the aid of a provincial newspaper.

How much these contemptuous allusions to Carlyle's vanity and desire for publicity, the bold repudiation of the solution itself, and the writer's persistent anonymity, nettled Carlyle may be guessed. In the same issue of 15 March there was a question he had submitted, to which no solution was ever sent in.[29] The next issue contained no reply from Carlyle to his antagonist, indicating that for the present at least he was abiding by the terms of his threat. All was quiet in the Mathematical Corner, until, in the *March 29* number several items appeared which delivered the *coup de grâce* to the whole correspondence. One of these was Carlyle's solution to a problem that had been submitted by "W.T.". The second was a

letter from "W.T." defending Carlyle and deploring the aggra-
vation of the dispute by the anonymous critic.

Sir, I hoped, after Mr Carlyle's letter in your paper of the 8th current, that the *new method*, as I now find it called, of solving mathematical questions, was set at rest, and am sorry to find it revived
by the solvers of Messrs W. and D's question of the 15th
inst.

The third item, a note by the Editor himself, reveals the fact
that Carlyle had not, after all, been able to remain silent.

The renewed attack of Messrs Walsh and Donald on Mr Carlyle,
has called forth from that gentleman a severe retaliation; but as
we are unwilling to encourage a *cacoëthes carpendi*, as Mr Carlyle
happily calls it, or to prolong a controversy which might in the end
produce irritation, we have taken the liberty of suppressing it.—
EDITOR.

This put an end to the mathematical correspondence in the
*Dumfries Courier* for some time. The Editor's assumption that
Carlyle's attackers were Messrs Walsh and Donald does not seem
to have been denied. Whether Carlyle's second rebuttal was more
rhetorical or less, more sharply vituperative or more temperate
and controlled, will never be known. Yet it does not seem to have
displeased the Editor-Minister of Ruthwell; there is in his note a
certain approval of the "severe retaliation" as well as affection for
its writer.[30] No blame is attached to the first rebuttal of 4 March,
only to the repeated attacks by Messrs W. and D. Much of the
trouble he knew had been caused by the fatal misprint, the rest by
their resentment of Carlyle's wit and mathematical prowess. But
only a Carlyle would enter the lists at full gallop and tilt at invisible windmills, to convert at one stroke a somewhat staid mathematical correspondence into a slashing polemic, and so end it.
Such a performance, though interesting to watch, could not but be
inappropriate to the quiet pages of the *Courier*. The game had
become a battle.

These letters to the *Courier* no doubt belong under the heading
of juvenilia, and, with their Carlylese, are of more stylistic than
mathematical importance. But they clearly establish his inchoate
ambition, his desire to become known, his sensitiveness to criti-

cism, his sometimes unrestrained truculence, even his difficulty with editors. It is clear too that his mathematical proclivities are geometrical and practical and that he uses Newtonian fluxions and symbols rather than the Cartesian calculus. When the Mathematical Column was revived in November 1816, problems being sent in to the Editor by ALPHA, S. Cowan, and others, Carlyle seems to have wanted to participate, for in his letters to Mitchell, who had become Mr Duncan's mathematical editor, he continued to send problems for nearly another three years.[31] Some of these may have been accepted. As his demonstrations grew more hasty (*CL*, I, 85–6) or careless (*CL*, I, 91, 101) it is evident that his fondness for problem-solving diminished; but at the same time his interest in geometry was broadening under Newton's influence into an interest in mathematics as related to the other sciences. Among his contributions to the *Courier* were two letter-essays on Thunder and Lightning, appropriate subjects, as has been remarked, for the "first published essay" of a writer like Carlyle.[32] He now read the *Principia* with more comprehension, and as his teaching days at Kirkcaldy drew to a close he was freer to consider how mathematics might be more than a game or means of support, might perhaps prove to be the vital part of a liberal education that Leslie had claimed, leading to a deeper understanding of man and society.

But at first it was a means of livelihood. He had earned money as a tutor at least as early as the summer of 1810 when at the age of fourteen he had taught a Major Davidson mathematics at Ecclefechan. With Leslie's recommendation he was nearly always able to eke out his slender resources by tutoring. His first job, as Teacher of Mathematics at Annan Academy in 1814, brought him £70 a year; his second, at the Burgh School, Kirkcaldy, in 1816, £80. When he resigned this position in October, 1818 ("I must cease to be a paedagogue", *CL*, I, 142–3), and went back to Edinburgh to prepare himself for a more attractive career, it was tutoring again, plus his savings, and some other employments, that supported him for the next six years. The Buller tutorship, with its £200 a year, made him financially independent from January 1822 to July 1824, but in 1818 no such windfall was in sight. Irving and Leslie helped him obtain pupils, while he looked, as it seems, in all directions for new opportunities. Though in his parents' eyes he was still supposed to be considering the ministry, he has long before "quitted all thoughts of the church"; and although any literary employment would be welcome he had told Mitchell that "To live by authorship was never my intention" (CL, I, 144). The question remained, what directions were possible? These were his hardest years. It must have been particularly mortifying when his revered Professor Leslie told him that "upon the whole . . . the best plan for *you* seems to be to learn the engineering business, and go to America" (CL, I, 158, 8 Jan., 1819). Though he had no desire to do either he did attend the classes in mineralogy and geology taught by Robert Jameson, Professor of Natural History, but he did not like that gentleman's "most crude theories" and faulted both his accuracy and the organization of his lectures. "Yesterday he explained the [colour] of the atmosphere, upon principles which argued a total ignorance of dioptrics. A knowledge of the external characters of minerals is all that I can hope to obtain from him."[33] Nevertheless he read works by French and German geologists, and then in order to be able to read "the illustrious Werner" in the original began his momentous study of the German language.[34] In February 1819, David Brewster commissioned him to translate a French article on "Some Compounds which depend on very Weak Affinities" by Jacob Berzelius for his *Edinburgh Philosophical Journal*, paying him promptly and honestly for this work, and also for two more scientific papers: a review of Hansteen's book on Magnetism, which was to be Carlyle's first published book review, and a translation of Mohs' German work on Crystallography and Mineralogy.[35] These engaged his scientific concerns, and exercised his power of independent scientific statement. With the Hansteen review he was happily involved in a discussion of the earth's magnetic forces, lines of force (*in*organic filaments), and the laws of controlling magnetic intensity. The experiments which had led Coulomb to the conclusion that the attraction between two particles is always as the square of the distance were, he observed, of doubtful scientific accuracy. Hansteen had now confirmed this conclusion by purely mathematical demonstration; but with perfect self-assurance, he rejects one of Hansteen's findings on the basis of his own knowledge of the parabola. As a whole, the review is a formal, neutral handling of a complex subject. But he concludes that "the whole science is involved in conjecture", and notes wryly that Professor Hansteen draws support for some of his arguments from one of "the sacred numbers of the Indians, Babylonians, Greeks and Egyptians": the number 432, and from the division in Brahminical mythology of the world's duration into four periods of $1 \times 432,000$ years, $2 \times 432,000$, $3 \times 432,000$ and $4 \times 432,000$ years, because these match (with some rounding of figures) Hansteen's own findings of the times taken by each of the four magnetic points to complete its circuit around its pole.[36]

A similar attempt at independent scientific discussion, done at the end of 1819 and meant for the *Edinburgh Review*, was his ill-fated review of what he long after referred to as Pictet's "mechanical *Theory of Gravitation*". Since Jeffrey neither accepted nor returned the manuscript it has been lost for ever, and the actual work Carlyle was reviewing has only recently been identified.[37] At about the same time he seems to have planned to write something on Hevelius's *Selenographia* (1647), and a life of Horrox—which came to nothing. Seeing now that all his skill and training in mathematics were failing to open up a career he attempted to train himself for the Law, but, enrolling in Hume's Scots Law class in the autumn of 1819, though he persevered, he could muster no interest in it, and was mercifully rescued the following March by Brewster's employing him to write the twenty odd *Edinburgh Encyclopedia* articles, which would give him some support and occupy much of his time during the next four years. Only two of the subjects assigned him directly involved mathematicians or scientists, Montucla and Pascal. Most were eighteenth-century historical figures, some were French philosophers (Pascal, Montesquieu, Montaigne), some merely geographical areas. Mungo Park was the only Scot. Brewster did not give him Newton. Yet the M's, N's, and P's served him well enough, for they enabled him to apprentice himself, before a public audience, in the biographical, historical, and journalistic essay, as well as in problems of researching and organizing materials and ideas. His concept of history was still light: it amused and instructed. The "Netherlands" gave him a chance to write history, and he wrote it like Hume and Robertson, an account of great men and celebrated events. In the "Nelson" he could describe his first hero, complete with a sort of conversion. The "Montesquieu" by its distinction of style and thought apparently drew the attention of Francis Jeffrey.[38] The "Montucla" briefly records the career of the French mathematical historian, without revealing anything of Carlyle's own mathematical interests. All the articles show what Lowell called "a certain security of judgement", and occasional flashes of Carlylean phrasing and imagery.

The "Pascal" deserves special attention not only because Pascal was philosopher, mathematician, physicist, and publicist all in one, but because it shows Carlyle's hand. His account of Pascal's life is, as Professor Shine observes, a significant indication of Carlyle's spiritual and intellectual development.[39] In his disapproval of Pascal's *"famous arithmetical machine"*, for example, as "a wonderful but useless proof of its author's ingenuity", we can hardly fail to detect the influence of Leslie: a calculating machine by-passes the mind. Leibnitz's "simpler calculating machine" is also disapproved in passing. And though he suspects as an exaggeration the report that Pascal as a boy had "actually discovered the truth of Euclid's thirty-second proposition" (that the three angles of a triangle are equal to two right angles) without any knowledge of Euclid, yet he describes Pascal's mathematical and scientific achievements with open admiration: the bold proof on the Puy-de-Dome of Toricelli's experiments with the mercury column, the "beautiful" invention of the Arithmetical Triangle which Leibnitz afterwards used in his development of the calculus, the discovery when he was 16 of the "Hexagonal Theorem", and his dramatic demonstration of the mathematics of the cycloid. Such scientific devotion in a devoutly religious man might be questionable, but Carlyle notes with sympathy that Pascal was encouraged to pursue and publish his findings "to show that the highest attainments in a science of strict reasoning were not incompatible with the humblest belief in the principles of religion" (p. 335). He admires Pascal also for continuing his work despite failing health and continual physical pain (cf. Carlyle's dyspepsia). Having recently experienced his own conversion he describes Pascal's conversion to Jansenism without disapproval, as if an attack on Jesuitism were as welcome as one on Atheism. He praises the *Provincial Letters* for their literary quality and formative effect upon the French language (p. 334). And he notes that even after that conversion the "speculations of early life resumed their sway [and] showed that his mathematical powers were diverted, not destroyed" (p. 334). With the quarrels between the Molinists and Jansenists Carlyle does not tarry: "Pascal's work is the main plank, by . . . which some memory of them still floats on the stream of time" (p. 334). But he refuses to deplore Pascal's religious passion or to associate it with insanity. Voltaire, remarking that "after the accident at Neuilly bridge, Pascal's head was deranged, . . . should have remembered, that as the external colouring of our feelings depends on the associations to which we are exposed, and is changed with all their changes, so the appearance of great intellect and lofty purposes, however modified and over clouded, is always entitled to the reverence and approval of every good man" (p. 335). It is a tender portrait. Though he would not express it here, he must have felt a kinship with Pascal; especially now when his intellectual allegiances were shifting and he was becoming more deeply involved in the main issues of Pascal's life, of knowledge and faith, science and religion, the head and the heart, issues that were still unresolved and a source of considerable perplexity to him. This can be seen in a remark following the one quoted above about the compatibility of "a science of strict reasoning" and religious belief (p. 335), that it was a precept for Pascal "that matters of faith are beyond the empire of reason". Well might Carlyle seek a resolution of his own problems redefining reason and relegating science to the lower realm of logic and the understanding.[40] Even when his views were finally matured and set, his mathematical interests, like Pascal's, would be "diverted, not destroyed". There was comfort, curiously, in observing that with all his intellectual attainments Pascal was not always rational; that the same genius that discovered the arithmetical triangle and produced the *Pensées* also made him keep an account of his near-death at Neuilly between the cloth and lining of his coat:

> It should excite not a smile but a sigh, to learn that Pascal believed in the miraculous cure of his niece by a relic at Port Royal; that he reckoned it necessary to appear cold toward his sisters, though he loved them deeply; or that in his latter years, he wore below his shirt an iron girdle studded with sharp points, which he pressed against the skin whenever any evil thought overtook him (p. 335).

While writing these articles for the *Edinburgh Encyclopedia* Carlyle was executing another assignment by Brewster, the translating of Legendre's *Geometry*. This work was, and still is, recognized by mathematicians as a distinguished one, and in Carlyle's translation it would go through many editions in England and America, so that one scholar credits him with an important place in the history of mathematics teaching and another marvels that "the famous Scottish litterateur" should have done it at all.[41] For Carlyle, however, it was an onerous job. He had agreed to undertake it before he knew about the Buller tutorship. Brewster would pay him only £50 for nearly seven months' work, at a time when, with Jane's encouragement, he was trying to devote his efforts to the writing of an original literary work.[42] The matter would not be worth further consideration but for the essay on Proportion which he wrote as the Introductory chapter. Whether Brewster asked him to do this is not known, but since he seems to have written it very rapidly—he later claimed in half a day, "a happy forenoon (Sunday, I fear!),"—it was perhaps his own idea.[43] It was done probably in July 1822, between *Edinburgh Encyclopaedia* articles, and while he was studying hard for a projected history of the Commonwealth. Like the Berzelius and Mohs translations, this one was hack-work and his letters contain frequent complaints, but, curiously, make no mention of the essay on Proportion which he afterwards remembered writing so easily and thought of with pleasure and pride.[44] Yet short though it is, it furnishes valuable clues to the connection between his early mathematical and his later, literary work.

The essay is a model of concision. Two introductory paragraphs explaining the relation of the essentially arithmetical subject of Proportion to geometry are followed by four definitions and some theorems with their corollaries. The doctrine of proportion, he announces in the opening sentence, does not belong exclusively to geometry, since its object is "to point out the relations which subsist among magnitudes in general, when viewed as *measured*, or represented by *numbers*"; it applies also to many other branches of knowledge. Thus, four magnitudes which are in proportion constitute an analogy, and the reasoning which is required to detect and demonstrate proportionality is analogous reasoning (p. xiv). The essay thus lays the groundwork for the extension of 'proportional' reasoning as used in mathematics to the use of analogous reasoning in other subjects. Carlyle takes considerable pains to establish the most difficult proportionalities, as where the terms are incommensurable. Ordinarily, he says, in order to demonstrate that two pairs of magnitudes are proportional, a common measure, or sub-multiple, must be found for each pair. When, however, the members of each pair are incommensurable, that is, have no common measure, the proportionality cannot be demonstrated so simply. This was the very difficulty that Euclid negotiated so "cumbrously" in his Fifth Book that it had to be omitted in most geometry texts. In an elaborate footnote (p. xi) Carlyle proposes a fractional method of obtaining a common measure, dividing successively smaller submultiples of one number of each pair into the other member so as to approximate a common measure, and thus diminishing the discrepancy "below any assigned magnitude". Then, "since the proportion still continues accurate at every successive approximation, we infer that it will, in like manner, continue accurate to the limit which we can approach indefinitely, though never actually reach". He also proposes a geometrical method, which constitutes an equally interesting analogy.[45] This brief foray into the realm of approximation and incommensurabilities assumes a special significance when we consider, among the characteristics of his later thought, his tendency to reason or argue by analogy, making intuitive leaps to find or to establish a condition among one set of terms which will then hold true for an analogous set of terms. Northrop Frye has noted the kinship between literature and mathematics, with their basic units of the metaphor and the equation: metaphor may be seen as a compressed equation, or analogy, the terms of which are either symbols or entities.[46] But in literature their proportional relationships will be more poetic than precise. So in *Sartor Resartus*, if Aprons give protection to the Nürnberg housewife so do the Police protect society; the clothes which cover our bodies wear out, as do the institutions of King and Clergy. The whole of *Sartor*, with its intricate symbolism, is an "infinitely complected" analogy, a working-out of the proportionality of things material and spiritual. It is an extensive example of Carlyle's analogic dialectic executed in large scale and small. Corresponding to the broad parallelism existing between the outer world and the inner are individual parallelisms:

> Thus is the Laystall, especially with its Rags or Clothes-rubbish, the grand Electric Battery, and Fountain-of-motion, from which and to which the Social Activities (like vitreous and resinous Electricities) circulate, in larger or smaller circles, through the mighty, billowy, stormtost Chaos of Life, which they keep alive! [47]

—where the Laystall "is to" (i.e. it circulates) material clothes as social activities "are to" (they animate) life—with Industry and the "electric battery" serving, so to speak, as submultiples in the proportion. The method of analogy may be used in argument, somewhat perilously, as Carlyle knew.[48] But it became a characteristic of his thought. Impatient of logical reasoning, he sought to establish proof by the transference of a truth which, recognized as a truth in one place, must be recognized as true in an analogous place. Yet analogy is not proof: for the "relation which is perceived to exist between two magnitudes of the same kind . . . appears to be a simple idea, and therefore unsusceptible of any good definition" (Legendre, p. xii). Rather, it is persuasion. Impatient also of the kind of sequential, phenomenal thinking that is usually required in narrative fiction, he found himself (no doubt for other reasons as well) unable to complete his *Wotton Reinfred*. What the essay "On Proportion" reveals most clearly is that the same intuitive, analogical thinking that characterized his mathematical demonstrations reappears in his later work. What he wanted in science as in literature, and had a peculiar talent for, was the flash of insight, the sudden perception of significant relation. Each flash was like an act of faith, bringing the discovery of a certitude, of a permanent, spiritual truth.

With the writing of the essay on Proportion, Carlyle brought to an end twelve years of mathematical activity. There is little doubt that by 1822 he considered himself launched on a literary career, though most insecurely and with no clear promise of success. It is not surprising then that he should for at least another ten years leave the mathematical door ajar. When opportunities arrived to apply for teaching positions he would apply. But his intellectual curiosity in mathematics and the sciences as they existed in his time, has all but died. For one thing, it is likely that he had reached his limit as a mathematical thinker. When in 1816 he was reading and attempting to understand Newton's *Principia* (*CL*, I, 79), it was "with considerable perserverance & little success", until he realized that he had too little knowledge of astronomy, whereupon he sent for a copy of Delambre's *Abrégé d'astronomie*, and in the meantime read a number of ancillary works, James Wood's *Elements of Optics*, John Robison's article on optics in the third edition of the *Encyclopaedia Britannica*, and Keill's *Introductio ad Veram Physicam*. Armed with these he read the Delambre when it arrived, with understanding enough, and then, presumably, returned to his study of the *Principia*. In spite of D. A. Wilson's statement that he now "saw with delight the *Principia* 'at his feet' " there is little evidence that he ever wholly mastered this difficult work. The following year, after attempting to read William Wallace's article on Fluxions in the *Britannica* he gave up, because he could not or would not take the time to understand the whole of this Newtonian branch of mathematics. "I wish I had it in my head—," he wrote Mitchell. "But, unless I quit my historical pursuits, it may be doubted whether this will ever happen" (*CL*, I, 112). In 1818 he read but could not understand Lagrange's *Mécanique analytique* (1788), Laplace's *Exposition du système du monde* (1796) and *Mécanique céleste* (1799–1825), and Bossut's *Mécanique* (1810) with its "integrals and differentials".[49] Though he still admired science, and advised Mitchell "you must not leave off Mathematics", he lamented his own lack of comprehension: "To see these truths, my good Robert—to *feel* them as one does the proportion of the sphere & cylinder! 'Tis a consummation devoutly to be wished—but not very likely ever to arrive. Sometimes, indeed . . . I say to myself—away with despondency—hast thou not a soul and a kind of understanding in it? And what more has any analyst of them all? But next morning, alas, when I consider my understanding—how coarse yet feeble it is."[50] After the *Principia* ceased to absorb him he was to advance no further in mathematical thought. He could teach, he could comprehend up to a point, but he could not create. In short, he could not go beyond Leslie's teaching. The mathematics in which he had been trained was in itself a hindrance. Having been taught to avoid analysis, he found it too difficult, and soon came to regard it with distaste on other grounds.

Carlyle does not attribute his loss of interest in mathematics to his own incapacity, or to the geometry-based mathematics he had been taught, but rather to what he regarded as the unphilosophical nature of all mathematical science. As with the solving of geometrical problems, though it exercised the mind and trained one to think, it was narrow and yielded little knowledge. "The worst of it is", he wrote while struggling with Wallace's *Fluxions*, "we are led to his conclusion, as it were thro a narrow lane— often, by its windings shutting from our view the object of our search—and never affording us a glimpse of the surrounding country" (*CL*, I, 112). His growing desire for a comprehensive understanding of man and the universe prompted him to renew his search in history and literature.[51] That he was not yet deeply attracted to history only added to the doubt and misery which darkened this period of his life and which was to culminate in his Leith Walk crisis. Among the complex of causes which brought on this crisis his disillusionment with mathematics must be counted an important one. By 1818 he feared that it would lead neither to the truth nor to the career he needed, and not until the autumn of 1820 would he find an equally absorbing interest in German literature. Nor was he to realize the full promise of the Germans until 1822, when he attained a deeper understanding of Goethe. Carlyle did not simply turn from mathematics to Goethe. There was the agonizingly empty period of his Everlasting No which lasted until his year at Hoddam Hill (1825–1826) and most probably even longer.[52]

Nevertheless he made the plunge early in 1821: "I must live by literature, at all hazards" (*CL*, I, 336) though he could not yet earn a living by it but must spend nearly a year translating the Legendre *Geometry* for Brewster. "Many a time I have wished that, when ruining my health with their poor lean triangles & sines & tangents & fluxions & calculi, I had but been writing any kind of doggerel" (*CL*, II, 116). He is here writing to Jane, whose love of poetry strongly influenced his decision to commit himself to a career of literature when his prospects were still so dim. It would not do to teach Jane mathematics; he must teach her literature, and must therefore be a writer himself. Thus practical circumstances played their part in drawing him away from mathematics. Only for reasons of security did he continue to apply for mathematical teaching positions;[53] only because his literary future was still perilous even in 1833 did he make that last effort to utilize his mathematical skill when he applied for the directorship of the Edinburgh Astronomical Observatory. Though he was qualified for this position, it lay far from his interests and would have entailed a drastic alteration in his career.

Even before he met Jane in June, 1821, a number of literary opportunities had brought encouragement and hope to his old literary ambitions. He reviewed Joanna Baillie's *Metrical Legends of Exalted Characters* for the October issue of Waugh's *New Edinburgh Review*, and wrote "Faustus" for the April 1822 issue. Later in 1822 he seems to have tried his hand at a (now lost) epistolary novel, at a short story, the "Cruthers and Jonson", and some poems. But these were not enough to sustain him either financially or intellectually. During the next five years (1822–1827) he would re-enact what he had done in mathematics, reading widely in order to comprehend, translating to earn money, and writing critical and biographical essays as apprenticeship for the original work he still hoped to do later. But when he attempted a novel, in *Wotton Reinfred*, he had to leave it unfinished at the eighth chapter. Not until he had thoroughly assimilated the Germans (1827–1829) did he find what he had sought in the study and pursuit of mathematics, a *Weltbild*, or philosophic picture of the world which compelled his belief.

To his friend Anna Montagu, after his failure to obtain the chairs of Moral Philosophy at London and St. Andrews, he wrote, "I accordingly came hither [Craigenputtoch]; still bent on 'professing Morals,' in one shape or another, but from a *chair* of my own, and to such audience as I myself could gather round me" (*CL*, IV, 391, 12 Aug. 1828). It was morals, then, that validated and ennobled literature, morals as part of a religious faith. The tradition of Dugald Stewart's course in Moral Philosophy at Edinburgh rose again, joining with Carlyle's religious training, to lead him to the pulpit for which his parents had educated him.

We may now ask what were the consequences of Carlyle's mathematical talent and training. The question cannot be answered precisely, for if we attempt to demonstrate that a mathematician necessarily thinks and writes differently from a physician we become involved in a complex of psychological theories not always

84

amenable to proof. Nor can we define how a man's training in one discipline will determine his ideas or modes of thought after he has adopted another discipline. In Carlyle's case the matter is still more elusive because he was never exclusively preoccupied with mathematics and science. While he was reading Franklin's *Treatise on Electricity* in 1813 he was also deep in Shakespeare. While winning honours in Leslie's mathematics classes he wrote, "Grant me that with a heart of independence, unseduced by the world's smiles, and unbending in its frowns, I may attain to literary fame" (Wilson, *Carlyle*, I, 93). We must remember that the same intellectual habits may arise from diverse disciplines, even from those of science and art. The same needs may be satisfied by them. What had drawn Carlyle to mathematics was intellectual excitement. Each demonstration was an adventure, each problem to be solved a challenge, each solution a conquering of the unknown. When with the Germans he encountered new philosophical questions these too were challenges, problems to be solved, theorems to be fitted into a larger whole. With social and political questions too his mind would seek clear solutions. Though mathematics lacked content he never lost his respect for its power of demonstration. Yet in one way he seriously misjudged it. When he discovered the superiority of Reason over the Understanding, it seemed obvious that mathematics belonged to the latter realm, that in dealing with "visibles" and "mensurables" it must be confined to mere logic. The fact that much mathematical reasoning involves intuition and requires an analogical imagination did not occur to him, even though he used both in his quadratic solution for Leslie's *Geometry*, and in his essay on Proportion for the Legendre. It was the analysts whom he and Leslie deplored who used logic; his own thinking, his perception of analogy and proportion, was an exercise of the very imagination and Reason which he denied to mathematics.

Such an attitude helps to explain Carlyle's increasingly ambivalent opinion of the sciences. He both dislikes and likes them. He will reject them but at the same time retain them as an ideal. After the Legendre translation his references to mathematics grow more critical. In *Wotton Reinfred* science is said to lead only to scepticism and doubt. Poor Wotton, "poring over thy Geometries and Stereometries, thy Fluxions direct and inverse, by the

Newtonian and Leibnitzian method", eventually discovered that "The *Principia* do but enlighten one small forecourt of the mind."[54] By 1829, in "Novalis", Carlyle adduced Leslie's old reprehension of analytical algebra in his own reprehension of "the higher mathematics", which is mechanical because "assisted with visible symbols, with safe *implements* for thinking" (*Works*, XXVII, 51). The same note is struck in "Signs of the Times": "The science of the age, in short, is physical, chemical, physiological; in all shapes mechanical. Our favourite Mathematics, the highly prized exponent of all these other sciences, has also become more and more mechanical" (*Works*, XXVII, 63–64). Yet Masson testifies that "to the end of his life . . . he would talk with great relish about mathematical matters" (Masson, 310). And Tyndall, we remember, said that "he was always in the advance of me, anticipating and enunciating what I was about to say". Mathematics and the physical sciences still claimed place as useful, even necessary, branches of knowledge. Furthermore he now had the example of Goethe, who sometimes said that he took less pride in his poetry than in his work as a scientist, his theory of colours and his discovery of the premaxillary bone. From Goethe and Novalis came authority for Carlyle's mature conviction that science, literature, philosophy, and religion were complementary, all related parts of a whole. If he could not fuse them, but must leave them separate, neither could Goethe. "I conceive mathematics", wrote Goethe, "as the most sublime and useful science so long as they are applied in their proper place; but I cannot commend the misuse of them in matters which do not belong in their sphere, and in which, noble science as they are, they seem to be mere nonsense."[55] In agreement with this position Carlyle believed that the Benthamites were misapplying mathematics in the sphere of morals.

Thus Carlyle believed on the one hand that the mathematical sciences, inherently limited to the logical manipulation of visibles and mensurables, have no value for the moral philosopher; and on the other hand that they are only being misapplied and *made* mechanical by the utilitarians. Science advances by laborious analysis and mechanical gathering of facts; "No Newton, by silent meditation, now discovers the system of the world from the falling of an apple" (*Works*, XXVII, 61–2). Carlyle reserves his respect for a pure science, an ideal mathematics, in which intellection is intuitive, proceeding rather by deduction than induction, and which cannot be corrupted by the mechanists. For this ideal he used, in 1829, the old term "mathesis", meaning the action of learning mathematical science in distinction to exhibiting it. The term connotes mental discipline, silent meditation the mystery of intuition. We may note an analogy with "poesis", the spontaneous 'making' of a poem. Both require genius. Its province is not the "higher mathematics", or even the lower in which he himself had been active, but abstract thought. The ideal mathesis could be found in Euclid, Pascal, Newton, and others who infused their thinking with moral or philosophical significance. To point the contrast, Carlyle now uses the term 'mathematics' pejoratively, to denote any limited or analytical extension of the older mathematical science, requiring a lesser talent. Thus, Novalis is "well-skilled in mathematics, and . . . fond of that science; but his is a far finer species of endowment than any required in mathematics, where the mind, from the very beginning of *Euclid* to the end of *Laplace* is assisted with visible symbols, with safe *implements* for thinking; nay at least in . . . the higher mathematics, has little more than a mechanical superintendence to exercise over these. This power of abstract meditation . . . with Novalis, is a much higher and rarer one; its element is not mathematics, but that *Mathesis*, of which . . . many a Great Calculist has not even a notion" (*Works*, XXVII, 51).

The postulation of a "mathesis" seems to increase and harden his opposition to science. Now all mathematicians are mere Calculists, dealing in counters, and falling short of truth. The *Principia* of Newton has been "swallowed up" in the *Mécanique céleste* of Laplace (*CL*, I, 233), and the *Mécanique* will in its turn be swallowed up because of its machinery. In another passage written at about the same time (1829) he grants them some worth, in an effort to be fair, but with the result that they are once again denounced in order to exalt the ideal. "Without undervaluing the wonderful results which a Lagrange or Laplace educes by means of it, we may remark, that their calculus, differential and integral, is little else than a more cunningly-constructed arithmetical mill;[56] where the factors being put in, are, as it were, ground into the true product, under cover, and without other effort on our part than steady turning of the handle. We have more Mathematics than ever; but less Mathesis" (*Works*, XXVII, 64). He clearly prefers the older mathematics which reached its conclusions the hard way to the newer and more intricate analysis, grinding its arithmetical mill. "Archimedes and Plato", he adds, "could not have read the *Mécanique Céleste*; but neither would the whole French Institute see aught in that saying 'God geometrises!' but a sentimental rodomontade" (*Works*, XXVII, 64). The calculus is calculated; "God geometrises" was intuited. In the right hands, mathematics may still move ahead towards mathesis: he calls Novalis "The German Pascal" (*Works*, XXVII, 53) because "both are mathematicians and naturalists, yet occupy themselves chiefly with Religion". Father Boscovich, the Croation astronomer and mathematician, was able "from merely mathematical considerations" to reach a kind of German Idealism (*Works*, XXVII, 23).

Furthermore he began to see the possibilities of this new Mathesis in his own development. Instead of rejecting science totally and appropriating German transcendentalism he could merge them in a philosophy which should utilize the best of both. After his long studies he had come at last to the point of creation. In February of this year he wrote in his Notebook:

> Has the mind its cycles and seasons like Nature, varying from the fermentation of *werden* to the clearness of *seyn*, and this again and again. . . . In my own case, I have traced two or three such vicissitudes; at present, if I mistake not, there is some such thing at hand for me.[57]

We cannot affirm that the notion of Mathesis was directly related to this new-found "clearness of *seyn*", but he did in the following year commence the writing of his "Thoughts on Clothes" which became *Sartor Resartus*. He did not define the notion but left its brief contexts in "Novalis" and "Signs of the Times" to adumbrate its meaning. Nor does he use the term again. It has served to name the antidote to chop-logic and gerund-grinding and to suggest that "science of the mind" which he had once hoped might arise to complement Newton's great science of "matter" (*CL*, I, 84). It had only partially arisen in such men as Pascal and Novalis, who had left their finest work in the fragmented form of "Thoughts" (*Works*, XXVII, 53). He clung to the hope that it might be rising in Germany, and might yet rise in England also, if the English could be shown the folly of mechanizing all their ways. The deeper signs of the times might not be faith in mechanism but a gradual realization that there is a superior Science of Dynamics, employing "the primary, unmodified forces and energies of man", and dealing with man's infinite rather than merely finite character. Although Carlyle heartily dislikes the Science of Mechanics he does not, despite his objurgations, reject it. Having been carried to excess, it needed to be brought back in balance with that of Dynamics. The two sciences should be complementary. Each is necessary to prevent excess of the other. The balance could be restored by a kind of thinking based on the inward, primary perceptions rather than on logic. Science had not originated in the schools and universities but "in the obscure closets of the Roger Bacons, Keplers, Newtons; in the workshops of the Fausts and the Watts" (*Works*, XXVII, 69). As these "gifted spirits" thought, so must Englishmen think again, in both the inward dynamical province and the outward mechanical. Science must be transcendentalized. It must, like mathematics in Leslie's teaching, become an integral part of the general culture.

After abandoning mathematics and the sciences for a literary career Carlyle retained an *altered* interest in them.[58] He continued to make levies upon them not only for imagery but also for concept. *Sartor Resartus* is studded with figures drawn from his scientific knowledge and mathematics gave him such central concepts as the fraction of life (*Sartor*, 191) and the Hyperbolic-Asymptotic shape of history (*Works*, XXVIII, 176). The very germination of *Sartor* was largely in mathematical terms: man is a living symbol and walks between two eternities and two infinitudes.[59] But the clearest consequence of his long interest and remarkable talent in mathematics seems to have been the analogical habit of mind which we see at work both in *Sartor* and in the earlier essay "On Proportion". It is obvious that many or most of his analogies are couched in symbolic terms and that the pervasive symbolism of *Sartor* can be expressed as a proportion or analogy. The use of symbol and analogy derives from many other sources than mathematics—art, philosophy, myth, anthropology—and there is no doubt that Carlyle's use of them had a diverse provenance; but his ten years of study under Professor Leslie's influence must be counted as one of the most important formative factors in his development. His analogizing imagination was stimulated, his powers of comprehension challenged. Subjected to the rigorous discipline of geometrical and algebraic study, he grew accustomed to reading things in terms of problems to be solved, puzzles to be understood, proportions to be perceived, analogies to be defined. With the final fixing of his interest on literature, his mathematical habits, instead of disappearing, continued in force to determine the special mode of thinking, arguing, and proving, that characterizes the critical and creative writing of his long career.

## NOTES

1. On 19 May 1820 Carlyle wrote to a friend, "I have nearly lost all relish for Mathematics, which some years ago I reckoned the loftiest pursuit of the human intellect," *CL*, I, 252. See also *Reminiscences* (Norton); Froude, *Life*, I, 25–6, 130; Wilson, *Carlyle*, I, 258. In his *Carlyle's Early Reading until 1934* (Lexington, Ky, 1953), p. 258, Hill Shine thinks that Newton's *Principia* at least ceased to be an engrossing interest after the Kirkcaldy period (1818). Jacques Cabeau believes that Carlyle's mathematical interests remained strong until 1826–7: *TC, ou le Prométhée enchaîné* (Paris, 1968), pp. 55f.
2. Nora Barlow, ed. *Autobiography of Charles Darwin* (New York, 1958), p. 114.
3. Herbert Spencer, *An Autobiography* (London, 1904), I, 231, *passim* and II, 248–9. But see the anonymous "Herbert Spencer: A Portrait", *Blackwood's Edin. Mag.*, 175 (1904), 110–16 for Carlyle's impact on Spencer.
4. Letter to *The Times*, 4 May 1881, p. 13. Tyndall denies that Carlyle was either incurious or hostile in respect to science and affirms Carlyle's later sympathy with evolution and admiration for Darwin. See also Tyndall's "On Personal Recollections of TC", *New Fragments* (London, 1892). Darwin, though he deplored Carlyle's "garrulity and haranguing at the dinner table", respected his power, his teaching of grand moral truths, and the vividness of his historical descriptions, "more vivid than Macaulay's". *An Autobiography*, p. 113.
5. *Ibid.*, p. 114.
6. A. De Morgan, *A Budget of Paradoxes* (London, 1872), p. 499.
7. H. V. Routh, *Towards the Twentieth Century* (Cambridge, 1937), p. 116.
8. The subject has received scant attention, except from mathematicians. In his *An Introduction to the History of Mathematics* (3rd ed. New York, 1969), pp. 73, 374, 410, Howard Eves credits Carlyle with the

solution of a difficult proposition for Leslie's *Geometry* (1817) and praises him for his translation of the Legendre *Geometry* (1822). Peter A. Wursthorn, in "The Position of TC in the History of Mathematics", *The Mathematical Teacher*, 59 (1966) 755–70, comments on the essay "On Proportion" which he wrote for the Legendre and gives further details of Carlyle's activities as a mathematician and teacher. Norman Gridgeman's "TC, geometer", *New Scientist*, 27 Nov. 1969, pp. 466–7, briefly lauds his mathematical bent at the expense of virtually all his literary work. Jacques Cabeau, *op. cit.*, has written perceptively about Carlyle's mathematical and scientific imagery, and notes the later postulation of "mathesis". See also Maxwell H. Goldberg, "Carlyle, Pictet and Jeffrey", *MLQ*, VII (1946) 291–6; Ian Campbell, "Carlyle, Pictet and Jeffrey Again", *Bibliotheck*, 7 (1974), 1–15, and Samuel Gill Barnes, "Formula for Faith: the Newtonian Pattern in the Transcendentalism of TC", Unpubl. Diss., Univ. of North Carolina, 1953.

9. Froude, *Life*, I, 25–6.
10. For an excellent discussion of this point see George Levine, "*Sartor Resartus* and the Balance of Fiction", *VS*, 8 (1964), 131–60. See also Carlisle Moore, "The Persistence of Carlyle's 'Everlasting No' ", *MP*, 54 (1957), 187–96.
11. Froude, *Life*, I, 26.
12. *The Prelude* (1805–6), lines 58–61.
13. According to Richard Olson, in his "Scottish Philosophy and Mathematics, 1750–1830", *Journal of the History of Ideas*, 32 (1971) 35–37, the Scottish philosopher and mathematician Thomas Reid had come very close to postulating a non-Euclidean Geometry with his "Geometry of Visibles". Carlyle knew Reid's work generally but not this in particular. *CL*, I, 343, 123.
14. In his *The Enchafed Flood* (New York, 1950) W. H. Auden opens his study of Romantic sea-imagery with Wordsworth's account of his dream of the Ishmael-Bedouin holding the "Stone" and the "Shell", with its imagery of the sea and the desert, and imagery to be found also in Carlyle's voyage-of-life and wasteland images in *Sartor*.
15. Olson, p. 29 n.1.
16. "Because the certainty of mathematical knowledge arises in large measure out of its connection with the primary qualities of matter rather than out of the hypothetical deductive nature of its reasoning alone, it is critical to the Common Sense philosophers that some power of the mind beyond mere reasoning be applied to assure that mathematical reasoning does not stray from its appropriate objects and that it is not extended beyond those circumstances to which it is appropriate. The Common Sense antagonism to algebraic or analytic mathematics arose in part out of this circumstance; for the extreme generality of algebraic symbolism seemed to make it far too easy . . . to fall into error." Olson, pp. 37–8. I am indebted to Olson for his full and convincing discussion of this point.
17. Olson, pp. 40–1.

18. When Carlyle went to the University in 1809, the course had been taken over by Thomas Brown (1778–1820), who, in this respect at least, seems to have taught it as Stewart had done. Carlyle, however, disliked him for "spouting poetry". David Masson, *Edinburgh Sketches* (London, 1892), p. 235.

19. Quoted in Olson, p. 42.

20. John Leslie, *Elements of Geometry and Plane Trigonometry* (Edinburgh 1817, 3rd edition), p. iii.

21. Leslie, p. 340. The solution that appears on pp. 340–1 is not Carlyle's but Pappus's more complex one; Carlyle's appears in the text, on pp. 176–7. Wursthorn calls it "remarkable in its originality, beautiful in its simplicity", *op. cit.*, p. 756. David Masson, who thought that the proposition had been given a geometrical solution before, may have had Pappus of Alexandria's in mind. (*Edinburgh Sketches*, p. 261, n.1.)

22. This is not surprising. Many Scottish ministers combined strong mathematical and scientific interests with their religious thought: e.g. Thomas Chalmers's *Astronomical Discourses* (1817), Edward Irving's early activities in mathematics and chemistry, and Henry Duncan's contributions in geology.

23. *CL*, I, lviii; Wilson, *Carlyle*, I, 155.

24. Olson, pp. 32, 34–5.

25. *Last Words of TC* (London, 1896), p. 22.

26. Wilson, *Carlyle*, I, 76; Wursthorn, p. 758.

27. Unpublished letters (NLS MS, 1764.11) from T. E. Hill to Carlyle, undated, about 24 Feb. 1814, given with the permission of the Librarian of the NLS.

28. All the passages from this mathematical correspondence in the *Courier* are quoted with the permission of the Librarian of the Ewart Public Library, Dumfries, Scotland. See C. R. Sanders' "Editing the Carlyle Letters; Problems and Opportunities", in *Editing Nineteenth Century Texts* (Toronto, 1967), pp. 84–6, and I, 8–9, for briefer accounts.

29. This seems to have been the only problem Carlyle submitted: "A and B are two ships at sea, distant from each other one mile, A east and B west; A sails east by north, at the rate of 7 knots per hour. At what rate per hour must B sail in the direction north-west, so that the locus of their centre of gravity may be a straight line?"

30. According to Wilson, *Carlyle*, I, 99, Carlyle probably did not meet the editor, Henry Duncan, until 24 October 1814, when he was invited to Ruthwell; but he had been made known to Duncan through such common acquaintances as Robert Mitchell and Edward Irving, and Duncan was later to give Carlyle commendatory letters of introduction to David Brewster and Bailie Waugh.—Wilson, *Carlyle*, I, 165.

31. *CL*, I, 91 n. 9, 113. He seems also to have continued working problems, both in the *Courier* and *The Literary and Statistical Magazine for Scotland*.

32. Issues of 6 June and 20 June 1815. See *CL*, I, 59, n. 10 and Wilson, *Carlyle*, I, 88. Though Carlyle called these "purely the effect of *ennui*",

they were inspired by a work he had read in 1813 and still admired, Franklin's *Treatise on Electricity*.

33. Carlyle attended Jameson's classes to the end, 14 April 1819, but wrote afterwards, "I am not calculated for being a mineralogist". *CL*, I, 150, 177.

34. Among those he read were A. J. F. M. Brochant de Villiers and Alexandre Brongniart; he does not mention his countryman James Hutton. *CL*, I, 162, 164, 177. On Carlyle's learning German, see *Correspondence between Goethe and Carlyle*, ed. C. E. Norton (London, 1887), pp. 156–7, and Shine, *Carlyle's Early Reading*, p. 53. For a recent discussion of this question see R. L. Tarr and I. Campbell, "Carlyle's Early Study of German, 1819–1821", *Illinois Quarterly*, 34 (1971), 19–27.

35. Carlyle read the Norwegian Professor Hansteen's work in a German translation; Moh's work was in German. Only two of the planned three parts of Carlyle's translation were published. *CL*, I, 168, 236, 240; David Brewster, ed., *Edinburgh Philosophical Journal*, 2 (1819), 63–7 and 243–53, for the Berzelius; 3 (1820), 124–38 and 4 (1821), 114–24, for the Hansteen; 2 (1820), 154–76, 317–42, and 4 (1821), 56–67, for the Mohs.

36. *Edinburgh Philosophical Journal*, vol. 3, pp. 117–21.

37. *Reminiscences* (Norton), II, 234; Wilson, *Carlyle*, I, 180. The credit for making this discovery goes to Ian Campbell of the University of Edinburgh. The book was, as Carlyle remembered, a French book but it was by Alfred Gautier, and was entitled *Essai Historique sur le Problème des Trois Corps* (Paris, 1817). Carlyle was reviewing, not Gautier's book, presumably, but Pictet's review of the book in the *Bibliothèque Universelle*, Série *Sciences*, V (1817), 253–75, which he edited in Geneva. See Campbell "Carlyle, Pictet and Jeffrey Again", *Bibliotheck*, 7 (1974), 1–15.

38. See S. R. Crockett, ed., *Montaigne and Other Essays* (London, 1897), p. xi.

39. Shine, *op. cit.*, p. 95. The "Pascal" appeared in volume 16, part II, pp. 332–5, of the *Edinburgh Encyclopaedia* (Edinburgh, 1830).

40. Hill Shine, *Carlyle's Fusion of Poetry, History, and Religion by 1834* (Chapel Hill, N.C., 1938), pp. 4–13, and *Carlyle's Early Reading*, p. 76.

41. Wursthorn, pp. 764–9; Eves, *op cit.*, p. 374.

42. *CL*, II, 80–1, 99–100. For this reason he asked a friend, then asked his brother, John, for help. John obliged with very acceptable portions of the translation, but it still took valuable time that he wanted for original work.

43. *Reminiscences* (Norton), II, 105–6.

44. Some doubt attached to Carlyle's composition of this essay, which was for a long time thought to have been done by a Scot named Galbraith. The evidence usually cited is Carlyle's own statement in the *Reminiscences*, II, 105–6: "I still remember a happy forenoon (Sunday, I fear!) in which I did a *Fifth Book* (or complete 'Doctrine of Proportion') for that work; complete really, and lucid, and yet one of the *briefest* ever known; it was begun and done that forenoon, and I have (except cor-

recting the press next week) never seen it since, but still feel as if it were right enough and felicitous in its kind!" In an unpublished letter dated 19 June 1869, written apparently to Augustus De Morgan (Univ. of London Library, A.L. 466/2) he wrote that he could not account for "the *Galbraith legend*" but that "I did undoubtedly translate the *Legendre's Geometry*, to which Dr. Brewster gave his name and nothing more." He makes no mention of the essay on Proportion, but quite apart from the *Reminiscences* the internal evidence of style and manner certifies his authorship beyond a doubt. Incidentally, his account in the *Reminiscences* errs in one detail: he calls the essay "*a Fifth Book*" of the *Geometry*, whereas it is the Introduction, occupying pages ix-xvi. Since he never saw the published book, apparently, he may not have known how Brewster finally placed it. Or, he could have been thinking of it as the Fifth Book of Euclid's *Elements*.

45. "If, for example, the first term A were the side of a square, B the second term being its diagonal, and the third term C = A+B the sum or the difference of the former two, there could exist no common measure between any of the terms . . . Nevertheless it is certain that, if C were made the side of a new square, and the diagonal were named D, the two lines C and D would stand related to each other in regard to their length, exactly as the lines A and B stand related to each other in regard to theirs: and though a line, measuring any one of the four, must of necessity be incapable of measuring any of the remaining three . . . yet these four lines are undoubtedly proportional, as truly as if they admitted any given number of common measures . . ." (p. xi).

46. Northrop Frye, *Anatomy of Criticism* (Princeton, 1957), p. 352f.

47. Harrold, *Sartor*, p. 45. Similar passages suggesting a four-way proportion are legion:

> *Call one a thief, and he will steal;* in an almost similar sense may we not perhaps say, *Call one Diogenes Teufelsdröckh, and he will open the Philosophy of Clothes* (*Sartor* 88).
>
> To breed a fresh Soul, is it not like brooding a fresh (celestial) Egg; wherein as yet all is formless, powerless; yet by degrees organic elements and fibres shoot through the watery albumen; and out of vague Sensation grows Thought, grows Fantasy and Force, and we have Philosophies, Dynasties, nay Poetries and Religions! (*Sartor* 88).
>
> Speech is of Time, Silence is of Eternity. (*Sartor* 219).
>
> Bees will not work except in darkness; Thought will not work except in Silence; neither will Virtue work except in Secrecy. (*Sartor* 219).

48. Thus Teufelsdröckh recognizes the danger of "sham Metaphors", and the English Editor repeatedly criticizes his "likening and similitudes", and "hyper-metaphorical style of writing, not to say of thinking", (*Sartor*, 73, 287, 293).

49. *CL*, I, 124–8. It may be noted that even Locke could not understand the mathematics of the *Principia*. However it may have been with Car-

lyle that he himself was unable to understand the *Instituzione Analitiche* by Donna Agnesi which he obtained through Leslie (*CL*, I, 138, 140), was unable to solve a difficult mathematical problem that Leslie submitted to him, and made no progress with Biot's *Traité de physique*. (*CL*, I, 158).

50. *CL*, I, 128. Masson wrote, "My recollection is that he used to connect the break-down of his health with his continued wrestlings with Newton's *Principia* even after he had left Kirkaldy for Edinburgh." *Edinburgh Sketches*, p. 282.

51. What he desiderates in mathematics is knowledge of "the grand secrets of Necessity and Freewill, of the Mind's vital or non-vital dependence on Matter, of our mysterious relations to Time and Space, to God, to the Universe". "Signs of the Times", *Works*, xxvii, 64.

52. See Carlisle Moore, "*Sartor Resartus* and the Problem of Carlyle's 'Conversion' ", *PMLA*, 70 (1955), 662–81.

53. From May to September 1820, he inquired through his friend Matthew Allen about a position tutoring a young man, who turned out to be subnormal. Carlyle rejected this in October (*CL*, I, 251–85 *passim*). In 1822 he was offered a Professorship of Mathematics at the Royal Military College at Sandhurst. (*CL*, II, 194, 208, 218, 287.) Though this offered security and comfort he decided by February 1823 to reject it because of his literary aspirations. In 1827 he actively sought to obtain Professorships in Moral Philosophy at the Universities of London (May 1827 to August 1828) and St Andrews (December 1827 to April 1828), which would have involved much mathematics. When these fell through in March or April 1828, he and Jane moved to Craigenputtoch.

54. *Last Words of TC*, pp. 3, 22–3.

55. Quoted in Asa C. Chandler's "Goethe and Science", *Rice Institute Pamphlet*, 19 (1932), p. 132.

56. Compare his disapproval, cited above, of Pascal's "arithmetical machine".

57. *Two Note Books of TC*, ed. C. E. Norton (New York, 1898), p. 132.

58. A further study of the place of Science in Carlyle's work is being completed by the present writer. It was attempted here only to examine his early concern with mathematics and some of the sciences before the writing of *Sartor*.

59. *Two Note Books of TC*, p. 136.

# 4

# Refractions of *Past and Present*

## by G. ROBERT STANGE

In spite of the sledgehammered preachments, the brilliant tableaux, the amiable flights of humour, Carlyle is difficult to know. One is in the habit of looking for a definable "position", a reconciliation of opposites, but this atheistical Calvinist will not reconcile the contradictions of his thought or the opposed tendencies of his art; his work is a constant dialectic, an almost reckless play of antithethical forces. The couplings, too numerous to list, can be found in any of his works: a passion for the past confronts journalistic contemporaneity; respect for the plodding accumulation of historical fact somehow lives with the wildest flights of fantastic artistry; contempt for the values of bourgeois society is made to lead to a systematic celebration of Captains of Industry. The whole business can be very irritating—as well as very charming. The clash of opposites produces a continual release of energy, a reassuring sense of life.

The special virtue of *Past and Present* rests, I think, in its accommodation of inherent oppositions to its structure and very language. As an example of Carlyle's historical method it is not as impressive as *The French Revolution*, and as a purely literary work not as affecting and ingenious as *Sartor Resartus*; but as an example of the range of Carlyle's interests, of the intersection of his literary and historical methods, I find it the most appealing—the most central of his works. If we consider it as a special kind of book, it turns out to be three things: an essay in "anti-history", a stylistic *tour de force*, and a tract for the times. To be orderly we must consider the work under these three heads, but it soon becomes clear that in every respect the distinction and power of *Past and Present* are in its exploitation of a stylistic idea.

## 1

Bracketed by the amateur zeal of the Camden Society (founded in 1838) and the austere precision of Bishop Stubbs' *Constitutional History* (published in 1874), *Past and Present* represents an important stage in the interpretation of the Middle Ages. The celebrated second book, "The Ancient Monk", is in form no more than a highly selective re-telling of *Chronica Jocelini de Brakelonda*, which had been published in 1840 as the thirteenth volume of the Camden Society publications. Detailed studies have been made, both of Carlyle's use of the chronicle and of his historical method.[1] It may not be necessary to repeat that, according to the received opinions of our own day—of the views, let us say, represented by the practice of Sir Lewis Namier—Carlyle was not writing history at all. What has not been sufficiently remarked is the degree to which he himself was aware of and even tended to exploit his anti-historical impulses. His approach to the twelfth century "world" of St Edmundsbury Monastery is resolutely modern; the choice of a medieval subject was, in 1843, very modish, and Carlyle's method was to maintain a double focus on his historical material. "Read it here", he tells his audience, "with ancient yet with modern eyes."[2] There is no attempt at the "objectivity" of more recent historians; we are never "immersed" in the past; neither events, institutions nor persons are given the quiddity of their thirteenth-century existence. There is, in fact, a stubborn avoidance of almost all the qualities of modern historical method, and yet "The Ancient Monk" continues to hold the reader's interest. If it does not give us an insight into the historical past, what—we must ask—does it do?

The answer might be that the finest achievement of Book II is in its expression of a sense of *process*. The modern writer is insistently before us, reading the old chronicle, reacting to it, moralizing on it, extending its meanings. He offers his readers a personal vision, dramatizes for them the way in which a committed, intellectually active man apprehends the materials of his art. Book II lives as a continuing reflection not on historiography, but on the possibility of our knowing the past. This open-ended form, the sense that expression is a process that never is completed, is part of the impulse of Romanticism which infused nineteenth century art. Carlyle's affinities, even when writing history, are with Browning and Dickens rather than with the elder Hallam or Stubbs. The protagonist of Book II is, I would suggest, not Abbot Samson, but Carlyle himself. Our attention is stimulated, our sympathies aroused by the writer's struggle to communicate to us the meaning he has found in Jocelyn's faded chronicle: out of the activity of expressing a historical insight Carlyle draws dramatic tension. This method of involving the reader in the creative process can be seen in the poetry of Browning and G. M. Hopkins. Hopkins, particularly, could make his subject the effort to realize a poetic insight, and by dramatizing the very act of writing poetry give to personal, ostensibly lyrical sensation an air of dramatic action:

> But how shall I . . . make me a room there:
> Reach me a. . . . Fancy, come faster—
> Strike you the sight of it? look at it loom there. . . .[3]

One effect of the dramatic impulse in both poetry and prose is to make the scene the module of construction. And indeed Carlyle as dramaturge often makes his effect by a succession of vivid pictures. This aspect of his writing was commented on from the beginning. Henry James, Sr, for example, remarked that Carlyle was not essentially a man of ideas; picturesqueness, he felt, was "the one key to his intellectual favour"; in order to sympathize he needed "visual contact".[4] And Carlyle himself insisted that it was an "indispensable condition" that the historian "*see* the things transacted, and picture them wholly as if they stood before our eyes".[5]

That Carlyle was faithful to this principle in writing *Past and Present* is affirmed by the most cursory consideration—either of the book itself or of one's recollections of it. Perhaps the most memorable episode of Book II is "The Election", the subject of Chapter VIII. It is worth noting how its climactic episode is conceived:

> What a Hall,—not imaginary in the least, but entirely real and indisputable, though so extremely dim to us; sunk in the deep dis-

tances of Night! The Winchester Manorhouse has fled bodily, like a Dream of the old Night; not Dryasdust himself can shew a wreck of it. House and people, royal and episcopal, lords and varlets, where are they? Why *there*, I say, Seven Centuries off; sunk *so* far in the Night, there they *are*; peep through the blankets of the old Night, and thou wilt see! King Henry himself is visibly there; a vivid, noble-looking man, with grizzled beard, in glittering uncertain costume; with earls round him, and bishops, and dignitaries, in the like. The Hall is large, and has for one thing an altar near it, —chapel and altar adjoining it; but what gilt seats, carved tables, carpeting of rush-cloth, what arras-hangings, and huge fire of logs: — alas, it has Human Life in it; and is not that the grand miracle, in what hangings or costume soever?—(pp. 79–80).

So far the author has given us a static setting, the paragraph that follows brings in the characters; they perform their actions and the scene is concluded as abruptly as if a curtain were lowered.

The literary skill represented by this galaxy of set pieces is stunning, but it is questionable whether they conduce to historical understanding. I think the only way the defender of Carlyle can answer the charge that he was a bad historian is to affirm that he was not a historian at all. He shows, in fact, none of the characteristics that mark serious historians of the most diverse schools. Not being, as James remarked, a man of ideas, he is not at all interested in making ideational patterns out of history; but he is equally unconcerned with either the forms or social effects of institutions. And unlike even the Romantic historians he is not attentive to the interaction of the private and public life—an obliquity which seems at first especially strange in view of the persistence of Carlyle's concept of the hero. However, I think it is the very supremacy of the heroic ideal that annihilates a concern for the complex interpretation of the individual life and the outer, public world. In Carlyle's view the heroic individual *makes* his universe: "The clear-beaming eyesight of Abbot Samson", for example, "is like *Fiat lux* in that inorganic waste whirlpool; penetrates gradually to all nooks, and of the chaos makes a *kosmos* or ordered world!" (p. 92). Elsewhere it is suggested that the "singular shape of a Man" and the "shape of a Time" are the same (p. 126), a view which hardly allows for the study of that web of influences and reactions which some of the more penetrating historians have

99

undertaken. For Carlyle the individuals who are worth writing about exist as discrete beings; all that matters in either past or present is the agon of the individual soul.

Such views, I repeat, make for bad history, but, in Carlyle's case, for intensely effective art. What he is interested in in *Past and Present* is, after all, not the Middle Ages, nor historical method, nor mind or thought, but an image, sensually evoked, of the past.

2

As a work of art *Past and Present* is a triumphant expression of the organic principle, an aesthetic tenet that Carlyle had encountered first in the work of the German critics, and then in the less admired redactions of Coleridge. By the 1830's, however, this notion had become so much a part of Romantic art that its metaphorical foundation was quite forgotten. Coleridge had said, "such as life is, such is the form", and the writers and artists of the new school were not inclined to doubt that in form all genuine art resembled a natural organism—even though such identification would be logically no more valid than the conception of the universe as a machine, or of a poem as an architectonic structure. But from the assumption that the reciprocal connection between art and nature was *real*, that true art was, in fact, *alive*, all other aspects of the organic principle developed. Abstraction, logical pattern, artistic rules are obviously to be contemned. In a truly organic creation there can be no distinction between form and content—an article of faith that led to the more elaborately figurative notion that in a work of art, as in the universe, the smallest part reflects the structure of the whole, and the other way around. A frequent means of illustrating this pleasing relationship was the leaf which repeats in small the structure of the tree. And since art is a natural process, always becoming, never being, it must reflect the dialectic of growth, and incorporate what were called the elementary opposites of existence. Such basic antitheses as the one and the many, odd and even, light and dark, right and left, provided a natural pattern for art.

A reader familiar with Carlyle will have observed that even this brief summary of the organic principle elicits some of his characteristic procedures. For example, a tree was one of the most commonly used symbols of natural growth and of the unity of disparate elements. In *Past and Present* Carlyle heightens this motif and by recurrent statement makes of the Life-tree Igdrasil the emblem of his book. It is first mentioned in the peroration of Book I:

> For the Present holds in it both the whole Past and the whole Future;—as the LIFE-TREE IGDRASIL, wide-waving, many-toned, has its roots down deep in the Death-kingdoms, among the oldest dead dust of men, and with its boughs reaches always beyond the stars; and in all times and places is one and the same Life-tree! (p. 38).

And again, toward the end of Book II there is an invocation of

> . . . The Life-tree Igdrasil, which waves round thee in this hour, whereof thou in this hour art portion, has its roots down deep in the oldest Death-Kingdoms; and grows; the Three Nornas, or *Times*, Past, Present, Future, watering it from the Sacred Well! (p. 129).

The last mention, almost an exact repetition, comes in the first chapter of the last book, "Horoscope".

The tree symbol which in poetry has stood for the unification of body, soul and spirit (*viz.* Tennyson's "Hesperides" and Yeats's "Among School Children") represents for Carlyle the unity of time and natural order. Since the three *Nornas* are also the tenses by which language is organized, syntax embodies the essential condition of being; the written work is made of living stuff, and like the life-tree has its roots among the dead dust of the past, grows in the present and reaches to the stars of the future ("Horoscope").

The whole book, as its title suggests, is based on a pattern of oppositions. The two experienced aspects of time, the known present and the past that the writer makes known to us, determine the ordering of the sections—a formal arrangement which suggests the penetration of the present by the values of the past, an act of realization which might bring about a better future. The large antithesis of the title is played out in a series of variations: smaller contrasts between law and anarchy, man and phantasm, heaven and hell, valetism and heroism, idleness and work, facts and semblances, jargon and genuine speech. Individual phrases and sentences tend to incorporate contraries: "Brief brawling Day, with its noisy phantasms, its poor paper-crowns tinsel-gilt, is gone; and divine everlasting Night, with her star-diadems, with her silences and her veracities, is come!" (p. 156). Such continual

101

oppositions are the mechanics of Carlyle's style; we move through his writing from one "wondrous Dualism" (p. 44) to another. The technique seems at first to resemble eighteenth-century antithetical prose, but the effect of Carlyle's method is altogether different. A writer like Gibbon, for example, holds the two elements of his sentences in a witty and pleasing balance. Each sentence—it is not extreme to say—is an image of reason, the syntax weighs the pro and the con, leads the well-conducted mind by normal, rational procedures to the truth. As aesthetic structures Gibbon's antithetical periods are analogous to the ordered symmetries of eighteenth-century architecture. But in Carlyle's writing there is no symmetry; the play of contraries is varied and dynamic, rudely jolting us into some new awareness. Often one element of an opposition is meant to annihilate the other: "It is very strange, the degree to which these truisms are forgotten in our days; how, in the ever-whirling chaos of Formulas, we have quietly lost sight of Fact" (p. 176). Or: "Observe, too, that this is all a modern affair; belongs not to the old heroic times, but to these dastard new times" (p. 156). Elsewhere the oppositions are fused: "O Mr. Bull, I look in that surly face of thine with a mixture of pity and laughter, yet also with wonder and veneration" (p. 160). Most characteristically, however, Carlyle's phrases seem designed to show how one term of an antithesis contains its opposite: "The cloudy-browed, thick-soled, opaque Practicality, with no logic utterance, in silence mainly, with here and there a low grunt or growl, has in him what transcends all logic—utterance: A Congruity with the Unuttered" (p. 159). The puns here are clever, but they lead to an illuminating paradox; the "cloudy-browed, thick-soled" Man of Practice is "dumb" in the proper Carlylean way, but he may have his head in the very heavens and be more durable of soul than his opposite number, the Man of Theory. The resolution of this sentence does not yield that pleasure in paradox that is a grace of Augustan prose; there is instead a rather solemn affirmation—opacity and silence are ultimately the only clear speech; the gross and earthy are the ethereal—statements such as this are closer to parable than they are to wit writing. Again and again one discovers that Carlyle's sentences re-enact the movement of discovery through transcendence.

Whereas the antithetical periods of Gibbon and other Augustan writers are discrete, each figuring a well-balanced world view, Carlyle's are part of a larger analogical structure. The sentence mirrors the chapter, the chapter the book. The architectural parallel to this style would be the Gothic of Abbot Samson's day, the aesthetic of which Carlyle could have found in Goethe's famous panegyric of Abbot Erwin, architect of Strasbourg Cathedral.

The image of the world projected by Carlyle's prose is of continual becoming, of ideas and things always being born out of their opposites. The sense of experience that Carlyle's writing leaves us with is suggested by Vico's term, "the coincidence of contraries". In shaping a work like *Past and Present* Carlyle would want his antitheses to be dictated by nature rather than by what seemed to him the mechanical rationalism of Augustan prose. It was his task to find a "living" form in which the relation between contraries is as that of the trunk of a tree to its flower, or of life to the death from which it has sprung.

The prose-texture of the non-historical sections of *Past and Present* has the density of good poetry. In a brief essay it is impossible to perform the kind of sentence by sentence analysis that such writing demands, yet by looking at the skeleton of imagery in a representative chapter it might be possible to suggest what rewards further study could bring. "Phenomena" is the first chapter of the third book, "The Modern Worker". The title picks up a minor but persistent motif in the first and second books, and Carlyle here prepares to work out the various implications of the word. It derives—we are meant to know—from the Greek verb which means "appear" or "show". In philosophical usage phenomena are objects known through the senses rather than through thought or intuition, and phenomenalism is the theory that there is no knowledge or existence outside the phenomenal world. In science phenomenology is the description of objects without interpretation, explanation or evaluation. In ordinary usage a phenomenon is simply any observable fact or event. As one or another meaning of the word is developed, all its connotations remain present as overtones.

After an abrupt, Browningesque beginning, the text of the chapter is set forth in the second paragraph: "We have quietly closed our eyes to the eternal Substance of things, and opened them only

103

to the Shows and Shams of things." The author then goes on to present, with phenomenological detachment, three appearances or shows, all occurring in the present but belonging to different epochs of history; each example is a procession which has lost all meaning, and in the conclusion all three are whirled together into one phantasmagoric rush toward the devouring gulf. Earlier in his book Carlyle had given a preliminary statement of this theme:

> What sight is more pathetic than that of poor multitudes of persons met to gaze at King's Progresses, Lord Mayors' Shows, and other gilt-gingerbread phenomena of the worshipful sort, in these times; each so eager to worship; each with a dim fatal sense of disappointment, finding that he cannot rightly here! (p. 55)

More ominously, and more than once, he had alluded to the destination of these processions: "We are rushing swiftly on the road to destruction; every hour bringing us nearer, until it be, in some measure, done" (p. 30). The streets over which these emblematic progresses proceed are both the "broad way" of the New Testament and a "life road" advancing "incessantly" toward "the firm-land's end" (p. 143).

The first of the "Phantasms riding with huge clatter along the streets, from end to end of our existence" (p. 137) is the rheumatic Pope, who, finding it laborious to kneel in his car in the procession on Corpus-Christi Day, has had constructed a "stuffed rump" or cloaked figure inside which he can sit with his hands and head extended, and so bless the Roman population.[7] The construction in which the "poor amphibious Pope" sits is merely a prop for what Carlyle calls "the Scenic Theory of Worship" and this bit of tourist lore comes to image the decay of the living, medieval Catholicism extolled in Book II. The Pope's frankness and wholeheartedness, which the author claims to admire, are employed in "Worshipping by stage-machinery; as if there were now, and could again be, in Nature no other" (p. 139).

The next degraded symbol, or "Phantasm walking the streets", appears in London rather than Rome, and resumes in one ludicrous image the inanity of a decadent aristocracy:

> The Champion of England, cased in iron or tin, rides into Westminster Hall, 'being lifted into his saddle with little assistance,' and there asks, If in the four quarters of the world, under the cope

of Heaven, is any man or demon that dare question the right of this King? Under the cope of Heaven no man makes intelligible answer, —as several men ought already to have done. Does not this Champion too know the world; that it is a huge Imposture, and bottomless Inanity, thatched over with bright cloth and other ingenious tissues? Him let us leave there, questioning all men and demons (pp. 140–1).

The final phenomenon is an empty symbol of the bourgeois world, the "great Hat seven-feet high, which now perambulates London streets" advertising the products of a hatter in the Strand. Carlyle's comment on this achievement of English Puffery can stand as a final judgment on the social utility of modern advertising:

> The Hatter in the Strand of London, instead of making better felt-hats than another, mounts a huge lath-and-plaster Hat, seven-feet high, upon wheels; sends a man to drive it through the streets; hoping to be saved *thereby*. He has not attempted to *make* better hats, as he was appointed by the Universe to do, and as with this ingenuity of his he could very probably have done; but his whole industry is turned to *persuade* us that he has made such (p. 141).

The three symbols of passing phenomena bring into focus a cluster of allusions that have appeared in earlier sections of *Past and Present*; but further, their congruity with each other enhances their meaning. Each example, available to any reader of the daily press, represents with factual precision a great ruling institution, two of which are beyond reconstruction, a third which may yet regain its value by honest work. All involve the use of an integument or artificial covering, a schema which—as *Sartor Resartus* sufficiently demonstrates—expresses a view not only of appearance and reality, but of truth and falsehood, and ultimately of the transcendental as opposed to the phenomenal world. Each artifice moves to the plaudits of the crowd, and each is hollow. But the most characteristic trick of Carlyle's humour is the fact that, though the symbols display themselves in the streets around us, they seem to belong to a mad, surreal world. In the conclusion to "Phenomena" the Pope, the Champion of England and the great Hat are swept up, along with other "unveracities", in a phantasmagoric procession that resembles some vision of Hieronymus Bosch. This is no longer merely a crowd-pleasing progress through the streets of Rome or

London, but a whole population advancing "toward the *firm-land's end*". The overtones now evoke the rush of the Gadarene swine, the frenzied procession of the lemmings:

> . . . the seven-feet Hat, and all things upwards to the very Champion cased in tin, begin to reel and flounder,—in Manchester Insurrections, Chartisms, Sliding-scales; the Law of Gravitation not forgetting to act. You advance incessantly towards the land's end; you are, literally enough, 'consuming the way.' Step after step, Twenty-seven Million unconscious men;—till you are *at* the land's end: till there is not Faithfulness enough among you any more; and the next step now is lifted *not* over land, but into air, over ocean-deeps and roaring abysses:—unless perhaps the Law of Gravitation have forgotten to act? (p. 144).

Even the kind of superficial account of Carlyle's prose that I have given suggests that, though his attitudes are essentially "Victorian", he belongs to a distinctive tradition. His literary structures are conceived in a very different way from those of Newman and Arnold, or even from those of his disciple Ruskin. A prose so densely allusive, organized according to an elaborate scheme of interwoven symbols, fiercely magnifying for satiric purposes the impedimenta of everyday life, finds itself on a line which extends—in English literature—from Swift to Joyce. If *A Tale of a Tub* is one of the ancestors of *Past and Present*, *Ulysses* is certainly its legitimate heir.

3

Considered as a social tract *Past and Present* turns out to have had an unexpectedly large influence. It has been used by thinkers on both the left and the right, and ultimately it appears to have succeeded by the force of its style, rather than by the weight of its social facts or the cogency of its arguments. The aspect of the book's influence which has been least commented on is its effect outside England. Within a year after its publication in April 1843, *Past and Present* had been treated to a review by Emerson and an extensive interpretation in German by Friedrich Engels.

It would be hard to conceive anything more perfervid than Emerson's essay in the *Dial*. For him the book is not only a "new poem", an "Iliad of English woes", but, "In its first aspect it is a political tract, and since Burke, since Milton, we have had nothing to compare with it."[8] Emerson seems determined to make the book all things to all men: "Every reader shall carry away something."[9] And though he comments on the disproportion of Carlyle's picture, "the habitual exaggeration of the tone",[10] he concludes that Carlyle's is the first style to express the richness of the modern world, the only "magnificent" style of his time.

Emerson's conceit that *Past and Present* was Carlyle's "poem" on England, and the *French Revolution* his poem on France became received opinion in the United States. As far as Carlylean attitudes were applied to a developing industrial society, they were derived from *Past and Present*. The great vision of Bury St Edmunds and of medieval organicism seems to have interested American readers only as "literature", but the social myth of Captains of Industry may be said to have found its natural home in the United States. In other quarters, particularly in the vague traditions of populist thought, the denunciation of a system in which the "cash-payment nexus" was the sole bond of human society became a part of the everyday vocabulary. It is worth noting, however, that this influence is purely rhetorical. Carlyle imposed in the most powerful way an attitude, a general receptiveness; he most emphatically did not communicate a connected set of ideas, or—much less—a system of thought. His singularity in this respect is felt if one compares his influence in America with that of John Mill, or even Ruskin. To his journal Emerson confided a remark about *Past and Present* which he kept out of his review; he observed that what Carlyle was "doing now for England & Europe" was "rhetoricizing the conspicuous objects".[11] It is a shrewd and quite complete definition.

Engels' admiration for Carlyle is less well known than Emerson's, but he may have spread the fame of *Past and Present* wider than any other commentator. His article, *"Die Lage Englands*; 'Past and Present' by Thomas Carlyle,"* was written in January 1844 and published immediately in the short-lived *Deutsch-Französische Jahrbücher* which Marx had initiated in Paris.[12] The essay, which has never been translated into English, is extraordinarily interesting; it is not only the first product of Engels' association with Marx, but—as its title suggests—is a kind of preliminary sketch for Engels' own book, *Die Lage der arbeitenden Klasses in*

*England*, which was published in Leipzig in 1845, but did not reach the English public until 1892.[13] One of the commentators on Marxist thought says that the young Engels "saw the English industrial situation . . . through the eyes of Thomas Carlyle".[14] In the light of Engels' first-hand experience of the factory system in Manchester and his close association with working-class people in England, the claim is hyperbolic; but it seems fair to regard Engels' book as one of the most important results of Carlyle's influence on other writers.

The degree of respect Engels shows for Carlyle's social views, and the warmth of his admiration for what he calls this "wonderfully beautiful" book come as a surprise from a writer whose political astringency and polemical fierceness are famous. It is revealing of Engels' own character that he begins his discussion by emphasizing the living, human quality of Carlyle's writing. Of all the books and pamphlets that have appeared in recent years, he finds Carlyle's the only one that strikes a humane note or expresses an essentially humanitarian point of view.[15] Carlyle is identified for Engels' continental readers as an interpreter of German literature, and is then placed politically—in a way that Disraeli might have appreciated—as being by origin a Tory, a party to which he always stands closer than he does to the Whigs. "So much is certain," Engels bitterly adds, "a Whig could never have written a book that was half so human as *Past and Present*."[16]

Though Engels tells his readers that he is simply going to proceed in an orderly way through the four parts of Carlyle's book, and then begins with long quotations from the first chapter, he manages to create the impression that the book is purely a social tract. He skips, for example, from the middle of the first book to the second chapter of the third, ignoring the whole medieval section. It is not, I think, that Engels wishes to conceal Carlyle's medievalism, or his religiosity, and to re-make him into a socialist critic, but rather that he is eager to give his readers the *usable* Carlyle, to translate a devastating vision of English industrial society. Addressing himself to the reactionary elements of Carlyle's thought, he points out that what Carlyle means by "atheism" is not disbelief in a personal God, but "disbelief in an inner essence of being (*Wesenhaftigkeit*), in the infinity of the universe, disbelief in inner reason (*Vernunft*), a despair of the human spirit and of truth". His struggle is not against disbelief in the revelations of the Bible, but against that "most terrible of unbeliefs, unbelief in the Bible of World-history".[17] Though Engels' interpretation errs in making Carlyle sound rationalist and humanistic, it seems to me to be closer to the truth than the views of those commentators who have insisted on Carlyle's theological bent, and evoked his vision of God. Nietzsche's remark that Carlyle was "an English atheist who made it a point of honour not to be one" has the virtue of avoiding by paradox both extremes of misinterpretation, but Engels' enthusiastic praise of the "humane" Carlyle affirms a side of the man that we may too often overlook.

Carlyle's yearning for an "Aristocracy of Talent" and his belief in Hero-worship are simply brushed aside by Engels as he moves into an extended interpretation of Carlyle as a pantheist, and indeed a *German* pantheist.[18] He relates his views to those of Goethe and accurately places him as "mehr schellingisch als hegelisch".[19] Having located Carlyle on ground where Engels feels at home he is then able to employ against him his own newly-forged ideological weapons. He attacks Carlyle and the whole tribe of German pantheists for their belief that a new religion could reconstitute a decaying society and a universe that has been deprived of meaning. Engels draws his arguments from the writings of Feuerbach, whose *Grundsätze der Philosophie der Zukunft* had been published in 1843, and of Bruno Bauer, both of whom he and Marx were shortly to attack with zeal.

Engels' discussion is, of course, an oversimplification, since it ignores the Calvinistic bases of Carlyle's views and implies that by taking a proper turn here and there he would emerge as a rational social critic. However, if the young Engels did not manage to penetrate in his definitions to the paradoxical heart of Carlyle's *Weltanschauung* where the forms of Calvinist belief, German metaphysics and a fierce social indignation play out their continual dialectic, he at least discussed Carlyle's work with a seriousness and sophistication that is not found anywhere else in the forties and fifties. There was not, to my knowledge, any British writer who considered Carlyle's work in so wide a philosophical context, and gave it such serious and informed attention.

But what is most admirable in Engels' essay is his reminder to us that as a social tract *Past and Present* is not merely an occasional pamphlet, but still an active, usable document, drawing on many currents of thought and belief. Engels need not have relied on Carlyle for his information about the condition of England. As his subsequent book shows, he had collected a great deal of data on his own, and by 1843 several writers had described "the perilous state of the land". The English book which has sometimes been associated with *Past and Present,* R. B. Seeley's *The Perils of the Nation; An Appeal to the Legislature, the Clergy, and the Higher and Middle Classes* (London, 1843), demonstrates how necessary literary art may be even to the communication of social statistics. Seeley's four-hundred-odd pages are marked by knowledge and deep (Evangelical) earnestness. His view of England is as dark as Carlyle's; for him England is "one vast mass of superficial splendour, covering a body of festering misery and discontent . . . however capital may have prospered, *the nation,* in a most important point, *has declined and decayed".*[20] Seeley quotes remarks made in the Commons by Buller and Lord Ashley (later Lord Shaftesbury), he refers to reports of the Commissioners of Enquiry and passes on a great deal of useful information about conditions of housing and sanitary regulations. But all of Seeley's shocking facts do not, somehow, startle or move us. His concern and obvious rectitude conduce finally to a kind of nagging dullness. Engels sums it all up when he insists that only Carlyle's book strikes the "menschliche Saiten". It is not just the note of humanity, it is the note of life. And it is this resonance, rather than the scope of his political views or the adequacy of his social documentation that gives Carlyle's tract for his times an indestructible energy.

## NOTES

1. Grace J. Calder, *The Writing of "Past and Present"* (New Haven, 1949) contains a great deal of valuable information. A. M. D. Hughes' edition of the work (Oxford, 1918) has an informative introduction and full annotation.
2. *Past and Present, Works,* X, 107, hereafter page references bracketed in text.

3. "The Wreck of the Deutschland", stanza 28.

4. See 'Some Personal Recollections of Carlyle", *The Literary Remains of Henry James*, ed. William James (Boston, 1885), pp. 429 and 425. A more extended study of this aspect of Carlyle is C. R. Sanders, "The Victorian Rembrandt: Carlyle's Portraits of His Contemporaries", *Bulletin of the John Rylands Library*, 39 (1957) 521–57.

5. *Letters of TC to John Stuart Mill and Robert Browning*, ed. A. Carlyle, (London, 1923), p. 83.

6. Goethe's essay, "Von deutscher Baukunst", was published in 1773 under the auspices of Herder, and is the most important early statement of the spiritual beauties of "Gothic" architecture—a term which Goethe consciously rescued from disrepute. See *Gedenkausgabe der Werke, Briefe und Gespräche*, ed. Ernst Beutler, 24 vols. (Zurich, 1949–50), *Schriften zur Kunst*, XIII, 16–26.

7. A number of travellers to Rome seem to have commented on this ingenious contrivance. Henry Crabb Robinson saw a Corpus Christi procession in 1830 and described with some wonder the artful chair by which the Pope "acts kneeling". *Diary, Reminiscences and Correspondence of Henry Crabb Robinson*, ed. T. Sadler (London, 1869), II, 469–70.

8. *"Past and Present"* in *Natural History of the Intellect*, in *The Complete Works of Ralph Waldo Emerson*, ed. Edward W. Emerson (Boston and New York, 1904), XII, 379. The original essay appeared in the *Dial*, 4 (July, 1843), 96–102.

9. *Natural History*, p. 380.

10. *Natural History*, p. 386.

11. *Journals and Miscellaneous Notebooks of Ralph Waldo Emerson*, ed. W. H. Gilman and J. E. Parsons (Cambridge, Mass., 1970), VIII, 408.

12. See Karl Marx-Friedrich Engels, *Werke* (Berlin, 1957), 525–49.

13. *The Condition of the Working Classes in England in 1844* (London, 1892) is a translation of a new continental edition published in Stuttgart in the same year.

14. Peter Demetz, *Marx, Engels and the Poets* (Chicago, 1967), p. 37.

15. *Werke*, p. 525.

16. *Werke*, p. 528.

17. *Werke*, p. 539.

18. *Werke*, p. 542.

19. *Werke*, p. 543. A much fuller discussion of Engels and Carlyle is to be found in Steven Marcus's *Engels, Manchester and the Working Class* (New York, 1974), pp. 102–12.

20. Seeley, pp. xvii, xxxviii–ix.

# 5

# Stern Hebrews Who Laugh: Further Thoughts on Carlyle and Dickens*

by GEORGE H. FORD

My subtitle, "Further Thoughts", relates to my having published a dozen pages on this topic, many years ago, a topic that has more recently gained prominence by its being extensively treated in books by Michael Goldberg and William Oddie, both appearing in 1972.[1] One of my friends, after reading these two full-length books on Carlyle and Dickens, complimented me by saying that it had been my good fortune not to have said too much on the topic. His compliment—if it was a compliment—haunts me now with a sense that it might have been well to follow Carlyle's gospel of silence and to say no more. I am, nevertheless, prompted to risk a return to the topic, or at least a phase of it, for Carlyle himself serves as a model of how hard to abide by is his gospel of silence.

Another comment on my previous discussion, less complimentary but more relevant, is by William Oddie who begins his book, *Dickens and Carlyle*, with a complaint about "the procedure adopted in one widely cited account of the relationship, by a scholar rightly held in some esteem". We learn later that this misguided scholar (however esteemed) is George Ford who made the mistake of remarking, in print, that the influence of Carlyle on the style of Dickens' later novels is "easily seen". Mr Oddie's objection, I now realize, is basically sound. The influence is *not*

* In its original form this essay was presented as a paper at a Modern Language Association conference in New York, December, 1974.

"easily seen". Furthermore the relationship between the two styles may perhaps not be a matter of influence. To "see" the influence, if it is there, would call for a lot of close work by stylistic experts, and although something will be said about style in what follows, my discussion will usually be of a more general nature and will deal with the question of stylistic affinities, which is more manageable than the question of direct influence. Moreover, this approach has the advantage of not involving us very much with priorities as such; instead it can be related to the question of affinities in general.

What were these affinities, and lack of affinities, that characterize this remarkable relationship? That from the time of his first meeting with Carlyle in 1840 Dickens was powerfully attracted by him is simply a fact for which we have plenty of documentation. Many of my undergraduates are bewildered by the story of this relationship; they find it incredible. And even older readers, as Edward Alexander remarks, are "embarrassed" by Carlyle's impact on an age of literature to which, nowadays, they otherwise feel well-disposed.[2] Yet the Victorian age and its literature will never be adequately understood without our trying to appreciate how that powerful magnet attracted everyone into its field in the 1840s, including those who later moved away from its field when it became too intense for them. In 1866, when Carlyle blew his whistle to assemble his team in defence of Governor Eyre (to which Dickens, of course, responded), it is most instructive to remember that the leaders of the opposing team, Mill and Huxley, had earlier been profoundly affected by Carlyle.[3] The commonplace I want to establish is that such writers as Ruskin or Browning or Arnold were attracted variously, and what we need to discriminate about Dickens is what areas of the magnetism attracted him and what parts, if any, repelled him. Their relationship was one of elective affinities, certainly, but also one of selective affinities.

In this regard we might ask what these two men talked about during the several times they met over a period of thirty years. I wish someone with the skills of a Walter Savage Landor or a Richard Howard could recreate such imaginary conversations for us, but I propose, instead, to consider what topics they probably did *not* talk about. The chief of these, it seems to me, would have been the art of the novel, or even, in much depth, Dickens' own novels.

Their first encounter gives a clue relating to my guess here. In 1837, Carlyle read *Pickwick* and described it in a letter: "thinner wash, with perceptible vestige of a flavour in it here and there was never offered to the human palate".[4] And in the following year, in his essay on Scott, he made another disparaging reference to *Pickwick*.[5] Three years later, when he met Dickens in person and generally liked him, one wonders whether he observed the amenities by complimenting the young novelist and perhaps making some allusion to the trial scene in *Pickwick*—a scene that in later life he was to enjoy with open-stopped hilarity. This was the procedure he was later to follow when *David Copperfield* was being published, and he delighted Dickens, when they met, by likening himself to that lone lorn creetur, Mrs Gummidge. What he privately thought about *David Copperfield* was disclosed in a letter recently published by Charles Sanders. In 1849, after disposing of Thackeray's *Pendennis* as "nonsense" Carlyle turns his pen on *Copperfield*:

> Dickens again is said to be flourishing beyond example with his present series of funambulisms [*Copperfield*, that is, is a rope-dance]:—I read one No of it (I am quite fallen behind) last night; innocent waterest of twaddle with a *suspicion* of geniality.[6]

Now I am not trying here to make Carlyle into a hypocrite; we all do this every day, as Molière's blunt speaker, Alceste, painfully discovered. What I am interested in speculating about, instead, is whether Carlyle ever told Dickens face to face about that thin wash and the rope-dancing. Despite his proverbial bluntness, I do not suppose that he did so. What he might have done, as he did with Meredith, was to recommend that Boz should turn to writing history instead of novels. "Man," he told Meredith, "ye suld write heestory! Ye hae a heestorian in ye!"[7] But that is not the same as saying, to Dickens' face, that *Dombey and Son* is a mere rope-dancing stunt, as Carlyle describes it in a fierce letter of 1847:

> Oh for a thousand sharp sickles in as many strong right hands . . . I poor devil have but one rough sickle, and a hand that will soon be weary . . . Dickens writes a *Dombey and Son*, Thackeray a

114

*Vanity Fair*; not *reapers* they, either of them! In fact the business of the rope-dancing goes to a great height.[8]

William Oddie concludes, in fact, that Dickens "never saw this side of Carlyle's feelings about him".[9]

Here I must part company. If Dickens did not know of Carlyle's contemptuous evaluation of specific novels of his, he must surely have known what the Master thought about novels in general. With Carlyle's early essays on History and Biography, or on Sir Walter Scott, Dickens is likely to have been familiar; in his library at Gad's Hill there were three different editions of the *Critical and Miscellaneous Essays* (1840, 1857, 1869–70). But even if Carlyle's early writings had been overlooked, Dickens could hardly have missed the *Latter-Day Pamphlets* (a copy of the 1850 edition was also in his library at Gad's Hill). And for a novelist as passionately dedicated to his craft as Dickens was, how would he have responded to the following passage from the pamphlet on "Jesuitism", with its fantastic blast against fiction and story-telling and Fine Arts that serve "to fib and dance":

> The Fine Arts . . . are to understand that they are sent hither not to fib and dance, but to speak and work; and . . . that God Almighty's *Facts* . . . are the one pabulum which will yield them any nourishment. . . . Fiction, I think, or idle falsity of any kind, was never tolerable, except in a world [of the indolent]. . . . Given an idle potentate, monster of opulence, gluttonous bloated Nawaub, of black colour or of white,—naturally he will have prating story-tellers to amuse his half-sleeping hours of rumination; if from his deep gross stomach . . . they can elicit any transient glow of interest, tragic or comic, especially any wrinkle of momentary laughter, however idle, great shall be their reward. Wits, story-tellers, ballad-singers, especially dancing-girls who understand their trade, are in much request with such a gluttonous half-sleeping . . . Monster of Opulence. A bevy of supple dancing-girls who with due mixture . . . of lascivious fire, will represent to him . . . the Loves of Vishnu, Loves of Adonis, Death of Psyche, Barber of Seville, or whatever nonsense there may be, according to time or country: these are the kind of artists fit for such an unfortunate stuffed stupefied Nawaub, in his hours of rumination. . . . Luxurious Europe, in its reading publics . . . is wholly one big ugly Nawaub of that kind; who has converted all the Fine Arts into after-dinner amusements.[10]

115

Now it might be said that the personal relationship of Dickens and Carlyle resembles that established between Boswell and Johnson, and that if Boswell learned to listen to Johnson's expressions of prejudice against Scotland, then surely Dickens could listen patiently to hair-raising diatribes such as this in which, in effect, Carlyle implies that the novelist's role is close to that of a whore as well as a liar. I cannot myself imagine that Dickens' response would be only a wry smile and a shrug.

It seems he responded in two ways, one that is clearly recognizable, and the other purely a matter of speculation. First, that if the writer cannot be an historian and is stuck with being a mere novelist, he can redeem some of the drawbacks of the rope-dancing profession by providing what Scott, in Carlyle's view, had failed to provide: [11] novels with a purpose (as Robert Colby calls them) in which a traditional story combines with social criticism and prophecy. From the time of his writing *The Chimes* in 1844, Dickens seems to have been aware of what was expected of him under the stern eyes of his great task-master. In many respects the role was thoroughly congenial to him. He had tasted power with his creation of Little Nell; he tasted power again, of a different order, with his creation of a Jarndyce and Jarndyce case, or a Circumlocution Office (which Carlyle admired) or a Coketown. And the task was made even more congenial because his view of the ills of society corresponded at so many points with Carlyle's view. It is remarkable how often the two writers draw from the same store of images to characterize corruption. Consider, for example, the stunning opening paragraph of *Bleak House*:

> As much mud in the streets, as if the waters had but newly retired from the face of the earth, and it would not be wonderful to meet a Megalosaurus, forty feet long or so, waddling like an elephantine lizard up Holborn Hill.

It may be noted that William Oddie prints a passage from this same paragraph of *Bleak House* in order to demonstrate that it has no similarities to Carlyle.[12] But let us look at a sentence from one of Carlyle's pamphlets, published in 1850, a year before Dickens began writing *Bleak House*. Carlyle is speaking of problems facing America:

New Spiritual Pythons, plently of them; enormous Megatherions, as ugly as were ever born of mud, loom huge and hideous out of the twilight Future in America.[13]

And in these same two works, as elsewhere, it is noteworthy how both writers resort to the image of fire as a cleansing agent. Carlyle cites a wit who commented: "That there was but one reform for the Foreign Office,—to set a live coal under it."[14] A year later Dickens concludes his chapter on Chancery iniquities by voicing the hope that the whole might be "burnt away in a great funeral pyre". Parenthetically, I should mention that similarities of this kind are, of course, most clearly in evidence in comparisons between *The French Revolution* and *A Tale of Two Cities*, but because this topic has been masterfully covered in Michael Goldberg's book and in William Oddie's, I am looking to other texts. Visions of an apocalyptic burning, as we might expect, are more prevalent in Carlyle. Of conditions in 1850 he speaks, characteristically, of "a bottomless volcano or universal powder-mine of most inflammable mutinous chaotic elements, separated from us by a thin earth-rind".[15] Dickens' scene of the fiery death of Krook, a year or so later, is one way of conveying the same sense. But the most recurrent image that they share is of contemporary society as a plague-infested "cess-pool", as Carlyle calls it. "British industrial existence", he writes, "seems fast becoming one huge poison-swamp of reeking pestilence physical and moral."[16] In *Bleak House*, as Michael Steig's article demonstrated, the dominant vision is an excremental one.[17] The same would apply to *Our Mutual Friend*, as a recent article by Avrom Fleishman indicates, although Fleishman's title, "The City and the River",[18] is less startling than Steig's. And it can surely be said that in *Little Dorrit*, again we are re-introduced to a cess-pool. Dickens' gruesome account of London, in that novel, with the Thames as a "deadly sewer" and its gutters reeking with "foul smells"[19] is in the same excremental vein. Tite Barnacle of the Circumlocution Office has a little house on a "hideous little street of . . . stables, and dung-hills".[20] Carlyle, earlier, had likened government offices to an Augean stable which he devoutly hoped Sir Robert Peel might clean away. Peel, he says, might go into that stable of King Augias, which appals human hearts, so rich is it, high-piled with the droppings of two-hundred years; and Hercules-like to load a thousand night-wagons from it, and . . . swash and shovel at it, and never leave it till the antique pavement . . . show itself clean again! [21]

All this indicates how congenial the role was for Dickens and why the younger writer can report to his mentor, in a letter of 1863: "I am always reading you faithfully and trying to go your way." [22] But was it really so congenial as all this seems to indicate? For, after all, even when the rope-dancer aspires to social criticism, he is still a rope-dancer. Perhaps in that letter of 1863 there is an undertone of discontent: "I am always reading you faithfully and *trying to go* your way." Did Dickens never protest that the role of "stern Hebrew", in which Carlyle wanted all writers to be cast, was not one to which he cared to be restricted? Tennyson, we know, spoke his mind about Carlyle when he remarked:

> About poetry or art Carlyle knew nothing. I would never have taken his word about either; but as an honest man, yes—on any subject in the world. [23]

My guess is that Dickens would have shared Tennyson's verdict, although, so far as I know, there is not a hint of formal evidence from reports of conversations or from letters so far published. Is it possible that his disaffection from parts of the stern Hebrew creed surfaced in his novels rather than in his correspondence?

The speculative trial balloon I'm launching here derives from my having been struck, some years ago, by the similarity between Carlyle's comment on Dickens and one of Mr Bounderby's recurring speeches in *Hard Times*. Dickens, Carlyle said, "thought men ought to be buttered up, and the world made soft and accommodating for them, and all sorts of fellows have turkey for their Christmas dinner". [24] This comment sounds curiously like Mr Bounderby's saying: "There's not a Hand in this town, Sir, . . . but has one ultimate object in life. That object is, to be fed on turtlesoup and venison with a gold spoon", [25] and perhaps this speech represents an impish expression of an area of disagreement between the two writers. A similar impishness is evident in a suppressed passage of *The Chimes*, which Michael Slater reprints in his edition of *The Christmas Books*. [26] Here Dickens has fun with Carlyle's well-known passage about Gurth's brass-collar in *Past and Present*. These, however, are minor. What I have been wondering about is something larger-scaled in their contrasting attitudes towards rope-dancing and how these might bear on *Hard Times*. It seems odd indeed that a novel dedicated to Thomas Carlyle should have as its chief reference point of virtue a circus. "People mutht be a amuthed [Thquire]. They can't be alwayth a learning, nor yet can't be alwayth a working . . ." says Mr Sleary, and perhaps that message is addressed not merely to the Utilitarian Gradgrind but to the Puritan Carlyle. And again when Dickens wrote to Charles Knight on this point he might have addressed his outburst to Carlyle:

> I earnestly entreat your attention to the point (I have been working upon it, weeks past, in *Hard Times*) . . . The English are . . . the hardest-worked people on whom the sun shines. Be content if, in their wretched intervals of pleasure, they read for amusement and do no worse. They are born at the oar, and they live and die at it. Good God, what would we have of them.[27]

If my guess here has any shred of validity, it may account for the curiously defensive tone that Dickens adopts when he writes to Carlyle about this novel. He seems almost to be trying to reassure him: "I know it contains nothing in which you do not think with me, for no man knows your books better than I."[28] And it may be significant that we have no record of Carlyle's response to *Hard Times*, as was pointed out by Richard Dunn in his article on the dedication for *Hard Times*.[29] All that we do have as record is a recently discovered letter from Jane Carlyle, hitherto unpublished, in which she comments upon the dedication (this letter, written to a friend, is undated):

> By the way, Dickens is going to dedicate *Hard Times* to Mr. C.! Moreover, he has invited us to spend a week with him at Boulogne. And that would be better than sitting in a pool of water in one's back-court—But, of course, we shan't go.[30]

The exclamation point here is a tantalizing item which could be interpreted in a variety of ways.

Dickens' feeling of disaffection may surface again in a more unexpected place in some of the awesome speeches of Mrs Clennam in *Little Dorrit*. Like Carlyle when he is wearing his Calvinist clothes and speaking of the rope-dancers, Mrs Clennam speaks of "those accursed snares which are called the arts". Might Carlyle, as he was reading this passage, pause and wonder whether his disciple was here kicking over the traces and off dancing with a rope again as he had done in *Hard Times?*

The comparison to Mrs Clennam is, of course, on further reflection, an absurd one, for Mrs Clennam never laughs. What is distinctive about Carlyle's Hebraic role is its admixture of colourful jocularity.

And it is this mixture, it seems to me, that is at the centre of the shared relationship of these two writers. In a short essay of 1852, *The Opera*, Carlyle offers a vivid example of the mixture. Once more he is out to attack the arts, but this time his attention is centred on the performance of an opera at the Haymarket, the frivolity of which he contrasts with the stern virtues of the Psalms of David. At the end, however, he offers a correction to the impression his essay may have developed. He is not, he says, recommending that England try to imitate the "fanatic Hebrews". His ideal, rather, is "Populations of stern faces, stern as any Hebrew, but capable withal of bursting into inextinguishable laughter on occasion."[31]

The saving clause about laughter is a crucial one, and the essay itself, in its grotesquely funny account of an opera, embodies the principle. Here is an example, his description of ballet dancers:

> The very ballet-girls, with their muslin saucers round them, were perhaps little short of miraculous, whirling and spinning there in strange mad vortexes, and then suddenly fixing themselves motionless, each upon her left or right great toe, with the other leg stretched out at an angle of ninety degrees,—as if you had suddenly pricked into the floor, by one of their points, . . . a multitudinous cohort of mad restlessly jumping and clipping scissors, and so bidden them rest, with opened blades, and stand still in the Devil's name![32]

Too many solemn readers of Carlyle forget what a funny writer he is, as G. B. Tennyson has reminded us.[33] As he himself noted in a letter to Mill: "I have under all my gloom, a genuine feeling of the *ludicrous*; and could have been the merriest of men, had I not been the sickliest and saddest."[34]

Surely here was one of the chief affinities between the two men and the two writers. If Landor were to have done one of his imaginary conversations, he would have to have left a lot of space on his pages for the shared *ho, ho, ho's*. If there were some topics to be skirted, there were plenty of others where mutual laughter could be shared, such as the misuse of statistics by the Utilitarians; laissez-faire; the indolence of the dandy: Parliamentary elections, oratory, and bungling; Charles II, and what Carlyle called, in *The Nigger Question*, "Exeter-Hallery and other tragic Tomfoolery".[35] The "vast blockheadism" they detected in the prosperous world of Mid-Victorian England provided them with a fun house. Their most obvious affinity, as I suggested earlier, is their shared vision of a sick society ("Merdle's complaint") and its attendant features of muddy corruption and foggy incompetence. The further affinity is their shared capacity to find the spectacle a field for laughter and colourful evocation. Consider, for example, Carlyle's treatment of the Second Reform Bill, a subject about which he feels passionate indignation. Yet in the midst of his apocalyptic prophecies, in *Shooting Niagara*, he indulges, as well, in what (as he says) the Germans call "mischief-joy". He finds a "secret satisfaction" that it is Disraeli who puts through the Bill:

> that he they call 'Dizzy' is to do it. . . . A superlative Hebrew Conjuror, spell-binding all the great Lords, great Parties, great Interests of England, to his hand in this manner, and leading them by the nose, like helpless mesmerized somnambulant cattle, to such issue, —did the world ever see a *flebile ludibrium* of such magnitude before?[36]

Now to labour a commonplace, this is totally unlike the way Mill writes, or Newman writes, or Mrs Gaskell writes. There is an element of "banter" here, as Carlyle himself called it,[37] which, combined with highly colourful language, constitutes the trademark of his writings, and of Dickens' also.

Of course, not all of Carlyle's writings or Dickens' writings are in this vein. When Dickens employs what we might call his soft style, jocularity and banter are absent.[38] Joyce, in *Ulysses*, points up this contrast in his stunning imitations of the two writers. Carlyle, whom Joyce obviously enjoys, is represented by a passage full of life and fun, but Dickens, whom Joyce disliked, is represented by a treacly imitation of the death of Dora Copperfield ("O Doady, loved one of old, faithful lifemate now it may never be again, that faroff time of the roses").[39] Trollope also played up the difference in *The Warden* by styling Dickens as Mr Popular Sentiment and Carlyle as Dr Pessimist Anticant. Trollope rightly treats them as a team of outsiders mutually at odds with the dominant temper of the 1850's, but his epithets also point to differences. It is when Carlyle and Dickens converge on anticant and corruption that their literary affinities become most discernible.

Finally, on the score of similarities, there is a witty essay by Sylvère Monod, recently published, on *Hard Times*, in which he asks the question, partly in jest: Who else, besides Dickens, could have written *Hard Times*? And he concludes, of course, that only Dickens could have written it.[40] Obviously I am not suggesting that Carlyle could have written it[41] (indeed, I have ventured to stress how un-Carlyle like is its circus theme), but I am suggesting that the manner of no other writer is as close to Dickens' hard style, in *Hard Times* and elsewhere, as is that of Carlyle.

### Supplementary Note: Carlyle's Letter on the Death of Dickens

Two sentences from a letter written by Carlyle in July 1870, on the occasion of Dickens' death, have often been cited by critics and biographers (see, e.g. Goldberg, p. 18). These sentences were first published by D. A. Wilson in *Carlyle in Old Age* (London 1934), p. 209. Apparently they must have been derived from an extract in a sale catalogue rather than from a complete copy of the letter itself.

The original letter, now in the Berg Collection of the New York Public Library, has been hitherto unpublished. It was located and transcribed for me by K. J. Fielding, as was the previously unpublished letter from Georgina Hogarth that prompted Carlyle to write. I am grateful to him for his generosity, and also to the Custodians of the Berg Collection for their kind permission to publish these two documents.

Something needs to be said about the circumstances under which the letters were written. According to the terms of Dickens' will, his sister-in-law, Georgina Hogarth, was to receive "all the little familiar objects from my writing-table and my room, and she will know what to do with those things". Soon after his death, Georgina began writing to various persons offering them mementos of their friendship with Dickens. Her letter to Carlyle was addressed to him in Dumfries where he had gone for a summer holiday, having left London in late June, subsequent to Dickens' funeral on 14 June.

The most noteworthy aspects of Georgina's letter and Carlyle's reply is the indication that the two men had not been meeting "very often" in Dickens' later years, and also, once again, the stress Carlyle makes on the qualities of Dickens the man rather than on the "talent" of the writer.

Both letters are written on mourning paper. The envelope for Georgina's is not postmarked, and her letter was presumably transmitted to Carlyle by Forster, co-executor of Dickens' estate.

The "two poor girls" referred to were Dickens' daughters: Mary Dickens and Kate (Mrs. Charles Allston Collins).

Gad's Hill
Monday—June 27th:

My dear Mr. Carlyle—

I have the charge under my dearest Brother-in-law's Will of distributing the "familiar objects" belonging to him amongst the friends who loved him. I had best tell you how very few the objects are, in proportion—and that I am obliged to offer the merest trifles to many.—But Mr. Forster assures me that I may venture to offer you one of the walking sticks which he constantly used— and that you will value it as a Memorial of your lost friend.—You did not meet very often of late years—but there was *no one* for whom he had a higher reverence and admiration besides a sincere personal affection than for yourself.—I hope you will not think it an impertinence in me to express this to you.—The two poor girls join me in sending respectful love to you—and I am always dear Mr. Carlyle

Most sincerely yours
Georgina Hogarth

The Hill, Dumfries, 4 july
1870

Dear Miss Hogarth,

I accept with a mournful gratitude, and many sad and tender

feelings, that little Memorial of the loved Friend who has suddenly departed,—gone the way wh*h* is that of us also, and "of all the Earth," from the beginning of things! —

It is almost thirty years since my acquaintance with him began; and on my side I may say every new meeting ripened it into more and more clear discern*t* (quite apart from his unique *talent*) of his rare and great worth as a brother man. A most correct, precise, clear-sighted, quietly decisive, just and loving man;—till at length he had grown to such recognit*n* with me as I have rarely had for any man of my time. This I can tell you three, for it is true, and will be welcome to you: to others less concerned I had as soon *not* speak on such a subject.

Poor Mrs Collins: poor Miss Dickens,—deep, deep is my pity for them, dear young souls; but what word can I say that will not awaken new tears! God bless you, all three,—I will say that and no more.

*Yrs* with many thanks & sympathies

T. Carlyle.

## NOTES

1. See George Ford, *Dickens and His Readers* (Princeton, 1955), pp. 88–92 etc.; Michael Goldberg, *Carlyle and Dickens* (Athens, Georgia, 1972); William Oddie, *Dickens and Carlyle* (London, 1972).
2. Alexander, "TC and D. H. Lawrence: A Parallel", *University of Toronto Quarterly (UTQ)*, 37 (1968), p. 248.
3. See, e.g., George Ford, "The Governor Eyre Case in England", *UTQ*, 18 (1948), 219–33, and also *Dickens and His Readers*, p. 91n. As further instance of the pervasive nature of Carlyle's influence, see N. John Hall, "Trollope and Carlyle", *NCF*, 26 (1972), pp. 197–205.
4. NLS MS, 531.7.
5. "Sir Walter Scott" (1838), *Works*, XXIX, 26.
6. C. R. Sanders, 'The Carlyles and Thackeray", in *Nineteenth-Century Literary Perspectives,* ed. Clyde de L. Ryals with the assistance of John Clubbe (Durham, N.C., 1974), p. 180.
7. See Ford, *Dickens and His Readers*, p. 89n.
8. Quoted by Oddie, p. 23.
9. Oddie, p. 21.
10. "Jesuitism" (1850), *Works*, XX, 322, 327–9.
11. On the Waverley Novels Carlyle comments: "Not profitable for doctrine, for reproof, for edification", *Works*, XXIX, 76.
12. Oddie, p. 37.
13. *LDP* (1850), *Works*, XX, 21. See also Goldberg, p. 61. For another

example of Carlyle-like passages in *Bleak House* see G. B. Tennyson's review of Oddie in *Dickens Studies Newsletter* (March, 1974), p. 27.

14. *Works*, XX, 111.

15. *Works*, XX, 7.

16. *Works*, XX, 27.

17. Steig, "Dickens' Excremental Vision", *VS*, 13 (1970), 339–54.

18. Fleishman, "The City and the River: Dickens's Symbolic Landscape", *Studies in the Later Dickens*, ed. Jean-Claude Amelric (Montpellier, 1973), pp. 111–32.

19. *Little Dorrit*, book 1, ch. 3.

20. *Little Dorrit*, book 1, ch. 10. Another example of the two writers' drawing from the same stores of images is their satirical references to varnish. In *Dorrit* (book 2, ch. 2) Mrs General "varnished the surface of every object that came under consideration. The more cracked it was, the more Mrs General varnished it." Ten years later, referring to the rottenness of English institutions, Carlyle comments: "Varnish, varnish; if a thing have grown so rotten that it yawns palpable, . . . bring out a new pot of varnish . . . and lay it on handsomely. Don't spare varnish. . . . Varnish alone is cheap and safe."—"Shooting Niagara: and After?" (1867), *Works*, XXX, 20.—I do not know whether Carlyle may have used the image of varnish in earlier writings.

21. *LDP*, *Works*, XX, 91–2.

22. *The Letters of Charles Dickens*, ed. W. Dexter (London, 1938), III, 348. Cf. note 28.

23. Hallam Tennyson, *Alfred Lord Tennyson, A Memoir* (London, 1897), II, 335.

24. Quoted by Ford, *Dickens and His Readers*, p. 91n.—Carlyle's attitude towards the Christmas feasting he witnessed in London was sometimes censorious and sometimes simply bewildered. In 1843, however, his distaste was overcome, for that season, by reading *A Christmas Carol*. As Thackeray reported, in *Fraser's*: "A Scotch philosopher, who nationally does not keep Christmas Day, on reading the book, sent out for a turkey, and asked two friends to dine—this is a fact!" See Philip Collins, *Dickens, The Critical Heritage* (London, 1971), p. 149. As Collins notes, Jane Carlyle was "overwhelmed" by her husband's "unwonted access of Christmas feeling . . . especially as she did not know how to stuff a turkey".

25. *Hard Times*, book 2, ch. 2.

26. *The Christmas Books*, ed. M. Slater (Harmondsworth, Mddx., 1971), I, Appendix A. Slater's discussion of the passages is in his "Carlyle and Jerrold" in *Dickens Centennial Essays*, ed. Ada Nisbet and Blake Nevius (Berkeley, 1971), pp. 191–2. Slater remarks: "In this case . . . he [Dickens] was not the 'pushover for Carlyle's bullying, sensational intellectual tone' that Angus Wilson finds him always to have been." See also a reviewer in *Fraser's* (1850) who contended that Dickens was generally a critic of Carlyle rather than a disciple, and who commented: "We even remember a passage in *Dombey and Son* which looks like

E                                   125

an overt declaration of war against the great priest of Hero-worship" (Collins, *Dickens, The Critical Heritage*, p. 248).

27. *The Letters of Dickens*, II, 548. See also Sheila M. Smith, "John Overs to Charles Dickens: A Working-Man's Letter and its Implications", *VS*, 18 (1974), 194–217. One of Overs' grievances about the lot of the working-man in the 1840's was the frustration of his wish to "enjoy myself on God's holyday". 'The horrible blasphemy of Parliament and the Saints", he notes, forbids such indulgence. "We tell you you must not, and shall not rest and be happy" (p. 207).

28. *Letters of Dickens*, II, 567.

29. R. J. Dunn, "Dickens, Carlyle, and the *Hard Times* Dedication", *Dickens Studies Newsletter*, 2 (1971), 90–2.

30. For locating and transcribing this letter, and also for information previously cited concerning Dickens' library at Gad's Hill, I am indebted to K. J. Fielding.

31. "The Opera" (1852), *Works*, XXIX, 402–3. See also Teufelsdröckh's laughter in *Sartor*, ed. Harrold, pp. 32–4.

32. *Works*, XXIX, 399.

33. See G. B. Tennyson, *Sartor Called Resartus* (Princeton, 1965), pp. 273–83.

34. NLS MS, 618.29.

35. "The Nigger Question" (1849), *Works*, XXIX, 367. The foibles of American life could be added to this list. Carlyle's response to the satire of "Yankeedoodledodom" in *Martin Chuzzlewit* was "loud assent, loud cachinnatory approval!" (*The Letters of Charles Dickens*, Pilgrim Edition [London, 1974], III, 542n). About *American Notes* he had also responded enthusiastically and wrote to Dickens telling him so (*ibid.*, pp. 356–7). His approval of *American Notes* may have been reinforced by Dickens' kindly reference to him (this passage seems to have been generally overlooked in discussions of the two writers). In praise of the Transcendentalists ("followers of my friend Mr. Carlyle") Dickens notes their "good healthful hearty disgust of Cant, and an aptitude to detect her in all the million varieties of her everlasting wardrobe".

36. "Shooting Niagara: and After?" (1867), *Works*, XXX, 11.

37. From a letter of 26 March 1842, quoted by Oddie, p. 26.

38. Concerning his hard public-style prose see George Ford, "Dickens and the Voices of Time", in *Dickens Centennial Essays*, ed. Nisbet and Nevius, pp. 50–5.

39. *Ulysses* (New York, 1936), p. 413.

40. See Monod, "*Hard Times*: An Undickensian Novel?" in Amelric, pp. 71–92.

41. Concerning Carlyle's problems as a writer of fiction, see George Levine, *The Boundaries of Fiction: Carlyle, Macaulay, Newman* (Princeton, 1968).

# 6

# Carlyle and Arnold: The Religious Issue

## by DAVID J. DeLAURA

1

Carlyle's later religious position, after 1834 and his more or less decisive move away from German transcendentalism, has never been fully detailed. Part of the reason lies in his failure to clarify his thought in the area, and part in a deliberate course of concealment as his theological position left him permanently outside the confines of even a broadly defined Christian orthodoxy. The usual view is that the implications of Carlyle's social and religious opinions were left ambiguous with the publication of *Cromwell*, and that only with the *Latter-Day Pamphlets* (1850) and *The Life of John Sterling* (1851) was the extremity of his views apparent. "The Negro Question", published in December 1849 and the precursor of the *Pamphlets*, gave, as Froude says, "universal offence. Many of his old admirers drew back after this, and 'walked no more with him'." (*Life*, IV, 26). But the actual story, which can only be sketched here, is more complicated.

A full account of the almost meteoric rise and fall of Carlyle's reputation between the publication of *The French Revolution* in 1837 and 1850, a period when many distressed young men were drinking deeply at the Carlylean well, would throw a good deal of light on the central issues of the troubled forties. Even among those who knew him personally and never failed to acknowledge his genius, doubts about the effect of Carlyle's teaching began very early. In 1844 Elizabeth Barrett, not yet Mrs Browning, shrewdly noted the equivocalness of his oracles in just such sensitive areas as religion and politics: ". . . the prophet of the Circle hath displayed a cloven tongue! —and peradventure the sincerity of his mode of expression in several works may at times have been questionable." But she thought that *Past and Present* (1843) had settled most doubts, and before most others she saw that no sect was to have Carlyle. She also saw that the apparent identification of Right and Might "has enabled any despot to show some sort of reasoning for any violent act". Miss Barrett was one of the first of many to indict Carlyle for a tone of dissatisfaction, "unhopefulness", and melancholy, and an "unfair method" of diminishing man "by comparison with space and time, and the miraculous round of things".[1] The next year, George Gilfillan was even friendlier to Carlyle's creedless religiosity, and praised him for giving in *Sartor* "the spiritual history of many thinking and sincere men of the time". But he repeated Elizabeth Barrett's charge that the "great moral fault" in *Heroes and Hero-Worship* (1841) is that Carlyle "idolizes energy and earnestness in themselves, and apart from the motives in which they move, and the ends to which they point". And in speaking of "Chartism" (1839) and *Past and Present*, he formulated what was to become the most frequent accusation against Carlyle in the coming years, that he has no remedy for "our political and social disease". "Does a difficulty occur? He shows every ordinary mode of solution to be false, but does not supply the true. . . . Or is it that he is only endowed with an energy of destruction and is rather a tornado to overturn, than an architect to build?"[2]

Nowhere was he more intensely read than among the Arnold-Clough circle at Oxford; but even there the growing doubts are manifest. As early as September 1847, Tom Arnold, Matthew's younger brother, wrote that Carlyle "is much to be pitied; having a philosophy that teaches him to be discontented with the life of other men, without shewing him how to attain to a higher".[3] Despite the public silence, Carlyle's darkening mood after 1845 was becoming well known among the wide range of literary and intellectual types with whom he associated in Cheyne Row, at the Ashburtons', and elsewhere. It was the revolutionary events in France, beginning in February 1848, that roused him from his morose lethargy, first to a high-prophetic welcome, and finally to the inevitable contemptuous rejection as the revolution sputtered out by the summer. For a moment he carried others with him, including Matthew Arnold and George Eliot.[4] But it was the Irish crisis that precipitated Carlyle's decisive swing toward the extremer authoritarianism of his later years. The four Irish articles of that spring, too little known even to Carlyle scholars, were immediately recognised as far more radical and inflammatory than Carlyle's previous recommendations of repressive force. Even Fonblanque and Ritoul, the sympathetic editors of the *Examiner* and the *Spectator*, where the articles appeared, insisted on trimming Carlyle's sails.[5] These essays alone would have provided plenty of basis for Arnold's judgment in September 1849, well before the "Nigger Question" in December, that Carlyle was a "moral desperado" (*LC*, p. 111).[6] But a month *before* the first of these new articles appeared, a slightly malicious Emerson reported on an evening party that included Thackeray, Samuel Wilberforce, and Charles Buller. "Carlyle declaimed a little in the style of that raven prophet who cried, 'Woe to Jerusalem,' just before its fall. But Carlyle finds little reception even in this company, where some were his warm friends. All his methods included a good deal of killing, and he does not see his way very clearly or far."[7] Emerson carried home a revealing vignette of the young men, "especially those holding liberal opinions", who "press to see him": "He treats them with contempt; they profess freedom and he stands for slavery; they praise republics and he likes the Russian Czar; they admire Cobden and free trade and he is a protectionist . . . they praise moral suasion, he goes for murder, money, capital punishment, and other pretty abominations of English law."[8]

The Irish articles provoked something between disgust and dismay. Mill answered the first one sternly, and Carlyle's friend Edward FitzGerald said, he "raves and foams, but has nothing to propose".[9] There can no longer, then, be any surprise that the Clough who had burlesqued Carlyle's style in the letter of 19 May beginning "Ichabod, Ichabod, the glory is departed" (*CC*, I, 207), should have asked the departing Emerson on the Liverpool docks in July: "What shall we do without you? Think where we are. Carlyle has led us all out into the desert, and has left us there."[10] It is not surprising, either, that J. A. Froude, not yet the singular

disciple of Carlyle he was to become, included in his autobiographical account in *The Nemesis of Faith* (published February
1849) of his wrestling-free from Tractarianism a more direct
attack on Carlyle: ". . . of all these modern writers, there is not
one who will boldly up and meet the question which lies the
nearest . . . to our hearts. Carlyle! Carlyle only raises questions
he cannot answer, and seems best contented if he can make the
rest of us as discontented as himself".[11] Young men like Arnold,
Clough, and Froude would also have heard a report from William
E. Forster, Carlyle's companion on the Irish tour in the summer
of 1849, who "was shocked at the almost exultation of Carlyle
at the wretchedness of the people".[12]

Well before the autumn of 1849, then, Carlyle was already
in the isolation he was to endure for the rest of his life, and
which he describes in a pathetic journal entry for November 11:
"In dissent from all the world; in black contradiction, deep as
the bases of my life, to all the philanthropic, emancipatory, constitutional, and other anarchic revolutionary jargon, with which
the world, so far as I can conceive, is now full" (Froude, *Life*,
IV, 22). "The Nigger Question" and *Latter-Day Pamphlets* turned
away almost all of "liberal" opinion, and most notably rent beyond repair the already strained friendship with Mill.[13] And yet,
though most of Carlyle's social and political prescriptions were
almost overnight and forever rejected by all sane Englishmen, it
should not be forgotten that a quite amazing range of even
Victorian freethinkers, including Mill, continued to speak of him
with something like affection, almost as if the later diatribes did
not count.[14]

2

Arnold's well-known description of Carlyle in 1883 as one of the
four "voices" at Oxford in the forties could almost have described
the change in his reputation between 1843 and 1850: "There
was the puissant voice of Carlyle; so sorely trained, over-used, and
mis-used since, but then fresh, comparatively sound, and reaching
our hearts with true, pathetic eloquence" (*DA*, pp. 142–3). The
poetry, the blazing genius, the largeness of moral and historical
vision—all these affected the sensitive young of all persuasions.
The decline of Carlyle's reputation as a political and social thinker

is the major subject of the evidence gathered above; but the reasons for the darkening of Carlyle's social vision from the mid-forties until the *Pamphlets* is not precisely the topic I want to deal with here.[15] It is somewhat harder to isolate Carlyle's decline as a specifically religious teacher, and the stages by which his position became known. Alert readers like Elizabeth Barrett saw his coming separation from all parties, and indeed from all brands of even liberal Christianity.[16] But many Anglicans, Dissenters, and Catholics had hoped, especially after *Past and Present* and *Cromwell*, that he was an ally. They were proved entirely mistaken.[17] The vitriol Carlyle poured over the religious world in "Jesuitism" (August 1850) could be seen simply as part of the vomiting-up mood of the *Pamphlets*; the religious issue as such was not quite directly engaged. But *Sterling*, his last meaningful public religious statement, separated Carlyle from every variety of contemporary religious thought. The new Broad Church party under the leadership of F. D. Maurice and Kingsley were especially offended to find Carlyle rejecting the Coleridgean defence of the Church, "that, by an intellectual legerdemain, uncertainties could be converted into certainties", and endorsing Sterling's discovery that "the Highgate philosophy was 'bottled moonshine' " (Froude, *Life*. IV, 69, 73). As Froude puts it, "From all that section of Illuminati who had hitherto believed themselves his admirers, he had cut himself off for ever, and, as a teacher, he was left without disciples, save a poor handful who had longed for such an utterance from him" (*Life*, IV, 75).

Gilfillan, this time reviewing *Sterling*, saw that Carlyle had openly revealed "the foregone conclusion, . . . long ago reached," that "he loves Christianity as little as he does its clergy". But, anticipating the modern difficulty in describing Carlyle's religious position, Gilfillan saw that Carlyle was even then "never so explicit as he should be" and that his religious opinions were "uncertain, vague, indefinite, perhaps not fully formed". He saw that the general public "are still in the dark as to his religious sentiments", and some still call him a Christian and even a "Puritan". Hurrying Carlyle off the stage perhaps a trifle prematurely, Gilfillan insists that Carlyle's "giant shadow is passing swiftly from off the face of the public mind. . . . It is *too late*. The gospel of negation has had its day, and served its generation, and must now give place to a better and nobler evangel."[18] At any rate, James Martineau was probably right in saying, in 1856, that although in a general way still influential, Carlyle's "specific action on the *religion* of the age . . . already belongs in a great measure to the past".[19]

This " 'Latter-Day Pamphlet' time", as Carlyle called it,[20] when he was revealing his final position in almost all matters, coincided exactly with the period of greatest spiritual struggle for the young Oxonians of Arnold's generation—the years of Clough's resignation of his Oriel fellowship, of Froude's *Nemesis*, and of Arnold's "Empedocles on Etna". These were obviously the "doubts and miseries" to which Arnold bitterly alluded in 1881: "It was very well for Mr. Carlyle to bid us have recourse, in our doubts and miseries, to earnestness and reality, and veracity and the everlasting yea, and generalities of that kind; Mr. Carlyle was a man of genius."[21] This, for the vague and useless *positive* side of Carlyle's message. Like others, Arnold chose the *Pamphlets* as the symbol of Carlyle's "furious" defects of tone and manner (*CPW*, III, 275). *Sterling* presented that younger generation with a different order of challenge. George Brimley, though hostile in saying Carlyle "has no right . . . to weaken or destroy a faith which he cannot or will not replace with a loftier", saw the importance of the book: "This life of Sterling will be useful to the class whose beliefs have given way before Mr. Carlyle's destroying energies; because it furnishes hints, not to be mistaken though not obtrusive, as to the extent to which they must be prepared to go if they would really be his disciples."[22] The years 1848–51 were an important turning point in English intellectual and spiritual life, and the series of shocks given by Carlyle to the intellectual community in these years helped to distinguish, harden, and spell out the implications of the tangled lines of earlier Victorian thought. After the convulsions of the Hungry Forties—Tractarian agonies, Chartist agitations, and revolutions across the face of Europe—England settled down in the fifties to a period of "opulence and peace".[23] To use a facetious shorthand, a whole generation married in the years around 1850, and adopted that Victorian panacea for spiritual doubt, domesticity—Arnold, Clough, Tom Arnold, Froude, as well as such non-Oxonians as Tennyson and Kingsley. More importantly for present purposes, it seems not to have been noted that, Arnold excepted, all the men of his circle—Clough, Tom Arnold, Froude, J. C. Shairp,[24] J. D. Coleridge—drew back from the Carlylean precipice and adopted by the early fifties one or another variety of Christianity, however liberal, or (in Clough's case) a near-Christian theism. It is Arnold's own remarkable independence of viewpoint (despite his own marriage, the inspectorship, and a quick decline in his poetic career) that allowed him to work out his own position more slowly, and to profit variously from Carlyle's example.

3

It may startle even to suggest that the Arnold who in 1857 called Carlyle "part man—of genius—part fanatic—and part tom-fool", and who two years later scornfully rejected "that regular Carlylean strain which we all know by heart and which the clear-headed among us have so utter a contempt for",[25] was in any positive way indebted to Carlyle's religious views. Moreover, Carlyle's name is almost entirely absent from Arnold's four major books of religious criticism published between 1870 and 1876. Still, as Mrs Tillotson and I have shown, both his poetry and his social views of the sixties are saturated with Carlylean phrasing, imagery, and ideas.[26] A likeness, if not debt, between the two even in religious views has occasionally been noted. Basil Willey has it that "Carlyle's position resembles that of Arnold in *Literature and Dogma*; it is so differently stated as to be hardly recognizable as similar, yet essentially it is so".[27] And one of Arnold's best-equipped clerical reviewers, J. Llewelyn Davies, reviewing *Literature and Dogma*, noted that although Carlyle was "in many respects unlike our preacher of mildness and sweet reasonableness", nevertheless his "conception of God and Christ" and his "feeling towards the Bible" are like Arnold's:

> As disciples of Goethe, they are both emancipated from *anthropomorphic* theology, but they have in common a profound reverence for righteousness and for the Old Testament which they did not learn from Goethe. To Mr. Carlyle as well as to Mr. Arnold, "God" is the enduring and awful power which makes for righteousness; and which causes that no unrighteousness shall prosper. The language of each about the religion of Christ is modelled mainly upon the type of Goethe's, and is more sympathetic towards it than

the ordinary tone of modern Liberalism. How far they would agree in their estimate of what Christ was, and in their judgment as to what he really said and what character he assumed, could only be conjectured, as Mr. Carlyle has thought it best to be silent on these questions.[28]

One of the best of Arnold's critics, R. H. Hutton, also pointed out that Arnold's lifelong presuppositions were exactly those of the 1840's, the period of Carlyle's greatest influence, when "certain premature scientific assumptions, . . . in vogue before the limits in which the uniformity of nature had been verified, had been at all carefully defined". Arnold belongs

> rather to the stoical than to the religious school—the school which magnifies self-dependence, and regards serene calm, not passionate worship, as the highest type of the moral life. And he was at Oxford too early, I think, for a full understanding of the limits within which alone the scientific conception of life can be said to be true. A little later, men came to see that scientific methods are really quite inapplicable to the sphere of moral truth, that the scientific assumption that whatever is true can be verified is, in the sense of the word 'verification' which science applies, a very serious blunder, and that such verification as we can get of moral truth is of a very different though I will not scruple to say no less satisfactory, kind from that which we expect to get of scientific truth. Mr. Arnold seems to have imbibed the prejudices of the scientific season of blossom, when the uniformity of nature first became a kind of gospel, . . . when Emerson's and Carlyle's imaginative scepticism first took hold of cultivated Englishmen. . . .

He finds Arnold's "immovable prejudices" revealed in his view that "miracles do not happen" or that "you can verify the secret of self-renunciation, the secret of Jesus, in the same sense in which you can verify the law of gravitation, one of the most astounding, and, I think, false assumptions of our day".[29]

Though hostile, Hutton is essentially correct. What we need to spell out is why Carlyle, more than Emerson or (as Davies saw) Goethe, remained a relevant influence, if not model, during Arnold's later "theological" period. First, Carlyle was both "religious" and independent. Arnold always proudly valued his own independence from all parties (he was a liberal of the future and his church the religion of the future); even his religion of the seventies is markedly original, in its intellectual radicalism combined with deep piety, and it falls outside the categories of the period. From his undergraduate days on, he keeps his distance from any variety of Christian orthodoxy, and even from any of the species of liberal and broad theology sponsored by such apparently natural allies as Jowett and Stanley and Maurice. For the lonely and eccentric Christian explorer like F. W. Newman or Colenso he can maintain an unpleasantly jeering and snobbish contempt. Most important, he is never tempted to join forces with the loose coalition of freethinkers of a newer generation who, following Mill especially, had put theological struggles behind them for good: Leslie Stephen, John Morley, Huxley. He is particularly Carlylean in sensing that the new "humanist" religions—in the wake of Saint-Simon, or Comte, or Feuerbach—had a dubious future.[30]

Both men were, in an important sense, both "religious" and "conservative" (*CPW*, VII, 398). They were doing the essential work of the nineteenth century—indeed of the modern world—in testing to see how much that was essential in the inherited religious consciousness could legitimately survive the collapse of the old institutions and of classical metaphysics. Despite Arnold's early interest in Eastern religions and Carlyle's flirtations with the German Idealists, both remained intellectually and emotionally what the categorizers call "ethical monotheists". They are also alike in the broad pattern of their spiritual careers: each gave up a childhood orthodoxy in the face of the apparently unanswerable rationalist arguments against a "personal" divinity, but each gradually assembled a "reconceived" Biblical religion. Both were "modernists" before that position became widely available in the pragmatist intellectual climate of the latter nineteenth century, and indeed Arnold's greater success in defining his position made him an important influence on the movement. Carlyle's "prophetic" character lay in his highly developed sense, which more and more religious people including the orthodox came to have, that some permanent change was overtaking man's religious consciousness, but that the whole traditional scheme of religious feelings and values could somehow be preserved—as Pater was to say, "the same, but different".[31] The central residue was the assertion of a shadowy providentialism, operative less and less in individual acts and lives than in some broad historical perspective. Carlyle passed on to Arnold a very Goethean fastidiousness about discussing the attributes of a "personal" God ("Wer darf Ihn nennen?"), although Carlyle would have conceded no future for even the redefined Christian Church that Arnold eventually sponsored.

Carlyle's "curious blending of stoicism, Hebraism, and transcendentialism", of which Harrold speaks,[32] left traces in Arnold's writings, but to these Arnold, though even more uncertain about divinity, added softer and more traditionally devotional elements. Carlyle, the "born Calvinist" whose faith had been shipwrecked by his reading in Gibbon, Hume, and the French Philosophes, went to the Germans, "seeking to reconstruct . . . a belief in the transcendent sovereignty of Right and in a world of immanent divine law". Though his career is unified by insistence on "the conception of moral right as the only reality, of the duty of obedience and 'self-annihilation', of the religious nature of work, of the organic unity of all things, and of the reality of heroes", by 1843 Carlyle's God was less the Divine Idea than "the Jehovah of eternal law and wrath".[33]

Arnold and his contemporaries would have had great difficulty in charting this change and simplification in Carlyle's religious thinking, partly because between 1837 and 1843 works of every period of his career became suddenly available, and because Carlyle's theological position remained inchoate and intellectually unclarified in any event. Nevertheless Arnold was particularly well situated to see that Carlyle had failed to make that Exodus from Houndsditch which he so urgently called for in the *Pamphlets* and *Sterling*.[34] Negatively, and as a programme for his own then highly tentative religious position, Arnold would not have disapproved of the attempt to remove from religion "this ghastly phantasm of Christianity", "Semitic forms now lying putrescent, dead and still unburied" (*LDP*, p. 68). Even in the seventies Arnold would have agreed that most of Christian theology had been a "broken-winged, self-strangled, monstrous . . . mass of incoherent incredibilities" (*LDP*, p. 289). Carlyle's programme would be acceptable, if not its tone: "The Jew old-clothes having now grown fairly pestilential, a poisonous incumbrance in the path of men, burn them up with revolutionary fire . . . but you shall not quit the place till you have gathered from their ashes what of gold or other enduring metal was sewed upon them, or woven in the tissue of them" (*LDP*, p. 330). Arnold's own less strenuous version of the Exodus was his approval in the sixties of the idea (endorsed by Teutonic sages like Humboldt, Bunsen, and Schleiermacher) of a Christianity stripped of its "alien Semitic" features and brought into line with "the opener, more flexible Indo-European genius".[35] In the forties and early fifties, while marking off his distance from all other positions and undergoing his own Exodus from Hounds-ditch, Arnold would have responded to Carlyle's image of the "tragic pilgrimage" required now of the honest man, "in defiance of pain and terror, to press resolutely across said deserts ["the howling deserts of Infidelity"] to the new firm lands of Faith be-yond" (*JS*, pp. 96, 60).[36]

But all this was negative if necessary, a stern preliminary to a more positive spiritual assertion. Here Arnold would have seen that the social dead end of the *Pamphlets* embodied a more general spiritual failure that also extended to *Sterling*. Carlisle Moore sug-gests that Carlyle felt, "but never admitted to himself openly, that there was a sort of second Everlasting Yea to struggle toward, a further faith and a more practical wisdom". It is "as if he felt there was a divine wisdom possible for him which he needed greater effort to find expression for".[37] It was probably not so much the intellectual deficiencies of Carlyle's vague theism that Arnold stepped back from, as a more fundamental failure in tone, spiritual "tact"—in short, love. At the very least, the "moral atmosphere" Arnold was "snuffing after" in September 1849 seems sufficiently different from the ferocities of Carlyle in these years. As Arnold says in the Yale MS, probably in the late forties: "I can-not conceal from myself the objection which really wounds and perplexes me from the religious side is that the service of reason is freezing to feeling, chilling to the religious mood. And feeling and the religious mood are eternally the deepest being of man, the ground of all joy and greatness for him."[38] And by 1853 he can say: "I would have others—most others stick to the old religious dogmas because I sincerely feel that this *warmth* is the great bless-ing, and this frigidity the great curse—and on the old religious road they have still the best chance of getting the one and avoid-ing the other" (*LC*, p. 143).[39]

Behind this is the larger and long-recognized "happiness" issue

137

that divided Arnold from Carlyle when Arnold came to formulate in the seventies his view that "Happiness is our being's end and aim", and that happiness is "the witness and sanction" of right conduct (*CPW*, VI, 195, 192).[40] But it is obvious that even before 1850 Arnold had rejected Carlyle as a model for his own slowly developing religious thought. The pose of austere but elevated aesthetic detachment experimented with in "Resignation" had obviously broken down by the time of Arnold's poems of distress in 1849 and 1850: "Empedocles", "Tristram and Iseult", "Obermann", and the Marguerite poems. Arnold had indeed incorporated "whole pages" of the argument of *Sartor Resartus* into the "sermon" of "Empedocles",[41] but even the minimalist doctrine,

> I say: Fear not! Life still
> Leaves human effort scope.
> But, since life teams with ill,
> Nurse no extravagant hope;
> Because thou must not dream, thou need'st not then despair!
>
> (I, ii, 422–6)

is obviously brought into question by Empedocles' (and implicitly Arnold's) inability to live in accordance with it. Carlyle is certainly one of the "masters of the mind" in "Stanzas from the Grande Chartreuse" (begun 1851), "At whose behest I long ago/ So much unlearnt, so much resigned . . ." (ll. 73–5). But there is surely a rebuke in the words Arnold used (in the first text, 1855) to describe the high but bleak ethical stance enjoined on him by his post-Christian teachers:

> For rigorous teachers seized my youth,
> And prun'd its faith and quench'd its fire,
> Showed me the pale cold star of Truth (ll. 67–9).

There may even be a reference to Carlyle in the faint vision of a future age, "More fortunate, alas! than we,/Which without hardness will be sage . . ." (ll. 158–9). Arnold's prescription in October 1852 of a poetry that should become "a complete magister vitae", "including . . . religion with poetry" (*LC*, p. 124), and the call in the Preface of 1853 for a poetry that should "inspirit and rejoice" (*CPW*, I, 2), though he was not yet prepared to supply such a poetry himself, are indications of a steady movement away from Carlyle and, in the last analysis, from the grimmer limitations imposed by modern naturalism.[42]

One way in which Carlyle did help Arnold in these years was in explaining the significance of the career of John Sterling. An important event for Carlyle and his public was J. C. Hare's publication in 1848 of Sterling's *Essays and Tales*, with a Life of the Author running to over 200 pages. Sterling, who had died in 1844 at the age of thirty-eight, had because of bad health and theological difficulties left a clerical calling for a career in editing and the writing of fiction and poetry. Hare implicitly presented the life, strongly influenced by the scepticism of Carlyle, as a tragedy of spiritual defeat. Beyond the inherent interest of the "emblematic" history (*JS*, p. 268) of this man, a "failure" after the brilliant promise of his youth at Cambridge, Hare's two volumes for the first time gave evidence of the extremity of Carlyle's later religious views, hitherto veiled from the public, but now frankly revealed in his correspondence with Sterling from the time of their meeting in 1834. Except for Hare's volumes, Carlyle might not have revealed so fully in "Jesuitism" and *Sterling* the depth of his religious frustration and alienation. His own life of Sterling is conceived as a corrective to Hare's account, and stresses the ambiguous "heroism" of his disciple's struggle to put off the Hebrew old-clothes of clericalism and theology. This was done primarily in justice, as Carlyle conceived it, to Sterling, attempting to rescue him from even liberal theologizers like Hare. In the process, Carlyle undoubtedly exaggerated Sterling's later scepticism and his rejection of religious interests.[43] But in presenting the unpublished letters that passed between himself and Sterling, Carlyle revealed much of his own position for the first time. The accidental timing of Hare's publication gave Carlyle the occasion for going as far as he ever was able in mapping out the Exodus from Houndsditch.

Arnold would have seen himself in Sterling, to some extent, and would have received sympathetically Carlyle's view that Sterling had saved his soul by removing himself from the "putridity, artificial gas and quaking bog" of contemporary theology (*JS*, p. 266). Arnold's own mood on the subject was not very different at the time. As he said of a book by F. W. Newman in May 1850, "It is a display of the theological mind, which I am accustomed to regard as a suffetation. . . . One would think to read him that enquiries into articles, biblical inspiration, etc., etc., were as much the natural functions of a man as to eat and copulate" (*LC*, p. 115). But Arnold would also have seen Clough in Sterling and may well have borrowed Carlyle's imagery and tone in describing the career of that later spiritual shipwreck. Arnold complained to Clough in 1853, "you would never take up your assiette [in life] as something determined final and unchangeable for you and proceed to work away on the basis of that" (*LC*, p. 130). We are told in "Thyrsis", rather vindictively, that Clough "could not rest"; he could not wait the passing of contemporary storms: "he is dead" (ll. 41, 49–50). Clough is the "cuckoo", a "Too quick despairer", a "light comet" (ll. 57, 61, 71). Even in conceding that he and Clough shared a "quest", Arnold insists on Clough's enfeebled and troubled state; too aware of the "storms" and contentions of present controversy, his muse "failed" (ll. 211, 214–15, 49, 224, 226). Carlyle, too, had presented Sterling as a creature of "impetuous velocity", "headlong alacrity", "rashness and impatience", who unsuccessfully sought guidance among the welter of modern "Professors of political, ecclesiastical, philosophical, commercial, general and particular Legerdemain". Though "high-strung", his was a "light and volatile" and "too-hasty soul", wanting in "due strength" (*JS*, pp. 84, 91, 234–5). Whatever the ties between the two portraits, Arnold sought to stabilize himself as neither Sterling nor Clough could. Independent, proud, and aloof, Arnold knew, above all, how to wait. His religious position was to be worked out very gradually, especially from 1862–63, when he turned his fuller attention to the religious situation.

4

Arnold's theology of the seventies was worked out in the context of surprisingly wide reading in theology and Biblical criticism.[44] Still, despite all his tergiversations with regard to Carlyle as a spiritual model, a good number of Carlyle's characteristic doctrines and habits of mind are detectable in Arnold's later religious writings, and they need detailing. Above all, there is the shared reluctance to "name" or define the divinity. As Sterling said of *Sartor* in the notable letter of 29 May 1835: "What we find everywhere, with an abundant use of the name God, is the conception of a formless Infinite . . .; of a high inscrutable Necessity, which it is the chief wisdom and virtue to submit to, which is the mysterious impersonal base of all Existence" (*JS*, p. 116). Harrold sees this as predictive of the nineteenth century's increasingly vague formulas like Arnold's *"the enduring power, not ourselves, which makes for righteousness".*[45] Sterling's charge that Carlyle did not acknowledge a "Living *Personal* God", a charge Arnold sustained in the seventies and firmly refused to repent of, was part of the nineteenth century's terror of Spinoza and "Pantheism", a line of thinking mediated to both Carlyle and Arnold by Goethe. Carlyle and Arnold were the true agnostics of the century, who refused to speculate on the nature of God; the label "agnostic" as applied by Huxley or Stephen to themselves was really a fig leaf for their atheism.[46] The result in both cases is a reliance on expressions like "the Eternal" and "the Eternal Power" to bridge the gap between a Spinozism they intellectually could not surrender and a deepening of the religious consciousness (especially in Arnold) they saw as emotionally necessary.[47] It also led to a self-protective jettisoning of the entire apparatus of theological speculation and dogma. Carlyle's contemptuous rejection of "Evidences, Counter-Evidences, Theologies and Rumours of Theologies" as a "world of rotten straw" and "wretched dead mediaeval monkeries and extinct traditions" (*JS*, pp. 125–26, 140–1), is not so far in tone from Arnold's analogizing of the Holy Trinity to the three Lord Shaftesburys (*CPW*, VI, 575–8), which gave so much offence.[48] Both men also resolutely put aside even "the larger hope" of personal immortality, that residual dogma of liberal Victorian religionists like Tennyson.[49]

Arnold's "natural experimental truth" of Christianity, which separated the "old forms" from their "essential contents" (*LECR*, pp. 174, 177), is in effect a more patient and more successful working out of the implications of Carlyle's "natural supernaturalism". Carlyle was as certain as Arnold that, in the traditional sense of the term, *"miracles do not happen"* (*CPW*, VI, 146; see VII, 368), and their discussion of miracles actually uses the same imagery.[50] In both, the playing off of "fact" and "reality" against "formula" and "symbol" (*LDP*, pp. 293–4) springs from the century's rationalist impulse to get behind all variable historical cultures to a permanent and universalistic (but finally fairly Christian) moral residue. But Arnold is, ultimately, less iconoclastic than Carlyle, or than some of Arnold's recent commentators would have him. The "old forms of Christian worship", "thrown out at a dimly-grasped truth", put in "approximative" language and now surrounded by "tender and profound sentiment", will survive as "poetry", a needful body of images and sentiments (*LECR*, pp. 177–8).[51] Arnold's new Christian is not nearly so naked as Carlyle's pilgrim in the desert. But both insisted that "a new religion" was a chimera: "you already have it," Carlyle declares, "have always had it!" (*LDP*, p. 333).[52] What was changed was the basis of proof for the older system of values, now that historical and metaphysical defences were failing it. Rationalism and an almost mystical iconoclasm join in Carlyle's call:

> A man's 'religion' consists not of the many things he is in doubt of and tries to believe, but of the few he is assured of, and has no need of effort for believing. His religion, whatever it may be, is a discerned fact, and coherent system of discerned facts to him; he stands fronting the worlds and the eternities upon it: to *doubt* of it is not permissible at all! He must verify or expel his doubts, convert them into certainty of Yes or No; or they will be the death of his religion (*LDP*, p. 313).

There is a very similar tone in Arnold's insistence that "Religion must be built on ideas about which there is no puzzle", and his doctrine that "the natural victoriousness of virtue, even in this world," rests on a "boundless certitude" based on "plain grounds of reason", rather than on Bishop Butler's alleged "imperfect evidence" of "probabilities" and "prudence" (*LECR*, pp. 294, 300–5; *CPW*, VI, 267–8).

Arnold's natural religion was to be "verified" not only in individual experience, but in "the whole history of the world to this day", which is "perpetually establishing the pre-eminence of righteousness". History is thus an "immense experimental proof" of the "necessity" of Christianity, "which the whole course of the world has steadily accumulated" (*CPW*, VI, 392, 397, 400). This important and often overlooked aspect of Arnold's religious thought, first developed in the concluding chapters of *Literature and Dogma* (1873), is perhaps his most explicit borrowing from Carlyle. "Is not God's Universe", Carlyle asks in *Sartor*, "a Symbol of the Godlike; is not Immensity a Temple; is not Man's History, and Men's History, a perpetual Evangel?" (*SR*, pp. 253–4). He comes closest to Arnold's point of view in *Past and Present*: "When a nation is unhappy, the old Prophet was right and not wrong in saying it: Ye have forgotten God, ye have quitted the ways of God, or ye would not have been unhappy" (*PP*, p. 28). They even coincide in the analogy they use for their Spinozistic deity operating in history. That "the great Soul of the World is just and not unjust", says Carlyle, "is not a figure of speech; this is a fact. The fact of Gravitation known to all animals, is not surer than this inner Fact . . ." (*PP*, p. 229). That there is "an eternal not ourselves that makes for righteousness", echoes Arnold, "is really a law of nature, collected from experience, just as much as the law of gravitation is" (*CPW*, VII, 191). There is a difference: Arnold is usually not very specific in his modern examples supporting his morality of history (except perhaps for the French defeat of 1871), whereas Carlyle is wildly elated, and soon depressed, by every revolutionary event up to at least 1848. Arnold would of course have been unreceptive to the associated view that Mights "forever will in this universe in the long run" mean Rights (*PP*, 191); and he might not have been surprised if he heard Carlyle's "cry of pain" to Froude about God's activities in history: "He does nothing" (*Life*, IV, 260). Both Arnold and Carlyle had a yearning for a City of God on earth, almost a theocracy; but of course Carlyle's vision of the "Drill-Sergeant" duke or earl doing the work of God by creating within his own domain a "superlative private Field-regiment" aiding Parliament in "warring-down" Anarchy ("Shooting Niagara", *CME*, XXX, 41, 43) is rather different in its implications from Arnold's final prophecy of the Kingdom of God as "an immense renovation and transformation of things" on earth, through the "dissolution" of the old order—"dissolution peaceful if we have virtue enough, violent if we are vicious, but still dissolution".[53]

The coincidences of attitude in religious and moral matters could be extended. Notably, there is Carlyle's view that literature is "the haven of expatriated spiritualisms" and that "the Fine Arts be if not religion, yet indissolubly united to it, dependent on it, vitally blended with it as body is with soul" (*LDP*, pp. 168, 319) —a view in a general way consonant with Arnold's more absolute prediction that "most of what passes with us for religion and philosophy will be replaced by poetry".[54] Even closer, perhaps, if not more pleasant, are Carlyle's screech against "a strange new religion, named of Universal Love", "a *new* astonishing Phallus-worship, with universal Balzac-Sand melodies and litanies" (*LDP*, pp. 80–1), and Arnold's protest against the Goddess Lubricity, who reigns at Paris, whose ideal is "the free development of our senses all round", and whose newer prophets are Hugo, Zola, and Renan.[55]

## 5

But, as I have suggested, Carlyle was less a source of particular doctrines than an influence, an ambience, almost a stain that Arnold never washed out of his thinking—as well as a positive model in his iconoclasm, and a negative one in his failure to march quite through the desert. Carlyle's later theism is simpler, if less articulated, than Arnold's: Carlyle is not the "English atheist, who made it a point of honour not to be one," that Nietzsche wittily called him, nor was his faith quite the "inextinguishable" flame that Basil Willey finds it.[56] The shrillness of his later appeals to a Calvinistic taskmaster God, though entirely sincere, and the frenzy with which he would smash all religious "forms", suggest to me a growing and terrifying doubt concerning the availability of the older varieties of transcendence, even as a vague force operating in history. Doubt and affirmation continue strong, and unresolved, to the end.

Arnold learned to live more serenely with his impalpable and gently affirmed divinity. A chief means for securing this serenity, and the centre of his theology, was his richly developed Christology. Carlyle, who insisted on a God of terror and fear, would have disdained Arnold's deity, stripped of such rough attributes. Carlyle's system, in Arnold's eyes, virtually came down to this: *I suffer, therefore I am.*[57] Both Carlyle and Arnold were attracted to Novalis's doctrine of Annihilation of Self (*Selbsttödtung*) and Goethe's recommendation of Renunciation (*Ent-*

*sagen*) (*Sartor*, pp. 186, 191; *LPD*, p. 303), and both sought to deepen them into something more authentically religious. But Arnold's "natural law of rule and suppression" brings not only Carlyle's pain and suffering, but joy and peace by "attachment" to Jesus, through his "method" of inwardness, his "secret" of self-renouncement, and his "temper" of mildness and sweetness.[58]

What Arnold had, and Carlyle lacked, was an authentic doctrine of conversion. Carlyle's own "conversion" in the twenties was rudimentary in content,[59] and like Evangelical conversion, had an underdeveloped sense of the ensuing spiritual life. As Willey says, in Carlyle's conversion "there is no contrition, no reliance upon grace or redeeming love, but on the contrary, much proud and passionate self-assertion. The emotion that follows release is hatred and defiance of the Devil, rather than love and gratitude towards God."[60] Although Arnold's doctrine of conversion also lacked to a large extent a traditional sense of sin and submission, he had an implicit theory of grace and he knew that religion must be located in the "central" or "buried" self, which by the seventies had become the "real" or "best" self. Arnold knew that the sense of the holy is deeply intertwined with man's possession of his own interiority. In contrast, Carlyle fled from and feared his own interior self and the chaos he would encounter there. He was right (and in this like Arnold and the Tractarians) in asserting that the self-preoccupation of a "morbid" Methodism (" 'Am I right? Am I wrong? Shall I be saved? Shall I not be damned?' ") was "but a new phasis of *Egoism*, stretched out into the Infinite" (*PP*, p. 117; see *CPW*, VI, 35–6). But there is something else revealed in a remark he made to Espinasse about his own avoidance of self-examination: "I never troubled myself . . . about my faults, it was only not struggling enough."[61] In Arnold's terms, Carlyle was not a "still, considerate mind", nor did he qualify for membership among the "children of the second birth" (*LC*, p. 110). The chasm that Carlyle fixes, in "Characteristics" (1831), between "the Voluntary and Conscious" and "the Involuntary and Unconscious" (*CME*, XXVIII, 10) is wider than the gap between Arnold's ordinary self and best self. In insisting that even in "the Moral sphere" not only is "self-contemplation" a "symptom of disease" and a form of "self-seeking", but "unconsciousness" is evidence of "wholeness" (*ibid.*, pp. 7–8), Carlyle was in effect renouncing that legitimate quest for self-knowledge and self-possession that is central in Arnold's career.[62]

Despite a strong mystical bent of his own,[63] Arnold refused to slip the leash of "ordinary" consciousness, however expanded and elevated. This is the limitation of his religious vision, but also a source of its continuing appeal. Carlyle predicted that spiritual seekers must face two centuries of "foul agnostic welter through the Stygian seas of mud" before they "pursue their *human* pilgrimage"; he would have viewed Arnold's serious concern with the residual value of the emotion, art, worship, and ethics of historical religion as a premature regression to the "superstitious terror" and "pestilential" old-clothes of mankind's now outgrown past (*LDP*, pp. 329–30). Carlyle's "naked" religiousness has its attractions, but very few followers. Arnold's position is logically vulnerable, and flawed by its shortsighted dependence on what proved to be orthodox Christianity's continually diminishing hold on the educated community. But it remains close to the implicit religious position of a large number of "humanistically" oriented people in the West who have not simply broken with man's religious past. In the nineteenth century England produced at least three men of original theological and religious genius—Coleridge, Newman, and F. D. Maurice. Outside of orthodoxy altogether, Arnold joins them in having created single-handedly one of the permanently available modern religious positions. For all his reservations about Carlyle's tone and temper, Arnold acknowledged to the end that the "scope and upshot of his teaching are true" (*DA*, p. 196). In working out his own religious views. Arnold was continuing not only his father's work, but curiously and problematically, Carlyle's too.

## NOTES

The following additional abbreviations are used:

CME:  *Critical and Miscellaneous Essays, Works*, XXVI–XXX.
JS:  *The Life of John Sterling, Works*, XI.
PP:  *Past and Present, Works*, X.
CC:  *The Correspondence of Arthur Hugh Clough*, ed. Frederick L. Mulhauser (Oxford, 1957).

CPW:   *Complete Prose Works of Matthew Arnold*, ed. R. H. Super (Ann Arbor, 1960–).

DA:    Matthew Arnold, *Discourses in America* (New York, 1924).

LC:    *Letters of Matthew Arnold to Arthur Hugh Clough*, ed. Howard Foster Lowry (London and New York, 1932).

LECR:  Matthew Arnold, *Last Essays on Church and Religion, in St Paul & Protestantism and Last Essays on Church and Religion*, 2 vols in one (New York, 1833).

NL:    *New Letters of TC*, ed. A. Carlyle, 2 vols (London, 1904).

1. R. H. Horne, *A New Spirit of the Age* (London, 1844), II, 270–3, 276. Dyer, p. 371, lists the essay as "largely Elizabeth Barrett's composition".

2. George Gilfillan, *A Gallery of Literary Portraits* (Edinburgh, 1845), pp. 124, 134, 136–7. J. B. Mozley, in a review of *Cromwell* in April 1846 (*Essays Historical and Theological* [London, 1878], pp. 229–37), delivered a strong blow against the doctrine of Might and Right, and Carlyle's emphasis on the "grandeval element of Power", "beyond the sphere and limits of morality".

3. *New Zealand Letters of Thomas Arnold the Younger* . . . (Auckland and London, 1967), p. 7.

4. I have explored Arnold's mood in the spring of 1848, and how he differed from both Carlyle and Clough, in "Matthew Arnold and the Nightmare of History", in *Victorian Poetry* (London, 1972). And see *The George Eliot Letters*, ed. Gordon S. Haight (New Haven, 1954), I, 252–3.

5. See *Life*, III, 437. The articles are collected in *Rescued Essays of TC*, ed. Percy Newberry (London, 1892).

6. In "Arnold and Carlyle", *PMLA*, 79 (March 1964), 104–5, I puzzled over the apparently sharp change in Arnold's views between March 1848 and September 1849. The evidence presented here suggests that the later view was long preparing in the minds of Carlyle's acquaintances, and that Arnold's mood of March 1848 was one of only temporary elation.

7. James Elliot Cabot, *A Memoir of Ralph Waldo Emerson* (Boston and New York, 1899), II, 530–1.

8. And so on through suppression of freedom of the press and "stringent government". See "Carlyle", in *The Complete Works of Ralph Waldo Emerson* (Boston and New York, 1883, 1904), X, 491–2; written in 1881, but incorporating a letter written shortly after the 1848 visit.

9. See Mill, in the *Examiner*, 13 May 1848, p. 107; and *Letters of Edward Fitzgerald* (London, 1910), I, 239, 4 May 1848. After listening to Carlyle dismiss the notion of immortality in Tennyson's presence, in May 1846, Fitzgerald reported: "Carlyle gets more wild, savage and unreasonable every day; and I do believe will turn mad." Wilson, *Carlyle*, III, 325–7. Tennyson, a good friend of Carlyle's, told Elizabeth Rundle in 1848: "You would like him for one day, but then get tired

of him; so vehement and destructive." See Sir Charles Tennyson, *Alfred Tennyson* (New York, 1949), p. 231.

10. Cited in Katherine Chorley, *Arthur Hugh Clough: The Uncommitted Mind* (Oxford, 1962), p. 132. In some versions, "the wilderness".

11. *The Nemesis of Faith*, ed. Moncure D. Conway (London, 1903), p. 23. For Carlyle's amusing reaction to the book ("a wretched mortal's vomiting up all his interior crudities, dubitations, and spiritual, agonising bellyaches, into the view of the public, and howling tragically") see *NL*, II, 59.

12. Ellis Yarnall, *Wordsworth and the Coleridges* (New York, 1899), p. 253. Forster became Matthew Arnold's brother-in-law in the summer of 1850.

13. See Mill's article, signed "D", in *Fraser's*, 41 (Jan. 1850), 25–31; and Edward Alexander, "Mill's Marginal Notes on Carlyle's 'Hudson's Statue'", *ELN*, 7 (December, 1969), 120–3. David Masson, in the *North British Review* (Nov. 1850), exactly caught the gathering mood: "For some years . . . a reaction has been in process against Mr Carlyle and his doctrines—a reaction, the elements of which were in existence before, but have only recently come together and assumed something like declared organization." See *TC, The Critical Heritage*, ed. J. P. Seigel (London, 1971), item 28, pp. 335–6.

14. See Mill's *Autobiography and Other Writings*, ed. Jack Stillinger (Boston, 1969), pp. 105–6; *Essays of George Eliot*, ed. Thomas Pinney (London, 1968), pp. 212–5; Leonard Huxley, *Life and Letters of Thomas Henry Huxley* (London and New York, 1903), I, 318, II, 172; Leslie Stephen, "Carlyle's Ethics", in *Hours in a Library* (London, 1899), III, 305, and *Some Early Impressions* (London, 1924), pp. 53–4, 105–9—the last explaining why undergraduates in the fifties turned for religious guidance from Carlyle to Maurice. As Stephen said in 1881 (Seigel, p. 485), "The character had a power quite independent of the special doctrines asserted."

15. The best account of both the personal and the public reasons for the tone of the *Pamphlets* is given in Chapters I and II of Evan A. Reiff's 1937 Iowa Dissertation, "Studies in Carlyle's *Latter-Day Pamphlets*".

16. The hostile William Sewell, in the *Quarterly* (Sept. 1840), had found "no profession of a definite Christianity" in Carlyle, and instead "a new profession of Pantheism". The equally High Church William Thomson, in the *Christian Remembrancer* (Aug. 1843), accused Carlyle of "an infidelity that dares not speak out", and says of *Heroes*, "*It is not a Christian Book.*" See Seigel, items 11 and 13. Kathleen Tillotson, in "Matthew Arnold and Carlyle" (*Mid-Victorian Studies* [London, 1965], p. 225 and n.), cites a phrase from the *British Quarterly Review*, 10 (Aug. 1849), 1–45, acknowledging Carlyle's standing as a critic, and by calling the article "strikingly representative of the contemporary view of Carlyle", implies that the article is favourable to Carlyle. In fact, with the exception of one paragraph from which she quotes (p. 42), the article is an elaborate attack on Carlyle's "onesidedness and exaggera-

ation" in all matters, and especially the "mischief" his religious views have done. In her fascinating study, *Novels of the Eighteen-Forties* (London, 1956), p. 152, Mrs Tillotson claims that, so pervasive was Carlyle's influence in the forties that, "even when such acceptance was shaken by *Latter-Day Pamphlets* at the end of the decade, Carlyle's power over men's minds did not wane". And citing Saintsbury (*Corrected Impressions*, 1895), misleadingly in my judgment, she declares, "Only towards the close of the century did it become usual to measure Carlyle by the content of his teaching. . . ." As the evidence of the present article suggests, her general view of the history of Carlyle's "influence" and reputation at mid-century requires numerous and careful qualifications.

17. On 26 Jan. 1850, early in the writing of the *Pamphlets*, Carlyle wrote (*NL*, II, 86–7): "All the twaddling *sects* of the country, from Swedenborgians to Jesuits, have for the last ten years been laying claim to 'T. Carlyle,' each for itself; and now they will find that the said 'T.' belongs to a sect of his own, which is worthy of instant damnation."

18. G. Gilfillan, *A Third Gallery of Portraits* (Edinburgh, 1854), pp. 313–27; originally in *Eclectic Review*, 7 (Nov. 1851), 717–29. The same assessment of Carlyle's total detachment from Christianity, even an "antichristian" spirit, was made by John Tulloch (*North British Review*, Feb. 1852), and the High Church *Christian Observer and Advocate* (April 1852); see Seigel, items 33 and 34.

19. "Personal Influence on Present Theology", in *Essays, Reviews and Addresses* (London, 1890), I, 266. No one seems to have made anything of Kingsley's remarkable letter of 5 April 1857, disclaiming adherence to Carlyle's "theology or quasi-theology", and declaring his "eternities" and "abysses" to be nothing to him but "clouds and wind put in the place of a personal God": see J. H. Rigg, *Modern Anglican Theology*, 1st ed. 1859 (3rd ed. London, Wesleyan Conference Office, 1880), p. 391, see also pp. 4–6, 116, 381–2, 414. Kingsley's three letters to Rigg—printed as two and with significant omissions—occur in *Charles Kingsley, His Letters and Memories of His Life*, ed. by His Wife, 2nd ed. (London, 1877), II, 22–3; the letters were further shortened, or even deleted, in later abridgements. In Nov. 1856 Kingsley expressed his wrath and disgust with Carlyle's "present phase, moral & intellectual"—though he later resumed friendly relations. See R. B. Martin, *The Dust of Combat, A Life of Charles Kingsley* (London, 1959), pp. 198–9.

20. *Reminiscences* (Froude), p. 449.

21. *Mixed Essays and Irish Essays and Others* (New York, 1904), p. 33.

22. George Brimley, "Carlyle's Life of Sterling", in *Essays* (1st ed. 1858; 3rd ed., London, 1882), pp. 247–9. Originally in *Spectator*, 24 (25 Oct. 1851), 1023–4.

23. See G. Kitson Clark, *The Making of Victorian England* (New York, 1967), p. 32.

24. Froude is an exception only in becoming an open "disciple" of Carlyle's. What his rationalistic Protestantism owes to Carlyle, apart from the notion of the Bible of History, is a different question, not much illuminated in W. H. Dunn, *James Anthony Froude, A Biography* (Oxford, 1961) I, 72–4, 97, 111–12, 201–2. J. C. Shairp, an unduly neglected minor critic, was to become Professor of Poetry at Oxford (1877–85). His withdrawal from Carlyle can be gathered from W. A. Knight, *Principal Shairp and His Friends* (London, 1888). Just what of Carlyle's message Clough retained after the forties needs further clarification. The fullest discussion is in Michael Timko, *Innocent Victorians* (Athens, Ohio, 1966).
25. R. B. Lowe, "Two Arnold Letters", *MP*, 52 (May 1855), 264; and *LC*, p. 151.
26. See nn. 6 and 16.
27. *Nineteenth Century Studies: Coleridge to Matthew Arnold* (London, 1955), p. 113.
28. "Mr Matthew Arnold's New Religion of the Bible", *Contemporary Review*, 21 (May 1873), 850–1.
29. *Essays on Some of the Modern Guides to English Thought in Matters of Faith* (London and New York, 1888), pp. 131–3.
30. "Progress", a poem of the early fifties, implies respect for some permanent relevance in "the old faiths" and a contempt for "the pride of life" of those moderns who are indifferent to "the fire within" and the need to *"be born again"*.
31. Not until Froude's *Life* appeared in the eighties would Arnold have been able to see even fragments of "Spiritual Optics", written in Nov. 1852, Carlyle's final and unsuccessful attempt to clarify his natural supernaturalism. The complete text is for the first time presented in Murray Baumgarten, "Carlyle and 'Spiritual Optics' ", *VS*, 11 (June 1968,) 503–22. In the "overturning" of the spiritual world, involving a new series of divineness "in man himself", "nothing that was divine, sublime, demonic, beautiful, or terrible is the least abolished for us". The ancient Jews were essentially right about Godhood, Providence, Judgment Day, the Eternal Soul of Right—even if they misattributed this scheme to the 'Great Jehovah and Creator" (Baumgarten, pp. 514, 516, 517). Unfortunately, Baumgarten treats the MS as a problem in rhetoric, without reference to its substance or significance, and thus fails to note that most of Carlyle's position here would have been evident to the alert reader of Carlyle's published prose of the period.
32. "The Mystical Element in Carlyle (1827–1834)", *MP*, 29 (May 1932), p. 463.
33. *Carlyle and German Thought, 1819–1834* (New Haven, 1934), pp. 235–7.
34. See Harrold, *Carlyle and German Thought*, p. 336: ". . . he never parted wholly from some of the thought-forms of dogmatic Christianity: he never made the 'exodus from Houndsditch.' Though the author of *Sartor Resartus*, he never adequately re-tailored his convictions. His failure to do so contributed one of the major elements in the 'Victorian compromise.' "

35. *CPW*, III, 301. See my *Hebrew and Hellene in Victorian England: Newman, Arnold, and Pater* (Austin, 1969), p. 172.
36. The pilgrimage Carlyle outlines is to be done in "darkness" and in "the raging gulf-currents": "Some arrive; a glorious few: many must be lost,—go down upon the floating wreck which they took for land" (*JS*, pp. 96–7). Is there a hint of this in the portrait of "the pale master" on the "spar-strewn deck" struck by the "tempest" in "A Summer Night" (published 1852)?

> And the sterner comes the roar
> Of sea and wind, and through the deepening gloom
> Fainter and fainter wreck and helmsman loom,
> And he too disappears, and comes no more.
> (Lines 70–3).

Or a hint of the pilgrimage in "Rugby Chapel": "Friends, who set forth at our side, / Falter, are lost in the storm. / We, we only are left!" (Lines 102–4, and see 117–8)?
37. "The Persistence of Carlyle's 'Everlasting Yea' ", *MP*, 54 (Feb. 1957), 196.
38. Cited in *The Poems of Matthew Arnold*, ed. Kenneth Allott (London, 1965), p. 262.
39. Even in the late forties Carlyle knew that the Exodus, "alas! is *impossible* as yet, tho it is the gist of all writings and wise books, I sometimes think—the goal to be wisely aimed at as the first for all of us. . . . But they that come out hitherto come in a state of brutal nakedness, scandalous mutation; and impartial bystanders say sorrowfully, 'Return rather, it is even better to return.' " Wilson, *Carlyle*, III, 409. Also, as Francis Espinasse reports (*Literary Recollections and Sketches* [London, 1893], p. 196), "in spite of all the harsh things that he wrote concerning the creed of orthodoxy, he recognised its hold on human nature, and said to me once, 'it will be a long time before they give it up' ".
40. See *PMLA*, 79 (1964), 126–7.
41. C. B. Tinker and H. F. Lowry, *The Poetry of Matthew Arnold: A Commentary* (London, 1940), p. 300. All quotations of Arnold's poetry are from *The Poetical Works of Matthew Arnold*, ed. C. B. Tinker and H. F. Lowry (London, 1950).
42. The shift in Arnold's poetry and poetics is summarized with admirable lucidity by K. Allott, in "A Background for 'Empedocles on Etna' ", *Essays and Studies*, NS 21 (1968), 80–100.
43. Good comments on the dialectic of the two books are given by William Blackburn, in "Carlyle and the Composition of *The Life of John Sterling*", *SP*, 44 (October 1947), 672–87. That Sterling's religious concerns continued strong to the end of his life is evident in Anne Kimball Tuell's excellent *John Sterling: A Representative Victorian* (New York, 1941). Though in my judgment he exaggerates in reading *Sterling*

151

as a "complete reversal" of the premises of *Sartor* and in totally "interiorizing" Carlyle's religious position in the book, Albert LaValley, *Carlyle and the Idea of the Modern* (New Haven and London, 1968), chapter 6, gives the book the most brilliant and searching treatment it has ever received.

44. The best account of Arnold's religious position and its sources is given in William Robbins's *The Ethical Idealism of Matthew Arnold* (London, 1959). His passing references to Carlyle (pp. 58, 123, 167) suggest no direct influence, only a general feeling for "the moral purposiveness of life".

45. Harrold, *Sartor*, p. 307. That Carlyle did not include his own evasive reply of June 4 (now in *Letters of TC to John Stuart Mill, John Sterling and Robert Browning*, ed. A. Carlyle [London, 1923], pp. 191–4) is indicative of his radical mood in 1851.

46. See Walter E. Houghton, "The Rhetoric of T. H. Huxley", *Univ. of Toronto Quarterly*, 18 (January 1949), 159–75.

47. For a fascinating discussion of Coleridge's inability (one I think he shared with Carlyle and Arnold) to relinquish either the "I am" of orthodox Christianity or the "it is" of Spinoza, see Thomas MacFarlane, *Coleridge and the Pantheist Tradition* (Oxford, 1969).

48. Arnold would have approved the sentence in Carlyle's reply to Sterling in June 1835: " 'Personal,' 'impersonal,' One, Three, what meaning can any mortal (after all) attach to them in reference to such an object?" (*Letters of TC*, p. 193).

49. See Carlyle to Tennyson in 1846: Wilson, *Carlyle*, III, 325–7; *CPW*, V, 171; VI, 232, 291, 403–4.

50. See the parallel passages on floating iron brought together by R. H. Super, in *The Time Spirit of Matthew Arnold* (Ann Arbor, 1970), pp. 70–1.

51. If Arnold read the letters of Sterling to his cousin William Coningham, first published in 1848, he saw a more "Christian" variant of the Carlylean discrimination predictive of his own later tone and vocabulary. In *Twelve Letters* (2nd ed. London, 1851), p. 14, Sterling contrasts "the moral and devotional side of Christianity" ("full of truth and goodness") with the present creed, and advocates "the combination of lax latitudinarianism as to the history of religion with earnest elevation of faith and feeling as to its eternal ideas". Morse Peckham's discussion of Carlyle's separation of the principle of "belief" from all particular "beliefs" (*Victorian Revolutionaries* [New York, 1970], chapter II) applies largely to Arnold, though Arnold saw more "permanent" values in the Judaeo-Christian experience.

52. See Arnold's scorn for reconstructed "religions of the future": *CPW*, III, 279–80.

53. *LECR*, p. 327; and "A Comment on Christmas", *Contemporary Review*, 47 (April, 1885), 472. John Holloway is suggestive on the difference in tone, though he underplays the seriousness and even danger of Arnold's later views: "All the apocalyptic quality of Carlyle's historical deter-

minism is gone; the trend of events is governed not by some ever-ready and apocalyptic hand, but by a gentle Platonic harmony between virtue, reason, and reality. The course of history is not grand, simple and mysterious, but neat and orderly, now one thing and now another, according to time and place." *The Victorian Sage* (1953; rpt. Hamden, Conn., 1962), p. 205.

54. *Essays in Criticism, Second Series* (London, 1896), p. 3. The link was mentioned in passing by Mrs Tillotson (*Mid-Victorian Studies*), p. 230; I have touched on the same idea in *PMLA*, 79, 117n., where I failed to note her earlier raising of the issue. The topic has received its most detailed treatment in Lawrence J. Starzyk, "Arnold and Carlyle" (*Criticism*, 12 [Fall, 1970], 281–300), which errs in my judgment by simplifying and overstating the identification of the two realms, especially in Carlyle. I have pursued the theme in "The Future of Poetry: A Context for Arnold and Carlyle", forthcoming in a Festschrift for Professor C. R. Sanders, ed. J. Clubbe (Duke Univ. Press).

55. See *CPW*, VI, 390–2; "Numbers", *DA*, pp. 49–62; "A Comment on Christmas", p. 470. Tennyson's "Locksley Hall Sixty Years After", with its "troughs of Zolaism", came later, in 1886.

56. From *The Twilight of the Gods: The Complete Works of Friedrich Nietzsche*, ed. Oscar Levy (Edinburgh, 1909–13), XVI, 70; Willey, p. 113. The best balanced modern presentation of Carlyle's theism can be found in the final chapter of G. B. Tennyson's *"Sartor" Called "Resartus"* (Princeton, 1965). I agree that Carlyle's conversion was not mere "glorification of his ego" (p. 325) and that in an important sense "his orientation remained basically Christian", but Tennyson tends to pull Carlyle to a more traditional position than the evidence warrants, even in the matter of the immortality of the soul (p. 328). On the imaginative ambience of Carlyle's theology, as well as his pride and contempt for ordinary mortals, R. H. Hutton, *Modern Guides* (n. 30, above), chapter I, remains of great value.

57. See A. O. J. Cockshut, *The Unbelievers: English Agnostic Thought, 1840–1890* (London, 1964), p. 133: "Carlyle valued unhappiness, because it seemed to show that *we don't fit*. It was better, he thought, to be a torn and bleeding animal body doomed to destruction between two wheels. Then, at least, one was alive."

58. *CPW*, VI, 295, 310, 299. And see "A Comment on Christmas", p. 472, where the annulment of self is made the condition of a broader "happiness in the common good".

59. See Harrold, "The Mystical Element" (n. 33, above), p. 463: "His 'purgation' amounted only to a Calvinistic rejection of worldly ease, and his 'illumination' never went further than 'a flash of rudimentary vision' into the 'otherness of natural things'. . . ." The long and complex process of Carlyle's "conversion" is studied in Carlisle Moore, "*Sartor Resartus* and the Problem of Carlyle's Conversion", *PMLA*, 70 (Sep. 1955), 662–81.

60. Willey, p. 115. C. R. Sanders, "The Question of Carlyle's 'Conversion' ",

*Victorian Newsletter*, No. 10 (Autumn 1956), p. 11, probably too strongly, places Carlyle's conversion in "a rebellious spirit and a determination to emancipate himself from all that would shackle his own ego". See also Cockshut, *The Unbelievers*, p. 135.

61. *Literary Recollections* (n. 39, above), pp. 196–7.

62. James Martineau saw some of this in 1856. Carlyle's rejection of "reflective thought", he says, is a rejection of "inwardness", and a "tragic paradox", springing "from a deep sense of the hatefulness of self-worship, and the barrenness of mere self-formation" (*Essays, Reviews and Addresses*, I, 269–70). And yet I agree with Mrs Tillotson (*Mid-Victorian Studies*, p. 238) that the fundamental image and point of Arnold's "The Buried Life" (published 1852) may have a source in Carlyle's words: "Of our Thinking, we might say, it is but the mere upper surface that we shape into articulate Thoughts;—underneath the region of argument and conscious discourse, lies the region of meditation; here, in its quiet mysterious depths, dwells what vital force is in us" (*CME*, XVIII, 4–5).

63. Arnold's rich contrast of the "voluntary, rational, and human world, of righteousness, moral choice, effort" and "the necessary, mystical, and divine world, of influence, sympathy, emotion" (*CPW*, III, 36–8) uses terms parallel to Carlyle's but though the second "element" stretches beyond "our own understanding and will" it too is none the less part of our "consciousness".

# 7

# Latter-Day Pamphlets: The Near Failure of Form and Vision

by JULES P. SEIGEL

Even serious readers of Victorian literature are apt to pass quickly over Carlyle's *Latter-Day Pamphlets*, briefly noting his attacks against the dogmas of progress, sacred nineteenth century institutions and minority groups, noting the aggressive and abusive tone and the seemingly chaotic structure of the work.[1] Often the *Pamphlets* are dismissed and perhaps, in the minds of many sensitive and otherwise sympathetic readers, for good reasons. Coming to the *Latter-Day Pamphlets* after two world wars, and the unbelievable Nazi holocaust, Carlyle's attacks against Jamaican blacks sitting idle, up to their ears in pumpkins, and Irish paupers too lazy to work, weary us. His strident talk of beneficent whips and leather along the backs of the unemployed in these times when all forms of individual life seem threatened set us on edge.[2] Yet we have no choice but to agree that the bloom held out by the promises of nineteenth century democracy has wilted, that the dogmas of democracy are upheld only by sacrifices, and that bureaucracy, democracy's offspring, has succeeded at producing as many evils as it has benefits. And Carlyle's criticism of the machinery and methodology of nineteenth century democracy in the *Pamphlets* has a bitter, cutting tone matched by no other prophetic voices of his time.

What actually were the reasons for such vitriolic outbursts, for this fierce and unbalanced work which, as David Masson said, brought the general antipathy towards Carlyle to a crisis and made him "unpopular with at least one half of the kingdom"? One explanation was that the Sage of Chelsea had taken to whisky; another, suggested by William B. Aytoun, was that the work was a product of a "diseased imagination".[3] Yet the *Pamphlets* do not, as Albert J. LaValley has shown, "represent a complete volte-face from his earlier political and social writings. They may be frightening in both what they say and how they say it, but they are still an outgrowth of Carlyle's earlier social writings" (pp. 279–80). One recognizes not only familiar language but also familiar themes: there is the continuing search for heroes, the call for action and not words (the need for silence), the necessity of work and redemption, attacks against the immorality of the economics of the day, against selfish beaverism and huckstering, against the foolishness of parliamentary reform rather than reform of the self, and against the hypocrisy of organized religion. His cutting satire in the *Pamphlets* lays bare evils still recognizable in the modern world, such as consumerism and the special rhetorics—bureaucratic and private—which exert unbelievable control over the people. Everything is, in Carlyle's words, either "Fit for the market; not fit" (p. 181). In his general exposure of the immorality of rhetoric—simply *lying*, as he puts it—he points to the corrosive effects it has in a modern democracy: "Words will not express what mischiefs the misuse of words has done, and is doing, in these heavy laden generations"[4] (p. 181). These familiar Carlylisms are expressed in his harshest and most direct style.

Yet his vision is intensified and his anxiety heightened. The language is violent as Carlyle agitates, urges and threatens. His voice becomes one of desperation as he strikes out trying to put down simultaneously all his disjointed and painful observations.[5] It is precisely this formlessness, a stylistic neurosis, that characterizes the *Pamphlets*. The familiar themes and images, however unsystematically presented, seem mainly held together by the urgency of the writer's voice, painfully haranguing, relentlessly arguing his readers into accepting his prophetic message. It is obvious that Carlyle's many personae (Jefferson Brick, Crabbe, Prime Minister, Benevolent Man, Future, and others) all have the same voice—authoritative, satirical, and aggressive. His is a sensibility marked by frustration; often grotesque, consistently angry. As George Levine has suggested, Carlyle has "identified himself with his creation, and Carlylese becomes the staple mode of expression at the same time as its sustaining tensions and its implicit faith in the possibilities of this world have broken down".[6]

Levine argues that the earlier works of Carlyle could survive artistic analysis, but he questions whether analysis could do anything for the inartistic *Latter-Day Pamphlets*. For him the *Pamphlets* are triumphs of negativism, unrelieved by the flexibility of the earlier and more obviously coherent works. Levine has noted this shift: "A style whose essence is the expression of a complicated vision of a dualistic universe and of the constant movement of all things in time from one pole to the other now becomes the vehicle for a proliferating and grotesque vision of evil in the world and of a diminishing and increasingly abstract vision of the ideals necessary to banish that evil" (p. 122). What has happened is that the "vision of the world is unrelievedly bleak and disillusioned. . . . Carlyle . . . is responding wildly and incoherently—and ineffectually—to all the aspects of his society which repel him" (pp 122–3). Fragmentation and splintering replace a sustained artistic and structural tension.

Carlyle's earlier fears of democracy were intensified by the outbreak of the revolutions of 1848, harbingers of inevitable democracy. These fears were then exaggerated by his growing awareness of the misery of Ireland. Together they represented the most fearful elements of an expanding democracy—an uncontrolled population without work, without direction, bereft of leadership, lost in social chaos and anarchy. It was the confusion and complexity of democracy which Carlyle now envisioned as a reality. Its great convulsions would inevitably destroy his essential vision of nature as a hierarchical structure—a simplistic and neatly ordered society and universe. To his Calvinistic sensibility democracy was also noisy and dirty—personally obnoxious:

> A world no longer habitable for quiet persons: a world which in these sad days is bursting into street-barricades, and pretty rapidly turning-out its "Honoured Men," as intrusive dogs are turned out, with a kettle tied to their tail. To Kings, Kaisers, Spiritual Papas and Holy Fathers, there is universal "*Apage!* Depart thou; go thou to the — Father of thee!" in a huge world-voice of mob-musketry and sooty execration, uglier than any ever heard before (p. 260).

F
157

The *Latter-Day Pamphlets* register a series of traumatic and fearful responses to a modern democratic culture. All the corollaries of democracy—decision by universal ballot, in particular, never a true way of electing the "best"—the greater distribution of "wealth", and the doctrines of progress, all become magnified and grotesquely distorted by an imagination which is able on the one hand to see the disease and corruption inherent in the political and economic systems themselves, but, on the other, is unable to dissociate that which it created itself from its own particular disoriented vision.

Carlyle's anxiety about Ireland was intensified by his visit there during July and August of 1849. Yet even before this he was well aware of the sick and starving Irish immigrants crowding their way into the industrial centres of Great Britain, where the population was already rising at an extraordinary rate. It is estimated that during these years "about a million of the Irish died and about a million fled overseas".[7] Carlyle clearly foresaw that such changes needed government, and that there were few countries like the United States, which at the present time "can do *without* governing,—every man being at least able to live, and move-off into the wilderness, let Congress jargon as it will . . . with mud soil enough and fierce sun enough in the Mississippi Valley alone to grow Indian corn for all the extant Posterity of Adam at this time;—what other country ever stood in such a case?" (p. 227). Neither crowded England nor starving Ireland was in such an enviable condition. Carlyle, in this mood of heightened anxiety, could practically hear the firing of muskets along Cheyne Row. His response was grim, calling for regimentation, to bring the "Captainless under due captaincy" (p. 36).

His aggressive stance in the face of advancing democracy and growing poverty, disease, and population derives more from his fear of the multiple unknowns inherent in these social phenomena than from any particular plan to stem the movements; though Carlyle does offer such concrete proposals in the *Latter-Day Pamphlets* as organized work forces or agricultural regiments to reclaim waste lands. Yet the *Pamphlets* are mainly his painfully-recorded responses; an answer to the crisis, and a search for some sort of artistic form to his response. In a strange way, Carlyle is both the prophet and the prophecy.

158

As early as two full years before the publication of the first pamphlet, Carlyle was struggling to embody his scattered and troubled thoughts into some kind of form. In a letter to his mother (26 Jan. 1848) he writes that as

> soon as my cold is quite gone, I have one or two bits of jobs that I must fall to. Not of much moment; but they will keep me going; a *big* job lies deep in the background, not yet shaped into any form, but likely to be heavy enough when it comes! (NLS).

The big job which would not shape itself was a source of anguish for Carlyle throughout 1848, 1849, and into much of 1850, as shown by many painful references in his letters. Froude tells us that Carlyle's journal contains virtually nothing for the four years preceding the February 1848 revolutions on the continent. But there was a flurry of activity early that February when Carlyle notes "a scheme of books" to be done: "Exodus from Houndsditch", "Ireland: Spiritual Sketches", "The Scavenger Age", and "Life of John Sterling". Only the life of Sterling made its way into a book.[8] It was, then, the revolutions of 24 February on the continent, and particularly in Paris, that began to harden Carlyle's thinking. His journal for 5 March announces a new scheme, the germ of the *Latter-Day Pamphlets*.

> Scheme of volume: *Democracy*. What one might have to say on it? (1) Inevitable now in all countries: regarded vulgarly as *the* solution. Reason why it cannot be so; something farther and ultimate. (2) Terrible disadvantage of the Talking Necessity; much to be said here. What this comes from. Properly an insincere character of mind. (3) Follows *deducible* out of that! *Howardism*. Regard every Abolition Principle man as your enemy, ye reformers. Let them insist not that punishment be abolished, but that it fall on the right heads. (4) *Fictions*, under which head come Cants, Phantasms, alas! Law, Gospel, Royalty itself. (5) Labour question. Necessity of government. Notion of voting to all is delirium. Only the vote of the wise is called for, an advantage ever to the voter himself. Rapid and inevitable progress of anarchy. Want of bearing *rule* in all private departments of life. Melancholy remedy: "Change as often as you like." (6) Though men insincere, not all equally so. A great choice. How to know a sincere man. Be sincere yourself. Career open to talent. This actually is the conclusion of the whole matter.
>
> Six things. It would make a volume. Shall I begin it? I am sick, lazy, and dispirited.[9]

Soon after (26 Mar.) Carlyle confesses to his sister Jean that he is thinking seriously of "some kind of Book,—poor wretch!—but the times with me too are not without their difficulties!" (NLS).

The revolutions held Carlyle's attention fast during these weeks. In a letter to Thomas Erskine (24 Mar. 1848), he sees them as a "spectacle of history", as "this immense explosion of Democracy", and as a time to be joyful yet a time for sadness. There is joy inasmuch as mortals "long towards justice and veracity", but sadness that "all the world, in its protest against False Government should find no remedy but that of rushing into No Government or anarchy (kinglessness)", which Carlyle takes this "republican universal suffragism to inevitably be". For Carlyle, violence is an almost inevitable corollary of universal democracy. In the same letter he remarks that an "abundance of *fighting* (probably enough in all kinds) one does see in store for them; and long years and generations of weltering confusion, miserable to contemplate, before anything can be *settled* again. Hardly since the invasion of the wild Teutons and wreck of the old Roman Empire has there been so strange a Europe, all turned topsy turvey, as we now see. What was at the top has come or is rapidly coming to the *bottom*, where indeed, such was its intrinsic quality, it deserved this long while past to be."[10] But the stable hierarchical order of Carlyle's reality is being threatened. The fearful posture of this letter foreshadows the familiar, anxious tone of the *Latter-Day Pamphlets*.

Because he was deeply disturbed, his whole psychological orientation threatened, he seems continually to refer to his desire to speak out and to write, but finds that his "heart is as if half-dead, and has no wish to speak any more, but to lie *silent*, if so might be, till it sank into the Divine silence, and were then at rest. Courage, however!"[11] Three days later, and after referring to a pleasant dinner with Sir Robert Peel, Carlyle once again records in his journal his response to the violence of the revolutions:

> N.B.—This night with Peel was the night in which Berlin city executed its last terrible battle (19th of March to Sunday Morning the 20th, five o'clock). While we sate there the streets of Berlin were all blazing with grapeshot and the war of enraged men. What is to become of all that? I have a book to write about it. Alas![12]

160

So, too, his journal entry for 5 April 1848 shows the unsettling combination of the times weighing heavily upon him and his anguishing over some kind of literary commentary: "The future for all countries fills me with a kind of horror. I have been scribbling, scribble, scribble—alas! it will be long before that makes a book. Persist however."[13]

Frustrated at his inability to decide what shape his response should take, Carlyle tried his hand at a series of articles.[14] They were troublesome to him, and he was well aware of the public outcry they would arouse. Yet he still wished to write a book as he says in his letter to his mother:

> I have a good many "Articles" still lying in me; and indeed I have been thinking of late seriously, whether I should not set up some little bit *Paper* of my own, and publish them there. But that is a little precarious . . . and I do not like it much. On the other hand, there is no Newspaper that can stand my articles; no *single* Newspaper that they would not blow the bottom out of in a short while! For example, the *Examiner* should have had all these three articles put together as one: but then poor little Lord John Russell is a pet of theirs, and I could not put them on doing such a thing; so had to cut the Articles in *three*. . . . At most, if nothing else will do, I can write the things in a *Book*; and really that is perhaps the *best* way, in other respects too, after all. (19 May 1848, NLS).

A year later (writing to his sister, 18 June 1849) he is still distressed over his inability to execute some singular composition and complains that all things have been "lying in a *fallow*, ill-conducted, unprofitable and ungainly state with me for one, which has impeded the discharge of a great many duties! My book has stood at a dead-lock, this long while. . . ." He complains further that his "*inner-man* (meaning both soul and *stomach* by that term) has been in a bad way" (NLS). It is interesting to see that even during the actual writing of the *Pamphlets*, he was still searching for the book. To his mother, he writes (11 May 1850):

> My last Pamphlet got on very badly,—there was so much bustling &c and my own bad nerves and liver were so put about. I do not yet know for certain how many more I shall have to write. I think sometimes of making out the dozen; but *ten* seem likelier for the present; nay something (a *cowardly* something) whispers occasionally. "If the thing grow *too* hot, you may finish with *eight*," which

161

is only one more now! What I have farther to say must grow into a *Book* in that case. But I think *ten* is the likelier. We must try to do and choose what is wisest for us! (NLS).

Yet Carlyle had lost his former hope of regeneration of the self in the face of social fragmentation. Throughout the *Pamphlets* there are points where Carlyle reasserts his earlier faith, but they appear sporadically and outside the consistent tone of accusation. The follies of democratic bureaucracy he dwells on continually irritated him. Prompted by a vision of a diseased society, Carlyle's stance becomes largely responsive and captious rather than synthetic and creative. The obnoxious elements he sees in society grate sharply on his senses, as shown by the imagery of excrement and slime. There is also recurring imagery of economics ("spiritual banknotes", "gold bullion of human culture", "nature keeps silently a most exact Savings-Bank") which jostles against imagery of technology (of railroad miracles: "The distances of London to Aberdeen, to Ostend, to Vienna, are still infinitely inadequate to me! Will you teach me the winged flight through Immensity, up to the Throne dark with excess of bright!" (p. 277) ). Every image is charged with the sense of a newly-emerging society, and with its overwhelming presence.

Carlyle found himself faced with a problem of epic dimension; its scope was nothing less than the known world; and he felt himself called upon to prophesy about it passionately. It was a subject of the immediate present, a subject yet of cosmic proportion, and a subject beyond the scope of biography or past history—both genres already familiar to Carlyle. In a way he was attempting to write a latter-day epic, but given his anxiety during these months and his anger and confusion, what finally emerges is a series of long pamphlets which participate in several literary styles, prophetic, satiric, and epic. Most obvious in tone is the voice of the Biblical prophet, condemning and exhorting.[15] This voice, however, fuses with that of the satirist, viciously and brutally laying bare to the bone with directness and often times with embarrassing incisiveness. It is a voice which may be compared to that of Eldridge Cleaver's in *Soul on Ice*, a work which, like the *Pamphlets*, engages in angry satire and the most acute name calling.[16]

Yet, still interesting, in certain ways, is the use Carlyle makes

162

of the traditional epic. The *Pamphlets* are clearly a continuation
of the epic theme of democracy which was so brilliantly and co-
herently handled in *The French Revolution*.[17] As most readers
notice there seems more coherence in the *Pamphlets* in terms of
texture (imagery and theme) and tone than there is in terms of
any formal structure, such as that of the epic. Yet there is also
an attempt, either consciously or unconsciously, to superimpose,
if nothing else, the sense of being epic. It may even be of significance that Carlyle made it clear that he wanted to write twelve
pamphlets, one for each month of the year, but also the number
of books that one finds in such secondary epics as the *Aeneid* and
*Paradise Lost*.[18]

Carlyle's personae have long, set speeches resembling those of
the epic, and yet they are all in the same voice—that of Carlyle
himself. The *Pamphlets*, in imagery and tone, collectively resemble
a descent into hell itself, though it is the hell of a democratically-
oriented society. It is both reminiscent of the epic and yet almost
a burlesque, for if the times had called for a mythic hero of the
calibre of Hercules, his modern counterpart has to be Robert Peel.
Carlyle's language, too, is not like the high style of the epic; rather
it is usually a satiric, biting, and oracular tone. Yet one might
say that Carlyle's audience is at one moment invited to feel awe
by the grim rehearsal of what he sees as the universal moral and
social decadence of the present, and then to respond to his ridicule. Finally, in the broad political sweep of the *Pamphlets*, he is
not unlike a modern epicist.

> The subject of all epic poetry might thus be said to be politics,
> but a politics not limited to society, a politics embracing the natural
> and the fabulous worlds, embracing even the moral or spiritual
> worlds they sometimes shadow forth, and involving ultimately the
> divine. The implications expand to suggest, if not frankly to assert,
> a cosmic power struggle.[19]

In the opening lines of *Paradise Lost*, Milton announces the
theme of his epic through the classic epic question and answer:

> Say first, for Heav'n hides nothing from thy view,
> Nor the deep Tract of Hell, say first what cause
> Mov'd our Grand Parents in that happy State,
> Favour'd of Heav'n so highly, to fall off

From their Creator, and transgress his Will
For one restraint, Lords of the World besides?
Who first seduc'd them to that fowl revolt?
Th' infernal Serpent; he it was, whose guile, . . . (I, 27–34)

In the first *Pamphlet* Carlyle rhetorically asks his modern epic question, indeed more prosaically, but clearly—in form and tone —similar:

What *is* Democracy; this huge inevitable Product of the Destinies, which is everywhere the portion of our Europe in these latter days? There lies the question for us. Whence comes it, this universal big black Democracy; whither tends it; what is the meaning of it? A meaning it must have, or it would not be here. If we can find the right meaning of it, we may, wisely submitting or wisely resisting and controlling, still hope to live in the midst of it; if we cannot find the right meaning, if we find only the wrong meaning or no meaning in it, to live will not be possible! (pp. 9–10).

For Milton the symbolic act of man's disobedience brought death to man and the loss of Eden. It is a personal sin which each man must subdue in order to regain paradise and overcome a hell which in Christian terms is individualized. So, too, Carlyle sees Democracy as demonic, symbolic of potential death, a force which once unleashed, it will "behove us to solve or die" (p. 9). He presents a myth of social degradation and alienation, and not chiefly religious alienation and personal death as in *Sartor*. He appeals for heroes:

Who will begin the long steep journey with us; who of living statesmen will snatch the standard, and say, like a hero on the forlorn-hope for his country, Forward! Or is there none; no one that can and dare? And our lot too, then, is Anarchy by barricade or ballot-box, and Social Death?—We will not think so (p. 169).

Societal death is seen throughout in the images of asphyxiation, the absence of lungs; his is a culture, as Carlyle puts it, slowly wheezing to death.

Carlyle's prophesying of a political apocalypse is also somewhat epical. The *Latter-Day Pamphlets* contain a sense of inevitable change; ultimate chaos seems always at hand. The whole world— from England, and the continent, to America—is on the brink of disaster. As Thomas Greene notes, the epic poet must attempt to "clear away an area he can apprehend, if not dominate, and commonly this area expands to fill the epic universe, to cover the known world and reach heaven and hell. Epic characteristically refuses to be hemmed in, in time as well as space; it raids the unknown and colonizes it. It is the imagination's manifesto, proclaiming the range of its grasp, or else it is the dream of the will, indulging its fantasies of power" (p. 10).

Although, then, there is no tightly structured development throughout the pages of the *Latter-Day Pamphlets* of the epic theme of Democracy, its presence is everywhere, affecting the actions of all the characters and all the institutions. Democracy has arrived and has been announced to the world in message after message; it is as if "all the populations of the world were rising or had risen into incendiary madness" (p. 153). In another metaphor Democracy is seen as some vital force rising from the bowels of the earth and forcing itself upon the political and social realities of the mid-nineteenth century world. Or, again, it is a bottomless volcano or "universal powder-mine of most inflammable mutinous chaotic elements, separated from us by a thin earth rind" (p. 7) and is fanned into anarchy by "students, young men of letters, advocates, editors, hot inexperienced enthusiasts, or fierce and justly bankrupt desperadoes" (p. 7).[20] Democracy is the "grand, alarming, imminent and indisputable Reality" (p. 9) and its problems must be solved or the world will die. No force seems at all able to drive it back to its elemental depths.

Society, indeed the Victorian world, is the scene of a cosmic night battle. Democracy, on the one hand, is a reality and will not retreat, and the laws of nature, on the other hand, are inflexible and hierarchical, as Carlyle sees them. What we have is a confrontation out of which Carlyle, in the overview of the *Latter-Day Pamphlets*, is unable to imagine a resynthesis along the lines of *Sartor Resartus*, *Past and Present*, or, for that matter, *The French Revolution*. This, it seems, is another basic reason that the *Pamphlets* appear so incohesive, disconcerting, and uneven. Carlyle, too, feels himself led towards personal disillusionment and self-destruction. Democracy is the devil, so to speak; it represents the present confusion, the complexity of modern life in confrontation with nature; and the staging area is the whole world:

Alas, on this side of the Atlantic and on that, Democracy, we apprehend, is forever impossible! So much, with certainty of loud astonished contradiction from all manner of men at present, but with sure appeal to the Law of Nature and the ever-abiding Fact, may be suggested and asserted once more. The Universe itself is a Monarchy and Hierarchy; large liberty of "voting" there, all manner of choice, utmost free-will, but with conditions inexorable and immeasurable annexed to every exercise of the same. A most free commonwealth of "voters"; but with Eternal Justice enforced by Almighty Power! (pp. 21–2).

Surely the resolution for Carlyle was not to be found in the ballot boxes which he felt would never be able to replace the natural hierarchy of God's world: the noble will always remain in high places, the ignoble in low:

To raise the Sham-Noblest and solemnly consecrate *him* by whatever method, new-devised, or slavishly adhered to from old wont, this, little as we may regard it, is, in all times and countries, a practical blasphemy, and Nature in no wise will forget it (p. 22).

His continued insistence on the futility of voting indicates the implacability of his position:

Vote it, revote it by overwhelming majorities, by jubilant unveracities or universalities; read it thrice or three hundred times, pass acts of parliament upon it till the statute book can hold no more,—it helps not a whit: The thing is not so, the thing is otherwise than so; and Adam's whole posterity, voting daily on it till the world finish, will not alter it a jot (p. 173).

The theme of the confrontation and the subsequent deadlock between Democracy and nature is reflected in Carlyle's language as well, which, although alluding to primitive animals, to Megatherions and Pythons, and mud-demons, suggests a reversal in the evolutionary process. It is as if civilization is not evolving but devolving into the primeval mud out of which it was bred. Democracy and its anarchical tendencies, its uncontrollability and unruliness, is represented by the "Irish Giant, named of Despair" who is advancing upon London, laying waste the English towns and villages:

I notice him in Piccadilly, blue-visaged, thatched in rags, a blue child on each arm; hunger-driven, wide mouthed, seeking whom

166

he may devour: he, missioned by the just Heavens, too truly and too sadly their 'divine missionary' come at last to *this* authoritative manner, will throw us all into Doubting Castle, I perceive! (p. 94).

The scope of Carlyle's epic theme goes beyond England even to America where he sees the battle *yet* to be fought. There is still time, but Democracy with its attendant horrors will inevitably come. The theme is epical in its limitlessness, prophetic in its tone:

> No! America too will have to strain its energies, in quite other fashion than this; to crack its sinews, and all-but break its heart, as the rest of us have had to do, in thousandfold wrestle with the Pythons and mud-demons, before it can become a habitation for the gods. America's battle is yet to fight; and we, sorrowful though nothing doubting, wish her strength for it. New Spiritual Pythons, plenty of them; enormous Megatherions, as ugly as were ever born of mud, loom huge and hideous out of the twilight Future on America; and she will have her own agony, and her own victory, but on other terms than she is yet quite aware of (pp. 20–1).

In terms of imagery the *Latter-Day Pamphlets* are consistently negative, and one might say that Carlyle is describing a true social hell, one which is viewed as near death, and slowly being asphyxiated. Throughout the *Pamphlets*, society is alluded to in classical terms as Stygian deeps, Phlegethon, and the mud of Lethe; yet the hell which emerges is modern. The *Pamphlets* describe a world of chaos, foul odours, vulgarity, filth, ultimate selfishness, characterized by slime, serpents, dung heaps, and finally the pig philosophy. The consciousness of the *Pamphlets* is one of pervasive contempt and disgust.[21] Yet there is some method in Carlyle's characterization of this living hell. What is suggested is a Dantesque vision, beginning with lesser or social evils and descending deeper into hell, to the source of all evil: spiritual evil, that point from which all social disorder emanates. This is symbolized by Jesuitism, the subject of the final pamphlet and the one which Carlyle felt was his best.

In "The Present Time", the first pamphlet, Carlyle circles the perimeter of hell. His descriptions are general and have an epical sweep to them. This is the *Pamphlet* which announces the theme of democracy, the advent of cosmic change. The following

*Pamphlets* particularize the social hell, the sickness and dehumanizing effects of institutions, and the move through the thin earth rind of "Parliaments" and "Downing Street", to the ultimate source of social corruption—egotism, selfishness—the stomach and the purse—as described in the eighth and last *Pamphlet*, "Jesuitism":

> the Human Species, as it were, unconsciously or consciously, gone all to one Sodality of Jesuitism: who will deliver us from the body of his death! It is in truth like death-in-life; a living criminal (as in the old Roman days) with a *corpse* lashed fast to him (p. 299).

The social institutions attacked throughout the *Pamphlets* are familiar—ineffective philanthropy ("Model Prisons", II); the dehumanizing effect of red tape ("Downing Street", III); mechanical rather than wise leadership ("New Downing Street", IV); hypocrisy of political rhetoric ("Stump Orator", V); uselessness of parliamentary government ("Parliaments", VI); worship of money ("Hudson's Statue", VII), and finally "Jesuitism" (VIII). The inhabitants of this social hell move centripetally from lesser to more serious sins: they range from ineffective bureaucrats such as Felicissimus Zero who gallops his thunder horse in circles and huckstering railroad kings such as George Hudson ("Copper Vishnu of the Scrip Ages") to Ignatius Loyola who inhabits the dead centre.

The centre of Carlyle's hellish vision is dominated by the pig philosophy, a form of metaphorical sensualism. All Carlyle's images of darkness, aggression, and confusion, mud-pythons, dung heaps, beaver intellect, "spiritual Vampires and obscene Nightmares" (p. 163), and the "world-wide jungle of redtape" (p. 87), are attached to this central image of the Pig Philosophy: *Schweinsche Weltansicht*, which, in effect, embraces the universe. The first principle of the Pig Philosophy states: "The Universe, so far as sane conjecture can go, is an immeasurable Swine's trough, consisting of solid and liquid, and of other contrasts and kinds; —especially consisting of attainable and unattainable, the latter in immensely greater quantities for most pigs" (p. 316). Pighood is the physical and mental condition of the world and, objectionable as it may seem, is the dominant image of the *Pamphlets* and the one toward which all others have been moving.

The universe, the "Swine's-trough", is a place where aggressive huckstering, the making of money, the Veritable Age of Gold reigns. In it man's duty is to consume ("to diminish the quantity of the unattainable and increase that of the attainable"); Paradise is the "unlimited attainability of Pig-wash; perfect fulfilment of one's wishes;" and justice is getting one's share of the "Swine's-trough" and "not any portion" of mine.[22] One's share is defined as whatever one can "contrive to get without being hanged or sent to the hulks". People become pigs and greedily engage in "consumerism". The system of consuming is, moreover, defended by a corrupt legal system of lawyers ("Servants of God"), and by a hypocritical church which itself is no longer able to distinguish between a heaven and a living hell. Harsh though Carlyle's satire may be, it is successful in magnifying the diseases of a capitalistic economy fostered by a growing democracy.

Seen another way, the world is poisoned, and Ignatius Loyola is the symbol of its having happened (p. 294); the dead world is seen as a "spiritual mummyhood"; the people are now devoted only to "cookery" and to "scrip", to prurient appetites, and to the acceptance of worn-out traditions as truth. The world has been infected by the "deadly virus of lying" and "prussic-acid and chloroform are poor to it" (p. 310). A fatal poison such as hydrocyanic acid or the fumes of chloroform—though actually able to destroy consciousness—are ineffective against the widespread disease of lying. In this same context Carlyle switches the image: "Jesuit chloroform stupefied us all" (p. 310). The human race is now "sunk like steeping flax under the wide-spread fetid Hell-waters,—in all spiritual respects dead, dead; voiceless towards Heaven for centuries back; merely sending up, in the form of mute prayer, such an odour as the angels never smelt before" (p. 311). It is a corrupt and foul world, rotten to the core, and a "detestable devil's poison circulates in the life-blood of mankind; taints with abominable deadly malady all that mankind do. Such a curse never fell on man before" (p. 265). Life is being destroyed:

> We of these late centuries have suffered as the sons of Adam never did before; hebetated, sunk under mountains of torpid leprosy; and studying to persuade ourselves that this is health (p. 312).

It is as if Carlyle has awakened from a dream and now faces the "consciousness of Jesuitism". It lies around him like the "valley of Jehoshaphat, . . . one nightmare wilderness, and wreck of deadmen's bones, this false modern world; and no rapt Ezekiel in prophetic vision imaged to himself things sadder, more horrible and terrible, than the eyes of men, if they *are* awake, may now deliberately see" (p. 313). Jesuitism, then, symbolizes the psychology of the new modern consciousness, now a reality.

There is, moreover, the contemptuous and bitter realization by Carlyle that Christian institutions have failed to embody a true belief for the modern world. They are blind, and their churchmen are pictured by Gathercoal (a "Yankee friend" of his) as apes " 'with their wretched blinking eyes, squatting round a fire which they cannot feed with new wood; which they say will last forever without new wood,—or, alas, which they say is going out forever: it is a sad sight!' " (p. 331). This criticism of Christian institutions is continued in what might loosely be called a modern heroic or epic metaphor. The language is oracular in tone and it is continued by Gathercoal in a passage at the end of the eighth and last pamphlet ("Jesuitism") which structurally balances the long opening set speech by the British Prime Minister at the end of the first pamphlet ("The Present Time"):

> The event at Bethlehem was of the Year One; but all years since that, eighteen hundred of them now, have been contributing new growth to it,—and see, there it stands: the Church! Touching the earth with one small point; springing out of one small seedgrain, rising out therefrom, ever higher, ever broader, high as the Heaven itself, broad till it overshadow the whole visible Heaven and Earth, and no star can be seen but through *it*. From such a seedgrain so has it grown; planted in the reverences and sacred opulences of the soul of mankind; fed continually by all the noblenesses of some forty generations of men. The world-tree of the Nations for so long!
>
> Alas, if its roots are now dead, and it have lost hold of the firm earth, or clear belief of mankind,—what, great as it is, can by possibility become of it? Shaken to and fro, in Jesuitisms, Gorham Controversies, and the storms of inevitable Fate, it must sway hither and thither; nod ever farther from the perpendicular; nod at last too far; and,—sweeping the Eternal Heavens clear of its old brown foliage and multitudinous rooks'-nests,—come to the ground with much confused crashing, and *disclose* the diurnal and nocturnal

Upper Lights again! The dead world-tree will have declared itself dead. It will lie there an imbroglio of torn boughs and ruined fragments, of bewildered splittings and wide-spread shivers: out of which the poor inhabitants must make what they can! (pp. 332–3).

The epic "hero" of the *Latter-Day Pamphlets* is Carlyle himself as he takes on the role of latter-day *Vates* and epicist.[23] His heroic mood must be seen in the familiar Carlylean context that all history was epic, that as long as societies remained "simple and in earnest" they knew unconsciously that their history was "Epic and Bible, the clouded struggling Image of a God's Presence, the action of heroes and god inspired men". Furthermore, the noble intellect who "could disenthral such divine image, and present it to them clear, unclouded, in visible coherency comprehensible to human thought, was felt to be a *Vates* and the chief of intellects". It was not necessary to ask that he write an epic or deliver a prophecy: "Nature herself compelled him" (p. 323).

It may be said that Carlyle himself was compelled to write the *Pamphlets*, and to deliver his prophecy. When he asks rhetorically, "Who are they, gifted from above, that will convert voluminous Dryasdust into an Epic and even a Bible?" (p. 326)—one must feel that Carlyle himself is assuming the role of epic poet and latter-day prophet. His contempt for the fine arts as they are shown in the *Pamphlets* rules out his contemporaries. If these are "Human Arts" at all, Carlyle writes, "where have they been woolgathering, these centuries long; wandering literally like creatures fallen mad!" (p. 326). As Carlyle has it, the fine arts have been converted into "after-dinner amusements; slave adjunct to the luxurious appetites" of one "big ugly Nawaub" (p. 328)—which all Europe has become.

His tone is strained to hoarseness, for if he has a covert "hero" it is Sir Robert Peel who is seen as the modern Hercules who must clean the bureaucratic Augean stables of layers of filth, corruption, of dead pedantries and accumulations of jungles of red tape and administrative droppings. Government, in fact, is a cesspool:

> Every one may remark what a hope animates the eyes of any circle, when it is reported or even confidently asserted, that Sir

Robert Peel has in his mind privately resolved to go, one day, into that stable of King Augias, which appals human hearts, so rich is it, high-piled with the droppings of two-hundred years; and Hercules-like to load a thousand night-wagons from it, and turn running water into it, and swash and shovel at it, and never leave it till the antique pavement, and real basis of the matter, show itself clean again! (pp. 91–2).

In another context Peel is called upon to lead England through the present morass, up the "long, steep journey" as if out of hell itself, and "snatch the standard"; and thus become a hero of his country (p. 169).

It would be easy to agree with Northrop Frye that Carlyle's style in general is "tantrum prose", the prose of denunciation, of propaganda, of rhetoric in which "we feel that the author's pen is running away with him . . ." As the prose grows more incoherent, writes Frye, the more it seems to express "emotion apart from or without intellect". It lapses into emotional jargon, consisting of "obsessive repetition of verbal formulas".[24] To a great extent this is true, but a close reading of Carlyle's *Pamphlets* shows that the writer, though angered, still has a certain control over the work. It is in essence the response of an outraged sensibility to modern madness. No reader of the *Pamphlets* can deny that Carlyle has anticipated the terrors of modernism, its nightmarish qualities, its insanity. If the *Pamphlets* are an overreaction, they nevertheless dramatize symbolically the consciousness of one man unable to cope with what he envisioned ultimately as the loneliness, the "restless gnawing ennui" (p. 335) of modern life. His responses were precipitous and spontaneous, angry and brutal, yet almost always conveying the sense of futility, of the loss of hope. Periodically Carlyle reasserted his older, hopeful visions in his direct addresses to the young men[25] of England, but these calls for redemption, for new and dedicated leaders, are lost in the overwhelming rhetorical structure of the work—a work which is unified by a myth of decadence and by a tone of impending crisis of total destruction and with virtually no hope of renovation. The inconclusiveness of Carlyle's vision—since structurally there is no myth of a future regenerated society—reveals the depth of his frustration. The *Pamphlets* are a prophetic warning, an ugly result of what has happened to one psychology when confronted with the new, the transitional, the relatively unknown:

> To the primitive man, whether he looked at moral rule, or even at physical fact, there was nothing not divine. Flame was the God Loki, etc.; this visible Universe was wholly the vesture of an Invisible Infinite; every event that occurred in it a symbol of the immediate presence of God. Which it intrinsically *is*, and forever will be, let poor stupid mortals remember or forget it! The difference is, not that God has withdrawn; but that men's minds have fallen hebetated, stupid, that their hearts are dead, awakening only to some life about meal-time and cookery-time; and their eyes are grown dim, blinkard, a kind of horn-eyes like those of owls, available chiefly for catching mice (p. 277).

It seems unlikely that if Carlyle had finished his twelve pamphlets he would have emerged from this vision of hell. He leaves himself, ironically, in the middle of things. To the many Victorians this work was deeply disappointing. It is decidedly negative: there is no tailor retailored. Rather we are left with the feeling that Carlyle's reality, his vision of England of 1850, was truly one of social and psychological chaos:

> we are not properly a society at all; we are a lost gregarious horde, with Kings of Scrip on this hand, and Famishing Connaughts and Distressed Needlewomen on that—presided over by the Anarch Old. A lost horde,—who, in bitter feeling of the intolerable injustice that presses upon all men, will not long be able to continue ever gregarious; but will have to split into street-barricades, and internecine battle with one another; and to fight, if wisdom for some new real *Peerage* be not granted us, till we all die, mutually butchered, and *so* rest,—so if not otherwise! (p. 283).

## NOTES

1. The best discussion of the *Latter-Day Pamphlets* is by Albert J. LaValley, *Carlyle and the Idea of the Modern* (New Haven, 1968). Several others are valuable: Louis Cazamian, *Carlyle*, trans. E. K. Brown (New York, 1932), pp. 240–55; Julian Symons' brief comments in *TC, The Life and Ideas of a Prophet* (New York, 1952); Evan A. Reiff, "Studies in Carlyle's *Latter-Day Pamphlets*" (unpublished dissertation, Univ. of Iowa, 1937), which is helpful in showing how the Irish tour during

the summer of 1849 helped to shape the *Pamphlets*; and Judith M. C. Miller, "TC's *Latter-Day Pamphlets*: An Analysis and a Defense" (unpublished dissertation, Univ. of Arizona, 1971).

2. The comments about Jamaican blacks come from Carlyle's "Occasional Discourse on the Negro Question", *Fraser's Magazine*, 40 (1849). I have excluded this pamphlet from my discussion of the *LDP* because Carlyle decided not to include it in the *Pamphlets* in two later collections of his works, the Library and the People's editions. In the first collected edition (1858), it was presented as a "Precursor to Latter-Day Pamphlets". It will also become clear from what follows that Carlyle thought of the *Pamphlets* as the eight pamphlets issued from February to August 1850. Each one sold for one shilling, and the bound volume for nine. According to *Dyer* (pp. 129–30) there were three British editions and one American in 1850. All quotations from the *Pamphlets* are from the *Works*, XX.

3. *North British Review*, 14 (1850); Froude, *Life*, IV, 36; and W. B. Aytoun in *Blackwood's Edin. Mag.*, 67 (1850). Masson was right. The *LDP* received more notice in the press than any other single work of Carlyle's. Most of the criticism, with some exceptions—American pro-slavers and radical journals, such as the *Examiner*—was hostile. See *TC, The Critical Heritage*, ed. Jules P. Seigel (London, 1971), and *Dyer*, pp. 485–532.

4. At one point he suggests that a plan of reform could be to "Cut from one generation, whether the current one or the next, all the tongues away, prohibiting Literature too; and appoint at least one generation to pass its life in silence" (p. 209).

5. In "Jesuitism", for instance, Carlyle explicitly writes: "My friend, I have to speak in crude language, the wretched times being dumb and deaf: and if thou find no truth under this but the phantom of an extinct Hebrew one, I at present cannot help it" (p. 235).

6. What Levine has suggested for "The Negro Question" holds true to varying degrees throughout the *LDP* themselves: "The use and abuse of Carlylese", in *The Art of Victorian Prose* (New York, 1968), p. 125.

7. G. Kitson Clark, *The Making of Victorian England* (Cambridge, 1962), p. 75. The figure may even be higher. See Oliver MacDonagh, "Irish Immigration to the United States of America and the British Colonies During the Famine", in *The Great Famine*, ed. R. Dudley Edwards and T. Desmond Williams (New York, 1957), pp. 319–87, esp. p. 329.

8. Froude, *Life*, III, 423.

9. Froude, *Life*, III, 429.

10. Froude, *Life*, III, 430–1, and compare: "Since the destruction of the old Roman Empire by inroad of the Northern Barbarians, I have known nothing similar" (*LDP*, p. 6).

11. Froude, *Life*, III, 432.

12. Froude, *Life*, III, 434.

13. Froude, *Life*, III, 435.

14. The pertinent articles that he had written were: "Louis Philippe"

(*Examiner*, 4 March 1848), "The Repeal of the Union" (*Examiner*, 29 April 1848), "Législation for Ireland" (*Examiner*, 13 May 1848), "Ireland and the British Chief Governor" (*Spectator*, 13 May 1848), "Irish Regiments of the New Era" (*Spectator*, 13 May 1848).

15. For a discussion of the interrelatedness of epic and Old Testament prophecy, see Brian Wilkie, *Romantic Poets and the Epic Tradition* (Madison, Wisc., 1965), esp. pp. 10–11. This study discusses epic as tradition rather than as genre and is valuable in showing what happened to the epic impulse during the early nineteenth century.

16. The comparison is not as strange as some might infer. The similarities between *Soul on Ice* (New York, 1968) and *Sartor* are even more striking—especially the account of Cleaver's conversion while in Folsom Prison; the chapter is called "On Becoming", a central theme in *Sartor*.

17. As will be obvious, my remarks about the epic tradition owe much to Albert J. LaValley's remarkable discussion of their use in his chapter on *The French Revolution*, esp. p. 141 ff. See also "The Epic Temper of Carlyle's Mind", in B. H. Lehman's *Carlyle's Theory of the Hero* (Durham, 1928), pp. 168–70, though the point is not developed. The opening lines of Mill's review of *The French Revolution* ("This is not so much a history as an epic poem") are echoed by Emerson and Thoreau. See *TC, The Critical Heritage*, pp. 52, 85, 290.

18. Froude, *Life*, IV, 28, and *New Letters of TC*, ed. A. Carlyle (London, 1904), II, 86. Because of the death of Peel and a general feeling of disgust, Carlyle could not go on with the twelve pamphlets as planned. The twelve became eight. Froude says how he heard Carlyle "loaded with bilious indignation flinging off the matter intended for the rest of the series which had been left unwritten, pouring out, for hours together, a torrent of sulphurous denunciation. No one could check him. If anyone tried contradiction, the cataract rose against the oracle till it rushed over it and drowned it" (Froude, *Life*, IV, 41).

19. Thomas M. Greene, *The Descent from Heaven: A Study of Epic Continuity* (New Haven, 1963), pp. 17–18, also quoted, LaValley, p. 141.

20. See LaValley (pp. 127–8) for a discussion of this image—"thin earth rind" as it appears in *The French Revolution*. The same image appears in "Ireland and the British Chief Governor": "No; and Europe has crashed together suddenly into the bottomless deeps, the thin earth rind, wholly artificial giving way beneath it; and welter now one huge Democracy." (*Rescued Essays of TC*, ed. P. Newberry [London, 1892], pp. 86–7).

21. LaValley, pp. 283–4. It resembles *Maud* and its paranoic narrator.

22. Cf. Harrold, *Sartor*, p. 232. " 'Call ye that a Society,' cries he again, 'where there is no longer any Social Idea extant. . . . Where each, isolated, regardless of his neighbour, turned against his neighbour, clutches what he can get, and cries "Mine!" and calls it Peace, because, in the cut-purse and cut-throat Scramble, no steel knives, but only a far cunninger sort, can be employed?' "

23. See John Lindberg, "The Decadence of Style: Symbolic Structure in Carlyle's Prose", *Studies in Scottish Literature*, 1 (1964), 192.
24. *Anatomy of Criticism* (Princeton, 1957), p. 328.
25. "Be not a Public Orator, thou brave young British man, thou that are now growing to be something; not a Stump-Orator, if thou canst help it. Appeal not to the vulgar, with its long ears and its seats in the Cabinet; not by spoken words to the vulgar; *hate* the profane vulgar, and bid it begone. Appeal by silent work, by silent suffering if there be no work, to the gods, who have nobler seats in the Cabinet for thee!" (p. 212). "Brave young friend, dear to me, and *known* too in a sense, though never seen nor to be seen by me,—you are, what I am not, in the happy case to learn to *be* something and to *do* something, instead of eloquently talking about what has been and was done and may be: The old are what they are, and will not alter; our hope is in you. England's hope, and the world's, is that there may once more be millions such, instead of units as now" (p. 213).

# 8

# Frederick the Great: "That Unutterable Horror of a Prussian Book"

by ARTHUR A. and VONNA H. ADRIAN

"What my next task is to be?" Carlyle pondered in a letter (29 October 1851) to Varnhagen von Ense, the German friend whose *Memoirs* he had reviewed in the *Westminster*.[1] Confident of yet "one other Book in me", he sought a subject to demonstrate further his hero theory. Discarding Luther as of too little interest in a non-theological age, he found himself drawn increasingly to Frederick II of Prussia, "the *last real King* we have had in Europe", he told Varnhagen. Though there was as yet no full-scale life of Frederick the Great in any language, Carlyle, perhaps by way of inviting Varnhagen's reassurance, professed some doubt that this king's future fame needed any help from an Englishman. Were he "a brave Prussian", however, he would attempt such a biography "forthwith".

A few days later (14 November 1851) he declared to Lady Ashburton that "Frederick, the more I know of him, pleases me the better; a Man and King whose love of *reality* was instinctive and supreme: that is his distinction among Men,—and truly it is one of the greatest and royallest, especially in days like ours".

This predilection for Frederick was of no recent origin. Indeed, Carlyle had long felt an affinity for all things Germanic. As a twenty-four-year old student of German he had expressed admiration for Frederick; later in *Sartor Resartus* he caused Andreas Futteral to exclaim of him, "*Das nenn ich mir einen König.* That

177

is what I call a King" (II, i). Again, assembling materials for his 1840 lectures, "On Heroes and Hero-Worship—from Odin to Robert Burns", he coupled Frederick with Luther. To Emerson (27 June 1835) he elucidated a point thus: "As the great Fritz said, when the battle had gone against him, 'Another time we will do better.' " Finally in 1845 (8 October) he told his wife that he was considering a trip to Berlin "to make more acquaintance with [Frederick] and his people". So by 1851 his intentions toward "Der Grosse Fritz" had actually been taking shape for several decades.

Why did this Prussian conqueror appeal so strongly to his would-be biographer? Though Carlyle's political convictions were obviously satisfied by Frederick's forceful government and his achievement in building a powerful nation and arousing the patriotism of its citizens, the initial attraction may have stemmed no less from certain personal circumstances and qualities which Carlyle shared with his hero. Royalty notwithstanding, Frederick can at times be seen as the *alter ego* of the humble Scottish stonemason's son.

Each came from a strict Protestant background, from which he broke away to become no atheist, but a free thinker, tolerant of all religions. In this each was influenced by Voltaire, who, said Carlyle, "gave the death-stab to modern Superstition" and became, with Frederick, "the celestial element of the poor Eighteenth Century".[2] Each retained from his heritage a sober frugality and an aversion to ostentation, frivolity, and fashion. Frederick, said Carlyle, was "a King . . . without the trappings of a King". True, as an adolescent Crown Prince he had affected a foppish and Frenchified hair style and wardrobe, but he soon sobered into the mould approved by his "heavy-footed practical" father—and Carlyle. As king, except on state occasions, he affected a "Spartan simplicity of vesture: no crown but an old military cocked hat— generally old, or trampled and kneaded into absolute *softness*, if new".[3] It was headgear no less eccentric which caused smiles in railway carriages and hoots in the park when Carlyle wore his white wideawake, at whose first appearance in 1836 his wife Jane had "shrieked, nay almost *grat* [wept]". That her husband rather vaunted himself on his sartorial independence is implied by the tone of his comment to her in 1857: "Think of riding most of the summer with the aristocracy of the county, whenever I went into Hyde Park, in a duffle jacket which literally was part of an old dressing gown a year gone. Is the like on record?"[4]

Though neither Frederick nor Carlyle permitted himself more recreation than necessary to keep in trim for work, each loved horses and riding, but detested hunting. (The spiders Carlyle killed in the back garden at 5 Cheyne Row were, he boasted, the only "game" he ever pursued.) Not pleasure but work was to each a gospel—held, preached, and practised throughout his life. Carlyle's constant insistence on work as man's only excuse for being, parallels Frederick's dictum, "Man is made to work."[5] Macaulay's remark that Frederick "loved labour for its own sake"[6] applies no less to the Calvinistic Carlyle, who, even as he lamented its rigours, embraced it as the ordained curse on Adam's sons.

To Carlyle it was highly satisfying to contemplate success won by dogged labour and determination in the face of repeated obstacles. "That unquenchableness is what has drawn Carlyle to [Frederick]," said Mark Rutherford.[7] This "wonderful plodding perseverance" which he attributed to the whole German race, he was himself to emulate, however impatiently, during his thirteen-year task, spinning out his manuscript "an inch a day"—or so he declared in typically exaggerated fashion. In such travail he must have felt particularly *bruderlich* toward his hero, that "most lone soul of man, . . . continually toiling forward, as if the brightest goal and heaven were near and in view" (V, xix, 395).

That the talk and correspondence of two such men, both copious letter writers, should not be graced by social trivia or decked by bombast is no surprise. Frederick, Carlyle reiterated, was a doer rather than an idle talker, one of those great silent men who are the salt of the earth. (To Carlyle, who uttered the Word, most men were given to uttering Wind.)

It seems only fitting that two such harsh souls should be visited by continuing dyspepsia and abdominal complaints, possibly related to their melancholy and misanthropic cast of mind. As if under compulsion to identify with his hero, Carlyle adds to his report of Frederick's brief attack of "something like apoplexy" ("hemi-plegia", according to Frederick himself) the conjecture that it was "probably indigestion . . . exasperated by over-fatigue". And again quoting Frederick on his haemorrhoids, he inserts the sympathetic

179

diagnosis "dreadful biliary affair", *biliary* being a favourite adjective to describe his own complaints (IV, xvi, 216; VI, xx, 64).

Though Carlyle's misanthropy was mingled with compassion, his inbred conviction of original sin led him to tell with obvious zest how Frederick once squelched a certain romantic who maintained that man is good by nature: "Alas, dear Sulzer, *Ach mein lieber Sulzer*, I see you don't know that damned race of creatures (*Er kennt nicht diese verdammte Race*) as I do!" (IV, xvi, 324).

Toward the female half of the *verdammte* human race Carlyle might have declared with Frederick that he was "no gallant". However different the origins and manifestations of his own lack of gallantry, Carlyle was constitutionally sympathetic with any man who shunned sentimental dalliance with women, single or *en masse*. As a husband, though, he was obviously superior to his hero, being genuinely devoted to his Jane. Yet certain parallels may be assumed. Frederick, according to his own statement, paid brief "tribute to Hymen" at the outset of his marriage.[6] It is an accepted opinion that Carlyle also paid his dues briefly—if at all. At any rate, both men remained childless. (But Jane Carlyle, perhaps unwilling to concede her husband's reputation for sexual indifference, is said to have protested to a friend, "My dear, if Mr Carlyle's digestion had been better, there is no telling what he might have done!"[9])

That the parallels between Frederick and his biographer are by no means exhausted in the foregoing paragraphs will be evident to all who have been struck by passages in *Frederick the Great* which might serve as well for autobiography, the traits stressed being those Carlyle found, or aspired to find, in himself. Even his rendering of his subject's countenance reflects not so much the Prussian king as what Carlyle saw in the mirror: "The face bears evidence of many sorrows, . . . of much hard labour done in this world, and seems to anticipate nothing but more still coming." There is the look of "pride, well tempered with cheery mockery of humour". As for the eyes, they show "a lambent outer radiance springing from some great inner sea of light and fire in the man" (I, i, 2). One is struck above all by the staunch aloneness of Carlyle and his hero, each a man of magnitude in, but not representative of, his century.

For all the initial attractions of his subject it was not without misgivings that Carlyle finally undertook what was to be his longest work, one to whose research and composition he was to give thirteen anguished years. In the first place, where could he gather information? Not in the British Museum, whose director, Anthony Panizzi, resented his charges of mismanagement—Panizzi, that social dilettante engaged in the "hollow dining and drinking Nonsense of so-called 'Literature' ".[10] To be sure, the Museum holdings included ample material on Frederick, which Carlyle might have examined in the general reading room, but he declined to expose himself to headaches from bad air, and distractions from noise and the freakish behaviour of certain readers. When he demanded instead a privileged place in the quiet of the King's Library, he was denied.[11] The refusal involved no serious deprivation, however, for he had at his behest faithful disciples to search out and copy documents in the British Museum, in the London State Paper Office, in German libraries and elsewhere.[12] Their slave labour, performed out of pure dedication to the "Master", indeed demonstrated a tenet of Carlylean doctrine: devoted obedience to the chosen *Übermensch*.

There followed a long period of vacillation and indecision, marked by lapses in hero-worship. Referring to Frederick as the "lean drill-sergeant of the World", Carlyle confessed to Lady Ashburton (16 February 1852), "I do not even grow to love him better: a really mediocre intellect, a hard withered Soul: great only in his invincible Courage, in his constant loyalty to truth and fact." Yet some four months later he could write to Varnhagen (6 June 1852), "I decidedly grow in love for my Hero, and go on; and can by no means decide to throw him up at this stage of the inquiry."

By now his scholar's conscience was urging a trip to Germany, yet he shrank from the "disgraceful wretchedness" that inevitably beset his travels. "On the whole," he wrote to Jane (13 August 1852), "there is nothing to drive me thither but a kind of shame, and a desire *not* to be a poor coward. . . . Really at heart I do not much love [Frederick]." (This some nine weeks after "I grow in love for my hero"!) On the eve of departure he announced to his brother John that he was now "*obliged* to go, there seems no honourable getting off from it" (18 August 1852).

Once abroad, his grim anticipations were realized. It was the old story: he could not sleep. German beds were impossible, their pillows shaped "like a *wedge* three feet broad". Worst of all, there were no bed curtains, and "in beds *without curtains* what Christian could give up the ghost?" The noise, too, was intolerable: loud voices in the street till midnight, the pealing of church bells, the watchman's horn with its "jackass" tone, "and a general Sanhedrin of all the dogs and cats of nature". Everywhere it was the same. "Confound . . . this abominable, sorrowful, shockingly expensive tour of Germany", he grumbled as he prepared to sail for home.[13]

For all his exertions and torments, the trip brought little reward. But "I saw where Frederick *had been*", he told his brother John, "—if that can do any good to me, I have acquired that" (3 October 1852). He might have added that after considerable search he had also acquired one graphic representation of Frederick which, he felt, revealed the inner man. (Some months later he was still fuming over the dearth of such portraits: "No mortal seemed to know of such a thing, or to be in the least want of it. . . . I said to myself a hundred times, the speaking, painting, dissertating, poetizing, most 'artistic' . . . German people, is *this* then all you can do to 'represent' a great man and hero, when the gods send you one?"[14])

But he still wavered. *"Eheu!"* he wrote in his Journal (5 December), "Shall I try Frederick, or not try him?" (Froude, *Life*, IV, 126); and to Charles Redwood, "He will walk the plank, I think, or has walked it, and I must try something else" (Wilson, *Carlyle*, IV, 453). Recalling his hero's death mask in Berlin, he pronounced it not so much "the face of a lean lion" as "alas, of a ditto *cat!* The lips are thin, and closed like pincers; a face that never yielded;—not the beautifullest kind of face. In fine why should *I* torment my domestic soul writing his foreign history?" Besides, Frederick "is not half or tenth part such a man as Cromwell, that one should swim and dive for him in that manner", he told his sister Jean (23 December 1852). The temptation to relinquish the task continued into the next year. "Very well," he told himself in March, "you have lived long without the 'Zollerns, they without you: why not continue to?"[15]

To his correspondents and his Journal he was to confide his doubts and struggles throughout the thirteen years that *Frederick* was in preparation. Actually he had wailed no less despairingly during his four-year labour on *Cromwell*; then, however, his doubts were mainly of his own powers: would the biographer be worthy of his noble subject? The question now was more disturbing: was the subject worthy of the biographer?

But in the end he resisted misgivings and began to write. The prospect looked dismal: "Only pain can now *drive* me through the subject; *led* and induced I shall never be", he told his brother John (20 May 1853). He professed no hope of proud success, only of "some day finishing" the task (Wilson, *Carlyle*, V, 34–5). As his health began to decline under the stress of work and worry his lamentations overflowed the letters and Journal for which he somehow found time. They even clogged his manuscript, delaying the progress of the narrative and adding considerably to its length.

He complained constantly of his source material—to Emerson, to his brother John, to Jane. The books he had ordered from Germany were mainly collections of dry facts, nothing but "the endless rubbish of dullards", he told Jane (23 July 1853). As he turned over tons of such matter he gave further release to his spleen by notebook jottings upon the offending volumes: "Dreadfully worthless!" "What perfectly worthless balderdash!" "Full of ignorance and mendacities." A few of his invectives attacked the unfortunate authors directly: "Oh you absurd old husky 'Psalmodist'—chanting in that dismal hypocritical manner . . . !" "You Dunce! Has cost me half an hour!" (This latter on being thrown off by a mistaken date.) One writer he dismissed as "dog gone mad . . . unfortunate barking individual"; another he addressed condescendingly, "You are rather a poor creature! thank you, however."[16]

Tribulations notwithstanding, by the summer of 1857 Carlyle was reading proof for the first two volumes. Encouragement came from Jane in Scotland, to whom the proof sheets were sent. "Oh, my dear!" she exclaimed, "What a magnificent book this is going to be! The best of all your books" (25 August 1857). (Not until later did she come to wish that Frederick had died in infancy.[17]) Though Carlyle called her "an excellent *encouraging* Goody" (25 August 1857), it was not in his nature to be sanguine, and the task was stretching ahead appallingly. Those first two volumes, by treating Frederick's forebears exhaustively, had failed to advance the hero beyond the status of Crown Prince.

And now, with Frederick's reign and military career looming ahead, Carlyle was forced, as Froude points out, "to make a special study, entirely new to him, of military science and the art of war".[18] For this he deemed it necessary to visit the various battlefields. In August of 1858, accordingly, he made his second tour of Germany. On his return he found himself so wretched and his "hand so out" that he could not take up composition again. One sleepless night he was visited by terror lest he should never finish the work. It was like the apparition of the Devil confronting Luther, or so he felt next morning. "Well, well, Herr Teufel," he resolved, "we will just go on as long as we are alive; and keep working all the same till thou do get us killed" (Wilson, *Carlyle*, V, 391).

But it was Jane whose life was soon to be endangered. Already in frail health, she had shared her husband's nervous anxiety over Frederick from the beginning and had suffered from his impatient temper—as he from hers. According to General John Sterling, who recalled a visit to Cheyne Row in 1859, she confided that her husband was then in despair over his waning respect for his hero.[19] In this same year she echoed his misgivings in a letter to his sister Jean (16 January): "He . . . ought never to have tried to make a silk purse out of a sow's ear." After her death Carlyle was to recall how "often enough it cut me to the heart to think what she was suffering by this book . . . and with what noble and perfect constancy she bore it all".[20]

As he doggedly inched his way toward the end of what he had condemned in 1859 as "that unutterable horror of a Prussian Book",[21] Jane's condition was gradually worsening. During 1864 her life was actually in jeopardy. But as the new year began she grew miraculously better, and Carlyle was fast approaching completion of his sixth and last volume. Perhaps the two circumstances were related. On a Sunday evening at the end of January he walked out with "a kind of solemn thankfulness" that he had written his last sentence: "Adieu, good readers; bad also, adieu."

In the months and even years to follow, well after he might presumably have recovered from his long toil, Carlyle was to lay his broken health and spirits at the charge of this last book, even more ruinous in its effect than his loneliness and remorse after

Jane's death in 1866. The tremors of his right hand worsened; his insomnia increased. His indigestion, by now "a fifty years story", had been "brought to a head by the unspeakable *Friedrich*", he declared in 1867, and would "evidently never much recover".[22] If, Carlylean exaggeration and the normal decline of age aside, the charge be at all admissible, one suspects continuing tension induced by a conflict peculiar to this book alone. That the hero king had proved harsh and unlovable—this might be freely admitted. But if he had also proved ignoble? Here Carlyle may have been forced into an embarrassing dilemma. Having early established his hero as worthy of reverence and emulation, and having seen this evaluation through the press in Volumes I and II, he had either to recant and destroy the unity of his work along with its intended didactic purpose, or take the saving course of suppressing or softening his growing distaste for the practical, able leader, whose duplicity, treachery, and rapacity were daily more apparent. Certain judgments of Frederick which he injected into letters and conversation, and, according to a later biographer of the Prussian king, even into the margins of books borrowed from the London Library, were omitted from his manuscript.[23] It was as if each bright coin of Frederick's virtues had its tarnished side, which Carlyle was obliged to turn up only briefly, if at all, for the reader's view. To resort to such jugglery and to justify his hero's conduct as an ignoble means to a noble goal—such manœuvring to demonstrate his own pet principle that "Right makes Might" should have strained that conscience which controls the Scots Presbyterian temper and digestive juices.

Carlyle's reputed confession in old age "that he had been mistaken about Frederick the Great", whom he now "found to be no worshipful man",[24] may be seen as the delayed acknowledgment of a revulsion he had earlier striven not to convey—perhaps not even to recognize fully. Consciously or not, he had employed a revealing phrase in a letter to Emerson (27 January 1867) when he looked back on *Frederick* as a "wrestle with . . . subterranean hydras". The torment inhering in such conflicts (and by implication, the easement of self-knowledge and confession) had already been recognized by the young Carlyle who wrote to Jane in 1835 (2 November), "It is a great misery . . . for a man to lie, even unconsciously, even to himself."

Inasmuch as this conflict, as well as the exigencies of organizing perplexing and chaotic material, had begun to torment him
before the first two volumes were submitted for publication, why
had Carlyle not abandoned "that unutterable horror" while there
was yet time to save himself? A tangle of motives, all typically
Carlylean, seems to have held him floundering, powerless to make
the break toward freedom. First of all, there were practical considerations. He had settled on producing some final major work
on the plea that it was for financial security in his old age, and
with so much time, labour, and money already expended on
Frederick, he balked at the waste involved in choosing another
subject more to his liking. He was therefore urged on by the same
frugal practicality he admired in his hero.

Besides, there was a moral, even religious, compulsion. To
abandon a difficult task was unmanful, abhorrent to the stern
religion of his childhood: Love not pleasure; love God and be
wretched. The more resistant one's work, the more its inherent
virtue. Then, too, there was his role of prophet to sustain, the
solemn role on which his fame depended. Here was his opportunity to reaffirm those cardinal principles imparted in his previous
works: the hero as a plain silent man of action, a reformer bringing order out of chaos, an ordained leader shaping the destiny
of a nation. Here was his opportunity to contrast the achievements
of "the *last real King* we have had in Europe" with the "do-
nothingness" of Victorian England's talk-happy Parliament and its
windy politicians. In short, here was his final opportunity for a
prophetic blast at his own mechanistic century, so like the godless eighteenth century, except that the latter had been miraculously saved by the emergence of the true king, the Able Man
("a long way till the *next*, I fear") whose dominion was not
based on "semblance" and whom the people therefore recognized
and obeyed. England too must develop the mystic "eye" to recognize and exalt some saving hero of her own.

Having bestowed such heroic stature on Frederick, Carlyle
must have surmised that his countrymen would hardly be persuaded to endorse his conception. Nineteenth-century England,
he knew, was too insular, too complacent to look for military
models beyond her own border. That "the ignorance of the English public in regards to Prussian things obstructs [Carlyle] more

than anything else" had already been pointed out by his brother John, who recognized that "the book must stand or fall on English ground".[25] In any case, English readers at all interested in Frederick could turn to Macaulay's clear and compact treatment, a review essay written in 1842, and find there a viewpoint more in harmony with their own. Instead of a hero, Macaulay had delineated a malicious practical joker, a blasphemer, a tyrannical military and civic leader, a plunderer, a deceiver—in short, an utter scoundrel. He had also hinted at Frederick's homosexuality —"vices from which history averts her eyes".[26] Basically, he had illumined facets of Frederick that Carlyle kept in semi-shadow, thus forearming the public against the heroic portrait. By glorifying so unpopular a man, Carlyle, as he must have seen, weakened any receptivity toward his central plan for an autocratic government of the earnest, dedicated, highly trained and able few, a concept increasingly unacceptable in an age of extending franchise. Accustomed, however, to crying his social and political doctrines into deaf ears, Carlyle seems to have trusted to some distant future for recognition. The present "English world's stupidity upon [Frederick]", he declared in his late years, "is a small matter to me. . . . Book is not quite zero, I perceive, but will be good for something by-and-by."[27]

Whatever the public's reservations about Carlyle's Prussian subject, the work sold amazingly well and contributed substantially to his prosperity.[28] From a few confirmed devotees—notably Froude in England and Emerson in America—came extravagant praise. Equal in enthusiasm but lacking their reverence was Swinburne, whose mildest epithet for Carlyle was "virulent old Arch-Quack of Chelsea". Yet when the final two volumes were due he declared himself "ravenous with expectation", having already delighted in the earlier four, whose hero was "more comprehensible to my heathen mind than any Puritan". It was "Frederick's clear, cold purity of pluck, looking neither upward nor around for any help or comfort" that captivated Swinburne.[29] One pictures this little red squirrel casting aside the dry husk of Carlyle's preachments to get at the rich kernel of his godless hero. The *Punch* staff, however, were less avid. Discussing the first two volumes at one of their weekly dinner meetings, they rendered the terse verdict: "A waste of labour."[30]

From the non-literary general public came respect inspired by the awesome research behind the work, its vast scope as a history of eighteenth-century Europe—and, of course, its author's status as England's "dear old Prophet Carlyle" (so Lady Ashburton had called him) whose thunder had long been esteemed and seldom heeded. It was this automatic respect which prompted *The Gentleman's Magazine* (December 1858) to pay exaggerated homage to Carlyle's work as a "faithful history" and "exquisite work of art", verdicts which it supported by further laudatory generalizations rather than by specific analysis or example. Certain judgments (for instance, "masterly arrangement of his vast mass of facts" and "matchless skill in condensation") were in direct opposition to those of the majority of commentators. For, though the importance of the work was generally conceded, its critical reception was less than enthusiastic. Reviewed by virtually all the leading journals, it received—with the exception noted above—little or no unqualified praise.

Repeatedly censured was the choice of hero, for, commented *Fraser's Magazine* (December 1858) with true English insularity, "It is difficult to care much about Frederick and his doings." Quoting Carlyle's own deprecating statement that "Frederick's ideal, compared with some, was low . . . and only worth much memory in the absence of better", *Blackwood's Edinburgh Magazine* (July 1865) asked, "Why not have sought better, then, Mr. Carlyle?" *The Saturday Review* (25 April 1865) also cited the history's constant patronizing tone in presenting Frederick as "a heathenish old brute [who] still fought and wrought so well that anything may be forgiven". Just how well he wrought was in the main ignored, though *The Times* (18 April 1865) did recognize the notable "domestic administration" through which Frederick "consolidated the Prussian State, repaired its losses in population and wealth, and soothed the very remembrance even of its scars". Most periodicals, however, inclined to the views expressed by *The British Quarterly Review* (January 1859), which accused Carlyle of portraying "the besotted qualities" of Frederick's character as "elevated instincts", of transforming "the passions of the tyrant" into "the virtues of a legislator", of exalting "a Bill Sykes in purple" as a "legitimate hero", and of confounding "the distinction of right and wrong". Calling this Carlyle's "most mischievous book", the October number followed with a similar condemnation: the work had trampled on "considerations of justice and truth as things too vulgar and commonplace to be taken into account when judging the actions of heroes". Similar dissent came from *The Quarterly Review* (April 1859), *The Cornhill Magazine* (July 1862), *The Athenaeum* (25 March 1865), *The Westminster Review* (July 1865), and *The North British Review* (September 1865). So, whether Carlyle exalted Frederick or apologized for him, the book was berated.

Especially offensive to Victorian complacency was Carlyle's scorn for his own nation and era. "Blessed with every comfort that liberty and enlightenment can confer, he sees in the fair, broad, honest face of England only a howling wilderness," accused *Blackwood's* (February 1859). *The Edinburgh Review* (October 1859) deplored his "elaborate ridicule of every institution and usage" of modern times. *The North British Review* (September 1865) concurred, charging him with painting the past "unduly bright" to emphasize "the inferiority of his country and time". This gave his history "a peculiar power to work mischief" on the public: "He stirs up doubt and discontent in their minds, and then abandons them to that unhallowed companionship."

But the victims of his sardonic mockery were by no means confined to his own country and time. Over the years Carlyle had cultivated a talent for derision, which he now exercised habitually and almost automatically, thereby incurring in turn the derision of reviewers who strained to outdo his own caustic tone. (To them one can only say, Thy tooth is not so keen.) One periodical, however, spoke so firmly and justly as to deserve somewhat extended treatment here. Having seen it in Scotland, Jane Carlyle wrote to her husband of "a review in the 'Cornhill' [July 1862] which would amuse you! Adoring your genius, but. . . ."[31]

This essay pronounced *Frederick* to be so "grotesquely original" as not to be subject to the usual criteria. "It must be accepted—or rejected—for what it is, and as it is: a book of strange power." The artist, so the reviewer asserted, must be allowed freedom to create as his genius dictates:

But the teacher is allowed no such license. And as a teacher there are two points upon which we think Carlyle is open to severe disapprobation. . . . The first of these is the painful excess of scorn, which poisons his graphic humour with cruelty and injustice. Scorn is an attitude perilous even to a mind like his, pernicious in its influence on weaker minds. Every serious man will at times be moved to indignant sarcasm at what is base. But in Carlyle, always too disposed to scorn, this attitude has become permanent, not occasional. It is no longer "shams" and charlatans that move his sardonic laughter; but much that is not base at all, good honest endeavour, is quizzed and nicknamed in contempt.

Among those inevitably made the butt of scorn, the writer mentions mathematicians and scientists: "We may allow him to estimate science as far inferior to 'spiritual insight' (somewhat misty as to what it *sees*), but we cannot forget that it is a very noble effort." Leibnitz and Maupertuis, for example, deserve better of Carlyle than repeated ridicule on the basis of the former's "long nose, bandy legs, and huge periwig (as if *those* were the most notable points in a great thinker!)" and of the latter's "big red face". These are "graphic, no doubt, but what is the sense or justice of it?" The perpetual mood of scorn is held to be as overdrawn as the "preposterous" worship of Carlyle's hero.

Attacked by a number of periodicals was the organization of material. *The North British Review* (September 1865) found the work prolix, confused, and out of proportion. *The Westminster Review* (July 1865) regretted that Carlyle had lost his "art of picturesque condensation, of loading his sentences with profound meaning and flashing out his thoughts in swift emphatic precision", a notable feature of his *French Revolution. The British Quarterly Review* (January 1859) accused him of merely taking his materials as they came to hand, without design or perspective. *The Quarterly Review* (April 1859) termed the book a mere "collection of sketches", which omitted "important details in some places" only to accumulate them "without mercy or evident reason . . . in others". Without its helpful index "it would be almost impossible to read the book through with profit". (Had the reviewer only known, this admirable index had been compiled as a labour of love by Carlyle's Chelsea neighbour and disciple, Henry Larkin.) The narrative was diffuse and "garbled", *The Quarterly* continued, as a result of the author's "running comments". The ratio of such interpolations to sound historical substance was summed up by *Blackwood's* (February 1859) charge that never had "the pennyworth of bread borne so small a proportion to the intolerable deal of sack". Also deplored by *The Dublin University Magazine* (July 1862) was the incoherence of Carlyle's "somersault mode of narration, wherein he emulates the springing kangaroo". In short, journalistic opinion agreed that Carlyle's peculiar organization imposed a grave burden on his readers.

But in the majority of negative criticisms Carlyle's unique style appears as an even greater culprit. The pungent flavour of "Carlylese", ever an acquired taste, seems to have turned unpalatable with the years, or with the concentrated six-volume dose. Thus many a reviewer complained of such grotesqueries as invented dialogue, elliptical fragments, the eternal invectives and apostrophes, the eccentric epithets staled by the repetition: *Windbags, Mud-Demons, Dryasdusts, Phantasm-Captains, Demon Newspapers, Enchanted Wiggeries*, and the hoary spokesmen *Teufelsdröckh, Smelfungus*, and *Sauerteig*. The initiated reader of Carlyle might grasp this terminology, but for the novice, so *Blackwood's* (February 1859) maintained, a glossary was needed. (Reviewers would have been wise to acknowledge a few of Carlyle's more successful epithets as well: for example, that for Frederick's pathetic Queen, *Her Serene Insipidity of Brunswick*.)

*The Edinburgh Review* (October 1859) was revolted by "the nauseous depths to which [Carlyle] drags his readers for metaphors". *Fraser's Magazine* (December 1858) pronounced his work "a curious mixture of phantasmagoria and anecdote, of riotous humour, incessant quaintness, extravagance of language, and painful exactness of detail". *The Saturday Review* (2 April 1864), another addict to a bland diet of everyday language, was thankful that "the ordinary chroniclers of current events do not write like Smelfungus". For, though it was "amusing at times to guess what on earth Mr. Carlyle can mean", success brought no reward but a mere "commonplace reflection . . . twisted into an odd but striking form of expression".

*The Athenaeum* (3 May 1862), however, tolerated the bewildering "extravagances" and "complications" of language in view of the vitality of Carlyle's characterizations and "military descriptions", noting that "his style, when he follows the army, marches with it, echoes its guns, reflects its bayonet gleams, is in harmony

191

with its wildest music". A later issue (12 March 1864) continues indulgent of the "intensely peculiar" expression, justly observing how "often the author's manner gives strength and picturesqueness to his matter". The consensus of journalistic opinion, however, was considerably less favourable to the vagaries of genius.

As with his earlier books Carlyle feigned to ignore critical opinion, except when "officious people" forced it upon him. Favourable or not, the reviews of *Frederick*, in so far as he noticed them, were dismissed as "no better . . . than the barking of dogs".[32] Nevertheless, the English rejection of his Prussian *alter ego* was in a sense a rejection of himself, and as such presumably held a degree of bitterness.

He must therefore, have been gratified by the response from Germany, where the work was immediately translated, widely circulated, and increasingly approved as the decade advanced. Its author was praised not only as an artist and epic historian, but also as a seer who had anticipated the rise of Germany and had prepared Europe for an expanding German Empire. Toward the end of the Franco-Prussian War, with a German victory assured, Carlyle therefore felt that a letter to *The Times* (18 November 1870) was called for to remind the English that "no nation ever had so bad a neighbour as Germany has had in France for the last 400 years; bad in all manner of ways; insolent, rapacious, insatiable, unappeasable, continually aggressive". Now he found it only just that this neighbour should have been dealt "so complete, instantaneous, and ignominious a smashing-down" by Germany, who would have been foolish "not to think of raising up some secure boundary-fence" between herself and her ancient enemy. He dwelt rapturously on the union of Prussian states that he had foreseen: "That noble, patient, deep, pious and solid Germany should at length be welded into a Nation and become Queen of the Continent instead of a vapouring, vainglorious, gesticulating, quarrelsome, restless and over-sensitive France, seems to me to be the hopefulest public fact that has occurred in my time" (*Works*, XXX, 52, 59).

Four years later Germany awarded Carlyle the Prussian Order of Merit, founded, appropriately enough, by Frederick himself. No doubt Carlyle was gratified. Yet he deprecated the honour in his usual manner, calling it a "sublime nonentity" and protesting that "had they sent me ¼lb. of good Tobacco the addition to my happiness had probably been suitabler and greater!"[33] The following year he was honoured by a note of congratulation from Bismarck on his eightieth birthday. He replied in German (10 December 1875) with keen appreciation, declaring, "What you are pleased to say of my poor history of your great King Frederich seems to me the fittest and most flattering utterance I have yet heard on this subject anywhere" (Wilson, *Carlyle*, VI, 374–5).

Actually, Bismarck's praise seems rather too general to be termed "the most pertinent . . . yet heard", consisting merely of the assurance that Carlyle's work had presented a full-length portrait, revealing Frederick to the German people like a living statue—"*wie eine lebende Bildsäule*". Carlyle's acknowledgment, however, becomes exempt from critical scrutiny when one notes that it was "with a great effort, painfully dictated" to his niece Mary, who had dutifully undertaken to answer "that wheelbarrowful" of birthday remembrances.[34]

Carlyle's letter to the *Times*, along with such subsequent evidences of his German connections and sympathies, brought on angry outbursts which reverberated into the next century, particularly during World Wars I and II. Writing to the *Nation* (14 September 1918) Stuart F. Sherman, in an article entitled "Carlyle and Kaiser Worship", recommended that the works of Carlyle be burned because of this bias. An unsigned contribution to the *National Review* (February 1923) accused him of being the "catspaw of the Hohenzollerns". And in 1927 Norwood Young held that Carlyle, by whitewashing Frederick's violence and fraud, had rendered judgments which even extreme Prussian admirers could not countenance. Such exaltation of "one of the worst men known to history", Young asserted, "came home to us in the terrible years of the Great War".[35] With World War II Carlyle was further discredited by association when the Nazis quoted him extensively in broadcasts beamed at Britain in the late thirties and early forties.

War-nurtured opinion aside, how has Carlyle's *Frederick* been regarded in this century? In 1929 Alec Wilson, unmoved by lingering post-war prejudice, but perhaps biased in favour of a fellow-Scot, said that this work surpassed other histories "as diamonds surpass coal" (V, 179). But another Scot, J. G. Robertson, well versed in German language and literature, declared it "doubtful if any of the acknowledged standard writings on Frederick in our day would have been essentially different had Carlyle never laboured".[36] True, the recent compact, objective, and popular treatment by Nancy Mitford does acknowledge Carlyle as a source: "a gold mine of information, both relevant and irrelevant" (p. 292), but obviously not as an influence on interpretation. With the exception of Norwood Young's notoriously anti-Carlylean *Life of Frederick the Great* (1919), other twentieth-century biographies of Frederick written or translated into English (Thaddeus, 1930; Veale, 1935; Gaxotte, 1941; Gooch, 1947; Reiners, 1960) acknowledge little or no more than the mere existence of Carlyle's work.

Other than professional historians, who are in any case armed against Carlyle's special pleading, the public today is for the most part too indifferent even to echo his 1859 damnation of the unfinished work as "that unutterable horror of a Prussian book". When years later in the gloom of his old age its author consigned it to "the belly of oblivion",[37] he was perhaps anticipating the position of Morse Peckham, who submits that this heroic book demands heroic readers, a species lacking today.[38] Granted, a firm grasp of eighteenth-century European history and its antecedents (even unto the tenth century) is a prerequisite to reading the work without floundering. To this must be added the diligence and patience to cope with the complexities of organization and the profusion of digressions. Those so equipped might, however, admit also to communion that small segment of readership, floundering but fascinated, which remains content with less than mastery.

Of such are those non-specialists, we who are neither historians, Carlylean scholars, nor thorough-going disciples of the prophet, but mainly devotees of a personality, one that in the beginning may call forth amusement and a measure of dissent, but finally respect, attention, and affection as well. We are those to whom the *Letters* must ever be the favourite among Carlyle's books. Thus we tend to value *Frederick* more as a revelation of its author than of its hero and his times. We consequently sieve the tough pulp to catch a pungent juice over which we linger. If we find the volume of such juice unmatched in Carlyle's previous work, it may be only because no earlier work approaches the length of *Frederick*. As for flavour, it cannot have been distilled from the author's zest, for unlike *The French Revolution*, this laboured work did not come "direct and flamingly from the heart". Yet flavour is notably present, tempting one to offer samples as an enticement to a first, or further, dip into plentitude.

Any collection of memorabilia might well include that vignette of the twelfth-century Frederick Barbarossa, "greatest of all the Kaisers . . . holding the reins of the world", who chained the rebellious Governor of Milan beneath his table and forced him to lie there "like a dog, for three days", till he complied. "Those", adds Carlyle approvingly, "were serious old times" (I, v, 76–7).

Frederick's father, too, that "solid, honest, if somewhat explosive bear" (I, iii, 30), is a source of delight, in whom we meet every parent who would have his offspring walk in his own footsteps, resembling him "as a little sixpence does a big half-crown". And in the youthful Fritz, wilfully bent on "French fopperies, flutings, and cockatoo fashions of hair", who could not then or ever become an exact copy of the paternal half-crown, we recognize and sympathize with the universal teenager (I, xii, 391).

As for Frederick's paternal grandmother, Queen Sophie Charlotte, we cannot forget her attempts "to draw water from that deep well" which was Leibnitz, and her failure to hoist anything but a "wet rope with cobwebs sticking to it . . . endless rope, and the bucket never coming to view" (I, iv, 35).

For the historical validity of these and other portraits we may care no more than we do for that of Shakespeare's Hotspur and Prince Hal. It is enough that they live, and enough that events are often re-created in such seeming actuality that we experience them with all our senses. Thus with each return to that rhythmic depiction of the advancing Prussian troops we are caught up in their "intricate, many-glancing tide . . . swift, correct as clockwork . . ., tornado-storm so beautifully hidden within it" (V, ii, 27). In like manner we witness the theatrical defiance of Maria Theresa, exultant on her hilltop; or the last hours of Frederick, attended by a shivering hound and a faithful hussar; or numerous other episodes. Opposed to dull textbook exposition, this method of Carlyle's is the essence of his virtue. Yet it is only an intermittent virtue, for such passages, composed *con amore*, mingle unevenly with series of disjointed paragraphs transcribed directly, though with disarming apology, from "rough Notebooks". This unevenness, along with ponderous jocularity, crusty rebuke ("pooh, you—!"), and footnotes combining documentation with damnation, are none the less savoured by the reader attuned to the quirks of Carlylean personality. Thus lured, he may grapple eventually with the titanic history entire.

But what of the book's future, that "by-and-by" which Carlyle foresaw in one of his rare moods of optimism?

That the reading public increasingly demands ease and brevity amounts to a prediction of further dwindling readership for such epics as *Frederick*. Along with ease and brevity the public also demands what it is pleased to term relevance, a quality which today's democratic society finds lacking in this history. But universal and eternal relevance is exactly what Carlyle himself regarded as the chief merit of his last work. And who can predict tomorrow's concept of relevance? As chaos and the decline of moral responsibility continue to blight our lives, who can say that the pendulum will not swing, however lamentably, toward the autocrat hero? Then, with the accompanying emergence of *Frederick* from "the belly of oblivion", we should doubtless find both governor and governed pursuing that unheroic method of mining the text for usable nuggets—such only as would sustain the authoritarian regime. Thus the prophecy in the final paragraph of Carlyle's history would be fulfilled: that "the Nations universally . . . bethink themselves of such a Man and his Function and Performance, with feelings far other than possible at present".

NOTES

1. Since letters cited will eventually be in *CL*, references are generally given only by date and name of addressee.
2. See Carlyle's "Voltaire" (1829) and letter to Emerson (25 June 1852).
3. *History of Friedrich the Second, Called Frederick the Great*, 6 vols (New York, 1859–66), I, i, 1. Subsequent references are to this edition and given in the text.
4. See Carlyle's letter (June 1836) to his brother John and another to Jane Carlyle (2 July 1857).
5. Nancy Mitford, *Frederick the Great* (New York, 1970), p. 247.

6. See his review essay on Thomas Campbell's *Frederick the Great and His Times* in *The Works of Lord Macaulay* (London, 1904), VI, 667.
7. W. Hale White (Mark Rutherford), *Letters to Three Friends* (London, 1924), p. 67.
8. Mitford, *Frederick*, p. 76.
9. See Margaret Oliphant's comments on Carlyle in *Macmillan's Magazine* for April 1881, pp. 487–95.
10. See Carlyle's letter to Varnhagen von Ense (6 June 1852).
11. Wilson, *Carlyle*, IV, 478–9.
12. *Ibid.*, V, 125.
13. See his letter to Jane Carlyle (9 Sep. 1852) and Wilson, *Carlyle*, IV, 442.
14. Letter to J. Marshall (13 March 1853), British Museum, Egerton MSS. 3032.1–33.
15. *Ibid.*
16. *"Carlyliana"; being the Opinions of TC on some books relating to the "History of Frederick the Great"* (London, privately printed, 1883).
17. Moncure D. Conway, *Autobiography* (Boston, 1904), pp. 394–5.
18. Froude, *Life*, IV, 86–7.
19. See Sterling's letter in the *Times*, 11 Jan. 1917.
20. See Carlyle's note in *Letters and Memorials of Jane Welsh Carlyle*, ed. J. A. Froude (London, 1883), p. 243.
21. Letter to Marshall (28 Nov. 1859), Egerton MS.
22. Letter to John Carlyle (31 Aug. 1867).
23. Norwood Young, *Carlyle, His Rise and Fall* (London, 1927), p. 294.
24. M. D. Conway, *TC* (New York, 1881), p. 105.
25. Letter to Marshall (13 Feb. 1857), Egerton MS.
26. *The Works of Lord Macaulay*, VI, 649.
27. Froude, *Life*, IV, 354.
28. Wilson, *Carlyle*, V, 328.
29. See his letters to Burne-Jones (15 May 1883) and Pauline, Lady Trevelyan (15 March 1865) in *The Swinburne Letters*, ed. Cecil Y. Lang (New Haven, 1959–62).
30. Diary of Henry Silver, entry for 10 Feb. 1859, in the *Punch* Library.
31. *Letters and Memorials of Jane Welsh Carlyle*, p. 102.
32. Froude, *Life*, IV, 228, quoting TC's Journal.
33. Letter to John Carlyle (14 Feb. 1874).
34. *Ibid.* (15 Dec. 1875).
35. *Carlyle, His Rise and Fall*, p. 366.
36. *Cambridge History of English Literature*, XIII, 20.
37. *Reminiscences* (Norton), I, 201.
38. *Victorian Revolutionaries* (New York, 1970), p. 45.

# 9

# *Frederick the Great*

## by MORSE PECKHAM

It is difficult to write about Carlyle's *History of Friedrich II of Prussia Called Frederick the Great,* for it seems a pointless and useless undertaking. Almost no one has read it, and it seems unlikely that anyone will read it because of a mere essay. Those who find this essay valuable will probably conclude that they are saved the trouble of reading the work; while those who dislike the essay will decide that it has not offered convincing reasons for undertaking the book itself. During the fifteen years since I first read it, constant inquiry among other Victorian scholars has not uncovered anyone else who has done so. In fact, one scholar who has written in some detail about it and with an air of considerable authority turned out only to have skimmed through it. Another, one who likewise found the work to be a failure, does not give me the impression that he has done more than a rapid skimming. When I recommend reading *Frederick* to other Victorian scholars, my enthusiasm is received with scepticism and more often than not a politely but barely concealed implication that my judgement is grotesque. To be sure, one friend to whom I recommended it did read it and, though he detested Carlyle, thought it to be a marvellous book. But then, he was not a Victorian scholar but a music critic, and besides he died not long thereafter.

I shall make no attempt, therefore, to argue that *Frederick* is a success or a failure, a great book or a poor one. When I first read it I felt that I was having one of the greatest and most thoroughly satisfying reading experiences of my life. My second reading was less agreeable, but it was done not at leisure but under deadline pressure. I look forward to reading it again, but at my ease and after I have retired. I think it is a fascinating and wonderful work. If one wants to understand Carlyle and the culture of the nineteenth century one should read it; if one wishes professional success and status, to read *Frederick* is clearly unnecessary, since so many Victorian scholars who enjoy both have not troubled to do so. Rather, I shall be concerned with certain rhetorical peculiarities in *Frederick* and in proposing explanations for them, since they raise interesting questions not only about Carlyle but also about the very nature of writing history.[1]

## 1

Approaching *Frederick* initially as a piece of historical discourse, one first notes the oddness of its proportions. Almost a third of the work is over before Friedrich succeeds to the throne. The last half of his reign takes up a little less than a tenth of the whole. Thus almost 60% of the work is concerned with the years from 1740 to 1763. This is the period of the Silesian Wars; Friedrich invaded Silesia in December, 1740, less than seven months after his accession. Moreover, Books I to III, almost 10%, are principally taken up with the history of Brandenburg and of the Hohenzollerns before the accession of Friedrich's father, Friedrich Wilhelm. Books IV to X, about 23%, ostensibly taken up with Friedrich's youth, are as much concerned with Friedrich Wilhelm as with his son. Thus anyone who wishes to read a balanced account of the career of Friedrich will be both disappointed and puzzled.

A clue to this way of laying out the work is to be found in the great space and immense detail devoted to Friedrich's campaigns and above all to his battles. Carlyle himself visited most of the battle-sites, and it is obvious that no one who had not done so could have written about the battles as he did. If he could not go to the field itself, he procured the most accurate and informative maps and descriptions he could lay his hands on. Two themes of the book emerge here, that of struggle and that of reality.

The theme of struggle emerges in the long accounts of the history of Brandenburg and of the Hohenzollerns, though it is not explicitly set forth until Book XXI. Carlyle is discussing the rapid recovery of Prussia from the devastations of the Third Silesian War:

> Prussia has been a meritorious Nation; and, however cut and ruined, is and was in a healthy state, capable of recovering soon. Prussia has defended itself against overwhelming odds,—brave Prussia; but the real soul of its merit was that of having merited such a King to command it. Without this King, all its valours, disciplines, resources of war, would have availed Prussia little. No wonder Prussia has still a loyalty to its great Friedrich, to its Hohenzollern Sovereigns generally. Without these Hohenzollerns, Prussia had been, what we long ago saw it, the unluckiest of German Provinces; and could never have had the pretension to exist as a Nation at all. Without this particular Hohenzollern, it had been trampled out again, after apparently succeeding. To have achieved a Friedrich the Second for King over it, was Prussia's grand merit (XXI, i, 8).

The interactions of Hohenzollerns and Brandenburg, the long history that lay behind the achievement of "Prussia's grand merit", is the theme of the first three books.[2] It is on the one hand the struggle of the Hohenzollerns to establish themselves, and on the other of the people of Brandenburg to establish themselves as an independent nation. The central theme is the struggle of Brandenburg and the Hohenzollerns to adapt themselves to each other, a struggle almost completed by Friedrich Wilhelm, who left to Friedrich an army and a disciplined population. In the Silesian wars Friedrich consummated the century-old struggle and created a modern nation.

Carlyle conceived of his task as the creation of an epic, the first true historical epic, although he was convinced that his cultural situation did not allow him to create that epic.

> Alas, the Ideal of History, as my friend Sauerteig knows, is very high; and it is not one serious man, but many successions of such, and whole serious generations of such, that can ever again build up History towards its old dignity. . . . "All History is an imprisoned Epic, nay an imprisoned Psalm and Prophecy," says Sauerteig there. . . . But I think all real *Poets*, to this hour, are Psalmists and Illiadists after their sort; and have in them a divine impatience of lies, a divine incapacity of living among lies. Likewise, which is a corollary, that the highest Shakspeare producible is properly the fittest Historian producible (I, i, 17–18).

Arms-and-the-man is the theme of epic, and to Friedrich the Electorate of Brandenburg and the Kingdom of Prussia were his arms, forged by his Hohenzollern ancestors.

But the joint struggle of electorate and family to realize themselves and each other was not enough to account for Friedrich. Not only must the arms be forged but also the man. Hence the long and lovingly detailed discourse on the reign of Friedrich Wilhelm, and on what, for Carlyle's purposes, was the real point of that reign, the fearful conflict between father and son, the result of which was the creation of a man and a king out of a sensitive, dilettantish, Francophile prince. It is therefore of great significance to the design of the work that Carlyle makes much of the reconciliation of father and son, of Friedrich's grief at his father's death, of his love for his father, and particularly of his continuation of his father's internal policies and administrative personnel. Thus by the end of the original first two volumes (Books I–VIII) both country and man are forged and ready for each other.

The next twelve months (IX–XX) are taken up almost entirely with the three Silesian wars, except for seven months of peace after the accession and two intervals of two and ten years (Books XI, XIV, and XVI). From these wars Friedrich and Prussia emerge, the one as finally a true King, the other as finally a true Nation. Book XXI, which Carlyle calls a "loose Appendix of Papers", is not a "finished Narrative" simply because to his theme such a finished narrative would be inappropriate. All that was needed was a demonstration that in the last twenty-three years of his reign, Friedrich truly ruled a consummated nation. The whole metaphysical point is to be found here.

In the chaos of the eighteenth century—that it was a chaos the French Revolution, to Carlyle, sufficiently proved—Friedrich had created an island of social order. Not that he was alone. Carlyle saw in that chaotic century of lies two other focal points of truth. One was Voltaire; the other was Pitt. Carlyle judged Voltaire to be no more perfect than Friedrich, yet he saw him as a counterpart. Voltaire had an intellectual grasp of his cultural situation; Friedrich, whom Carlyle saw as intellectually superficial, nevertheless had a practical, non-intellectual grasp of a similar sort. Pitt stands on the sidelines; he helps Friedrich, but his help is validated by his intelligence in grasping that America must be

English not French, France, of course, being at once the most brilliant and the most corrupt of eighteenth-century nations. America is presented as the hope of the future; Pitt was great because he saw that hope as something that would be destroyed if France controlled America.

Further, Carlyle saw the nineteenth century as the inheritor and the continuator of the collapse of eighteenth century culture in the French Revolution. The first chapter of Book I begins with that theme and the first chapter of the final book reiterates it, "New Act,—or, we may call it New *Part*; Drama of World History, Part Third" (XXI, i, 2). This is not a casual remark here, but a proper introduction to that Book. The work cannot be allowed to end triumphantly, heroically, in a blaze of Friedrich's glory. Friedrich, it is true, created an island of order, but it was bound to be temporary, since it came toward the close of Part II of World-History. The world in which Carlyle was living was the opening chaos of Part III. That is why the true Historical Epic lay far in the future, why Carlyle could not write it. To do so it would be necessary to understand the meaning of Part III, and though Carlyle guesses at it—("unappeasable Revolt against Sham-Governors and Sham-Teachers,—which I do charitably define to be a Search, most unconscious, yet in deadly earnest, for true Governors and Teachers")—the result of that search cannot be envisioned. Friedrich, he implies in the next sentence, is not particularly significant for what he did, but that he existed may be of the highest relevance. At the beginning of Book I Carlyle writes, "To many it appears certain there are to be no Kings of any sort, no Government more; less and less need of them henceforth, New Era having come" (I, i, 16). At the beginning of Book XXI he defines Part III of World-History as "the breaking-out of universal mankind into Anarchy, into the faith and practice of No-Government" (p. 2). That is why he says in Book I, "My hopes of presenting, in this Last of the Kings, an exemplar to my contemporaries, I confess, are not high" (I, i, 17). In short, if Carlyle has understood World-History, true Governors and true Teachers—political and moral agents of social control and management—will arise; if he has not, mankind will find a way of living satisfactorily without social control and management. Since Carlyle cannot be sure of how the problem is to be resolved, if at all, he cannot write a true Histori-

cal Epic, since such an epic would require an understanding of
the meaning of World-History. He can only show the struggle,
he can only demonstrate how one man became a true King, but he
cannot be sure that such struggle and becoming can really be useful. (I cannot forbear interpolating that, disagreeable as the notion
may be, I cannot imagine mankind without techniques of social
control and management. My reason is that notions of society
without social control and management are founded upon love,
but love, in all its forms, appears to me to be the most stringent
and oppressive of the various modes of social control and management. Possibly Carlyle was hinting at this when he proposed that
Part II of World History began with Christ and ended with the
French Revolution.) The future, then, may not need such exemp-
lars as Friedrich, or, on the contrary, it may need them but be
unable to use them. From this point of view the real hero
of *Frederick* is Carlyle himself, for he engaged in and persisted in
the immense struggle to complete the work without any confidence that it was worth completing. This is the difference between
the redemptionist Carlyle (and Marx) of the 1830's and 1840's
and the Carlyle of *Frederick*.

The theme of *Frederick*, then, is the theme of all Carlyle's work
from before 1830: the struggle to create order out of chaos, and
the struggle to penetrate through shams and lies to reality. However, the notion that that penetration is redemptive is now gone
or at best has suffered a severe attrition. What had sustained
Carlyle so long, up to *Latter-Day Pamphlets*, was the conviction
that the penetration through lies and shams revealed the reality
of the world as a symbol of the divine, or that the hero was a
symbol and instrument of the divine. All this has disappeared
from Frederick. We hear often enough about the Laws of Nature
and the Laws of God, but we are not informed precisely what
those laws are, except that they tend on the whole to be disagreeable, and except that the heroic man can face their disagreeable-
ness and act in spite of it. Indeed, Carlyle's conception of God
becomes remarkably like that of Kierkegaard's at much the same
time: from the belief in God no moral or metaphysical propo-
sitions can be deduced. The only reality the not very intelligent or
perceptive Friedrich was capable of was the reality of creating an
island of order, in the chaos of the eighteenth century, the reality

of knowing what he wanted; yet his island was to be washed away by the French Revolution. The best Carlyle can suggest is that Friedrich's achievement enabled Prussia to survive several inferior Kings, the French Revolution, and Napoleon. Thus the marked difference between *Frederick* and the works of the 1830's and 1840's is not sufficiently explained (and to my mind not at all explained) by postulating failing powers or loss of "creativity" (whatever that is). One must recognize a radical difference of vision. Recent writers on *Frederick* have been young (and platitudinously liberal). Their rejection of the work may, possibly, be a function of their youth (and their ideology), not of their critical insight nor of their social comprehension.

2

A second oddity of Frederick is typographical. A very large portion is in small print. It was the result of a very idiosyncratic decision, and I have never seen it discussed, though it seems impossible that it has never been commented on. Why did Carlyle set up this additional barrier to the reader?[3]

Many of these small-print passages are, to be sure, quotations from letters and other documents, but most of them are not. Some of them are summaries of documents; others are elaborations of minor points; for only a few of them is there any suggestion that they can be profitably skipped by all but persevering and determined readers. A sampling of how they are introduced will be of some interest. "Says one whose Note-books I have got" (I, i, 58); "says one of my old Papers" (I, i, 75); "the following Excerpt" (I, i, 77); "perhaps I had better subjoin a List (V, i, 15); "the following stray Note" (V, iii, 31); "accept this Note, or Summary" (V, iii, 39); "a most small Anecdote, but then an indisputably certain one" (V, v, 48); "One glance I may perhaps commend to the reader, out of these multifarious Notebooks in my possession" (IX, vi, 78); "excerpted from multifarious old Notebooks" (IX, viii, 91); "the following chronological phenomena of the Polish Election" (IX, viii, 95); "As to the History of Schlesien . . . I notice . . . Three Epochs" (XII, i, 4); "Read this Note" (XII, ii, 17); "says an Excerpt I have made" (XII, ii, 20); "and this of Smelfungus" (XVI, iii, 233); "I have something to quote, as abridged and distilled from various sources" [it is not a quotation] (XVI, vi, 273); "says a certain Author" [unidentified] (XVI, viii, 306); "take this brief Note" (XVIII, vii, 228); two paragraphs without introduction, but placed in quotes (XVIII, viii, 264); "Smelfungus takes him up, with a twitch" (XVIII, ix, 304); "For our poor objects, here is a Summary, which may suffice" (XX, v, 299); "some glances into the Turk War, I grieve to say, are become inevitable to us!" (XXI, iv, 100); "a rough brief Note" (XXI, v, 132); "Here, saved from my poor friend Smelfungus (nobody knows how much of him I suppress), is a brief jotting, in the form of rough *memoranda*, if it be permissible" (XXI, v, 181).

A thorough study of all the small-print passages, the categories into which they fall, and their various introductions, when present, as they usually are, might be of considerable interest, but probably would not change drastically the impression one gets from a thorough reading of the entire work. One group, as suggested, consists of direct quotations from letters and other documents. Here the small print is clearly a typographical convention. The effect of the other group, however, is quite different. For these passages Carlyle has innovated not merely a typographical convention but one that may properly be called a rhetorical one. The effect is by no means one that indicates that the material is skippable or unessential in any way. Often enough the effect is quite the contrary; it is an effect of emphasis. There seem to be two quite different functions, subordination, and superordination.

In the first category are materials which only remotely impinge upon Friedrich, events which affect his activities and his purposes, but only indirectly, though some other agency. Although it is not in small print, the following passage gives some clue to this function. It is about the Italian War from 1742 to 1748. "War of which we propose to say almost nothing; but must request the reader to imagine it, all along, as influential on our specific affairs" (XIV, ii, 381). And every now and then there is a reminder that it is indeed going on, and occasionally more than a reminder, sometimes in small-print passages. Excellent examples of this kind of subordination are to be found in the accounts of Wolfe in Canada (Books XVIII and XIX). What Carlyle was attempting to do is clear enough. To carry out his theme of Friedrich creating an island of order in the European chaos of the eighteenth century, he had to present that chaos both vividly and in considerable detail. To feel Friedrich's struggle, the reader has to feel as intimately what he was struggling against. The effect is certainly precisely that. As the reader continues to burrow his way through the book, gradually he gains, as several readers at the time noticed, an extraordinarily comprehensive and detailed imaginative grasp of the political life of Europe during the twenty-three years of Friedrich's role as Friedrich Agonistes, not Carlyle's own epithet but justified by the identification of Friedrich with Samson Agonistes in Book I (p. 5). From this tremendous detail emerges a pattern of forces marshalled against him, at various times and in various combinations, England, France, Austria (above all), Russia and Sweden. I know of no sustained historical discourse, even of much lesser length, in which the general contours of political and military events emerge with such grandeur and clarity. The convention of subordination by small print certainly, I think, contributes greatly to this. Such a passage is to the large print as a subordinate clause is to an independent clause. The equivalent of a logical articulation is achieved in large-scale historical articulation.

The second category, superordination, is equally important. The effect is cinematic, a close-up, together with a slowing down of the tempo of narration. A more appropriate nineteenth-century term would be "vignette". One of Carlyle's constant minor themes is the difficulty of getting a clear picture of Friedrich, or of his contemporaries, such as Voltaire or Czar Peter III. Just as Friedrich's effort was to penetrate through the shams and lies and illusions of the eighteenth century, so Carlyle presents himself as engaged in an equivalent struggle to penetrate through the mass of documents and formal histories—subsumed under the imaginary Prussian historian Dryasdust—to get at the living reality of a human being. The large-print discourse, then, carries forward the events in a more or less normal historical rhetoric, but it is apparent that Carlyle recognizes such narrative rhetoric as an abstraction, a simplification, a reduction to a spurious order of the infinitely complex interactions of human beings. The small-print superordination not only serves, then, to penetrate through that abstraction and to offer relief from it, but also—and this is the most important effect—to reveal its abstract character.

Moreover, the conventions of rhetorical articulation of sub-ordination and superordination effected by small print are them-selves part of a larger and even more interesting rhetorical strategy, the dissolution of the narrator into a group of narrators. First, of course, is "I". This is the modest struggling historian, attempting to set forth clearly the history of Friedrich, to disentangle immense complications, such as the Schleswig-Holstein question, or the case of the Miller Arnold, to present clearly what cannot be presented clearly, a battle, to explain the movements in Friedrich's campaigns. Above all—and this is of the highest importance—the "I" is struggling with an immense accumulation of documents. This "I" often calls himself "Editor". This not only emphasizes the physical presence of the documents but also links Frederick with Carlyle's truly editorial role in *Cromwell* and with the fictitious editor of *Sartor Resartus*, also struggling with a confused mass of miscellaneous documents from which he has to construct some kind of meaning. Closely related to this primary "I", and almost identifiable with him, is the "I" of some previous stage in the construction of the book. This former "I" has left behind him note-books, scraps of paper, annotated maps, and so forth, which the current "I" uses. Part of the humour of the current "I" is the pleasure he takes in burning up materials he no longer needs. More remote is an unnamed "predecessor", transparently Carlyle himself. Dramatized in this figure is the experience every researcher has of feeling that his earlier notes must have been made by someone else, a justified feeling, since as one studies and writes one does become a different figure. Still more remote is the unnamed tourist, transparently again Carlyle himself. Here also is dramatized the feeling that the historian in his study, consulting his notes and his documents, is not the same man as the historian in the field, actively engaged in examining the battleground, or the palace, or the gardens, or the portrait. All these figures are anonymous, and each indicates a different and psychologically accurate relation of the historian to his materials.

Over against these are two named figures, each with quite a different function. "Sauerteig" is the author of the discussion of Ideal History, of the identification of history with imprisoned epic, quoted above. "Sauerteig" means yeast, or leaven. He is the ultimate interpreter not of history itself but of the historian's activity. He is the meta-historian. At the opposite pole is "Smelfungus", presumably meaning "smelling of the mould of ancient documents". He is the polar opposite of Sauerteig. He is the researcher; he occasionally seems to be Joseph Neuberg, Carlyle's immensely valuable assistant. He is spoken of with contempt and affection, and with sorrow for his endless and often profitless efforts, for he often produces the useless or the barely usable. He is, therefore, a useful means of subordination, a way of bringing in material of very peripheral interest, which is, however, at least above the level of the negligible, though often enough he turns up with that as well. These two figures likewise indicate psychologically accurate relations of the historian to his materials.

Against these named and nameless figures is the enemy of all of them, Dryasdust. He is not only the unimaginative, non-interpretative historian, usually Prussian; he is not even competent and reliable in presenting his materials. He is particularly incompetent—and he often gets cursed for this—in providing indices; either they are non-existent or they are bad. Thus he is as unimaginative in comprehending the relation of the historian to his documents as he is uncomprehending of the extreme pole of the competent construction of historical discourse—meta-history, the role of Sauerteig. Dryasdust cannot give a rational account of a sequence of events of any complexity; he cannot even construct a simple chronological table of such a sequence. He is entirely overwhelmed by the maelstrom of historical documentation; he himself is only caught up in the perpetual whirlwind in the dustbin of historical documents. He is therefore a constant threat to the other narrators; without knowing it, he continuously undermines and subverts the activity of constructing a historical discourse. And he too is an aspect of Carlyle, of the narrator of the narrators, as he is of any historian.

This dissolution of the narrator into a variety of roles is of the highest interest. It is a device which, without compromising *Frederick* as historical discourse, nevertheless pulls it into the general field of art. The narrator, as increasingly in the novels of the time, *Vanity Fair* for example, the "I" is not a category with a fixed and stable set of attributes.[4] He becomes something like the central figure of a major work of fiction, a proper-name category with a constantly changing set of attributes for which there is no attribute which subsumes the remaining attributes into a coherence. Thus the narrator resembles not only the narrator of sophisticated fiction but also the narrator of many lyric poems and of the informal essay. This dissolved narrator, in fact, tends to become more interesting, because of attributional discontinuity, than Friedrich himself, who shows greater attributional stability and coherence than Friedrich Wilhelm, his father, a character recognized by some of Carlyle's contemporaries as one of the great creations of English literature.

This attributional dissolution of the narrator into various named roles is on the central line of Romanticism, the separation between self and role, as George Herbert Mead pointed out many years ago. The usual procedure in Romantic fictions of one sort or another, including poetry, is the creation of an anti-role, the Bohemian, the Artist, the Dandy, the Virtuoso, and the Historian.[5] The anti-role establishes and defines the self, which, of course, is a pure concept and has no empirical existence, or at best is a feeling-state, a sense of continuity as one shifts from one social role to another. In dissolving and subdividing the anti-Role of the Historian, Carlyle has gone one step further in this, anticipating Nietzsche, who insisted that the effort to create a coherent interpretation of his thousands of aphorisms and paragraphs would be a profound miscomprehension of what he was trying to do. Carlyle has shown the similarity of the construction of anti-Roles to the construction of socially validated roles. The self, as it were, can manifest itself only in roles, and from this point of view, even the creation of an anti-Role itself belongs to the socialization process. The personality is thus revealed not as a manifestation or embodiment of the self but as part of the social world from which the self is alienated. This is again an instance of the radical difference between the redemptionist Carlyle of the years before *Latter-Day Pamphlets* and the Carlyle of *Frederick*.

Nevertheless, the continuity of the self behind the roles is symbolized. The prose style is that symbolization; for whatever role is being played, even a minor role not yet mentioned, the Translator, there is a stylistic continuity. However, that continu-

209

ity is by no means identical with the style of Carlyle's previous writings. It is different from the style of *Latter-Day Pamphlets*, in which appears an unusually high percentage of complex sentences. On the other hand, *Frederick* shares with the *French Revolution* and *Latter-Day Pamphlets* a most unusually high percentage of sentence-fragments. Again, only *Past and Present* and *Latter-Day Pamphlets* show a higher average of expressive punctuation marks than *Frederick*, to which the average in *Heroes and Hero-Worship* is equal. The latter, of course, was designed for public presentation in lectures, and *Past and Present* was written after several years of public lecturing. *Latter-Day Pamphlets*, on the other hand, was specifically polemic, designed to bring about changes in attitudes and action. Sentence-fragments and expressive punctuation are the marks of a style aimed at oral delivery. The self underlying the various roles in *Frederick* can be usefully categorized as a man speaking to other men, but a man separated from other men by an alienation more thorough-going than at any previous stage in Carlyle's life. Thus the style of *Frederick* is often more like Carlyle's journal style than is the style of any of his other published works. This is perfectly consonant with the implications drawn above from the passages on No-Government, and with the conviction that the true Historical Epic cannot be written at the present time by anyone.[6]

But this is not all, for that alienation is further dramatized by the narrator's alienation from the task he is engaged on, the construction of a history of Friedrich. That this alienation was perfectly sincere is indicated by Carlyle's journal entries at the time. That sincerity, however, is of no importance; the evidence for it serves little more than to support a rhetorical analysis developed from other evidence. It is more interesting that the alienation from the task itself is consonant with Carlyle's lack of conviction that the whole enormous effort was worth the trouble it was taking to do it. All of the devices so far discussed are employed to dramatize that alienation from the effort. *Frederick* is unique in the way it forces on the reader an awareness of the narrator's struggle with documents and with previous histories on this and related subjects. Everyone who attempts to construct a discourse from primary and secondary materials and from his own notes experiences that struggle; but the normal and socially validated attributes of the scholarly narrator's role are the suppression of that awareness, the presentation of an air of quiet confidence, and a dramatization of perfect competence, even though in fact the author is constantly trembling with professional anxiety. The competence of the scholar and the historian is one of those shams and illusions and lies, one of those "unveracities", which Carlyle is attacking. This is often dramatized amusingly, as when the narrator admits he has lost a note, or has inadvertently destroyed it, or can no longer locate the source of a quotation or a reference. The highly unsatisfactory and fundamentally incompetent behavioural processes of the scholar and historian are thus brought out into the open. Perhaps this is why younger scholar-critics have rejected *Frederick*. Their professional ambitions and longings for validated professional status do not permit them to become aware of and examine the illusory and unveracious attributes of the social role they are playing. That incompetence and wasted effort are fundamental attributes of humanity is neither an attractive nor a sustaining notion. Nevertheless, it sustained Carlyle through the immense struggle of writing *Frederick*. It is worth speculating on how this could have been the case.

### 3

In the first place Carlyle saw the ultimate task of the historian as the interpretation of historical events:

> That the man of rhythmic nature will feel more and more his vocation towards the Interpretation of Fact; since only in the vital centre of that, could we once get thither, lies all real melody; and that he will become, he, once again, the Historian of events,— bewildered Dryasdust having at last the happiness to be his servant, and to have some guidance from him. Which will be blessed indeed. For the present, Dryasdust strikes me like a hapless Nigger gone masterless: Nigger totally unfit for self-guidance; yet without master good or bad; and whose feats in that capacity no god or man can rejoice in.
>
> History, with faithful Genius at the top and faithful Industry at the bottom, will then be capable of being written. History will then actually *be* written,—the inspired gift of God employing itself to illuminate the dark ways of God (I, i, 19).

This is spoken by Sauerteig, the yeast of historical discourse, the metaphysical historian. In this passage two things are to be noted: interpretation as the ultimate task of history, and the insistence that though history may be the gift of God which illuminates the dark ways of God, the time for the exercise of that gift has not yet come. This is Sauerteig's hope. The fact that it resides in the realm of hope, however, suggests something about how Carlyle was able to sustain himself. The central epistemological thesis of Romanticism, not often uttered but constantly exemplified, is the irresolvable tension between subject and object. In this passage the hope for the future historian appears to be, for history at least, that the interpretation of fact, the illumination of the dark ways of God, will ultimately involve a resolution of subject and object. But it is to be remembered that this is Sauerteig speaking, and that Sauerteig is a role. Thus what he says is displaced from Carlyle's own position. A hope is offered, to be sure, but the ultimate Romantic position of non-resolution of subject and object is not ultimately compromised. It is as if Carlyle were stating that Sauerteig's hope has its primary attractiveness in its emotional satisfaction, that such satisfaction cannot be rejected simply because it is satisfying, but also that it cannot be accepted on the same grounds either. This is one of the more subtle Romantic epistemological strategies, one at which Browning was particularly adept. "The tension between subject and object is irresolvable, but insofar as that proposition is itself object, it is necessary to maintain an irresolvable tension between the subject and that proposition as object." It was a very Hegelian way of considering the problem.

*Frederick*, then, rests upon an historian's alienation from his task of constructing an historical discourse, but the task could be, in spite of that, continued since it was sustained by the Romantic epistemology of subject-object tension. That alienation, moreover, particularly as it is manifest through the reader's intense awareness of the historian's unsatisfactory struggle with the documents and already existing instances of historical discourse, raises a further question about historical discourse which cannot be answered in terms of the Romantic epistemology, at least as it had developed for Carlyle and his contemporaries. That question is, What is historical discourse, really? Now there is a fallacy in Sauerteig's remarks, a fallacy revealed by the actual discourse of *Frederick*. The historian does not in fact interpret fact, that is, historical events. He interprets documents and historical discourses. Carlyle seems to have some self-conscious inkling of this. He urged the student of history to seek for portraits, just as he himself collected all the portraits of Friedrich he could acquire. The portrait, he said, was "a small lighted *candle*, by which the Biographies could for the first time be read with some human interpretation".[7] Though I do not know of any passage in which he spelled it out or even hinted at it, other than this one, here, at any rate, Carlyle seems to have had some notion that there is a profound difference between interpreting fact and interpreting documents. The latter, the historian's task, is the interpretation of language before him, not of events in the past. The past is inaccessible; only language is accessible. The historian constructs a linguistic discourse which is related, somehow or other, to a selected assemblage of discourses, a package of discourses held together by the wrappings of the package, not by internal affiliation. Their affinities are elected, but the historian does the electing.

History, then, is language about language, language that refers to language. A notion of history thus is properly subsumed by a notion of language, and the question, "What is history?" resolves itself into the question, "What is language?" One can find a way into this maze by focusing upon the term "refer". Now it seems to be reasonably clear that language does not refer. "Refer" when applied to language is a metaphor. Human beings refer; *language* does not do anything. It consists of signs to which human beings respond. Furthermore, responses to particular signs are not stable over time nor at any given moment, since to any single sign an indefinably wide range of responses is always possible. Further, human beings *learn* how to respond to signs and learn, with considerable imprecision, what responses to a given sign or set of signs are appropriate in a given situation or set of situations. Like Fritz Mauthner, and others before him, I think the most adequate resolution of this problem is to define language as instructions or directions for performance, effective only for those who have been previously instructed how to respond to those directions, even when the proper response is to produce further linguistic utter-

213

ances. Such a position avoids completely any notion of immanent meaning and accepts fully both conventionality of meaning and the imprecision (that is, the constant flow of innovation) which is characteristic of responses to language. Much else remains to be said about historical discourse, but a conclusion about history from this notion of language can serve to explain the extraordinary and unique character of *Frederick*. A historical discourse is a set of instructions for reading primary and secondary documents originating in the past. The drama of *Frederick* is the drama of an historian struggling to learn how to read his documents.

The charm of historical discourse is its capacity to elude our human demands for the probable, a demand to which fiction is disgracefully obedient. If one likes to read history, merely for the sake of reading history, Carlyle's *History of Friedrich II of Prussia* offers a hugely enjoyable experience. Beyond that it derives a further interest because it raises questions of great interest both about historical writing in Carlyle's own cultural situation and about the philosophy of history, or more precisely, the philosophy of historical discourse.

### NOTES

1. A few bibliographical details may be of some interest, particularly since the first edition is less frequently encountered, in my experience, than the Centenary Edition.
*First edition:* Vol. I, Books I–V, pp. 634, 1858; Vol. II, Books VI–X, pp. 694 (with index to p. 712), 1858; Vol. III, Books XI–XIV, pp. 759 (index to p. 770), 1862; Vol. IV, Books XV–XVII, pp. 615 (index to p. 632), 1864; Vol. V, Books XVIII–XIX, pp. 639, 1865; Vol. VI, Books XX–XXI, pp. 698 (index to p. 781), 1865. The total pages (excluding indices) amount to 4,039. The first instalment (Books I–X, 1858) ends with the death of Friedrich's father, Friedrich Wilhelm; the second instalment (Books XI–XIV, 1862) recounts the events through the First Silesian War and Friedrich's subsequent two years of peace; the third instalment (Books XV–XVII, 1864) carries the account through the Second Silesian War, Friedrich's ten years of peace, and the first year (to March, 1757) of the Third Silesian or Seven Years' War; the fourth instalment (Books XVIII–XXI) concludes that war (1762) and in Book XXI gives a summary of Friedrich's last years (1763–1786).
*Centenary Edition:* Vol. I, Books I–IV, pp. 435, 1897; Vol. II, Books

V–VIII, pp, 406, 1897; Vol III, Books IX–XI, pp. 413, 1897; Vol. IV, Books XII–XIV, pp. 501, 1898; Vol. V, Books XV–XVI, pp. 410, 1898; Vol. VI, Books XVII–XVIII, pp. 435, 1898; Vol. VII, Books XIX–XX, pp. 494, 1898; Vol. VIII, Book XXI, pp. 321 (index to p. 390), 1898. Total pages (excluding index): 3,415.

The work is about the same length as Gibbon's masterpiece. Comparison is difficult because so many passages in *Frederick* are in smaller type. References in the text are (by Book, chapter and page) to the *Works*, XII–XIX.

2. Here "Prussia" means what it meant when Carlyle was writing, all the territory of the former Electorate of Brandenburg. As King of Prussia Friedrich was in fact *King* only of E. Prussia, separated from Brandenburg by W. Prussia, acquired in 1772 by the first Polish partition (except for Danzig).

3. The large print yields about 2,160 characters to the page; the small print about 2,910. If 900 pages in the Centenary edition are in small print, and if those pages were printed in the larger type, there would be about 300 pages more than the present 3,415, an additional bulk of less than 9 per cent. Since 900 is probably too high a figure, though not extremely far off, a reasonable guess would be that if the entire book were presented in the large-type font, not including the index, it would grow by about 7 per cent or perhaps 240 pages. In the original edition there might have been about 300 additional pages, or 50 pages per volume. The cost of paper might have been responsible for the decision to print much of the book in small type, but the book was so splendid and even luxurious a piece of publishing that this explanation is most unlikely. The immediate model was probably Macaulay's *History of England*. The decision to use smaller type may have been the publisher's, but, in view of Carlyle's fame and prestige, it seems most likely to have been Carlyle's.

4. See my "Discontinuity in Fiction", *The Triumph of Romanticism, Collected Essays* (Columbia, S.C., 1970), pp. 318–40.

5. See my "The Dilemma of a Century", *id.*, pp. 36–57.

6. I owe the above information to the kindness of Professor Robert Lee Oakman III of the University of South Carolina, who has allowed me to use his unpublished dissertation, *Syntax in the Prose Style of TC, A Quantitative, Linguistic Analysis*, Indiana Univ. 1971. Professor Oakman is not responsible for my statement about Carlyle's journal style.

7. "Project of a National Exhibition of Scottish Portraits", *Works*, XXIX, 405.

# 10

# Carlyle's Pen Portraits of Queen Victoria and Prince Albert

by C. R. SANDERS

Despite his many expressions of scorn for aesthetics and what he called "dilettantism", some of Carlyle's deepest instincts were those of an artist, and it is a great mistake not to assume that usually he quite consciously wrote as an artist. *Sartor Resartus* is a combination of several literary genres deliberately brought into harmony with one another; *The French Revolution* unites history treated philosophically with what Carlyle thought of as an epic poem in prose, with echoes of Homer recently read in Greek ringing in his ears as he wrote; the "Death of Edward Irving" he himself spoke of as a kind of classical funeral oration, like that in Shakespeare which Antony delivers over Caesar's dead body; and he never grew weary of reading, writing, and theorizing about biography as an art form, the complex function of symbols, and the mysterious powers and problems of language.

He was least an artist when he wrote about his health, denounced the people or institutions which he disliked, moralized, prophesied, or preached. He was most an artist when his eyes came into play and when his intellect interpreted and his imagination shaped what he had actually seen. There can be little doubt that he was one of the greatest picture writers of all time or that, deliberately setting out early in his life to make for posterity as full, vivid, vital, and trustworthy a record of his time as possible, he deserved the title which his contemporaries gave him and which has continued to be accepted, that of the "Victorian Rembrandt".[1] His purpose here was linked in his mind with the important part that he played in bringing about the establishment of National Portrait Galleries in England and Scotland.

Perhaps none of his pen portraits is more interesting to examine with artistic technique in mind than those which he made of Queen Victoria and Prince Albert. Like the thirty or forty other major pen portraits produced by Carlyle, they create their effect and gradually build up the precise conceptions and images he wished to suggest through an accumulative process, as over a long period of years he saw the subjects of his portraits from time to time, corresponding to the way in which a painter requires a series of sittings by his subject before he finishes his portrait. In Carlyle's work, as in a painter's, as his subjects presented themselves from various points of view he modified the general conception, with such changes of line, colour, tone, and emphasis as seemed needful. Yet each new view of his subjects was remarkably fresh, and each new stroke of the pen in recording his impressions seems uncontrived and spontaneous.

One of the most striking powers which Carlyle exercises in drawing his pen portraits, even those of his Queen and Prince, is that of intellectual and artistic dominance. This he achieves in considerable part through the extensive use of diminutives. The young Victoria is a "poor little thing" or "poor little lassie" or "poor little Queen" or "unhappy little child" or "her little Majesty taking her bit departure for Windsor". Carlyle refers to "this little wedding of hers" and describes her as "small, sonsy and modest,—and has the ugliest task, I should say, of all girls in these Isles". Similarly, Prince Albert is "a sensible lad". Nicknames have the same function, as in Carlyle's well-known longer works. The Queen is "poor little Victory" or "little Queen Victory".

Dominance in Carlyle carries with it the right to evaluate and judge. All of his portraits, like most of those by Chaucer, Browning, and Yeats, are appraisal portraits. His subjects are not merely described but are weighed on the scales of his philosophy of life. More than once Carlyle expresses very serious misgivings about the young Victoria's ability to play her role of Queen well. On one occasion when some of her subjects cheer for the Queen as she passes along the street but one refuses to do so and says, "I vont holler!" Carlyle adds, "Neither did I holler at all." When he read a newspaper story indicating that the Queen had been unjust and even stupid in dealing with one of her maids of honour, he commented, "The little Queen behaved like a hapless little fool." Sometimes these judgments take the rather unpleasant form of direful predictions concerning the future of England under such rulers, whether the ruler be Queen Victoria or her son the Prince of Wales.

The dislike of Dandyism and worldly glitter which is often expressed in his longer works also appears in his pen portraits. He is somewhat scornful about the pageantry of Victoria's marriage as "Victory's gilt coach and other gilt coaches drive out". He cares little for the spectacle of the Coronation Procession: "Crowds and mummery are not agreeable to me"; and he describes what he sees as "all gilding, velvet and grandeur". He is just as scornful in commenting on the Glass Palace during the summer of 1851 and speaks of it as a mass of insignificant ostentation under the sponsorship of "King Cole, Prince Albert and Company". In their indictment of Vanity Fair Carlyle and Thackeray have much in common.

If at times Carlyle's evaluations seem too narrow and Puritanical and if he appears to carry the principle of dominance too far, he makes amends by a wealth of convincingly real pictorial detail, by the life with which all his portraits are endowed, by the skill with which they are clearly related to the life of their time and its significant events, by the extent to which his subjects are made to reveal their own inner nature in dramatic action, and by the deep strain of compassion in Carlyle's own nature which usually leads him to identify his subjects with himself as fellow creatures sharing in the common lot of humanity with all its suffering and all its joys. As one reads through his portraits of Victoria and Albert arranged chronologically, one senses a progression through a series of chance glimpses, explosive comments, quick, valid perceptions mixed with prejudice, flashes of light illuminating not only the subjects themselves but to a considerable extent the whole Victorian Age in the background—all moving in a kind of crescendo toward two scenes fully acted out and fully painted in which the real Carlyle meets the real Prince Albert and the real Queen in clear light where there is no distortion and where Carlyle's sense of proportion, perspective, emphasis, and balance has now made its last needful adjustment. Something very much like this takes place in the development of the pen portrait of Coleridge, which reaches its final stage in *The Life of John Sterling*, and in nearly all of his other major pen portraits.

Nothing could be more vivid or memorable than the pictorial details, almost Chaucer-like in their quality, which Carlyle gives us. Albert has a "well-built figure of near my own height, florid *blond* face (with fair hair); but the eyes were much better than I had fancied; a pair of strong steady eyes, with a good healthy briskness in them"; and he wears "loose greyish clothes". At the time of her meeting with Carlyle, Victoria comes "gliding into the room in a sort of swimming way, no feet visible"; and after the meeting she "sailed out as if moving on skates". In 1867 she "still looks plump and almost young (in spite of one broad wrinkle that shows in each cheek *occasionally*)". She is "all gentle, all sincere-looking, unembarrassing, rather attractive even;— *makes* you feel too (if you have sense in you) that she is Queen". Details in the setting are not overlooked: the tea-cups are of "sublime patterns", but the coffee is "very black and muddy". In earlier glimpses of the Queen, Carlyle's use of picturesque Scottish words do much to spice his descriptions and make them fresh and vivid. Touches of humour often enliven his portraits. At least one appears in those of Victoria and Albert when Victoria is misled by Sir James Clark into "mistaking the wind and protuberance of a certain maid of honour's *digestive* apparatus for something in the *generative* (Gott in Himmel!)".

As in all his other writings, Carlyle here places a very high value on good manners. Prince Albert when he meets Carlyle is a model of courtesy and as he leaves mentions Carlyle's works and backs out as a token of recognition of Carlyle's eminence as a writer; and Carlyle writes of Queen Victoria, "It is impossible to imagine a *politer* little woman."

The use of metaphor also counts for much in these pen portraits. The young Queen's throne is a "frail cockle on the black bottomless deluges".[2] At the time when frenzied young men were shooting at the Queen, Carlyle, though fully aware of the need for social and economic reform in that day, declares that the would-be assassins were like "a man that wanted the steeple pulled down" but who had to be content with flinging "a stone at the gilt weathercock". The Crystal Palace, though sponsored by Prince Albert, is the emblem of the "profoundest Orcus, or belly of Chaos itself". He describes the "deep bow of us male monsters" when the Queen appears; and Mrs George Grote is spoken of as "a tall old Gearpole" ["Irish-weaver implement"—T.C.].

Carlyle's subjects are never placed in a vacuum, and the social and economic background against which they are presented and which often involves them in dramatic interplay with the incidents and forces of their times is never artificial or contrived in such a manner as to suggest a mere stage setting. As we observe the young Queen, trembling with fear and sometimes even weeping, we learn that she has many enemies among the Tories. We sympathize with her when she cannot even take a ride in her carriage without being shot at by young fanatics. We also sympathize with Prince Albert when false rumours damage his reputation and during his unpopularity about 1854. We admire him when he joins forces with Carlyle in establishing National Portrait Galleries and when he shows a lively, informed, and intelligent interest in German studies and German culture. We assay the quality of the Queen's taste in terms of the part she had in determining the architecture of the Albert Memorial; and we admire her as she listens patiently to Carlyle's discourse on Scottish history and lore. Questions concerning England's relation to France, Germany, Russia, and India are also an integral part of the background.

Extremely important in Carlyle's delineations of his subjects is the skilful use of other persons bearing somewhat the same relation to them that the supporting characters in drama bear to the principal members of the cast. His technique here strongly suggests that of Boswell, whose *Johnson* was a lifetime favourite with him. In Carlyle's portraits, Victoria, "poor little fool", quarrels with her mother, puts the aggressive and formidable Mrs George Grote in her place, cuts short Professor Grote when he threatens to lose himself and others in labyrinths of erudition, pretends politely to listen for a time to Sir Charles Lyell's discourse on geology, asks Robert Browning, who was at work on *The Ring and the Book*, "Writing anything?" and then like Pontius Pilate turns quickly away without waiting for an answer, finds her own excellent manners greatly enhanced by the personal charm and corresponding excellent manners of Lady Augusta Stanley, and her own attractiveness enhanced by the loveliness of her daughter Princess Louise. Yet the threatening incompetence of the Prince of Wales and what Carlyle considers the questionable activities of Alfred Ernest Albert, Queen Victoria's second son, rise like clouds upon the horizon. Prince Albert, at times idealistic and visionary, appears at a great disadvantage when contrasted with Arkwright, whose head was full of practicality and common sense. On the other hand, a Prince Albert ready to sponsor such an admirable project as a National Portrait Gallery is greatly to be preferred to a Sir Anthony Panizzi, Keeper of Printed Books in the British Museum, who, Carlyle believed, was concerned altogether with the kind of librarianship that stressed ostentatious exhibitionism and impressive statistics relating to the annual budget and other administrative matters.

But the quality that gives the greatest value to Carlyle's pen portraits is their humanity and the sense of human kinship which he feels with his subjects, often accompanied by a feeling of deep compassion for them. The young Queen during the trying early years of her reign is "a sister situated as mortal seldom was". In 1838 he writes: "Poor Queen. She is much to be pitied." Prince Albert is far from being a mere figurehead but is "truly a handsome flourishing man and Prince" who after his meeting with Carlyle at Windsor was spoken of as "the young Brother Mortal I had just been speaking to". It is significant that the banker-poet Samuel Rogers, not usually associated with sentimentalism, rises greatly in Carlyle's esteem when, in the period of the Queen's early unpopularity, he defends young people in general and the young Queen in particular. The bond between Carlyle and the Queen is greatly strengthened by deep sorrow. Her gracious message sent to him after the death of his wife in 1866, is expressed in terms of her own sense of loss when her husband died about five years before. And his chief thought as he describes for his sister his meeting with the Queen is what the meeting would have meant to Jane, if she could have been alive to know about it.

So much then for comment and analysis. Let us now read the pen portraits themselves in chronological sequence and see how they move toward a kind of climax when Carlyle meets first Prince Albert and then the Queen. What follows these meetings is brief, mere epilogue, as the years and distant memories close in on an old man who had seen much and served his Queen and country well.

*TC to Margaret A. Carlyle, 9 November 1837:*
We heard nothing of Queen Victoria and her dinner yesterday except the jowling of the bells.[3]

*TC to Alexander Carlyle, 26 November 1837:*
I enclose a Portrait of Queen Victoria poor little thing, whom I have never seen yet; they say it is as like her as another. It will need pasting together at the edges (the edging will); it was too big to go into the letter,—or, lo, Jane has done it with no need of pasting![4]

*TC to John A. Carlyle, 12 April 1838:*
Going thro' the Green Park, I saw her little Majesty, taking her bit of departure for Windsor. I had seen her another day at Hyde Park Corner coming in from the daily ride. She is decidedly a pretty-looking little creature; health, clearness, graceful timidity looking out from her young face; "frail cockle on the black bottomless deluges," one could not help some interest in her, as in a sister situated as mortal seldom was. The crowd yesterday, some two thousand strong, of loungers and children, uttered no sound whatever, except a kind of thin-spread interjection *"Aihh!"* from the infantile part of it, one old Flunkey in tarnished laced hat was the only creature I saw salute, he got a bow in return all to himself. Poor little Victory![5]

*TC to Margaret A. Carlyle, 12 April 1838:*
Yesterday, going thro' one of the Parks, I saw the poor little Queen. She was in an open carriage, preceded by three or four swift red-coated troopers; all off for Windsor just as I happened to pass. Another carriage, or carriages, followed; with maids of honour &c: the whole drove very fast. It seemed to me the poor little Queen was a bit modest nice sonsy little lassie; blue eyes, light hair, fine white skin; of extremely small stature: she looked timid, anxious, almost frightened; for the people looked at her in perfect silence; one old liveryman alone touched his hat to her: I was heartily sorry for the poor bairn,—tho' perhaps she might have said as Parson Swan did, *"Greet* not for me brethren; for verily yea verily I greet not for myself." It is a strange thing to look at the fashion of this world![6]

*TC to Jean Carlyle Aitken, 6 July 1838:*

A Miss Fergus[7] from Kirkcaldy was here staying: I had to accompany her to see the Coronation Procession; we had been invited to the Montagues' window, but shd not otherwise have gone. I had even a "ticket to the Abbey" (a thing infinitely precious), but gave that decidedly away. Crowds and mummery are not agreeable to me. The Procession was all gilding, velvet and grandeur; the poor little Queen seemed to have been *greeting* [weeping]: we could not but wish the poor little lassie well; she is small, sonsy and modest, —and has the ugliest task, I should say, of all girls in these Isles.[8]

*TC at a dinner given by Richard Monckton Milnes in 1838:*

Poor Queen! She is much to be pitied. She is at an age when she would hardly be trusted with the choosing of a bonnet, and she is called to a task from which an archangel might have shrunk?[9]

*TC to John A. Carlyle, 16 April 1839:*

Sir James [Clark] has got into a scrape lately and led the Queen-kin into one; mistaking the wind and protuberance of a certain maid of honour's *digestive* apparatus for something in the *generative* (Gott in Himmel!), and quite roughly requesting said maid of honour to *confess!* The little Queen behaved like a hapless little fool,—and indeed looks like one now (very strikingly since last year, to my sense), and seems very generally to be thought one. Unhappy little child.[10]

*TC to Margaret A. Carlyle, 11 February 1840:*

Yesterday the idle portion of the Town was in a sort of flurry owing to the marriage of little Queen Victory. I had to go out to breakfast with an ancient Notable of this place, one named Rogers the Poet and Banker; my way lay past little Victory's Palace, and a perceptible crowd was gathering there even then, which went on increasing all the time till I returned (about one o'clock); streams of idle *gomerils* [block-heads] flowing in from all quarters, to see one knows not what,—perhaps Victory's gilt coach and other gilt coaches drive out, for that would be all! It was a wet day too, of bitter heavy showers, and abundant mud: I steered, by a small circuit, out of their road altogether, and except the clanking of some bells in the after part of the day heard no more of it. Poor little thing, I wish her marriage all prosperity too;—but it is her business, not mine. She has many enemies among the Tories, who repeat all kinds of spiteful things about her; she seems also to have abundance of obstinate temper, and no great overplus of sense:

I see too clearly great misery lying in store for her, if she live some years; and Prince Albert, I can tell him, has got no sinecure by the end! As for him, they say he is a sensible lad; which circumstance may be of much service here: he burst into tears, in leaving his little native Coburg, a small quiet town, like Annan for example; poor fellow, he thought I suppose how he was bidding adieu to *quiet* there, and would probably never know *it* any more, whatever else he might know![11]

*TC to John A. Carlyle, 15 February 1840:*

I did attend Rogers's Dinner, as appointed. . . . I decidedly liked Rogers a little better. His love of young people is itself a good sign. He defended the poor little Queen, and her fooleries and piques and pettings in this little wedding of hers.[12]

*TC to Alexander Carlyle, 17 February 1840:*

Queen Victory has got her bit wedding over; the people are all accusing her, poor little dear, how she has quarrelled with her mother, openly insulted her; how she has done this and that! I am heartily sorry for her, poor little fool; but for the poor little fool's *Twenty Millions of people* I am infinitely sorrier. Bad days are coming, as I often *spae* [foretell].[13]

*TC to Margaret A. Carlyle, 4 June 1842:*

It was precisely on that Wednesday [2 June] that the Queen had been shot at. These are bad times for Kings and Queens. This young blackguard, it seems, is *not* mad at all; was in great want, and so forth; it is said they will hang him. Such facts indicate that even among the lowest classes of people, Queenship and Kingship are fast growing out of date.[14]

*TC to Margaret A. Carlyle, 4 July 1842:*

On Saturday night it was publicly made known that [John] Francis, the man who last shot at the Queen, was not to be hanged, but to be sent to Botany Bay, or some such punishment. Well, yesterday about noon, as the Queen went to St. James' Chapel, a third individual [John William Bean] presented his pistol at the Majesty of England, but was struck down and seized before he could fire it; he and another who seemed to be in concert with him are both laid up. There is no doubt of the fact. The two are both "young" men; we have yet heard nothing more of them than that. The person who struck down the pistol (and with it the man, so vehement was he) is said to be a gentleman's flunkey; but I do not know that for certain and have seen no newspaper yet. . . . Are not these strange times? The people are sick of their misgovernment, and the blackguards among them shoot at the poor Queen: as a man that wanted the steeple pulled down might at least fling a stone at the gilt weathercock. The poor little Queen has a horrid business of it,—cannot take a drive in HER *clatch* without risk of being shot![15]

*TC to Jane Welsh Carlyle, [13 August 1842]:*
   Yesterday I did not see Charles Buller; on arriving at Charing Cross I found the Parliament just *then* in its agonies, and that there was no chance of him at the Temple. I stept down rather, to look at the Queen for an instant. She did pass, she and Albert, looking very much frightened, red in the face; but none shot at the poor little thing, some even gave a kind of encouraging cheer. "No, me? *I vont holler!*" said some of the populace near me; neither did I *holler* at all.[16]

*TC to Joseph Neuberg, 25 July 1851:*
   To look once at this Glass Palace was (if you forgot all else) perceptibly pleasant; but to have gone to study, to think, or to learn anything in it, would almost have driven a serious man mad. Who can bear to look on *Chaos*, however gilded the specimens shown? Very empty persons only! "Improvement in Manufactures?" I have often said: "The grandest specific set of improvements ever made in manufactures were effected not in a big Glass Soapbubble, presided over by Prince Albert and the General Assembly of Prurient Windbags out of all countries, but under the torn hat, once, of a Lancashire Pedlar [Richard Arkwright] selling washballs and cheap razors thro' the Hill-country,—Pedlar and Barber who chanced to have a head that he could employ in *thinking* under said Hat!"[17]

*TC to Jane Welsh Carlyle, 10 September 1851:*
   I had no idea till late times what a *bottomless* fund of darkness there is in the human animal, especially when congregated in masses, and set to build "Crystal Palaces" &c under King Cole, Prince Albert and Company! The profoundest Orcus, or belly of Chaos itself, this *is* the emblem of them.[18]

*TC to Lord Ashburton, 8 September 1853:*
   Edward Hyde, the great Chancellor, first Earl of Clarendon, is the only Englishman I have ever heard of attempting seriously to

form a Gallery of English Portraits. . . . I have no hesitation in asserting that of all Galleries whatsoever the one that has in Nature the *best* right to exist on English Funds were a Gallery of Portraits of Historical English. If the Prince Consort would be pleased to take up this important and neglected Enterprise, I love to persuade myself he has the means both inward and outward of doing much to accomplish it. . . . That the Prince himself should be Sovereign of the thing,—the Prince, or somebody possessing the qualities of mind which I privately ascribe to the Prince;—who should do the operation in much more silence than is common: this seems to me to be an essential condition. From Committees and After-Dinner Oratory,—alas, what can we expect? We know these sad entities, some of us; and all of us are beginning to know,—to our cost! And if the Parliament would give no money on these terms, I believe, even in that worst case, the Prince might make more real progress with money he could spare of his own, than with the Parliamentary money granted on the common terms. And just as George the Third's modest, solid and excellent Library is *worth* far more than Panizzi's huge expensive unsound and ostentatious one, and calls forth a blessing yet on the faithful and really human soul of that simple King (instead of a *non-blessing* on certain other *in*human, pedant, and merely showman souls),—so might the Prince's Gallery of English Portraits, conducted even on his own resources if he could get no other on fair terms, be a blessing and a credit to this country.[19]

*TC to Lady Ashburton, 11 January 1854:*

Come, then; and comfort poor Prince Albert, who is really getting into turbid water at present. Poor soul: Louis XVI said once, "What have I done to be so loved?" Thou (probably) "what to be so hated?" The answer in both, "Nothing!"[20]

*TC to John A. Carlyle, 27 January 1854:*

Abundance of rumour still abt Prince Albert (poor soul), but no sensible person that I meet takes the least share(?) in it.[21]

*TC to Lady Ashburton, 9 November 1854:*

Yesterday I went to Windsor, as arranged; was met on [all?] hands by the due facilities; had in fact good success, and much reason to thank the beneficent individualities who made all roads so smooth for me there. The Collection of Engraved Portraits, Miniatures &c &c far exceeds, in quantity and quality any I had ever had access to; . . . a larger proportion were of interest to me, in my present affair [the writing of *Frederick the Great*], than I could at all have expected. . . . Glover is an intelligent handy cheerful man, of London-Offical nature; not wanting in what learning is needful to him; . . . he was civility itself to me. . . . I had four very good hours there, and saw much that I shall remember: the only thing was, I *talked* a great deal too much (having acquired no art of keeping silence, even when I wanted to do so, fool that I am!),—and flurried all my nerves, even had there been no other mischief in it!

Towards 4 o'clock there came a light footstep to the door; I still busy among 100 Frederick Portraits did not look up, till Glover said, "Prince Albert!"—and there in fact was his Royal Highness, come for a sight of the monster before he went;—bowing very graciously, and not advancing till I bowed. Truly a handsome flourishing man and Prince; extremely polite (in the English way too);—and with a far better pair of *eyes* than I had given him credit for in the distance. We had a very pretty little dialogue: about Frederick's Portraits first (and your despised Picture now turned to the wall at Bath House, the original of which is well known to H.R.H., came in among other things); after which, by a step or two, we got into the Saxon genealogies, Elector Frederick the Wise, Martin Luther, Wartburg, Coburg, and had the whole world free before us! Very fair indeed: but a noiseless, almost voiceless *waiter* glided in just at this time, out of whom I caught the words, "gone out to the Terrace";—whereupon, after a minute or so, his R.H., our Dialogue winding itself up in some tolerable way, gracefully vanished (back foremost, as I noticed, the courteous man!), and I saw him no more. That was about the finale of my day; and I need not deny, was a pleasant, not a painful one,—and left me with a multiplicity of thoughts, inarticulate and other, about the young Brother Mortal I had just been speaking to; thoughts surely not of an ungrateful unrecognizing nature, whatever else they might be in the confused and confusing epochs of the world!——— That is the history of my day; which I thought good to lay at your Ladyship's feet, that you may see how "the pleasure of the Lord prospers in your hand," when you do kindnesses to your friends.[22]

*TC to Jean Carlyle Aitken, 10 November 1854:*
The day before yesterday I went to Windsor; for the sake of innumerable Portraits, Engravings, Miniatures &c which I had got access to there. It is some 20 and odd miles off: one of the beautifullest Palaces,—for situation &c much the beautifullest I ever saw.

Built on a sheer steep Hill (high for those parts, and beautifully *clothed*); commanding an immense plain, the richest in the Island; with Oak forests, with the River, with &c &c to all lengths. I regarded little or nothing of that; but proceeded straight to my Print rooms, where a Mr. Glover, the "Librarian" of the place, was extremely kind to me, and I saw really a great many things that may be useful in my operations; and had four diligent and goodish hours out of a day. I mean to go back when the weather is brighter (for Pictures and old eyes), and when "the Court" is not there. Towards 4 o'clock, while I was busy with a hundred Prints of *Frederick*, there came a soft step to the door; I did not look up till Glover said, "Prince Albert!"—and there in truth was the handsome young gentleman, very jolly and handsome in his loose greyish clothes, standing in the door; not advancing till I bowed. His figure and general face were well known to me, well-built figure of near my own height, florid *blond* face (with fair hair); but the *eyes* were much better than I had fancied; a pair of strong steady eyes, with a good healthy briskness in them. He was civility itself, and in a fine simple fashion: a sensible man withal. We talked first of Fred*k*'s Portraits; then went, by a step or two, into the *Saxon genealogy* line, into the Wartburg, Coburg, Luther, Frederick the Wise (that is the Prince who caught up Luther, put him safe into the Wartburg; he is *Ancestor* of Albert); we had there abundant scope of talk, and went on very well, the Prince shewing me a Portrait he had copied of "Fred*k* the Wise" (not ill done), telling of a Luther Autograph he had (from Coburg, and a joke appended to the getting of it there),—when a *domestic* glided in upon us, murmured something, of which I heard, "gone out to the Terrace!" (Queen out, wants you,—he had been in Town all morning)—whereupon, in a minute or two, our Dialogue winding itself up in some tolerable way, P*ce* Albert (prince of Courtesy) bowed himself out, back foremost and with some indistinct mention of "your *Works*," which did not much affect me; and so ended our interview. I had had an indistinct questionable anticipation of some such thing all day; but tho*t* too I was safe, having *met* his carriage on the railway as I came. However, it was managed as you hear; and I was not ill pleased with it, nor had any reason,—*well* pleased to have it over as you may fancy.[23]

*TC to John A. Carlyle, 10 November 1854:*
The day before yesterday I was at Windsor, looking into Portraits, Prints, Miniatures &c (by private favour),—saw many a

thing; and at length "the Prince" himself, with whom there was a pleasant enough little Dialogue; of which you shall know all the particulars one day, if you like. *Hat nichts zu bedeuten.* I returned home, much flurried by my day's travel and activity; and have had a worse dose of cold ever since.[24]

*TC to Lady Ashburton, 18 November 1854:*
There should really be a place found for that picture of the Boy Frederick Drumming: yes indeed! there are 3 or 4 prints of it at Windsor, all rather coarse and bad; the Prince Consort suggested the original at Charlottenburg (as yet ignorant that there was a first-rate Copy in these parts).[25]

*TC to John Forster, 5 July 1855:*
By the bye, thinking about Lemoin[n]e yes[terday?] I reflected, before getting home, that he seemed to have no *evidence* whatever, beyond his own surmise and suspicion, of Prince Albert's having interfered at all in the matter of the *Débats* Paragraph or Article? Knowing to what length suspicion can go in the mind of an angry Frenchman, I incline to think Lemoin[n]e most probably altogether mistaken, and Louis Napoleon (in whom I have traced much of the *Housebreaker* talent, touches of the Truculent-Flunkey, and nothing of the Heroic hitherto) probably himself the *sole* author of that Lemoin[n]e operation. "To put down the Press in France": what good or evil can the Press of France do to that poor Gentleman? The Press of England, not put down or *puttable*, is what he hangs on!— Give him the benefit of this doubt I charge you; think not *worse* of your Prince than you were wont, except upon new *evidence.*[26]

*TC to Lord Ashburton, 18 January 1856:* after Prince Albert through Lord Ashburton had offered to lend Carlyle his copy of Clausewitz, *On War*, 3 vols (1833):
I suppose it is not seemly for the like of me to thank H.R.H. the Prince Consort in word or message of any kind; but I hope you will, on some good occasion, indicate for me how sensible I am to this mark of humanity in high places.[27]

*TC in conversation with William Knighton, 28 November 1855:* in reply to the question "Is there yet any hope for England?":
None; *for a hundred years we have been going downhill fast, losing faith and hope. What kind of a boy is this that is to be our King of England next? The German race we have imported from*

*the Continent has been a heavy, stupid race. Prince Albert is an exception.* He looks forward, I think, and is preparing for what he foresees—that those boys of his will live in troublesome times; but he cannot say so, of course.[28]

*Conversations of Sir Charles Gavan Duffy with Carlyle, ca. 1865:*
I [Duffy] asked who was responsible for the disappointing effect of the Albert Memorial. The person to be contented, he said, was the Queen. She lived in such an atmosphere of courtly exaggeration that she ceased to comprehend the true relation and proportion of things. Hence the tremendous outcry over Prince Albert, who was in no respect a very remarkable man. He had a certain practical German sense in him too, which prevented him from running counter to the feelings of the English people, but that was all. He was very ill-liked among the aristocracy who came into personal relations with him. Queen Victoria had a preternaturally good time of it with the English people, owing a good deal to reaction from the hatred which George IV had excited. Her son, one might fear, would pay the penalty in a stormy and perilous reign. He gave no promise of being a man fit to perform the tremendous task appointed him to do, and indeed one looked in vain anywhere just now for the man who would lead England back to better ways than she had fallen into in our time.[29]

*Lady Augusta Stanley to Dr John A. Carlyle:* soon after the Queen had received news of Jane Welsh Carlyle's death:
Osborne: April 30, 1866.
Dear Dr. Carlyle,—I was here when the news of the terrible calamity with which your brother has been visited reached Her Majesty, and was received by her with feelings of sympathy and regret, all the more keen from the lively interest with which the Queen had so recently followed proceedings in Edinburgh. Her Majesty expressed a wish that, as soon as I could do so, I should convey to Mr. Carlyle the expression of these feelings, and the assurance of her sorrowful understanding of a grief which she herself, alas! knows too well.
It was with heartfelt interest that the Queen heard yesterday that Mr. Carlyle had been able to make the effort to return to his desolate home, and that you are with him.[30]

*TC's reply to Lady Augusta Stanley:*
Chelsea: May 1, 1866.
Dear Lady Augusta,—The gracious mark of Her Majesty's sym-

pathy touches me with many feelings, sad and yet beautiful and high. Will you in the proper manner, with my humblest respects, express to Her Majesty my profound sense of her great goodness to me, in this the day of my calamity. I can write to nobody. It is best for me at present when I do not even speak to anybody.[31]

*TC to Sir Henry Parkes, 27 April 1868:*
One set of Newspapers seemed to be filled with the Duke of Edinburgh [Alfred Ernest Albert (1844–1900), 2nd son of Queen Victoria] and his to me thrice-unimportant speakings and doings. These I took no interest in at all, and indeed fled from, as from an afflictive object. I am sorry you have spent £100,000 on that young gentleman, and am much afraid it won't pay! Our "Statesmen" (if we have still any such animal among us) had, most probably, nothing to do with that mission of him to the Antipodes [as commander of the *Galatea* on a world cruise, 1867–71]; it must have been Mamma, merely, and the wish to be rid of him for a while.—Yesterday there came a "telegram" to the effect that some of you had shot him at Sydney (poor soul), not quite killed him but tried it; which I found agitating several people,—tho' not much me, in its present state of mere telegram and uncertain rumour. Poor England will have to prepare herself for quite other disasters, atrocities and brute anarchisms at home and abroad, even if it be true![32]

*TC to John A. Carlyle, 6 March 1869:*
Hoho! Here is Froude;—and there was one great thing of all to tell you: interview with Sacred Maj*ty*, Thursday last, at "The Deanery" by an appoint*t* a week before. I one of four,—and I may partly think the main one perhaps. Sacred M*y* was very good; thing altog*r* decidedly insignif*t*, do *tiresome*; and *worsened* a kind of cold I had (and am still dropping with on this very sheet). Ab*t* all wh*h* I will not say a word more, unless specifically *desired* by some of you![33]

*TC to Jean Carlyle Aitken, 11 March 1869:*
"Interview" took place this day gone a week; nearly a week before that, the Dean and Dean*ess* (who is called Lady Augusta Stanley, once *Bruce*, an active hard and busy little woman) drove up here, and, in a solemnly mysterious, though half quizzical manner, invited me for Thursday, 4th, 5 P.M.:—Must come, a very "high or indeed highest person has long been desirous," etc., etc. I

231

saw well enough it was the Queen incognita; and briefly agreed to come. "Half past 4 COME *you!*" and then went their ways.

Walking up at the set time, I was there ushered into a long Drawingroom in their monastic edifice. I found no Stanley there; only at the farther end, a tall old *Gearpole* of a Mrs. Grote,—the most wooden woman I know in London or the world, who thinks herself very clever, etc.—the sight of whom taught me to expect others; as accordingly, in a few minutes, fell out. Grote and Wife, Sir Charles Lyell and ditto, Browning and myself, these I saw were to be our party. "Better than bargain!" "These will take the edge off the thing, if edge it have!"—which it hadn't, nor threatened to have.

The Stanleys and we were all in a flow of talk, and some flunkies had done setting coffee-pots, tea-cups of sublime patterns, when Her Majesty, punctual to the minute, glided softly in, escorted by her Dame in waiting (a Dowager Duchess of Athol), and by the Princess Louise, decidedly a very pretty young lady, and *clever* too, as I found in speaking to her afterwards.

The Queen came softly forward, a kindly little smile on her face; gently shook hands with all three women, gently acknowledged with a nod the silent deep bow of us male monsters; and directly in her presence everybody was if at ease again. She is a comely little lady, with a pair of kind clear and intelligent grey eyes; still looks plump and almost young (in spite of one broad wrinkle that shows in each cheek *occasionally*); has a fine soft low voice; soft indeed her whole manner is and melodiously perfect; it is impossible to imagine a *politer* little woman. Nothing the least imperious; all gentle, all *sincere*-looking, unembarrassing, rather attractive even;—*makes* you feel too (if you have sense in you) that she is Queen.

After a little word to each of us in succession as we stood,—to me it was, "Sorry you did not see my Daughter," Princess of Prussia (or "she sorry," perhaps?), which led us into Potsdam, Berlin, etc., for an instant or two; to Sir Charles Lyell[34] I heard her say, "Gold in Sutherland," but quickly and delicately cut him *short* in responding; to Browning, "Are you writing anything?" (he had just been publishing the absurdest of things! [nothing less than *The Ring and the Book*]); to Grote [35] I did not hear what she said: but it was touch-and-go with everybody; Majesty visibly *without* interest or nearly so of her *own*. This done, Coffee (very black and muddy) was handed round; Queen and Three women taking seats (Queen in the corner of a sofa, Lady Deaness in opposite corner, Mrs. Grote in a chair *intrusively close* to Majesty, Lady Lyell modestly at the *diagonal* corner); we others obliged to stand, and hover within call. Coffee fairly done, Lady Augusta called me gently to "come and speak with Her Majesty." I obeyed, first asking, as an old infirmish man, Majesty's permission to *sit*, which was graciously conceded. Nothing of the least significance was said, nor *needed*; however my bit of dialogue went very well. "What part of Scotland I came from?" "Dumfriesshire (where Majesty might as well go some time); Carlisle, *i.e., Caer-Lewel*, a place about the antiquity of King Solomon (according to Milton, whereat Majesty smiled); Border-Ballads (and even old Jamie Pool slightly alluded to,—not by name!); Glasgow, and even Grandfather's ride thither,—ending in mere *psalms* and streets *vacant* at half-past nine P.M.;—hard sound and genuine Presbyterian *root* of what has now shot up to be such a monstrously ugly Cabbage-tree and Hemlock-tree!" All which Her Majesty seemed to take rather well.

Whereupon Mrs Grote rose, and good-naturedly brought forward her Husband to her own chair, *cheek by jowl* with her Majesty, who evidently did not care a straw for him; but kindly asked, "Writing anything?" and one heard "Aristotle, now that I have done with Plato," etc., etc.—but only for a minimum of time. Majesty herself (I think àpropos of some question of my *shaking hand*) said something about her own difficulty in writing by dictation, which brought forward Lady Lyell and Husband, mutually used to the operation. After which, talk becoming trivial, Majesty gracefully retired,—Lady Augusta with her,—and in ten minutes more, returned to receive our farewell bows; which, too, she did very prettily; and sailed out as if moving on skates, and bending her head towards us with a smile. By the Underground Railway I was home before seven, and out of the adventure, with only a headache of little moment.

Froude tells me there are foolish *myths* about the poor business; especially about my share of it; but this is the real truth;—*worth* to me, in strict speech all but nothing; the *myths* even less than nothing.[36]

*TC's entry in his "Journal," 15 March 1869:*
It was Thursday, 4th March, 5–6.30 P.M., when this pretty "Interview" took place. Queen was really very gracious and pretty in her demeanour throughout: *rose* gently in my esteem, by everything that happened, did not fall in any point. Sister Jean has got a brief sketch of the thing,—on her earnest request. The "Interview" was quietly very mournful to me; the one point of real interest a sombre thought, "Alas, how it would have cheered *Her* bright soul (for my

233

sake), had she been here!" To me, with such prospects close ahead, it could not be much, and did indeed approximate to melancholy well-meant *zero*.[37]

*Disraeli to TC, 27 December 1874:*

I have advised the Queen to offer to confer a baronetcy on Mr. Tennyson, and the same distinction should be at your command, if you liked it. But I have remembered that, like myself, you are childless, and may not care for hereditary honors. I have therefore made up my mind, if agreeable to yourself, to recommend Her Majesty to confer on you the highest distinction for merit at her command, and which, I believe, has never yet been conferred by her except for direct services to the State. And that is the Grand Cross of the Bath.

I will speak with frankness on another point. It is not well that, in the sunset of life, you should be disturbed by common cares. I see no reason why a great author should not receive from the nation a pension as well as a lawyer and a statesman. Unfortunately the personal power of Her Majesty in this respect is limited; but still it is in the Queen's capacity to settle on an individual an amount equal to a good fellowship, and which was cheerfully accepted and enjoyed by the great spirit of Johnson, and the pure integrity of Southey.[38]

*TC to Disraeli, 29 December 1874:*

Yesterday, to my great surprise, I had the honour to receive your letter containing a magnificent proposal for my benefit, which will be memorable to me for the rest of my life. Allow me to say that the letter, both in purport and expression, is worthy to be called magnanimous and noble, that it is without example in my own poor history; and I think it is unexampled, too, in the history of governing persons towards men of letters at the present, as at any time; and that I will carefully preserve it as one of the things precious to memory and heart. A real treasure or benefit *it*, independent of all results from it.

This said to yourself and reposited with many feelings in my own grateful mind, I have only to add that your splendid and generous proposals for my practical behoof must not any of them take effect; that titles of honour are, in all degrees of them, out of keeping with the tenour of my own poor existence hitherto in this epoch of the world, and would be an encumberance, not a furtherance to me; that as to money, it has, after long years of rigorous and frugal, but also (thank God, and those that are gone before me) not degrading poverty, become in this latter time amply abundant, even superabundant; more of it, too, now a hindrance, not a help to me; so that royal or other bounty would be more than thrown away in my case; and in brief, that except the feeling of your fine and noble conduct on this occasion, which is a real and permanent possession, there cannot be anything to be done that would not now be a sorrow rather than a pleasure.[39]

*TC to John A. Carlyle, 1 January 1875:*

You would have been surprised, all of you, to have found unexpectedly your poor old Brother Tom converted into Sir Tom, Bart., but, alas, there was no danger at any moment of such a catastrophe. I do however truly admire the magnanimity of Dizzy in regard to me: he is the only man I almost never spoke of except with contempt, and if there is anything of scurrility anywhere chargeable against me, I am sorry to own he is the subject of it; and yet see, here he comes with a pan of hot coals for my guilty head![40]

*TC in conversation with Mrs Anstruther, summer 1878:*

He [Disraeli] has done great harm to the Queen, persuading her to believe anything. Then by giving her this title of Empress of India he secured her good will. "Peace with honour" indeed! There is no peace at all. He has provoked the enmity of Russia, instead of conciliating her and gaining a friend and a powerful ally.[41]

\*    \*    \*

Thus it was that the independent spirit and the critical mind, indispensable to a true artist, remained with Carlyle to the very last. That he was able to maintain them consistently testifies not merely to his great talent as an artist and integrity as a person but to the high quality of British democracy in his day, which granted privileges touching the Monarchy itself to a gifted writer of very humble Scottish origin. Ben Jonson, the Elizabethan writer most like him in temper, tone, courage, and vigorous, rough-grained individualism, would never have spoken of his Queen with the freedom or with the tenderness with which Carlyle spoke of his.

## NOTES

1. See my "The Victorian Rembrandt: Carlyle's Portraits of His Contemporaries", *Bulletin of the John Rylands Library*, 39 (March 1957)

521–57. Since I wrote this article I have discovered that John Sterling and Friedrich Althaus, were also among Carlyle's contemporaries who compared him with Rembrandt. Interestingly enough, the common element in the two which both stress is humour. Possibly the earliest comparison of Carlyle with Rembrandt is to be found in a passage in John Sterling's "Carlyle's Works", *London and Westminster Review*, 33 (1839), 20: "It becomes evident why the humorous lies so near as has often been remarked to the pathetic and sublime: how they pass into each other by perpetual undulations and successions, with a play and interfusion of vital energy from one to the other: so that the homely farce of a Rembrandt and a Bunyan, of a Hogarth and a Fielding, lies under and supports conceptions of which the tenderness and lofty passion will never fade from human hearts." For Althaus, see "Thomas Carlyle. Eine Biographische-Literarische Charakteristik", *Unsere Zeit*, II (July 1866), 23.

2. Quoted by Carlyle: untraced but possibly from an old ballad.

3. NLS, MS 520.62. William IV was succeeded by Victoria on 20 June 1837.

4. Edwin W. Marrs, Jr., *The Letters of TC to His Brother Alexander* (Cambridge, Mass., 1968), p. 432.

5. NLS, MS 523.57.

6. NLS, MS 520.70.

7. Elizabeth Fergus, who later married Comte Carlo de Pepoli.

8. NLS, MS 511.52.

9. From the *Autobiography* of Sir Archibald Alison, I, 413, quoted in Wilson, *Carlyle*, III, 47.

10. NLS, MS 523.63.

11. NLS, MS 520.89.

12. NLS, MS 523.74.

13. Marrs, p. 478. According to Lytton Strachey, Victoria broke away from the influence of her mother, the Duchess of Kent, soon after she became Queen. See *Queen Victoria* (London, 1921), pp. 73–4. Friction with the Tories rose in part from the Queen's insistence that the nation settle £50,000 a year on Prince Albert at a time when there was much poverty in the country.

14. C. T. Copeland, *Letters of TC to His Youngest Sister* (Boston and New York, 1899), p. 125.

15. Copeland, pp. 127–8. Queen Victoria was first shot at on 10 June 1840 by a youth of eighteen named Edward Oxford, son of a mulatto jeweller of Birmingham. Oxford was later declared insane. In 1882 the Queen was shot at by a youth named Roderick Maclean. Strachey writes: "This was the last of a series of seven attempts upon the Queen, attempts which, taking place at sporadic intervals over a period of forty years, resembled one another in a curious manner. All, with a single exception, were perpetrated by adolescents, whose motives were apparently not murderous, since, save in the case of Maclean, none of their pistols was loaded" (pp. 375–6).

16. NLS, MS 611.108. From 1842 to 1851 Carlyle seems to have had few glimpses of the Queen and Prince. We know, however, that he and the Queen attended the same performance of Bulwer-Lytton's *Richelieu*, produced by Macready in 1848. Carlyle declared at the time that he felt quite sorry for the Queen, condemned to sit and see a king as wicked, weak, and contemptible as Louis XIII in this play. On 15 May of the same year he and Queen Victoria saw the same performance of another play, Dickens and his friends playing in *The Merry Wives of Windsor*. See Francis Espinasse, *Literary Recollections and Sketches* (New York, 1893), p. 267; and Edgar Johnson, *Charles Dickens* (New York, 1952), II, 646.

17. NLS, MS 551.18.

18. NLS, MS 613.348.

19. Wilson, *Carlyle*, V, 42–3. This passage is part of a much longer prospectus on the subject sent in an envelope addressed to Lady Ashburton and labelled "For Lord Ashburton (on a rainy day)".

20. Supporters of Palmerston helped to spread wild rumours concerning what many believed was Prince Albert's Prussian-like high-handedness in his desire to dominate the government and, near the outbreak of the Crimean War, his leaning toward Russia. See the broadside entitled "Lovely Albert" in Strachey, pp. 242–3.

21. NLS, MS 524.95.

22. MS., the Marquess of Northampton.

23. NLS, MS 515.89.

24. NLS, MS 515.88. See also Carlyle's note in J. A. Froude, *Letters and Memorials of Jane Welsh Carlyle* (London, 1883), II, 249.

25. MS, The Marquess of Northampton. For a copy of "The Little Drummer", see Carlyle's *Frederick the Great*, in *Works*, XII, opp. p. 370, with Carlyle's comment on the merits of the picture and of the Ashburton's copy on p. 372.

26. MS, Victoria and Albert Museum. John Marguerite Émile Lemoinne, (1815–92), French journalist, was on the staff of the *Journal des Débats* from 1840 to 1892. John Forster (1812–76), best known for his biography of Dickens, edited the *Examiner* from 1847 to 1855.

27. MS, the Marquess of Northampton. According to Wilson, Sir James Stephen told Carlyle that when Prince Albert proposed a pension for Carlyle during the years when George Hamilton Gordon, fourth Earl of Aberdeen (1784–1860) was Prime Minister (1852–55), Aberdeen shuddered, shook his head, and said that such a thing was impossible because of Carlyle's "heterodoxy" (*Carlyle*, III, 265).

28. Wilson, *Carlyle*, V, 255.

29. *Conversations with Carlyle* (London, 1896), p. 229.

30. Froude, *Life*, IV, 320–1.

31. *Ibid.*, p. 321.

32. MS., Mitchell Library, Sydney, Australia.

33. NLS, MS 526.88.

34. Distinguished British geologist (1797–1875), often regarded as the father of modern geology.

35. George Grote (1794–1871), English banker, historian, and educator, best known for his *History of Greece* (1846–56).

36. A. Carlyle, ed., *New Letters of TC* (London and New York, 1904), II, 252–5. "The Court Circular", 13 March 1869, carried the following item: "Her Majesty on Thursday last had the pleasure of becoming personally acquainted with two of the most distinguished writers of the age—Mr. Carlyle and Mr. Browning. These eminent men—who, so far as intellect is concerned, stand head and shoulders above their contemporaries—were invited to meet the Queen at the residence of the Dean of Westminster." Quoted by Betty Miller, *Robert Browning: A Portrait* (London, 1952), pp. 246–7. Wilson says that after the Queen and Carlyle had talked the Queen told Browning, "What a very singular person Mr. Carlyle is!" *Carlyle*, VI, 186; quoted from C. E. Norton's *Journal*, 23 March 1869. Later in telling Ruskin and Joan Severn about his meeting with the Queen, Carlyle said that after describing to her the beauties of Galloway he got his chair on her dress and had to move it. *Praeterita, Works*, ed. Cook and Wedderburn (London and New York, 1909), XXXV, 539–40. According to Wilson, Mrs Anna Maria Pickering wrote that the Queen was much affronted with Carlyle for asking permission to be seated and declared that she would see no more literary men but that she later not only had an interview with Dickens but was charming to him. Wilson comments that she had probably not read the beautiful story of how Frederick the Great insisted that old Ziethen take a chair "while he himself remained standing before him". *Carlyle*, VI, 187–8. For Carlyle's statement that "the Queen came gliding into the room in a sort of swimming way, no feet visible", see *ibid.*, p. 184.

37. A. Carlyle, ed., *New Letters of TC* (London and New York, 1904), II, 255–6n.

38. Wilson, *Carlyle*, VI, 343–4.

39. *Ibid.*, pp. 344–5. Carlyle believed that the Countess of Derby had been chiefly influential in having the honour offered to him. For an incomplete text of his letter to her, 30 Dec. 1874, see Froude, *Life*, IV, 431–2.

40. Wilson, *Carlyle*, VI, 345.

41. *Ibid.*, p. 429. Several related details may be added. After Carlyle's interview with the Queen in 1869, Princess Louise came to see him at Cheyne Row and presented him with a portrait she had made of the historian J. L. Motley. Gerald Blunt once asked Carlyle, "Do you think the Queen has read your books?" Carlyle replied, "She may have read many books, but I do not think she has read mine." In Carlyle's extreme old age Sir Bartle Frere wrote him to request an interview for the Prince of Wales, Albert Edward. Carlyle denied the request, saying, "I am too old. He might as well come and see my poor old dead body." *Ibid.*, pp. 187, 458.

# 11

# Froude and Carlyle: Some New Considerations

by K. J. FIELDING

Of all writers on Carlyle the most quoted and the least liked is James Anthony Froude. Able, bitter, contentious and tactless, he has left his mark on the study of Carlyle, not simply in the way he used the papers that came into his hands but in the manner in which his own opinions and personality appear in his selection and in what he says himself. The impression he leaves is not entirely an unlikeable one. Yet his chief fault is not simply that he is rather an inaccurate editor, but that he so strongly leaves the impression of being untrustworthy.

There are several excuses to be made for him. He was hasty because he persuaded himself that his duty to write a biography was onerous but unsought. He is clear and decisive even when he is wrong, many of his editorial mistakes are forgivable, and it is now really much less important that he omits, misreads, changes punctuation and capitalization, or even that he garbles texts, than that he relies too heavily on what Carlyle had to say about himself in his journals and his letters. Yet there should be no question of thinking that this treatment of texts, facts and evidence was acceptable according to the usual standards of his time, though there might have been a better case for this if he had not insisted that he meant to set a new standard of truth telling, and that he was not a conventional romantic biographer. He claimed to give "a complete account" of Carlyle's "character", in which "there should be no reserve, and therefore I have practised none".[1] But

239

for this kind of work Froude had neither the sympathy, the knowledge, the nerve, the judgment, nor the time.

Even so, Froude has his champions, especially his most recent biographer, Waldo Hilary Dunn. It was even Dunn's belief that Froude "far surpassed Carlyle", and that "in the final analysis" he "emerges as an outstandingly more able and representative man".[2] Yet his biography is more than partisan. Whether in his study of *Froude and Carlyle* (1930) or in his biography (2 vols, 1961, 1963) Froude can do no wrong. "I have found", wrote Dunn, "no reason to question any of Froude's statements"[3]; and no less complacently, between his own first and second book, "no reason to necessitate any revision".[4]

Now the accuracy and character of Froude and the disputes that arose almost immediately after the publication of his edition of Carlyle's *Reminiscences* and his *Life* are almost nothing in themselves. They matter only because, if we are to understand Carlyle, it may be helpful to be clear about the authority of those who wrote about him. For myself, I find that, although Froude is sometimes right in matters of dispute, almost everything he says is open to question; he contradicts himself; and he even sometimes seems to be unaware of what he is saying. However unpleasant and petty the disputes that arose between Froude and others after he had written on Carlyle, they raise certain questions about his reliability as a biographer. For Froude still stands in our way. His is still the standard *Life*; he is the authority for the text of the passages he provides from Carlyle's journal; and he has given us a decisive portrait of Carlyle which has firsthand authority. As biographer, he had the use of all Carlyle's private papers, some of which are now inaccessible. Many of his own papers were destroyed. However open to criticism, therefore, his biography will always be indispensable.

A recent discovery of legal papers associated with Carlyle's Will, his manuscripts and copyrights, allows questions to be raised which not only bear upon Froude but which affect his interpretation of Carlyle. The documents are musty and confused, they carry us into the middle of one of the most undignified squabbles in literature, but they also allow us a chance to re-assess the more important issues involved. Waldo Dunn, secure in unrestricted access to the Froude family papers, professed to regret that the

240

question of who owned the literary manuscripts Carlyle left behind him at death had never come into court. The one person whom it would have been disastrous to put into the witness-box was Froude, and possibly the man to see this most clearly was his own friend and co-executor Sir James Fitzjames Stephen, the eminent lawyer, critic and judge.

My own interest in this began with my discovery of these legal papers. After joining the editorship of the new Carlyle *Collected Letters* in 1967, I looked at his Will to trace the history of some of his papers. (It is convenient that, though there are various manuscripts and printed copies, the text of the Will is correctly given in Froude's *My Relations with Carlyle* [1903]). From the names of the witnesses I saw who the solicitors were who had drawn it up; and, as they happened to be the same as Charles Dickens's, I did then what I had done with Dickens fifteen years earlier: wrote to the firm and then went up to London to see them.

I was not quite so fortunate as I had been before, but I was allowed to examine a large deed-box and to remove it to the temporary keeping of the National Library of Scotland. Examination showed that what it chiefly contained was correspondence with Carlyle's executors, Froude and Sir James Fitzjames Stephen. Much of it was the old unseemly story, familiar from Froude's *Relations* and the rejoinder to it, *The Nemesis of Froude* (1903) by Alexander Carlyle and Sir James Crichton-Browne, and I do not mean to go over every detail of the affair again. Nor, in what is retold, when there are corrections to previous accounts, shall I explicitly point them all out. Earlier biographers are unreliable, and the notes should be enough to show how this account derives from the new papers. It is certainly different from the one given by Froude.[5]

It is necessary to begin by turning to Carlyle's Will (dated 6 February 1873) which was no doubt drawn up with some contempt for lawyers and according to his own ideas about wording. What mainly concerns us is the disposal of his literary papers; but, especially with the original documents before us, it is impossible for a biographer to disregard this as the last expression of Carlyle's *will*, so emphatically is it stamped with his character yet so incompetent as a testament of his wishes. It bears his mark strongly, from its opening insistence that he is to be buried at Ecclefechan with his parents "since I cannot be laid in the Grave at Haddington" with Jane, to the signatures of the witnesses at the end: John Hare, Butler at Palace Gate House (residence of John Forster) and Frederic Ouvry, Solicitor, from whose offices I had collected the papers.

The question of who were to be the executors and trustees was important: one was John Forster, Carlyle's old friend and trusted adviser in business matters, and the other his brother, Dr John Aitken Carlyle. The Will then states that if John dies first his place is to be taken by the youngest brother, James Carlyle; and, if Forster is unable to act, his place is to be taken by "my friend", James Anthony Froude.

Certain dispositions are made next: some small sums of money, books for Harvard, and Carlyle's watch to his Canadian nephew, Thomas Carlyle. Then it disposes of the rest of the property, at the same time characterizing (in a typically Carlylean way) all those who were to be most closely connected with his uncertain intentions. For the Will shows itself to be, in all its associations and expressions, not at all like the formal drafting of a lawyer but as the personal utterance of Carlyle; so that, even when he comes to deal with the most important question of the disposal of his books, copyrights, manuscripts and papers, it continues in the same discursive personal tone.

Dr John Carlyle, "my ever dear and helpful Brother", is said to have no need of help or money. As a result he is left the lease of the Chelsea house and all its contents except those "herein-after bequeathed specifically"; and, simply as a "memento", he is to have the remainder of "my small and indeed almost pathetic collection of books". Yet later, as we see below, with two special exceptions, he was to have "My other manuscripts". There is thus already some uncertainty about what is meant by a *manuscript*, which may be anything from an unpublished holograph (written with publication in mind), or family letters and papers. Meanwhile, Carlyle goes on to write of one or two of them in particular:

My manuscript entitled "Letters and Memorials of Jane Welsh Carlyle" is to me naturally, in my now bereaved state, of endless value, though of what value to others I cannot in the least clearly judge; and indeed for the last four years am imperatively forbidden

242

to write farther on it, or even to look further into it. Of that manuscript my kind considerate and ever faithful friend James Anthony Froude (as he has lovingly promised me) takes precious charge in my stead. To him therefore I give it with whatever other fartherances and elucidations may be possible, and I solemnly request of him to do his best and wisest in the matter, as I feel assured he will. There is incidentally a quantity of Autobiographic Record in my notes to this Manuscript; but except as subsidiary and elucidative of the text I really put no value on such. Express biography of me I had really rather that there should be none. James Anthony Froude, John Forster and my Brother John will make earnest survey of the Manuscript and its subsidiaries there or elsewhere, in respect to this as well as to its other bearings; their united candour and partiality, taking always James Anthony Froude's practicality along with it, will evidently furnish a better judgment than mine can be. The Manuscript is by no means ready for publication; nay the questions How, When (after what delay, seven, ten years) it, or any portion of it, should be published, are still dark to me; but on all such points James Froude's practical summing up and decision is to be taken as mine. The imperfect Copy of the said Manuscript which is among my papers with the original letters I give to my niece Mary Carlyle Aitken, to whom also dear little soul, I bequeath Five hundred pounds for the loving care and unwearied patience and helpfulness she has shown me in these my last solitary and infirm years. To her also I give at her choice, whatever Memorials of the Dear Departed One she has seen me silently preserving here, especially the table in the Drawing-Room at which I now write and the little Child's Chair (in the China Closet) which latter to my eyes has always a brightness as of Time's Morning and a sadness as of Death and Eternity when I look on it; and which, with the other dear Article, I have the weak wish to preserve in loving hands yet awhile when I am gone. My other manuscripts I leave to my Brother John. They are with one exception of no moment to me. I have never seen any of them since they were written. One of them is a set of fragments about James the First . . . But neither this latter nor perhaps any of the others is worth printing. On this point however my Brother can take counsel with John Forster and James Anthony Froude and do what is then judged fittest. . . . In regard to all business matters about my Books . . . Copy rights, Editions and dealings with Booksellers . . . John Forster's advice is to be taken as supreme and complete, better than my own could ever have been. His faithful wise and ever punctual care about all that has been a miracle of generous helpfulness, literally invaluable to me in that field of things. Thanks, poor thanks, are all that I can return, alas! I give the residue of my personal estate to my Trustees before named. . . .

The remainder of the estate is then divided between Carlyle's five remaining brothers and sisters, or, if they were to die before him, their children at the age of 21. These were the two other brothers, Alexander and James, and the three sisters, Mrs Austin, Jean Aitken, and Janet Hanning. This specifically and most importantly includes Carlyle's copyrights which were thus part of the astate under the direction of his trustees:

Finally:

> To my dear friends John Forster and James Anthony Froude (Masson too I should remember in this moment and perhaps some others) I have nothing to leave that could be in the least worthy of them but if they, or any of them, could find among my reliques a Memorial they would like, who of Men could deserve it better. No man at this time. . . .

So there is Carlyle in 1873, at the age of seventy-seven, setting down his wishes in mainly clear and obviously personal terms. Had he died then, with John Forster as his executor, there would have been no difficulties. For Forster was a remarkable man, a powerful and efficient literary agent, who had been acting for many years as Carlyle's adviser in dealings with publishers; he had been a good friend of Jane's, and he was both discreet and dominant enough to have ensured that no disputes would have persisted between any of the parties. But Forster died in 1876, and Dr John Carlyle in 1878. Conditions changed, new executors were needed, and I think we may accept what Froude says in the *Life*, that Carlyle—realizing that there were sure to be biographies whether authorized or not—asked Froude to tell the story of his life. In fact, it seems that as early as 1873 he began to deposit some of his papers with him.

Yet then (in November 1878) at the age of eighty-three and without Forster to advise him, Carlyle added a codicil to his Will, dictating the terms to a clerk who no doubt submitted it to Frederic Ouvry for advice. But Ouvry was an old man himself who was to die a year after Carlyle, and so Carlyle's intentions, never entirely clear, were left more confused than ever. His first idea, in fact, had been to keep the matter mainly to himself, and it was only because of the prudence of his niece, Mary Aitken, that the solicitors were informed. She wrote:

> 30 Oct. 1878
>
> . . . Mr. Carlyle, my Uncle, being anxious to add a Codicil to his Will directing that what he has bequeathed to his Brother, Dr. Carlyle, should on the death of Dr. Carlyle revert to me or to my heirs, I should be much obliged if you would send a Clerk able to take down his directions, either tomorrow or on Friday the 1st. Nov. . . .
>
> Mr. Carlyle's own wish is that I myself write out this Codicil; but I think it a better and more satisfactory plan to make this application to you.

New executors and trustees were to be appointed: first Froude, once more, and then Sir James Fitzjames Stephen. Stephen was a most forceful man, in his younger days he had been a brilliantly unfair critic contributing mainly to the *Saturday Review*, an advocate of devastating one-sidedness and really superior power. He was an historian of criminal law, and author of *Liberty, Equality and Fraternity* (1873) written in answer to Mill. He is mentioned only once in Froude's *Life of Carlyle*, in reference to a speech at Edinburgh which Carlyle found "a very curious piece of work indeed", though he thought Stephen "very honest . . . with a huge, heavy streak of work in him".[6] At the same time, Stephen was an illiberal man who seems to have meant to be just but who was often blinded by his own powers of advocacy. Between the signing of the codicil and Carlyle's death he was made a High Court judge, and in all the disputes that follow he was naturally respected because of his position and the clarity and tenacity of his arguments. He was also a personal friend of Froude.

So, in the codicil, the gift of the drawing-room table was withdrawn from Mary Aitken and transferred to Stephen: "I know he will accept it as a distinguished mark of my esteem. He knows it belonged to my honoured Father in Law and his daughter, And that I have written all my Books on it except only Schiller." In its place Mary was given a Screen: "She knows by whom it was made and I wish her to accept it as a testimony of the trust I repose in her and as a mark of my esteem for her honourable veracious and faithful character and a memorial of all the kind and ever faithful service she has done me."

*The Times* (9 April) made much of its amusement at the airs with which Carlyle bequeathed "his old watch or his writing table as if it were a big estate with a title attached". It noticed a touch of self-idolatry, and saw the "curious will" as a sign of "the ultimate judgement to be pronounced on his character. . . . A reaction is now in operation. . . . Counterblasts, loud and decided, are about to be blown"; Froude's editing of the *Reminiscences* may have set it off but, whatever the cause, "Let the counterblast blow." The *Times* leader on the "curious will" is itself a curious reaction.

A more practical and immediate difficulty for the new executors was that the new codicil was extremely vague about Carlyle's papers and copyrights. It will be remembered that, with the exception of Carlyle's annotated "Letters and Memorials of Jane Welsh Carlyle" (bequeathed to Froude), the "imperfect Copy" (i.e. original MSS) of the same work and some of Jane's other original letters (bequeathed to Mary), all Carlyle's other papers had originally been left to Brother John. This was specifically stated: he was to have "My other Manuscripts" *and* the contents of Cheyne Row. This time neither manuscripts nor papers were specifically mentioned, although everything previously left to John (except the lease of the house itself) was left "to my Niece Mary Carlyle Aitken", who was to receive "all such of my Furniture plate linen china books prints pictures and other effects [therein] . . .".

Had all of Carlyle's papers been left undisturbed at Cheyne Row, it would presumably have been clear that they were to go to Mary with the rest of its contents. If one supposes that she were not to have had the contents, or if the papers were arguably not among the "contents" since some were placed elsewhere, then they would have belonged to the estate, and thus to the residuary legatees who were Carlyle's brothers and sisters, or their children. In both cases the copyright (controlled by the executors) would have been theirs and not Mary's. But there are a number of problems we ought to be clear about if we are to understand the behaviour of Froude and Mary Aitken Carlyle.[7]

The first of these is that (by 1878) Carlyle had entrusted—at different times—a large number of papers to Froude, and that neither he nor Froude had made a written note of the terms on which they were passed over. Meanwhile, the ageing Carlyle had told Mary that they were *hers*, and that the papers in Froude's hands were ultimately to be returned to her. Although this was repeated before witnesses, it was apparently not until 1879 that this was made clear to Froude who then willingly accepted it. But once again there was no written record, and neither Froude nor Mary was sure what Carlyle had said to the other. Secondly, arising from the uncertainty of ownership, there were problems of copyright which are almost equally confused. Finally the position was further complicated by the variety of manuscripts involved. Among these were: (i) the composite manuscript of the *Reminiscences*, which was among the papers belonging to Mary but entrusted to Froude,[8] which with Carlyle's assent was already in proof as he was dying and published within a month of his death; (ii) the mass of journals, letters and papers, so carefully preserved by Carlyle, which were also apparently Mary's though temporarily with Froude; and (iii), there were "The Letters and Memorials of Jane Welsh Carlyle", the fair copy of which with some of Jane's letters was certainly bequeathed to Froude with the consequent presumption that the copyright was his although even here there were complications. How far, for instance, Froude might stretch the bequest of manuscripts "farthering and elucidating" the *Memorials* was quite undefined, and it must remain uncertain whether his copyright in the "fair copy" (in Mary's hand) might be affected by the bequest to Mary of what was the original autograph manuscript, even though it was known to Carlyle as "the imperfect copy of the same Memorials . . . with the original letters".

Involved as all this may appear, there can be no full understanding of the relations of Froude to Carlyle without them, and certainly they are essential to understanding the tussle for control of the Carlyle archive between Froude and Carlyle's niece Mary.

Mary Aitken was the daughter of Carlyle's younger sister Jean who lived in Dumfries; and, after he paid a visit to her in the summer of 1868, she returned to London with her uncle as his secretary and companion for the rest of his life. She and her mother are barely mentioned in Froude's last two volumes, neither is indexed, and her presence in Cheyne Row is ignored: her name is given twice, in quotations from Carlyle, and she is mentioned once merely as an anonymous "someone to write for him" (II, 416). Yet the part she played in Cheyne Row can be seen more clearly in such a record as William Allingham's *Diary* (London, 1907), or the reports of other visitors. For Mary remained with her uncle even after her marriage with her cousin Alexander Carlyle in 1879, they cheerfully accepted his company even when they went away on their honeymoon, and her first child was born at Cheyne Row, where "our baby" was a source of pride and wonder to his great-uncle. Obviously, at the time of her uncle's death, no one knew him more intimately.

Yet during Carlyle's lifetime Froude (and perhaps her uncle too) usually regarded Mary with masculine condescension. In his eighties Carlyle still writes of his niece as "dear little soul", and Froude's term for her (even within his own family) was "the little girl".[9] Yet when Carlyle died she was a married woman of about thirty-five, whose correspondence shows that she was both intelligent and sensible. Twelve years with Carlyle had taught her a great deal. She expresses herself well, and she was clearly at ease with the distinguished friends of his old age.[10] Letters about her uncle's business affairs are not only in her hand, but were frequently left for her to word, even for example in dealing with Frederic Chapman on copyright. Yet Mary and Alexander Carlyle were obviously aware of Froude's air of patronizing aloofness; and of their uncle's friends we find that it was only Froude who disagreed with them. The situation between Mary, Froude and Alexander was probably already a sensitive one to be exacerbated by the terms of the Will. It is true that they were apparently on friendly enough terms just after Carlyle's death when (after an initial misunderstanding) Mary was ready to write, "Mr. Froude has been uniformly kind and generous to me" (22 Feb. 1881). But, once their disagreements had grown, Froude was to write resentfully to Ouvry's partner, Farrer:

> I blame myself for all this mass of confusion, but it rose from this single cause: that I told Carlyle (when he told me that Mary C. had been very violent with him about the small provision that was made for her) that he might feel easy about her future, for I

248

would treat her as if she were a daughter of my own. One does not look for this slippery treatment from a woman to whom one has undertaken to be a quasi guardian (20 Oct. 1881).

The difficulty was that Mary did not want or need a guardian, and as soon as she was allowed to read a copy of the *Reminiscences* she was clear that if a guardian was needed for anyone it was Froude. For though Froude was editor of the *Reminescences*, the manuscript and copyright (as he eventually conceded) were hers.

Yet no prior consideration before Carlyle's death had been given to the copyright question, nor to the division of profits to come from publishing the *Memorials*, the *Reminiscences* or the biography; at least, none on which there was any written memorandum. In the disagreements that followed it was accepted, without much dispute, that Carlyle had meant the gift of the papers to make up to Mary for the rather slight provision he had otherwise made for her.[11] Legally, if Mary could establish that the manuscripts of the *Reminiscences* had been given her with the other papers, then the *prima facie* assumption would be that the copyright was hers also; and the same was true of anything written by Carlyle in the main group of papers. But this had all been left uncertain. It rested on her word, on comments by Carlyle in front of others, and on Froude's intermittent admissions—followed by his retractions. There was nothing written.

Carlyle himself had been too old and tired to bother with it, and he had simply exerted himself to leave it in the hands of someone he thought well-disposed. Rather similarly, he allowed Froude to cast himself in the role of reluctant biographer, while stating in the Will "express biography of me I had really rather that there should be none". Froude even asserts that he had not known he was to be an executor.[12] He thus had every reason to complain, as he did vehemently, that he had been put in a false position. At the same time he was at fault for letting it happen. He bemoans the fact, for example, that when entrusted with the papers he was given no inventory; yet he took none himself. He was ex-editor of *Fraser's* and an established writer who cannot have been innocent about copyright. No doubt he fully intended to be generous, but he was the kind of man who expected to be trusted even when he made mistakes. Even his friend Sir James Stephen was soon reduced to writing to their solicitor in exasperation, "Froude seems to me to have no idea of the legal effect of anything" (24 Oct. 1881).

Carlyle died on 4 February 1881, and in less than ten days Froude wrote to *The Times* to say that the *Reminiscences* would be out within a few weeks. All of them, he stressed, except the essay on Mrs Carlyle, would be printed "exactly as Mr. Carlyle left them". Mary Carlyle then made a friendly objection to Froude's remark in the same letter that Carlyle's papers had been "made over" to him; and as a result he wrote again on 25 February to say that they "belong to his niece . . . to whom he directed me to return them". Even so, when the book was published, there was no reference to Mary in the Preface either as owner of the manuscript or copyright and, until they were reminded, the publishers did not send her a copy of the book. Yet, when Mary consulted the executors' solicitor about the copyright, he confirmed, "Mr. Froude does not question your right to it" (28 April). Mary was deeply concerned: not so much about the payment as about how the work had been edited, and it was soon made clear to her that she was generally held to be involved. For some of the *Reminiscences* refer to old friends of Carlyle whom he had written about with the same scathing intimacy he used in his private letters and journals. It was obviously raspingly painful to their surviving relatives, and Froude admits that Carlyle had warned him to take care. The result was that the daughters of both Lord Jeffrey and Mrs Basil Montagu wrote promptly to complain—not to Froude, but to Mary.

It is not new that the *Reminiscences* caused offence, since it has always been known that Froude not only gave pain but so offended the families of some of Carlyle's correspondents that letters were destroyed. It is now clearer why they objected so strongly; and what we can now see, for the first time, is how Mary was involved and that it was the beginning of their differences.

Mrs Montagu's daughter was Anne Benson Procter. Mary had sent her protest on to Ouvry with a copy of her reply (8 March 1881), and presumably he sent it to Froude. Mrs Procter evidently met the comments on her mother and step-father by saying that she would publish a selection of Carlyle's letters to her parents which would make an entirely different impression. Mary tried to dissuade her, but whatever reply Mrs Procter received from Froude she went on to issue a pamphlet of *Letters Addressed to Mrs. Basil Montagu and B. W. Procter by Mr. Thomas Carlyle*, prefaced by her justification. Carlyle's comments in his essay on Edward Irving are dismissed as "shameful", "malicious" and "malignant lies". He had come to London as a "raw young Scotchman", her parents had befriended him, and yet while accepting their hospitality he had written falsely about them and left his comments to be published after his death. His satiric comments were, in fact, made not only on her parents but on step-brothers and sisters, and apparently kept for publication while Mrs Procter remained on friendly calling terms with Carlyle. His remarks *are*, in the circumstances, quite unforgivable and Mrs Procter's reply is entirely justified.

At the time Mary sent on Mrs Procter's first letter she still had not read the *Reminiscences* but, once she had received a copy, she mildly complained to Ouvry that she "understood it well enough. It is a grievous pity that such things should have been printed a month after my Uncle's death. It was Mr Froude's *'reticence'* which he most of all trusted; this hurrying-off to the market-place with everybody's dirty linen shews with what results. But I suppose it is no use to speak of it" (9 March 1881).

Mrs Procter delayed a month in publishing her reply, and then sent it to other interested parties. Among them may have been Mrs Empson, daughter of Lord Jeffrey, who had been honoured by an essay to himself. Some of it a daughter might have been proud of, but there is another side to it: the work is tinged with contempt, and it is not only frank about Jeffrey's "habit of flirting . . . like a lap-dog", but calls Mrs Empson's children "of strange Edinburgh type", her husband "long-winded" and "jargoning", and herself "abstruse, timid, enthusiastic", "perhaps . . . jealous", and "a morbidly shy kind of creature" with "the air of a . . . spoiled child". Carlyle also remarks of Jeffrey's letters to himself and Jane, that he has lost sight of them, at which point Froude cheerfully breaks in, "All preserved and in my possession.—Editor." It was to recover these letters that Mrs Empson first wrote to Froude, then Mary:

You cannot fail to understand that the tone of Mr. Carlyle's "Reminiscences" . . . must have greatly shocked and amazed me. It will not surprise you that . . . I cannot bear the idea of any letter of my father's . . . appearing in any publication referred to by Mr. Carlyle—& that I feel it absolutely needful to have them in my possession. On writing to Mr. Froude to reclaim them, he tells me that it is from you, I must ask them, & that if you are willing he will return them without delay. I now write to ask this & under the circumstances I think it impossible you should refuse it.[13]

There was no legal obligation for their return, but Mary wrote to Ouvry:

It is natural enough that she should ask to have her Father's letters sent to her, not knowing to what uses they may be put & I am most willing she should receive them, but it is not less natural that I or any member of my Uncle's family should find it most painful to have another similar work to Mrs. Procter's published from these materials (9 April 1881).

Froude was evidently forbidden to print any of Jeffrey's letters in the biography, and presumably he sent back those that he had sorted out; the result of his frankness, apparently, was that it not only lost the letters for himself and Mary, but the Carlyle-Jeffrey correspondence was destroyed.

Certainly Mrs Empson was not appeased, since in 1887 Mary was unwise enough to write to her again to present her with a copy of the corrected edition, edited for her by Charles Eliot Norton. By then she was even optimistic enough to hope that Mrs Empson might let her have copies of any Carlyle letters she might still possess. But although some important omissions had been made, Mrs Empson sent the book back, since "for obvious reasons I should not wish to have it in the house". She went on:

I was greatly shocked when Froude published those Reminiscences as I consider my Father deeply wronged. . . . The account given of his London life is also quite untrue—how untrue probably no one but myself, now alive, knows. . . . I wrote to Froude to express my sense of injury—his only explanation was that he had not thought I was alive. I leave you to judge how this could satisfy me or my daughters. . . . As to the relations between my father & your uncle which you tell me you wish to verify I do not think that there is anything more to be said than that my father had a very considerable friendship for Carlyle & his wife (a friendship which I even at that day regretted—a regret which these Rem. certainly abundantly justify.)[14]

Obviously this response to her uncle and his work dismayed Mary. Her own papers are now mainly unavailable or not preserved, but there is something to show that several friends were amazed at Froude's lack of judgment. One of them remarks that it seemed as though "private persons have *no* feelings to be hurt";[15] and David Masson ends his review of the *Reminiscences* in the *Scotsman* (9 March) by saying that "as a whole, it must honestly be said that its publication . . . is a mistake"—one for which he blames the editor. Froude confesses that the book was received "with a violence of censure for which I was quite unprepared"; yet in writing *My Relations With Carlyle* he omits the reasons and seems quite unable to see how acutely it concerned Mary.

Her answer was to ask Ouvry whether, since the copyright was hers, she could not either suppress Froude's edition or publicly correct his "blunders, as he has in many cases made my uncle say exactly the contrary of what he has written to me. I shall also be obliged by Mr. Froude's returning to me 'the imperfect copy' of the Ms. called Jane Welsh Carlyle, which is bequeathed to me by Uncle's Will. My haste to claim this will be excused by Mr. Froude's own in printing it" (27 April). Since Froude had acknowledged that the copyright *was* hers, she discovered that though nothing could be done about the first edition she could certainly see to it that there were no more, and that it might even be possible to bring out a corrected version, as she did subsequently. Froude, who had also "forgotten" to return her copy of part of the chapter on Jane Welsh Carlyle, was extremely disturbed, and the dispute grew hotter.

Once Mary was able to read her "imperfect copy" she was even more upset than Froude, and there was a new bout of letters in *The Times*. Her first (5 May) points out that Carlyle had left written instructions on the manuscript that it was not to be printed without "fit editing", and that when he was dead "fit editing" would probably be impossible. Froude replied (6 May) to say that these instructions had been countermanded by what Carlyle had said to him personally and in the Will. Mary's response (7

May) was to point out that the Will had also implied that, though he was to have the final decision, he would be wise to take advice—and that he should be willing to take it now. Clearly Froude was offended at public exposure by "the little girl"; and so, merely reserving the manuscripts explicitly bequeathed him, he publicly stated that:

> The remaining papers, which I was directed to return to Mrs. Alexander Carlyle as soon as I had done with them, I will restore at once to any responsible person whom she will empower to receive them from me. . . . [She] can have them all when she pleases (*Times*, 9 May).

This was crucial but, as he confessed to Stephen, he had simply replied in a fit of irritation without any intention of giving up the biography "the greater part" of which he said he had already written.

Much of the rest of the story has already been published in the accounts by Froude, by Alexander Carlyle and by Waldo Dunn: it is their *interpretation* which needs re-examination rather than a questioning of the facts. In Waldo Dunn's life of Froude, for example, he speaks of Mary's behaviour as "virtual blackmail", and he is blindly unable to account for her concern about the manuscripts except by supposing that she coveted their "probably large monetary value".[16] He seems entirely ignorant of the fact that they were actually her own manuscripts, that they had been given to her, that Froude admitted it, she was able to produce witnesses, and that it would have been strange if she had not seen their value. He says nothing about the way in which she was willing to return the Jeffrey letters to Mrs Empson, and he ignores the fact that she offered to give up £1,500 due to her for the first edition of the book if Froude would relinquish the biography and return her papers immediately. Dunn made a mean charge, and is particularly foolish in saying that as Carlyle "had disposed of the matter in his Will, he doubtless thought it unnecessary to do anything further".[17]

For the position was clear: Froude had publicly stated that the papers were Mary's and that she could have them when she pleased. Her solicitors sent for them immediately—and Froude withdrew his undertaking. Obviously he had had second thoughts

and was restrained from his folly by Sir James Stephen. The day
on which Mary sent for her papers, Froude wrote a distraught
letter to his solicitors:

> . . . So far as I am individually concerned she can have them at
> once—but a question occurs to me which as an Executor I have to
> consider. Whose are those papers at the moment?—They were sent
> to me six years ago without a word as to their future destination,
> and I was told to burn freely. Two years ago Mr. C. told me that
> when I was done with them I was to give them to Mary C. But he
> has not left them to Mary C. in his Will. Marys right seems to
> devolve through use—am *I* in law the present owner? or are the
> Papers part of the general Estate.
>
> Kindly give me what guidance you can. Mary C. must have them
> somehow but I have to mind what I am about—if they belong to
> the general Estate I require (do I not?) Sir James Stephens assent
> (11 May).

The message had got through from Stephen. If he and Froude refused to admit that the papers had been given to Mary, then they
must be regarded as belonging to the general Estate, whatever the
verbal understanding with Carlyle, whatever promises had been
given, and whether the other members of the Carlyle family wished to
deprive Mary of them or not. The "blackmail" is in the other hand.

The next day Froude drew up what seems to be a more formal
letter based on instructions from Stephen—it is formal because
it is to the executors' solicitors and meant to provide them with a
better basis for negotiation:

> . . . You have only to assure me that the papers which I was to
> return to Mrs. Carlyle are in law hers and I shall give them up with
> pleasure.
>
> But I must make one further provision. The papers were given
> to me to make use of for Carlyle's Biography. I have been for 8
> years at work on them and a certain use I mean to make of them.
> It will not be much but it will be something.
>
> I cannot hereafter have a claim raised that I have no right to
> make this or that extract from Carlyle's or Mrs. Carlyle's journals
> or from letters. The journals and letters were put in my hands that
> I might make such extracts. Carlyle's memory is as dear to me as it
> can possibly be to Mrs. A. Carlyle.
>
> I honoured and loved him above all other men that I ever knew

or shall know. It is my duty to show him as he was & no life known to me will bear a Sterner Scrutiny. But he wished—especially wished—his faults to be known. They were nothing, amount to nothing, in the great balance of his qualities. But such as they are they must be described.—-Surely by no unfriendly hand (12 May).[18]

His claim to have been working on the letters for six years has been advanced to eight: it may well have been less. His private admission that Carlyle had told him to give the papers to Mary (because they were hers) is replaced by a challenge to her to establish that her uncle had given them to her formally The rhetoric is heightened, "Mary C." is even called "Mrs. A. Carlyle", and he seeks to change the grounds for disagreement. Up to this point the objections had mainly been to his reckless manner of "editing" which hurt Carlyle only because it made him seem so treacherous a friend. It was Carlyle's acquaintances (dead or alive) who were to suffer from Froude's devotion to the "truth". Now he takes his stand on its being his positive duty to show Carlyle's faults as well. We must not be unfair to Froude; but this is the point at which the breach between Froude and Mary Carlyle was complete and at which a new round of negotiations was to begin.

The "practicality" of Froude could not stand being challenged, and his place as a negotiator had to be taken by Sir James Stephen. As might be expected Stephen's tactics, if doubtfully fair, were sound in law. He knew that there could be no written record of the gift of papers, if for no other reason than that with a partially paralysed hand Carlyle had long found it impossible to write, for this was why Mary had been needed as a secretary. So that even though, in due course, Mary's solicitors were able to show that it was well understood that the papers were hers, Stephen protected Froude by resolutely refusing to admit it. His instructions to counsel were far from impartial or complete, and he chose to argue that it was uncertain whether the papers had been given to Froude or Mary. His own duty as executor, he maintained, was to protect the rights of the residuary legatees; and he continued to maintain this even when it was clear that those whose interests he claimed to represent did not want him to. Then, even though he had no intention of letting the case go to court, both he and Froude were ready to use this as a threat, which means in fact that it was they who were putting pressure on Mary though they knew that whatever the law might be they could hardly set aside Carlyle's express wishes. It was perfectly clear to Froude's party that there was no real problem about his being allowed to complete the *Life*; but, as the *Reminiscences* had already shown, the crunch might well come when the original documents could be checked against the way he had used them. So that, although private, public, spoken and written promises had all been made that the papers were Mary's and a first instalment had been given up, Stephen refused to concede that this was so in law until Froude was guaranteed all the time he needed and until he could exact some concession to secure Froude literary control over the *Reminiscences*. It is this which the bulk of the new papers, the old ones used by Dunn, and all the small print in the appendix to *The Nemesis of Froude* are really about. Their monetary value had nothing to do with it; it was a struggle for the control of the Carlyle archive arising from lack of faith in Froude.

Unfortunately, as the dispute dragged on years later, it even brought up questions about Carlyle's sexual competence, his marriage, and the way he and Jane treated each other. According to Froude much of this had been in his mind from the moment he undertook to write the *Life*. He had been told various stories on the doubtful authority of Geraldine Jewsbury which he could hardly have meant to repeat about the old man when he accepted his task.[19] But it seems that the more he was rattled by criticism from Carlyle's family and friends, the more determined he grew to make the most of his story. His final two volumes are written in a different tone from the first two; and Froude at last resorted to the old trick of leaving his own account to be published after his death. As a result many of the details of this story, pathetic in themselves, have been discussed to the pitch of absurdity: especially, *did* Carlyle, in a fit of temper, once bruise Jane's wrists or arms? We don't know; and if he did it is not clear how it was to excuse Froude. The whole subject eventually drifted into gossip. The only new point about this in the Farrer-Stephen papers is that, as early as 1884 Froude evidently believed that he was bothered by it:

. . . I dread a controversy which may force me to tell an incident that has been my greatest difficulty from the beginning.—*Once* only once that I know of, the quarrelling led to actual physical violence, and there is an allusion to it in the part of Mrs. C's journal which I have suppressed. The effect would be miserable if this were known —It has been a weight on my own neck for the last 13 years (28 Oct. 1884).

Froude did not in fact "know" anything except from Geraldine Jewsbury, and he was to keep the dreaded secret by leaving it for his children to publish. It is typical of Froude that, in spite of his declared ambitions as a biographer, he did not know when to tell the "truth" and when to be silent. Apart from this he was innocent enough but overcome by the responsibility.*

I do not want to go over the old ground. The essential weakness both of Froude's case and character can be seen in the fact that he and Stephen were reluctantly forced to yield to Mary. When not flustered by opposition they always recognized that Carlyle meant her to have his papers, and that he had even given them to her in effect in his own lifetime. They could hardly do otherwise in the face of two written statements of Froude made when Carlyle was living:—"I perfectly understood that all the papers were to be returned to you when I had done with them" (10 Feb. 1880), and, "It has, however, long been settled that you were to have the entire collection when I had done with it" (12 Feb. 1880).[20] Yet it was with the utmost unwillingness that they ultimately lost control over them. Throughout the remainder of 1881 Froude threatened to compel Mary to resort to the law to establish her claim, and Stephen and the solicitors had to restrain him. There were many good reasons, the main one being that the question was a moral as well as a legal one in which Froude would show up badly, and there was the other consideration that (though ready to support Froude) Stephen was not prepared to accept liability for any legal expenses that might result from actions to satisfy his friend's hurt pride. Nor can he have been confident about how Froude's contradictions would have stood cross-examination. Legal brinkmanship continued, therefore, until a frail compromise was reached.

---

* In fairness to Froude, he *was* accused of having torn a page out of one of Jane's journals, which he had not done. This meant that his children could save their father's posthumous reputation at the expense of his "loved and honoured friend" by publishing the manuscript (*My Relations With Carlyle*) which he had left them for the purpose.

In brief its terms were: (*i*) that Mary should have the copyright of the *Reminiscences* but that, somehow, Froude was to be thought of as having reserved "literary control"; (*ii*) Mary was to be given an inventory of the papers, "with a Memorandum, that subject to Mr. Froude's right to make use of them for the purpose of his biography they belong to Mrs. Carlyle,"—accepted, although the inventory was to be a sketchy one and she may never have received the memorandum; (*iii*) Froude was to keep what had been specifically bequeathed to him; (*iv*) the papers were to be returned to Mrs Carlyle as soon as Froude had done with them for writing the biography;—all accepted, with the stipulation that Froude should have time to correct the second edition, and with some uncertainty about what letters and notebooks of Jane's he might keep. The terms were arrived at by correspondence and were never drawn up in a single document. One can sense that everyone but Froude was relieved to be reaching a workable compromise. There was a temporary lull, therefore, as some of the papers were sent back and the biography completed.

Yet once the papers were in her hands, Mary's position was stronger. She went on to arrange for Norton's edition of the *Reminiscences* in America, and even to persuade Froude to agree to an English edition as well.[21] In time, Alexander Carlyle also brought out the *New Letters and Memorials of Jane Welsh Carlyle* (1903). Alexander Carlyle and Norton were to devote much of their lives to the Carlyle papers and to demonstrating the editorial sins of Froude. Though not blameless for pursuing him in this way, it must be understood that Froude was oddly careless in the way he treated texts. It is true that he lamely offered to correct later editions if he could be allowed to consult the papers again; but the fact is that if the letters and journals quoted in his biography were to have been edited to exact standards the whole edition would have to have been reset, which would have been impossible. His disdain for Mary and Alexander Carlyle had left its mark and their response is understandable. His defeat left him exasperated and unhappy.

There are letters to William Allingham, among other unused papers in the National Library of Scotland, which suggest that he also suffered from Froude, and that he and his wife shared Mary's opinion.[22] They imply that little would have been lost if Froude had carried out his threat to give up writing the biography, since an exchange for Allingham could well have been for the better. They also thought that (at Mary's request) he might have edited some of Carlyle's miscellaneous unpublished papers.[23] No reader of the *Diary* can have closed it without an affection for its writer and Mary may well have had him in mind as a biographer. In 1870 he had noted, "Mary tells me she said to her Uncle—'People say Mr. Allingham is to be your Boswell', and he replied, 'Well let him try it. He's very accurate' " (p. 202). We have only Mary's side of a limited series of letters, but we find her writing to him quite cheerfully about "the Froude affair". By 22 October 1881, for example, she reports on the second phase, after Stephen has taken over, that she has come to believe him "worse than Froude. . . . He plants his portly figure between Froude and me", determined to wrest a concession. What she says is perfectly clear and consistent; and yet Allingham pacifically advised her how to avoid an open conflict (as she had intended) and she did as he said. But both Froude's accounts and the paper he persuaded Sir James Stephen to write for him are biased and incomplete; and although Sir James never lost his air of judicial impartiality in his letters, Froude reveals both his weakness and his better nature.

In 1882 we find him at last ready to give up more of the papers after publishing his first two volumes: they included letters up to 1835, "Edward Irving's letters, Mrs. Basil Montagu's letters, and a few others" (Froude to Farrer, 20 May). Evidently there were still some delays, but he was anxious now to have everything settled:

> . . . As soon as I have finished my own work and published what I mean to publish Mrs. Carlyle shall have *everything*—such of "Jane Welsh Carlyle's" letters diaries &c as I do *not* mean to publish as well as all the rest,—because hereafter a complete edition of the whole of the MSS.—I mean the whole remains of both Carlyle & his wife—will certainly be demanded—and the papers ought to be kept together (18 July 1882).

For Froude's sake it would be better to stop here, where he shows that he appreciates the papers' importance and even means to be magnanimous, but perhaps the strain of finishing was too much for him. When he had completed the last two volumes he wrote to Farrer again:

My work is done.—It is time for the long talked of dinner, when you & I and Stephen can celebrate the close of our adventures in this matter. . . .

The Letters &c. will now be given up to Mary Carlyle. I must however go over my extracts & quotations in a last examination to make certain that no errors have crept in. It occurs to me that perhaps it might be well if *some one of your people* was to go over them with me. I have to do with a dangerous & very vindictive person, very reckless of statement and unscrupulous in the accusations which she may bring. It will be easy for her when the Papers are in her hands to insist that this & that is wrongly quoted and I shall have no means of setting myself right. She is at this moment bringing out in America a rival edition of the *Reminiscences* although I have always refused to allow her any literary control of it.

Think over my suggestion—& when you come here we can talk about it (26 Oct. 1884).


He seems to have forgotten that (if he wanted to) he could have kept the papers for a second, corrected edition; yet Froude may have already realized that, in a sense, his work was beyond correction. No law clerk could help him, and it remains astonishing that he was so careless about detail even when he was afraid to be caught out. At the same time his friends seem to have persuaded him to take a little longer, and perhaps the text we now have is one that (by his standards) *had* been guardedly corrected. For, by November, he still had the papers and was distressed to discover that Mary was demanding them:

. . . I have answered that the Biography has first to be completely revised but that I told you that they would be in your hands before Xmas. At the same time by bringing out this Edition of the Reminiscences in America she has broken the promise which she made me in her uncle's life time to make no use of these Papers without consulting me. I was satisfied with that promise & therefore said nothing to him on the subject—as I otherwise might have done. I have therefore been thinking seriously whether we might apply for power to deposit the whole Collection in the British Museum where they would be open to every one. You and Stephen can judge whether this would be possible. To me it would be a quite infinite relief (Froude to Farrer, 8 Nov. 1884).

261

Froude begins to seem almost unbalanced. It can hardly pass that here is a further admission that the manuscript of the *Reminiscences* was meant to be Mary's, and presumably the whole collection—always subject to his paternal supervision—and that he is not to be bound by his promises though she ought to have kept hers. Even with the celebration dinner in view, Farrer's heart must have sunk to find that his client still somehow believed that, to teach Mary a lesson, an uncertain "power" might be applied for to withhold her papers. Ultimately, of course, Mary and Alexander Carlyle needed no prompting to see that most of them went to the National Library of Scotland.

In this account I have tried to give the story with a respect for the facts, but without pretence that its conclusions are impartial though I hope they are fair. Froude has already been described as careless, inaccurate, patronizing, and so lacking in judgment as sometimes to be unbalanced. He was not dishonest, but he lacked self-understanding so badly that he easily gives that impression. His abilities were remarkable, but it is not too much to say that in some ways he was a fool. Mary Carlyle appears to have been determined, intelligent and truthful. Sir James Stephen was always an advocate, acting strictly within the law but ready to suppress the truth to support his cause. There is no point in whipping up controversy: these conclusions are re-stated because we have no clear or accurate biography of Froude. Mary Aitken Carlyle was not mercenary, as Dunn decided; she did not marry hastily in order to get her dying uncle's papers into her hands, as Froude's daughter suggested to Dunn; she wanted what was hers, but she did not "nag", "badger", "blackmail", tell lies, or act like a "she-demon", as Dunn tells his readers or as Froude told his friends.

Apart from this, what difference does it make to our knowledge of Carlyle and Froude? Perhaps a considerable one, although some of the implications remain to be thought about. At the simplest biographical level we know rather more about them both, and in a most general way we are able to make a better estimate of Froude's biography. Its chief value remains, like many Victorian biographies, as a repository of documents; and certainly a re-examination of the *Life* makes one see why control of the papers was so essential to Froude. It is mainly the work of the Carlyles, and most of Froude's task lay in arrangement and copying, though it was accepted that he should have the entire receipts of payment from the publishers even though they were Mary's papers. He confessed himself, "it may be said that I . . . have thus produced no 'Life', but only the materials for a 'Life' ". The same, of course, is true of the *Reminiscences,* which were edited by Froude only in the sense that he had them copied for the printer. Yet *both* Froude *and* Mary deserve our gratitude for respecting the papers that were entrusted to them. Carlyle had occasionally thrown out the injunction to select and burn, but whether in Froude's indiscretion or his wisdom he faithfully preserved them. It is fortunate for us that John Forster died before his friend, since had he lived to act as an executor he would have thinned them remorselessly.[25]

The disputes may also remind us how opinionated Froude could be, and how this may have distorted our view of Carlyle. We also notice how curiously he divided his volumes. When he began, the first two volumes were designed as *Thomas Carlyle, A History of the First Forty Years of His Life 1795–1835,* which is logical provided one thinks of a man's maturity and old age as needing about the same space as his youth and childhood. The final two volumes had to be *A History of His Life in London, 1834–1881.* But of *Life in London* the first volume covers the period from 1835-1848, leaving for the last one the years 1849 to 1881, the period when material is still abundant, when Froude knew him personally, but when he inevitably ran out of space. For Froude was decidedly a disciple of Carlyle's later period, and so what we have is a biography placing a disproportionate emphasis on Carlyle's early life written from the point of view of someone whose sympathies and special knowledge belong to the later period. Froude, for example, is far more interested in the ageing Carlyle's self-styled "remorse" about Jane than his early radicalism. The circumstances of the quarrel about the papers may also have affected the second half of the biography not only by reinforcing the commitment to finish in two volumes, but by tempting him to rely even more on direct quotation (at which he was weakest) and to make less of personal knowledge than he might.

Yet his two letters about the importance of keeping the collection together suggest that by the time he had finished he had begun to see their enormous value. No doubt he was well able to arrive at this conclusion himself; but it is also abundantly clear that although Carlyle was sometimes worried about their publication his remarks about burning them were largely affectation. Discussing the subject with a friend of Mazzini shortly after the latter's death, he approved of Mazzini's habit of burning all intimate letters as soon as possible, but to her surprise disagreed with it as a general rule.[26] It is self-evident not only from his enormous accumulation of correspondence, but the care with which they were kept and annotated. He was a prose-poet of memory who had come to be doubtful of immortality and overwhelmed by the need to reassure himself of the existence of those he had known and loved. No less, in his letters and journals and in everything he wrote, he had the pleasure and discomfort of feeling that he did so for posterity. His self-concern is enormous, and at times hateful to him, hence the instructions to "burn", "express biography of me I had really rather that there should be none", and the outburst to Allingham (*Diary*, p. 196), "Write my autobiography? I would as soon think of cutting my throat with my pen-knife!" But he may well have realized, at other times, that he was a short-range thinker with a supreme power of expression, often capable of his best in speech, diary and correspondence, but too self-questioning to write anything which was fully self-consistent and self-developing in design.

Certainly this is suggested by one path his reputation has taken. For though volumes of the *Collected Letters* have only recently begun to appear, other collections of the Carlyles' letters have long attracted more interest than his major works, and new collections such as those of the letters to Emerson and to his brother Alexander have been given an editorial treatment that fresh editions of the works now lack.[27] The Carlyles' observations in letters, journals and contemporary comment of all kinds are what possibly give them at present their largest claim on our attention.

Yet Carlyle is more than a Victorian Pepys or Boswell; he deserved his reputation as a great writer in his own time, and he saw more deeply into men and society than either. But even his major works have some of the same qualities we find in his papers: they are a collection of sure and rapid insights, not easily connected unless he found the right subject or related them to himself. The swift and compact accumulation of observations is the principle of Carlyle's composition, as well as the process of his thought. He may make a fantasy in this way as with *Sartor*, or he may devise a quasi-epic structure for the *Pamphlets*, but he is so concerned with the actual that any theory he takes up disintegrates as he worries at it. When troubles of his own time press directly on himself he can turn to and deal with them. But essentially he is a critic: able to write with wonderful expressiveness and insight even in the wilds of Craigenputtoch if he is provided with the twenty-six volumes of Diderot or the complete works of Voltaire, reliant on translation to begin writing, pleased to find a master in Goethe, but as an original artist never completely satisfying. It is this which gnaws at him. History is his refuge, and it is in his historical studies that he is most original, working painfully over the French Revolution, Cromwell and Frederick until he masters them by finding a pattern in their events or imposing one on them of his own.

"All books", he says, "are in the long run historical documents." He chooses to write histories because, hard as he finds it, he believes that only in writing could he feel himself fully come *alive*. Yet he finds that his insight comes partly in proportion to the difficulties surmounted and so, whatever the task (as with *The French Revolution*), he feels he must grapple with it, "seize it, crush the secret out of it, and make or mar".[28] He speaks of his plight as a writer facing the life of Cromwell:

> For many months there has been no writing here. Alas! what was there to write? About myself, nothing: or less if that was possible. I have not got one word to stand upon paper in regard to Oliver. . . . I seem to myself at present, and for a long while past, to be sunk deep, fifty miles deep, below the region of articulation, and, if I ever rise to speak again, must raise whole continents with me. . . . I am, as it were, without a language. . . . I wish often I could write rhyme. . . .[29]

Poetry he could never write because he could not bring himself to speak of contemporary poetry as anything *but* rhyme. His general philosophy was to declare that no general philosophy was possible, and his outlook when faced with creating anything not centred on himself was almost blank. The only difference between the Everlasting No and the Everlasting Yea is self-will. Listing various

schemes for books, he notes: "Life consists, as it were, in the sift-
ing of huge rubbish-mounds, and the choosing from them, with
ever more or less error, what is golden and vital to us."[30] About
the same time, he declares: "Neither does Art &c., in the smallest
hold out with me. In fact, that concern has all gone down with me
like ice too thin on a muddy pond. I do not believe in 'Art.' "[31]
After writing *Heroes*: "I sometimes feel as if I had lost the art of
writing altogether; as if I were a dumb man. . . . I do lead a most
self-secluded, entirely lonesome existence. 'How is each so lonely in
the wide grave of the All?' says Richter."[32] It is not *all* Carlylean
"exaggeration". He sees the desperate nature of being a writer,
and that he is dependent on rousing himself into a state destructive to his "nerves"; yet, finally, because so few will listen to him
after 1850, he turns to *Friedrich II of Prussia*, making supreme
demands on himself and his readers.

*The French Revolution* is a great exception for which reasons
might be given, but, apart from this, it is arguable that Carlyle's tremendous powers produced works which were fragmentary—though
no doubt his fragments are greater achievements than most men's
life-work. Yet it is in his private papers that he often expressed
himself best because (to use his own terms) they are about *himself*, and this is what he believed in—*himself*. This is not always
enough, even for Carlyle; but a justification can be found near the
start of his published *Cromwell*: they "hang there in the dark abysses
of the Past; if like a star almost extinct, yet like a real star. . . .
These Letters will convince any man that the Past did exist!"[34]

Illustration from *Punch's Almanac* (31 Dec. 1881), showing that
March 1881 had been memorable for Froude's besmirching Carlyle on
publishing the *Reminiscences*.

NOTES

1. Froude, *Life*, III, 4 and 7.
2. Dunn, *James Anthony Froude, A Biography, 1818–1856* (Oxford, 1961), I, 9.
3. Dunn, *Froude, A Biography, 1857–1894* (1963), II, 472. There are pointed comments on Dunn and Froude by Gertrude Himmelfarb, *Victorian Minds* (London, 1968), "James Anthony Froude: A Forgotten Worthy", pp. 236–48.
4. Dunn, *Froude, A Biography*, II, 477–8.
5. NLS, MS. Acc. 5074, referred to hereafter as the Farrer-Stephen papers. I am greatly indebted to the kindness of Messrs Farrer & Co. The papers include many letters, some autograph, others legal copies, and several in both forms; but there is no point in distinguishing for the present purpose between originals and accurate legal copies, so that citation only by date means that the text is taken from these papers.
6. Froude, *Life*, IV, 423, where Carlyle's rather odd comments on Stephen's speech mean that he was contemptuous of his relative moderation in willingness to tolerate parliamentary government.
7. In judgment on legal points I have been guided by the present extensive papers, such previously published documents as those in the appendix to *The Nemesis of Froude*, and W. A. Copinger, *The Law of Copyright in Works of Literature and Art* (London, 1870, 2nd edn 1881).
8. The manuscript of the *Reminiscences* is a composite one, including the chapter on TC's father, "James Carlyle", written in January 1832; chapters on Edward Irving, Lord Jeffrey and others, written in 1866–7; and pieces combined to make the chapter on Jane Welsh Carlyle, mainly written in 1866. The latter is much more in the form of a journal than either Froude or Norton allow us to suppose. All but "James Carlyle" are in NLS. There is nothing to be gained by distinguishing between the different parts of the MS at every reference.
9. Dunn, *Froude, A Biography*, II, 483.
10. See especially NLS, MS 1777, but there are many other miscellaneous letters of Mary Carlyle in NLS.
11. The bequest to Mary by the codicil of the lease of the house in Cheyne Row, previously left to Dr John Carlyle, was convenient but almost worthless; its probate value was nil, since with only 2¼ years of the lease to run its rentable value was balanced by the cost of putting it into good condition again at the end of the lease.—Farrer-Stephen papers.
12. *My Relations with Carlyle*, p. 29. Froude falls into the dilemma of bemoaning that Carlyle did not tell him about his intentions, and denouncing "the absurdity" of the supposition "that I, being in constant and confidential communication with Carlyle, did not know his wishes".—Quoted, Dunn, *Life of Froude*, II, 491. A similar contradiction is noted by *Dyer*, p. 215, in Froude's claim to have consulted Carlyle

on various questions while also saying that (at this time) Carlyle was incapable of understanding what they meant.

13. NLS, MS 1777.113. Froude again admits Mary's right to possession.

14. NLS, MS 1777.163, 29 June.

15. NLS, MS 1777.121, unidentified correspondent from Forres (15 May 1881) who also asks, "Was Froude his *secret* enemy or what? or is it the overweaning conceit which gets naturally into the blood of all writers."

16. Dunn, *Life of Froude*, "blackmail", II, 486; "monetary value", II, 476, and Dunn, *Froude and Carlyle*, p. 30.

17. Dunn, *Life of Froude*, II, 477.

18. Froude was rather taken with the wording of the last paragraph; Stephen obligingly quoted it back to him, when he wrote his "privately printed" letter for Froude to distribute in self-justification (*The Late Mr. Carlyle's Papers*, 1886, reprinted in *My Relations*), and Froude used some of it again, as if a fresh thought, in writing to Lady Derby, as quoted by Herbert Paul, *Life of Froude* (London, 1905), p. 329.

19. Not necessarily because Geraldine Jewsbury was a bad witness, but her evidence was unwritten, came orally from Mrs Carlyle, was repeated (presumably as a broken confidence) to Froude, and is unverifiable. Yet she *may* be right.

20. These letters are quoted and referred to in *Nemesis*, pp. 87 and 140–1, were never denied by Froude, and were accepted by Dunn in *Froude and Carlyle*. (It needs to be appreciated that whereas I have worked mainly from the Farrer-Stephen papers, Dunn worked exclusively from the Froude family set of documents, and that there is still probably a Mary Carlyle set in existence (part given in *Nemesis*) among which the originals to these may still be found.)

21. Dunn, *Froude and Carlyle*, pp. 91–5.

22. NLS. MS 3823.

23. The proposal to edit some of the unpublished papers for *Fraser's* had occurred to Allingham and Mary previously, in 1876, but Mary (to whom Allingham recognized they belonged) changed her mind.— *Nemesis*, p. 144.

24. *Life*, I, xv.

25. By analogy with his treatment of both the Dickens papers and his own: see K. J. Fielding, "New Letters from Charles Dickens to John Forster, How They Were Found", *Boston University Studies* in English, II (1956), 140–9.

26. *Nemesis*, p. 145.

27. *The Correspondence of Emerson and Carlyle*, ed. J. Slater (New York, 1968), and *The Letters of TC to His Brother Alexander*, ed. E. W. Marrs, Jr. (Cambridge, Mass., 1968).

28. *Life*, II, 466.

29. *Life*, III, 279.

30. *Life*, III, 422–3.

31. *Life*, III, 421. Compare, for example, two entries in the Forster manu-

script: "What is 'Art'? I confess myself entirely unable to say. For my own share, I have as good as no Art: —more pity" (f. 95 v.); "Why look on revolutions? Are men never great but in revolution? Why, truly, yes occasionally; and yet oftenest enough also, far oftenest in these last times, *no they are not great!* They are not great, in these poor ages of ours, I think, but little rather; an *ignarum pecus*; driven, or driving, to pasture, to market,—not at all in the heroic manner. It is in great moments only, when life and death hang in the balance that men become veracious, sincere. I for one admire veracity; it is real deeds however rude, not mimetic grimaces of deeds however elegant, that I should wish to look upon" (f. 170, about 19 Oct. 1841).

32. *Life*, III, 195.
33. *Life*, IV, 85.
34. *Works*, VI, 77.

# Contributors

ARTHUR A. ADRIAN is Emeritus Professor of English, Case-Western Reserve University, and the author of *Georgina Hogarth and the Dickens Circle* and *Mark Lemon: First Editor of Punch*; he is married to VONNA H. ADRIAN, poet and Lecturer in English (retired), Case Western Reserve University and Cleveland Institute of Art.

JOHN CLUBBE is Associate Professor of English, Duke University, author of *Victorian Forerunner: The Later Career of Thomas Hood*, editor of *Selected Poems of Thomas Hood*, an assistant-editor of the Carlyle *Collected Letters*, and editor of *Two Reminiscences of Thomas Carlyle*.

DAVID J. DeLAURA is Avalon Foundation Professor in the Humanities, University of Pennsylvania, author of *Hebrew and Hellene in Victorian England: Newman, Arnold and Pater*, and editor of Newman's *Apologia Pro Vita Sua* and *Victorian Prose: A Guide to Research*.

K. J. FIELDING is Saintsbury Professor of English, University of Edinburgh, author of *Charles Dickens: A Critical Introduction*, editor of Dickens's *Speeches*, and associate-editor of Dickens's *Letters* (Pilgrim edn vol. I) and of the Carlyle *Collected Letters*.

GEORGE H. FORD is Professor of English, University of Rochester, author of *Keats and the Victorians*, *Dickens and His Readers*, and *Double Measure, A Study of the Novels and Stories of D. H. Lawrence*, and co-editor of the Norton *Hard Times* and *Bleak House*, and one of the editors of the *Norton Anthology of English Literature*.

CARLISLE MOORE is Professor of English, University of Oregon, author of the Carlyle chapter in *English Romantic Poets and Essayists*, "Carlyle and Fiction, 1822–34" (in *Nineteenth Century Studies*, ed. H. Davis *et al*), "*Sartor Resartus* and the Problem of Carlyle's 'Conversion'" (PMLA, 1955), and "The Persistence of Carlyle's 'Everlasting Yea'", MP (1957) and other studies in Romantic and Victorian literature.

271

MORSE PECKHAM is Distinguished Professor of English and Comparative Literature, University of South Carolina, and author of *Beyond the Tragic Vision, Man's Rage for Chaos, Art and Pornography, The Triumph of Romanticism,* and *Victorian Revolutionaries,* and editor of Darwin, Browning and Swinburne.

CHARLES RICHARD SANDERS is Emeritus Professor of English, Duke University, author of *Coleridge and the Broad Church Movement, The Strachey Family, Lytton Strachey: His Mind and Art,* editor of an abridgement of Malory's *Morte D'Arthur,* and General-editor of the Duke-Edinburgh edition of the Carlyle *Collected Letters.*

JULES P. SEIGEL is Associate Professor of English, University of Rhode Island, editor of *Thomas Carlyle: The Critical Heritage,* and author of several articles on Victorian literature.

G. ROBERT STANGE is Professor of English, Tufts University, and is author of *Matthew Arnold: The Poet as Humanist,* and editor of *The Poetry of Coleridge,* and co-editor of *Victorian Poetry and Poetics.*

RODGER L. TARR is Associate Professor of English, Illinois State University, editor of *A Bibliography of English Language Articles on Thomas Carlyle: 1900–1965,* and author of articles on Carlyle, Dickens, and related topics.

G. B. TENNYSON is Professor of English, University of California, Los Angeles, and author of *"Sartor" Called "Resartus,"* editor of *A Carlyle Reader,* and until recently of *Nineteenth-Century Fiction,* and author of the Carlyle chapter in *Victorian Prose: A Guide to Research.* He is co-editor of *Victorian Literature: Prose and Poetry.*

# Index

*Writers and their works are entered under the authors' names, although a few titles are given in addition. Other titles are of works by Carlyle. For Carlyle himself see the chronology, pp. 11–12; for topics with which he was concerned, and stylistic devices, see alphabetically separate entries. Most secondary material has been indexed, but not always repeatedly when only cited in the notes.*

279

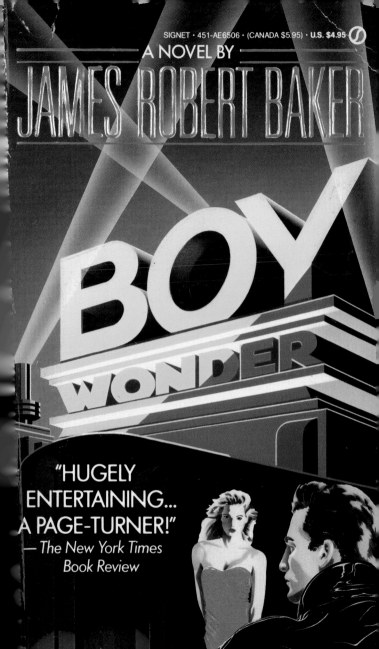

# BOY WONDER

# BOY
# WONDER

**James Robert Baker**

A SIGNET BOOK

## NEW AMERICAN LIBRARY

A DIVISION OF PENGUIN BOOKS USA INC.

## PUBLISHER'S NOTE

This book is a work of fiction. Names, characters, places, and incidents
either are the product of the author's imagination or are used fictitiously,
and any resemblance to actual persons, living or dead, events, or locales is
entirely coincidental.

NAL BOOKS ARE AVAILABLE AT QUANTITY DISCOUNTS
WHEN USED TO PROMOTE PRODUCTS OR SERVICES.
FOR INFORMATION PLEASE WRITE TO PREMIUM MARKETING DIVISION,
NEW AMERICAN LIBRARY, 1633 BROADWAY,
NEW YORK, NEW YORK 10019.

*Boy Wonder* previously appeared in an NAL BOOKS hardcover edition
published by New American Library, and was simultaneously published in
Canada by The New American Library of Canada Limited (now Penguin
Books Canada Limited).

SIGNET TRADEMARK REG. U.S. PAT. OFF. AND FOREIGN COUNTRIES
REGISTERED TRADEMARK—MARCA REGISTRADA
HECHO EN DRESDEN, TN, U.S.A.

SIGNET, SIGNET CLASSIC, MENTOR, ONYX, PLUME, MERIDIAN
and NAL BOOKS are published by New American Library, a division of
Penguin Books USA Inc., 1633 Broadway, New York, New York 10019

First Signet Printing, January, 1990

1  2  3  4  5  6  7  8  9

PRINTED IN THE UNITED STATES OF AMERICA

*For John*

# ACKNOWLEDGMENTS

This oral history of Shark Trager—a man whom Edmund R. Frye once described as "arguably *the* quintessential Hollywood wunder-kind producer of the last quarter of the twentieth century, and therefore almost certainly the definitive narcissistic genius-as-monster of an atrophying art form's, if not an entire civilization's, final phase"—this *print documentary* would have been impossible without the candor of a great many people, most of whom speak in these pages with a bracing, forthright and often moving eloquence. A few who, for reasons of structure, "ended up on the cutting floor" nonetheless have earned my gratitude for their honesty, however redundant it at times proved to be. For the few who chose *not* to participate, and luckily none was crucial, I can only offer my regretful understanding, tempered in a few instances with a certain contempt where, it seems, reticence was grounded less in a desire for privacy than a wish to produce an independent "quickie" confessional, exploiting a sometimes ephemeral, not to say fleetingly sexual, involvement with Shark Trager—a predictable trend in the light of Trager's controversial life, immense popularity, equally immense vilification, and sudden spectacular death.

To be fair the list of those I should thank would have to include everyone I interviewed. But I owe considerable special debts to Greg Spivey, Neal Ridges, Woody Hazzard, Brian Straight, Drake Brewster, Simone Gatane, Kenny Roberts, Lorna

Trager, Brad Jenkins and Narges Pahlavi-Bardahl. Elliot and Sue Bernstein, two of our most respected and prestigious film producers, were especially warm and generous; as a result of the time we spent together on this endeavor they have become two of my dearest friends. If anyone was justified in wishing *not* to relive the pain of the past, surely it was another gifted producer, Carol Van Der Hof; she is a brave and charming woman. My hat is off to Mac Trager; I know how difficult it was for Mac to dwell at such length upon the son he had come to loathe so intensely. Yet key scenes of Shark's boyhood would have remained blank film without Mac's careful recollections.

Finally there is one person without whose candor this book would have been unthinkable. For if there was a ''Rosebud'' in Shark Trager's life—to use an obvious but wholly appropriate analogy—it was surely not a sled but a woman. There are no words to properly thank Kathy Petro. She is a warm, intelligent, tender and funny and indelibly beautiful survivor.

James Robert Baker
*Los Angeles, 1988*

# Contents

# 1/ Gun Crazy
## (1950–1957)

### Buzz Payne

You bet I remember the night Shark was born. I was sixteen and had just gone to work at the Flying Wing Drive-In in Costa Mesa. I helped at the snackbar during intermission and the rest of the time I rode a bicycle around through the cars, using a flashlight to discourage too much carrying on, since Mr. Krogfoss the manager liked a family atmosphere. I hadn't seen much yet except a lot of kissing, though I was both afraid and kind of hoping that sooner or later I was going to see a whole lot more. So when I heard this woman moaning in the back of a Chrysler I got pretty shook up. Just moaning and groaning, like some guy was really letting her have it. I went up and shined my light in the window like I was supposed to, and almost crashed my bike, 'cause it was this woman having a baby.

### Myrtle Butts

It was a hard pregnancy for my sister, being so frail and all. I'd come out from Nebraska while she was in her seventh month, not long after my husband Jop got killed in a cropdusting accident. I'd called Winnie and sobbed on the phone, and she'd said, "Come on out to California and start over, Sis. That's what Mac and I did." So I slept on their sun porch while I grieved over Jop and looked for work.

Winnie was no spring chicken when she had Shark, you know. She was almost forty, though Mac thought she was thirty-five. Winnie had her heart set on a girl, but Mac wanted a boy—Lord, how they'd squabble over that! Winnie was a whiner, you know. And Mac was always on a low boil. Whining and boiling. After two months of that my nerves were a wreck.

The night Shark was born Mac and Winnie argued over what to watch on TV. Mac wanted to watch wrestling, Winnie liked that Goldberg show, but Mac didn't go for Jews. He didn't go for anyone, you know. Negroes and Jews and what-all. He really went for that Joe McCarthy though. So Winnie finally said, "All right, Mac, you watch your wrestling, Myrtle and I are going to the show."

That drive-in was new then and I remember it was packed. Some shoot-'em-up movie, not my cup of tea. Winnie kept smoking—she really went for those Chesterfields. "Mac makes me so mad," she kept saying, till that old Chrysler was so filled up with smoke I had to roll down my window. People didn't know then that pregnant women shouldn't smoke.

The baby wasn't due for a few more weeks, but I was still worried that Winnie was in such a tizzy. "I'll go get us some Coca-Colas," I said, and got out to go to the snackbar.

On my way back I heard Winnie moaning and dropped those Coca-Colas and ran. There she was in the back seat, Shark sliding out into this young man's hands.

## Buzz Payne

Suddenly this baby was just coming out of her and I had to catch it. "Get Mr. Krogfoss," I yelled. But people started laughing and tooting their horns. I don't know what they thought, the way that woman was moaning.

Finally the lights came up, making it hard for people to see the screen, so they started yelling, "What the hell is going on?" 'cause it was right at the good part where somebody was about to be killed.

"A woman's having a baby," I yelled. "Somebody get Mr. Krogfoss!"

## Greg Spivey

Shark once told me they were showing the B-movie film noir *Gun Crazy* at the drive-in the night he was born. He claimed he remembered it, which is preposterous, of course. But that's what he said—that the first thing he saw in this world was not even real life but a motion picture.

One afternoon in 1979 we screened *Gun Crazy* as part of the preparation for *Red Surf,* and I asked him, half-jokingly, "So which scene was playing when you popped out the womb, Shark?"

He smiled, then a few minutes later said, "This is it here, the first thing I ever saw."

It was the climax of the film, where the guy shoots the girl and the cops shoot him.

## Mac Trager

They called me from the hospital and said, "Mr. Trager, your wife's just given birth to a healthy baby boy." I'd been half-asleep, but I dashed right out and jumped in the pickup. On my way to the hospital I had a head-on collision on Pacific Coast Highway. It was the other guy's fault—he crossed the line. Luckily for me he was in an MG, so all I got was some cuts from flying glass. He died though, and later I came to wonder if it hadn't been an omen.

## Kenny Roberts

We lived across the street from the Tragers on Mackerel Drive. When you say Newport Beach, people think of yachts and sports cars and fine beach homes, which is all true—but not Mackerel Drive. It was within the city limits, but it might as well have been Pacoima. Well, maybe not that bad. But Mackerel Drive was definitely on the wrong side of PCH—no ocean view, just a crummy little suburban street with trees that dropped these berries that stained the sidewalks and ruined people's paint jobs and everything else. The Tragers had this tract house with a white rock roof, and they'd painted the stucco this bright, almost Day-Glo aqua blue that really pissed off all the neighbors. It was a deliberate eyesore that stood out from all the other timidly pastel houses. But then it was the 1950s, wasn't it? All you could do was paint your house a bright color in a pathetic little stab at defiance.

## Myrtle Butts

That house was always a mess and it got even worse once Winnie came down with that lifting disease. I forget what they called it now, but she was so weak she had to rest all the time. And she couldn't lift anything if it weighed much more than a pound. She'd open a can of Campbell's soup and be so exhausted she'd have to go lay down. That ruled out the vacuum cleaner and the scrub pail.

## Kenny Roberts

Yes, Winnie's lifting ailment. I don't remember what it was called either. I don't think anybody does. It was one of those ailments you could only have in the fifties. Of course, it was psychosomatic. Her silent, inarticulate protest against a dull, stifling life.

## Mac Trager

It was bullshit. There was nothing wrong with her except in her mind. I see that now, though at the time I indulged her. "All right, Winnie," I'd say. "Go stretch out in the den and watch 'I Love Lucy.' I'll do the housework." Then I'd run that vacuum a minute before I said, "To hell with this! Does John Wayne do housework?" He used to come into the station, you know.

## Kenny Roberts

Mac had the Shell station down on PCH. He always seemed to be there till all hours of the night, probably to get away from Winnie. She was a whiner, you know. That's my earliest memory of Shark's mother. A frightened, whiny semi-invalid coming out to get the paper in a ratty floral housecoat. Not the Sunday paper though, she couldn't lift that. "Hon-*eeyy?*" she'd whine pathetically. Voices carried in the summer with all the windows open. "Hon*eeeyyy?*" And Mac would bark: "What the *hell* is it now!" He was this gruff ex-navy guy with a

14

steel-gray flattop, a mean, stocky man who looked a lot like Glenn Ford.

## Myrtle Butts

I had my own place for a while, but I moved back to Mackerel Drive when Shark was six months old since it had reached the point where Winnie could no longer care for him. At first she could still lift him and bottle feed him, then one day she dropped Shark in the rumpus room. Shark hit his head on that linoleum floor, Mac rushed him to the hospital, but it turned out not to be serious.

So I slept on the sun porch and played nursemaid to Shark, though we were still calling him Gale then. I'm not sure where Winnie got that name, though I do know she really went for that Gale Gordon on "Our Miss Brooks." "What a fine gentleman he is!" she would say.

"You're going to turn my boy into a fruit," Mac would say. "Gale's a broad's name."

"So is Marion," Winnie would say, "and that's John Wayne's real name. You don't think he's that way, do you?"

That steamed Mac something awful. He looked up to John Wayne in a big way.

## Mac Trager

I loved the man, I'm not ashamed to admit it. He stood rock-hard for Americanism at a time when our great country was under attack from enemies both within and without. I still get misty-eyed when I think about Duke Wayne. That's why I feel a terrible rage even to this day when I remember why he quit coming into the station. I hate to recall how close I came that afternoon to killing my wife and only son.

## Myrtle Butts

It was a beautiful Sunday afternoon and I had taken Winnie and Shark out for a drive. Shark was in the little baby seat in that old Chrysler, and Winnie was all bundled up in a pink coat and scarf even though it was warm, with that cupid lipstick she tried to do like Lucille Ball's. We were passing the station when Mac saw us and waved, so I pulled in. Only then did we realize that the tall man standing by his new Cadillac convertible was none other than John Wayne! Well, I almost died, never having seen a real movie star before. Mac insisted we get out and met Mr. Wayne, who owned a house down by the beach. I was just as flustered as a mare. But Winnie turned cross and moody, which embarrassed Mac, though he tried not to show it. Mr. Wayne was gracious, though I could tell he was eager to move on. Then Mac saw my camera, this old Kodak kind you had to hold at your waist and look down into. So he said, "Let's take a picture."

Well, I didn't want to, I could feel the tension in the air between Mac and Winnie. But Mac hissed at her to get out of the car and bring the baby over, even though he knew she couldn't lift the child. "Honey, I can't," Winnie whined. So Mac finally picked up Shark, and then Mr. Wayne took him and said, "Cute little fella." And Mac got the camera and made Mr. Wayne and Winnie stand in the hot sun by the Cadillac forever while he tried to get the camera right. Mr. Wayne started to perspire in the sun and Shark began crying, and Winnie started getting a weak attack. Mac finally snapped the picture, but Shark went potty in his diapers, and Mr. Wayne could tell and tried to hand the baby back to Winnie. But Winnie dropped Shark and he fell into the convertible. He wasn't hurt because he landed on the seat, but his diaper came off and he got some B.M. on Mr. Wayne's nice new upholstery. Mac flew into a terrible rage, saying horrible things to Winnie, while John Wayne just wiped off his car seat with one of those blue paper towels, and got in and drove off without saying a word.

## Elliot Bernstein

As Shark described it in high school, one of his earliest "directly experiential memories" involved his "mother, a hot car, a gila monster and a nuclear blast."

## Myrtle Butts

We'd all gone to a hotel in the desert, where Winnie got an awful sunburn when she fell asleep by the pool. She was all bundled up, but her hands and her face around her sunglasses were just red as a beet.

She was still in pain the next morning as Mac drove out along a desert road to a place where we could watch the A-bomb test that was planned.

When we reached the spot Mac got out, while I stayed in the car with Winnie and Shark, who was almost three years old then.

"Now you make damn sure they don't look," Mac said to me and walked a ways away to set up his Polaroid Land Camera on its tripod.

The bomb was supposed to go off at twelve o'clock noon way off across the desert but we'd got there early. Mac put on his war surplus goggles and got his camera all set and then we all waited, but that car was hot. The sun was pounding down and I started to perspire, and Shark got cranky and Winnie started looking funny, licking her dry lips, so I got out and went to Mac.

"Mac, the car's too hot," I said.

"Goddamn it, Myrtle, it's almost time," he snapped, without taking his eyes off the viewfinder.

Before I could say another word Shark let out a scream.

## Elliot Bernstein

Shark was in the front seat of the car, his mother in the back, where she suddenly began "keening breathlessly in terror." Shark looked over the seat and saw a large black and orange gila monster crawling over Winnie's leg. Apparently, the desert reptile had gotten into the car the night before and gone undetected until then. Shark had no idea what a gila monster was, that it was in fact highly poisonous. But instinctively, he said, "When that fat, ugly, foot-long thing flopped between my mother's rigid pedalpusher-clad thighs, I yelled, 'Daddy, Daddy, Daddy!'"

## Myrtle Butts

"Shut that kid up, shut him up, shut him up," Mac barked at me as I hurried back to the car. When I saw that lizard between Winnie's legs I let out a scream they must've heard in Reno.

Just as Mac turned from the camera the whole sky behind him flashed white. "Oh God, woman, cover their eyes!" he yelled, and I threw myself on Shark, grabbing Winnie by the hair, pulling her head down.

The whole ground quaked. I thought we'd gone in too close and were going to die.

## Elliot Bernstein

Shark remembered Myrtle's "humongous spongy bazooms crushing my face," then a glimpse of his father "frantically snapping pictures of the rising mushroom cloud."

## Mac Trager

I got some pictures of it, some good pictures of it. Black and white though. It was before Polaroid made color.

## Myrtle Butts

Mac finally came and used a rolled-up map to flick that lizard out of the car. He yelled at me for almost letting Winnie and Shark look at the blast, and slapped Winnie 'cause by then she'd gone all hysterical.

"And you shut your trap, mister!" he yelled at Shark who was scared and crying too. Then he ran back and took some more pictures.

## Elliot Bernstein

Shark remembered his father telling him as they drove off, "You almost made your mother go blind."

Not understanding, Shark began to cry again, and Mac yelled, "Shut up, you little pansy. I'm telling you for the last time!"

Shark held in his tears, and they drove on in silence, "everybody holding everything in." In a while Mac had to squirt water on the windshield and run the wipers to clean away the ash.

## Myrtle Butts

As we drove off all this soot started coming down. "Oh my Lord, Mac," I said. "You don't think it's radioactive?"

"No," he said crossly. "I've told you twelve times already,

we're well outside the limit. It's dust, that's all. Those things kick up some dust.''

But in a minute he said, ''Goddamn it, Myrtle, will you close your windwing?''

## Kenny Roberts

One day Shark and I were playing in my backyard—we must have been about three or four, and he was wearing a new Hopalong Cassidy cowboy outfit—when he put down his cap gun and innocently opened his trousers to pick at a white Band-Aid wrapped around his penis.

## Myrtle Butts

Mac had this old wire recorder—like a tape recorder except it used spools of thin wire instead of tape—which he used to record Senator McCarthy off the TV set. He kept all the neatly labeled little spools in a metal fishing tackle box—''in case there's a fire,'' he said. And one day he came in and found Shark playing with the spools on the rumpus room floor. They were all unraveled, the wires all snarled, and Mac saw red.

He yanked Shark up and started spanking him so fast he didn't notice that one of those snarls of wire had gotten into Shark's baggy shorts and snagged his little you-know-what. Do I have to say the word? His penis.

I was in the kitchen when I heard Shark screaming bloody murder and raced into the rumpus room.

''Oh my Lord, Mac,'' I cried when I saw what had happened. ''Stop, you're about to tear off his—''

Praise the Lord, Mac stopped in time, and there was no real harm done. I think the worst part was taking off that Band-Aid. Did Shark ever squeal when Mac did that!

## Kenny Roberts

My parents felt sorry for Shark. I think that's why they started letting him come over all the time. Plus I was an only child as well—spoiled rotten I might add. I had everything but a playmate. My parents came to regret their hospitality though, because they became virtual babysitters, especially after Gladys entered the picture.

## Myrtle Butts

I moved out after Mac made the pass at me. He was a drinker, you know. He liked that wrestling and that Brew 1O2, a cheap beer he just drank by the gallon. One night after Winnie had gone to bed we were watching the Gleason show in the rumpus room when he said, "Myrtle, why don't you make us some hot-buttered popcorn?"

So I did, but when I came back with it he said, "How 'bout it?" and tried to pull me down onto the recliner with him, and I spilled popcorn everywhere.

I said, "Mac, it's not right, you're married to my sister." And he started to cry. It was the only time I ever saw Mac Trager cry, and it was just too awful for words.

He sobbed and said there'd been no love for years, even before Winnie got weak, that the night they'd conceived Shark Winnie was sleeping, or pretending to be, and there'd been nothing since. Then he described what he did in the bathroom to satisfy himself till I covered my ears and said, "Please stop."

I packed my bags in the morning. Not long after that Gladys moved in. Lord, what a scandal that caused!


## Kenny Roberts

Gladys was this trashy blonde. She looked like Gloria Grahame with that same cupid lipstick thing Winnie tried to do, only Winnie always botched it. Gladys wore these tight pedalpushers and tight blouses with Peter Pan collars and had these incredibly pointy tits that caused gasps of flustered shock when she pushed a shopping cart through the Alpha Beta. And the perfume! A scent that just screamed cheap. She was supposed to be a nurse or something, but everybody knew what she was. The word my parents used was *tramp*.


## Gladys Frazer

I met Mac in '55 not long after I left my third husband. I had this stupid little Nash Metropolitan that broke down one night on the coast highway, so I footed it back to the last whistle stop, which was Newport Beach. Jerks kept pulling up beside me, offering me a lift—I had a good body in those days and knew it—but I told 'em what they could do.

Mac was just closing up as I reached his Shell station and there was something about him I liked right away. He was good-looking, a little like the movie star Glenn Ford. But more than that he just seemed, I dunno, solid. We drove back to my car in his pickup truck. He took one look at my engine and said it was done for. Then he offered to drive me into Long Beach back to this sailor I'd just left.

On the way we stopped for a six-pack of Brew 102, which we drank as he drove and told me about his wife and kid.

"What you need is a live-in nurse," I said. "Too bad I don't do that anymore."

Then he said, "Where'd you get that shiner?"

"From this sailor you're taking me to," I said.

So we laughed, then he turned up this road and said, "I haven't slept with a woman in over four years."

At the end of the road was an old gun emplacement from World War II, put there in case the Japanese ever attacked, but they'd removed the guns by then. We parked there. It was a warm night.

"Shark? That's a funny name for a kid," I said as we finished the beers. "How come you called him that?"

" 'Cause the first time I ever took my boy fishing that's what we caught," Mac said.

Then we made love standing up in one of the concrete slots where the big guns used to be.

## Myrtle Butts

I'd heard that Gladys had moved in but I could barely believe such a thing. So one afternoon I went by to see for myself. As I pulled up to the house I heard loud, exotic music playing—you know, that Martin Denny. I rang the bell but I don't suppose they heard me. So I let myself in.

The first thing I saw was poor little Shark on the rumpus room floor before the TV. He was wearing a spaceman's helmet, a big plastic fishbowl sort of thing, just like the one worn by that Captain Jet on TV. Except for that helmet, which was smeared with peanut butter and jelly, the child was not wearing a stitch!

"Where is your father?" I said, absolutely livid.

"In the garage," Shark said.

Well! Mac was in the garage all right. And so was that woman—her toreador pants hanging from the fin of that new Buick Mac had just bought. More than that I do not wish to describe.

I marched back in the house straight to Winnie's room, and found her sitting up in bed, watching her own portable TV. "Do you know what is going on in your house?" I said.

She looked up at me and smiled this funny smile and said, "I love him." And I saw that she meant the handsome game show host on TV. Then she smiled again, a sweet, peaceful smile just like a saint, and I knew she'd finally gone round the bend.

## Mac Trager

It was a grim time. I'd always known in my heart that Winnie's condition was but a symptom of a far more profound and progressive mental illness. And I had loved her once, I don't care what anyone says.

Naturally, she hated Gladys on sight, though Gladys tried to tend to her needs. Gladys had been a nurse at one time, the facts will bear me out on that. But Winnie said terrible things to both Gladys and me, and then she just seemed to shut down.

## Kenny Roberts

People were so hard-up for excitement in the fifties that what was happening at the Tragers really seemed like a big deal. I remember, when Shark and I started kindergarten Gladys would sometimes drive us, though my parents were under considerable pressure to take a dim view of her. My parents had voted for Stevenson, you see, and prided themselves on being "open-minded." But the rest of the neighborhood was hardcore Ike and felt compelled to act scandalized by the "shameless adultery" taking place in our otherwise tediously wholesome community. "How can you let *that woman* drive your son to school?" other parents said to me.

In retrospect it was like something out of a lurid James M. Cain novel. Overheated suburban sex, the make-up-for-lost-time syndrome—at least in Mac's case. After school Gladys would quickly deposit Shark at my house so she and Mac could go fuck hanging from the pole lamp while the neighbors watered their flowers far too frequently and gasped in titillated shock when they heard Gladys's orgasmic cries coming from the Trager house. God only knows what Shark overheard or saw when he was at home.

## Gladys Frazer

One evening Mac and Shark and I were watching "Father Knows Best" when a pleasant neighbor lady came to Robert Young's door. "I'll bet she wants to give him a blow job," Shark said as Robert Young let the woman in.

Mac turned his head to Shark in slow-motion. "*What* did you say?"

Shark cringed. "Nothing."

But Mac grabbed him and just spanked the living daylights out of him. "Don't you *ever* use talk like that in this house," Mac yelled.

"Mac, stop, for God's sake," I said. "He's just a child. He didn't know what he was saying."

I felt awful because I had a pretty fair idea where Shark had heard that expression. Mac's favorite trick was to come up and hug me from behind in the kitchen and whisper: "What say you give me one of your prize-winning before-dinner blow jobs?" He was not the world's most romantic man.

## Mac Trager

I know what you're going to hear, that I was having sex with Gladys hanging from the rafters till it finally drove poor Winnie off the deep end. Well, it wasn't like that. I had certain needs and Gladys tended to them, but we were always discreet. When I realized the Pillsburys next door might be able to see her giving me a b.j. on the service porch, I made it a point to draw the shades the next time.

Seriously though, I wish I'd done something about Winnie sooner, but for a long time I still thought she was faking. She'd stare at that TV all day long and refuse to acknowledge me when I entered the room. But unlike the true catatonic she continued to chainsmoke. And she ate like a horse, though never in my presence. But I'd leave a plate of food and when I came back later it would be licked clean, and she'd be sitting there staring blankly at "Ozzie and Harriet," smoking an after-dinner Chesterfield.

And then, just like that, she could snap right out of it. She wouldn't speak for weeks and then suddenly she'd say in a normal tone of voice, "Mac, honey, would you please bring me the *TV Guide?*"

## Gladys Frazer

The doctor came to see Winnie—they still made house calls in those days—and said it might be the change of life. He prescribed some pills, which seemed to help a little—at least we tried to believe they did. We started bringing her out of her room, propping her up at the breakfast table. She still had that funny smile, like an idiot almost. By then she'd got over her fight with me. I brushed her hair and did her nails and bathed her just like you would a child or a retarded person.

It was my idea to take her along to Disneyland the day we went.

## Elliot Bernstein

It was Shark's first visit to the Magic Kingdom, and I don't suppose I have to tell you what Disneyland was like for a kid in those days. It was really the ultimate thrill.

Mac took Shark on a lot of the rides. "It was undoubtedly the best day of my early childhood," Shark said. So strong was his capacity for fantasy that he was nearly able to block out his mother's painful presence—"a specter shuffling up Main Street on Gladys's arm, a vegetable in pedalpushers and harlequin sunglasses with a smeary red idiot grin."

## Gladys Frazer

"Mac, we should go," I said in Tomorrowland. "Winnie's getting tired." By that point we'd been stomping around for three hours,

But Mac said no. "Not till my boy and I go to the moon."

## Kenny Roberts

In the line for the Moon Trip attraction, Shark and Mac ran into the Weltys, a family who lived one block over on Bonito

Drive. It was Mr. and Mrs. Welty and the twins, Christopher and Christine—or Chris and Christy as they were known—who were also six years old and in the first grade with Shark and me. They were these perfect blond, blue-eyed twins, and the Weltys were absolutely *the* most perfect family in the neighborhood. Ray Welty was this incredibly "nice guy" type of dad—smiley, genial, completely Robert Young. And Mrs. Welty—God, I think her name was actually June—was just perfect perfect perfect.

They had recently put in a swimming pool, and I remember Shark and I going over there once with a bunch of other neighborhood kids, and everything was so great, the Weltys were so loving and joyful, that it made Shark sad. "I wish I lived here," he said to me in the pool. "I wish Mr. and Mrs. Welty were my parents."

He also developed kind of a crush on Christy—that sort of airy, innocent first-grade kind of thing. She was extremely precocious and believed in UFOs.

"Someday the saucers are going to come and take me back to my real parents," she said on the playground one day. Which, when you stop and think about it, is really pretty weird, considering how perfect her parents were.

### Elliot Bernstein

During the Disneyland moon trip Shark sat beside Christy Welty, a girl from his first grade he had a crush on. When the plastic seats began vibrating as part of the rocket trip simulation Shark experienced a "transcendent elation, a visceral excitement mixed with dreamy feelings towards Christy, which was really the peak moment of my life up to that point."

Stepping out of the moon trip attraction Shark and his father were abruptly brought back down to earth.

### Gladys Frazer

"I can't find Winnie," I told Mac. "I left her sitting right here on the Coca-Cola Terrace. When I came back with the drinks she was gone."

Well, we looked all around but we couldn't see her anywhere. Mac started getting mad. "Why the *hell* didn't you watch her?"

We walked around Tomorrowland, Mac tugging Shark along, getting madder and madder. "Bringing her was your idea, Gladys. I hope you're happy now."

"She's got to be here somewhere," I said.

Then we heard a young boy say to someone, "Guess what? There's some crazy lady in the Monsanto house taking off all her clothes."

## Mac Trager

I have no idea what she thought she was trying to prove. But there she was, naked as a jaybird in the House of the Future while everybody and their mother gawked.

## Gladys Frazer

She was just standing there in the futuristic living room stark naked, holding out her hands like a madonna with the peaceful smile of a saint.

People were giggling and had funny looks in their eyes.

Mac was furious. He picked up her clothes and threw them at her, telling her to get dressed.

"Mac, she's not responsible," I said, and led her back into the streamlined kitchen where I helped her back into her clothes. By then she seemed confused.

Some park people came and threatened to have Winnie arrested. But they soon saw that she was crazy and let us call the hospital instead. Then we couldn't find Shark. We realized he'd disappeared as soon as we heard about Winnie.

## Kenny Roberts

Shark couldn't handle what his mother was doing. While Mac and Gladys were rushing to the House of the Future, Shark took off in the opposite direction and caught up with the Weltys.

"My father says I'm supposed to go home with you," Shark told Mr. Welty.

Mr. Welty assumed Shark just meant a ride. And though he didn't understand entirely he took Shark along when they left.

But when they pulled up to the Trager house, which was still dark, Shark said, "No. My father wants me to live at your house."

Well, the Weltys realized something was wrong, so they took Shark to their house, and finally reached Mac later that night.

## Mac Trager

I was furious and worried sick by the time Ray Welty called and said Shark was over there. Disneyland was closed by then and we knew Shark wasn't there. We were beginning to think he'd been kidnapped.

If that wasn't enough I'd also had to deal with having Winnie committed.

## Gladys Frazer

The ambulance backed right up to Tomorrowland and took her straight to the mental ward in Santa Ana.

## Mac Trager

She was in the hospital for about two weeks, and the doctors couldn't figure it out either. One of 'em said, "We could give her a lobotomy," and I said, "Why bother? The way she sits around like a bump on a log it's like she's already had one."

So they gave her electroshock and a hysterectomy instead.

## Gladys Frazer

After the hospital she was actually worse. She sat in her room and stared at the TV like she didn't even see it, and I had to feed her like a baby.

## Kenny Roberts

I think Shark tried hard to lose himself in a fantasy world so he could forget what was going on with his mother. You know how you can transform reality when you're a child? Shark did that, pretending he was Flash Gordon—that old Buster Crabbe serial was running on TV in those days. In his imagination he was Flash and Christy Welty was Dale. She wasn't playing though—it was strictly Shark's fantasy. She was completely stand-offish, constantly snubbing him, only playing with other girls. But he'd say things like, "Someday I'm going to rescue her, and then she'll be different."

Then one day the Welty twins didn't come to school and Mrs. Healy, our first-grade teacher, said, "I have a very sad announcement, class. Yesterday evening, both Chris and Christy stepped onto a rainbow."

"*What?*" I said to Shark. I wasn't familiar with the expression.

"She means they're dead," Shark said.

## Gladys Frazer

It was a terrible tragedy. The Weltys had a swimming pool and somehow while Mrs. Welty was in the kitchen fixing dinner and Mr. Welty was on the phone, the twins drowned.

## Kenny Roberts

There was always something kind of weird about it. Just the fact that both of them drowned. The theory at the time was that one had tried to save the other, and in panic they'd drowned each other—which happens, I guess. But it just seemed very strange to me.

At recess after we heard about it Shark was very disturbed. That was probably why he forgot it was Friday, and when the air-raid siren went off at ten o'clock, which it always did in those days, he thought it was really a nuclear attack and peed in his pants.

## Gladys Frazer

The school called and said Shark had had an accident and I'd have to come and get him and change his clothes. So I did and he was very embarrassed. "I thought it was real," he said. "I thought we were all going to die."

"I know. It's all right," I said, and got him changed and drove him back to school.

When Mac came home that evening and I told him what had happened he saw red. "Oh Christ, that's the limit," he said.

"He couldn't help it, Mac. He thought the bombs were

28

falling," I said, and tried to explain about the Welty twins drowning, since I knew that was part of Shark's distress.

But Mac wouldn't listen. "Out to the garage," he said to Shark.

Mac kept a paddle out there, and Shark started bawling as Mac dragged him out through the sliding glass door. Then I heard Mac say, "Goddamn it!"

He'd tripped on Shark's toy truck on the patio, and Shark had got away.

## Kenny Roberts

Shark ran up Mackerel Drive. He had a pretty good headstart on his father but as he rounded the corner he looked back and saw Mac coming. Shark ducked up the alley and hid there. In a minute his father reached the alley, but not seeing him, continued on to Bonito Drive.

Shark ran on up the alley, his heart pounding, and as he passed the Welty house he heard someone splashing in the pool. Though he wasn't sure why, he said, that splashing sound—the knowledge that someone was using the pool—made his blood run cold.

He looked through the fence and saw Mr. and Mrs. Welty swimming in the pool—the pool where the day before Chris and Christy had drowned. He said they weren't saying anything to each other, they were just silently swimming. Shark got a very funny feeling because they didn't seem particularly sad.

Then they climbed out, first Mrs. Welty and then Mr. Welty, and they were both naked. Shark had never seen a naked adult before—he knew he shouldn't be looking. They dried off and lit cigarettes, never taking their eyes off each other, but still not saying a word.

Suddenly Shark stepped on a twig and the Weltys heard it. As they looked at the fence with alarm he took off in terror.

He ran to the end of the block, and then ran up Eel Road. In those days there was nothing on the other side of Eel Road except a field. And in the night sky above the field Shark saw it.

## Elliot Bernstein

A band of flashing lights. He knew instantly that it wasn't an airplane or a helicopter. It was hovering in the night sky, silently hovering. There was only one thing it *could* be. Shark would always describe that moment as "one of the most truly ecstatic of my life." After having been exposed to so many movie flying saucers, but always believing, you know, that it was essentially bullshit—now to actually *see one*. To see plainly and clearly what could be explained in no other way.

Shark was mesmerized. Then he heard running footsteps closing on him. But he wouldn't take his eyes off the craft in the sky. He knew why it had come. "Here I am," he said silently, knowing they could read his thoughts. "I'm ready, please take me. Please." He heard the footsteps getting closer. "Please save me. I don't care if you have scaly skin and huge exposed brains, it doesn't matter, as long as you take me away from here."

But the craft did not descend. And Mac grabbed him. "Now you're really going to get it, mister."

As his father began spanking him Shark at last identified the flying object. It was the Goodyear blimp—with a moving band of lights wrapped around it, the bulbs spelling out an advertising slogan for a popular product of the day. *No Bugs, M'Lady Shelf and Drawer Paper*, it said.

## Kenny Roberts

All things considered, Shark and Gladys seemed to get along pretty well. But then she indulged him tremendously. He ate what he wanted, when he wanted. But no matter how many times he gorged himself on Bosco and Three Musketeers, no matter how intense his fantasy life, I believe his mother's continuing deterioration affected him deeply. I think he was profoundly enraged at his father, but at seven years of age there wasn't much he could do about it.

Only once do I recall Shark's submerged resentment toward Gladys surfacing in a truly lethal way—though his chief aim may well have been to simply get at his father by depriving him of his tawdry sex obsession. Gladys was up on a ladder in her skin-tight pedalpushers hanging Christmas tree lights along the eaves of the house, giggling and wriggling as Mac held her hips—when suddenly, there was little Shark, pedaling directly toward the ladder on his tricycle, head lowered for the kill. At the last second Mac saw him coming and kicked over the tricycle, causing Shark to crash face-first on the lawn. He cut his chin pretty bad on a sprinkler-head—that's where that scar came from. I can still see him lying there bleeding on the dichondra while his father gave him hell.

That was the year that Winnie stepped onto a rainbow.

## Mac Trager

Winnie wasn't getting any better, and a few days before Christmas the doctor came to see her and agreed she should be permanently committed. Those arrangements were in the process of being made when the man upstairs called her number.

## Greg Spivey

Shark told me the story of his mother's death the Christmas Eve we got drunk together in Beirut during the filming of *Blue Light* in 1983. That it was Christmas Eve brought it back, no doubt, and as the tale unfolded I could easily see why he'd repressed it for years, for it was surely the most heart-rending Christmas story I had ever heard.

He described how as a little boy he'd go into his mother's room, toward the end I guess, and talk to her, trying to get her to respond. But she wouldn't, or couldn't. And then finally on Christmas Eve she did.

Shark said his father and Gladys were in the rumpus room that night watching TV, and there was a Christmas tree in the living room but his mother had never come out of her room to see it. And so, remembering how in previous years she'd loved the holidays, how they'd been her only joy in a neurotic, psychosomatic life, he went to her bedside and said, "Mommy, come look at the Christmas tree."

At that his mother smiled at him, Shark said, seeing him really for the first time in months. She smiled like a saint and said, "My precious baby." And Shark, who was seven then, led his mother into the living room and she looked at the brightly lit tree and there were tears in her eyes.

Then she looked at the bare tip of the tree and said, "Why, there's no angel." Then she smiled at Shark and said, "*You* can be my angel."

She led Shark back into her bedroom and dressed him in a long flowing white nightgown of hers so that he might roughly resemble a Christmas tree angel. And then, with floating, dreamy motions, she placed one of her hats, a white hat, on Shark's head. "Now you are mother's angel," she said, and lightly hugged him to her.

At that precise moment Shark's father burst into the room, wordlessly grabbing Shark by the arm, tearing off the nightgown, tearing off the hat. Then Mac threw Winnie back across the bed, slapping her again and again, until Gladys came in and pulled him off.

Shark, who didn't understand what was going on at all, ran to his mother, crying, "Mommy, Mommy." And Mac, still without saying a word, yanked Shark away from his mother, shoved him into his own bedroom, and slammed the door.

Shark said he was terrified all night and didn't sleep at all. He had no idea what he'd done or what his mother had done. All night he lay awake listening for the arrival of the one person he knew he could count on to provide at least momentary solace. But Santa Claus passed by the Trager house that night.

Then shortly after dawn, when Shark should have been excitedly anticipating opening his gifts, Mac returned. He threw open the door, glared about the room, then walked out.

He was looking for Winnie. It appeared she'd run off. But a few minutes after Mac left the room Shark heard Gladys scream.

## Gladys Frazer

It was a terrible thing to do to a child on Christmas Eve.

Of course, you know Mac was something of a bigot. I didn't dare tell him my second husband had been Jewish. Or that I'd once made love to a black jazz musician in New Orleans. He would have dropped me like a hot potato if he'd known about that.

More than anything he hated homosexuals though. That was the worst thing, along with being a Communist—since both could happen to anyone regardless of skin color or religion. And he'd heard somewhere that mothers made their sons go that way by dressing them as girls.

## Mac Trager

I admit I lost my temper, but I'm glad I did. It may have been the thing that stopped my son from going queer. And in that case it was worth it.

## Gladys Frazer

It was an awful night. When Mac and I finally went to bed he wanted to make love, but I didn't. After what had happened I just wasn't in the mood.

I got up once to check on Winnie. She was sleeping and did not appear to be injured, though when Mac was hitting her those slaps were loud. She was supposed to go into the hospital the day after Christmas. That had been my idea—to at least wait until after we'd opened the gifts, if only for Shark's sake.

When I went to her room in the morning she was gone.

We thought she might still be in the neighborhood, so we got in the car. There was this freezer in the garage, the flat kind with the door on top, and as we were backing out I noticed all this frozen food defrosting on the work bench, packages of peas and venison Mac had shot on a hunting trip, and I got a sick feeling in the pit of my stomach.

"Stop the car, Mac," I said and got out.

Then he saw the food and started to get angry. "What the hell. My venison! Has she completely lost her mind?"

Then I opened the freezer and there was Winnie inside. That was when I screamed.

## Greg Spivey

Shark ran out to the garage and his father said, "Don't look in there," but he did.

He said his mother was naked and her skin was very pale. Her eyes were closed and she looked peaceful. Shark said it wasn't terrible or gross at all, there was no sense of indignity or indecency, that on the contrary she looked like an angel, as if her lifeless body were reflecting where her soul had gone. Shark said he felt very peaceful looking at her and was barely aware of Gladys screaming hysterically behind him.

## Kenny Roberts

I was opening presents when we saw the ambulance pulled up across the street. Soon everyone on Mackerel Drive was out in the street to see what had happened, and I heard someone say, "Winnie crawled in the freezer and died."

I caught a few other comments to the effect that it was Mac's fault this had happened—what he and Gladys were doing was bound to lead to something like this. You know how people are.

I went up the Tragers' driveway as the ambulance attendants were removing Winnie's body on a stretcher. She was covered with a sheet but one foot was sticking out. I remember the chipped red polish on her toenails.

I saw Mac with his arm around Gladys on the patio swing. She looked numb. Then I saw Shark alone in the living room, his back to me as I approached the sliding glass door. He was opening his presents under the tree.

When he saw me he smiled with a strange cheerfulness as if nothing at all had happened, and said, "Look what I got."

It was a Viewfinder. I looked into it and saw an eerie tableau of the Cisco Kid and Pancho on their horses, both of which looked stuffed.

# 2 / **Vertigo**
## (1957–1961)

## Myrtle Butts

Gladys left not long after Winnie's death, which was the best thing she ever did.

## Gladys Frazer

I just couldn't take it, the way people looked at me at the local supermarket, and the things they said. Even the checker: "If you had any shame, you'd clear out."

And Mac wouldn't talk to me. You know how men get. He wouldn't say a word except, "Pass the salt."

Then one day he said, "My boy and I are going hunting." And I said, "Fine, but don't expect me to be here when you get back."

The last time I saw Mac he was backing out in that pickup, his rifle in the back window, Shark there beside him in his coonskin cap. The next day I caught the bus to Long Beach.

## Kenny Roberts

Once Gladys left, people started to forgive Mac. It was like he was paying for what he'd done by being lonely again. People were so small minded in the fifties, don't you think? Making everybody pay for every crummy little thrill.

Mac felt guilty too, I guess, 'cause it was about that time that he started going to the Skylark Methodist Church, dropping Shark off at Sunday School, which my parents forced me to attend as well.

Sometimes I almost wish I'd been raised a Catholic, terror at least being more interesting than tedium. If there is a purgatory it must resemble a Methodist Church basement with old ladies moving biblical figures around on a feltboard in overpowering waves of sweet perfume. Jesus Christ and the reek of gardenias. Shark and I always sat together, talking and giggling like evil schoolgirls. Don't misread that—it was entirely innocent, we were only seven years old. But I see now that adults were already beginning to look at us as if there might be something "unhealthy" going on.

## Myrtle Butts

I was heartened when I heard that Mac had begun attending church, and pleased when I heard he'd taken a fancy to Evelyn Burns, since she was certainly cut from a different strip than that Gladys.

## Mac Trager

I did seek the comfort of the Lord after Winnie's demise, not out of guilt but simply because it was something I'd neglected. I had always had a deep faith in God and country, but had somehow felt I was too rough-hewn for church. Then I reflected on the fact that John Wayne went, and he was a man, so I gave it a try. I can't say I didn't feel awkward at first, but there was a certain serenity to be derived from it, and I believe it helped Shark too. He was troubled by his mother's death and had begun to put on weight, though it was far from the problem it eventually became.

I just couldn't be both father and mother to Shark, and I believed at the time the Lord sensed that. Those thoughts were in my mind, I know, the sunny Sunday morning the pastor introduced me to Evelyn Burns.

## Evelyn Burns

My husband, Fred, whom I had worshipped, had passed away the previous spring after a long, excruciating bout with cancer. Toward the end his testicles had swollen up like footballs. It was ghastly and terrible and in grief I had turned to God.

I was not that impressed with Mac on first meeting. He was goodlooking in a way, a little like Glenn Ford only more rough-hewn. But I'd heard things about him. I knew he had that Shell station, and in fact saw grease under his fingernails, and frankly felt I was a cut above that. Fred had been an executive at Petro-Chem in Costa Mesa, and we'd lived in a lovely home on Lido Isle, which sadly I had been forced to sell. When the proper time came for me to consider the possibility of remarriage I planned to look for a man still on his way up, not one pumping gas at the bottom of the ladder. But God, it would seem, had other ideas.

## Kenny Roberts

Evelyn Burns took over our Sunday school class when one of the old ladies died. She was maybe thirty-five, though she looked much younger, a radiant vision of wholesome purity with a face and smile like Loretta Young. She was one sick cunt though.

## Mac Trager

The next time I spoke to Evelyn was after Shark's prank. I was walking to the car with Shark after church when Evelyn came up and said, "Mr. Trager, can I have a word with you?"

Then she held up a flat piece of rough brown plastic and said Shark had put it on her Bible. "What is it?" I said. "It's plastic vomit," she said.

"Why did you do that?" I said to Shark.

"Because she makes me sick," he said, and I whacked his head right there in the parking lot.

Then I dropped Shark off and met Evelyn for coffee.

## Kenny Roberts

Shark just had this aversion to Evelyn right from the start, like he sensed she was a phony or something. Then when Mac started going out with her a lot, Shark just went nuts.

## Mac Trager

Evelyn was a stunning woman, as beautiful as Loretta Young, radiating a similar kind of goodness and decency. I knew of her late husband Fred because of his work on behalf of Americanism and was a bit intimidated by that at first. I'd heard him speak a few times and he was a real dynamo. So was Evelyn.

One Sunday after church I stopped by the small apartment she had on Pacific Coast Highway, and I laughed out loud and said, "Yes!" when I found out that she knew the score on the Reds and the niggers and the Jews.

## Kenny Roberts

She was a grassroots American fascist just like her husband. I don't mean conservative, I'm talking Zionist conspiracies and blacks are monkeys trying to mongrelize the white race and the whole sick bit. It wouldn't surprise me to learn that Mac and Evelyn never actually had sex, but just lay in bed listening to Mac's old wire recordings of Joseph McCarthy's speeches.

Shark had inherited his mother's portable TV, which he and I watched in his bedroom all the time. The local stations seemed to show a lot of old costume adventure movies on weekend afternoons in those days. Shark liked the Errol Flynn stuff especially, *The Sea Hawk, Captain Blood*. One Saturday we were watching some piece of dreck with Louis Hayward when Shark heard Evelyn talking with Mac in the living room and he just went crazy. He started pacing around in circles, groaning as Evelyn cackled in the living room. Then he buried his head under the pillow and pounded the bed. I guess he sensed what was coming.

## Mac Trager

I proposed to Evelyn on the second anniversary of Joe McCarthy's death. I took her out to a fancy prime rib restaurant and we drank a champagne toast to a man I have always considered a true American martyr, and then I popped the question. She was such a fine, decent woman, not a cheap piece of trash like Gladys had been, that I suppose I wasn't sure I deserved her. But she smiled and said yes, though we had yet to sleep together, and did not until the honeymoon. She was that kind of gal.

## Kenny Roberts

Mac took Evelyn back to the house and together they told Shark they were going to get married. But things quickly turned ugly with Shark hitting Evelyn, you know, pounding her with his fists at about cunt level, saying, "I hate you, I hate you," until Mac whacked him and sent him to his room.

That night Shark climbed out his bedroom window and ran away. He was gone for nearly a week, and since he was only eight years old the cops were out looking for him, and it was quite a big deal.

They finally found him in the Balboa Theater. He had slipped in during a Saturday kiddie matinee and hidden in the balcony, which was closed off in those days. At night after everyone had gone he would gorge himself at the concession counter—which was what had finally precipitated a thorough search of the premises. *Vertigo* was playing there that week. He told me he watched it something like twenty-four times.

## Mac Trager

I was hopping mad as I brought Shark home. "You are going to pay a price for the worry you've put us through," I told him.

"What are you going to do?" he said.

"I don't know yet," I told him. "I haven't decided. I'll think of something while Evelyn and I are on our honeymoon. You'd better be trembling, mister. 'Cause it is going to be bad."

Then I left him in the care of the Roberts. Why I ever did that I don't know.

## Kenny Roberts

It was Easter break when Mac and Evelyn belatedly went on their honeymoon, driving up the coast somewhere—though Berchtesgaden would have been more appropriate. One evening my parents took us to the Flying Wing Drive-In to see a movie I hated at the time, but which I rather like now, Orson Welles's *Touch of Evil*. It's a dark film, aggressively grotesque and bizarre, and at that point I was addicted to the sunny escapist world of musical comedies, you see. Shark, however, was galvanized by the film, responding to it as if it were somehow an exact representation of his inner state at the time—or so it seems in retrospect. I remember him chuckling cynically throughout the movie—a cynical eight-year-old!—chuckling in a way that mirrored Orson Welles's exhausted chuckle in the film, chuckling like a fat and evil old man as he wolfed down Milk Duds. Shark had quite a weight problem by then.

A few days later my parents took us to see *Gigi* and I was in rapture. I gushed about it for hours afterwards, asking Shark if he didn't agree it was the best movie either one of us had ever seen. He shrugged. "It's okay for what it is," he said.

Regardless, he did indulge my favorite pastime, which was lip-syncing showtunes before the dining room mirror. I would play *South Pacific* and *Carousel* and *Gigi,* and Shark and I would perform these little playlets for our own amusement, just having a gay old time. Actually, it was innocent, at least on Shark's part. It's funny, but in retrospect I see he always played the guy. Without even thinking, he would just instinctively do the Rossano Brazzi part while I would instinctively go for Mary Martin or whoever. But we were completely naive. We had no idea we were playing a dangerous gender role game.

Then one warm afternoon we were listening to *Oklahoma!* in the rumpus room as my parents lay sunning out by the pool. Shark and I were in our bikini swimsuits, which probably made it look even worse. Gordon MacCrae and Shirley Jones were singing their duet of "People Will Say We're In Love," Shark lip-syncing MacCrae's deep masculine voice as he held me in his arms while I batted my eyelashes repulsively camping it up as Shirley, when suddenly Evelyn walked in. She and Mac had come back from their honeymoon a day early.

The look she gave us could have killed bugs. Suddenly I just knew we'd been doing something terrible, something evil, though I didn't really know what it was exactly. In a fury, Evelyn tore the needle from the record, scratching it. The way she glared at me made my skin crawl. It was the first time I'd ever felt real hatred from anyone. She stormed out to my parents. Shark and I couldn't hear what she said to them, but my parents looked puzzled and then frightened.

Evelyn stormed back through the house and across the street to get Mac. Then Mac stormed in and yanked Shark by the arm all the way across the street.

The upshot was that Shark and I were forbidden to play with each other ever again.

## Evelyn Burns

I saw right away that Shark's friendship with the Roberts boy was abnormal, so Mac ended it. He was determined that Shark would grow up to be normal, but after the Roberts boy left the picture Shark sulked and put on weight and refused to make new friends.

I tried to get along with Shark. The day I moved in, Mac and I sat him down and I said, "Listen, I know I'll never replace your mother . . ."

And Shark said, "You're right, you won't, you whore."

Mac hit Shark and he ran to his room. Later that night he tried to kill himself. Or so he said.

## Mac Trager

He took a bottle of Sleep-Eze but nothing really happened. We wouldn't even have known if he hadn't told us. In the morning he came out with the empty bottle and said, "I took all of these last night. If she doesn't leave the house, next time I'll use one of your guns."

Evelyn sighed and said, "I've heard everything now."

I figured it was bullshit. But I did lock up my guns.

## Evelyn Burns

Those two years with Mac were a nightmare. I don't know why I stayed as long as I did. Shark would barely speak to me at all. If I asked him a question he'd say, ''Yip,'' or ''Nope,'' the minimum possible. I could feel his hatred every time I stepped into that house.

Mac and I had our own problems though. He was in the mood all the time and I wasn't. I tried explaining to Mac that I couldn't do the deed without seeing Fred in his last days with his testicles swollen up like footballs. But Mac wouldn't listen. I went along for a while till the migraines started. Then I took this medication that did something to my skin so that it was painful to be touched.

## Mac Trager

I worshiped Evelyn but she was cold as a fish. Then the headaches started and I watched the marriage slowly die.

## Greg Spivey

Shark told me that the single high point during the years his father was married to Evelyn was the afternoon Mac took him to *The Searchers* at the Balboa Theater. Evelyn was out of town visiting relatives at the time, the marriage was already shaky, and in retrospect Shark said he realized Mac had begun drinking early in the day in a fit of self-pity and was drunk as he and Shark arrived at the theater just as the John Ford classic was beginning. Shark told me he felt that his father's intoxication accounted for what then occurred, a simple action rendered extraordinary by its utter absence from Shark's young life. As the two of them watched John Wayne move across the sweeping vistas on the CinemaScope screen Mac put his arm around his son and Shark rested his head against his father's chest.

Well, at the very end of the movie—which to my mind is one of the truly poignant moments in American film—where John Wayne stands framed in the doorway, watching the re-united family enter the house which he can never enter, then turns to the bright western vista, the comfort of family and culture forever denied him as he rides away eternally alone—

just at that point, Shark told me, his father said in a choked-up voice, "That's you and me, son. We're both gonna end up like that someday."

Shark didn't understand what his father meant at the time. "But I do now," he told me twenty years later.

## Mac Trager

Shark told me once in the late seventies that the one time he really felt close to me as a kid was when I took him to see Duke Wayne in *The Searchers*. I told him I had fond recollections of it as well. But the truth was the whole thing was pretty much a blank. I'd been drunk as a skunk that afternoon.

## Evelyn Burns

Despite its side effects, the migraine medication did allow me to function, and in 1959 I took a full-time job at the local Republican headquarters, so I could be in on the ground floor of Dick Nixon's campaign.

## Jeannie Goodhew

I used to babysit Shark, and I'm not sure to this day which of us was more lonely or miserable. We both had weight problems, and that's all we ever did: sit there and watch TV and stuff our faces. He liked those old movies they showed at night when the kids were supposed to be in bed. *Double Indemnity*, I remember that one. "I'm not sure you should watch this," I said. "It may be too adult." In those days people thought those characters were amoral.

There was one with Farley Granger where a carousel flew apart at the end. Shark really liked that.

His parents weren't getting along. His dad was always working late at the gas station, and his stepmother was always off doing something in politics somewhere.

## Herbert Banton

Shark was in my sixth-grade class at Pizarro Elementary School and you could see he was a boy in trouble. He was fat and had no friends and the other kids made fun of him. His nickname was "The Blob," and the more his peers ridiculed him, the more obese he became, in a viciously circular attempt to further insulate himself from their ever-escalating cruelty. His work was listless and barely adequate. Here was a boy who had already given up on life, a fact driven home by the paper he turned in on what he'd done over Easter vacation. "I thought of different ways to kill myself," he wrote, and then listed fifty separate ways. It was clearly a cry for help. I called his parents in for a conference.

## Mac Trager

Shark had turned into a fat sack of lazy shit, it was as simple as that. We met some yo-yo teacher of his who spouted out a lot of psychological crap. But I knew what Shark needed.

## Herbert Banton

The conference was a disaster. As Mac Trager listened to my expression of concern his face grew redder and redder. Then he began punching his fist in his palm, plainly a nervous, compulsive gesture which nonetheless made me uneasy.

I showed the stepmother the suicide essay. She skimmed it, quickly losing interest, and began asking me very pointed political questions. Did I teach Americanism, that sort of thing. I said, "Mr. and Mrs. Trager, your son needs psychiatric help."

Mac Trager said, "This is horseshit," and they left.

## Jeannie Goodhew

It was so sad. I used to drop Shark off at the kiddie matinee at the Balboa Theater. When I came to pick him up, he would be waiting there on the bus bench in front of the theater all alone. He was huge by then and so depressed he would barely even talk to me.

Then one afternoon the Balboa manager caught me and said Shark had broken a seat and would not be allowed in the theater again unless he lost a great deal of weight. "We can't risk being sued if he hurts himself," the manager said.

Shark was glum and said very little, but inside he must have been humiliated. On the way home he did his Alfred Hitchcock impression. He could even make his face look like Hitchcock's, and of course with the weight . . . But it wasn't funny, there was something despairing about it.

I think the only thing that saved him was that his stepmother finally left.

## Lorna Trager

Evelyn was gung-ho for Nixon in 1960, and during the campaign there was some kind of coffee klatsch that Nixon dropped in on to thank all these Republican women who were working on his behalf. Evelyn was pretty high up in the organization by then, the head of some committee, and the way I heard it, right in the middle of the coffee klatsch, with all these people standing around, Evelyn said to Nixon, "Off the record, Dick, once you're elected what are you going to do about the kikes?"

Well, everybody just dropped their load, because that kind of thing wasn't said anymore. Supposedly, Nixon just laughed as if Evelyn was joking, then said, "Say, who baked this cake?"

But later he sent down the word that he wanted that woman out of the campaign, and the next day Evelyn was fired.

## Mac Trager

The day Evelyn got fired from the Nixon campaign she came home and went completely berserk. At first it was just the Reds and the Jews and Nixon's "spineless advisors" she was mad at. I said, "Honey, I know," and tried to put my arms around her and she turned into a banshee. She said things to me then I could never forgive, even though I knew she was distraught. "You bore me," she said. "You make me sick, you always have."

Well, I hit her and told her to get out of the house and she left. I heard the car start and ran out to the street and said, "Oh no, you don't. You can walk." So we fought for the car keys, then she got out and walked, screaming, "You're no good in bed," for all the neighbors to hear.

As I walked back to the house I saw Shark watching from his bedroom window. "Are you happy now?" I said. By then several neighbors had come out to watch.

Shark just looked at me and pulled down his window shade. I could hear some old movie on his TV.

## Lorna Trager

Mac was worried for a long time that Evelyn was going to take him to the cleaners. All he had was the station and that house. But Mac was funny. Once she was gone he wanted her back. She'd gone to Texas and he began calling her when he got drunk. But she met some Texas oilman and said, "I don't want anything you have, Mac. Just don't call me anymore." Then she got a new number.

Mac was bitter. I was bitter then too, since my husband Phil had left me for a younger woman in Kansas City. I hadn't seen my brother in almost ten years when Mac invited me out to California in 1961. I arrived that winter and slept on a little cot on the sun porch.

Shark and I hit it off right away.

# 3 / The Thrill
of It All
(1962–1965)

## Brad Jenkins

I was Shark's best friend in junior high. We moved into the
house across the street on Mackerel Drive when the Roberts
moved out. I know Shark and Kenny Roberts had been friends
at one time. I only saw Kenny once, but he acted just like a
sissy. You could tell he was going to grow up to be a fruit.

I was tall for my age and had a bad acne problem. I got the
nickname "Pus," which I hated, but it stuck. I was into math
and science, and then after I met Shark, movies. We went to
the show all the time.

## Lorna Trager

Shark became best friends with Pus Jenkins, who'd moved in
across the street where the homo boy used to live. Mac had a
thing about homos, you know. I heard once he'd had a bad
experience in a hobo jungle when he was a boy during the

Depression. He was worried about Shark's new friendship with Pus until he eavesdropped on them talking in the backyard one day. They were talking dirty but about girls, you know. So Mac turned to me and said, "I guess it's all right."

## Brad Jenkins

Shark liked Lorna. I guess everybody did. She wasn't too bright but she had a sunny disposition. She was pretty but not in a cheap way. She would always be out watering the flowers, or hanging clothes on the line, singing some tra-la song. And sometimes when the sun was behind her you could see through her dress.

## Greg Spivey

Shark liked to say that his early childhood had been a "dark, grim, black and white era, about as much fun as an FBI surveillance film." But when his aunt came to live in the house "a luminous new WarnerColor age began." He felt that she'd literally saved his life and "probably prevented me from hating all women for all time."

## Brad Jenkins

I think Lorna gave him his first movie camera.

## Lorna Trager

It was my idea. Mac wanted to give him a set of barbells. But I said, "Oh come on, Mac. Let's pop for this Bell and Howell. It's Christmas. Don't you want to have some movies of the tree?"

## Brad Jenkins

It was an eight-millimeter camera, not even Super 8—I don't think Super 8 was even around yet. Right away, Shark really got into it. And he didn't just do home movie stuff. Right from the start he tried to make real movies with plots and so forth, using other kids in the neighborhood. He was still fat, but that camera brought him out of his shell.

## Julie Ferguson

I was in one of Shark's silent movies. I played a girl who saw a flying saucer land. He used this old pie tin for the saucer. Twenty years later when my husband and I went to see *Blue Light* and they showed the scene with the girl who sees the flying saucers, I said, "My God, Burt, that's me."

## Brad Jenkins

We both liked science fiction movies. *Forbidden Planet, Earth vs. the Flying Saucers, War of the Worlds*—the kind of movies they showed at the Balboa Theater Saturday matinee. Shark and I would leave the theater and he'd talk about the movies all the way home. Then he'd make films of kids screaming and pointing, then cut to a shot of a Martian made out of red clay climbing out between two pie tins. Those movies were pretty good when you think that he couldn't even do any editing, except what he did just by choosing what he shot.

## Mac Trager

I took a dim view of the camera from the start. It was just a way for his sick imagination to run wild when he should have been doing something physical. He was in some special P.E. class for spastics and queers because of his weight. When I found out about the queers I lowered the boom.

## Lorna Trager

Mac sent Shark to a doctor who put him on a diet that included taking pills. In those days people didn't know as much about speed as they do now.

## Brad Jenkins

Shark started losing weight as if by magic. He was glad, but I think it scared him too. By then he was used to being the fat kid all the time. Plus he was starting to develop. You know, his voice changed and he got hair and a man's dick. As the weight came off, his dad had him switched back to regular P.E. and put him on a crash sports course.

## Lorna Trager

I was glad to see Shark lose the weight. But I think Mac pushed him too hard. Mac would do things like throw a football at Shark when he wasn't looking, shouting, "Catch!" too late. When the football hit Shark in the head, Mac would shout, "Come on, you pantywaist. On your toes!"

It got so that Shark would flinch when Mac just walked in the room.

## Brad Jenkins

Shark's dad pushed him real hard. Shark started getting muscles but he was nervous and jumpy all the time. He was still making these little science fiction movies, but if somebody screwed up he'd lose his temper real quick. So after a while the other kids didn't want to do it anymore.

Then one day he said, "Come on, let's go see *Psycho*, it's playing with *The Birds*. I wanna check out that shower scene again."

Well, I got kind of excited because *Psycho* was forbidden. My parents wouldn't let me go see it back when it first came out because they'd heard it was too extreme. So we went off and saw it, sneaking in through this exit door. We watched it a whole bunch of times so that Shark could look at the editing. We watched it until it really *did* something to me, and Shark lost all interest in science fiction. "I'm going to make a movie like that," he said. And one afternoon he tried to get Julie Ferguson to take off her clothes in the shower.

## Julie Ferguson

Shark tricked me into coming over to his house. There was no one there but Pus and him, and Shark took out his camera. "Come on, Julie, take off your clothes," he said with a funny look in his eye. When I said no he said, "Come on. Janet Leigh did it."

When I said, "No, she didn't, that was a movie," Shark picked up this knife.

## Brad Jenkins

I don't think Shark ever intended to stab her or anything. He just wanted his way. But I made him put down the knife and Julie ran out of the house. Nothing ever happened. If she told her parents, they decided to drop it.

I thought about it later though, the look on her face when she saw that knife, and it made me hot.

## Greg Spivey

According to Shark, he was playing sick to get out of taking a test the Friday President Kennedy was shot. He was home in bed, "masturbating to a *Nugget* magazine," and just about to "pop," using his term for it, when his aunt, watching daytime TV elsewhere in the house, cried out: "Oh God, no, no!"

Shark was subsequently "awed by the sense of history taking place," and exasperated because his portable TV had been temporarily taken away from him as punishment for bad grades, and his father, who'd never liked the president, obstinately refused to watch the extensive television coverage of the assassination's aftermath. "All the networks were live that weekend," Shark recalled, "but my father stayed tuned to a cheesy local channel showing 'Highway Patrol' reruns and 1930s B westerns. If I hadn't been over at the Jenkins' Sunday morning I would've missed seeing Oswald bite the dust."

Shark confessed to "an illicit ambivalence" about that weekend. "As terrible as it was that Kennedy had been killed, the national trauma did provide an exhilarating sense of heightened reality, a feeling that life had broken free of its humdrum everyday restraints, that something had really *happened*. In an innocent adolescent way I guess I just found it very good drama and was so jacked up I barely slept the entire weekend, taking more of my weight control pills than usual, since I'd discovered they increased my alertness, though I knew nothing at the time about speed."

## Brad Jenkins

Shark spent most of that weekend watching TV at our house. When Oswald got it, Shark clapped his hands and said, "Man, this is *wild!* I wonder who's gonna get it *next!*" And my parents kind of looked at him.

## Lorna Trager

I could see the diet pills were affecting Shark's mind. He was jumpy all the time and started mumbling to himself. I talked to Mac but he said, "Aw hell, there's nothing wrong with him that running a few more laps won't cure."

## Brad Jenkins

Shark really changed in junior high. He kept getting more muscles and hair on his chest and got one of the biggest dicks around. He was sex obsessed too. He told me he beat off five times a day. We would talk about different girls at school and I began to feel jealous because sometimes the girls would look at him, but they never looked at me except to throw up because of my acne.

Shark started dressing like a hood too. At Cortez Junior High there were hoods and soshes. The hoods wore white T-shirts and unwashed blue Levis while the sosh guys wore white Levis and Madras shirts. The hoods came from our neighborhood and the even worse area up by Costa Mesa while the soshes lived down in the nice houses by the beach. Shark went around with a rubber in his wallet saying, "I'm gonna get me some socialite ass."

It was about that time that he first saw Kathy Petro.

## Paige Petro

We bought the place in Newport Beach in '64 so Jack could be near the Costa Mesa plant, which was expanding then. It was a stunning house, a showplace really, which we needed since we entertained. How I adored it, I truly did. The view, the sunsets! The ocean breeze! Orange County was the future then, the ideal place to raise a family.

## Neal Ridges

There was an obsessively repeated tracking shot in Shark's notorious "non-linear" student film which, he told me in the late seventies, came as close as anything he'd ever put on celluloid to capturing his first impression of Kathy Petro. Although I had known nothing of Kathy Petro per se when I'd served as his student "line-producer" on the film in 1968, it was obvious from Shark's driven perfectionism as we set up the shot that he was bent on recreating a key moment of his life.

It took us an entire day to get that shot. The silver Mercedes had to sweep into the gas station at just the right speed, so that it appeared to be floating. The father who was driving—the Jack Petro figure—had to remain in darkness despite the bright sunlight of the Newport Beach day. His blonde daughter however, occupying the passenger seat, had to appear to "glow from within." That was hard to achieve. But we finally did it with a carefully adjusted sun-gun.

It was an extraordinary, near-hallucinatory shot, and it did capture the quasi-religious tone Shark wanted to impart to that "first enraptured emanation of love."

The silver Mercedes floats up to the pumps, the camera tracking in on the luminous teen angel, so fresh, so white, so light and pretty. So blindingly blonde. So sunny, so cheerful, so rich and privileged, yet so innocent and unconceited. Startling green eyes and a sunshine smile, a California smile. Sweetly delicate peachfrost mouth. She places a nearly empty cream soda bottle to her lusciously pearlescent peach lips, and you can almost *taste* the vanilla as she takes a final swallow. Now she smiles at the camera—at young Shark in his father's gas station—she smiles so cheerfully, so good-naturedly, not stuckup at all. "Hi," she says, holding out the empty cream soda bottle. "Could you do something with this?" she laughs lightly, infectiously, as if to indicate she doesn't mean to impose.

"Hi. Could you do something with this?" Again and again that shot replayed, at least two dozen times, a compulsive leitmotif of Shark's first sound film, as it was, I believe, and would always remain, of his mental and emotional life.

## Kathy Petro

I remembered that first encounter later, of course. But at the time Shark made no special impression on me. He was just some hoody boy at the gas station I asked to take my cream soda bottle. If I smiled at him I certainly didn't mean anything by it. I tried to be nice to everyone in those days. The golden rule and all that.

## Brad Jenkins

Once Shark and I walked past this big house on the Balboa peninsula, a big Spanish-style place with a tile roof and a silver Mercedes-Benz in the court beyond the iron gate. "I'm in love with the girl who lives there," he said.

Later I found out the Petros had moved in there. Jack Petro owned Petro-Chem and knew John Wayne and all these big Republicans. He was a millionaire many times over.

## Neal Ridges

Shark said he became "actively obsessed" with Kathy Petro right from that very first encounter. He began dreaming of her at night, fantasizing about her. "If I'd seen the future," he told me, "I would have kept that cream soda bottle she handed me with her peachfrost lipstick on the rim as the ultimate icon of my life."

In retrospect he admitted that the speed he was taking had probably contributed to his fixation. "Speed is very mental. It makes it easy to stay locked on one thing." At the time, of course, he didn't really understand what his "appetite pills" were doing to him. But even without the speed, Shark contended, "I would still have lost my heart forever on a sunny summer afternoon."

Sometimes he would ride his bicycle past the Petro house in the evening, looking up at the windows, imagining what Kathy might be doing at that moment. He would visualize her seated at her vanity, applying her peachfrost lipstick, and instead of perfume the air would be laced with the scent of vanilla, the cream soda flavor Shark would then and forever always associate with Kathy Petro. He had already switched from Coke to cream soda, in fact virtually subsisting on little more than the soft drink and his Obetrol tablets.

One evening at sunset, he said, as he peddled past the Petro house he saw Kathy in an upstairs window. She was naked behind the diaphanous curtain as she prepared to dress and Shark was so mesmerized he crashed his bicycle into a parked car, severely bruising his leg.

## Brad Jenkins

Shark and I were walking along the strand by the yacht club one day when he saw Kathy Petro coming up the landing from her father's boat. The way we were walking we were going to cross her path in about half a minute, and Shark whispered to me, "This is it. Disappear."

By then I was already sick of hearing about her, 'cause Shark talked about her all the time, even though they'd only met once at his dad's station. But he said he thought about her when he jerked off at night, and he knew she was thinking about him too. I told him he was crazy and he got mad. "You wait and see," he said. "It's just a matter of time."

So I stood there on the strand, pretending to look out at the boats, and let Shark go on ahead alone. He crossed her path as she reached the strand and she almost kept going. Then she stopped and she and Shark talked but it looked like she was in a hurry to continue on.

## Kathy Petro

He startled me that day, I guess. I was in this extra-good mood, when suddenly he stepped in my path like a dark cloud blocking out the sun. He wasn't bad-looking exactly, but into this hoody thing I found very unappetizing. He tried making this awful, tense small talk, like was I going to Cortez Junior High in the fall and so forth, and something about him really made me uncomfortable. Not scared exactly, just, I don't know, repelled. He had this starving dog look in his eyes.

Finally Daddy called to me from the boat, which gave me an excuse to get away.

"Who was that?" Daddy said.

"I don't know," I told him.

## Brad Jenkins

When Shark came back I asked him what happened. ''She wants me,'' he said.

''Yeah, I could tell.''

''What do you know, Brad?''

''I know she's out of your league,'' I said.

Shark exploded. ''You don't know shit, you ugly geek. But I know one thing. I'm never going to get to first base with a stomach-turning creep like you lurking in the background. So take a hike, Brad. Okay? Get lost.''

He really hurt my feelings that day. He apologized a few days later and we were friends again, but it was never really the same.


## Neal Ridges

According to Shark, the kiss in *Tropics*—that swirling preposterously delirious shot of the lovers' juicy, sweaty faces, all Gauguin colors and crypto-von Sternbergian South Seas pictorialism—came the closest of any kiss in any of his films to conveying the ''nearly unbearable rapture'' of his first experience with Kathy.

It happened at the Flying Wing Drive-In on a Friday night late in the summer of 1964. Shark had gone there with a carload of older guys to drink beer and watch Ann Margaret in *Kitten with a Whip*. But the co-feature was still playing, Doris Day's unctuous vehicle, *The Thrill of It All,* when a new car swept in and Shark saw Kathy Petro in the passenger seat.

His heart started pounding, but several minutes passed before he got up the nerve to get out and approach the car, which had parked several rows down. As he did he saw the driver, an older girl friend of Kathy's, going off with a boy to another car, leaving Kathy to watch the movie alone.

Shark stepped to Kathy's window and said, ''Hi.'' He said she looked at him ''dreamily,'' and sighed but didn't speak. And although he'd been prepared to strike up a conversation, he suddenly realized with a stunning, galvanizing clarity that she didn't want him to, that it wasn't even necessary, that she did in fact want him as much as he wanted her. That what she wanted right then in that moment was simply for him to kiss her. And so he did.

He kissed her through the window, long and deeply, and she

moaned. More excited than he'd ever been, Shark broke the kiss long enough to go around to the driver's side and climb into the car, where the kiss resumed despite the window-speaker counterpoint of a "classic Doris Day fit of mock-indignation in response to some 'wolfish male's' advances"—a seemingly inconsequential detail of considerable significance, I think. Kathy moaned meltingly, and Shark soon had a rock-hard erection, and knew that the time had come. But as he reached under her skirt, Kathy abruptly snapped out of her trance. "Oh my God, what are you doing? What am *I* doing? Oh no, look, you shouldn't be here. Oh, Jeez, here comes my girl friend."

That last remark jolted Shark sufficiently that he climbed out of the car, quickly pulling out his shirt tail to hide his erection, only then realizing that Kathy's girl friend was nowhere to be seen. Confused, he tried to open the car door again, but Kathy pushed down the lock a second before he could. Then she rolled up her window, locking the passenger door too.

"Look, I'm sorry," Shark said, thinking it was simply that he'd gone too far.

But Kathy wouldn't look at him. "Please go away," she said, covering her face in embarrassment. "Please just go away."

Shark walked a ways away, then lingered, watching the car for a while, hurt and angry, but most of all confused. "Her refusal to look at me," Shark told me fifteen years later, "that was the thing that really killed me. One minute she's giving me everything I've ever wanted. And the next it's like she's saying I'm a total piece of shit."

## Kathy Petro

That night was so strange. I had this sinus problem and had taken an antihistamine which really knocked me for a loop. I shouldn't have even gone out, but I was curious about *Kitten with a Whip*, which was supposed to be racy and everything. But I was so woozy from the antihistamine I couldn't even follow the plot of that Doris Day film.

I didn't really even know what was happening at first when Shark started kissing me, I swear. Suddenly it was just happening and it felt good and everything, and the next thing I knew he was in the car. But when he touched my you-know-what, it was just like a bucket of ice water in the face. 'Cause I was fourteen and still a virgin and everything and suddenly realized: Oh my God, I can't do this, not with him. My reputation would be ruined forever.

## Brad Jenkins

"She fucked with my head," Shark said one day at Cortez Junior High as we watched Kathy Petro crossing the quad. "But I still want her."

Then a few weeks later he approached her at lunch. She was with her blonde girl friends and Shark was only there a minute. He came back pissed off, and the blonde girls were laughing at him behind his back.

## Kathy Petro

I tried to just block the drive-in incident out of my mind. Fortunately, I didn't have any classes with Shark. When I did see him at a distance I felt this flush of embarrassment though. At times like that I'd wish he'd just go away to some other school.

Then one day he came up and asked if I'd like to go see the Beatles' movie *Help!* "No," I said, just like that. It was at lunch and my girl friends were there and I was afraid he would say something about the drive-in. He was so hoody and everything I didn't want anyone to even think for a minute I would even consider going out with him, let alone anything else.

"Why not?" he said.

"Isn't it obvious?" I said. "I don't go out with boys like you."

"Why are you making it so hard?" he said, which scared me a little for some reason.

"Look, I'm just trying to eat my lunch, okay? Do you mind?"

At that he walked away.

Later I thought: It's too bad in a way. He could be cute if he weren't so hoody. If we were on a desert island it might not be that bad. But we weren't. Besides, even if we were it might not be that great, 'cause he had a look in his eyes that made me think he might actually be a little crazy.

## Lorna Trager

Two policemen woke me up with their pounding on the door one morning. I got Shark out of bed and as soon as he saw the policemen he started shaking. Mac got up and when the cops told him what Shark had done he saw red. The cops went into Shark's bedroom and took all his movie film, and then they took him down to the station.

## Kathy Petro

I'll never forget it. We were watching "Bonanza" in the den when the phone rang and Daddy went into the other room to answer it. In a minute he came back as white as a sheet. "Jack, what on earth?" my mother said.

When he told us I kind of went into shock at first. Then I started screaming.

## Brad Jenkins

Shark told me later that one night he'd been thinking about Kathy and without really knowing why he just got up from his bed and got his movie camera and walked on down to her house. When he got there he saw a light on in her window, and the gate was open so he went into the court and climbed up the trellis to the balcony of her bedroom.

He saw her through the curtains, trying to decide what to wear that night, a Rolling Stones record playing on her 45 player. She was just wearing panties and a bra, he said, holding up these different dresses, looking at herself in the mirror, pausing every once in a while to take a hit off a bottle of cream soda.

Shark said he just watched her for a long time like he was spellbound. He said he loved her so much he felt like he could almost be content just looking at her forever. Finally though he lifted his camera and started to film her as she bounced around the room, singing to the records, modeling different clothes.

Then suddenly a record ended and the whirring sound of the camera seemed loud. Right then she started toward the balcony and Shark was sure she'd heard the camera and was going to catch him.

But she turned at the last minute and went into her own private bathroom. So Shark stepped over to the bathroom window, which was high up, the bottom of it fogged but the top part clear, so he could look right in and see Kathy.

He said she finished off this bottle of cream soda and then took off her bra and panties like she was going to take a bath, but she sat down on this pink velvet chair instead. Then she started doing things. You know, dirty things. And she finally used that cream soda bottle to do something real dirty.

Shark said he didn't want to film her doing that, 'cause he knew it was real wrong, but it was like he couldn't stop himself. By then there was more music playing so she didn't hear the camera, and his finger pressed the trigger till all the film was shot.

He said that what he wanted to do was open the window and crawl on in. But he knew that would really freak her out. So he left instead. Climbing down from the balcony, he was shaking so much with both fear and excitement he almost dropped the camera.

Then he was scared to get the film developed, 'cause back in those days anything dirty was still a big deal. Finally a week later he shot some more film of boats and took it all into Doolittle Camera. "Got some good boat stuff," he told Mr. Doolittle. But he said his heart was pounding.

When Mr. Doolittle developed the film he recognized Kathy with the cream soda bottle and called Jack Petro. Jack Petro called the cops.

## Kathy Petro

The worst part was not knowing who'd seen the film. I could never go into Doolittle Camera again, knowing that rabbity little man had seen me like that. I asked Daddy if the cops looked at the film, and he said, "No, they gave it to me and I destroyed it." I didn't have the courage to ask him if *he'd* looked at it. I guess I didn't want to know. Years later Mom told me he had, just so he could see how bad it was.

## Paige Petro

It was a terrible ordeal for Kathy, who was just so unaware of the perverse, awful things people can do to one another in this world. It was definitely a dark cloud. But we did all we could to make sure it passed as quickly as possible.

## Lorna Trager

Once the cops were sure Shark's other movies weren't dirty, they were ready to let him go. They called around dinner time to say Mac could come down and get him.

"I'll tell you what, Gus," Mac said on the phone to this one cop he kind of knew. "Why don't you keep him till morning? That boy's been headed for trouble for a long time now, and this goddamn movie thing's the limit. Maybe a night behind bars'll teach him a lesson."

It didn't seem like that bad a thing since Shark was alone in the juvenile section of the city hall jail. But then this cop suggested another idea that would *really* put the fear of God into Shark.

## Elliot Bernstein

The way Shark described it, he was alone in the juvenile hall section of the Newport Beach jail, "with nothing to do, nothing to read except the graffiti," when he heard the doors opening and assumed they were finally coming to release him. He felt both relief and apprehension, anticipating a severe paddling from Mac once he got home. But his fear of that survivable ordeal was quickly overridden by an incalculably greater terror.

"Come on, buddy boy. Not that way, this way," the cop said, steering Shark back through the station to a waiting prisoner transport van.

"But you're letting me go, aren't you?" Shark said. "My dad must be waiting in the front—"

"I don't know about any dad," the cop said with a chuckle. "We're shipping your ass to the big house. Let's see how tough you are in County Jail."

Shark began to hyperventilate.

## Lorna Trager

The idea was to take Shark to the Orange County Jail and put him through the admission procedure, all the while acting like they were going to put him in with the hardened adult prisoners, but not really do it. They told Mac they could lead Shark through the cellblock and let the adult prisoners verbally taunt him so he would know what lay in store for him if he didn't straighten out.

But somewhere along the line somebody got their signals crossed, because the cops called Mac in the morning and said, "Mr. Trager, we're having some trouble locating your son."

## Woody Hazzard

Shark would never really talk about what had happened in County Jail except to say he'd seen "some very bad things."

## Lorna Trager

Mac was upset to the point of being kind of numb. The cops called back in a little while and said, "It's all right, Mr. Trager. We've found him."

"Is he . . . still my boy?" Mac said into the phone. His face was ashen.

## Mac Trager

I felt like hell. I only intended to scare him, that's all. I didn't want to hear what had happened, I didn't want to know.

"I've got to go down and open the station," I said to my sister. "You'll have to swing by the jail and pick him up."

## Lorna Trager

I felt awful for Shark. They said he was all right, that he hadn't been hurt, but he seemed too quiet. As we walked to the car outside the jail some prisoners started hooting from the windows, yelling awful things at Shark, things I blocked out of my mind, they were so awful. They said things to me too. I think they thought I was his mother.

We were both silent for a long time in the car. He stared out the window.

"Look," I finally said. "Your father didn't mean for you to be thrown in with those men—"

"What are you talking about?" he said softly, but clearly surprised.

I saw I should've kept my mouth shut. But it was too late, so I went on and told him about Mac's plan to teach him a lesson.

He hardly said a word, and his expression was blank, but I could tell he was shaken.

Then I said something stupid, trying to cover up my own bad feelings, I guess. "Anyway, that doesn't excuse what you did. How could you make that awful dirty movie? To violate someone's privacy like that—"

We were stopped at a red light and suddenly he bolted from the car.

## Elliot Bernstein

Shark hitchhiked down Pacific Coast Highway, "running blind," he said. He had no idea where he was going, but home and his father were out of the question.

He never really told me what happened in County Jail, except to say he'd seen things that made him wonder "if man's so-called higher ideals aren't just a thin veneer of self-serving lies."

His last ride let him off in Laguna Beach, where he saw that the Surf Theater was playing a revival of *Rebel Without a Cause*. Although he'd seen the film on TV—the inferior, smeary "scanned" version, chopped up with commercials, that played in the early sixties—Shark had never really connected with the movie. He'd been too young to appreciate or identify with James Dean at the time of the young actor's death and initial stardom in the fifties and had even scoffed at the older guys who went around trying to act like Dean. His attitude had been: "He was just some young hayseed actor who died, too bad, but what's the big fuckin' deal?"

He was about to find out. He bought a ticket and entered the Surf Theater, and would forever describe the next hundred minutes in religious terms. Watching the film on TV had been like "looking at a newsprint photo of the Sistine Chapel ceiling." Experiencing *Rebel Without a Cause* in its "full luminous mythic wide-screen WarnerColor grandeur" was "transcendent," "redemptive," "resurrective." As he sat there in the darkened theater a scant few hours after the worst terror of his life, he accepted James Dean into his soul "much as, I suppose, a born-again Christian must accept Jesus Christ into his heart."

As the film reached its climax, and Sal Mineo died on the observatory steps, Shark wept. "I felt as if I *were* Sal Mineo," he said, "but also Dean. In the end more Dean, the survivor, than Mineo, the martyr. But a *part* of me died on those observatory steps."

He also identified the character of Judy with Kathy Petro, though it irritated him that Natalie Wood wasn't blonde. "But I felt that perhaps Kathy had a girlish crush on her father, as Natalie did on hers in the film. Perhaps *that* explained why Kathy had rebuffed me. And of course I still believed, despite what had happened, that as Jim Stark introduced Judy to his father over Plato's body, the day would come when I would introduce Kathy to my dad over the part of me which had died."

Only as the film ended and the lights came up did Shark realize there was just a handful of people in the theater for this early show. Somewhere towards the back he heard a girl weeping, reflecting his own silent tears.

Shark left the theater in a transported state, "revived and refreshed and determined to go home.

"I was fourteen," he said. "Practically speaking, there was not much else I could do. But stepping into the brisk night air I felt I had the strength to go on, to face my father, to do what I needed to do for the next few years so that when I did leave it would be to go off and make movies as indelible as the one I'd just seen."

As Shark walked around the corner he ran into the girl he'd heard crying in the theater, still with tears on her cheeks, though she was angry as well now, since her Vespa motor scooter wouldn't start. She was a Japanese/American girl, and Shark was immediately struck by her "simple, delicate beauty, matched to the sense of keen but gentle intelligence in her eyes."

Shark smiled and offered to take a look at her Vespa, though he in fact knew nothing about mechanics at the time. He noticed a paperback book stuck under the elastic on the rear part of the seat—a dog-eared copy of *Zen Flesh, Zen Bones*—and began asking her about it as he wriggled her spark plugs. Judy Oshima was somewhat skeptical of Shark at first, but then he said something that amused her, and for the first he heard her infectious laugh.

## Lorna Trager

I'd insisted we call the police to report that Shark had run off. I was afraid he might try and kill himself.

"He damn well better not," Mac said.

I was sick with worry. Finally, around midnight we heard a car outside, then Shark coming up to the door, singing that Beatles "Love Me Do" song.

Mac was furious. "Where the hell have you been?"

I went and hugged Shark, hoping that would stop Mac from flying off the handle. "Shark honey, are you all right?"

"I'm fine," he said, like nothing had happened. "I just went to a movie, that's all."

# 4 / Blonde on Blonde
## (1965–1967)

### Elliot Bernstein

According to Shark, his first evening with Judy Oshima began on a heavily verbal note. "I'd eaten another Obetrol part way through *Rebel*," he recalled a few years later, "so I was in a real chatterbox, Dean Moriarty mode. We must have stood there outside the Surf Theater for a good half hour yakking away while I dicked around with her Vespa."

When it became clear the Vespa wasn't going to start, Shark offered to help her push it home, an offer she accepted since home was several miles away, and uphill, in Laguna Canyon. As they walked up the road, Shark pushing the scooter, their intense conversation continued. "I think Judy was probably contact high from my speed vibes," Shark said.

The Oshimas lived in a small house behind the Canyon Nursery where George Oshima worked. As Shark and Judy came up to the house they heard George inside muttering angrily to himself in Japanese, and Judy motioned Shark to stop.

"It's no good, he's drunk," she said. The idea had been for Mr. Oshima to give Shark a ride home in return for his helping Judy with the Vespa.

"But my mother's due home soon," Judy told Shark. "She can get me the keys to the car. Come on, we can wait in the tree house."

In the tree house, which served as Judy's bedroom, she and Shark drank tea and began to make out. Suddenly they were disturbed by the sounds of Judy's father reeling into the patio below.

George Oshima was a genuinely tragic figure. Although he and Miko had both been born in California, after Pearl Harbor they had been interned, like thousands of other Japanese/ Americans, in a relocation camp for the duration of the war, George forced to sell the modest but profitable fruit farm he'd developed in Costa Mesa for far less than its worth. By the time the Oshimas gained their freedom their immaculately tended orange and lemon groves were gone, replaced by the Brutalist bunkers and stinking expulsions of the PetroChem plant. George never recovered, financially or emotionally. He became an alcoholic, and in retrospect that may not have been the only thing affecting his brain. He was the insecticide man at the Canyon Nursery. For twenty-five years, until a few months before his death from cancer, he inhaled those fumes on a daily basis as he sprayed the lawns and gardens of the wealthy with a variety of chemical solvents, including the nerve-damaging and virulently carcinogenic Herb-Ex D4 manufactured by Petro-Chem, a compound finally banned in 1981.

Shark and Judy peered down from the tree house, Shark startled to see that George was waving a ceremonial sword. He staggered drunkenly about the patio, cursing in Japanese as he lashed out at the air, until at last he stumbled and fell to the ground, where he lay jerking "as if the whiskey he'd drunk had been laced with Raid."

Shark and Judy climbed down from the tree house and helped George to his feet. "He was gone, in another world," Shark said. "It was incredibly sad."

As they helped George to bed, Judy's mother came in. Only then, when he saw Miko, did Shark realize the Oshimas were the same Japanese couple who'd had a run-in with his father in the late fifties.

And Miko recognized Shark as Mac Trager's son—she had

probably seen him working at the gas station where the painful scene with Mac had occurred.

"I want this boy out of our house," Miko said.

## Lorna Trager

Mac had a special hatred for the Japanese because of his wartime experience. When he was in the navy he was on one of those aircraft carriers that had got attacked by kamikazes. He'd watched his best friend, a fellow sailor named Gene, get killed by a crashing kamikaze plane.

## Gil Shirley

One afternoon in '59 when I was pumping gas for Mac Trager we seen this Japanese gal get out of an old Ford and head for the ladies room. It was okay by me, but Mac saw red. "She's using the crapper and she didn't even buy gas," he said. But that was just an excuse. The main thing was he hated all Japanese.

"Hey," he said to her through the ladies room door. "No-buy-gas-o, no-can-use-o." He tried the knob but she had the door locked.

"I'll only be a minute," she said through the door in perfect English.

"No nip-o shit-o," Mac said and kicked the door. "I mean it, you slit-eyed yellow monkey, this ain't *Teahouse of the August Moon*. Vacate now or I'll clean your Jap butt out of there with a flame thrower."

Mac kicked the door again, and right then George Oshima just sprung out of nowhere and *jumped him*. They both hit the ground and it was real bad for a while, like a genuine fight to the death, but me and Bud finally pulled 'em apart. Mrs. Oshima came out of the john, looking real shook up.

"Get off my property, you fuckin' nip," Mac shouted at George, so mad he turned the words around when he said: "And take that cunt-eyed slit with you."

"You're *dead*," George yelled at him. "I'm gonna come back and *kill* you!"

But that was it.

68

## Elliot Bernstein

Shark's first evening with Judy, indeed the relationship itself, appeared to be ending abruptly as Mrs. Oshima sent him packing. But he had only walked a short ways along the canyon road when Judy pulled up beside him in the family car—she'd grabbed the keys while her mother wasn't looking.

"Aren't you going to catch hell from your mom?" Shark said as they parked at the beach.

"Yes, but I don't care," Judy replied and they began making out again. Eventually, Shark opened her blouse and wanted to go even further. Although Judy wanted to as well, with a typical clear-headedness she declined since neither she nor Shark were prepared.

"God, I wish I weren't leaving for Stanford in the morning," Judy said.

It would be another year before their paths crossed again.

## Brad Jenkins

Shark's dad took away his camera after what he did to Kathy Petro. And he took all Shark's movies too. When Shark discovered that his movies were gone he went to his dad and asked for them back.

"It's too late," his dad said. "I've already thrown them away."

Shark got so mad he thought about breaking into the locked closet where he knew his dad kept his guns. "I'd like to blow his goddamn head off," he said.

"If you decide to really do it," I told him, "let me know. That's something I'd like to see."

It was about that time that they sent him to a shrink.

## Lorna Trager

The psychiatrist was my idea. Mac wanted to send Shark to a military school till he found out how much it was going to cost. The doctor was cheaper. He zeroed in on the speed right away.

## Raymond Dahl, M.D.

Shark came to me in a borderline psychotic state resulting from the overuse of Obetrol, a powerful amphetamine. I withdrew him in increments with the help of Valium, and Dalmane for sleep.

In therapy he was alternately sullen and sarcastic, and categorically refused to discuss the incident of camera voyeurism which had precipitated his coming to me. He displayed a profound ambivalence towards his parents—especially his late mother Winifred whose suicide he subconsciously interpreted as a form of abandonment. His father was a cold and dominating authority figure with an obsessive need to assert a masculinity he secretly doubted. The women in Shark's life, on the other hand, had either been smotherers or pamperers, or anal-retentive obsessive-compulsives and castraters, or in one case a pathologically lewd nymphomaniac he'd been encouraged to think of as a "substitute mother." In short, here was a teenage boy whose psyche was already stretched to the snapping point, whose only release lay in a fantasy life of the most intensely onanistic sort.

## Brad Jenkins

Shark told me the shrink kept trying to steer him back to the subject of beating off.

## Raymond Dahl, M.D.

Shark was a compulsive masturbator, massaging his youthful penis to the point of orgasm as frequently as five times a day. This concerned me a great deal as a symptom of far more profound psychic aberrances. But when I tried to discuss the issue with Mac Trager, he terminated Shark's therapy.

## Mac Trager

This yo-yo tried to tell me Shark jacked off too much. And I said, I'm paying this asshole fifty bucks a crack so he and Shark can sit around and talk about jerking off? Who's jerking off who? To hell with this!

## Lorna Trager

Things were better for a while though, once Shark got off the speed. I think he saw himself how close he'd come to really going crazy and maybe doing something a lot worse than making a peeping-Tom movie, and it sobered him a lot.

That last spring at Cortez his grades picked up. And when he started at Balboa High he really started studying. He had quite a high IQ, you know. Not gifted, but close to it. For a long time there things ran pretty smooth. I took it as a good sign when he made friends with the Bernstein boy, since he was real bright too. Mac didn't feel that way though.

## Elliot Bernstein

I became friends with Shark our sophomore year at Balboa High. We were in gym and social studies together, then we started eating lunch together and hanging out a lot. I thought of myself as the school intellectual in those days, though in retrospect it was that terribly pretentious, adolescent sort of thing. But I read—Beckett, Burroughs, the *Evergreen Review*, and philosophy: Sartre, Husserl, Kierkegaard—and got Shark reading "seriously" too. We began having passionate "meaning of life" discussions that would go on for hours as we walked along the suburban streets of Newport Beach at night. "But that is precisely the *point* of phenomenology!" one of us might cry as we passed a house, catching a glimpse of "The Beverly Hillbillies" on TV. "To perceive the *thing itself*, free of discursive ideation. Which is precisely the goal of Zen!"

We lived on Squid Drive, a few blocks over from Shark's. My parents were not well off. My father had a small tailor shop on PCH, my mother was a bitter failed novelist. But my parents were relatively permissive, so Shark and I spent a lot of time at my place. I had moved into the garage, where we could play the stereo almost as loud as we wanted. It was the time of the Beatles and the Rolling Stones and Dylan, and we listened to that stuff till the records wore out. *Highway 61 Revisited*, I remember, had a profound effect on Shark. The first time I played it he became enraged, saying it was sick, that I'd "raped" his mind. Later, he made a complete turnaround, saying it was the greatest record ever made by man, and listened to it obsessively, endlessly quoting the lyrics. That was after we'd begun smoking dope, of course.

I never went to Shark's house at all because of his father's antiSemitism.

## Brad Jenkins

Shark changed in high school. We were still kind of friendly at first. But once he started hanging out with Elliot Bernstein he became this big intellectual and tried to get me to become one too. He gave me books to read, like Camus' *The Stranger*. When I said that book was sick he said I was stupid, and we had this big argument and quit being friends. It hurt my feelings a lot at the time, since he'd been my only real friend. Without one single friend in the brutal world of Balboa High my grip on reality soon became quite relaxed.

## Elliot Bernstein

Shark and I started going to foreign films at the Surf Theater in Laguna Beach. They showed the latest Fellini and Bergman, and there'd be special weekend screenings of films like *October* and Carl Dryer's *Passion of Joan of Arc*. Afterwards we'd have heated discussions at the local Norm's Coffee Shop about what these films meant and how they were made.

I recall a particularly volatile debate over the merits of Jean-Claude Citroen's *Angel Street*. I considered it an essentially third-rate New Wave genre hommage, far inferior to either *Breathless* or *Shoot the Piano Player*, but Shark disagreed violently, quoting extensively from Sonya Heinz' rapturous review. By then he was something of a Sonya Heinz fanatic, tearing through each new piece in the hard-to-get *French Quarterly Review* as if it were an urgent dispatch from the frontline of cinema.

"*Angel Street* transcends genre!" Shark cried, pounding the table at Norm's. "Citroen is the only pure genius working in film today. I would gladly sacrifice one of my eyes if the one that was left could see as he sees." *Angel Street*, of course, was the last Citroen film with what we normally think of as a plot.

Shark told me about the eight-millimeter films he'd made in junior high which his father had destroyed, and spoke of his determination to get a "real" sixteen-millimeter camera. By then he was working part-time at the Jack in the Box and saving his money toward that end.

He'd never really said much about the peeping-Tom movie of Kathy Petro, assuming correctly that I'd heard about the incident. "It was a mistake," he said once. "The speed made me do it, I was nuts then." Despite his attempt to dismiss the matter as a nearly forgotten aberration, I sensed from a few occasions when we happened to see Kathy Petro on campus that his feelings about her were not all in the past.

## Greg Spivey

Shark liked to say that Elliot saved his life. "There was nothing to read at our house except right-wing hate tracts and back issues of *Guns and Ammo*. Nobody ever talked about *ideas*. Elliot introduced me to the world of the mind, and that set me free. If I hadn't met him I would probably have become just like my father."

## Elliot Bernstein

One night Shark and I went to the Surf Theater for a midnight screening of *Last Year at Marienbad*. The film was several years old at that point but Shark had never seen it, and I was curious to see what he'd make of it.

The lights were just about to go down when Kathy Petro and her current boyfriend came in and, oblivious to Shark's presence, took the two seats directly in front of ours. Presently, they began cuddling and cooing in one another's ears. I looked at Shark. He was staring at the blank screen, trying not to look at Kathy and her beau, which was virtually impossible. And he had begun to perspire.

By the time the film started Shark was pouring sweat, just imploding, Kathy and this blond jock sharing little impulsive kisses now, still completely unaware of Shark's presence. I was tempted to whisper to Shark, "Do you want to move?" But he was wound up so tightly by then, I was afraid to do or say anything at all.

Predictably enough, Kathy and her boyfriend soon grew restless with the film. He was your typical suntanned moron, and to be honest in my opinion in those days Kathy wasn't much more. I could certainly appreciate why Shark found her attractive physically. But she struck me as real zero, a pretty face masking a numbing vacuity.

The couple began talking, "I don't get it." "This is weird." "I can't follow this." "This is irritating." Then they'd start

73

making out. Then they'd stop kissing and complain some more. Kissing and complaining, it just went on and on. And Shark was still sweating, but he'd also begun to tremble and had a near-demented look in his eye. Finally, during one of their kissing interludes, with a really terrifying abruptness Shark kicked the back of Kathy's seat and said: "If you want to fuck go somewhere else. This is a movie theater."

Well, I'll never forget the look on Kathy Petro's face. It was fear initially, shock and fear. But that gave way to . . . How to describe it? It was almost as if she'd *expected* something like this to happen eventually. As if, though she and Shark had had no contact for nearly a year, she *knew* on some level that it wasn't over, that in some incomprehensible and probably terrible way their fates were irrevocably intertwined.

Her boyfriend jumped up and did the manly thing. "How dare you talk to my girlfriend like that," or some such shit. And people began yelling: "Sit down!" By then Shark was on his feet too, but the standoff was brief. Kathy said something like, "Come on, it's not worth it." And she and surfer boy went off like they were going to sit somewere else. But I think they just left, because when the film was over I looked around and didn't see them.

Shark was still mad as we left the theater. "That bitch, that cunt," he said as we walked up the street, and he was still looking around for her, I didn't know what to say, it was so crazy. The way he was acting you'd have thought they'd been passionate lovers who'd just recently broken up.

## Kathy Petro

The incident at the Surf Theater was exactly the kind of thing I'd always feared. I'd see Shark around campus from time to time and just completely ignore him, and sometimes walk out of my way to avoid him. But I couldn't help but notice the way he was still looking at me. Not like he was angry exactly, or was going to do anything to hurt me. But it was like I had really hurt *him,* and his glance seemed to say: How could you? I just wanted to forget what had happened completely. Thank God we ran with completely different crowds and everything.

It was awful though because word had got around about the movie and all that, except you know how people exaggerate. There were even people saying they'd actually seen the movie, which of course was impossible. Though in time I guess people did get tired of talking about it, and moved on to other gossip. But it was definitely a cross I had to bear.

## Elliot Bernstein

The summer of '66 was really idyllic, a kind of ultimate California summer. Shark was pumping gas at his dad's station and I had a boxboy job at the Alpha Beta, but we still managed to spend a lot of time at the beach. Before I met Shark I'd had this phobia about exposing my body, some bit of craziness I'd picked up from my parents, but Shark convinced me my body was fine and before long I was as sun-baked as any surfer. We'd lay there and look at the girls, the conversation drifting inexorably from Sartre to snatch. We were both sixteen and hadn't been laid yet and it was starting to drive us insane.

We met Woody Hazzard, which was something of a turning point, the night Debbi Henderson got him fired from the Taco Bell.

## Woody Hazzard

I was eighteen then and I lived with my mom in this place she'd got from the divorce, this bitchin beach house on the Balboa peninsula right up the street from the Petro place. I was working nights at the Taco Bell and one night while Shark and Elliot were there I got into this thing with the manager after Debbi Henderson told him I spit in her burrito. I didn't really spit in her burrito, I just said I did to make her crazy while she was taking a big bite. She was this real square little blonde goodie-two-shoes type I really wanted to ball, but since I couldn't I teased her instead. But the manager had the hots for her too and took her side and canned me.

Shark and Elliot took my side, saying, "Yeah, that guy's a dip," and "Debbi's a cunt," till we all started laughing. So I invited them back to the house to get high. By then I had the whole house to myself since my mom was up in L.A. having a hot affair with her lawyer.

Shark and Elliot started coming over all the time, to get loaded and stuff, because that summer was rapidly turning into this big nonstop party. I'd heard about Shark's movie thing with Kathy Petro, but I just thought it was funny—it was probably part of what made me think Shark was cool. I mean, at the time he looked real square with short hair and so forth. But anybody who'd do something like that had to be intense, right?

We'd sit around on this weird blue shag carpet in the living room with the stereo pumping the Rolling Stones and smoke Mexican dope till we were stupefied. And there would be girls around—I'd been getting laid since junior high. But it was only too obvious that Shark and Elliot had not yet found a way to cross that border.

Then one night Shark came by with Judy Oshima and it was clear with one look at the smile on his face that she'd stamped his passport.

## Elliot Bernstein

One afternoon in late August Shark was working at his dad's station when Judy Oshima pulled in to gas up her Vespa. Although Shark admitted he "hadn't really thought about her much" in the year since their first encounter, he felt the rapport and excitement of that night return as they made small talk while he filled her tank, the heat of their eye contact giving Shark a "pounding erection."

"What the hell were you saying to that nip?" Mac asked him after Judy sped off.

Shark stared at his father, then turned and walked away, whispering "Moron" under his breath.

"What did you say? Did you say something?" Mac said, going after Shark, whacking his head.

After work Shark hitchhiked up to Judy's despite a sudden freak tropical rain storm. Her parents were visiting relatives up north, in one of Miko Oshima's ill-fated attempts to get George to stop drinking, and Judy had the canyon house to herself. Shark was soaked by the time he arrived. "You'd better get out of those damp clothes," Judy said, the last words either of them spoke before losing their virginity. It was the beginning of a poignantly resonant, if tragically brief, affair.

## Haiku Poem by Shark Trager, August 1966

*For Judy*
   dogs bark at thunder

76

a peach drops in your tree house
rain on your Vespa

## Woody Hazzard

Everybody loved Judy Oshima, it was impossible not to. She was beautiful, but more than that she had this spirit about her, this sense of joy. She was friendly to everybody, not in a sappy way like a flowerchild, but like in this totally present way. She was always *right here,* in the moment, instead of being off in her thoughts somewhere like most people are. I guess that came from her Zen thing.

## Elliot Bernstein

Judy introduced Shark to Zen meditation, which she had been practicing for several years at this point. When Shark got his VW bug they began driving up to Los Angeles on the weekends, where they would go to the Zen Center and then sometimes take in a film at the Toho La Brea where all the Japanese films played at the time. Shark reported being "wiped out" by Kursosawa's *Throne of Blood,* and "blown away" by *Naked Youth* from the iconoclastic young director Nagisa Oshima, to whom Judy was related. She was extremely supportive of Shark's cinematic ambitions, and there was a good deal of talk of their someday going to Japan to practice Zen Buddhism in its most conducive setting and perhaps find work in the film industry there.

These jaunts were undertaken with considerable subterfuge at first, since Miko Oshima would not have stood for her daughter going out with Mac Trager's son. But in September, despite her mother's protests, Judy took a leave-of-absence from Stanford, ostensibly to reassess her life direction, and using the money she'd saved from a summer waitress job, rented a small apartment on the Balboa peninsula, which was quickly converted into a spare, white-walled minimalist love nest. Clearly, her real motive for postponing college was to continue the affair with Shark. It was obvious to everyone how deeply she'd fallen in love with him.

I suppose all told they were only together for three or four months, but in those days that was somehow a lot longer than it is now. Knowing his father's special hatred for the Japanese—

and for the Oshimas in particular—Shark's way of dealing with the potential for disaster was interesting. On the one hand he was fairly circumspect, telling his father he was staying over at Woody's when in fact he was spending the night with Judy. On the other, he barely took his hands off Judy in public, and they were all over town. He had to know it was just a matter of time until word got back to Mac.

But towards the end I remember getting a strong impression that Shark was growing tired of Judy, as if the novelty, the exoticism, was wearing off. With a sense of the pain it was going to cause, I began to suspect that he was in fact still obsessed with Kathy Petro, and he confirmed this one day. "I'm very fond of Judy, but I don't love her," he admitted. "I like her as a friend, but sexually I think I may be using her. She's wild in bed, but most of the time we're together I imagine I'm with Kathy. And when the sex is especially good, it kills me because all I can do is think: Why can't I be having these sensations with Kathy?"

A few nights later Shark had stopped by Woody's on his way to Judy's when the telephone rang and we learned that she'd been killed.

## Woody Hazzard

She was on her Vespa when a Petro-Chem tank truck hit her on PCH. They said she was killed instantly. It was never established who was to blame. The Petro-Chem truck driver said she ran a stop sign. But at least one witness said the Petro-Chem driver was deliberately riding her tail, like coming on to her— "Hey, baby. Where you going on your scooter, sweet thing?" —when she stopped for a red light but he didn't.

## Elliot Bernstein

Shark and I tried to attend Judy's funeral but Miko Oshima blocked the way. It was obvious she'd learned of Shark and Judy's affair. "I don't want you here," she told Shark. "Somehow this is your fault. You're just like your father."

After that rebuff, Shark and I stopped at the Norm's Coffee Shop in Laguna. Shark hadn't wept, he seemed numb, stunned. I guess we all were. "I should have said yes," he said as we sat staring at our coffees in the orange vinyl booth.

I asked him what he meant.

He said Judy had stopped by the gas station the evening she'd died, knowing Shark was on duty alone there till closing time. They had laughed and kissed and made plans for later. "I love you," she'd said lightly by way of parting, adding, "Do you love me?"

"Before I could answer I heard a car pulling in," Shark recounted. "When I saw that it was my father in his Buick my blood ran cold and I couldn't speak. I couldn't even say one word: 'Yes.' I watched Judy's expression change as she saw the fear in my eyes. I felt my father's hatred like a hot wind on my back, and I hated myself for being afraid. But I cringed when my father called my name, and watched Judy get on her Vespa and squeal away . . ."

For the first time Shark seemed about to cry.

"Shark, it's not your fault. These things happen."

"Elliot, if I'd said 'Yes,' she wouldn't have squealed away. A difference of even a few seconds—"

"Shark, you're not God."

He was still anguished when we parted that night.

But the next time I saw him, a few days later at Woody's, his mood had completely changed. He was smoking a joint with another girl, joking and flirting with her, although Judy had been dead less than a week. I convinced myself his pain was so great he'd had to repress it.

Later that evening he drew me aside in the kitchen and said, "By the way, our discussion at Norm's the other night—that never happened, all right?"


## Lorna Trager

I knew Shark was seeing the Oshima girl. I'd heard talk about it, and one afternoon I saw them holding hands on the pier. But I didn't say anything to Mac.

When she was killed in that crash, I saw what it did to Shark and tried to get him to open up about it one day when Mac was out. "You really loved her, didn't you?" I said. "Why don't you just cry? Men cry, you know."

"I don't want to talk about it," he said and walked out of the room.

## Woody Hazzard

Judy's death definitely put a damper on the holidays. Shark totally stopped his Zen meditation and got kind of manic for a while, like he couldn't let himself think about what had happened. He was still like that a month or so later when he and Elliot and I drove down to Tijuana.

## Elliot Bernstein

Shark and I didn't know it was a dope run until we reached Tijuana and Woody went off to score. It wasn't the first time he'd done it, either. He had hollowed-out places behind the panels of his deliberately innocuous Oldsmobile. I almost crapped when I realized what he was up to since I'd heard some real horror stories about Mexican jails. Shark was scared too but tried not to show it. He was determined not to be a pussy in Woody's eyes. But I'm sure our fear of what might happen in the morning inspired our extreme drunkenness that night at Tijuana's notorious Blue Fox.

## Woody Hazzard

The Blue Fox was legendary for having these raunchy sex shows. These really horrendous Mexican women would come out dancing, and then strip and bump their snatches right up in your face, while this sleazy MC said, "It's chowtime! Come and eat Maria!"

And if there happened to be a guy in the first row wearing glasses . . .

## Elliot Bernstein

I wore thick Coke-bottle glasses in those days before they perfected contacts. Well, by the time the "show" started Woody and Shark and I were just blitzed on our butts, literally falling off our chairs. So the girls came out to this grungy mariachi striptease music, and we'd never seen anything like it—at least Shark and I hadn't. Just cheap and vile, yet incredibly exhilarating!

One particularly obese "dancer" gyrated over to me, doing her bump and grind routine practically in my face. I was so naive I actually imagined that contact with the audience wasn't permitted. So I was stunned when she suddenly took off my glasses and before I could object actually placed them inside her vagina! Then she snapped her fingers, lewdly undulating her crotch before my awestruck face, and said: "No hands."

Well, of course, I was far too dumbfounded to take her depraved hint.

## Woody Hazzard

Suddenly Elliot was going down on this big Mexican babe to retrieve his glasses, and even after he did, he just kept chowing down like a starving man. Everybody was hooting and yowling, going totally apeshit, when suddenly I looked up and saw that Shark was stealing the show.

He was up on the stage just fucking the shit out of this young Mexican woman, who seemed like she might be pretty even though she was made up to look like a real whore. You know, fierce eyes and she's doing this whole fierce number: "Oohh, baby. *Yeah*, give it to me." Like really acting out everybody's fantasy of rowdy sex to the max.

And Shark's just fixated, like fucking her real slow with long, deep thrusts, like totally getting off on everybody watching. So everybody starts cheering him on, and then right at the last minute he pulls out just as he comes about a quart.

## Elliot Bernstein

It was quite a performance.

## Woody Hazzard

We were all sick with hangovers in the morning. But I was almost glad in a way because I was too ill to worry much about the border. So we started back and we were kidding Shark about the night before when he said, "Yeah, I'm gonna fuck the living shit out of her, just fuck and fuck and fuck her until one of us drops dead." Which I just took as meaningless bravado, you know? Like he was saying, Yeah, I'm gonna come back here every weekend from now on.

So we crossed the border with absolutely no problem, since we were in this very square Oldsmobile, and we were all taking pains to look equally square. Then north of San Diego when we were sure there weren't any narcs tailing us or anything, Shark said, "Pull over."

"Why?" I said.

Shark looked over his shoulder and said, "Juanita?"

And from the trunk came this muffled voice: "Si."

## Elliot Bernstein

Juanita got into the back seat with Shark and they fooled around all the way into Newport Beach, and in daylight this girl was really tough looking. But Shark was clearly obsessed, with a driven look in his eye, and he wanted Woody to put Juanita up at his house on the peninsula.

## Woody Hazzard

I said, forget it, Jack. No way.

## Elliot Bernstein

So we dropped them off at Shark's. It was about three in the afternoon and nobody was home, but it was just crazy. Shark was acting as if he really thought he could smuggle Juanita into his bedroom and hide her there and nobody would ever know.

He told me later that she'd spent the night. They'd stayed in his bedroom, and when Lorna came home and then Mac, Shark told them he was sick with the flu. Then he and Juanita had fucked all night till she was exhausted and fed up. Because Shark had lied to her to get her to come back with him, saying he was a lot richer than he was, promising to put her up in an oceanfront house and all that, and now she knew the score.

So in the morning while Shark was still sleeping Juanita got up and dressed and stalked out of the house right past Lorna and Mac who were completely blown out. But Mac was probably pleased, since he didn't know about Shark's affair with Judy, and had always had an irrational fear that Shark was going to become gay.

## Lorna Trager

I was flabbergasted to see that cheap Mexican girl in the house.

## Mac Trager

I was relieved to see that his urges were normal. But when he told me where he'd met her I lowered the boom.

## Elliot Bernstein

Mac Trager was a very strange, sick man. Shark told me that after the night with Juanita, Mac made him lower his pants every day for a week so Mac could inspect Shark's dick to see if it was dripping.

## Lorna Trager

Not long after Shark spent the night with that Mexican girl something happened between Mac and him out in the garage. I still don't know what it was. But Mac came in looking white as a sheet, and Shark ran off up the driveway and didn't come back for three days.

For a long time after that Mac just seemed broken, as if Shark had said something to him that cut him to the quick.

## Elliot Bernstein

Mac wanted to look at Shark's dick again—that's what happened. It was several weeks after the Juanita incident, and Shark was working in the garage when Mac stepped in and said: "Drop 'em, mister. Drip check."

Well, Shark had had enough. He exploded and yelled something like: "Not this time. You've ogled my dick for the last time, you latent homo!"

Mac was too wiped out to even get mad, Shark said—which was worse than anything, because it made Shark see that a remark made purely for its inflammatory impact might actually contain a kernel of truth!

Shark went to stay at Woody's for several days after that.

## Mac Trager

Shark and I had an argument in the garage one day. We both got pretty riled up. But he said some things to me no son should ever say to his father. I tried to forgive him, but I don't think I ever really did.

## Lorna Trager

It wasn't long after that business with Shark that Mac made a pass at me and I had to move out. He was drinking more than usual and we were watching "Green Acres" one night when he said, "Why don't you make us some Jiffy Pop?"

So I went into the kitchen and was standing there at the stove when he slipped his arms around me from behind. I jumped and said, "My God, Mac. I'm your sister, have you lost your mind?"

And he said, "Nobody will know."

And I said, "You *have* lost your mind."

And he said, "It's all right as long as you don't have a baby. I'll wear a rubber, how 'bout it?"

And I covered my ears and said, "This is sick."

Then he broke down and started sobbing and said, "I haven't slept with a woman in over six years, not since Evelyn left."

And I said, "Well, Mac, that's not my problem."

I left that night.

## Elliot Bernstein

After Mac and Lorna had a fight and she moved out, Shark described his father as having fallen into a deep depression, drinking heavily and barely talking to him at all. "It's too grim, I can't take it there anymore," Shark said, and virtually moved into Woody's.

There was still a lot of partying, but Shark was always meticulous about his homework. He refused to light a joint until he was satisfied that his assignments were completed at a "B + level or higher." There was a calculation to Shark I'd never seen before, a capacity for coldly analytical judgment that could be unnerving. In a time when the greatest virtue was to live in the *now*, Shark was definitely thinking ahead. "I'm going to get out of here," he said, meaning Orange County. "I'm not going to end up like my father."

It was during our junior year that the really heavy dope dealing started.

## Woody Hazzard

At first it was just grass. We made more runs down to Mexico. Grass had really caught on by then, so we were dealing to everybody. I mean, we were the big connection in Newport Beach.

We had a close call once in Tijuana though, when Shark ran into Juanita on the street. She started cussing him out in Spanish and her boyfriend or pimp or whoever he was pulled a knife. Mexico was getting freaky, we were afraid somebody was going to set us up. So pretty soon we started leaning more toward acid, making runs up to San Francisco.

## Elliot Bernstein

We started taking acid at Woody's place. By that time his mother had virtually abandoned the house to him. I think she sensed what was going on there but didn't know how to deal with it.

Shark had his own bedroom with a view of the sea. He had affairs with different girls, but it was all light, party-time action. He was technically friendly, even jokey, but increasingly there seemed to be a part of him nobody could reach. I believed at the time that on some level he was still mourning Judy. Several girls got crushes on him and couldn't understand why he so quickly lost interest. I recall a girl crying on the sofa, "What's wrong with me? Why doesn't he love me?"

One night a bunch of us dropped acid and listened to records, you know, the Byrds, *Blonde on Blonde*, the Beatles—a typical sixties scene. And eventually Shark retired to his room with a girl named Cindi or Candi or something like that. But at dawn I saw him standing out on his balcony, alone.

He was looking off up the beach, sipping a bottle of cream soda. Sound carried at that hour, and you could hear laughter, bright girlish laughter, coming from beyond the wall that hid the Petro house.

## Woody Hazzard

Shark was really the businessman. I had the contacts but Shark made the deals and kept track of everything. He just had a knack for it. I was too laid back to be a really tough negotiator, especially in a time where everybody tried so hard to "mellow." But Shark didn't give a shit if people thought he was uptight or not. We split the profits fifty-fifty. We made a lot.

## Elliot Bernstein

In early 1967 Shark bought a new Camaro Z/28, a special limited edition with horrendous horsepower. It was silver, a stunning car, and you could hear it for blocks. A real head turner in the golden age of muscle cars. It impressed the girls, and everybody.

## Mac Trager

Let me put it this way. I knew he didn't pay for that car by doing "odd jobs." I tried not to think about it. But I told him, "When the cops finally arrest you, you can have that Hazzard fella or that Jew boy post your bail, cause I won't."

## Elliot Bernstein

That winter Woody and I put together a group called Black Light. I sold my old Martin and bought a Stratocaster, and Woody got a primo set of drums. Fred and Stu Dilday, who were twin brothers, had graduated from Balboa High with Woody a couple of years before, and had already been in a couple of other groups. We rehearsed at Woody's and at first we sucked. We made Blue Cheer seem accomplished. I wrote and sang the songs, which were dark and twisted. We wanted to be a kind of West Coast Velvet Underground. Soon, even though we still pretty much sucked, we began to get gigs locally in Orange County. Light shows were in then, which was part of the reason that Shark bought a camera.

It was a sixteen-millimeter Arriflex, and he shot the works, buying sophisticated lens and accessories, spending thousands of dollars. At first he shot a lot of pseudo-surrealistic acid-trip stuff, which we incorporated into our light show. Some of it wasn't bad—Shark definitely had a knack—though I imagine it would look terribly dated now. He would use whoever was around, creating these dreamlike Felliniesque episodes, though as time went on—after we'd seen a few D.A. Pennebaker documentaries at the Surf Theater—he began going for a more gritily "realistic" cinema verité approach.

One night he was running some footage he'd just got back from the lab—projecting it on Woody's living room wall—when suddenly the verité stuff of the band gave way to a telephoto shot of Kathy Petro sunning nude on a patio of the Petro house. She was with Jeff Stuben, a Balboa High quarterback from a wealthy Newport family, and he was also nude. As I watched in astonishment Kathy and Jeff began to have sex. Then Shark, who had been on the phone in the other room, came back and looked very freaked-out when he saw what was being projected—he clearly hadn't intended to show it—and immediately snapped off the projector. As it happened, of the people who were there that night, Woody and I were the only ones from the immediate area who were able to recognize Kathy Petro and understand that Shark had "done it again."

I figured out later that the only way he could have got that telephoto shot was to climb up to the very highest and most precarious point of Woody's tile roof.

It was hard to avoid the drug analogy: that Shark was a psychic junkie who had briefly cleaned up and experienced the beginnings of true happiness with Judy Oshima. But that serene happiness had come too easily and bored him, his craving for the unattainable had never really left him, and with Judy's death he had returned with an abject inevitability to his mainline blonde obsession.

## Woody Hazzard

Shark had decided he wanted to go to film school and his first choice was USC. His grades were good enough that he could have got a scholarship—he played things very clean and straight at school. But when he heard that Kathy Petro was going to go to USC, he didn't even apply. "It's pointless," he said. "Her dad would make sure I didn't get accepted." Which was not even paranoid, since about that same time they'd announced there was going to be a new building named after Jack Petro at USC.

So Shark applied to UCLA instead.

Then I guess it was during the Easter break in '67 that Kathy came to the house.

## Elliot Bernstein

Shark and I were alone in the house, smoking dope and listening to *Between the Buttons* as we watched the sunset, when suddenly there was a knock. We weren't expecting anyone, and we'd been getting a little paranoid lately. There'd been so much traffic Shark and Woody were sure the cops were on to them and had quit keeping large quantities of dope in the house. So Shark collected the joints with an eye on the bathroom while I looked through the peephole in the front door. When I saw that it was Kathy I opened the door a crack.

"Hi. Is Woody here?" she said.

"No, he isn't," I replied. And before I could say anything else Shark opened the door all the way.

"What do you want?" he said very neutrally.

There was a long look between them which I still to this day am not sure how to read. She certainly didn't seem afraid of him, I'll say that.

Finally Kathy said in that wholesomely sun-drenched way she had—I mean she could talk about shit and make it sound like apple pie—she said, "Well, I just heard you guys might have some LSD."

"We might," Shark said, and indicated his bedroom. She hesitated, then followed him in. Shark left his bedroom door slightly ajar.

## Kathy Petro

To be honest I didn't want to go to Woody's at all. But Jeff Stuben, this guy I was going with then, had never taken acid, and so finally I said, "Okay, I think I know where we can score."

Later I'd wonder if that had just been an excuse. I had heard Shark was living there, I knew I might see him.

I don't know. I'd changed for one thing. And so had Shark. I'd seen him a few times roaring around in that Camaro he had, which I thought was really cool. Anyway, it was the sixties, you know what I mean? All the artificial barriers were breaking down, drugs—especially acid—kind of uniting everybody.

Shark *was* good-looking. I think it had occurred to me: Gee, you know, it's too bad that thing with the movie happened. But was it really that big a deal? Or was I just buying into my parents' values if I thought so?

I hate to say this, because I'm not for judging people solely on their looks. Other values are important. But if Shark had been a creep I might've felt less forgiving.

This is going to sound kinky, I know, but sometimes I would think about him filming me with that camera, you know, in the years after it happened, and it would excite me. It was like a fantasy or something. Like this really handsome guy watching me with a camera while I you-know-what. And I'd think: Gee, what if he'd put the camera down and climbed in the window? Well, if he *really* had I would probably have come unglued. But later I'd think about what might have happened and kind of imagine certain things.

I think what he did affected me in more ways than I knew at the time.

## Elliot Bernstein

Shark and Kathy were only in the bedroom a few minutes. Then he walked her out to the street. They stood there talking a while longer, and she appeared to admire his Camaro.

## Kathy Petro

Shark seemed really nice that day, which was maybe what I'd secretly been curious about. He sold me two tabs of acid, this orange sunshine acid everybody was taking then, and we even joked a little, though I think both of us were very cautious.

He certainly didn't try and push anything, and I made a point not to lead him on in any way. I mean, I just said, "Goodbye," not "See you later," or anything that implied any future at all. But a part of me was thinking, you know: Gee.

So I was just killed by what happened.

## Woody Hazzard

Shark and I were alone in the house when a little after midnight the cops smashed down the front door. We had some grass which I managed to flush in time. But I didn't know until after they booked us that Shark had been holding twenty tabs of acid, which he'd managed to swallow before the cops slapped on the cuffs.

## Elliot Bernstein

I was home in bed with the flu when Woody woke me at one in the morning to say he and Shark had been busted. He was calling from the jail, frantic because he couldn't reach his drug attorney. "The house is clean, they can't hold us," he said. "But we gotta get out of here quick, man! Because Shark's coming on to ten thousand mics." Which was, you know, a lot.

Well, I finally reached the attorney, but he couldn't get Woody and Shark released till morning. They spent the night in the drunk tank where, Woody told me later, he literally held Shark down all night, gagging him with a blanket while the drunks watched in awe. "I thought he was going to fucking explode, man," Woody said.

The cops were extremely pissed off and really tore the house apart looking for evidence. They definitely held Woody and Shark responsible for what had happened to Jeff Stuben.

## Kathy Petro

I guess it goes without saying that it was up to then the single worst night of my life. But I never really blamed Shark, though naturally all the parents did. If anything, I blamed myself since I was the one who'd given Jeff Stuben the acid. Not that he hadn't wanted it. He'd been badgering me about it for weeks. Something in me always sensed that Jeff might not be able to handle it. I only wish I'd listened to that little voice of doubt.

His parents were in Hawaii for Easter, so we dropped at his place, this really stunning house on Balboa Beach. The setting was perfect—it wasn't the setting. We were cuddling on the shag, listening to Donovan as the acid started coming on. Right away it began going badly for Jeff. He started holding his head, saying, "I feel like I'm losing my ego, I don't like this!"

I tried holding him, saying, "Don't fight it, Jeff. Just go with the flow." I put on the Beatles, you know, *Revolver*. But nothing helped.

Then he went to the bathroom and I heard this terrible crash.

90

I ran in and saw that he'd smashed the mirror with his head. There was blood everywhere. Now *I* started to freak, and said, "Jeff, here, use this towel." But he ran outside and that's where it happened.

There was this eucalyptus tree in the yard that had fallen down during a rain storm, and they'd been cutting it up to take it away. There was this chainsaw lying there, and Jeff picked it up and pulled the cord and it started buzzing. He just looked possessed by this time, and I was totally freaked out because I'd never been around violence before. I think his hormones were wrong or something because of playing so much football. He was just filled with all this aggression. I said, "Jeff, put that down, it's all right." For some reason I wasn't afraid that he'd hurt *me* with the chainsaw. So I took a step towards him. That's when he lifted up the chainsaw and cut off his own head.

Well, you know, first I barfed. I mean, what else could I do? And then I started screaming till the neighbors came.

I guess he didn't really cut all the way through his neck, but you could have fooled me at the time. There was blood squirting everywhere like in one of those awful Japanese samurai movies. He was dead long before the ambulance arrived.

Then Daddy came and I was completely flipped out, just screaming hysterically till Daddy slapped me and I told him where we got the acid.

## Elliot Bernstein

Shark's mind was completely gone by the time he and Woody were released on bail. We took him to a friend's apartment and gave him some Thorazine. We thought he might be permanently damaged. But he slept all day and then seemed to be all right.

When we told him what had happened to Jeff Stuben he was awed at first, then incredulous—and ultimately rather darkly and coldly amused. He certainly didn't feel responsible. His attitude seemed to be: *Of course,* Jeff was precisely the sort of penultimate square you could expect to have a bad acid trip. I recall the way Shark smiled. Years later I noted DeNiro doing a similarly thin, wry smile in, I think it was *The Godfather, Part Two,* as he heard of the death of one of his rivals.

## Woody Hazzard

It was real bad for a while. The parents really wanted to throw the book at us, but the cops had fucked up by neglecting to plant any evidence. Shark had really saved us by swallowing that acid. So there was nothing they could do to us.

But it was definitely the end of an era. A weird vibe was sweeping over the Orange County beach cities because there'd already been a couple of murders of young blond couples, what eventually became known as the Surf Killer murders, though it would be another six months and twelve victims later before they finally caught Brad Jenkins. But even though it was only June there was already this sense that, at least in Orange County, the fabled endless summer was over.

My mom made plans to sell the house, and Shark's dad told him, "You can stay till you graduate. Then you are on your own." Which was fine with Shark since he'd been accepted at UCLA.

Elliot convinced me and Stu and Fred that Black Light had a better chance if we went up to Frisco, where all kinds of groups were getting attention then. The week after graduation we were all set to leave, planning to hit the Monterey Pop Festival on the way up north, when we had this farewell breakfast with Shark one morning at Huck Finn's.

## Kathy Petro

I was just totally wrecked by what had happened to Jeff. I kept having these nightmares about it. I'd wake up screaming till Daddy came in and slapped me. Then finally this shrink put me on some Thorazine-type drug. But I was still just fragmented. It was decided I should spend the summer at a friend's villa in Spain just recuperating and thinking positive thoughts. The morning I was going to leave we all went out for breakfast at Huckleberry Finn's.

## Elliot Bernstein

Huckleberry Finn's Family Restaurant was a huge, dementedly quaint Americana-style place on PCH, very conservative, a popular spot for well-dressed families to go for brunch after church. My hair was pretty long then, which was a tense issue at the time, especially in Orange County. Well, they let Shark and Woody and me in, but not without a few dirty looks. It was a buffet, so we got in line with the staid, conservative family people. But it wasn't until we had got our food and were sitting down that we saw the Petros at a table across the room.

## Woody Hazzard

I knew something was gonna happen. Shark wouldn't take his eyes off the Petros. Off Kathy. She looked out of it that morning, completely withdrawn like she was on Thorazine or something. She ate like a zombie. Mrs. Petro was trying to ignore us. But Lance,* their asshole son, and Kathy's dad were drilling us with total hate.

## Elliot Bernstein

Finally Kathy got up to go to the buffet table. And Lance, who was maybe twenty then, a big man like his father, got up too and accompanied Kathy, as if to protect her. And Shark got up before either Woody or I could stop him.

## Kathy Petro

I was just numb that day, I barely even knew where I was. But suddenly Shark was there, trying to say something to me, I don't even know what. Then the next thing I knew he and Lance were fighting.

## Woody Hazzard

It wasn't much of a fight really. But Shark fell back into the buffet table, and it made a lot of noise when all this silver shit fell. I pulled Shark away and Jack Petro restrained Lance. And Mrs. Petro was kind of shielding Kathy, who was cringing.

*Lance Petro would be dead within a year, succumbing to a rare form of liver cancer linked a decade later to Sol-Vex PPD, a popular pesticide manufactured by Petro-Chem. As Kathy recalls, "Daddy believed Lance should learn the business from the ground up. I can still see my brother coming in all sweaty, his bare torso glistening with that sweet-smelling chemical frost, after a hard day's work hosing down the vats."

And then the maitre d' was there, telling us we had to leave. So Elliot and I steered Shark toward the door, but by then his nose was bleeding. So when we reached the entry area Shark ducked into the men's room to get some paper towels for his nose.

## Elliot Bernstein

Woody and I were waiting for Shark by the door when suddenly we heard screams and crashing in the dining room, and Jack Petro yelling, "You goddamn punk!"

We rushed in and saw Jack Petro just beating the living shit out of Shark, who was stumbling through the tables—stumbling because his pants were down around his ankles! Apparently, Shark had been taking a leak in the men's room when Jack Petro came in and saw him and completely flipped out, grabbing Shark before he even had a chance to button up his fly. Shark had tried to escape back through the dining room, his Levis slipping down, as Jack beat him every step of the way. By the time we reached him Shark could barely see, his face was cut and bleeding so severely, and Jack Petro was just completely insane, kicking Shark in the ribs when he fell, as if he quite literally intended to stomp Shark to death. People were going crazy.

Woody and I jumped Jack, and then Lance came at us. And then, somehow, it was over, all of us spent and panting for breath. There was poor Shark on the floor with his pants down in front of everybody—he never wore underwear. Woody and I helped him to his feet, and pulled up his pants, and got him out of there.

## Paige Petro

It is not my favorite memory. But I did sympathize with Jack's vehemence. This young man had tried twice to ruin our daughter's life. If I'd known what was coming I might have entered that fray myself.

## Woody Hazzard

Shark really got creamed. It wasn't a fair fight, what with Shark with his pants down. And Jack Petro was a big man, you know, like John Wayne or Ronald Reagan, while Shark was five-ten and maybe 14O at the time. Petro was in his fifties but he kept himself in shape.

Shark was getting stitched up in the emergency room when he went into this revenge riff: "I'm not going to forget this. Someday he's going to pay for this. I'm going to destroy that rotten old pig."

I understood how he felt but figured it was just talk, because Jack Petro had so much money and power it was kind of like saying you were going to get even with God.

# 5 / *East of Eden*
## (1967–1968)

**Letter from Shark Trager to**
**Elliot Bernstein, July 14, 1967**

Hey, bro:

The gods of Hollywood are already smiling upon me. I'm writing this letter from my bitchin new pad, a cruddy little A-frame in Sherman Oaks. Do you detect a note of inconsistency there? Yeah, you do. This place is a dump. The faucets drip, there are cobwebs in the rafters—and there's a scurrying sound under the floorboards I don't even want to think about. Then why is it so bitchin? Sixty bucks a month for one thing. But that's not the main reason I snatched (ooohhh yeah!) this place up.

It's the knowledge of who once lived in these walls, once slept on a mattress in the loft where I now sleep, once cooked on the cruddy stove, took a leak in the toilet, jerked off in the shower, parked his '55 Porsche Speedster in the shaded driveway. (Did I just give it away?)

## Neal Ridges

I met Shark in the summer of '67 right after he moved into the James Dean house in Sherman Oaks. It was a rundown A-frame on an overgrown lot and at first I thought he was bullshitting about Dean having lived there. But he wasn't. It was really the place Dean had leased and lived in right up to the day he died.

Shark became a bit obsessed about that. We'd be sitting there smoking dope and he'd point to the bathroom and say, "Just think, Dean shaved in that mirror the last morning of his life."

It actually became a bit spooky. It was a time when people were taking a lot of acid and believed in "vibes," that a house most definitely absorbed the psychic energy of its previous occupants. So when Shark told me he sometimes heard disembodied sobbing in the night—"Dean was in pain when he lived here; he was on the threshold of becoming mythic and it was tearing him apart"—I did not dismiss it out of hand.

I was working on my thesis film project at UCLA that summer, and Shark pumped me at great length about how the film school worked. It was clear he had no interest in a college degree. He just wanted to take advantage of the film school's facilities to make a movie that would propel him out of academia into the real world.

## Frank Forte

I was teaching a Project Two sixteen-millimeter production class when Shark approached me requesting admission. According to the rules he should have begun like everyone else with the Project One class, which was eight-millimeter. But when he showed me his films I was more than impressed. Arty, some of it, pseudo-Felliniesque, but extremely well done. And the verité material—at least I *thought* it was verité. When he told me it was "acted" I was stunned! To be blunt I thought he might well be our generation's Orson Welles. And I believed in art then, we all did—it had something to do with the times, I suppose. I waived the requirements, the departmental rules be damned. If he was a genius, we needed him now. The walls of academia were crumbling. Revolution was here.

## Neal Ridges

It was a volatile time and the film school was heavily radicalized. Plot was out, "story" was considered a bourgeois conceit. Nobody talked about money, about Hollywood "deals" or ambition. Hollywood was seen as corrupt. The studios could only make films like *The Green Berets,* or smarmy youth culture rip-offs concocted by middle-aged producers who fantasized about fucking hippie girls. We were in it for art and to change the world. The cinema of "escape" was dead.

Our idols were Godard, Truffaut, Resnais, Chabrol, Rivette, and above all, Jean-Claude Citroen.*

Shark caught the fever, primarily from Simone Gatane, I think. Simone was a stunningly beautiful and high-breasted, chain-smoking, nail-biting Critical Studies major from France. It was well known that she and Jean-Claude Citroen had once been lovers.

## Simone Gatane

I met Shark one day in the Steenbeck room, where I was working on a shot-by-shot analysis of *The Nutty Professor*— laughing out loud, clapping my hands in joy at the multiplicity of meanings in this subversive masterpiece of Jerry Lewis— when Shark spilled hot chocolate on the front of my blouse.

Naturally, I initially hated him for this. But when he apologized and told me he lived in James Dean's house we went there and made love into the night.

I soon moved in, for I found him stimulating as a lover, though his intellect was quite crude. I would speak of Bazin, for example, and he would laugh and say, "I don't care about these concepts, Simone. I want to *make* movies, not *talk* about the nature of film."

This would anger me and I would say, "Oh, now you're

---

*Whose great-uncle, incidentally, was French car king Andre Citroen. In a brief 1939 *scandale*, Jean-Claude sought to have the family name removed from all of the automobiles (both retroactively and in the future), on the grounds that the vehicles were "violent embodiments of capitalism," and "aesthetically absurd." The case was dismissed as soon as the complainant's age was ascertained; the future *enfant terrible* of the *nouvelle vague* was then nine.

posturing, you're trying to play the primitive." And he would get quite mad. Then we would make love.

One night we saw *Neon City*, Jean-Claude's 1966 hommage and blow of death to American film noir. It had only then finally reached America and Shark was profoundly astonished. He had long admired Jean-Claude's early "narrative" films, but as Shark himself said as we left the theater, "This is a cinema *beyond* cinema! If only I knew how he dared to take such a quantum leap!"

That very night I saw to it that Shark read Jean-Claude's seminal essay, "The Death of Film as 'Entertainment,' " and it changed him forever. "Yes, yes, of course, I see now!" he cried, as we spoke with great zeal of Jean-Claude's revolutionary cinema far into the night, until at last near dawn we made love. Shark then took the conventional script he was working on and completely revised it in accordance with Jean-Claude's radical dictums. "I am going to do with the bedroom farce what Jean-Claude did with film noir," he said. "It's time somebody went for Doris Day's throat."

## Neal Ridges

Most Project Twos were shorts, running maybe twenty minutes at most. But it soon became apparent that Shark was planning to shoot what amounted to a feature. When I finally saw the script I was floored. It was completely insane, a viciously satiric, deconstructive anti-"sex comedy" set in Newport Beach. The title, an obvious play on one of the key films of the genre, was *Pillow Fuck*.

## Frank Forte

I considered the script unfilmable, less for reasons of "taste," than economics. I don't think Shark had ever written a script before and it was filled with intricate camera directions, elaborate tracking shots and the like. "Jesus, Shark," I said. "This is going to cost you at least twenty thousand dollars." Which in 1968 was a lot.

## Simone Gatane

When Shark realized how much the film was going to cost he almost gave up on it. Then he said, "I know that this film was meant to be. I am going to proceed with pre-production. The cash *will* materialize.''

So he began lining up the student crew and auditioning actors from the Theater Arts department. But I became concerned, especially after the cameraman mentioned that Shark had said if all else failed he would rob a series of ''imperialist banks.'' In those days that was not crime, but a political act.

Luckily, it never came to that.

## Neal Ridges

Shortly before the actual shooting began, at a time when if anything he should have been scrounging for cash, Shark pulled up to Melnitz Hall in a primo restored 1955 Speedster. White, like you-know-who's. I asked him how much he'd paid for it and he said three thousand. ''Jesus, where are you getting your money?'' I asked him.

He just smiled and said, ''You don't want to know.''

## Elliot Bernstein

I called Shark from San Francisco in February to say I was coming down for the weekend to visit my parents, and hoped we might get together. ''You should stick around,'' he said. ''I'm going to be shooting in Newport Beach next week.'' Then he explained that through a third party he'd taken a two-week lease on the house next door to the Petro's.

When I arrived in L.A. a few days later and saw the Porsche, I said, ''Are you dealing again?''

He said, ''Yeah, but not dope.''

What then, I asked him.

''Plastic explosives,'' he said.

## Warren Dray

Simone Gatane introduced me to Shark one night at the Nuart Theater. We were all standing in line for Jean-Claude Citroen's *Honeymoon in Algiers* when Simone recognized me despite my disguise, in retrospect a rather pathetic black dye job and horn-rimmed glasses. I was already a fugitive then as a result of a troop train bombing up north. I knew Simone from UCLA where I'd been a film major before coming to see how pointless all that was.

After the film the three of us went to a dimly lit Mexican restaurant where I spoke bitterly of the impotence of art.

"But this is precisely what Jean-Claude is saying," Simone asserted. "That is why *Honeymoon in Algiers* has no 'meaning' according to the bourgeois or 'literary' notion of art. Because it is *film*. And film *as* film is *only* film, *not* something other *than* film."

Shark was very quiet, something clearly on his mind. When Simone left us for a moment to use the restroom, Shark looked at me and said, "Would *you* do what they did in the film?"

I knew he meant the sequence where the Algerian freedom fighters had butchered the smugly complacent bourgeois newlyweds.

"Yes," I said. "If it would stop the war."

Shark considered this, then said, "What if it would only mean saving a few thousand lives? Perhaps even just a few hundred Vietnamese babies from napalm?"

"Why are you asking me this?" I said, sensing correctly that the question was far from rhetorical.

"Because I have some privileged information," Shark said. "And enough plastique to blow Mount Rushmore off the map."

I looked around and noticed a couple at the next table who appeared to be eavesdropping. "Let's talk about this later," I said.


## Darrel Tyrone

One day Simone calls me and says, "Darrel, my boyfriend's casting a student movie at UCLA and he's looking for someone to play a black terrorist."

So I say, "Simone, I *am* a black terrorist. I don't act in no honky movies no more."

And she says, "I know. That's why I thought of you. 'Cause this film is cool."

So I go out to Shark's place in Sherman Oaks, and the whole thing sounds like bullshit to me 'cause he don't have the money. Then this white chick comes by I get to tie up and rape in the script. So I say okay, and get this white chick's number so maybe we can get together and rehearse.

Then two nights later the pigs bust down my mother's door in Watts and shoot the lady in the spleen. They lookin' for me and a few other brothers, 'cause they hear we got some plastic explosives and plan to blow up Parker Center in revenge for their offing two other brothers they said offed a pig.

When we hear about this we go right away to where we stashed the explosives, since my mother knows where that is too. We got most of it loaded when we see the flashing lights. A high-speed freeway chase ensues. We're in a GTO so the pigs can't catch us. But on the Ventura Freeway we start running out of gas. "Get off here!" I shout to Lamel when I see the Sherman Oaks exit sign.

We reach Shark's house but there's nobody home. So we pull up the driveway, parking out of sight behind the house, while meanwhile the pigs are screaming up and down the streets. "We leave the car here," I say to Lamel, "and come back later when the pigs clear out."

So we set out on foot. Somewhere near Encino they close in on us, about fifteen pigs with their shotguns leveled at our heads.

## Simone Gatane

I received a call from Darrel Tyrone's attorney, saying, "Look, there's a hot GTO filled with plastic explosives parked in your driveway. You'd better get rid of it."

I said, "Yes, I know. My boyfriend is out looking at it right now. Do you mean all of that stuff piled in the backseat could blow up any time?"

## Warren Dray

It was a sizable cache, though not worth the twenty thousand in requisitioned pig money we paid Shark. But we were desperate to strike a blow against the American Empire, and there was enough destruction there for a number of operations. The first blow—which Shark suggested—was too good to pass up. Along with the explosives he provided two hand-drawn maps: one of the Petro-Chem complex in Costa Mesa showing the unit where the napalm was manufactured, and the other a diagram of the Petros' pig residence in Newport Beach.

The only thing Shark asked was that we hold off till after the 27th, when his filming at the house next door to the Petro winter palace would be done.


## Simone Gatane

I swear, I knew nothing of Warren Dray's terrorist plan. Shark left in the GTO the night Darrel's attorney called, returning several hours later on foot. "I left that explosives-filled car on a side street in Pacoima," he said, assuring me he had wiped it clean of his prints.

When not long after Shark announced that his film financing was "in place," I asked him how it was possible.

"Oh, I'm using my dope-dealing savings," he said.

"But I've seen your bank book," I said. "You have less than four thousand."

"Oh, no, I remembered another account," he said. "I guess I opened it on acid and then forgot. Isn't that something?"

I agreed that it was.


## Elliot Bernstein

I told Shark he was crazy to film next door to the Petros. But he said it had to be there, the script called for Newport Beach. When I visited him at the Dean house a few days before filming began, things were already in high gear, people coming and going, consulting Shark on the details—it was almost as elaborate as a regular film.

And then the amphetamine arrived. Well, Shark was never able to handle speed, not that that ever stopped him from taking it. Soon everybody was just possessed and I knew something bad was going to happen.

"Come on, stick around," Shark said, and even offered me a part in the film as a soldier returning from Vietnam to find his wife being kept as a sex slave by a black guy.

"My hair's too long to play a soldier," I said, and split for San Francisco.

## Simone Gatane

We began filming on a Friday morning, all of us having sneaked into the leased house as inconspicuously as possible. How exciting it was to be making this subversive film clandestinely in the very heart of the rancid American dream!

Shark worked feverishly, brutalizing the cast and crew. But no one minded for here was clearly a genius at work! He shot virtually in sequence, the film beginning normally enough. The first reel might easily have been mistaken for an insipid hommage to the films of Ross Hunter. Then, inexorably, all expectations are undermined until "logic" and "sanity" no longer remain.

## Janet Bundy

I played the lead. I have to tell you it's not something I would do again today. I became a feminist a few years later, but at the time . . . Well, you've got to understand, it was the sixties. The sexual revolution and all that. The body—and nudity—were *in*. To think I actually thought it was art!

## Neal Ridges

Shark really put Janet through the ringer.

## Janet Bundy

My name in the film was variously Brenda, Jan, Doris, Kit, Tammy, and tellingly, Kathy. It was part of the intentional confusion of the script that all the other characters called me by different names.

## Neal Ridges

Ron, the black acting student Shark got to replace Darrel Tyrone, was gay. Between takes he amused us with letter-perfect impressions of Dionne Warwicke and Diana Ross. There was a sequence where he was supposed to tie Janet to a lawnchair and then subject her to an interminable racial/political/sexual diatribe. It was an Eldridge Cleaver sort of thing, but

Ron was irredeemably effeminate. "Look, you white ruling class bitch," he'd whine prissily. "I've got half a mind to just fuck the living shit out of you, except I know that's what you secretly want. All you honky snatches do is sit under your hair-dryers all day dreaming of a big, mean nigger cock."

Well, I didn't think the scene was supposed to be funny. But when I mentioned it to Shark, he said, "It's better this way. It'll twist people's heads even more."

## Simone Gatane

The shoot was going fine, we were even ahead of schedule, when one night Shark was ready for a take and we couldn't find Janet. Then we looked out to the street and saw her smoking a cigarette and talking to a blonde girl who had pulled up to the house next door.

## Kathy Petro

I was living in a sorority house near USC then, but still came home on weekends a lot, and as I pulled up that night I couldn't help but notice all the bright lights in the courtyard of the Kenneys' house next door. I knew they'd gone to the islands and leased it out, so naturally I was curious. I saw this girl smoking a cigarette, wrapped in a blanket against the chill, and just looking incredibly bedraggled. "Hi. What's going on?" I said.

And she said, "He's crazy."

"Who?" I said.

Then I saw Shark.

## Warren Dray

We'd been watching the Petro-Chem plant for a week, and we'd checked out the Petro house on the Balboa peninsula too. As far as we could tell Shark's maps were accurate. Then while watching the plant we observed on two separate occasions massive shipments of napalm going out.

"This is fucked," I told the others. "Babies are going to have their skin burned off while we wait for Shark to finish his stupid fucking movie. Art never changed anything, and it's not going to now. Fuck waiting. Let's do it. Tonight.''

## Neal Ridges

We were ready for a take on the courtyard scene when Shark saw Kathy Petro at the gate. At the time I didn't understand how closely the courtyard scene was modeled on a real life event.

## Kathy Petro

I saw Shark and the camera and the movie lights but I just couldn't believe he was there. It was just too crazy. And he looked at me, you know, the way he *always* looked at me, as if every meeting we ever had was somehow *inevitable*.

Then before I could even react or anything, somebody started up this chainsaw! Well, you can *imagine* what that sound did to me! I could never go to any of those chainsaw movies that came out in the seventies, never, never, never. Because *that sound* just *did* something to me.

Then I saw that they had this muscular male dummy made out of flesh-colored plastic. The head was on a hinge or something, which they were trying to cover with makeup. And there was a pump device for the blood, you know? But the pump wasn't working right, and the blood was just kind of trickling down the dummy's chest from the neck. And then something blew and the blood started squirting every which way, just like it had in real life with Jeff Stuben. And I just started screaming.

## Warren Dray

The plan was to kidnap Jack Petro and force him to admit us to the plant. That was to be no problem since he owned the fucking place. Shark pointed out, and I completely agreed, that if Jack Petro went up with his napalm it would be a warning to the other pig industrialists that their money and influence would not protect them either.

We decided on our own not to leave any witnesses. As for any janitors or night watchmen we might run into, we believed that people were responsible for their actions. There were no "good Germans" only taking orders. The same went for Petro's pig wife, the society bitch Paige. If she happened to be home the night we came for her hubbie she was due to be gutted. That went double for Petro's decadent daughter. If she was wriggling around that fascist household I would personally off that pampered blonde piglet.


## Paige Petro

Jack and I were watching a late movie in the den when we heard Kathy scream outside. We knew the Kenneys had leased their place next door, but the properties were really quite private. We certainly had no idea Shark was there. Jack wouldn't have stood for it, needless to say.


## Warren Dray

We pulled around the corner and suddenly there were cop cars parked at the Petro house dead ahead. We almost shit but we couldn't make a U-turn without attracting attention. "Stay cool, just keep going," I said to Randy who was at the microbus wheel.

We drove at a normal pace past the house where Shark was filming and saw cops in the courtyard under the movie lights. Then as we passed the Petro place we caught a glimpse of Jack and Paige comforting their sobbing debutante in a touching pig family tableau.

"Let's grease 'em," Randy said, his hand going to his AK-47. "Let's grease 'em now."

"Fuck, are you crazy?" I said. "There must be thirty pigs."

"Randy's right," Gretchen said from the backseat, fingering her own weapon. "Let's off 'em all." And her lover Luanne said, *"Yeah!"*

But several cops were already checking us out, microbuses being inherently suspicious. I stuck the barrel of my AK-47 in Randy's ribs. "Keep going at a slow pace or I'll blow your Marxist/Leninist guts out," I said, then glared at Gretchen: "And I'll blow off your radical lesbian head."

We kept going.

## Neal Ridges

The cops shut us down, and told us to clear out, since we didn't have a location permit. Shark argued that we didn't need one since it was private property, and the cops threatened to take us all in. I imagine that was what Jack Petro was pushing for. At one point Shark started over to the Petro house; if he'd encountered Jack Petro I'm sure there would have been a bad scene. But the Petro gate was closed by then. Her parents had taken Kathy inside.

## Kathy Petro

Mom took me up to my bedroom, and I was just kind of whimpering by then, so she left me there, I guess thinking that the worst was over. But no sooner had she left than I just flipped out again and started whirling around the room, screaming like an insane dervish. That was when Daddy came in, and trying to restrain me so I wouldn't hurt myself, yanked my arm so hard he dislocated my shoulder. A bunch of ligaments were torn and everything, and even though it healed it acted up for years to come, causing me intense pain, which led to some very bad things.

For a long time whenever I felt that horrible pain in my shoulder I cursed Shark, even though technically it was Daddy who had caused the injury.

## Neal Ridges

Shark was furious about losing the beach house since the film was nearly half shot at that point, and he didn't have the money to reshoot everything at a new location. Everyone assumed the film was lost until Shark decided the apparent disaster was actually a blessing in disguise. He would complete the film at a new location, then cut everything together, even though in a number of instances that meant the location would change from shot to shot within the same sequence. "It's a major opportunity to gut some of the most oppressive 'rules' of cinema," he said.

He found a beach house in Venice, a sterile modern place absolutely unlike the tropical Spanish ambiance of the house in

Newport Beach. The only thing the two locations had in common was an ocean view.

## Simone Gatane

So much of filmmaking entails exploiting chance. But only a genius would have dared such a leap.

## Warren Dray

I caught up with Shark the night after the Newport Beach fiasco, wanting to find out what the fuck happened. And when he found out we'd jumped the gun he flipped.

"You stupid fucking moron," he yelled at me. *"You would've killed Kathy!"* At that time I had no idea he was fixated on her.

"You blew it," he said. "It's off." Then he threatened to warn Jack Petro and even call the FBI. When he mentioned the feds I went through the roof.

"Listen, you capitalist ass-licker," I said, jamming my gun under his chin. "You're in this way over your head. This isn't a movie, you simpering shit. This is a real gun with real bullets . . ."

Simone interceded, pushing my gun away from Shark's face. "Don't you see? This is precisely what they want, for us to fight among ourselves."

As it turned out we soon lost all interest in the Petro plan in favor of a much, much juicier target. A few weeks after the Newport Beach fiasco, Randy and I came back from casing a certain rather well-known Orange County theme park only to discover that Gretchen and Luanne had split with all the plastic explosives, leaving a note that said they were severing all contact with men.

## Neal Ridges

We wrapped in May and I smelled disaster. I'd seen the rough footage and, the mismatched locations aside, the acting was wretched. Of course "good acting" was a bourgeois concept. But still . . .

Shark wanted to have the film finished in time for the June

screenings in Melnitz Hall. Because of the delay caused by the location change that gave him less than a month. He got a new supply of speed and a stock of cream soda—have you ever tasted that stuff warm?—and worked around the clock in his editing room until his nerves were shot. If somebody laughed in the hall he'd step out in a rage, his eyes like Hitler's. "Shut up, goddamn you! How dare you disturb my concentration when I'm creating great art!"

I mean, it would've been funny if he hadn't been dead serious.

## Simone Gatane

Shark poured his heart and soul into *Pillow Fuck*. I know because I would come to see him and say, "Shark, you haven't slept for many days, please come home." And he would yell at me and slam the editing room door in my face.

## Neal Ridges

I believe he was nearly finished when he learned that Jean-Claude Citroen was coming to UCLA in June to screen one of his own films. This sent Shark into a complete frenzy. "No, this isn't right, I've got to redo it." He began tearing off splices, frantically searching for lost trims. Have you ever seen someone short-circuiting on speed? He was in a state of total panic because of course you know Citroen was his idol.

## Simone Gatane

When Jean-Claude arrived in Los Angeles, he let the studio put him in a bungalow at the Beverly Hills Hotel so that he could experience firsthand the decadence of Hollywood and thus knowingly attack the capitalist factory of "entertainment." Though we had been lovers once, that was many years before, when I was fourteen. But when I saw Jean-Claude in his bungalow we made love together for old times' sake. Afterwards, as we smoked in bed, I said, "Oh, by the way. My boyfriend is screening his film tonight."

## Neal Ridges

I remember the screening only too well. It started late because of the mob scene caused by Jean-Claude Citroen's arrival. Students crowded around him in the Melnitz Hall foyer, asking urgent, pointed questions about the future of cinema, a subject about which Jean-Claude always had a great deal to say. He was with Simone, who'd picked him up at his hotel, and I kept trying to get her eye, because Shark was just inside the theater, coming completely unglued. He looked terrible. I think he'd literally been up for a week, only hours before completing the final sound mix. His eyes, God. Like a character the actor Brad Dourif might play.

Finally, Simone steered Jean-Claude into the theater and introduced him to Shark, who could barely speak he was so exhausted, his voice little more than a hoarse whisper. Shark tried to express how much Citroen's *Neon City* had affected him. While Jean-Claude acknowledged Shark's admiration, he remained polite and reserved to the point of skepticism, as if he meant to indicate to Shark that he did not intend to let their mutual friendship with Simone color his critical reaction to Shark's film in any way—he took the art form of cinema that seriously. Given Jean-Claude's body of brilliant, unforgivingly incisive film criticism, I don't think Shark expected anything less.

At last everyone was seated and the lights went down. As they did I noticed Jean-Claude's hand sliding over Simone's knee.

Contrary to my earlier fears, based in part on Shark's occasional empathic references to Erich von Stroheim, the final cut of *Pillow Fuck* ran a concise ninety minutes. It was really a masterpiece of romantic deconstruction, beginning with an episode of coy telephone banter à la *Pillow Talk,* which quickly degenerated into obscenity and dementia. Needless to say there was no "plot," but simply a series of grating and increasingly fragmented vignettes, some of which were unmotivatedly violent, others intentionally tedious and repetitious, still others purposefully stupid and stultifying. I found that the "bad acting" worked after all. What in a Hollywood film would have been a kind of virtuoso Oscar-fodder acting moment became instead merely nauseating. The editing was aggressively chaotic or "bad," a senseless, arrhythmic jumble of jump cuts, pointless zooms, deliberately mismatched continuity—including of course the everchanging location. "Oh really?" Janet would say, smoking a cigarette in Newport Beach. "Yes," Ron would reply as the film cut to a shot of him in the beach house in Venice. Then cut back to Janet, sans cigarette, sitting now, not standing as before, nodding, in a different dress.

A few people walked out, the squarer students. Everyone else was galvanized—or at least awed.

I glanced at Jean-Claude during one of Ron's political harangues to see how he was taking it. The harangue was intentionally illogical, of course, an insane blend of Marxist and fascist cliché, while Jean-Claude was himself a grimly "serious" Marxist, so I thought this might be a touchy moment. But he was smiling with pleasure. Then I noticed that his hand had disappeared under Simone's miniskirt.

When the film ended there was silence. Then a thunderous standing ovation. I have no doubt it was one of the great moments of Shark's life. Vindication. Shark smiled wanly despite his exhaustion. Inevitably, he turned to Jean-Claude. We all held our breath, waiting for Jean-Claude's reaction. Finally, after an excruciating pause, Jean-Claude said to Shark, "I understand you live in the house of James Dean."

Shark smiled a bit shakily and said, "Yes. I'm having some people over. Would you care to join us?"

## Simone Gatane

"He hasn't told me what he thought of my film yet," Shark said to me at the party, indicating Jean-Claude across the room in deep discussion with Janet Bundy and another girl.

"Perhaps you shouldn't press it," I said to Shark, sensing correctly that Jean-Claude's opinion meant far too much to him.

By then it had become all too apparent that Jean-Claude was deliberately avoiding his host. So finally Shark tossed back yet another glass of wine—how he was still on his feet I have no idea—and stepped up to Jean-Claude. I cringed as I saw the look of helpless longing and anger on Shark's drawn face.

## Neal Ridges

"So what do you think of my movie?" Shark said to Jean-Claude, loud enough for most of the room to hear.

"I'm sorry, what?" Jean-Claude said, torn from his conversation with the girls.

Shark repeated his question. And Jean-Claude looked right past him to the large French *Giant* poster on the wall.

"Ah, *Géant*," Jean-Claude said. "Dean moved into this house as he finished that film. Only to die in a matter of what? Days?"

Shark responded, his voice cracking with rage: "I don't want to talk about James Dean, man! I want to know what you thought of my fucking movie!"

"It was shit," Jean-Claude said, and several people gasped. "You're a moron, a poseur, you have no talent. You're not even mediocre, you're an incompetent fraud. An excreter of fake art, which is the worst kind, a cancerous tumor of capitalism which must be excised. You're a phony, a thief, a debased cinematic plagiarist, you will never do anything worthwhile. Anyone who spews out such drivel would be better off putting a bullet through his head."

I don't know, perhaps it was the James Dean aura of the house, but Shark's reaction reminded me of nothing so much as Dean's response to Raymond Massey's rejection in *East of Eden*—you know, the scene where Cal tries to give his father the money? It was like that, just awful, Shark reeling around the room in total incoherent agony. Just excruciatingly painful—if it had been a film, unwatchable. And no one knew what to do or say. Simone looked helpless. Finally, still groaning in unrelievable emotional pain, Shark reeled out the door. A moment later we heard the Porsche roaring out of the driveway.

## Simone Gatane

I ran out after Shark but it was too late. In that Porsche like James Dean's he was screaming up the street.

## Neal Ridges

Naturally, it occurred to us that Shark might try to kill himself. Later that night—after Jean-Claude had attacked a few of us who'd belatedly come to Shark's defense, and then he and everyone else had left—Simone said, "Neal, where did James Dean die?"

"On the highway to Paso Robles, I think."

We got out a map and located the highway, and set out in my VW bug at something like three in the morning.

I soon had second thoughts. "But Dean's death was an accident," I told Simone as we approached the Grapevine. "He broadsided somebody. How could Shark possibly hope to copy that fluke event? If he's really hot to kill himself I'm not at all sure he'll bother to drive all this way."

"He won't mind the drive," Simone said. "I know how his mind works, Neal. He will find the exact place where it happened and broadside someone there. And what's more, I'll bet they'll be driving a car just like the one Dean hit back in 1955."

It struck me as unlikely. But she certainly knew Shark more intimately than I did.

We reached the place where Dean had died around ten that morning. A super-highway had replaced the original road, and there was no intersection anymore. But there were still chunks of the old road running parallel to the highway, weeds growing up through the broken asphalt. Affixed to a tree near the old road we found a commemorative plaque identifying the spot where the crash had occurred thirteen years before.

"Maybe Shark stopped for breakfast at a roadside cafe," Simone said. So we waited—even though we both knew by then it was logistically impossible for Shark to reenact the crash no matter how badly he might have wanted to.

Finally around two I said, "Simone, this is inane." And we drove back to L.A.

For three days we heard nothing. I stayed with Simone who was literally sick with worry. Finally, we learned from Elliot Bernstein that Shark had sought refuge with his father.

## Mac Trager

I hadn't seen my boy in a good nine months when he showed up late one night. I was watching Duke Wayne on TV in *Big Jim McLain,* feeling lonesome as hell, when I heard the door-bell ring.

Shark looked beat and said, all choked up, "Dad—I want to come home."

For some reason it got to me—I guess I'd been drinking some. It was all I could do not to cry like a goddamn girl.

"Come on in, son," I said. "Come on in and pop yourself a brew."

He fell asleep in that old green recliner with a can of beer in his hand.

## Elliot Bernstein

Shark called me in San Francisco from his father's the day after the UCLA screening. We made small talk for a while before he finally told me what had happened with Jean-Claude Citroen. Although he tried to make light of it he was clearly in a state of deep psychic pain. When he began making quips about "pulling a Hemingway" with his dad's shotgun I tried to keep him talking. But he began giggling distractedly—a bit like James Dean I remember thinking at the time—and then abruptly hung up.

## Mac Trager

He was in a bad way. I knew it had something to do with that student movie he'd made. I'd heard abut the deal next door to the Petros'. I figured he'd done something sick again and had to pay the price. And I could tell just by looking at him that he'd been on that speed drug. I should've kicked him out, but he got to my soft spot the way a lost, starving dog would.

## Elliot Bernstein

I tried calling Shark back at his father's, until it became obvious the phone was off the hook. I was quite concerned by then, imagining his brains decorating the rumpus room. I considered alerting the Newport Beach police, but thought better of that, and called Simone instead.

"Simone, he's at his dad's with a gun," I told her.

"No, he's here," Simone told me. Perhaps two hours had passed since I'd spoken to Shark. "He's sleeping like a baby in the James Dean loft."

## Mac Trager

I was under the impression that we'd had a good talk that evening. We drank some beers, and Shark said he was going to quit college, which was horseshit anyway, and come back to work for me at the station.

"We're a lot alike," I said to my boy. "Like father, like son."

I went out for another six-pack, but when I got back he was gone. Just like that. No note, no nothing. So I drank that six-pack myself and said: All right then, *to hell with you!*

## Neal Ridges

I was with Simone in the A-frame when we heard Shark's Porsche pulling into the driveway. Simone and I had just finished having sex—there'd always been an attraction—and we dressed hurriedly as Shark came in the door. We weren't fast enough though. We were still in the loft—and in those days before VCRs there was little else we could have been doing up there *besides* having sex.

Shark entered and saw us but didn't seem to care at all. He was almost scarily calm, as if he'd done some very serious soul searching in the last three days, as if he'd given up a terrible struggle and in so doing found peace. Precisely because of this aura of surrender neither Simone nor I were at all prepared for what happened next.

Shark picked up the film cans that held *Pillow Fuck*, the work print, the answer print and—I realized with horror and incredulity—the original negative. I sensed he was not going to take them to a vault for safekeeping.

## Simone Gatane

"What are you doing? Oh my God, no!" I yelled at Shark, as I tried to find my blouse. By the time Neal and I followed Shark outside he was squirting lighter fluid on the open film cans.

## Neal Ridges

He was giggling—a kind of tortured Dean giggle—as he drenched the film with lighter fluid, holding the can at crotch-level so that there was a kind of unmistakable piss symbolism.

Simone tried to stop him from striking the match.

"*Noooooo*," Shark whined, as he pushed Simone away,

sounding less like Dean now than Montgomery Clift. "Jean-Claude was *right!* It *is* shit!"

Shark tossed the match and the film ignited in the driveway as he groaned like an animal in agony, tears rolling down his grimacing face.

## Elliot Bernstein

I spoke to Shark on the phone a week or so after he destroyed his film, and the conversation disturbed me a great deal. He was no longer suicidal per se, but he was mentally fragmented, burned out, rambling endlessly.

He'd left his father's, he said, "because there's a part of me that really wants to kill him. He's a bigot, he drove my mother to suicide, and he totally fucked me up for life. Sometimes it's all I can do," Shark added with heavy sarcasm, "to remember that he's still my dear old dad."

He was nearly broke, he said, though he made it clear he wasn't asking for help. Simone had gone back to France, he was losing the James Dean house, and his primo Speedster had "blown up on the freeway," forcing him to sell it for a fraction of what he'd paid.

"Where are you going then?" I asked.

He didn't answer, rambling on instead about the last half hour of *Giant,* how they'd receded Dean's hairline when he played Jett Rink as an old man. The way Shark was muttering reminded me *of* Jett Rink in that terrible, lonely banquet room scene that marked Dean's last moment on film.

"Look, Shark, when you know where you're going to be, let me know," I said finally and got off the phone, since I was paying for the call.

# 6/Planet of the Apes (1968)

## Neal Ridges

Shark got a part-time job at the UCLA Film Archives that summer and moved in a dumpy apartment in Venice. The campus was relatively deserted during those months, but I was there several days a week, fine-tuning my thesis film project, and sometimes gave Shark a lift home since he no longer had a car.

He changed radically that summer and it was all for the worse. He got fat for one thing, putting on maybe thirty pounds from eating junk food, which I suppose was all he could afford. Still, it was disgusting to watch him stuff five Der Wienerschnitzel kraut dogs in his mouth one right after the other like a starving pig. He let his hair and beard grow long until he looked like a blond Jim Morrison. Remember Morrison after he went to seed? That was Shark in the summer of '68.

## Frank Forte

I saw Shark occasionally that summer and he'd become a disgusting slob. His hair and clothes were dirty—it went far beyond the hippie look of the time. He'd just ceased to care about his body and begun living entirely in his mind. His eyes had a kind of burning, Rasputin intensity as he lumbered through the corridors of Melnitz Hall, always with a number of dog-eared Critical Studies texts under his arm—Kracauer's *Theory of Film: The Redemption of Physical Reality* and the like.

One night I saw him at the Ray-Mar Theater in Mar Vista, which had just gone revival, using a pen-light to furiously scribble notes throughout a Jean-Claude Citroen double bill—*Neon City* and *Renée's Breath*. He was mumbling angrily to himself as he wrote until several other patrons shushed him. Clearly, he was researching a critique of Citroen's oeuvre, and was bent on intellectual revenge.

## Eric Sievers

I worked with Shark in the film archives that summer. We were cataloging a cache of silent nitrate footage, which was badly decomposed and therefore extremely dangerous to work with. We were on a razor's edge of anxiety about it, and one day Shark actually came in *smoking!* Smoking and mindlessly flicking ash! He should have been fired on the spot.

But I think we all felt sorry for him. I know I did. I hadn't seen *Pillow Fuck,* but I'd certainly heard about it, and about the horrific aftermath. Anyone who'd destroy his own art . . . I don't know. In a way it was romantic—inevitably, you thought of Rimbaud—and yet it spoke of such pain. You could see that Shark was hurting, which in itself frightened a lot of people away. And his criticism of others was as merciless as Jean-Claude Citroen's had been of him.

Once after work we went upstairs to one of the screening rooms to watch the rough cut of a girl student's film. Well, it wasn't very good, but I mean she'd been working on it for months. So everybody was polite except Shark who asked her, "Where are you from?"

"Nebraska," she said.

And Shark said, "You're a zero. You should go back."

Well, she started to cry. It was just shitty, gratuitous cruelty on Shark's part, and there were many other similar instances of that sort of thing.

## Neal Ridges

I stopped by Shark's one afternoon on my way to the beach. I'd never been inside before, and the building was indeed forbidding. Venice was a slum in those days, well before the gentrification of the seventies, and that rundown brick apartment house at Brooks and Speedway was a cesspool of burntout bikers and junkies.

Shark's room had an ocean view, though you'd never have known it. He had a ratty blanket tacked permanently over the window since the bright sunlight "hurt his eyes," he said. He sat on his lumpy bed, his lumpy body surrounded by fast-food debris and a dozen notepads, as he told me he was going to "annihilate" Jean-Claude Citroen. When I asked him how he hoped to do that he showed me a rough draft of a critical essay he was confident *Jump Cut* would publish.

Well, some of it was brilliant. But most of it was a demented screed. Every coolly rational critical point was invariably mired in a swamp of the most obviously personal vindictive bitterness, deranged diatribes which ran on for pages, rendering the essay completely unpublishable. That Shark didn't see that truly made me fear for his mind.

## Eric Sievers

It must have been about the middle of the summer that Tom Field stopped by the archives one afternoon. I remember, Shark was watching *Kiss Me Deadly* on the Steenbeck when Tom walked in, and the two of them immediately plunged into an animated discussion of film noir that went on for hours. Then they left together still talking up a storm. It was amazing, the first time I'd ever seen Shark really excited and enthusiastic in a positive way. Obviously the beginning of an important friendship. Sad in a way too, because more than anyone I'd ever known—and more that summer than ever before—Tom Field radiated an aura of premature doom.

## Neal Ridges

Tom Field had graduated a few years before and was really one of the bright lights of the film school. He was brilliant, absolutely brilliant. His thesis film, *Icons,* a kind of pseudo-verité *Citizen Kane* story of a rock star who commits suicide at the peak of his fame, was astounding. He'd won a number of festival awards with it and gone straight from UCLA into a studio development deal. And it was at that crucial point, sadly, that his health had given out. He'd had a severe recurrence of a childhood ailment, which had forced him to stay in bed for a year.

At the time he and Shark became friends Tom was back on his feet again but remained frail. He was, besides being brilliant, incredibly handsome, though in a delicate, almost feminine way. Poetic is the word, I suppose. He had the aura of a doomed poet—too sensitive, too beautiful for this coarse world.

Shark and Tom were soon together constantly, so much so that there began to be talk. There had always been rumors that Tom might be bisexual—though I think those were bred largely of either wishful thinking or envy, the desire to denigrate his genius in some way.

I never seriously thought that Shark and Tom were actually having sex, though the relationship was clearly intense—intense and exclusionary. They had a way of speaking a kind of private, intimate code, the way lovers do really, which was part of what fanned the rumors. One day in August Shark told me, as if it were a closely guarded secret, that he and Tom were writing a screenplay together.

## Eric Sievers

I never believed the gay rumors. It's possible Tom may have experimented at some time in his life, but there was something totally asexual about Shark that summer—his body was just something that carried around his mind.

I'm sure his rapport with Tom was strictly mental, which is not to say there weren't some rather bizarre subtextual elements. I didn't realize it at the time, because I had yet to see Kathy Petro. But when I did see her a few years later I have to tell you I experienced quite a jolt. My God, I thought, looking at her face on the cover of a magazine. She could be Tom Field in drag.

## Neal Ridges

There was definitely a resemblance, though I would describe it as more generic than mirrorlike. Tom had Kathy Petro's blonde hair, the exact same shade of pale blonde. He had her skin coloring, her green eyes. They were of a similar *type,* in the sense that people will speak of being attracted to a certain type.

Look, anything's possible. I have no way of knowing what was really going on in Shark's mind, either consciously or subconsciously, anymore than I or anyone will ever really know what happened the day Tom Field died.

## Janet Bundy

I hadn't seen Shark for a couple of months, not since the *Pillow Fuck* screening, when I picked him up hitchhiking in Venice one day. I almost didn't stop, not recognizing him at first because of his beard and weight. "Janet, you've got to take me to UCLA," he said. "It's a matter of life and death."

On the way he explained that Tom Field had got the news that afternoon that the studio he had a deal with had decided to dump him. Then his agent had done the same thing, saying he had decided that Tom, however talented, was "a loser." Tom was devastated and had called Shark to say he was going to kill himself, mentioning that someone shooting a film on campus was using a real gun as a prop.

Even at the time I sensed that wasn't the whole story though. For one thing Shark's face was scraped, his lower lip swollen as if he'd just been in a fight. I'd heard some funny stories about Shark and Tom, which I'd tried not to believe.

When we reached Melnitz Hall, Shark barged right into the sound stage, ignoring the red light, spoiling a take. He was still looking around for the prop gun when we heard a shot in the archives and Eric Sievers crying, "Oh God, no! No no no!"

## Eric Sievers

Tom came in that afternoon and asked if he could look at *Touch of Evil*. I was busy and said sure, and he went and got the film. He knew where it was since he'd studied it endlessly. It was his favorite Orson Welles film, if not his favorite film period. Later, I would recall that he seemed a bit moody, and remember noticing was that his knuckles were skinned as if he'd been in a recent fight.

I didn't give him much thought at the time though. I was painstakingly cleaning a nitrate print of *Greed*, and nearly jumped out of my skin when the gun went off less than six feet away in the Steenbeck room.

## Janet Bundy

Shark and I rushed into the archives and there was Tom Field slumped over the flatbed. The gun was on the floor at his feet. It had been loaded with live ammunition so they could film a realistic close-up of it firing. There was blood everywhere.

## Eric Sievers

As we went to Tom I couldn't help but notice the ending of *Touch of Evil* playing on the flatbed screen: a grotesquely bloated Orson Welles, shot by his partner, collapsing into the garbage-strewn waters of a Venice canal. Then a shot of Marlene Dietrich delivering her famous deadpan eulogy: "He was some kind of a man." Which she qualifies, with heavy poignance: "What does it matter what you say about people?"

At just that point the film ground to a halt, Tom Field's blood spreading like a magnified light-show effect over the close-up of Dietrich on the screen.

I looked at Shark. His expression was blank—stunned, I like to think—as he simply turned and walked out the door.

## Elliot Bernstein

As it happened I came to L.A. about a week after Tom Field killed himself. I stopped by the UCLA Film Archives hoping to catch Shark, and Eric Sievers told me about the suicide. Shark had left the day it happened and had not been back since.

I went to Shark's Venice address. The apartment was empty, recently cleaned out, the landlady still angry about the mess Shark had left behind. It appeared he had simply taken off the night of Tom's death without bothering to return for any of his possessions, which were mostly books and papers.

As I was leaving the building I saw a screenplay in the trash with Shark's and Tom Field's name on it. All I knew of Tom Field at that point was the little Shark had written: that Tom was a gifted film-maker and a great guy, that they were working on something "incredible" together.

Impulsively, I took the script, perhaps curious to see how incredible it in fact was.

## Neal Ridges

When Shark disappeared after Tom Field's death a lot of people feared the worst. Though it was true that Tom had lost his studio deal and his agent on the same day, the rumors of a fight—or to be blunt, a lovers' quarrel—between Shark and Tom spread. And now Shark, it was thought, might have drowned himself or OD'ed somewhere so that he could join Tom in death.

## Elliot Bernstein

I was jolted when I read the script—which was called *Canyons* then—shortly after I returned to San Francisco. It was obvious that the main characters were modeled on Kathy Petro and Jean-Claude Citroen. It was essentially the story of a young California woman, blonde and rich with an industrialist father, who has an affair with a famous French auteur in Los Angeles. They lease a house in the Hollywood Hills which they use as their love nest. Then, while the director is away on location, the young woman and several of her friends are brutally murdered by a gang of psychotic hippies who break into the house on a random killing spree.

The script I read was a heavily annotated first draft. You could see that someone, probably Tom, had been afraid the film director might too closely resemble Citroen. As a result his name (Jean-Paul Peugeot originally) and nationality had been tentatively changed here and there, in one case making him Italian, in another Polish.

The violence was extreme by 1968 standards, though "artful," I suppose—if you consider the climax of *The Wild Bunch* artful. At the time I read the script I believed it was simply a wishful fantasy, Shark's way of exorcising his anger towards both Kathy and Citroen, the two people who had hurt him most, by placing them together in an imagined scenario.

Then a week or so later I saw a photo in *Look* magazine of Kathy Petro on Jean-Claude's arm. Eventually I learned that Shark had seen similar photos before he and Tom wrote the script.

## Kathy Petro

Paris in the springtime, I mean any springtime, what can you say? But Paris in the spring of 1968—well, talk about being where *la action* was! Barricades and Pouilly Fuisse, tear gas and *chocolat soufflé [sic]*. What a time to be young and *now* and free!

I was in this little cafe one night where Hemingway used to go when Jean-Claude came in. I'd never been a big fan of his movies, mainly because I didn't understand them. I mean, I'd always liked stories, and still do, so shoot me, okay?

So I was there with *my* friends and he came in with *his* friends and right away he looked at me with, you know, *that look*. Well, he was almost forty then, so I mean, my God. Then he asked somebody who I was and they must have said: Oh, her father's Jack Petro of Petro-Chem, the people who make the napalm and everything. Because suddenly he got this severe look and marched right over and just totally dressed me down. "Your father's a war criminal. Your sports car is fueled with the blood of the Third World, your college tuition is paid with the scorched skin of babies." He just went on and on, saying all these horrible things to me, until finally I broke down and cried.

"Look, I can't help what Daddy does," I said and ran out into the street.

And he came out after me, saying, "Wait, wait, you're right. It's not your fault. Please forgive me, I didn't mean to make you cry."

He brushed back my hair and caught one of my tears with his finger. And then, very gently, he kissed me.

## Drake Brewster

Although I'd done a few drugs at one time, I was no fucking hippie and couldn't stand that bunch. So when I saw this grungy long-hair hitchhiking on the highway in Santa Barbara I had no intention of stopping. But suddenly the asshole stepped right in front of my car.

I veered to avoid him and hit the brakes. "You goddamn stupid fuck," I yelled back at him. And he reeled around like a goddamn drunk, so I threw it in park and jumped out.

"You fuckheaded dork," I said, about to waste him when he started whimpering like a fucking girl. It was so pathetic I just shook my head and said, "Man, I'm not even gonna dirty my hands on you."

Then he said, "I just lost my brother."

I see now he meant it in that bullshit hippie sense, like: we're all brothers. But at the time I thought he meant his *brother* and got a premonition. "What do you mean, man? In 'Nam?"

"Yeah," he said. "That's right. In fuckin' 'Nam, man."

I see now he meant it in the sense that the war was everywhere, so that everywhere was 'Nam. More of that hippie shit. But at the time it fuckin' moved me, man, since I'd lost my own brother over there in '65.

"Where you goin'?" I asked him.

"I don't know," he said. He looked like a poor fuckin' dog.

"Come on," I said. It was two in the morning. "You can sleep on my floor tonight."

I was living in this guest house then behind a big mansion in Montecito owned by an old Nazi. I mean a real German Nazi from World War II. I told Shark about that as we pulled up and he said, "So are you a Nazi too?" He meant my brown uniform.

"No. I'm a security guard," I said.

The next day was a Sunday and he'd got some sleep but I could see he was still pretty fucked up with grief. "Come on, the sun's out," I said. And we drove around

Montecito in this old Nova I had, looking at all the rich people's homes.

"Boy, this place makes Beverly Hills look sick," he said.

"Damn straight," I said. "And the criminals know it too."

"What do you mean?" he said.

"See that house?" I said. "Couple of Mexicans shot the owner two weeks ago. All they got was an old clock. Too bad that was my night off." I opened the glove compartment so he could see my piece.

"You ever killed anyone?" he said.

"Not yet," I told him. "But last year I shot off a black guy's thumb."

That night we went to Taco Bell. There were two girls there, both interested in me—until they saw this grungy animal I was with. That irritated me, but when we got back to my place and drank a few beers and talked a lot more I had to admit Shark was not a bad guy.

He said he'd had to get out of L.A. because that city was a jungle.

"Yeah, you can get eaten alive in a jungle," I told him. "Especially when you're a fat fuckin' slob panting for breath like you." I told it like it was, since I worked out with weights and took good care of my body and couldn't stand slobs, I had no sympathy at all.

"I guess I have let myself go to seed," he said.

"Man, that's an understatement. Lift your shirt."

I was gonna let him have it about this fat fuckin' gut he had. But we ended up just laughing and I let him off the hook.

He told me he was broke and I said, "You might be in luck, a fella just quit. Do you have a clean record?"

He said he did.

## Ernie Post

I managed the Santa Barbara office of Island Security then, and I hired Shark Trager on Drake's recommendation. Shark seemed like a level-headed young man to me, with something of a weight problem, but basically clean-cut.

## Drake Brewster

Before I took Shark in to meet the boss I gave him a haircut, short as short could be, right down to the scalp. I shaved that dirty beard off too, since I knew how to handle a straight edge. I liked the body builder look for myself, without all that dirty hair, so I was smooth all over except for my butt. It's hard to shave your own butt, so I slapped on some lather and handed Shark the razor.

"Are you crazy?" he said and started to laugh.

Well, I saw red and we had our first fight. I pinned him to the carpet the way you might pin a child. "I've seen some fat sacks of shit," I said, "but you take the cake."

## Ernie Post

Shark said he'd been in the ROTC and knew guns. So I told Drake, "Okay, go down and get him his permit and you break him in."

## Drake Brewster

We got Shark a uniform but it was a joke. "Man, you're a lard-ass," I said. "We gotta do something about you."

So I switched him to a high protein diet and made him jog every morning with me. Then I took him to the gym. He was panting and begging for mercy but I was brutal. "Come on, you fuckin' pussy," I'd yell when he wanted to quit.

The weight started coming off and he got some definition but only cause I whipped him like a goddamn horse. On our days off I took him to the pistol range and showed him how to handle my .357. The first time he fired it he flinched and I said, "Christ, man, you fire that thing like a goddamn fruit." I kept riding his ass till he got pretty good.

I showed him the route, pointing out what to watch for, strange cars and what-not. It was a pretty boring job unless you caught an in-progress, so a lot of the time we just talked about snatch. He told me about some French bitch who sounded like a real cunt, and about some other girl he still had the hots for. "Someday I'm gonna get her," he said once in a strange kind of voice that was filled with both anger and heavy-duty longing.

So I said, "Get her? What do you mean? Fuck her or kill her?"

I laughed and he blew up, saying, "Shut your stupid fucking mouth, Drake."

Well, nobody calls me stupid, so I hit him and we almost drove up onto this doctor's lawn.

Another time while we were jogging he said he'd gone to UCLA. "No wonder you were going crazy," I said. "All that shit they teach at college."

Then he set me straight about the guy who'd died the night we met being just a friend instead of an actual brother. When he said it was suicide, I said, "Man, that's a pussy's way out."

Shark said, "No, you don't understand. He was an artist and they drove him to it."

I said, "Fuck that shit. He was a loser. Only losers kill themselves like fucking little babies. Winners don't pull shit like that. That's what makes this country great."

We got into it on politics at first, 'cause he liked to spout this rancid radical shit this French bitch had filled him up with. But one day we passed some flowerchild types in Goleta and I said, "Look at those pukes. When all this *love* shit's over with, they're gonna go home to mommy and daddy. But where are you gonna go?"

Then one afternoon while he was spotting me at the gym he said the guy that had killed himself was a queer.

"How do you know that?" I said, feeling real nervous all of a sudden.

"Because he said he loved me," Shark said. And several other guys heard and gave us both funny looks. And I thought: Uh-oh, am I living with a fag?

"But I told him to get lost," Shark added. And I went: Pshew!

A while later in the showers he said, "You know I've been thinking. I think you're right. Tom *was* a pussy. If you can't stand the heat—"

"Damn straight," I said. "It's fuck or be fucked."

Just then a black guy stepped into the shower just as Shark stepped back, and they accidentally brushed. When Shrk saw the guy was black he almost flipped. "Watch it, Sambo," he said, and there was almost a fight.

But the black guy shook his head and said, "Man, forget you."

Shark had a real problem with black guys.

"Yeah, it's a brutal world," I said as we drove back through Montecito. "Look at all these houses. You think the people who live in these houses got rich by taking it up the ass?"

We both laughed at that. Then we passed a couple of young babes in hot pants. "You see that one on the left, she's dying for it," I said. "They look like sisters to me. One for each of us. I wish they'd cut up that alley."

"Why?" Shark said.

"Cause I'm kind of into rape," I told him.

## Elliot Bernstein

I'd heard nothing from Shark for over a month when he wrote me a letter from Santa Barbara saying he was working for a security patrol company and did not intend to return to UCLA in the fall. He said he'd quit drugs and was getting himself into shape "for combat," which struck me as a curious figure of speech since he had always been so passionately opposed to the war. What followed was even more disturbing. Less political than philosophical it was a kind of crypto-Nietzschean rant. Life is a jungle, the survival of the fittest, that sort of thing. The primacy of the will, the mandate of the strong to subjugate the weak—a brutal, insane philosophy which I mistook at first for parody. It was only as I came to his commentary on Tom Field that I realized how serious he was.

"Tom could never have made it in Hollywood," Shark wrote. "And he saw that himself. That's the reason he took the quick way out. Seen in this light his suicide was not cowardly, but was in fact the bravest act of his life. Tom was an artist but he was also a weakling. He was like a delicate poetess, Emily Dickinson, thrown into the Roman Colosseum. He was still shrinking from the sword with which he might have defended himself when they cast their nets and came in for the kill. This may sound heartless and self-serving, but I like to think that the weak, feminine, timid side of my own nature died when Tom pulled that trigger. Whenever I feel like pussing out I hope I'll see his bleeding head on that flatbed and remember what happens to 'suffering artistes.' "

I was extremely put off by this radical shift in Shark's weltanschauung, and showed the letter to Sue, whom I'd been living with for several months at that point. "I don't know what's going on with him," I told her. "This is not the Shark I used to know. Or perhaps one I want to know."

"He's been through a lot," Sue said. I had told her a great deal about Shark by then, though she had yet to read his and Tom's screenplay.

She read it that night. When she was done she came into the living room of our place on Haight Street and said, "This is the most farout script I've ever read." She laughed with the joy of a great discovery. "I'm going to send it to Dad."

## Drake Brewster

One night after we went to see *Planet of the Apes*, I turned Shark on to my philosophy of Zen rape. "The bitches want it," I told him. "That's the bottom line. And if you're a man you'll let 'em have it. That's what makes the world run. Everything else—society, the law, good manners—is all horseshit. Real men can take whatever they want. And if you're *real*, if you stay locked into the present on that animal vibe, the bitches won't complain. That's what I've found."

Up to then I'd nailed maybe seven separate babes, but not even one had gone and told the cops.

"Take her for example," I said as we saw some nurse getting off a bus. "I could nail her right now and she wouldn't do shit."

"You're crazy," Shark said. "You could go to prison."

"You're a pussy," I told him. "Watch this."

I made a U and pulled up behind the nurse as she walked toward an apartment building. "Come on, we can take turns," I said, thinking it would be a gas for us to watch each other fuck.

"You're nuts," Shark said.

"Quit saying that," I told him, cause I was getting turned on.

Then this nurse looked back and saw us in the car and started walking fast. By then I had a hard-on.

I pulled up and was about to jump out when she reached her door and this big Mexican dude came out.

"Damn, I hate it when this happens," I said, pulling out. "She had a nice ass too."

So we drove home and I jacked off, but I still felt frustrated and half-blamed Shark. If he hadn't been there giving me static, sure as shit I would've nailed that nurse before she even knew what hit her.

## Elliot Bernstein

Sue and I met backstage at the Avalon after a gig and it was love at first sight. She was extraordinary, lithe with incredible legs, a stunning face with a large sensuous mouth, coal-black hair down her back, just a beauty. And intelligent! Really, her mind blew me away as much as anything. Her wit, her infectious joie de vivre.

She was still enrolled at Berkeley then. But it was 1968, you know, so the idea of actually attending classes and worrying about grades and all that just seemed incredibly unimportant. We spent the weekend together, dropping acid, and in the idiom of the day, we just merged. We barely spoke. Verbal communication was unnecessary, for we had entered a realm of tactile language, composing Italian sonnets and Dostoyevskian novels in and about one another's bodies.

Finally though, I had to drive her back to Berkeley to pick up a check she was expecting from home. That was when I first learned who her father was.

## Sue Schlockmann

I was really embarrassed in those days about the kind of films Dad made. Of course film itself was cool, so if the subject came up I tended to color the truth. "Yes, my father runs a film company. He imports foreign films." The foreign film thing always sounded good. Maybe they'd think he was Janus or somebody, bringing Bergman films to the States. I'd usually change the subject at that point, because once I said Regal Pictures there would be this sneer that just killed me.

"Regal Pictures? Don't they make all those sleazy biker movies? And import those cheesy Asian caged-women flicks?"

I'd just be mortified because Regal was synonymous with the bottom of the barrel. I mean, let's face it, Dad made Roger Corman and AIP look like class operations. At least some of those B-films were kind of cool in a way, with a young Jack Nicholson or at least a name has-been. But Regal made Z-movies with sub-SAG morons no one had ever seen before or would ever see again.

Not that Dad cared as long as his films made money, and they almost always did. But 1968 had been a bad year. That was why I knew he'd consider Shark's script. He'd had high hopes for a depressing turd of a film called *Stews on Wheels*, and when it died he became despondent. He'd spent more than usual on advertising—I can still see the poster illustration of the buxom stewardesses scattering in terror as the grungy bikers roar up the aisles of the 747 on their Harley-Davidsons, with the tag: "They quit smiling the night the Angels ripped off their wings"—but still nobody came.

"I don't know, maybe I've lost touch," he'd said to me. "I don't know what these kids today want."

"Do this script, Dad," I told him on the phone the night I read Shark's screenplay. "It's cool and it's now, and it makes a statement about America that people of my generation will relate to. Plus—since I know this is important to you—it will also make a bundle." And then I told him, "Dad, if you don't screw it up it could even be art."

I knew that would get to him because by then he'd made so much money that it was really only a symbol. He'd talked cautiously for some time about someday mounting a "really class production," one that would give him the one thing that no amount of crass profit could provide: respectability.

I called him a week after I mailed the script and he said, "I couldn't finish it, I found it repellent. I don't mind turn-on violence, but this is turn-*off* violence, which is a whole other thing. These boys are sick. They should be in a mental hospital."

"One of them's already dead," I told him. "But the other one's a genius. At least that's what I hear."

He changed the subject and I didn't press it since at the time I'd spent my allowance on grass and acid and, you know, needed a few more dollars for food.

## Woody Hazzard

Black Light played all over the bay area but for a long time nobody would sign us, cause they said we were "too dark." All these candyass psychedelic groups were being signed right and left and I got depressed, and when we didn't have a gig I just stayed in bed with Rat, this girl I was living with in a Sausalito houseboat.

Then suddenly in December this hot producer signed us. He said we were gonna be the next Doors. The studio dates were set in L.A., and Elliot and Sue and I drove down together in my VW, stopping to visit Shark in Santa Barbara on the way.

I don't think any of us were prepared for his roommate. The second I laid eyes on him I knew he was nuts.

## Elliot Bernstein

Shark was out when we arrived. But Drake was sitting there in the living room watching "McHale's Navy" in his jockstrap, one leg over the arm of the chair as he rubbed his gun against the pouch of his jock. I thought at first we'd come to the wrong guest house. Then Shark pulled up in Drake's Nova.

## Sue Schlockmann

I had a bad feeling about Drake right from the start. The gun-in-the-crotch business . . . I don't know. This was a few years before the women's movement and all the talk about sexism and machismo, so my reaction was not intellectual. It was just a gut feeling this guy was the enemy.

When Shark arrived he led us into the house and introduced us to Drake, who was glum and surly and refused to put on any clothes even after Shark asked him to. Drake muttered something like, "It's my fuckin' house," and strutted around in nothing but his supporter for the rest of the evening. He did have a pretty spectacular body, but his whole narcissistic thing was really a bore.

## Woody Hazzard

Shark invited us to stay over, so I put my sleeping bag on the floor. Shark took the sofa and let Elliot and Sue use his bed on the service porch since they were still into this heavy sex thing. They went to bed early, partially I think to get away from Drake.

Then Shark and Drake and I smoked some dope, which Drake said he hadn't done in a long time. He said he'd taken peyote years before and had been hip when the word still meant something. Then he talked about how great Vietnam was, and at first I thought he was joking. But he wasn't, and he went into this incredible riff about how it must be like taking peyote to be in a battle, that it must be an "incredible rush to kill a man," that he'd heard it was better than sex.

"So why haven't you joined up?" I said.

And he said he wished he had because now it was too late. All the "pussy peaceniks" had fucked it up, making it impossible to "get off good over there."

I kept looking at Shark, trying to catch his eye 'cause I was sure he had to know his roommate was crazy. But every time I looked at Shark he quickly looked away.

## Sue Schlockmann

The next day was a Sunday, a beautiful warm day, and since the guys weren't due in L.A. until Tuesday there was no real rush to move on. Drake had already gone to the gym by the time we got up, and Elliot and Wood went off to find some guy who might have some speed for the sessions. "Come on, grab a towel," Shark said to me. "Let's hit the beach."

Soon Shark and I were walking out across the toasty white sands of a stunning little cove which we had all to ourselves. "No need for tan lines," Shark said, and I suppressed a gasp as he pulled off his shorts.

This is going to sound corny, I know, but in many ways Shark was like a god back then. At least that's how he struck me that shimmering afternoon. With his blond hair and blue eyes, his golden skin and Greek statue physique—he was like a surfer or a Marine or maybe even a Viking.

And his talk was brilliant—though he could have been speaking Sanskrit and I would have still hung on every word. Soon I was topless and then bottomless myself, and I felt as if I'd taken acid, though in fact it had been nearly a week since I had.

There was a coolness to Shark however. Though our intellectual rapport was instantaneous he showed absolutely no sign of romantic interest. Of course I was going with one of his best friends. But still, you know, you can tell if there is repressed desire if you're really looking for it. And I was.

At the time I knew little of Kathy Petro. Elliot had mentioned in passing that the character of Karen in *Canyons* was based on a girl Shark had once known. I didn't really understand what that meant, though it was clear from the script that she must have hurt him deeply for him to imagine her murder as intensely as he had.

Eventually I steered the conversation toward film. Shark winced when I mentioned UCLA. It was obvious that wound was still healing. Then I revealed who my father was and, thank God, he didn't sneer. Instead he became bleak. "I don't care about movies anymore," he said. "I'm finished with that."

At that point I told him I'd read his script and for a moment I saw a look of real fear in his eyes. He was astonished when I explained that Elliot had retrieved the script from the trash in Venice and it had now gone all the way to Dad. For a second I thought he was going to be angry. Instead he laughed. "My God, that's funny, that's really funny. Our supposed masterpiece ends up going to Sam Schlockmann! Tom would fucking shit!"

Well, that remark cut me. Shark saw that he'd been thoughtless and immediately apologized, then asked almost timidly, "So . . . what does he think of it?" I saw his naked longing for approval—even from someone he respected as little as Dad.

I was still hurt and angry though, and tempted to say, "He thinks it's shit, below even him. So there!" But I couldn't bare to hurt Shark when I sensed how badly, on so many different levels, he'd already been hurt.

"He's still reading it," I lied.

Shark said nothing.

"*I* like it," I said, "I think if it's done right it could be art."

Shark snorted. "Then you're blind. There's a reason that script ended up in the trash."

Then he rolled away from me and I studied his tan back. God, I did want him that first afternoon.


## Drake Brewster

I'd just about had it with Shark even before his fucking hippie friends came by. There was this little bitch in the big house, this old Nazi's niece, who used to wriggle her ass up the driveway after tennis. One day I was watching her through the window and I rubbed my crotch and said to Shark, "Man, if I don't shoot soon I'm gonna go crazy. Come on, man. Let's nail that little snatch right now."

And Shark said, "Man, you're crazy."

And I said, "Shit. You won't even fuck a Nazi. Man, I'd sure hate to be fighting next to you in World War II."

Then he called me stupid again and I chased him into the bedroom and threw him on the floor. I pinned him down and said, "Man, I've got half a mind to cram my dick down your throat just on general principle."

At that he threw me and pinned *me* down and said, "Don't you ever fuck with me again or I'll kill you."

I nodded okay and tried to act scared, but inside I was secretly smiling. Thanks to me, this guy who'd started out as a fat sack of shit that could've turned into a homo or a loser was now a real nobullshit man like me.

Then a few days later I found a newspaper ad section with a few rentals circled on it. Some friend, right? He's gonna move out and he doesn't even tell me. I was all set to call him on it the night his hippie friends came by.

Those pukes made my blood boil. When I came back from the gym that Sunday and saw that their shit was still there I wanted to kill. I was alone in the house fixing myself a protein drink when I saw that black-haired hippie bitch coming back from the beach.


## Sue Schlockmann

As Shark and I reached the driveway he went over to check the mailbox and I continued on to the guest house, eager to take a shower. I guess Drake saw me coming and thought I was alone.

I came in through the kitchen and the second I saw him standing there in his gym shorts I sensed what was going to happen. I tried to pass him and he grabbed me and forced me back against the sink. I fought him, but he was stronger, and he was just about to do it when Shark came in.

Drake froze and looked at Shark. Shark appeared stunned. Then Drake said, "Get in line, bro. Sloppy seconds."

Drake laughed and for a second I thought: Oh my God, Shark isn't going to help me, it's some sort of male thing. And for what seemed an eternity Shark didn't move, even as Drake turned his attention back to me.

Drake was just about to do it when Shark finally grabbed him, saying "Drake, let her go."

The two of them went at it, a grunting red-faced struggle, until both of them hit the floor. Then Drake got on top of Shark, pinning him down on his stomach. Drake's thing was still out, you know, as he abruptly tore down Shark's cut-offs, exposing Shark's buttocks. "Okay then," Drake said, "in that case I'll give it to *you*."

I tried to pull Drake off of Shark but he knocked me away. Then—thank God—Elliot and Woody barreled into the room and stopped Drake before he actually managed to do it to Shark. They pulled Drake to his feet, pinning his arms behind his back. By then he was like an animal—I'll never forget that insane red face—and both he and Shark were pouring sweat.

Shark got up, and refastened his cut-offs as best he could. Breathing hard he said to Elliot and Woody, "Let him go."

They released Drake, assuming as I did that the violence was over. But with a sudden ferocity that caught us all off-guard Shark laid into Drake, slugging him in the stomach and face again and again in a total rage, until Elliot and Woody managed to restrain him. By the time they did Drake was a bloody-faced mess beaten back into the corner.

## Woody Hazzard

It was a bad scene. Shark really wasted Drake. If we hadn't stopped him I'm sure he would've literally killed Drake.

## Elliot Bernstein

Sue was emotionally devastated. I took her outside while Shark packed his things, and there on the patio I said something incredibly stupid.

"Didn't you realize this might provoke him?" I said, indicating the sheer and skimpy bikini she was wearing. I'd never say anything like that now. But in those days people didn't really know what rape was.

"You asshole," she said, and pulled away from me.

## Woody Hazzard

I helped Shark take his stuff out to the car. No way was he gonna stay there after what had happened. Drake was in the bathroom, mopping the blood off his face as Shark picked up a few final things.

"Hey, Shark," Drake called in this weirdly casual voice as if nothing that serious had happened. "Hey, Shark, can you run down to the drugstore? Looks like we're all out of mercurochrome, bro."

Shark didn't answer, but I remember there was almost a look of sadness on his face. Then he said, almost gently—too gently, I think, for Drake to hear, "Hey Drake. Thanks for . . ." But his voice trailed off, and then he snorted and said to me, "Fuck it. Let's go." And we left.

# 7 / Sex Kill à Go-Go (1968–1969)

## Elliot Bernstein

Sue spent the entire drive down to L.A. talking film with Shark. Her attitude was so unctuously idolatrous you might have thought Shark was some sort of teenage Ingmar Bergman. Clearly, she was trying to make me jealous, but I refused to play that stupid game.

When we reached L.A. we dropped Shark off at Neal Ridges's place in Santa Monica. Then Sue—now in a cunty mood—and Woody and I met up with the Dilday twins at the Tropicana Motel in Hollywood. The first day in the recording studio Sue and I blew up at each other, and she ran home to mommy and daddy in Beverly Hills.

## Sue Schlockmann

I hated being at home again back in my stupid Princess Anderson bedroom. I hated that kitsch Greco-Roman house on a street behind the Beverly Hills Hotel where all the houses were kitsch something. I moped and sulked, angry at Elliot, my Dad mad at me since by then he knew I'd screwed up at Berkeley.

Then one day Shark called. "I want my script back," he said adamantly. "I want it back right now."

I called Dad right away at the studio. And after checking around he called back and said someone had given the script to Nigel Blore.

## Sam Schlockmann

Nigel Blore had run into trouble after being a British boy wonder. He'd made *The Hard Life* in '60, which wasn't too bad. Black and white, British losers, you know the kind of picture. Good camera work but downbeat—I skipped the last reel. I don't like to be depressed, I don't think audiences do either. Maybe that's why his other movies went down the toilet, including *Method to Her Modness*—lousy title—which he shot for a bundle in Spain in '67. After that he couldn't get arrested—till I gave him a break since he was willing to work for scale.

## Neal Ridges

Shark had been staying at my place a few days when he announced as I came in one afternoon, "Guess what? Nigel Blore wants to direct my screenplay."

Shark's tone was so neutral I wasn't sure how to respond. Was this good news or bad? Nigel Blore had been something of an auteur in the early sixties. But after *Method to Her Modness* he was considered washed-up.

"So how do you feel about it?" I asked Shark.

He shrugged and laughed. "It's Writer Guild scale." Which in those days was something like six thousand dollars for a low-budget script.

## Sue Schlockmann

Nigel Blore was totally wrong for the project. He'd been good in his own "kitchen sink" element. But *Method to Her Modness* was just nauseating drivel, a complete misinterpretation of what the sixties were all about. It was so wretched it made *Myra Breckinridge* look like a film by Satyajit Ray.

As soon as I realized Dad was actually going to buy the script for Nigel I called Shark and said, "You've got to meet me at the beach house at once," meaning Dad's house on the Gold Coast in Santa Monica, which was closed up then. Shark and I could meet there and talk without anyone knowing.

## Elliot Bernstein

I felt bad about my fight with Sue and called her one afternoon at her parents'. "Oh, she just left," the Schlockmanns' black maid told me. "She's going to the beach house, Mister Bernstein. You know where that is?"

## Sue Schlockmann

Shark and I entered the beach house living room and I opened the drapes, bathing the room in bright sunlight. The Gold Coast is to my mind *the* choice beach in L.A., a broad vista of pure white sand and blue sea without the fires and slides and distance of Malibu. And what a history. Selznick, Thalberg and all the other giants—they'd all had houses there. John Kennedy had conducted his trysts with Marilyn at the Lawford house a few doors down. It was funny, but even in those first few minutes with Shark in that house I had a premonition we were going to live together there.

"Look, I know you're a genius," I told him. "It's something I sense intuitively, as well as a rational judgment I make on the hard evidence of your screenplay, and what I've heard about *Pillow Fuck,* your legendary student film. You went to bat for me in Santa Barbara, Shark. If you want me to I'll go to bat for you now with Dad. This may be your only chance. *You* should direct *Canyons*. My gut instinct tells me that this could be your *Breathless,* if not your *Citizen Kane.*"

Shark said nothing for a long time. His back was to the

window and the glare was so bright his expression was hidden in shadow. When at last he spoke he sounded old, old and scarred, even though at the time he was just nineteen. "I'll never direct another film," he said.

"Don't be foolish," I said. "Just because you had one bad experience—"

"You don't understand," he interrupted.

"Oh, yes I do," I said. "You're chicken—"

"Shut up," he said.

"No, I won't shut up," I replied. "I'll never shut up. I'm going to go on believing in you even if you don't quite believe in yourself. I know what happened with Jean-Claude Citroen—"

At that he grabbed my face—that is, he squeezed my cheeks between his thumb and fingers so that my mouth resembled that of a fish.

"This is not a subject I care to discuss with you," he said.

Our eyes met. Then he kissed my fish mouth, and soon we were stuck together like two ravenous kissing fish. Inexorably, we drifted to the sofa. We were making love there when Elliot walked in.

## Elliot Bernstein

I said nothing to either of them. What could I say? I simply turned and walked out.

A few hours later I felt a terrible burning rage, which I quickly suppressed. Jealousy was considered very uncool in those days. We should all love one another without being possessive, it was felt. People changed partners in the dance of life. I see now what damage I did to myself by swallowing the fury I felt toward both of them, but in those days I was beatific whatever the cost.

Once our album was finished we decided to relocate in L.A. And so I would visit Shark and Sue—once a lover, but now a "dear friend"—after Shark moved into the beach house with her.

## Sue Schlockmann

For a long time my parents weren't aware that Shark was living in the beach house with me. They thought I was there by myself, trying to "get my head together." My mother was fairly conventional about morality—which is to say she just didn't want to know. And Dad wouldn't have thought much of my living with Shark, especially after their disastrous first meeting.

Shark went to see Dad and Nigel Blore at the studio right after Dad bought the script, since both he and Nigel felt it needed some minor revision. Sadly, the moment when I might have convinced Dad to let Shark direct the script seemed to have passed. Given Shark's pained reaction to that possibility, I hadn't mentioned it to him again. For as fine as *Canyons* was, I had no doubt his mind would soon be fired with an even greater directorial vision.

The meeting with Dad and Nigel was supposed to be a positive, celebratory, "let's make a movie" sort of thing. But the minute Shark stepped into Dad's office he took a breath of Dad's cigar smoke and felt sick to his stomach. Dad was still in that terrible place in Palms with the noisy window air-conditioners. Even though the room was frigid, Shark said, the cigar smoke was just hanging in the air.

As Dad began to talk Shark said he almost laughed, because here was this "living three-dimensional cliché of the ultimate sleazebag Hollywood producer." (That designation stung me, though sadly I knew in my heart it was true.) Then Nigel began gushing effusively, "You're a gifted writer, it's an astonishing story, a fantastic script," when Shark stood abruptly with a snide, denigrating, "This is a joke," and walked out.

Dad was furious. "Who does he think he is? That arrogant punk. He's a nobody, fuck him." He was ready to kill the project then and there.

But Nigel interceded, making excuses for Shark's behavior. "James Dean was like that, you know. The boy may be a genius. Rudeness goes with the territory."

So Dad, who was desperate for a hit and had no more confidence in his own instincts, said what the hell and went ahead with the film.

## Elliot Bernstein

One day I stopped by the beach house and Shark and Sue were arguing. "You insulted my father," Sue said.

"That's impossible," Shark replied. "You can't insult an old hack like your dad."

"Then I guess you don't want this, do you?" Sue grabbed Shark's screenplay check from Regal Pictures and tore it up in front of him.

Shark saw red and smacked Sue across the face. I intervened on her behalf, and she screamed at me, "Elliot, stay out of it!"

So I said, "Okay, fuck you both," and left.

Shark called the next day and apologized, mentioning that Sue had got her father to authorize a new check.

It was about that time that an FBI agent came around to see Shark. He'd registered for the draft in Santa Barbara, but had neglected to inform the board of his change of address, and the G-man told him to report for a physical or else.

## Woody Hazzard

Shark told me he didn't have sex with Sue, or jerk off or anything, for like two weeks before his physical, and when the day came he didn't wear any underwear, knowing full well that all the guys had to strip down to their underwear to go through the procedure. So there was Shark walking around with his folder totally naked. Then, he said, he used all his powers of concentration to imagine he was having excruciating sex with Kathy Petro so that he got this huge fuckin' hard-on, and the army doctors and everybody became totally disturbed. They put him in the line to see the shrink, and while he was standing there, without touching himself or anything, he like totally shot off all over the place, getting jiz on the guy in front of him in line.

Everybody went apeshit, and they figured Shark was gay, so they stamped him 4-F and sent him home.

## Sue Schlockmann

At the time I believed Shark had avoided the draft because he had a "John Kennedy-like back problem," though I would have been for anything that kept him from being turned into cannon fodder for that obscene war.

Early 1969 proved to be a difficult period though. Shark was irritable and directionless with too much time on his hands. With the money from the screenplay he didn't have to work. So he read a lot—books on Zen Buddhism especially—and we made love a lot, with the exception of a two-week period when his back was bothering him, and went for long walks on the beach. But he was restless.

The sex was quite good, though he held back emotionally. In an odd way I think that only increased my love for him. There was still such a sense that he'd been hurt so badly—by this Kathy person. And yet Shark was so beautiful in those days, with such an untapped depth of tenderness, that I was certain in time he would surely see how much I loved him and let down his guard and love me.

Once I hinted at the real possibility that if *Canyons* did well Dad might let Shark direct his next script, and Shark flared. "Fuck Hollywood," he said. "I don't care about any of that. There are other things in life beside movies, you know."

But one day I noticed that along with *The Three Pillars of Zen* he was also reading a paperback copy of *Memo from David O. Selznick*.

I was getting restless myself. As good as the sex was it began to seem like that was all Shark ever wanted to do. So in March I went to work as Dad's story editor, though the job was something of a joke. By the time a script reached Regal it was falling out of its binder, was generally wretched, and often genuinely psychopathic. Stories by geeks in Texas about women eaten alive by armadillos and the like. Very depressing.

Which I suppose was why I had such high hopes for *Canyons*. If Nigel Blore could relocate his pure artistic flame, the film might be another *Bonnie and Clyde*. Violent to be sure, but esthetically so.

*Canyons* rolled in April of '69. At the end of the first week I attended the dailies and actually threw up in the screening room.

## Woody Hazzard

I was visiting Shark at the beach house when Sue flew in and said, "My God, I'm sick. Nigel Blore is ruining your script."

Shark snorted cynically, as if to say: So what did you expect?

I asked Sue what she meant and she said she was sick to her stomach in the screening room. "Why?" I said. "Because of the violence?"

"No," she said. "Because it's *Method to Her Modness* all over again."

Then she described how Blore was turning it into a cheesy psychedelic "art" movie, adding a bunch of disconnected visual stuff that wasn't in the script. For example, in the scene where the murders were taking place, instead of showing the violence he'd cut to a shot of a go-go dancing dwarf with this zoom going in and out, in and out real fast—which was the part that had made Sue sick.

"Let me talk to Dad," she said to Shark. "It may not be too late." Meaning that Shark might still be able to replace Nigel as the director.

But Shark stared out at the ocean and said, "Somebody else wrote that script, I didn't. I don't know what it's about anymore, nor do I care." Then he turned and looked at Sue and said in a cold, scary voice, "Both the losers who wrote that script are dead."

## Sue Schlockmann

I couldn't bear to attend the dailies again, but it wasn't really necessary because word soon spread that *Canyons*, even by Regal standards, was a dog. Dad could have stopped the production but he didn't. He'd come back from the dailies shaking his head and tell me, "It's not even shit." Which translated meant it was arty as opposed to trashy—perhaps *that* was why he didn't pull the plug. "I don't know, is this what the kids want now?" he'd say with a terrible lost expression.

And Nigel *was* staying on schedule. He was shooting what was in the script, it was just that he was shooting so much more. But he was working so fast, and in a sense so ingeniously, that the film was still holding to its budget. I suppose from Nigel's point of view it was his last chance to make what he considered great art and as a result he was remorselessly brutal with the cast and crew and by all accounts completely possessed.

Nigel had made a number of seemingly minor adjustments to

the script, many of which would eventually prove to be uncannily resonant choices indeed—though the most horrifying, thank God, had been avoided. Just prior to principle photography, Nigel had come up with the brilliant idea of making Daisy Withers, who'd been cast as the young blonde wife, pregnant. "It'll jack up the jeopardy," Nigel had enthused. "Look at *Rosemary's Baby.*"

Dad, I'm sorry to say, had been on the verge of agreeing, grateful I suppose that Nigel was still making concessions to such outmoded conventions as jeopardy and suspense, but I'd argued against it in the only terms Dad would understand. "If you make Daisy pregnant she'll lose her sex appeal. You don't want that, do you?" The idea was dropped.

The final week of shooting was on location at a house in Coldwater Canyon, and that was where the shit finally hit the fan.

## Sam Schlockmann

It's bad when you can't trust your instincts. I'd look at Nigel's rushes and think, this shit makes me sick. But if it's what the kids want . . .

Then he's shooting the murders up in Coldwater Canyon and he says: I wanna do the pigs. What pigs, Nigel? I say. There are no pigs in the script. Well, by now I'm used to that. He's done second unit go-go dancing dwarves, hunchbacked ballerinas, pinheaded debutantes—what he likes to call "surrealism." Fine. But pigs? I get a bad feeling. What do you mean, Nigel? He wants these pigs to fly across the swimming pool. He wants real pigs with wings attached. What are you saying, Nigel? You want a matte shot? No, he says. Live. I say how, Nigel? He says we run a wire through the pigs' mouths and out their assholes, then slide 'em down the wire across the pool. I say how do you keep 'em upright? He says we weight down their feet. I say Nigel that sounds painful for the pigs, there's gonna be a lot of squealing. He says I know, that's what I want. I say Nigel it sounds cruel. He says it's art and besides we'll get it in one take, we've got no choice. Why's that? I say. Because I'm gonna put a charge on each pig, he says, and when they reach the far side of the pool I'm gonna blow 'em up.

You're a sick man, Nigel, I told him. Go home, you're off the picture.

## Sue Schlockmann

An hour after Dad fired him over the phone we learned that Nigel was still shooting, claiming that contractually Dad *couldn't* fire him. So we drove up to the location on a remote cul-de-sac in Coldwater Canyon, Dad primed for a confrontation.

When Dad picked up a megaphone and told the crew it was over Nigel went berserk. He called Dad every name in the book and threatened him with a Directors' Guild suit as the cast and crew stood around smirking. By then they all hated Nigel and thought he was completely insane.

Finally Nigel stormed off and got into his Jaguar, and at first it wouldn't start. He sat there pounding the wheel, pouring sweat, and you couldn't help but feel sorry for him. At last the car started. "You haven't heard the last of me," he yelled at Dad and tore out.

Not more than a minute later we heard a terrible crash.

## Elliot Bernstein

I was smoking dope with Shark at the beach house when Sue came in and said, "Nigel Blore is dead. He had a head-on collision in Coldwater Canyon."

Shark was stunned and silent as Sue explained that Sam had been forced to fire Nigel, and that Nigel's devastation over that event had doubtless been a factor in his death.

Finally Shark said, "What's going to happen to the film?"

"I suppose Dad's going to write it off," Sue said bleakly. "It's crap. Unsavable. Which is a pity." She looked at Shark. "In the right hands it might have really been something."

I think Shark waited a day or two before he went to see Sam Schlockmann.

## Minnie Schlockmann

Sam felt so bad about Nigel Blore's death. "I should've canned him sooner," he said sadly. Then he got mad and said, "Why did I hire him in the first place? That goddamn limey jerk."

Then he fell into a deep depression. "I'm too old for this

business, Minnie. It's a kids' business now. Maybe it's time to bail out.''

He was still depressed when Shark came to the door that Sunday afternoon. Shark was wearing a neatly starched white shirt and tie and was very polite and pleasant. ''Good afternoon, Mrs. Schlockmann. Do you suppose I could have a word with your husband?''

Well, I knew Sam's first meeting with Shark had not been good. But Shark was so charming I said, ''Yes, why don't you come in. Sam's out on the patio.''

I watched from the window as Shark went out to Sam, who did not look happy to see him at all. They began talking. I was too far away to hear what was said, but in a little while Sam's scowl gave way to a smile. Then he laughed at something Shark said and saw me in the window. ''Minnie,'' he called. ''Why don't you bring our guest some wine?''

## Sue Schlockmann

It was nearly midnight when Shark came in drunk, and I was mad as blazes. I'd cooked a meal that I'd had to throw out, and to be honest at that point I was insanely possessive and suspicious. ''How was she?'' I said.

''I was with your father,'' Shark said, and I was incredulous.

It turned out they'd been together since one that afternoon, getting drunk, then driving down to the studio where they looked at all the rushes of the film.

''I'm going to save the picture,'' Shark said. Then he went into the bathroom and threw up because he and Dad had been drinking Manischevitz all day, and Shark could never take sweet wine.

## Woody Hazzard

''I jacked him off shamelessly, man,'' Shark told me a few days after Sam put him in charge of cutting the picture. ''I had to be careful not to go too far. If I'd said I thought *Stews on Wheels* was art he would've known I was stroking him. So I used the veiled sexual approach. Regal Pictures represents 'rugged, masculine filmmaking, hard, assertive action pictures with a tough no-bullshit forward thrust.' The stupid old fart ate it with a spoon.''

"Do you really think you can save the picture?'' I asked Shark. And suddenly he quit gloating, like he was afraid he'd revealed too much. He turned real sober and serious and said, "Yes, I think so, Woody. And I believe passionately that Black Lights' music is going to be a major factor in my attempt to shape this film into something resembling art.''

By that time, you see, our album had stiffed and our label was talking of dropping us. So we were only too willing to let Regal have a bunch of our songs for use in the film.

## Sue Schlockmann

I was thrilled at first. If anyone could restore the film to its original concept, surely it was Shark. Amid all the artsy dreck the performances were not at all bad. Daisy Withers was especially convincing. Her protracted running-through-the-house-from-the-killers routine could have degenerated into giddy camp histrionics so easily. But Daisy made you absolutely believe her terror, as she ducked through door after door, hiding in the vestibule, then doubling back around as the knife-wielding hippie girls inexorably closed in. Sadly, it was Daisy's last movie role. Though I'm sure she didn't know it yet, botched silicone implants had resulted in malignant tumors in both of her breasts. Rather than face the double mastectomy she felt would end her career she took a lethal overdose of pills in 1970, allegedly inspired by the example of the starlet-with-breast-cancer in Jacqueline Suzann's *Valley of the Dolls*, a paperback copy of which was found beside her body.

Playing opposite Daisy, Reggie Bingum was quite good as Clay, the fashionable young designer who, still in love with Daisy's character, pays her a visit that hot summer night when he knows her auteur husband is away, and ends up paying the ultimate price for his obsession. Linda Carlisle was perfect as Andrea Grey, the British tea heiress, who is stabbed again and again on the lawn. All of the performances were actually quite naturalistic and believable. I was convinced that once Shark cut away the fat we might yet have a spare and serious crime drama in the realistic vein of *In Cold Blood*.

But I began to worry when he wouldn't let me see what he

was doing. He was practically living at the studio, working with the editors till all hours of the night, and he made it quite clear that the editing room was "off-limits." I tried to attribute this attitude to nerves, or his abhorrence of criticism. Then too I knew he had begun taking speed to stave off his fatigue, and that was certainly a factor in his irritability.

Then one afternoon I heard he was "shooting some inserts" on one of the soundstages. I was puzzled since he'd said nothing about it, so I went over to see what was going on. I arrived just in time to see an extremely realistic miniskirted dummy being gutted. A knife would go in and what I presume were cow's intestines would spill out on the floor. "No, no, no, *cut*," Shark yelled, without seeing me there. "I don't believe how *fake* that looked! Come on, people, this isn't a comedy! Let's try it again."

I ran from the soundstage in shock and disgust, with no more illusions about what sort of film it was going to be.

## Sam Schlockmann

I asked Shark to pick up some gore because Nigel had been too squeamish. Gore's funny. I don't know what it is, but a lot of guys get carried away, and Shark definitely did. Even after the trims I knew we'd get an X. But in '69 an X wasn't the kiss of death it is today.

## Sue Schlockmann

"It's done," Shark announced as he came in one night, as if he had committed some terrible but inevitable and necessary crime. He dropped on the bed, exhausted. "Your dad likes my new title too," he said.

"What new title?"

"*Sex Kill à Go-Go,*" he said, and laughed a terrible, bitter laugh.

I went to the studio screening a few days later, but walked out ten minutes into the film.

## Elliot Bernstein

We let Shark use our music in the film because he led us to believe it was going to be an artistic statement sort of film.

Violent, but toward a lofty end, like an Arthur Penn film or something.

So we were angry when we saw what a piece of shit it was. By then it was too late to get our music back, and we didn't really even say that much to Shark because at the time we believed he didn't really know how bad the film was. But of course he knew. He had coldly and deliberately turned the film into the garish trash Sam wanted.

## Sam Schlockmann

I knew we had a winner when the exhibitors went gaga, especially the boys from the South. "This is the sickest piece of shit I've ever seen," one of 'em said. Which translated meant: Big bucks.

We opened wide in the last week of August with no press screenings. What do you think, I'm stupid? By the time the critics organized a lynch mob we would have cleaned up and blown town. Not that your typical drive-in redneck pays much attention to Vincent Canby.

I smelled success. The timing was right for this kind of picture. I knew the first weekend would be a killer. I had no way of knowing how true that would be in more ways than one.

## Sue Schlockmann

The print ads were revolting. A chic couple strung from the beams of a living room ceiling, the woman's breasts about to pop from her blouse as a crazed bearded hippie threatens to cut off her buttons with a Bowie knife. And the tag: "To their friends they were rich, young, and beautiful. To their killers they were just a bunch of pigs."

I told Shark I thought it was tasteless and sick.

"Gee, I'm sorry you feel that way," he said. "Since I'm the one who thought it up."

"I hope you know what you're doing to yourself," I said. But I knew I was on precarious ground. Who was I, after all, to accuse Shark of whoring himself when my entire life-style was funded from the proceeds of the biggest whore in town.

Secretly though I was beginning to wonder if his fabled

153

UCLA student film had really been as great as people said. Perhaps he had less in common with Orson Welles than he did with Russ Meyer.

Still, I loved him—though I see now how much that had to do with sex. He'd been too tired to make love during the editing period. But with the film in the can we resumed with a vengeance. He was good. To be blunt he knew how to use his hands and his mouth. And in those days I tended to romanticize all that.

## Sam Schlockmann

We opened on a Wednesday, and the film left the gate like somebody'd fired a blowtorch up its ass. Even the matinees were packed, and it just kept building. There were lines around the block at the walk-ins, and the drive-ins were packed. It was the biggest opening we'd ever had. Whether it was the ads, or the word-of-mouth or what, I don't know. You can drive yourself nuts trying to figure these things. I know, 'cause I spent the next ten years doing just that.

## Sue Schlockmann

Shark was elated when the film began breaking records. He was still resting at the beach house, but was constantly on the phone to Dad. I was happy for him, and of course for Dad too. I was just sorry their success had to come from such an odious and amoral piece of artless crud.

By Friday night Shark was actually kind of manic, feeling giddily omnipotent. "Let us remember this night, Sue," he said, "as the first major victory on the road to my conquest of Hollywood. This is my Beer Hall Putsch!"

I was startled by the Nazi reference, despite the ironic manner in which he'd made it. I'm quite sure Shark didn't realize at the time, anymore than I did, that Hitler's Beer Hall Putsch had actually failed.

I suppose there are peak sexual moments in every life, and who knows why they occur when they do. But that Friday night with Shark was certainly one of mine. I won't be pornographic. Even now I can't bring myself to cheapen that experience by describing it in detail. I will say only that I did not fall asleep until the dawn's first light, and by then I was dreamily exhausted and satisfied as I had never been before.

I woke up in the early afternoon, the bed empty beside me. I heard Shark on the phone in the other room, though I couldn't make out what he was saying. Presently he came back into the bedroom, a sundrenched Greek god, though I could have sworn he looked ill.

"Who died?" I said as a joke.

And Shark smiled and came down the bed, taking me in his arms. I'll never forget how I felt that dazingly hot August afternoon as he kissed me so sweetly and said, at long last, the words I so wanted to hear.

"I love you, Sue. It scares me to say it because as you've undoubtedly deduced my heart has been broken severely in the past. But I can't play it safe any longer. I love you, and I want to marry you, Sue."

We left for Mexico late that afternoon.


## Elliot Bernstein

Subconsciously, I don't think I ever forgave Shark for marrying Sue that weekend in what amounted to a crass and desperate act of self-preservation.


## Sue Schlockmann

We were married in Ensenada by a seedy little man with extremely bad teeth and a linty blue suit. We were pretty looped on margaritas by the time the ceremony took place, both of us weaving and slurring our vows. We thought it was quite hilarious at the time. In retrospect it was strictly F. Scott and Zelda—which is to say, sad.

The motel was even sadder, though that sequence too seemed delightfully madcap at the time. We drank toasts to the cockroaches and laughed hysterically when, as we made love, the bed collapsed. Several times I voiced a desire to call my parents and break the news. But Shark would always laugh and pull me from the door back to the bed.

## Minnie Schlockmann

From Saturday till Monday we heard absolutely nothing, and we were worried sick. It's hard to imagine now how terrified everyone was that weekend. That murders like that could occur right there in Beverly Hills!

## Sue Schlockmann

We got back to the beach house in Santa Monica around eleven Monday morning. We hadn't seen any newspapers or heard the news on the radio—Shark made sure we didn't, I see now. When I saw Elliot's Renault and Woody's VW parked at the house I sensed that something odd was going on.

Elliot and Woody came running out to meet us as we parked, both saying they'd been afraid something might have happened to us. At first I didn't understand what was clearly a paranoid overreaction. Then Woody described what had happened Friday night at Sharon Tate's.

## Elliot Bernstein

I felt gut-punched when Shark mentioned that he and Sue had got married. I was stunned because I knew in my heart I still loved her. I said very little as Woody told them about the Cielo Drive murders. Later I would remember that although Shark acted astonished, as if he was hearing about the killings for the first time, his performance was not quite convincing.

## Sue Schlockmann

As Woody described the Tate murders detail by detail I began to feel as if I were peaking on bad acid. Because, you know, the parallels between what happened on Cielo Drive and the plot of *Sex Kill à Go-Go* were just too numerous to mention. The isolated house in the canyon, the beautiful young blonde woman married to the foreign director—French originally, modeled on Jean-Claude Citroen, though fearing that similarity was too close, Shark had made the director and his visiting friends, dear God, Polish instead.

And of course there were hippie killers in the movie—even

some of their nicknames proved similar to the Manson family members who were arrested several months later. The degree of prescience was really quite terrifying. You couldn't avoid the thought that the movie had in some bizarre mystical way actually *caused* the murders. As crazy as that sounds now, it made perfect sense in the summer of 1969 that art, or even trash, could affect real life.

Shark got right on the phone to Dad. It didn't take long to confirm that in fact Dad had done what he had no choice but to do.

## Sam Schlockmann

It broke my heart to pull the film. But it was a matter of taste and pressure from the community. It was like you'd made a movie about a fictitious U.S. president who got bumped off in Dallas and opened wide on November 20th of 1963.

I have to admit when I read about the Tate girl and her friends up there and saw the similarities, it even spooked me. I turned to Minnie and said, "You know, for the first time in my life I feel unclean." Then I picked up the phone and said, "Yank it."

## Woody Hazzard

Shark told me years later that he'd heard about the Tate murders early Saturday morning, and that the only reason he married Sue was because he thought Sam might freak out and dump him. Shark said he saw right away all the similarities between the film and what had happened, and knew Sam would have to pull it, and figured Sam's great comeback success was going to turn into a "terrible, odious debacle," and his first reaction would be to blame it all on Shark.

Knowing what a piece of shit the film was, Shark had made sure his name was nowhere near it, even using a pseudonym for the shared screenplay credit. "But if Sam decided to make me the scapegoat and went public about my true role in *Sex Kill*," Shark said, "I knew it could contaminate me and destroy my career when it had just barely begun."

Shark felt that if he was married to Sue, Sam would be compelled to temper his anger.

He also knew Sam had a bad heart. "Once Sam checked out, his studio and fortune would be effectively mine, since everything would go to Minnie and Sue, and I had both of them wrapped around my finger."

## Sam Schlockmann

I didn't blame Shark for what happened. Far from it. It was his instinct, I felt, his marketing genius, that had taken us as far as we'd gone.

Once the Mansons were arrested I began to see the whole matter in a much clearer light. It was, after all, just a freak coincidence. Say you make a movie that has a car crash, then somebody leaves the theater and crashes their car. Do you blame the movie? It was proved eventually that none of the Mansons had seen *Sex Kill à Go-Go*. I would bet good money they never even saw the ad.

I figured this out eventually, but the first few days after I pulled the picture I was extremely depressed. I was low when Shark and Sue came by the house and told us they'd been married in Mexico. Minnie started bawling, but I smiled cause I saw the dark clouds lifting. I had warm feelings for Shark, you see. I felt like we'd built this beautiful ship, the Titanic maybe, that had struck an iceberg on its maiden voyage. But we could build another ship. And another.

"Welcome to the family," I said, and we all drank a toast. Then I gave my new son-in-law his first studio deal.

# 8/ No Fat Chicks
## (1969–1972)

### Paige Petro

I suppose the early seventies were really Kathy's time, weren't they, if we truly believe we're only young once. Kathy was surely at her best in those years, and America was thirsting for the sunny goodness she personified—especially after the dark excesses of the previous decade.

### Kathy Petro

The early seventies were really my time, I guess, if as Mom likes to say you're only young once. I certainly had fun, I'll say that. No matter what happened, or what strange things I saw—for much of the world is sadly not at all like Southern California—nothing ever really seemed to spoil my mood for long.

Once in Italy, in some little village near Naples, Jean-Claude made me look at this deformed person in a cardboard box. It was just this little creature with no arms or legs and a funny-shaped head. At first I thought it was a strange doll or something. Then it moved and I said to Jean-Claude, "Oh my God, I'm going to be ill."

And Jean-Claude said, "This is what happens when your father's chemicals affect the unborn."

But I just felt like he'd deliberately polluted my mind. "Look, Jean-Claude," I said. "You can't blame *Daddy* for *that!*"

I saw Jean-Claude for almost two years, but it was very off and on, because I was having too much fun to be tied down to any one man. I considered modeling fun at the time, even though the hours could be long, and boy, did I get tired standing on my feet! But everybody was always so nice to me, I still don't know exactly why. Except in those days I tried to be nice to everyone, whether they were a famous movie star or just a simple Spanish peasant. People were just people as far as I was concerned.

I knew Jean-Claude was in love with me. And I admired his creative genius, but he was just too old to take seriously. I inspired him though, he told me that in so many words, and he was just always pursuing me. I'd have sex with him every so often. But in those days I found it hard to concentrate on sex with anybody. I can't explain it, but right in the middle of sex I'd always start thinking of something else, like: Oh, I should do my nails tonight. Or I'd think of a funny scene in a movie and start to laugh. Or I'd think of some song I liked and start to hum it. I don't know, I didn't dislike sex, but I just couldn't keep my attention focused on it. Mostly my feeling was: Let's get it over with so we can go out.

I never really mentioned Shark to Jean-Claude because it was something I just didn't like to think about. Those years were blessedly Shark-free. The present was so full, the past seldom crossed my mind. And Jean-Claude never told me about humiliating Shark at UCLA because I guess it just wasn't that big a deal to him.

Jean-Claude could be really cruel if he sensed competition. I saw him savage several young men who idolized him and longed for his approval—as I learned later he'd once savaged Shark. Mostly I wouldn't understand what he was saying to them though, because it would either be in French, which I never really mastered, or even in English it would be this intellectual talk I could never make heads or tails of. But there was a rumor that one young man had gone out and jumped off a bridge right after Jean-Claude dressed him down.

Jean-Claude was always trying to start an argument with me. "Why must you be so American?" he'd say.

And I'd say, "Because, Jean-Claude, I *am* American."

Then he'd talk politics until I said, *"You're boring me!"*

Then he'd explode and start to leave. But he'd always stop as he reached the door and turn and say, "Oh Kathy! Only you can do this to me."

Then he'd come back and kiss me and we'd make love.

Then one day in Paris he attacked me for having my picture on *Time* magazine, which in a way was kind of the summit of my whole modeling career. It did make me nervous though, in a way I didn't totally understand. There was just this feeling that *Time* was for politicians and Gandhi or something. But the only reason I was on the cover was because I'd been on so many other covers in such a short period of time. Because I was "Super-Model Kathy Petro." So I was feeling a little insecure and out of my element, and Jean-Claude stormed in and went straight for my throat.

"Look at this!" he shouted, waving the magazine at me. "You've turned yourself into the ultimate product, a celebrity, you're ruined. With this you've created a psycho-visual loop which is bound to destroy you and give you cancer. You are made of paper now, a smile, a face and nothing more. Famous for being famous, the ultimate capitalist decadence."

He just went on and on until I was sobbing. Finally when he wouldn't stop I threw my hairbrush at him and cried, "Why are you doing this to me? This is how I make my living. Why are you doing this now?"

He wouldn't tell me. He just walked out the door and this time he didn't come back. Later I found out why he was so mad. He thought *he* was going to be on the cover of *Time* that week. But they'd bumped him at the last minute, deciding that it was the seventies and he was *out* and I was *in*.


## Sue Schlockmann

I remember the period when Kathy Petro seemed to be on every magazine cover. I assumed that Shark saw those magazines as well, though we never discussed it. That is, he never mentioned her name, and despite my curiosity I never asked him directly about her.

Once as we lolled in bed after especially good sex I told him about a boy who'd broken my heart in junior high, thinking he might in turn tell me about his similar experience with Kathy. But when I was finished he just said, "Yeah, it's tough when shit like that happens," and got up to make some calls.

Then one afternoon he came into the den in a rage. "Why are we subscribing to this piece of shit?" he yelled, waving a copy of *Time* magazine. "These fucks are still apologizing for the war." He went on and on about *Time*'s politics, which was in itself odd since by that time Shark considered himself post-political.

Of course it was the issue with Kathy's picture on the cover.

## Elliot Bernstein

Black Light disbanded in the spring of 1970 after the Dilday twins OD'ed on heroin one night in San Antonio right before a gig. Woody and I were jolted. We didn't even know they were using smack. But there they were, two blue bodies side by side on a ratty backstage sofa. I think that night Woody and I both knew beyond any doubt that the sixties were really over.

I came back to L.A. and cut my hair and thought about going to law school. But instead I went to work for Shark, and in so doing began my Hollywood career.

## Sue Schlockmann

Dad gave Shark quite a generous deal. He got the biggest office at the Palms studio, except for Dad's. He had both the office and the Santa Monica beach house redone with authentic thirties rattan furniture, potted palms and ceiling fans—that tropical decor which at the time had not yet been done to death. We'd taken mescaline one night and watched a couple of von Sternberg movies in the basement screening room, *Morocco* and *Shanghai Express*, both of which gave Shark a series of "sustained mental orgasms"—I believe that's how his infatuation with the "exotic" began. Soon he was buying up old Hawaiian shirts, which he wore with baggy khakis and a short 1930s haircut a decade before Indiana Jones.

He also had a vintage soft drink machine installed in the beach house foyer, which he stocked with his beloved cream soda. He was virtually always nursing a bottle. That taste was always in his mouth. Even now when I smell or taste vanilla it triggers a sense-memory of Shark's kisses.

One weekend he procured some cocaine, which was just becoming fashionable then, and wrote the screenplay of *Tropics* in two days flat. On Monday morning he showed the script to Dad.

## Sam Schlockmann

I could tell by page five there was no way we could do it. It was period for one thing, 1930s, and called for filming at a South Seas locale. Beyond that it was boring. Amelia Earhart and her navigator stranded on an island. All they do is talk. Should they or shouldn't they? Ten years pass, I'm not kidding, and they still haven't. Then finally they're about to. By now it's 1950. Just as they kiss there's a nuclear explosion. Turns out they're on an island right next to Bikini Atoll.

I told Shark, "Look, it's too expensive. It's at least two million, which is four times more than I've ever spent on a picture."

He said it would still turn a profit. So I said, "Okay, look, we'll talk about it later. Maybe if you can solve *Redneck Scum* . . ."

## Elliot Bernstein

I went to work as Shark's story editor, which of course meant that I was working closely with Sue. Initially I thought I could handle it, but it soon became apparent I could not.

One night as Sue and I were working late coordinating the revisions on *Redneck Scum* I impulsively tried to kiss her.

"Don't ever do that again, Elliot," she said. "Or I'll have to tell Shark."

I should have quit then, I suppose. But she didn't tell Shark what had happened, and he promoted me to associate producer, which gave me my first hands-on filmmaking experience—a trial by fire with *Redneck Scum*.

## Sue Schlockmann

*Redneck Scum* was one of Dad's pet projects. The script had been around for years, revised to the point of total incoherence. Every time Dad read a new version he'd shake his head and say, "I just don't understand why we can't get this thing to work. I know it's a money maker."

Shark completely rewrote the script in one night and Dad approved it the next day. That was the last script Shark ever personally wrote. Of course, he knew it was a piece of shit and wisely used a pseudonym.

## Elliot Bernstein

We shot *Redneck Scum* in something like ten days on a ranch near Lancaster that was supposed to be the Mississippi delta. The lighting was so bad I don't think anyone could tell the difference. It was a *Baby Doll* rip-off, only extremely violent. Libidinous white trash girl kept prisoner in her bedroom by her cretinous father, gangraped by morons and bikers, everybody blown away at the end. It cleaned up though.

Sam was grateful but he still wouldn't do *Tropics*.

## Sue Schlockmann

In late 1970 Shark bought a shelved Taiwanese film about a bunch of topless girls in a bamboo jungle prison. He had new dialogue dubbed in without bothering to get a translation, and for a while he wanted to call it *Caged Twats*.

## Sam Schlockmann

Shark showed me the artwork with the title *Caged Twats* and I said, "Shark, let's go for a walk."

We walked around the lot and I told him, "Shark, we can't put a word like twat on a marquee, it's a dirty word."

He said, "But it's the seventies. All those barriers have broken down now."

I said, "I may be an old man, but twat's still a dirty word. It's dirty in the South. It's dirty here in L.A. I guarantee you, the *Times* will refuse the ad."

We went back to our offices. In a while Shark calls through the door: "Sam, take line two."

So I do and it's Charles Champlin, who in those days was the big movie critic at the L.A. *Times*. And Champlin says that Shark called him and the *Times* would have no objection to running an ad for *Caged Twats,* because twat is basically just a somewhat bawdy expression of American slang. So I say, "Thanks, Chuck." But after I hang up I call him right back. But the real Charles Champlin's voice is different and he doesn't know what the hell I'm talking about.

## Elliot Bernstein

Sam finally agreed to call it *Slit Bamboo,* which was suggestive without being blatantly obscene. Shark always referred to the film as *Bamboo Slits*.

I don't know why I stayed at Regal. The situation was becoming incredibly painful. We were doing this utter shit, and the proximity to Sue was killing me. And then during the *Tract House She-Devils* period Sue began to put on weight—lots of it—and that was horrible to witness as well. She was still insisting that she and Shark were happy, but in her heart I'm sure she knew that their marriage was a lie.

And by then Shark was far from the friend I'd once known. Though I didn't want to see it he had already begun to put into practice the crazed crypto-Nietzschean philosophy he'd begun spouting in his letters from Santa Barbara. He was becoming a powerfreak, an egomaniac screamer, the epitome of everything we'd smirked at as crass and uptight a few years before.

And yet he did have a terrible charisma. He was honest, he didn't kid himself, he knew what we were doing was shit. And he still spoke with a kind of messianic idealism of someday making great films that would matter. Indeed, his commitment to that abstract goal seemed to grow in intensity the more corrupted he became. You wanted to believe he might yet do something astonishing. Perhaps a brutal jungle mentality was necessary to get the job done. Hollywood was not a tea party for poets after all. A true artist needed toughness and low cunning to survive, and Shark had plenty of both.

## Sue Schlockmann

The sex stopped first, *then* I started eating—that was the chronology, I see that now. But at the time I let Shark confuse me into believing it was the other way around. As I became fat he'd say I was no longer attractive, and then in frustration I'd eat even more. He was always working late, months passed and he didn't even touch me. And I stuffed down my hurt and anger with pies and ice cream and cookies till I ballooned up to two-ten, which on my five-four frame was more than plump.

Shark's sarcasm was merciless. "Jesus, you're turning into a real sow, you know that?" he'd say when we were alone. Once he made an oinking sound as I was coming up the hall with several other people.

Then one day Shark and I and several others were walking to our cars in the studio parking lot. Shark had recently purchased a Porsche Cabriolet and when I saw the bumper sticker he'd placed on it I truly wanted to die. NO FAT CHICKS it said. The car had been there like that all day. Everyone on the lot must have seen that slogan and known it referred to me. Humiliated, I ran back to my office in tears.

## Elliot Bernstein

One afternoon Sue broke down over lunch. It was just the two of us at a Mexican restaurant not far from the studio and she alone had ordered enough for two people. She'd just inhaled the enchiladas and was wolfing down a burrito when she began to sob uncontrollably. Everyone looked and I was embarrassed for her, so I paid and quickly got her outside.

In the parking lot she told me how severely Shark had been emotionally abusing her over the weight issue, and how they hadn't slept together for nearly six months. She was just abject and I'm afraid I didn't handle it very well. She finally grabbed me and said, "Oh, Elliot, why didn't I stay with you?"

You've got to understand she was just huge then, in a floral muumuu stained at the moment with burrito sauce, as was her chin. "Elliot," she pleaded cloyingly, and as much as I loved her—loved the Sue that was hiding somewhere beneath those layers of fat—I recoiled.

"Sue, please." I pried her fingers from my shirt.

She was silent as we drove back onto the lot, angered by my rejection. As I parked she got out without saying a word and vanished. A minute later I looked out the window and saw her screeching off in her Mercedes convertible.

I was worried but afraid to tell Shark what had happened. Perhaps it was nothing, she'd just gone for a drive. I tried to concentrate on the script I was reading, Neal Ridges's *Desert of the Daylight Kill*. Since Neal was a friend of Shark's from UCLA, I tried to be forgiving, but I found the script extremely irritating. Arty in the worst sense of the word. Stilted, laconic dialogue, an incredibly vacant, boring story of lovers on the run. Murders in the desert set to Verdi. In truth I was so subliminally worried about Sue I don't think I would have liked anything I read that afternoon.

Shark stepped in around three. "Where's Sue?"

"I don't know," I told him. "She left after lunch."

"She was probably still hungry," he said and laughed. Then he picked up Neal's script which he hadn't seen yet.

"It's got some serious problems," I told him. And he laughed as if he were sure it did, and took it back to his office.

An hour later he stepped back in with Neal's script in his hand. *"This,"* he said, "is our ticket out of here."

At first I thought he was joking. Then I saw that he wasn't. Then the phone rang and we found out that Sue had just tried to kill herself.

## Sue Schlockmann

The dam just burst that day. For two years I'd been living on lies, telling myself that Shark really loved me, when I knew it wasn't true.

I drove back to the beach house in a black-out state. God only knows why I didn't crash on the freeway. Once inside the house I just went insane. I looked at all that rattan crap and knew he cared more about that *stuff* than he did about me. I

167

started breaking furniture and tore his beloved *Blonde Venus* poster of Dietrich from its frame and ripped it to shreds.

I was crazy as I found myself in the garage. As fate would have it his Porsche was there that afternoon. He'd been about to leave that morning when he saw that one of the tires was flat, so he'd ridden in with me. The keys were still in the ignition. I wanted to destroy that car, but there wasn't a sledgehammer around. So in my crazy sorrow and rage I tried to destroy myself instead.

## Elliot Bernstein

It wasn't Sue's time, thank God. One of the neighbors had noticed the exhaust coming out of the cracks around the garage door and called the police. By the time Shark and I arrived they were loading Sue into an ambulance, after having given her oxygen to save her.

Shark was furious. He began yelling at her. "You stupid pig. You fat, dumb twat. What the fuck were you trying to do?"

I'd had it. "Shark, shut your goddamn mouth," I said, pulling him from the ambulance. He swung and hit me, splitting my lip.

He glared at me, ready to strike again, and I had a true moment of clarity, finally admitting to myself what I'd denied for far too long. He didn't give a shit about Sue. Or me either. Or anybody. If this was Hollywood, then fuck it. Life was too short.

I stood there by the garage, still trembling with adrenaline, as the ambulance took Sue away. Shark had gone in by then, and I heard him explode anew as he discovered the damage in the house. As I turned to leave I saw for the first time the NO FAT CHICKS bumper sticker on his Porsche.

"My God, you fucking animal," I thought out loud. "You drove her to it."

## Minnie Schlockmann

Sam and I were about to step into Sue's hospital room when Shark came dashing up the hall and said, "Please. Let me see her first."

## Sue Schlockmann

Shark kneeled at my bedside and wept against my hand. "I'm so sorry, baby, I love you so much. That's why I got mad. I wouldn't get mad like that if I didn't love you. Oh my God, I almost lost you."

He was very convincing. Shark was nothing if not a good actor. I started crying too.

Then my parents came in. I was so embarrassed about what I'd done.

## Sam Schlockmann

We were all upset. Shark drew Minnie and me aside in the hospital hallway and told us Sue had done some damage to her mind with drugs back in her Berkeley days. He said she'd taken some LSD and drugs like that, which I'd always suspected, knowing that a lot of kids did that then. Shark explained that she'd had flashbacks and episodes of depression, but they would pass if she got the right care.

Minnie and I were upset. We wanted to believe Shark when he said he'd take care of our daughter. He told us how much he loved her, and that he knew a doctor who could help her emotionally and at the same time help her deal with her weight. Shark walked us to our car and we felt reassured.

He could talk a good line.

# 9 / **White Desert** (1972–1973)

## Sue Schlockmann

Shark sent me to see Dr. Rinker, a psychiatrist on Bedford Drive. He was about sixty and very distinguished-looking, and I'd heard nothing bad about him at the time. I just poured my heart out to him and he was very compassionate. Then he wrote a prescription, saying it would help me lose weight. It was for Desoxyn, which of course I knew was speed. But I'd never really taken much speed and thought I could handle it. How I deluded myself, repressing the crushing insights that had precipitated my suicide attempt, believing yet again that if I simply lost weight my dream marriage might somehow be saved.

Well, I lost weight all right. But I also lost my mind.

## Elliot Bernstein

I left a message with Shark's service, saying I was quitting. I didn't want to talk to him ever again. Then I went in on a Sunday to clean out my desk. Apparently the guard called Shark and told him I was there, because on my way out Shark and Sue pulled up in his Porsche. I couldn't help noticing that the NO FAT CHICKS bumper sticker had been hastily removed.

Shark begged me to stay, repeating that Neal's script, which he'd renamed *White Desert*, was going to be our ticket out of exploitation-land. He'd convinced Sue of this as well. "El, don't give up right before the miracle," she said.

Well, I was dumbfounded. I see now they were both into heavy denial, trying to pretend that their personal problems were somehow the result of the kind of dispiriting crap we were churning out. And I suppose I was still naive enough to believe in the redemptive power of art. For whatever reason, I stayed.

And things were better for a while. Shark got the green light from Sam to produce *White Desert*, and there was a tremendous surge of energy and enthusiasm, especially from Sue. She began to shed the pounds, so consumed with *White Desert* that food no longer mattered. I knew she was speeding, of course. Once her prescription ran out and she went right through the ceiling, screeching into the phone to the nurse at her Beverly Hills doctor's office. "You tell that fucking asshole I need a refill and I need it now!"

## Neal Ridges

I was deeply ambivalent about Shark buying my screenplay. On the one hand I was just starting out so any sale at all was a positive step. But Regal Pictures—I mean, it was just one rung above writing for TV. When Shark told me he had big plans to make it a "breakthrough film" I was heartened, but knew there'd be problems. Nobody decent would work for Regal.

## Elliot Bernstein

Shark approached a number of top directors, people like Altman and I think Sam Peckinpah and Arthur Penn. Several were interested in the script, but not as a Regal production, not even after Shark's highpowered "breakthrough film" pitch.

Then he went to several big stars, but the same thing happened. So he stopped before he'd gone through everybody, and went to Sam.

## Sam Schlockmann

Right from the start *White Desert* felt like a winner. It was a simple, straightforward story with a love angle and enough violence to hold your average viewer's attention through even the artiest camera work. It could be that rare breed, both an audience and critical success. So I was hurt and saddened when Shark came to me with his proposal.

## Sue Schlockmann

I'll never forgive Shark for what he did to Dad then, though at the time I was callous enough to go along. I blame the speed for that. It destroys your sense of humanity.

## Elliot Bernstein

Shark convinced Sam to surreptitiously finance *White Desert* through a complex series of dummy corporations and a prestigious European bank. The deal was set up so Sam would eventually get a large chunk of any profits from *White Desert*, but no one except the accountants would know. Shark told Sam they would have to manufacture a falling-out for the trades, and Shark would have to publicly trash Sam in order to gain the credibility he needed to mount *White Desert*.

Initially, I found it quite astonishing that Sam would so easily agree to such an insulting arrangement.

## Sam Schlockmann

Shark said Sue's recovery depended on making *White Desert*. "She's pouring her soul into it, working twenty-hour days. If this project bites the dust I'm afraid Sue might too."

I let the bum have his way because I loved my daughter.

## *Hollywood Daily*, April 9, 1972

"TRAGER GOES INDIE, LASHES REGAL"

Producer Shark Trager announced an abrupt departure from Regal Pictures yesterday to set up an indie company, Balboa Productions. According to Trager, who is only twenty-one, "I'm fed up with the soul-destroying crud I've been forced to churn out at Regal. Working on films like *Redneck Scum* and *Tract House She-Devils* left me demoralized and physically sick. But I'm young enough to rebound, and make the kind of serious artistic and commercially successful films that have always made our industry great."

Trager, who is married to Regal topper Sam Schlockmann's daughter Susan, plans to house Balboa Productions in the Gower Studios. First on Lido's slate, per Trager, is *White Desert,* described as a "violent love story" set in the American Southwest, but "metaphorically about our involvement in Vietnam."

## Neal Ridges

I don't know where Shark got the Vietnam angle, though everybody said that sort of thing at the time. Actually the story was based on a real-life incident that occurred in Arizona in 1964. These incestuous brother and sister twins, who were clinical idiots, themselves the product of incest, killed a family in Tuscan and went on a joyride in the family's station wagon, running down a number of tourists in Monument Valley before they were both shot in the head. I did a rewrite and Shark made me lose the brother and sister angle—he didn't think people were ready to deal with incest yet—though we retained the couple's clinical idiocy because Shark felt that did make them "more sympathetic." He saw them as "innocents, mindlessly controlled by the consumerism and instant gratification depicted in ads and the media." I was disturbed by this watering down at first, afraid we might be "going Hollywood." But when Jack Hardin came on as director, I was ecstatic, all my apprehensions swept away.

## Sue Schlockmann

Jack Hardin had just scored critically with *Scalp Cody and Wanda McBride,* one of the last truly great revisionist westerns —he was just the perfect choice to direct *White Desert.* He was young, handsome, extremely virile and masculine, with the lean, spare artistic sensibility the project called for. I worked quite closely with him in the pre-production phase, and it became quite obvious something extraordinary was about to happen.

## Elliot Bernstein

Jack Hardin was a complete asshole in cowboy boots and Stetson—affecting the whole western thing even though he came from Ohio or someplace. I hated him on sight and he hated me. He was hot then, however, and he was talented, so I tried to think of the picture.

Then one night I walked into Sue's office and she and Hardin were having sex on the floor. She'd lost a lot of weight by then. She was back to being lithe, leggy Sue.

"Elliot," she said, "please don't tell Shark."

In deep pain I stepped out and closed the door.

## Sue Schlockmann

Yes, I had an affair with Jack Hardin, and it was rather animalistic. I was a bit crazed by that time because of the speed, and I sure wasn't getting laid at home! Here I'd lost all this weight and Shark was still a cold fish.

"I'm exhausted," he'd say. "I don't even think I can get it up, honey."

Well, Jack Hardin could!

## Elliot Bernstein

Principal photography began in July of 1972 in Tuscan and it was hellish from the start, the temperature rising to 115. It was Jack's idea to cast unknowns in the leads, though we could've got almost anybody, mainly because of Jack. At one point Shark was talking Ali MacGraw for the girl, and I said, "Can she play an idiot?" I don't remember what Shark said. We talked about Tim Bottoms and a few other young actors who were hot then for the guy, but Mike and Julie were really perfect, we knew that as soon as we saw them. They auditioned on different days, but when Shark saw Julie he said, "My God, she could be a twin of that guy we saw yesterday, what was his name?" So we cast them mainly because of the eerie resemblance.

It was not until late into the production, after we'd shot the notoriously "graphic" love scenes, that we discovered that they were in fact brother and sister.

## Neal Ridges

Shark had me change some details about the family that got killed, he said for legal reasons. And when I visited the location, they were shooting the murders. They had the father lying "gutted" on the floor in front of a wrestling match on TV, and the mother was dead in the kitchen covered with blood and right-wing hate tracts. I was stunned when I first saw her because she was a deadringer for Loretta Young—but the Loretta Young of the thirties. I mean, I knew it wasn't *really* Loretta Young.

Then Elliot told me, "That's Evelyn, Shark's ex-stepmother." And he said the father was Mac.

## Sue Schlockmann

Arizona was crazy because we were all there. I mean, Shark was there as executive producer. And Elliot and I were co-producing. And I knew Elliot was still in love with me, but I just couldn't say no to Jack.

Then at some point I began to go psychotic from the speed. I was hearing voices, and everything people said took on a double meaning. And through all that Jack Hardin was just using me. I didn't see it at the time, I was so used to being used. But he was literally fucking me for inspiration. They'd be lighting a shot and he'd say, "Sue, the trailer." So we'd go in there, ostensibly to go over some production details, and he'd just screw me brutally, as if I were some sort of outlet for his nervous tension. He was the kind of guy who believed he had to fuck a lot to be creative.

Finally one day I just came unglued.

## Elliot Bernstein

Everybody knew Jack was fucking Sue silly, including Shark. I'd glare at him every time Jack and Sue went off to the trailer, as if to say: Christ, aren't you going to do something?

Obviously he wasn't. Obviously he didn't care. The dailies were astonishing, that was all he cared about.

Then one afternoon we heard Sue yelling obscenities at Jack in the trailer. Then glass broke and Jack moaned, "Oh no. Oh no."

Well, I just assumed he'd done something to Sue. But a moment later he staggered out of the trailer, holding his bleeding stomach.

## Sue Schlockmann

I don't remember breaking the beer bottle and jabbing him with it, I really don't. I was so crazy and paranoid I didn't know what I was doing.

## Elliot Bernstein

For me it was Sue's suicide attempt all over again—except this time she'd turned her anger outwards. But Shark was just as clearly responsible for this. I was literally imploding with pent-up rage at him. But we had to get Jack to a hospital. Sue was completely hysterical by then, and Shark said, "Elliot, get her out of here now. Take her back to L.A."

## Neal Ridges

I was on the set when Sue jabbed Jack. Shark was crazy at first. There was a lot of blood and he was afraid Jack was going to die. "Please don't do this to me," Shark actually said to him at one point. Once we got Jack to the hospital and realized his injury, while grisly, was far from terminal, Shark began to worry about the publicity. He threatened the cast and crew that if any of them talked he'd destroy them. Then he called Elliot who'd taken Sue back to L.A. and said, "I want that bitch locked up in a psycho ward until we've wrapped this film."

## Elliot Bernstein

I was not about to place Sue in a mental hospital, when what she clearly needed more than medical attention was love. I stayed with her at the beach house, with the help of Thorazine and Librium carefully withdrawing her from speed.

As I did, her sanity returned. Finally one morning she slipped her arms around me and said, "Oh Elliot, I was such a fool to leave you."

Well, this time I did not recoil from her.

## Sue Schlockmann

I now see my marriage to Shark Trager as the saddest, sickest episode of my life—an example of what happens when you marry strictly on the basis of fantasy and sex. Elliot is my true, destined mate in this life—supportive, loving, gentle. Shark was the emotionally masochistic daydream of a lonely young woman with very low self-esteem. That young woman—thank God—has since learned to love herself.

## Neal Ridges

I went with Shark to see Jack in the hospital, and Jack raved on and on about Sue, "That bitch is fucking insane, she nearly killed me," and Shark agreed with everything he said.

"Yeah, she was too much for me a long time ago, man,"

Shark commented wryly. "I guess she turned out to be too much for you too."

They ended up laughing about the whole thing—like a couple of cowboys who'd both tried to tame the same horse and been thrown.

Then at the wrap party the shit hit the fan with Mike and Julie.

## Virgil Homer

I played one of the state troopers in *White Desert*. It was no secret to any of us that Mike was banging Julie off camera as well as on, so I was not surprised when I came upon them in a state of undress in the back seat of a car during the wrap party there in Monument Valley. I was backing off when Mike pulled up his pants and said, "It's okay, Virgil, we're all done. Stick around and have a drink."

So I did, and they told me how they were real-life twins who'd killed their parents.

At first I thought they were pulling my leg. Then after a while I didn't. "We're just *into* each other," Mike said, and they were still kind of feeling each other up. They said their parents hadn't understood, and wanted to know what I thought.

"It's fine by me," I said, and stuck around till we finished the bottle. Then I went and talked to Jack and Shark.

## Neal Ridges

Shark just completely shit when Virgil repeated what Mike and Julie had told him, and Jack turned white as a sheet. We all knew *White Desert* was going to be a very great film, and we all saw it going down the toilet if what Mike and Julie had said was true.

Shark sent Virgil back to get some more details so we could check to see if it was true, but by that time Virgil was shaking. He did it though. "Where'd you say you killed your folks? I guess you had to change your names after that, huh? What did you say your real name was?"

Shark checked it as soon as we got back to L.A. Their real name was McBurney, Jon and Jan McBurney from Eloise, Indiana. They'd crushed their parents against the side of a barn with a tractor, slamming them repeatedly until they were both squashed like bugs. Then, like so many other midwestern fugitives, they'd come to Hollywood.

It was grim news. Shark was deeply depressed, and Jack was nearly suicidal—here was his masterwork and it looked like we might have to shelve it. It was as if we'd been flying as high as any plane had ever flown, and suddenly our engines had gone out.

Shark paced in his Gower Gulch office and inevitably hit upon the idea of exploiting the truth. See actual killers portraying actual killers! See twin-like idiot lovers played by real-life incestuous twins!

But Jack wouldn't go for it. "I don't want people to see the film for those reasons," he said. "If you go that route you might as well be back working for Sam."

We all fell into silent thought until Shark said suddenly, "I've got an idea. Why don't we pay somebody to shoot Mike and Julie in the head? They can die in real life as they did in the movie."

Of course, it wasn't a serious suggestion, and right after that the meeting ended. As Jack and I were walking up the corridor to his office, a production assistant came up to him and said, "You'd better brace yourself. Mike and Julie are dead."

Well, I reeled. Though I knew the feeling wasn't rational, I half-expected to hear that Mike and Julie had been shot in the head.

## Sue Schlockmann

I was in bed with Elliot when we heard about the plane crash that killed Mike and Julie. I hadn't talked to Shark in weeks, not since the jabbing incident, but I knew he was back in L.A. I knew he'd be devastated, so I called him.

"It's a terrible tragedy," he said. "But they will not be forgotten, not with what we've got on film." Then he said it was a shame they died before they'd done the looping. "But then, the same thing happened with James Dean on *Giant* and that turned out okay."

## Neal Ridges

Shark had trouble containing his elation. Of course, he used the

Dean analogy. Their demise was the best possible luck for us, provided the truth could be contained. There were only a handful of us who knew that Mike and Julie were actually twins who'd killed their parents.

"But when the film comes out, won't somebody recognize them?" I said.

"Eloise, Indiana, is a small town, I've already checked," Shark said. "But just to play it safe, we'll lose the whole state."

"But somebody who knew them is bound to see a magazine photo, especially if the film does well," I said. "Maybe we should just 'fess up now."

At that Shark exploded. "Listen, you spineless pussy, honesty never got anyone anything in this town. You know where all the honest people are? They're all jacking off in their beer in some crummy little apartment on Yucca Avenue, wondering why they never made it. If anybody loses his nerve on this, you or Jack or Virgil or anybody, you are going to be *dead* in this town, do you understand me? You'll spend the rest of your lives playing with yourselves in a third floor walk-up in the Arbuckle Arms at Ivar and Yucca."

## Sue Schlockmann

Elliot and I heard that Shark had taken a bungalow at the Chateau Marmont, where he slept between three-day work marathons with Jack and the editor, and that he'd begun using a lot of cocaine.

## Neal Ridges

It was a crazy schizoid time because the film just kept getting better and better as Jack cut it. But all the while there was the sense that everything could blow up at any moment if the truth about Mike and Julie came out. There were already magazine pieces on them, because they were young and attractive and then suddenly dead, which struck everybody's fancy. I think on a largely unconscious level they became emblematic of the whole sixties thing, which was also dying. Of course, the media used their fake biographical information, which Shark had checked as well, and Mike and Julie had been fairly ingenious. That we all continued to think of them as Mike and Julie, rather than Jon and Jan, is perhaps an indication of how effectively they'd remade themselves. They had developed incredibly intricate false backgrounds: born in midwestern towns destroyed by floods and tornados respectively, so that hospital and school records had been lost, both of them drifting through a series of anonymous foster homes and obscure odd jobs after having been abandoned by relatives who had since vanished—their manufactured pasts were virtually uncheckable.

Still we held our breath. All it would take was one Indiana farm girl twanging, "My God, it's them! The McBurney twins! The ones who squashed their parents with a tractor!"

But Shark walked this tightrope over the abyss in a state of unnerving calm, cocaine having replaced the harsh amphetamine acceleration of his UCLA days. Shark thought of cocaine as his "wonder drug" in those days—in retrospect, how naive we all were about its ultimate effects. A toot or two of his snow and Shark was in perfect *control*, down to the slightest vocal inflection.

He knew just what to say to get his way with Jack, which wasn't easy because Jack had a tremendous ego. But in terms of the final editing and every other crucial post-production question Shark won every point. Not that Jack or anyone else really minded, since what'd we'd all accomplished together truly transcended ego the way a collaborative art form can but seldom does.

When I saw the answer print I wept. The film was that good.

## Elliot Bernstein

Sue and I were lolling on the beach one afternoon when we looked up and saw Shark. We were both apprehensive—you could see he was coked to the gills—yet as he approached us he exuded cordiality. What then occurred was a classic example of well-Vaselined Shark Trager audacity. He said he bore neither Sue nor me any hard feelings and hoped we would all continue to be friends. Of course, he understood that she'd want a divorce, and that would be no problem, though he did want the house—which had been a wedding present from Sam and was really their only asset—for, he said, "mystical reasons." I took this as an allusion to the lingering vibrations of Selznick and

Thalberg which, at least for Shark, still infused that stretch of Gold Coast beach.

He made the house, which was worth perhaps four hundred thousand in '72 dollars, sound trivial compared to the inevitable megabuck profits from *White Desert,* and he offered Sue gross points in the film as her share of the divorce settlement. He was quite convincing and Sue nearly agreed on the spot, until I intervened, saying, "Honey, you should really discuss this with your attorney."

Well, for just a moment Shark appeared ready to go for my throat. Then he laughed expansively and invited us to a screening of the film.

## Sue Schlockmann

The film just blew me away. In 1973 I was still naive enough to believe that genuine art would be acknowledged in the marketplace. So I let Shark keep the house.

## Elliot Bernstein

We were all bowled over by the finished film. The screening Sue and I attended was truly cathartic. Sue and Jack made up, both apologizing, Sue tearfully. It all seemed worth it—Sue's psychosis, Jack's stab wound—since the end result was a milestone in American cinema. I wept at the end, where the state troopers shoot Mike and Julie in the head, thinking: God, these two beautiful young kids—how many people who live to be ninety come anywhere near achieving the grace and purity preserved here forever in these few precious pieces of time?

I hugged Shark after the screening. "Goddamn it, you've done it," I said. "You really have."

## Neal Ridges

It was a time of very great elation—until Shark screened the film for Benjamin Klieg, the president of Mastodon Pictures. Klieg had personally requested the screening, telling Shark he'd heard some "truly astonishing things" about *White Desert.* Shark assured us he had no intention of accepting Ben's offer, however generous it was, since Mastodon, known in the industry as "the dreck factory," had the least prestige of any of the majors. But a juicy offer from Mastodon would definitely provide leverage with the other studios.

Ben remained poker-faced throughout the screening, Shark said. But he was so sure Ben "had to know" how well the film was going to do that he began talking really outrageous terms as soon as the lights came up.

But Klieg stood abruptly and said, "Look—I think we're gonna pass on this."

Shark was speechless. And then he wanted to kill Klieg. "This fucking dinosaur, this tight-assed ancient fuck, is telling me this film's not commercial!"

But he held his tongue. Shark wasn't stupid. Dreck factory or not, Mastodon was a studio to be reckoned with, and Ben Klieg was one of the two or three most powerful men in town.

But Shark was shaken. He knew word of Mastodon's pass would spread quickly, and he feared that Ben Klieg was going to personally bad-mouth the film as well. "He hates me," Shark said. "I could see it in his dead fish eyes. He envies my youth, my virility, my vision. He's going to spread the word that this film is too bizarre, or too arty or too violent or too something—he's going to scare everybody else off if we don't act fast."

Shark called me at two o'clock that morning. "Do you have a passport?" he said. I told him yes and asked why. "Because we're taking this fucking movie to Cannes."

# 10 / **Cannes**
## (1973)

### Cindi Dinkler

I was fifteen in 1973 and I thought Kathy Petro was really cool.
I used to study her pictures and copy her hairstyle, and then
when she started doing the Sun-Ray makeup ads I started
buying Sun-Ray lipstick and eyeliner and all that, and everybody was always saying how much I looked like her. So
naturally when Babcock's department store in Encino had this
Kathy Petro look-alike contest I entered. I couldn't even believe it when I won!

It was just so cool, and then right there at Babcock's this guy
came up and laid this line on me about being a big Hollywood
producer. I thought he was kidding at first because he was so
young, but he *was* cute so I gave him my number. Then he
called and asked me out, and my parents were fighting so I
said: Well, okay. Then he took me to a movie studio and we
watched *White Desert* and when his name came on the screen I
knew he wasn't lying about being a producer.

Then he said, "How'd you like to go to France?" And I said, "What about school?" He said, "Play hooky." And I said, "I'd better ask my parents."

But we left without telling them.

## Elliot Bernstein

Sue and I nearly crapped when we saw Cindi. Shark had already been in Cannes several days when we arrived. We entered his suite at the Carlton without knocking—the door was ajar—and there he was on the balcony with Cindi, both of them naked. In the noisiest, sloppiest manner imaginable, Shark was going down on her.

## Sue Schlockmann

I reeled. At first I thought she *was* Kathy Petro—the resemblance was really frightening. Then I realized she was much too young to actually be Kathy—*much* too young. It was insane. Shark was jeopardizing everything we'd worked for, for a cheap and futile exercise in sexual nostalgia.

## Neal Ridges

I took a dim view of Cindi's presence since she was so obviously underage. Lest people think it was a case of exploitation, it should be said it was obvious to us all that Cindi had been around. She was a knowing, calculating Valley Lolita, a tough little nymphet who knew just what she wanted, and she had Shark wrapped around her finger—though I doubt that she had a clue as to the real meaning of his attraction to her. When she told me where she'd met Shark, I got a bad premonition, since I knew they'd conducted those Kathy Petro look-alike contests in many cities all across the country.

Ultimately though, I had little time to think about the situation. I was too busy helping Jack push the film.

## Elliot Bernstein

I quickly became exasperated with Shark. He was spending all
his time with Cindi, just locked into her in this cloying sexual
way at the very time we needed him most. We wanted the film
to be shown in competition, and we were about to succeed in
that even though it required an extraordinary last-minute jury
approval. But an aura was growing about *White Desert*, you
could almost say a kind of frenzy. An unprecedented wave of
anticipation was building. And then the worst thing possible
happened.

Just as we were about to screen the film for the jury in our
bid for inclusion in the prize category, we were told that one of
the jury members had taken ill, necessitating a last-minute
replacement. Barely had these words been translated for us than
the new juror arrived breathlessly from Paris. It was Jean-
Claude Citroen.

## Neal Ridges

I finally found Shark on a small deserted beach where he and
Cindi were going at it as if there were no tomorrow. "Maybe
you'd like to know that Jean-Claude Citroen just scuttled your
film," I said.

Well, Shark froze. "What are you talking about?"

I explained that Jean-Claude had persuaded the other jury
members to bar the film from competition.

I thought Shark was going to have a stroke. His face turned
red, his entire body seemed to turn red, he began hyperventilating.
Cindi was worried too. "Shark, are you okay? Shark?"

It would have been funny had it been a film. A real case of
overacting—Charles Bronson about to go on the warpath. He
started toward his rented Renault like a naked red killing
machine.

## Elliot Bernstein

I saw Shark on the Carlton terrace and he was just possessed.
"Where is he?" he said, scanning the crowd. It was a mob
scene, you know Cannes.

"I don't know," I said, though I'd just seen Citroen chatting with Godard and Bertolucci a few minutes earlier.

"Let it go," I told Shark, and explained that Jack and I were already making arrangements for the film to be shown out of competition. "Jean-Claude can't stop *White Desert*. You wait and see, Shark. We're not finished yet."

## Cindi Dinkler

I don't know if I fell in love with Shark exactly or what. But France was really cool and we did a lot of coke, and that was cool too. Then suddenly after some French guy put down his movie, Shark just lost interest in me totally, and I got really bored.

## Neal Ridges

The night of the screening we were all crazy. As we walked down to the Palais Shark said, "By the way, somebody should find out what happened to Cindi." He said he hadn't seen her since the night before, and her billfold and clothes were still in the room. "Everything but her bikini."

We had no time to worry about it. The Palais theater was packed and you could feel the expectation. It seemed as if every major figure in film was present—name someone and they were there. Jack was trembling, his cowboy cool disintegrating. As the lights went down I gripped Jack's arm, and Sue squeezed my hand. Down the row Shark watched the screen with a face of stone, the stark white titles reflected in his dark glasses, which he wore for the duration of the film.

## Simone Gatane

I ran into Jean-Claude in Cannes soon after he had Jack Hardin's film barred from the competition, and he savaged it mercilessly. "It is pure shit. If it were allowed to compete we might as well open the doors to American TV shows as well, and place *The Conformist* against 'Bonanza,' or *Cries and Whispers* against 'My Mother the Car.' "

"But you laughed at 'My Mother the Car' in L.A., don't you remember?" I said to him.

187

"Yes. But it's not art."

"Are you sure you don't hate this film merely because Shark produced it?" I said.

"No, it's shit. Go see for yourself."

So I did.

## Sue Schlockmann

It was the strangest screening I've ever attended. For a hundred minutes there was literally not a sound. I swear, there was not a single cough, a single movement in a seat, let alone a whispered comment or a gasp or a snort or a laugh. There was not a single walkout, and I tell you as well, there was not a single mental vibration. Usually, even if the audience is quiet you can feel how they're responding. But that audience in Cannes was absolutely blank. They had entered the film, they were *inside White Desert*, they had *become* the motion picture to such an extent that as viewers, *as perceivers*, they had ceased to exist.

## Neal Ridges

It's true, there was a feeling of vacancy in the theater, a sense of silent spatiality, which was precisely what I'd striven to suggest in the script, and precisely what Jack had placed on the screen. The genius of *White Desert* is that in a very real sense the screen—*as* a "screen," and all that that implies—is simply removed.

I was fearful as the film reached its conclusion. When you go that far you're never sure how people are going to take it. They can feel used—soul-robbed or mind-raped—and hate you afterward for what you've shown them about themselves.

## Elliot Bernstein

I've seen quite a few standing ovations since that night in Cannes in 1973, but never one like that. The audience applauded for twenty minutes—I timed it. Jack was flicking tears from his eyes—it was his moment of course. We all had damp eyes— Sue, Neal, Shark.

## Neal Ridges

The applause went on so long I had time to reflect. Jack rightfully took the glory, but so much of the picture's genius did rest with Mike and Julie AKA Jon and Jan, those poor gifted if twisted twins. I hoped no one would ever discover the truth about them. Nothing should taint what they'd given us all here.

As I looked at Shark I felt a terrible poignance. In a rare moment of genuine self-effacement he had his arm around Jack, rubbing his shoulder, granting him all of the credit.

But I couldn't help thinking of Shark's *Pillow Fuck*, that ingenious, insane lost masterpiece, the chances he'd taken back then, chances he himself would never take again. For he had been hurt so badly then.

Then I glanced back and saw the man who had done the damage.

## Simone Gatane

I had been clapping so long my palms were sore when Jean-Claude tapped my shoulder. I was on the aisle in the back and he had just come in. He appeared quite puzzled.

"What's going on?" he said. "Why aren't they showing the Chabrol film, it should have started five minutes ago."

Then suddenly he saw Shark and realized what was going on. I will never forget the look that came to his face.

## Elliot Bernstein

Toward the end of the ovation I caught sight of Jean-Claude Citroen standing just inside the door. He was pale and profoundly shaken. Of course, his own career was in trouble by that time, his radical anti-narrative didacticism having passed out of vogue. *White Desert* was indisputably an art film, and yet it had a "story," which no doubt infuriated Jean-Claude on a theoretical level—though I'm sure the devastation he felt was occurring on a much less rational plane.

Later, I wished I'd pointed him out to Shark, so that Shark might have seen how thoroughly he'd won. Jean-Claude was beaten, there was no need for further revenge. Instead, I steered

Shark's attention away from the door, afraid if he saw Jean-Claude something might happen that would spoil this ecstatic moment.

## Simone Gatane

I went up to Shark and we embraced cathartically. As we did he said, "Have you seen Jean-Claude?" And I saw a terrible look in Shark's eye.

"No," I told Shark, "not for many years." Though, you know, I had seen him less than one minute before. Now when I looked back, thank God, he had gone.

## Elliot Bernstein

As you know, *White Desert* received a special award, the Palme Noir—there was just no way they could allow Jack's genius to go unacknowledged. It was a joyful, magnificent moment when Jack's long-time idol, Pierre La Douche, warmly presented him with the award, and the next few days were spent fielding the avalanche of distribution offers. Shark held off, growing increasingly testy and temperamental. I thought the cocaine might be catching up with him. Then too there was the matter of Cindi. She had been missing for several days by then, and I was beginning to wonder if our moment of glory might yet degenerate into the scandal of an underage corpse on the beach. We had people looking everywhere for her to no avail.

But Shark seemed more interested in finding Jean-Claude Citroen. He actually grabbed Eric Rohmer by the lapels in the Majestic bar when he overheard the director relating a conversation he'd had with Citroen the previous evening. "Where is he?" Shark demanded. "Where is he staying?" It was quite embarrassing.

I managed to calm Shark, and later he told me, "It's all right. I just want to *talk* to Jean-Claude, that's all." I almost believed that—I knew he'd been carrying on an imaginary mental debate with Jean-Claude for years. But I feared Shark's temper, his short fuse even shorter than usual thanks to the cocaine. I breathed a sigh of relief when we heard that Jean-Claude had left Cannes.

Then one afternoon Shark and Jack and Neal set out for Saint-Tropez to see Derek Horus.

## Neal Ridges

Jack and I had a script idea that was somewhat akin to *Performance*, about a rock star living in seclusion in L.A. Since Jagger had already done that turn, Derek Horus was the obvious next choice. In '73, remember, Down in Flames was one of the top superstar rock groups, right up there with the Stones and Led Zeppelin—though tragedy would render their time in the sun quite brief. They'd taken an indefinite break from touring that spring, and we knew that Derek was fielding film offers. Jack called him cold and it turned out that Derek was crazy about Jack's western. And the fact that he'd just won the Palme Noir didn't hurt.

Shark and Jack and I arrived at Derek's villa one sunny afternoon, and the meeting could not have gone better. Derek cut quite a figure, his blond hair running down to his lower back, shirtless as always in lowcut bellbottoms, tight with no underwear. He brought out some astonishingly good dope and soon all of us were riffing, throwing out script ideas, on this tremendous elating roll, just convinced this was going to be the best film ever made. Shark and Derek especially fell into immediate sync, their creative rapport instantaneous and ecstatic, so much so that both of them reacted with considerable irritation when Derek's girlfriend of the moment called from the next room in a grating, whiny voice: "Honey? Have you seen my stash? *Hon-ey?*"

Everyone turned to look as Kathy Petro stepped through the door.

## Kathy Petro

I could not believe Shark was really there. I mean, here I was on the Côte d'Azur, which is a long way from Newport Beach, and who shows up but the last person in the whole world I ever want to see again. Derek tried to introduce me, and I just said, "Look, I just really do not want to deal with this."

So I didn't. I just went and found my stash, and went straight upstairs and skin-popped some heroin, which I thought

I was using just recreationally that spring. Boy, was I stupid as it turned out.

## Neal Ridges

It was a stunning moment when Shark saw Kathy, a Hitchcock moment—Shark's expression like James Stewart's in *Vertigo* when Kim Novak steps out of the shadows transformed.

Then track in on Kathy, wearing a micro-bikini, very tan, very fresh, very Kathy Petro: the patented California Look—except that, you couldn't help but notice, so skimpy was her bikini bottom, there were tell-tale injection bruises in the otherwise flawless flesh of either cheek.

Kathy took one look at Shark and stormed out, leaving Derek quite puzzled.

Shark was so shaken he completely spaced out, which effectively trashed the mood of the meeting. Jack didn't understand what had happened, he didn't know about Shark's past with Kathy. I was the only one who could begin to imagine what was going on in Shark's mind. I saw the way he was now looking at Derek. A few minutes before Derek had been an icon of cool, but now he was evil, the Satanic rock star working a terrible black magic on Kathy, leading her into addiction and ruination. I could almost hear Shark's thoughts as he glared at Derek: You fucking scumbag, what have you done to my Kathy, I should kill you, you evil pig.

The vibes got so bad I knew we had to get out of there before something happened. Jack felt it too. I got Shark up, and by now he looked literally psychotic. We were moving toward the door, but Derek didn't understand what had gone wrong. Maybe he just thought the dope had made Shark paranoid, because he kept cajoling Shark, trying to loosen him up again, trying to get him to laugh, and I wanted to say: Back off, man, just let us go.

Then, just as we reached the door, a Jaguar pulled up to the house. Jean-Claude Citroen got out and came around to open the passenger door for Cindi, who'd been missing for five days then. The auteur had quite a smile on his face until he saw Shark.

## Kathy Petro

Granted I was nodding, just floating on this smack high which I thought was so harmless—Jeez, was I dumb!—when I looked out the window and saw Jean-Claude and this girl getting out of a car below, and thought: God, how weird! Because this girl looked *just like me*—I mean, a lot of girls did then, kind of, because they were copying my look, but she *really* looked like me, you know what I mean? And I thought: Oh my God, does this mean Jean-Claude's doing that awful *Vertigo* number? Like only being attracted to girls he can remake in my image and everything? Because obsession is such a bore!

Then I saw Shark coming out and, well, I guess you know what happened then.


## Neal Ridges

The second Jean-Claude saw Shark he got a trapped-animal look, because he knew what was going to happen. He didn't have time to get back into the car, so his feet made tracks. I've never seen anyone take off so fast, and Shark was after him like a bullet.

Shark chased Jean-Claude down along the path to the beach, it was quite a long chase, with the rest of us running along after Shark. Shark chased him out along the water's edge. Jean-Claude was lithe and on fire with adrenaline, but Shark finally caught him at the nude beach. By the time the rest of us got there Shark was just beating the living shit out of Jean-Claude.


## Simone Gatane

As it happened I was there on the Saint-Tropez nude beach sunning myself with my new boyfriend. When suddenly we looked up and there was Shark kicking a fallen man in the face. The man's face was so bloody that at first I could not even tell it was Jean-Claude. People were screaming and covering themselves with towels, it was so horrible.

## Neal Ridges

We finally pulled Shark away from Jean-Claude, but that was no easy task, because Shark was like a man on angel dust. It took all of us to subdue him, and then he turned on Derek, calling him a "demonic snake" and demanding that he "let Kathy go," as if it were obvious that she was with Derek against her will.

Jean-Claude was wasted. He was conscious but his jaw was broken, his face was red pulp, and he was feeling around in the blood-soaked sand for several of his teeth. When Cindi saw him she became hysterical.

## Cindi Dinkler

I was on acid. I'd run into Jean-Claude on the beach at Cannes after Shark started ignoring me—I thought Jean-Claude was really cool since he reminded me of my real father. We had sex and everything and he kept calling me his Lolita, which at the time I thought was a French term of affection—years later I saw the movie on TV with Sue Lyon. Then we took all this acid and the whole Riviera turned into something like you'd see at Disneyland. Then suddenly Shark was just killing him, and there was all this blood and violence where minutes before there'd been nothing but naked French bodies. I just freaked.

## Kathy Petro

By the time I got down to the beach it was all over, and I mean, Jean-Claude was just a mess. It almost made me sick even from a distance—I stayed back by the path so Shark wouldn't see me. Then suddenly this girl who looked so much like me came running back up the path, kind of keening.

## Cindi Dinkler

I thought I was hallucinating at first when I ran into Kathy Petro, I just couldn't believe she was really there in France. Then I looked and looked and saw that she was real. Then I went kind of crazy, like I thought she'd stolen my identity or something, this weird acid thing. So I started to scratch her, saying, "Give me back my soul, you bitch."

## Neal Ridges

It was just sheer insanity. The next thing we knew Cindi was attacking Kathy, and Derek and Jack went to intervene. Simone was there too, and had called an ambulance for Jean-Claude. Somehow I managed to get Shark back to the car.

## Elliot Bernstein

Sue and I were checking out of the Carlton when Neal and Jack returned with Shark. Shark was in pretty bad shape emotionally—he hadn't slept for days and was muttering angrily under his breath. Far from satisfying his desire for revenge, the beating he'd given Jean-Claude had only whetted his appetite for blood. "I should have killed him," he kept saying. "I want to go back, the job's not done." We knew we had to get him out of the country.

There was just one loose end. We dispatched Sue to round up Cindi.

## Sue Schlockmann

It was the last favor I did for my soon-to-be-ex-husband. I drove down to Saint-Tropez and found the poor girl trembling in the bushes near the nude beach as the sun was going down. I gave her some Valium and on the drive back to Cannes she became lucid again and mentioned in passing that her folks were sure going to be mad when she got home since they had no idea where she'd gone. "They probably think I got kidnapped or something," she said, clearly relishing the likelihood that they were worried sick.

I cursed Shark, certain our moment of triumph was about to give way to scandal.

Then when we got back to Cannes everybody was going crazy because Shark had disappeared.

## Kathy Petro

It must have been about nine o'clock that night and things had finally quieted down. Derek and I had quarreled though and weren't speaking, so I decided to do some more junk. I went into the upstairs bathroom and was right in the process of popping myself in the rear-end—I was still telling myself I wasn't a junkie since I didn't mainline, if you can believe that!—when suddenly there was this tap on the window. I looked over my shoulder and saw Shark in the window and I just almost died! I mean, I went into this whole big flashback to the peeping-Tom movie thing in Newport Beach. Here I was in the bathroom again, and there he was at the window again! At first I was too stunned to even speak. Then he pushed open the window and started to crawl in, saying, "Kathy, I've come to rescue you, it's all right." But I just started screaming. He said, "No, no, Kathy, don't scream." But I couldn't stop, and Derek came running in and saw Shark in the window, and then went to get his gun. And for some reason, as much as I hated Shark I didn't want to see him dead, so I said, "Get out of here, you asshole. Derek's getting his gun."

Shark saw I wasn't kidding, and suddenly he looked at me in a way that both frightened me and touched something strange and unfulfilled in me too. "You're the love of my life," he said. "Do you know that?"

And I said, "Get out of here," because Derek was coming. And Shark took off.

## Elliot Bernstein

We were all frantic. We'd even alerted the hospital in Nice where they'd taken Jean-Claude, afraid Shark might be on his way there to "finish the job." Then suddenly he walked in. He was dead on his feet, exhausted but oddly calm. "Let's go home," he said.

On the plane he told me he'd gone to see Kathy, but his mood was still tranquil, acceptant. "It's all right now," he said. "I know that she loves me. And she'll be by my side when the time is right. In the meantime, Elliot—" Here he squeezed my arm. "—we have much to do, much to do."

"Get some sleep, Shark," I told him. But the rest of the

flight he stared out the window, though there was nothing out there but black sky, and I could see his thin, serene smile reflected in the glass.

## Sue Schlockmann

Cindi sat beside me, leafing through magazines and singing Rolling Stones songs under her breath all the way into L.A. At one point she came upon a cheerful fashion photo of Kathy, and observed to me, "You know, she may have a nice smile. But underneath it she's slime."

I was too tired and disgusted to respond with more than a grunt.

## Neal Ridges

We were all aware of the potential for disaster with Cindi, and somehow it fell to me to drop her off at her parents' house in L.A. We'd checked the papers upon landing, there was nothing about a missing girl. Still, I half-expected to be surrounded by cop cars when I pulled up to her house. It was all in my head though. Nothing happened. Nothing ever happened.

## Cindi Dinkler

My parents were assholes and drunks who didn't give a shit what I did. When I walked in my stepdad said, "Oh, are *you* back?" So I said, "Yeah, but I went to France, which is further than you'll ever go, loser." My stepdad called me a liar. Then when I showed him the stamp on my passport he slapped me hard across the face.

Later, I tried calling Shark a whole bunch of times, but every time I did he had either just stepped out or else he was in some kind of meeting.

# 11 / The Condoist
## (1973–1975)

## Mac Trager

I saw that *White Desert* movie one night at the Balboa Theater. I went by myself and sat in the back and got madder and madder, gripping the arms of the seat so hard that my knuckles hurt. 'Cause everyone there was snickering at the parents—that smirking, superior kind of thing, you know?—even as the parents got cut up and killed by the young retarded couple. And it didn't take a genius to see that those parents were copied from Evelyn and me.

## Evelyn Burns

A friend called from Fort Worth and said, "Evelyn, you know that former stepson of yours, the one you bragged was a Hollywood producer? Well, I just saw his movie, and all I can say is, if I were you I'd sue."

Well, I looked to see where the movie was playing, but it was already gone. I guess it didn't do very well, now did it? Not long after I finally saw it on TV a few years later I suffered my first stroke.

## Elliot Bernstein

The very first day back at the Gower Studios Sue and I heard Shark explode in his office: "Goddamn it! Oh, *fuck* no!"

We rushed in to see what was wrong, and Shark threw a sheaf of legal papers at Sue and yelled at her, "You fuck-cunt! You and your fuck-cunt father! I should've ripped the guts out of both of you!"

Well, I snapped, and decked Shark, a nice clip to the jaw. Just one blow, and he didn't return it, he was much too stunned for that. He held his jaw and looked at me, and for a moment I thought he was actually going to cry. He really thought I'd gratuitously turned on him, you see. He had absolutely no concept of how long-suffering I had been.

"You are out of my life, Elliot," he said finally, his voice trembling. "I don't ever want to see you again." Then he indicated Sue without looking at her. "And take that fuck-cunt with you."

Well, it turned out he'd read the fine print in his financial agreement with Sam.

## Sue Schlockmann

It was no way to say good-bye. But I have to say that when I found out what Dad had done I understood Shark's anger.

## Neal Ridges

The deal was almost indecipherably complex, but what it amounted to was that if *White Desert* went even slightly over budget—and it did just that, by something like two thousand dollars—Shark would owe Sam, through the European bank and a string of dummy corporations, the entire cost of the production plus interest plus all the moneys Shark had been advanced to set up Balboa Productions. The contract provided Shark a 48-hour "window"—long since past at the point he discovered the fine print—in which he could pay Sam off before a "triple-budget clause" went into effect. Shark would then owe Sam three times the cost of the film. The film had come in at roughly two million, which meant Shark owed Sam six million, plus interest and penalties and various odds and ends which came to another four million. He owed Sam ten million dollars, and even if he could pay it Sam would *still* assume ownership of the film.*

## Sam Schlockmann

You could say I had the last laugh.

## Neal Ridges

The day after Shark attacked Sue and Elliot, Sam Schlockmann came in for the kill. The phones went dead at Balboa Productions, they came for the furniture. Shark was enraged and humiliated, and the whole thing became a legal and financial nightmare. There were lawsuits and counter suits. Simultaneously, Shark's divorce from Sue was going through, and on that count at least he got what he wanted. In the rush of elation after the initial screening of *White Desert* Sue had signed an iron-clad property settlement agreement giving Shark the Gold Coast beach house.

But it was doubtful he was going to be enjoying it for long if he didn't reach a cease-fire with Sam. Shark had to deal and deal fast to save his own skin. I could understand that.

The full-page ad in *Hollywood Today*, thanking his "men-

---

*In the wake of this contractual debacle Shark enlisted the services of Jerry Bratman, the high-powered "attorney to the stars," who represented him in all his legal affairs until 1981. From 1983 on, Shark was represented by Steven "Little Barracuda" Ging, who took over many of Bratman's clients after the older attorney was machine-gunned in a Las Vegas casino parking lot in a still unsolved murder. The labyrinthine deals of Shark Trager might themselves form the basis of an intriguing book on the financial workings of Hollywood. Unfortunately, Shark's files "vanished" within hours of his death, an event about which Steven Ging, despite his role as executor of Shark's estate, claims to know nothing. Ging is among those who declined to be interviewed for this book.

tor'' Sam Schlockmann ''for his keen intelligence and artistic guidance'' in helping to bring *White Desert* to the screen, was a virtual retraction and public apology, as unctuous as his previous trashing of Sam had been harsh. The day the ad ran, Shark called to confirm the obvious: a deal had been reached with Sam.

It devastated me—and it literally killed Jack!—when we found out what the deal was. Mastodon Pictures was bailing Shark out as the first step of a generous multi-picture production deal. They had reached a settlement with Sam for an undisclosed sum and assumed outright ownership of *White Desert*—an act, we all felt, which was tantamount to giving K-mart exclusive rights to sell the works of Picasso.

## Bill Kemmer

I was a vice-president in charge of production at Mastodon then and had seen *White Desert* at its extraordinary premier at Cannes. I'd been overwhelmed, and made our acquiring the film a personal crusade, even when I realized it meant throwing a rather expensive cut of meat to Sam Schlockmann. I put my career on the line, giving Ben Klieg no peace until he agreed. I sensed correctly that *White Desert* wouldn't make money—it was an art picture in a time when art pictures were dying—but at the very least it would bring us a shot of sorely needed prestige.

More importantly it would bring us Shark. ''He's a genius,'' I told Ben, ''another Thalberg. Whatever you may think of *White Desert,* or of Shark Trager as a personality, he is the future of this business. If we don't bail him out, somebody else will. And we'll be kicking ourselves a few years down the line when he's pouring millions into someone else's coffers.''

## Sonya Heinz, *French Quarterly Review,* Summer 1973

Not since last year's *Last Tango in Paris* has there been a movie that redefines an art form the way Jack Hardin's *White Desert* does. With a loose, zingy, wigged-out abandon Hardin takes both violence and eroticism to the point where they become the same thing, which is something only a young film genius—Welles was one—can do. This isn't the coy, ditsy, tuned-out sex we've come to expect in Hollywood movies, this is sex the way it really is: ugly, mean and violent. At the same time Hardin's violence has a thick, sweaty, pendulous sensuality, a sinewy wised-up cowboy wooziness. This is rapturous cathartic violence, the kind that makes you understand why some people prefer violent movies to actually having sex. Jack Hardin is a virile young Peckinpah on mescaline. He's likely to become the Sam Shepard of film if the studios don't destroy him first. That danger is real. With the businessmen taking over Hollywood again, *White Desert* may be the last true American art film we see in some time.

## Neal Ridges

It *was* an art film. It should have been opened slowly and carefully with a hip, intelligent ad campaign, all of which Mastodon was incapable of comprehending. Let's face it, of any of the majors they were the crassest, junkiest studio. They only knew how to spew out mass-produced crap—greasy french fry movies for the malls. Which was just what they did with *White Desert*.

But to push it as a comedy was truly unforgivable.

## Bill Kemmer

I always knew the ad campaign was a mistake. But when we sneaked it in Bakersfield, and the audience laughed, the marketing people took over and I lost control.

## Neal Ridges

I'll never forget the day Jack first saw the ad. The busy cartoonish illustration and the intentional play on *Bonnie and Clyde*'s famous tag: "They were young, they were stupid, they killed a bunch of funny people." And the legend:

WHITE DESERT. A Crazy Kinda Comedy.

Jack was too destroyed to even get angry. He sat slumped in one of the few chairs left in the Gower Gulch office—it was the day Shark was moving into his new offices at Mastodon—and finally looked up at me with tears in his eyes, which was itself shocking, because Jack was a very macho guy. "You know, I can take anything except being laughed at," he said.

## Bill Kemmer

It was a crazy kinda flop. Most of the audience came expecting a comedy and left angry and confused. The film actually did okay in the hipper houses where the Cannes prize carried some weight. And of course it had a long afterlife as a cult film—I think it finally broke even in 1979.

It was sad though about Jack Hardin. Because there was a man with talent.

## Elliot Bernstein

For a long time I held Shark responsible for Jack's death. Even though Jack technically drank himself to death in Arizona, we all felt that he'd died of a broken heart.

## Neal Ridges

My first thought when I heard the news of Jack's death was to blame Shark. In retrospect though, I think both Jack and the film were essentially victims of the seventies. Despite his tough-guy exterior Jack was emotionally frail. When people laughed at his masterpiece it simply crushed his spirit. He should've seen what was coming, the vapidity which would dominate that decade in American film. He should have gone to Europe where people understood his kind of movie. But like so many of us he had Hollywood dreams. And in the end they killed him.

Whatever else you might say of Shark, he knew how to swim with the tide.

## Bill Kemmer

Ben Klieg never stopped hating *White Desert*—though he pretended to have changed his mind—but he genuinely reversed his opinion of Shark, especially when the story got out about how viciously Shark had mangled Jean-Claude Citroen.

"It was artsy assholes like him who almost destroyed this industry," Ben said of Citroen. "Thank God all that shit's over now, and we can get back to the business of making movies."

The crucial meeting between Ben and Shark occurred over lunch at Chasen's. Ben came into my office afterwards beaming, as he hadn't beamed in some time, and said, "You know, Bill, you were right. Shark Trager is—what's the expression?—a cool drink of water. I see blue skies ahead."

The expense of settling with Sam Schlockmann aside, the deal Ben gave Shark was quite lavish.

The first project Shark chose to develop was a treatment dashed off by Mrs. Benjamin Klieg, a truly wretched idea that had been lying around the story department for years. You know Jean Klieg, the quintessential L.A. socialite, the dilettante who is always coming up with a "fabulous movie idea." Well, you don't tell the boss's wife to stick to charity work. We had a foot-thick file full of worthless Jean Klieg notes.

But Shark said, "This is it, this is my next movie." It was *The Condoist*.


## Neal Ridges

When Shark showed me Jean Klieg's treatment I guffawed. When he asked me to write the script I was insulted. But when he said he would pay me two hundred thousand dollars to write it—well, what would you have done?

I suppressed the bad feelings I had toward Shark about Jack Hardin's death and with what I termed resilience swallowed my bitterness over *White Desert*'s fate, and plunged into *The Condoist* with zeal—like any young whore just starting out.

Shark kept little more than the title. Immediately I saw that the new story had strong autobiographical elements. That is to say, he intended the wife who would be terrorized by voodoo zealots to strongly resemble Kathy Petro.

Then he added a Derek Horus figure. The condo where the wife and her husband were vacationing in the Bahamas would be haunted by the tortured ghost of a dead British rock star.

204

The condoist himself, the leisure-suited real estate tycoon-cum-"spiritual detective," initially resembled Shark, though he eventually decided that the condoist should be played by a much older man—Ernest Borgnine and Lorne Greene were both mentioned. Shark anticipated a TV series derived from the movie, and believed that middle America preferred her episodic heroes "square and stout."

Shark's ideas changed from day to day—he was doing a lot of cocaine. And the script became increasingly bizarre, an eclectic brew of contradictory occult elements—voodoo and demons, ghosts, vampires, telepathy, black magic, poltergeists, you name it. I was constantly rewriting, juggling his whims, trying to maintain some semblance of logic and plausibility.

Finally I'd had it and told Shark I quit—I'd gone far beyond the number of revisions called for in my contract.

"You can't quit now," Shark responded in his enormous office on the fourteenth floor of the Mastodon Building. He'd had the space remodeled to resemble Raymond Massey's office in *The Fountainhead*, a severe retro-Expressionist decor he sardonically termed "forties crypto-fascist."

"Shark, I'm exhausted and befuddled," I told him. "The script's not getting any better, it's getting worse."

"You're a pussy," he said without warning. "You're a pussy and a loser, and a no-talent fuckheaded schmuck."

Well, I sensed he was coked, but that was no excuse.

"Why don't you eat shit," I said, and started for the door.

I heard him coming around from behind his desk to head me off. "I should've done this five years ago," he said, "when I caught you fucking Simone in my loft in Sherman Oaks!"

He pulled me around in the doorway and swung at me, but I jumped back and he hit the heavy crypto-Frank Lloyd Wright door with his fist. It was extremely painful for him—he broke several bones in his hand.

"Good-bye, Shark," I said, and as I walked out past his stunning young secretaries I actually felt sorry for him. He was riding a tremendous elating wave of pure Hollywood power all right, but I had been the last of his true friends.

## Jean Klieg

I adored Shark initially. What a charming young man he seemed! Naturally I was flattered that he'd chosen one of my humble musings as the basis of his first film for Ben.

However I must say I was disturbed when I saw Neal Ridge's screenplay. About the violence more than anything.

But Shark assured us he had in mind a tasteful, stylish thriller with major stars. And then of course he approached our dear friend Lawrence Granger, surely one of our finest directors.

## Neal Ridges

I was sick with disgust and laughter when I heard Larry Granger was going to direct. Of all the tired old hacks! He hadn't had a hit since *Romanesque* in 1959. But he still played tennis with Ben Klieg.

Shark's lips were brown with dinosaur shit.

## Lawrence Granger

Frankly, I never understood the sixties, and I hadn't cared for *White Desert* at all. So I went to see Shark with some apprehension, which was quickly allayed. For here was a businessman, neat, articulate, in a finely tailored British suit, good shoes. Clearly a man of taste and style who appreciated fine art and literature—I recall our shared admiration of both Whistler and Henry James.

"I'll do it," I said. "When do we start?"

"Don't you want to read the script first?" he said, and we had quite a good laugh about that. I suppose that gives you some idea how enthusiastic I initially was.

## Bill Kemmer

The script was incoherent, and I personally found some of the more sensational elements distasteful. But the genre was hot, and we knew Friedkin was doing *The Exorcist* complete with piss and masturbation and the works.

The squashing scene bothered me though—you know, where

206

the piano drops on Anthony Cray. The script said something like, "His guts go flying every which way as if the piano were a shoe that had stepped on a bug."

"Tony Cray's a ponderous old bore," Shark said. "America secretly longs to see him crushed like a bug."

"What about Laura's decapitation?" I said. By then we knew we had Laura String for the mother, but she was such a fine and distinguished actress, I mean right up there with Helen Hayes, that I felt a little crummy about it.

"She's a twat," Shark said. "A right-wing cooze who fingered her friends during the witchhunts and deserves a thorough trashing. When those steel jaws grab her head and rip it off America's gonna pee in its pants with secret glee."

## Lawrence Granger

I was high on Ali MacGraw for the lead, but Shark insisted the actress must be blonde. I proposed Faye Dunaway, but he shook his head. "Not California enough," he said.

"It's a pity we can't get that Petro girl," I quipped. "She's certainly California."

Shark absolutely froze. "You fuck," he said, which I considered in very poor form. "What are you trying to do to me? How dare you try and fuck with my head?"

At the time, you see, I knew absolutely nothing of his, shall we say, *obsession avec la femme Petro [sic]*. I merely assumed that he'd heard she'd recently been cast in a film. That proved not to be the case, however. For as I mentioned the occurrence his anger soared to new heights—though I thankfully was no longer its object.

Trembling with fury he buzzed his secretary Mrs. Clive: "Find out everything you can about *Manhattan Holiday*," he said to her urgently. "Andreji Pavlavo . . . whatever that Yugoslavian idiot's name is, he's directing it in New York."

## Kathy Petro

Derek and I finally had this really awful fight, and he gave me this big black eye even though he knew I had to do a *Vogue* session the very next day. So I said, "Look, I really don't think I need this," and left even though I was afraid I might be just a teensy-weensy bit strung out on smack. Boy, was I right about that!

On the plane to New York I went into withdrawal. I had chills and sweats, my teeth were chattering just like one of those sets of toy false teeth! And this really nice man, who was Andreji Pavlavojac, sat down next to me and put a blanket around me and held me all the way into Kennedy. He wasn't much to look at, I mean compared to Derek, but he just exuded this niceness which to be honest I hadn't felt from anyone in I don't know how long. I just felt safe with him for some reason, and I heard one of the other passengers say, "Oh, you know he's the Yugoslavian Woody Allen."

## Bill Kemmer

Andreji Pavlavojac had come to the West from Yugoslavia in the late sixties, to France initially, where he had directed several modest comedies including *Papa Always Said So,* a substantial art-house hit in the States, which had finally brought him to America to make *Manhattan Holiday.* Shark was obsessed with seeing a script, which I couldn't provide since the picture was an indie production—there just weren't any copies of the script floating around like there are with most major Hollywood pictures.

Then Shark wanted the picture "killed."

"There must be some way to stop it," he said. "Call in some favors, Bill. Scare off the backers."

*"Why?"* I wanted to know.

"Because I'm developing a property that's just like it," Shark said.

"How do you know if you haven't seen the script?" I asked him.

"I know. I've heard enough about it to know that."

Much later I realized his real motive was jealousy. For by then it was known that not only had Kathy Petro been cast as the romantic lead opposite Andreji—like Woody Allen to whom he was so frequently compared, Andreji was directing himself— but Kathy and the Yugoslavian wunderkind were simultaneously engaged in a passionate real-life affair.

## Kathy Petro

Andreji really saved my life then. He took me straight to this
private clinic up in Connecticut and got me off junk, and just
kept all the *Vogue* and agency people and everybody else at
bay. He'd come and visit me and we'd walk around the grounds
and he was so adorable in that little Mets baseball cap he
always wore.

Then he showed me the script for *Manhattan Holiday*, which
was just this sweet, light-hearted little romantic comedy, and
when he said he wanted me to play the lead girl I thought at
first he was joking.

"Andreji," I said. "I've never *acted*. I'm not an actress."

"Yes, but you have sometheeng," he said. "A special
sometheeng, Kathy. How do you say? A spark."

I just giggled like a schoolgirl 'cause his accent was so
charming. How could I say no to a man who made me feel so
good inside?

## Bill Kemmer

I finally convinced Shark there was nothing we could do to stop
Pavlavojac's film. "There are only so many ideas floating
around in the air. He grabbed it first, Shark. Those are the
breaks."

Of course, by that time we had far more urgent matters to
tend to. *The Condoist* had a start date and we still hadn't cast
the female lead. Then literally at the last minute, Shark came
up with Karen Quall. I'm still not sure where he found her.

## Carl Stook

I was with Westwood Detective then, and Shark Trager hired
us to track down all the winners of the Kathy Petro look-alike
contests nationwide and compile dossiers on each of the girls.
It seemed a bit eccentric, but then he was a Hollywood producer, so we assumed he was looking for a certain type for a
film.

## Karen Quall

I was a senior in high school in Kansas City when I won the Kathy Petro look-alike contest there, then I came to Los Angeles to go to UCLA and study theater arts.

One day I had just finished doing a scene from *Romeo and Juliet* in the UCLA theater when Shark approached me. "How would you like to be in a major motion picture?" he said.

I did a double-take and recognized him from a photo I'd seen in *Variety*. I remembered the photo because he was so good-looking and so young and yet so successful that I'd thought at the time: God, I wish a producer like *that* would pull the casting couch routine on me.

So it was like a dream come true—and I didn't even have to sleep with him to get the role.

We did have lots of sex later though, after the film started. And at first anyway it was really great!

## Lawrence Granger

I found Karen quite the comely beauty, if somewhat eerily reminiscent of Kathy Petro. Her acting abilities were crude at best, but then let's be honest, *The Condoist* did not require the virtuoso skills of, say, an Audrey Hepburn or a Deborah Kerr. Karen was bright and cheery, and therefore we would care when she was brutally terrorized.

Last but not least we cast the condoist himself. I wanted Sir Laurence Olivier though Shark favored William Conrad of television's "Cannon." In the end we compromised and gave the part to Bud Squat, who had for many seasons charmed America as the mean but lovable male nursemaid in the situation comedy, "The Dinkleberry Brood." The cameras rolled in late October of 1973 on location in enchanting Jamaica.

## Bill Kemmer

I flew down to Jamaica with the film company, and upon our arrival an incident occurred which really marked the beginning of my disillusionment with Shark. No sooner had we all cleared Customs than Shark relieved his secretary Mrs. Clive of a metal briefcase she'd been carrying. In his hotel room that night Shark opened the briefcase and removed a false bottom to reveal an enormous amount of cocaine.

Well, of course Mrs. Clive had no idea she'd been risking arrest, and I considered it unconscionable. Here was an infinitely decorous Englishwoman then in her early sixties, a legendary Hollywood secretary who as a young woman had worked for both Irving Thalberg and David Selznick, which was of course why Shark had lured her from retirement—as a kind of "good luck mascot," he said—only to turn her into his unwitting drug mule!

## Cynthia Clive

That's absurd. Shark could never have done such a thing to me. Obviously, Bill Kemmer had his own reasons for denigrating Shark now, but I shall not allow him to involve me in his lies.

I cannot say I was wholly unaware of Shark's use of cocaine. Everyone knew why Gramps came around.* Initially, I was perhaps guilty of romanticizing the practice somewhat. Freud had partaken of the stimulant, hadn't he? And Sherlock Holmes. It seemed a harmless vice, one that went with the territory. Perhaps every genius from time to time required an extra bit of zip.

I suppose it must be said as well that I was initially quite taken with Shark, and it was never any secret to me why. He bore quite a strong resemblance—in the first few years especially, before the drugs began to age him—to the man I still considered the love of my life, though our affair, my last, had been quite brief that glorious summer of *The Dawn Patrol*, the year before the war. How like a youthful, rakishly charming Errol Flynn Shark was that autumn of *The Condoist* in Jamaica.

## Karen Quall

Everything was great at first. Lawrence Granger was just wonderful, so kind and considerate. But then he and Shark started to get into it because Shark had this vision of the film.

*Veteran character actor Ernie "Gramps" Prichett, known for his wry chuckle and homespun manner in such classic films as *Dustbowl Dina* and *This Blessed Town*. Allegedly one of Hollywoods most likable and reliable drug dealers until his death by dismemberment in 1981.

Then I fell in love with Mark LeManns, who was playing my husband in the movie. And that caused tension because Mark fell in love with me too, even though by then I was having all this sex with Shark.

## Bill Kemmer

I flew down in January because Larry Granger was threatening to walk off the picture. "Shark said things to me which I can neither forgive nor forget," Larry said.

It seemed that Shark had exploded one evening at the dailies, calling Larry a "fatuous, insipid hack" in front of the actors and crew. "This is supposed to be a visceral, wrenching thriller, you silly old fool! Not Holly Golightly skipping down Park Avenue with Fred Astaire."

Then in a blind rage Shark had stayed up all night drawing up an intricate storyboard for the rest of the film.

"Shoot this, you dodo," Shark told Larry in the morning. "Or you'll never do another picture."

Larry had called Ben Klieg in quite a state.

## Jean Klieg

Shark called us from Jamaica to explain that Larry was suffering an emotional breakdown. This was sad news, but not a complete surprise, for Larry had been treated for alcoholism and emotional problems in the sixties.

"Don't worry though," Shark said. "I intend to ignore his ravings and do whatever it takes to hold this picture together."

No sooner had Shark hung up than Larry called, and indeed his grip on reason seemed tenuous at best.

## Karen Quall

At first sex with Shark was really super. Then one night after we'd got it on he just looked at me a long time in this strange appraising way, as if he were suddenly dissatisfied with me. I had these freckles on my breasts, you know? And he said, "You shouldn't have these freckles. It spoils the effect."

212

"What effect?" I said. "What do you mean?" But he wouldn't tell me.

I didn't know then he had this thing about Kathy Petro, but I did know I was supposed to look like her in the film. I learned from makeup and wardrobe that he'd given them pictures of Kathy and said, "I want Karen to look like this."

## Lawrence Granger

I found myself taking Valiums simply to get through the picture. I followed Shark's storyboard, but it was all I could do to keep a tap on my rage.

Then William Rickard, the fine black actor, who was to portray Dr. Voo, contracted a virus and had to be flown home. And Shark replaced him with Man Lafitte, a Haitian non-actor, who was already on payroll as our "voodoo adviser," though I had avoided him like the devil—which was precisely what he was. A genuinely frightening man!

## Karen Quall

When I found out I was going to be ravaged by Man Lafitte I almost died. He'd been hanging around the set from day one, though the first time I saw him I thought he was some poor local derelict and told the AD he should be removed. "He's Shark's buddy," the AD said.

And it was true. He and Shark were always going off to the trailer together, ostensibly to discuss voodoo, but really I assumed to do coke or smoke dope.

Man Lafitte was just filthy, he never bathed. You could tell when he'd been around because his smell lingered. "You're not going to touch me," I'd tell Shark. "Not until you wash your hands and air out this trailer."

I pleaded with Shark to get a real actor to play Dr. Voo. But he said, "Man's perfect. His eyes are filled with a terror and insanity that no actor could ever fake."

That was true enough.

## Mark LeManns

I thought I was in love with Karen, and when I heard Man Lafitte was going to play Dr. Voo, which meant he would actually kiss her and maul her bare breasts, I saw red. I marched straight to Shark's trailer, but before I could knock I saw Shark in there with that grungy Haitian varmint. Man was muttering something in dialect, then he jabbed a pin into the chest of the voodoo doll he held. I couldn't help noticing the doll was wearing a little crudely fashioned Mets baseball cap.

## Kathy Petro

Andreji and I were alone in this loft in SoHo where he was editing *Manhattan Holiday,* looking at some footage on the Moviola when Derek Horus burst in. Well, Derek was drunk and crazy and he wanted me back. Andreji told him to leave, and Derek started shoving Andreji. Then he grabbed Andreji, who was much smaller, by the lapels and started slapping him around, and it was just sheer sadism. "Derek, stop it," I said. But Derek just laughed, and then he took Andreji's Mets baseball cap and put it on and started mugging and doing this vicious impression of Andreji's accent. When suddenly without warning Derek grabbed his chest and reeled back and crashed through the window, falling six stories to the street below.

Later they said he'd had a massive heart attack.

## Karen Quall

We started doing the scene where Man Lafitte had to attack me, and on the first take he tore open my blouse and started mauling my bare breasts. He smelled horrible, there was dirt under his fingernails, and he was mumbling this voodoo mumbo-jumbo right in my face and he had really awful breath. When he began rutting against me, and I felt his big, hard thing rubbing through his filthy pants right up against my bare thigh, I just lost it and started screaming.

Larry yelled, "Cut!" But Shark yelled, "No! Keep rolling!"

Finally Mark intervened and spoiled the end of the take. Shark used the take right up to that point though—he had to because I wouldn't do it again.

Then, thank God, Man Lafitte disappeared.

## Mark LeManns

I asked Shark where his friend had gone and he said, "Back to Haiti." Then he smiled ironically, as if he knew something I didn't. The stereo in his trailer was blasting a Down in Flames album, I remember, as a kind of requiem for Derek Horus, whom we'd heard had died of a heart attack the day before in New York.

## Bill Kemmer

Several months after *The Condoist* wrapped, Shark came into my office at Mastodon looking frightened and pale. "We've got to take care of this or we could be in big trouble," he said and showed me a letter.

It was barely legible on greasy, stained paper but the gist of it was: "You send me one more check for fifty thousand dollar or you will lose your sex tool, Shark." It was signed Man Lafitte with a Haiti address, and a P.S. "I have your pube hairs, friend, so don't jerk me."

It was clearly some sort of crackpot voodoo threat, but Shark appeared genuinely shaken.

"What should we do?" I asked him.

"Either put out a contract on him or issue a check."

Well, by then we sensed that *The Condoist* was going to be a blockbuster. So I issued the check.

## Lawrence Granger

Poor sweet Karen! What an ordeal that film was for her. Dear Laura String and Tony Cray—what a joy to work with both of them again, though sadly how times, and tastes, had changed. Frankly, I was thankful Shark had storyboarded the decapitation and squashing sequences. I delegated that unsavory business to the second unit director, a brash and eager young man thirty years my junior, and proclaimed for all to hear, "As far as *I'm* concerned, that's a wrap."

# 12 / **Boy Wonder**
(1975)

## Greg Spivey

Shark hired me as his story editor in early '75, while he was in post-production on *The Condoist*. I was a couple of years out of USC film school, and had been scraping by as a freelance story analyst, when it came to Shark's attention that I had been the only reader in Hollywood to give the first-draft screenplay of *Angel's Flight* a positive report. When the film was eventually made, and surpassed *Chinatown* as the top-grossing Los Angeles period film of all time, Shark tracked me down and called me in for a meeting. I'd been there maybe ten minutes, we'd made little more than jokey small talk, when he offered to make me his "right-hand man."

I couldn't believe my good fortune. How could I possibly know it was the beginning of a professional and personal relationship that would eventually cost me two marriages, my sense of humor and self-esteem, and permanently damage my

216

physical health. Whether or not it was worth it is still a very difficult question. Shark Trager did have his upside, and in 1975 that was all I saw. His energy, his magnetism, the heady sense of being "where the action was." Shark wasn't just hot then, he was the hottest producer in town, since the advance word on *The Condoist* was that it was going to be a megahit, which of course is what came to pass—though I don't think even Shark was prepared for the magnitude of the success. He really had only one serious bit of competition. I don't think he ever forgave Steven [Spielberg] for making *Jaws* the same year.

## Malcolm Stale, *The New Adlai Review*, June 23, 1975

*The Condoist* is a whacking good thriller. Beats *Jaws* by a country mile as top-notch summer entertainment. Lawrence Granger is back with a stylish vengeance. Not since *Romanesque* have we enjoyed this sort of good old-fashioned cinematic vim and verve. Bud Squat is surprisingly effective in the title role. Laura String and Anthony Cray are by turns wickedly delicious and utterly delightful. Newcomer Karen Quall steals the film with her pert desirability and fresh-scrubbed "California girl" charm. The film does have its violent moments but Granger tends to these with such incomparably good taste that only the most squeamish could possibly be offended. A five-star crackerjack movie. They just don't come any better than this.

## Bill Kemmer

I suppose it's no secret the film saved the studio. We were in deep financial shit after a string of flops in the early seventies, and had a great deal more riding on *The Condoist* than most people knew at the time. But Ben knew. And he also knew that Shark had single-handedly saved the picture. Left in Larry Granger's hands it would have degenerated into unreleasable drivel, so it would be difficult to convey the true depth of Ben's gratitude.

But he still wouldn't let Shark make *Tropics,* his Amelia Earhart "fantasy romance." He was diplomatic with Shark, citing the most recent budget which was something like eighteen million. But privately he told me, "The script's so bad it defies comprehension. But every so-called genius has at least one truly terrible idea. It's part of my job to see that Shark doesn't embarrass himself. Or us."

## Greg Spivey

*Tropics* did represent a blind spot on Shark's part. It was awful, an interminable, stickily romantic, cliché-riddled exercise in delayed gratification that was guaranteed to infuriate any audience. I was truly at a loss for words when he told he was determined to make it his next film.

Of course I see now why he was so irrationally attached to the project. The entire story was a metaphor for his thwarted longing for Kathy Petro. He projected himself into the role of Frederick Noonan, Earhart's adoring if taciturn navigator. How he ever came to associate Kathy with the famed aviatrix really confounds understanding though—have any two women ever been more dissimilar? Of course on a purely emotional level the Earhart myth does possess an intrinsic sadness, doesn't it? A yearning for the past, which when you think about it is rather poignant—that Shark at twenty-five was already steeped in a nostalgia for a love that had never really even existed, except in his mind.

## Jean Klieg

We very nearly lost Shark over *Tropics*. He stormed into Ben's office, which no one ever did, not into *Ben's* office, and *demanded* that Ben greenlight *Tropics* or else. *The Codoist* had just passed the hundred million mark, so Shark no doubt believed Ben would cave in.

Well, he didn't know my husband. No one told *Ben Klieg* what to do.

Then Shark made the mistake of insulting me. *"Tropics will* make money," he yelled at Ben. "*Of course,* it's excessively romantic, but that's *a plus*. Who do you think decides which movie a couple's going to see? Ask that cow you're married to."

At that Ben rose up behind his desk on the twenty-first floor of the Mastodon Building, a towering figure of indignation against the vertiginous view of L.A. "Now you see here, you young punk! Nobody calls the woman I love a cow! You'd really better watch it, Shark. You may be riding a wave but you could sink like a stone if people ever found out certain things about you.''

"What things?" Shark asked, clearly shaken.

"Everyone has a past," Ben said, cryptically. He was bluffing, of course. But he was fairly certain Shark had done something in the sixties he wasn't too proud of. In those days, you know, a lot of people Shark's age were rather frantically trying to cover their tracks.

## Greg Spivey

I remember well Shark's extreme anxiety after that meeting. Without really wanting it I suppose I had already become his chief confidant and ''best friend''—in effect taking Elliot Bernstein's place.

"What can Ben know about me?" Shark said.

"What have you done?" I said, jokingly.

But Shark looked at me with real fear in his eyes.

Not long after that he had the beach house swept for electronic bugs. One Saturday I was there for a story conference when he said, "Let's go for a walk."

Once we were out on the beach—away from the hidden microphones—he said, "You know, Greg, I think I may have killed a man."

I was jolted for a moment, thinking maybe he really had, a drunken hit-and-run perhaps, something he couldn't completely remember. So I was relieved when he told me about the voodoo curse which had been directed at Andreji Pavlavojac but which had by fluke, Shark believed, caused Derek Horus' death.

"But Shark, voodoo's bullshit. Derek Horus' heart attack could only have been a coincidence."

"But he was wearing Andreji's baseball cap," Shark said. "Just like Man Lafitte's doll."

"Was it your intention to give Andreji a heart attack?" I said.

"No!" he replied, almost hysterically. "I just wanted to make him impotent. But Man Lafitte stabbed the doll in the heart not the penis. I realized too late that the doll Man Lafitte used didn't even *have* a penis. Greg, I fucked up bad."

219

"Shark," I said. "You're overwrought. Maybe you should take a vacation. God knows, you've earned it."

What I really wanted to say was you should get off the cocaine. It was obvious Shark had an addict's personality. Once he took to anything there was never enough of it.

## Cynthia Clive

As Shark's cocaine usage escalated it became increasingly difficult to regard his partaking of the drug as a romantically mischievous vice. I found myself cringing when I saw Gramps coming, no longer charmed by his folksy manner, knowing full well what a new delivery meant. And God forbid Gramps should be late! Shark's impatience had became chronic, one could barely complete a sentence without his interrupting, and by noon his voice would be hoarse from shouting into the telephone.

His temper could be frightful. We'd been trying to reach Robert Redford for days, when finally I got him on hold. "Shark, Redford on two," I called, and no sooner had they said hello than I accidentally pressed the wrong button and disconnected them. Shark stormed out to my desk. I shan't repeat the stream of obscenities he uttered.* Suffice it to say I stood trembling and said, "Never, in all my years in Hollywood, has anyone ever spoken to me as you just have. Not Mr. Thalberg, even at his testiest. Not even Mr. Selznick, when I occasionally lost my way in his furiously dictated memoranda. I have worked for the giants, Mr. Trager. But you, sir, are a very small man."

I tendered my resignation on the spot, and departed posthaste lest he see my tears.

An enormous bouquet of red roses was waiting on my Brentwood doorstep when I arrived home less than thirty minutes later. Shark appeared at the door an hour or so after that, at sunset. The light, I shall never forget, was a soft, nostalgic orange, such as one finds in the title sequence of Mr. Selznick's

---

*According to Julie Dess, an assistant secretary, it went something like this: "You stupid English cooze. You idiotic British twitch-box. You soft-headed, kidney pie-brained old sow. You cocksucking Queen Victoria, you simpering third-rate Deborah Kerr."

masterpiece.† Never had Shark more resembled the youthful Errol Flynn than he did then bathed in that poignant glow.

"I am so sorry, Mrs. Clive," he said with a boyish, touching earnestness. "I swear upon my mother Winnie's grave, if you come back I shall never from this day forward speak to you in any but the most civilized, respectful and kindly tones."

And you know, right up until the end, he never did. (*weeping*) I'm sorry.

## Greg Spivey

Almost losing Mrs. Clive gave Shark a certain pause. "I still feel like stabbing my tongue with an icepick when I think of the things I said to her," he told me. "She's really quite dear to me, you know."

But his cocaine-fueled rage at everyone else reached new heights. "Then choke on my rod, you cocksucking whore," I heard him yell over the phone to a hot young director he'd grown tired of trying to woo. Later that same afternoon he flared in a meeting and threw his telephone at one of the town's most powerful agents, yelling, "You're trying to gouge me, you fuck. I'll give you a *real* gouge." The cord stopped the phone an inch from the fellow's face, but everyone present was shaken—including Shark. The next morning he said, "Greg you're right, I've got to get out of town, I've got to cool out. One way or another, I've got to stop this goddamn brain."

Well, I was relieved, preferring to ignore the darker implications of what he'd said. But when he simply vanished, telling no one where he was going or when he'd be back, and several days passed without his even checking in by phone, there began to be a great deal of concern.

## Betty Ray

I was working at a Jack in the Box in Monterey, California, when Shark pulled up to the window in this fantastic Porsche. Right away he started coming on and I finally gave him my number because the cars behind his were honking.

He called that night and we went out and ended up spending the weekend together in this super-expensive oceanview hotel

†She can only mean *Gone With the Wind*.

221

suite in Carmel. I was nineteen then and had never done anything like that before, but he was so handsome and charming I couldn't say no. And when he told me he had produced *The Condoist* I was really impressed, since except for *Jaws* that was about the biggest movie around.

He was really sweet and a very good lover—better than I'd ever known up to then—and we walked on the beach and went to that mission where Kim Novak fell from the tower in *Vertigo*. We even climbed up to the top of the tower, though we weren't supposed to, and really caught hell from some nun.

I'd told Shark about winning this Kathy Petro look-alike contest, so when he saw that her movie *Manhattan Holiday* was playing in Carmel he said, "Let's go."

Even though the movie took place in New York City, it seemed almost like some foreign film, especially with that funny little guy in the baseball cap who played the lead opposite Kathy. He had a real thick accent. It was hard to believe that Kathy was supposed to be in love with him, since he was so dumpy and all. And Kathy just stunk. I mean her acting was so bad I really felt sorry for her. I guess Shark did too. He kept shaking his head and looking really sad.

He didn't tell me that he knew her or anything though.

## Kathy Petro

The reviews really killed me, and they hurt Andreji too. They accused him of being dazzled by me, and not being able to see what a bad actress I was and that sort of thing. Andreji kept picking at me, critiquing my performance after the fact in this compulsive post mortem that seemed to go on forever. "Kathy, if you'd only listened to me when I say, 'Take it down.' " Or we'd be watching the movie for the thirty-fourth time and he'd say, "See? Here, I tell you not to be so wooden. But look how stiff you are!" Finally I just exploded and said, "I never wanted to do it in the first place." So we ended up having this big blow-out on Fifth Avenue and I ran off up the street in tears.

I just felt so rotten I didn't want to do anything. Then some photographer at a party offered me some junk, and I broke into a cold sweat. That was when I knew I had to get out of New York.

Dad had this place on Maui, a beautiful little house in Hana just up the road from where Charles Lindbergh went to live the last years of his life in solitude and sorrow. So I went there, to be alone.

I see now there must have been an item about it somewhere. You know, "Super-model Kathy Petro goes into seclusion on Maui to lick her wounds."

## Betty Ray

The way it ended with Shark was really strange. We stopped at this market in Carmel to get some stuff for a picnic—it must have been Monday morning, I remember we were both raw and exhausted—and he went over to the newsstand while I went to get the food. A minute later I glanced out the window and saw him running to his Porsche. By the time I reached the door he was already pulling away. As I stood there, angry and confused, I noticed this *People* magazine on the floor by the newsstand, opened to a picture of Kathy Petro. It was just some little story about now she'd washed out as an actress and gone into seclusion somewhere.

## Bill Kemmer

I was with Ben and several other executives in Ben's office, and we were all frantic about Shark, really afraid he might have gone off and OD'ed somewhere—Ben was even saying, "If I'd known *Tropics* meant *that* much to him . . ."—when Shark burst into the room.

"*Hail!* just went into turnaround, right?" he yelled with an infectious enthusiasm that instantly told us how unfounded our worry had been.

"Yes, I think it did," I said. "Didn't it, Ben?"

After topping the best-seller lists for thirty weeks, Richard Dreckley's novel *Hail!* had gone through development at half the studios in town. Despite the story's photogenic Maui location, the film remained unmade for a variety of reasons, not least of which was the concept's essential preposterousness.

Ben nodded cautiously. "Yes, I believe Universal just passed."

"Get it!" Shark yelled. "It's our next blockbuster!"

I tried to dissuade Ben. But when the marketing people ran a plot synopsis through the computer and projected domestic rentals of *at least* a hundred million my objections fell on deaf ears.

## Greg Spivey

It was decided that *Hail!* would be Mastodon's big picture for Christmas, which meant that we had to move fast. Structurally, it was your basic disaster film: an all-star cast trapped at a posh island resort during a horrendous freak hail storm. The concept itself of course marked the reducto ad absurdum of an exhausted genre. Earthquakes, burning skyscrapers, tidal waves, capsized ships, bees—everything but hail had been done. And there were technical as well as esthetic reasons for this. The special effects were going to be a tough, expensive nut to crack. The script called for hail stones the size of basketballs to come crashing down through hotel skylights, to pulverize sunbathers on the beach like meteorites, and to crush people in their cars.

Shark brought Frank Gleese on to direct and whip the script into shape, and together they flew to Maui in June to scout locations.

## Frank Gleese

I may be one of the few people in Hollywood who can honestly say he always got along beautifully with Shark. But then I've always believed in the collaborative nature of the filmmaking process and find prima donna egotism extremely wasteful and tedious.

## Greg Spivey

Frank Gleese was a true director for the seventies, that is to say a colossally overpaid hack, a colorless, styleless, dutiful mediocrity—in short just the sort of director Shark needed if he were to stamp his own vision on *Hail!*

## Frank Gleese

Shark and I quickly chose the Kalahali resort complex on Maui as the principle location for *Hail!* The resort was new then, sprawling and gleaming, precisely the sort of clean, modern look we were after. We imagined the miniatures, and the special effects shots where the tanned and screaming teens would be bludgeoned with hailstones on the picturesque beach. We studied the stupendous skylight over the lobby, picturing the mob of tourists keening hysterically under the bombardment of hail and shattered glass, and knew it would work.

The next day Shark and I planned to drive out to the Haleakala crater. I came down to the lobby in the morning only to be told he'd already taken off by himself in the Jeep.

## Kathy Petro

Hana's so great cause it's so primitive. It's not all trashy and built up with tacky resorts like the rest of Maui. It's the way all the islands were fifty years ago. Just one road in and a dinky little airfield, and even the grocery store is primitive too. Staples, no gourmet deli.

Which was fine with me. I was so happy in that ramshackle house. I felt like I was relaxing for the first time in years. The air was so warm and heavy, and the house was so private, most of the time I wore little more than my clogs. The storms would come and go—God, the spectacular cascading view down to the ocean, kind of like Big Sur only better! I can barely describe the serenity I felt as I whiled away the balmy days cooking brown rice in the buff, and lolling for hours in the hammock, wearing nothing but my glasses as I savored the poetry of Rod McKuen.

I had dozed off one afternoon midway through *Listen to the Warm* when a voice called my name, jolting me awake. I looked up to see Shark peering through the front door back in the house.

"Kathy?"

In terror I grabbed my sarong, though not before he saw me in the all-together as he stepped into the house. "What are you doing here? How dare you come here?" I said, panic welling up in me. The house was so isolated, screaming wouldn't help.

"Take it easy," he said, coming closer. "I just want to talk to you." His voice was calm but he had that look in his eyes.

"Why can't you just leave me alone?" I said. "You have no right to come here."

"I have every right, Kathy," he said, and my skin crawled—even as another part of me was strangely excited. His shirt was

225

open. He did have a good body. But I thought: Wait, this is crazy. I can't be attracted to this man, not after all he's put me through. I'm not that sick, I'm not!

So I said, "Please, just go."

He smiled and said, "Look, I don't blame you for hating me, Kathy. But let me make up for the things I've done. Let me make you a star."

"I am a star," I said. "I don't need you, or anyone, for that."

"I mean, a movie star, a *real* movie star."

Well, that touched a nerve. I didn't even want to think about movies ever again. "This is crazy," I said. "I don't even know why I'm talking to you. Get out."

But he had this script and he tried to hand it to me. "This is going to be my masterpiece," he said, and I saw it was *Tropics*. "I want you to play Amelia Earhart."

"You're crazy," I said. "Haven't you seen *Manhattan Holiday?*"

"I saw it," he said. "You were wretched. But that wasn't your fault. I know about film, Kathy. I can turn you into another Dietrich or Garbo."

I could tell from his manner that he was coked. I figured he was capable of anything so I said, "Okay, give me the script, I'll read it," just to get rid of him.

"It's about us," he said, as he handed it to me, and for some reason that remark just twisted my insides.

"What do you mean, *us?* There is no us, Shark. There never has been, except in your mind. I can't stand you, I hate you, you make me sick, you always have." Then I just went crazy and started hitting him with the script, screaming more things at him, until he finally stopped me, holding both my wrists.

Our faces were close and then, inevitably, he kissed me. But I pulled my mouth from his and spit in his face. Well, that jolted him, and I could see he was mad. So when he let go of one of my wrists to wipe off his face I broke away.

I ran out across the porch and out across this big grassy field overlooking the ocean, and he was right behind me. I was really more scared than I had ever been, not sure if he was going to rape me or kill me or both.

Suddenly I came to the edge of the cliff, and there was nothing but the crashing surf and the rocks far below. I whirled around as Shark approached me. "If you come any closer, I swear I'll jump," I said.

He stopped a few feet from me. We were both out of breath, our hearts pounding.

"I don't believe you'd do that," he said finally.

"Touch me and see what happens," I said.

"That sounds more like an invitation than a threat," he said, and smiled rakishly, which enraged me.

"I hate you so much," I said. "You're the only person in this world I've ever really hated."

"That's not what I see in your eyes," he said, and took a step towards me, opening his arms.

I stepped back. "I'm not kidding, I'll jump."

"I don't believe you," he said.

Then, just as he took another step towards me, I looked past him and saw Daddy up on the windy hill, just towering above us, the wind whipping his white slacks, and even at a hundred yards I could just feel his searing rage.

I was so startled by Daddy's presence that when I stepped back again from Shark I almost fell. Shark grabbed my arm in time. I guess he saved my life, though for a long time I refused to think of it that way, since after all he was the one who'd driven me right up to the edge of that cliff in the first place.

When Shark saw Daddy he let go of my arm as if I were suddenly no longer there. He just glared at Daddy, who was starting down the hill, glaring at Shark with the same kind of hatred, his fists clenched.

"Please, don't do anything, Shark," I said, because even though Daddy still looked strong, he'd had a bypass operation.

But Shark was already in an attack mode, no doubt flashing back on the time Daddy beat him to a pulp in Huckleberry Finn's Family Restaurant. Then before I could say another word, they were charging each other like angry rams.

It was no contest because of Daddy's condition. Shark slugged Daddy in the stomach, knocking his wind out. Then he pushed him back against a tree and kind of pinned him there, and just started smashing Dad's face in. Shark was just berserk, I knew Daddy was going to end up like Jean-Claude if I didn't stop it. So I pulled Shark away, my sarong slipping open as I did, so that my bare breasts pressed against Shark's bare muscular chest, as Daddy slumped to the ground.

"Please, go," I said to Shark. But my nipples were hard and a part of me wanted him. Crazy as it sounds, a part of me wanted him right there in front of Daddy.

And I could see he wanted me more than anyone had ever wanted me, or ever would.

Then we heard voices back in the house. My mom and several other people who had come on this surprise visit with Daddy.

Shark glanced down at Daddy and said, "You'd better get him stitched up." Then he kissed me gently on the mouth and said, "So long, funny face," and took off as my mom and the others came out.

## Greg Spivey

*Hail!* rolled on Maui in July. Despite its complexity, the filming went fairly smoothly. An extra looked up when he shouldn't have, and lost an eye to a plastic hailstone, and one of our has-been matinee idol stars was nearly arrested for having sex with an underage Hawaiian girl. But Frank Gleese kept the film on schedule.

Then one afternoon Dean Sutter arrived and I realized something was up. I knew Dean from USC, where he'd directed a prize-winning short, then gone to Europe where he'd made an art film in Spain. I assumed he was there to discuss a future project with Shark, but both he and Shark were very furtive and secretive—neither would tell me what was going on.

Then we had a break and the three of us drove out to Hana.

We reached a remote house and Shark said, "Wait here," and walked up to the house.

As Dean and I waited in the Jeep, I said, "What are we doing here?"

"Scouting locations," he said.

"Locations for what?"

Again, the furtive air. *"Tropics,"* he said.

"What are you saying? That Klieg actually approved that?"

"Not exactly," Dean said.

Then he explained how they were going to shoot it on the sly, hiding the cost in the *Hail!* budget.

"Shark's a genius," Dean said, and tooted some cocaine. "He planned it this way from the beginning." He said that a small cast and crew for *Tropics* was due to arrive next week.

"This is insanity," I told him. "You're jeopardizing your career."

"Art means taking risks," Dean said, and offered me the vial.

228

I went to the house to find Shark.

The place was closed up tightly. I found Shark sitting on the porch, holding a soiled sarong and a weather-beaten book of Rod McKuen poetry, seemingly lost in thought.

## Dean Sutter

I knew we could get into fairly serious trouble, but then you always can when you're really making art, and *Tropics* was a script I wanted to do. I was always aware that Shark took the story seriously, that it represented a romantic bent of his personality that he did not realize was kitsch. In this sense he was very much like Selznick, and I went along, humoring him as it were, though I always saw *Tropics* as a coolly ironic hommage —a kind of blissfully neo-von Sternbergian orgy of deadpan narcotic camp.

## Greg Spivey

"You can't hope to get away with this," I told Shark.

"I don't expect to," he said. "But by the time Ben finds out about it, it'll be too late to stop it. And if he tries . . ."

Well, of course, Ben found out.

## Bill Kemmer

I was aghast, we all were, when we discovered what Shark was doing. I think *Tropics* had been shooting for a week in Hana, even as *Hail!* continued filming on the other side of the island, when our spies confirmed Shark's incomprehensible audacity.

Ben was livid. But also fearful of scandal. It made us all look very bad that Shark had been able to hide the entire cost of *Tropics* in the *Hail!* budget without anyone noticing.

Ben and I flew to Maui, then spent three hours simmering in the Kalahali complex waiting for Shark to return from the *Tropics* location. The infuriating thing was that *Hail!* was still rolling smoothly and the footage we'd seen was sensational.

Ben was near the explosion point when Shark finally pulled up in his muddy Jeep. "You goddamn son of a bitch," he yelled at Shark.

"Look at it this way, Ben," Shark said, jauntily. "You're getting two films for the price of one."

"Nobody pulls this kind of crap on me," Ben said. "I don't care who you think you are, mister, I'm going to destroy you."

"No, you're not," Shark said, turning lethal. "You're going to kiss my ass, old man. You're going to kiss my ass and sing my praises—when you take home your seven-figure bonus next year after *Hail!* goes through the ceiling."

"You son of a bitch!" Ben yelled again. "I'm pulling the plug on that piece of shit you're shooting in Hana right now!"

"No, you're not," Shark said.

"And you're off *Hail!*," Ben added. "The next film you make is going to be a Super 8 production in Soledad prison."

Shark paused for effect, and then simply said, "Ben . . . the negative."

Ben didn't get it at first, then he did, and a tremor ran through him. "You son of a bitch," he said, but this time his voice was weak and shaky.

We checked and found out it was true. All the film shot so far had been shipped back to L.A. for processing, then removed by Shark's people to an unknown location.

Ben knew Shark was crazy enough to destroy the *Hail!* negative if it came to that. Ben was abject, nearly suicidal. His own career was at stake. Finally, he said to me, "I'll speak to George [*McSlot, chairman of World Leisure Petroleum, the parent company, Ed.*] and tell him I approved *Tropics* on a wild hunch. Prepare the announcements. We'll cover our tracks."

## Dean Sutter

I only had one real blow-up with Shark, and that was over the length of our female star Jane Hegel's hair. I'd had it cut short, like Earhart's, and the first time Shark saw her he went through the roof. "What have done? Where's her hair?"

Jane had had long blonde hair when we'd cast her, but I said, "Shark, it's the nineteen-thirties. Do you want her to look like Kathy Petro?"

At the time I knew nothing of his past with Kathy.

He exploded, calling me every name in the book.

"Then fuck you," I said. "You don't like what I'm doing, *you* direct the picture."

This stunned him into silence. It was obvious I'd touched an old wound. He apologized profusely, blaming his irritability on cocaine, and basically left me alone after that.

## Paige Petro

Shark gave Jack quite a licking on Maui, though I suppose it looked worse than it was. Jack's face was just ghastly for several weeks. I was all for pressing charges, and shutting down Shark's films. Jack certainly had enough clout in the islands to make life there quite painful for Shark.

But Jack did nothing—except glare accusingly at Kathy, as she stalked about petulantly, refusing to acknowledge him. "I can't believe I am back in this house," she would say, as if Newport Beach were a prison. "I'm twenty-five and I'm back in this goddamn house."

Of course Jack did have his mind on other things. It was the beginning of the cancer suits. Suddenly it was chic to blame chemicals for everything. Within a few years the empire Jack had built from the ground up would be besieged from all sides.

## Kathy Petro

I couldn't even look at Daddy without thinking about how he'd seen me with my bare nipples pressed against Shark's chest, and without thinking how for a second I'd really been ready to have sex with Shark right there in front of my own father! God, I felt so sick.

But I had no place else to go. I'd spent all my modeling money on junk, except for the two hundred thousand I'd loaned Andreji to finish *Manhattan Holiday*. Fat chance I'd ever see any of *that* again!

And suddenly nobody wanted me anymore. The agency dropped me, saying I was overexposed. "Your time is past," they said. "This is Cheryl Tiegs's time now." And I'd see Cheryl Tiegs on a magazine cover and think: You rotten bitch, you stole my job.

I even started thinking: Gee, maybe I *should've* done *Tropics*. Then I'd think: What's wrong with me, am I crazy? Then I started having all these dreams about Shark.

## C. Glibb, *Face* Magazine, September 2, 1975

FROM "SHARK TRAGER: HOLLYWOOD'S NEWEST BOY WONDER"

He's young, he's good-looking, and he's sitting on top

of the world. In a town where you're only as good as your latest picture, Shark Trager is *hot*—this year's definitive Hollywood wunderkind. At twenty-five, the producer of this summer's blockbuster *The Condoist* is out to top himself with not one but two new pictures filming concurrently on Maui: *Hail!*, a "big splashy thrill-packed all-star disaster epic for the whole family," and *Tropics*, a "serious romantic fantasy for young couples everywhere."

How does it feel to be a mega-success at such a young age? "Mighty fine," quips the magnetic go-getter with a rakish grin. "I've got everything I've ever wanted, almost, and I'm ecstatic! Who says material things aren't important? I've got a spectacular beach house, the Porsche of my dreams, top-of-the-line you-name-it—and it's all a gas! People who try and trash success are just sore losers."

And in the love life department Trager's not complaining either. "Power is a major turn-on, there's no doubt about it. I need a steam shovel to keep away the babes. If I didn't pace myself I'd be doing nothing but you-know-what twenty-four hours a day.

"But movies are my life," asserts the self-confessed workaholic. "People fail you eventually, but movies never do. They're like dreams."

Do we detect a wistful tone in Trager's voice? "Oh, maybe. There are still a few things money can't buy, I suppose."

Like what, for instance?

Before Trager can answer the phone interrupts. Juggling two productions on the island paradise isn't easy.

"I love the phone," Trager says a minute later with a half dozen calls on hold. "It's like sex to me. Movies are like sex, too."

And what's sex like?

"Like going to the movies," the boy wonder retorts.

With an attitude like that, it's a good bet Shark Trager's going to be around for some time.

## Bill Kemmer

Both *Hail!* and *Tropics* wrapped in September, and Shark took *Tropics* to a secret Los Angeles location for editing, afraid Ben might attempt to seize it once the *Hail!* negative was in Mastodon's hands.

I will say this. However thinly he may have been spreading himself, Shark's meticulous zeal to see that *Hail!* was ready for its scheduled Christmas release was unrelenting.

## Cynthia Clive

Shark worked ceaselessly, going without sleep for days, until he was reduced to a state of hallucinatory agony, such as a handsome RAF bombardier might know toward the end of a ceaseless string of air assaults against the industrial might of Hitler's Germany.

One morning he was so exhausted I insisted he let me drive him home. He yammered all the way in my ancient Renault—in retrospect I imagine he'd been taking cocaine to stay awake but had consumed a sedative of some sort to counteract the stimulant's jangling effect in anticipation of sleep. He went on at great length about a woman he vainly loved, who was anonymous at first, then confessionally revealed to be Kathy Petro. I tried not to listen, sensing correctly that he would regret these personal revelations later, but there was no stopping him.

As we streamed down the freeway he said, "You know, Mrs. Clive, you remind me a great deal of Lorna, my aunt. You're a bit older of course, but you're physically quite similar. Oddly enough, I believe that Lorna is the single woman in this world whom I have neither loved nor hated, but simply cared for."

At that Shark rested his head in my lap as I drove and fell soundly asleep like a child.

# 13 / **Scars**
## (1975–1976)

### Bill Kemmer

As much as Ben wanted *Hail!* to succeed for the obvious
business reasons, on a purely emotional level I think he was
secretly praying it would fail so miserably that it would spell
Shark's demise as a Hollywood power. "If this turkey doesn't
fly," Ben confided to me on the eve of *Hail!'s* massive release,
"Shark Trager is going to be standing under it. And I'm going
to make sure everybody sees him covered with feathers and
entrails and blood."

It didn't turn out quite that way, of course. By the time it
was all over *Hail!* had become the top-grossing film in the
history of Mastodon Pictures, despite generally negative reviews.

### Barry Crown, "*A.M. America*," DBC-TV, December 20, 1975

Big, dull and boring. Like a tired ride at Disneyland, *Hail!* is no fun at all. Unbelievably crummy considering how much it cost. The special effects are cheesy, the acting listless, the direction nonexistent, the concept preposterous, the overall results indescribably depressing. Vacantly, blandly, dismally bad. On my one-to-ten scale, gets a *minus seven!* It stank! I hated it! If you go, and incredibly there were long lines when I saw it, don't say I didn't warn you.

## Jean Klieg

The film was "review-proof," wasn't it? As Ben was always fond of pointing out, there were "a lot more average schmucks buying tickets than critics." And there was certainly no dissuading the schmucks that winter.

Privately Ben deplored Shark, even as he was compelled to publicly laud him as the maker of *Hail!* "I've got a bad feeling about Shark," he said to me once. "Not just because of the *Tropics* extortion, but just a bad feeling in general. I think someday Shark may do something truly and colossally unconscionable."

I asked Ben to elaborate, but he simply looked out the window at our Bel-Air grounds and shook his head as one might, anticipating the horrors of, say, World War III.

## Bill Kemmer

Through some miracle the true story behind the making of *Tropics* never saw light. I believe Ben called in some favors with people in the trades. There was talk, of course, but we had covered ourselves, exploiting the relative novelty of "two films shooting at once." Besides, in a business as financially baroque as ours it's probably beyond the power of any single mind to ever pin down where all the money is coming from and where it's all going.

As much as Ben loathed *Tropics* he didn't try to quash it. He didn't have to. The problems were all intrinsic to the film itself.

## Dean Sutter

When I showed Shark my cut he exploded. "You stupid, ignorant fuck, you've ruined it. This is shit. I'm going to see that you never direct another picture."

Well, I was exhausted and flew off the handle. I'm not a physical person, so I was astonished to find myself grappling with Shark on the floor of the screening room. The next thing I knew he was actually *biting into my forearm*. You can still see the scar.

## Greg Spivey

Shark told me later he'd lost control in the fight with Dean, though the fight itself had been planned. He just wanted an excuse to get rid of Dean so that he could cut *Tropics* himself. Which he did, endlessly. He just couldn't get it right. But then nobody could have. The performances weren't the problem. It was the script, the whole concept of the film itself, that sucked. I tried to tell him this tactfully, but he wouldn't hear it.

Eventually, after months of trying to save the film in the editing room, Shark simply ran out of steam. He never admitted defeat in so many words, but the work prints were put in storage. And so his von Sternberg hommage died with a whimper, his rotten mango romance, it seemed, permanently shelved.

There followed a long stretch—actually most of 1976—during which Shark did little more than rest on his laurels. We had a number of projects in various stages of development, but there was an unspoken sense that none of them was really *it*.

One of the oddest projects was the "Riviera romance" Shark insisted on calling *The Thrill of It All*. The story, which went through a number of permutations, was something of a pastiche of Hitchcock's *To Catch a Thief* and *Rear Window,* and the Michael Powell cult film *Peeping Tom:* a voyeuristic Saint-Tropez catburglar spying on a blonde model inadvertently photographs a murder. Shark drove the writer crazy with new plot twists and changes, before finally abandoning the idea after Universal refused to let him use the title of their 1963 Doris Day film. "There's no point to doing it if I can't use that title," Shark said, which I didn't understand at all. Of course, about that time he discovered the British art-rock group Roxy Music, which became his favorite group from that point on, and they had a song called "The Thrill of It All," which Shark played obsessively at home and in his car. It was a strange, calamitous, driven song, the lyrics speaking of hopeless romantic loss and subsequent dissipation—spiritually about as far removed from a Doris Day comedy as you could get.

There were other scripts, other deals, but nothing held Shark's interest for long. There were weeks on end where he didn't even bother to come into the studio. Of course his old high school friend was back in the picture by then.

## Woody Hazzard

The early seventies had been a bad time for me. I got busted in Mexico with a hundred keys of grass, and did eighteen months in a rathole Chihuahua prison before being returned to the U.S. as part of a prisoner-exchange deal. Then I did another nine months at Chino before I got paroled. I was in real bad shape when I called Shark from a phone booth in L.A. and he invited me out to the beach house.

I ended up staying there for over a year. At first I was a little intimidated, cause he had all these heavy-weight movie star types running in and out of there day and night. But I got into the swing of it soon enough. In a lot of ways it was like a replay of our summer at my mom's place in Newport, except instead of surfer girls we had starlets. Instead of acid and grass, we had bushels of Thai sticks and huge fucking mounds of cocaine.

Talk about bitchin summers, man, I couldn't believe it. After two and a half years in the joint I was starved for snatch—to say I made up for lost time wouldn't quite describe it. I don't know what Shark's excuse was. But we had more pussy than we even knew what to do with!

Of course every girl in town was dying to fuck Shark, since he was the man of the hour. And even though he still liked the blondes the best—especially if they looked the least bit like Kathy—he had 'em coming and going in all sizes, shapes and colors. I guess in some ways Shark had put a lot of his sex drive into his work up to then—maybe that was *his* excuse— and now he was reaping the rewards.

So I wouldn't feel like a freeloader he hired me on as his assistant/bodyguard, but the whole concept of money no longer even seemed to matter. I remember seeing a check from Mastodon once, either profits from *Hail!* or *The Condoist*, for the sum of fourteen million dollars and change. It was just sitting on his desk, man!—this check for fourteen million dollars! —along with the gas and electricity bills.

He had servants—there was a great Swedish cook for a while—but they were always quitting because a lot of the times during the day Shark went around without any clothes on, and then he'd be fucking some starlet on the dining room table or something. He got off on that, being something of an exhibitionist. Then when he hired Lupe that really got out of hand.

## Lupe Sepulveda

I was new in Los Angeles from Mexico when Shark hired me as his live-in maid. I had a nice room above the garage. Then right away he started making love to me, which I didn't mind because he was very handsome. But then he promised many things that turned out to be lies.

## Woody Hazzard

Lupe was stunning, though she did have a tough edge. Visually, she really could have been an actress—but who knew if she could act? I think Shark fed her a line about a remake of *Ramona*, this time with a real Hispanic girl in the Loretta Young part. He promised to give her a screen test and all that and proceeded to just fuck her senseless. I mean, it was sex-object city. I'm sure a lot of the attraction was based on the fact that Lupe did greatly resemble Juanita, the young whore he'd fucked on the Blue Fox stage in Tijuana and smuggled across the border in my car trunk in '66. Shark was always a glutton for nostalgia.

One day he was giving it to Lupe dog-style on the balcony, which wasn't too cool since it was a crowded day at the beach, and anyone who happened to look back up at the house could've seen what they were doing. I was lying by the pool below when he called to me, "Hey, bro. Check it out." I looked up just as he withdrew from Lupe and fired off this huge fuckin' load in a big arc through the air.

When she and Shark weren't getting it on Lupe was still doing the housework, but I sensed she was getting sick of waiting for her screen test, and that sooner or later something bad was going to come down.

## Grey Spivey

In the fall of '76 Shark became briefly obsessed with developing a "prestige literary property." He was hungry for Academy recognition. Despite the gargantuan success of *The Condoist* and *Hail!* neither film had garnered more than a few technical award nominations. I understand a recording of his side of one of our phone discussions from that period exists.

## Shark Trager, *Audio Cassette*, October 2, 1976

Greg-O. How's it hangin', you get laid last night? Yeah, I've had her. You're more generous than I am. Talked to Ben? Yeah, that figures. I wonder how much it would cost to have a 747 crash into his office. No, I'm hot for Jean. Don't be so sure, I saw her number on the Polo Lounge men's room wall. "For the meanest blow job north of Sunset—" *(laughs)* Greg, I've got Ovitz on two, let me put you on the speaker-phone and give you my notes. *Finnegans Wake:* Pass. Irish shit always goes down the toilet. *Pale Fire:* great title, but I'm not sure who we're rooting for. *Gravity's Rainbow:* maybe, if Bill Goldman can find the spine of the tale. *Catcher in the Rye:* up the offer to one million five. *Naked Lunch:* John Milius might bring it off, but do this decade's kids know the title? It sounds like a Crown International picture. *On the Road:* yes, if we can make it contemporary. Neal Cassidy as a disco fanatic, driving cross country to a big dance contest. It needs a sure-fire *Rocky* ending. *Giles Goat-Boy:* pass. Sounds like a Disney film. *Humbolt's Gift:* yes, if we can snag Robby Benson for the lead. *Our Lady of the Flowers:* send this to Steven [Spielberg]. If his UFO yarn's the dog I hear it is, he might like a change of pace. Greg, I've got Laddie, Michael Eisner, Sidney Korchak, Swifty Lazar, Nicholson's people, and Annette Funicello on hold—gotta go, kiddo. Oh, hey—track down *The Searchers*, will you? Ciao.''

## Neal Ridges

I had fallen on hard times since writing *The Condoist* which despite its phenomenal success had earned me nothing—thanks to the trickery of the studio accountants. I'd had a few bullshit development deals, but was basically scrounging. So I swallowed my pride when Greg Spivey called and said Shark was eager to discuss a "remake of *The Searchers*."

The day I arrived at the beach house the door was open and I caught a glimpse of Shark going down on his Mexican maid in the kitchen. It was a kind of real-life porno situation. She was wearing one of those short, frilly French maid costumes, and no panties.

"I'll come back another time," I said when Shark saw me.

But he just laughed, and wiped his chin, and said, "No, that's okay, Neal, this can wait. Come on in."

Well, he was in good spirits, but the girl Lupe wasn't—I picked up those vibes right away. With considerable charm Shark asked my forgiveness for his "inexcusable behavior" during *The Condoist* writing period, which he attributed to "pressure, low-grade cocaine and creative nerves." I accepted his apology, and his praise of my "unique filmic genius," and we began to discuss the new project. It soon became apparent that what he had in mind was less a remake of *The Searchers* than simply another of the "updates" of the basic *Searchers* plot that were so popular at the time. It would be an "urban version," Shark said, with the "racial aspect" of the original brought to the fore. The girl Debbie, abducted by Indians in the original, would be kidnapped by black men and taken to live in Watts.

As we talked Lupe began banging pots and pans and angrily slamming cupboard doors in the kitchen. Several times Shark shouted, "Hey, I'm in a meeting." But the noise continued, until at last she began breaking plates.

In a rage Shark stormed in the kitchen, and there were heated words, hers in Spanish. Then Shark groaned, and staggered back into the room, bleeding from the stomach. She came at him with the knife again—a serrated steak knife—which I managed to get away from her. Then Shark collapsed in a pool of blood, as Lupe, sobbing now, held his head. "Oh God, what have I done!" she wailed. "Please don't die, Shark, I'm so sorry! Oh God, why couldn't you just love me!"

## Woody Hazzard

I was out surfing the day Lupe stabbed Shark, but I rushed to the hospital as soon as I found out. It was an evil jagged wound but they said Shark was going to make it.

He could've had Lupe charged with attempted murder, of course, but instead he chose to cover for her. He told the cops he'd been running past her to answer the phone when she turned abruptly with the knife in her hand and accidentally poked him.

Later I asked him why he let her off.

"Because I had it coming," he said, and smiled. "I knew she was in love with me. But to me she was just an incredibly wild and hot little fuck."

Then he looked at the scar on his stomach—we were catching some rays by the pool—and smiled again and said, "It was worth it."

But he seemed changed. The partying tapered off radically after that. He didn't care if I brought girls around, but he started keeping to himself again.

Then one day he said, "I'm sick of sitting in the sun. My brain's starting to atrophy. It's time to make another movie."

## Lupe Sepulveda

This guy called me from Shark's studio and said, Here's ten thousand dollars, get out of town. I said, I don't want your money, I want a screen test for *Ramona*. He said there was no *Ramona,* so I took the money and moved to Santa Barbara and began going to night school there.

It turned out to be a blessing. I earned a business degree, became a U.S. citizen, and today have my own company, Ramona Industries, manufacturing douche bags and related products. In my spare time I am a poet, a gifted painter and a serious, dedicated female body builder.

It would be many years before I saw Shark again, and it would not be as I imagined it.

## Bill Kemmer

We handled the maid, and kept the incident out of the papers. It was a blessing in the long run, of course, because it had a sobering effect on Shark and brought him back to work.

We were quite troubled at first though by Neal Ridges's neo-*Searchers* script *Scar,* which Shark insisted must be his next film.

## Neal Ridges

I always thought the idea sucked, but I was sick of eating macaroni. I felt it was racist for one thing, especially the scenes where "Duke White," the neo-John Wayne uncle character in the script, starts tearing up Watts in search of his niece "Nattie" —played by Natalie Wood, you may recall, in the original. The first draft was virtually a scene-for-scene transliteration of the Ford classic, and I found Shark's new version both ridiculous and extremely offensive to write. The women's jail episode, for example, where the cops show Duke several white girl prisoners who've been "shacked up" with black male criminals—in the original John Wayne encountered a group of white pioneer women whose years in Indian captivity had driven them insane. "If she's still alive, *this* is what your niece will be like," the cop tells Duke. *"Now* can you tell me you still want to find her?" At which point the white girls, their hair frizzed out in horrendous Afros, begin screeching in black ghetto dialect: "What you lookin' at, mothuhfuckuh? Fuck yo' face, you jiveass honky," as we track in on our conservative protagonist's look of unfathomable horror.

Our white-bread hero goes on to shoot out a dead drug dealer's eyes and so forth and wins his showdown with the evil pimp Scar. But when the ultimate moment of truth comes, and he chases his Negroized niece back into a Watts riot-gutted Pioneer fried chicken outlet, he's so unhinged from the infernal rhythm & blues sex-beat pulverizing his Rotarian brain than instead of rescuing the girl, in a convulsion of libidinous fury *he rapes her.*

I argued vehemently against this ending, citing the original. "Shark, if you do this the audience will kill you. You can't have them identify with Duke for ninety minutes only to have him rape his own niece in the last reel. Use your common sense. If Ethan had raped Debbie in the original it would have utterly subverted the entire meaning of the film. It was *crucial* that he said, 'Debbie, let's go home,' not 'Straddle this, you dirty little squaw.' "

"But he *wanted* to fuck her," Shark contended vehemently. "Run the film, Neal! Look at the scene!"

Well, it's one of the classic moments in American film—there's no one right way to read that scene. "Okay, Shark," I said. "You're the producer, if that's what you want, that's what you'll get. But I'm warning you."

## Bill Kemmer

After I read the script I met with Shark and said, "Shark, I don't understand this. I know you're not a racist. Like most of us who came of age in the sixties you're probably a liberal or a post-political humanist or something like that, and yet this is the most virulently racist script I've ever read."

Well, he exploded, saying the script wasn't racist, the character was, and was I so stupid I couldn't tell the difference?

"*I* can tell the difference," I told him, "because I am an intelligent educated person who understands the nature and purpose of art. But I'm not sure the average moviegoer will perceive the distinction. Face it, America is sitting on a volcano of barely suppressed racial animosity. I'm afraid there'd be white girls attacked in the ladies rooms and black men strung up against the drive-in screens in the wake of this inflammatory tract."

"It's not a tract," Shark said angrily. "It's based on my father. My father's a racist, I'm not. But it's not just my father, it's all fathers. All fathers are racists. Isn't yours?"

Well, he was. But I hardly saw what that had to do with the script. Shark was clearly irrational, the victim of volatile and unresolved subjective forces.

"Shark, there's no way we can make this movie," I said calmly. And he stormed out, muttering, "Fucking dildo executives," under his breath.

We were all very concerned. Then the next afternoon he burst into my office and said, "Bill? Problem solved. Forget the black angle. She's kidnapped by lesbians."

At the time it struck us all as a brilliant solution. We knew from Marketing that demographically lesbians, unlike blacks, were a group we could easily afford to offend.

## Neal Ridges

I was ecstatic when Shark came up with the lesbian angle. Lesbianism was a subject that had long fascinated me, though I was the first to admit that I, as a heterosexual male, could not really presume to understand what it was for two beautiful women to make sensuous love to one another. But I saw the script as suddenly giving us a chance to provide a non-judgmental, perhaps even tastefully erotic, glimpse into the exotic netherworld of sex between dreamy young women without men.

The Scar character *would* have to be a stoutly masculine mean-tempered "diesel dyke" in coveralls and flannel shirt, but I felt I could impart a kind of humanity even to her.

## Greg Spivey

Everybody was crazy about the lesbian draft—except me. Not that it wasn't well-written, but I'd lived in the bay area for a while, and knew what could happen when you got a radical lesbian mad.

## Woody Hazzard

The afternoon the studio rejected the black version of Shark's *Searchers* script he came home in a rage. He tossed back some Valiums with his cream soda but still didn't calm down. Finally he said, "I gotta get out of here, I'm going for a drive," and took off in his Porsche.

I know now he drove down to Newport Beach.

## Kathy Petro

I found out later what happened, that apparently Shark was just driving through the neighborhood, upset about his script rejection and trying to blow off steam, when he saw Beth and me coming out of my parents' house. It was the day I was moving to Beth's, which Shark could tell, since Beth and I were putting a bunch of my clothes in her car.

When we left Shark followed us to Beth's house in Laguna Beach. And when it got dark he sneaked up to the house and looked in the window and saw Beth and me making love.

## Woody Hazzard

I remember the first day on the set in Joshua Tree—they were doing the scene where the gang of lesbians on motorcycles surround the family's Winnebago. And when I saw how they'd done up Marcia Reed I almost shit. Because, you know, they'd given her that patented Kathy Petro California Look.

"You're still weirded out about her, aren't you?" I said to Shark later in his trailer as we shared a joint.

"Who?" he said.

"You know who," I said. "Kathy, man."

"I don't want to talk about it," he said, and looked at me kind of suspiciously. See, one night when we were drunk he'd told me about seeing her on Maui and wasting Jack Petro, and how Kathy's nipples had got hard against his chest and all that—but he was so drunk I don't think he remembered for sure how much he'd really told me.

"This is kind of a low blow, though," I said, referring to the picture. "Especially if she was finally starting to have second thoughts about you. 'Cause when she sees this movie she's gonna know you're trying to imply that she's a dyke."

Shark stared out the window. "She *is* a dyke," he said.

## Kathy Petro

I don't know. It was a funny time for me. I don't think I was ever really a lesbian, not like Beth was, but I just got so sick of being back with my parents.

And that whole thing with Shark on Maui just really confused me. In a way I still hated him, but then I would have these dreams where he'd be making love to me in this really wonderful way—like something you've wanted for years was finally happening, that kind of sex—and then I'd wake up and be mad at myself, thinking: Why am I dreaming this?

Then sometimes I'd get mad at Shark, thinking: So if he wants me so bad, how come he didn't take me away with him after he wasted Daddy on Maui? That was his big chance, my mom couldn't have stopped him. And for that matter, why hadn't he tried harder to save me from Derek in Saint-Tropez? True, Derek had a gun, but if Shark had really been determined he could have fought Derek for the gun or something, couldn't he?

Was it possible he just liked *wanting* me but didn't really want to *have* me? Was I like some kind of fish he liked to hook and fight to reel in, only to cut the line at the last minute so he could do it all over again? Was that it, was it something like that? Or something else? I didn't know, and thinking about it just gave me a giant headache.

Then I met Beth and we just hit it off right away. She worked in a pottery shop in Laguna and seemed really artistic and bohemian and we talked for hours in her quaint little house, drinking herb tea and listening to Holly Near records. She was very frank about her lesbianism, which was no big deal to me, and she was also a feminist and made a very powerful case about how my whole life had been controlled by men. I mean, I could really see it, being a model and all, and the thing with Derek where he hit me and everything—Beth was really enraged when I told her about *that*. She even knocked my romantic affair with Andreji, saying, "You were just a fetish for him, a masturbatory icon, otherwise known in male religion as a madonna."

At first I just started staying over at her place, and we'd sleep in the same bed without touching. Then we started holding each other. Then more happened, and I can't really say it was bad or anything. But I think mostly I just wanted to get out of my parents' house.

## Marcia Reed

*Scar* was supposed to be my big break. I always had mixed feelings about the role of Nattie, because of the lesbianism mainly, but my mother convinced me it was exactly the kind of daring debut that could turn me into a major Hollywood star overnight.

I loved Steve Riley, he was just a dream director, but I hated Shark from the very start. He wanted me to have this Kathy Petro look, but I said, "Come on, she's past it. I don't want to look like some washed-up old model." That really infuriated him, and Greg Spivey told me later in strict confidence that Shark had had some kind of thing for Kathy Petro and I should never, ever mention her name again.

But Shark kept baiting me, treating me as if I were actually the character I was playing. It was kind of disguised as a joke but you could tell he really hated me. Like he'd sing, "Hey there, lesbo girl," to the tune of "Georgie Girl." Then he'd get really crude, saying, "Hello, muff-diver." Or: "Here comes the pussy-bumper." Or: "Someone bring Marcia a toothpick. I think she's got some cunt hair stuck between her teeth."

Finally, I walked right up to him and said, "If all guys were like you, Shark, I *would* go lesbian."

He hauled off to slap me, but Steve stopped his hand.

## Bill Kemmer

There was some friction on the set, which was actually a good thing. Some of the best films come out of a charged combative atmosphere, and *Scar* looked to be a case in point. I was on the set in Victorville—watching Steve Riley shoot the scene in the lesbian bar where Burt Grady, delivering an Oscar caliber performance as Duke Manmann the protagonist uncle, has disguised himself as a bull dyke and first encounters his niece being ordered about by Wanda Gerkin, doing a brilliant, hair-raising turn as the domineering Scar—when someone tapped my shoulder and said there was an urgent call from Ben.

Right up to that point Ben had been gung-ho on the picture. I knew he shared my opinion that the dailies were astonishing, so naturally I was floored by what he had to say. In a stunned daze I went to Shark and Steve, feeling especially bad for Steve since this was his directorial debut. "We're dead," I told them. "It's over. Ben has just ordered an immediate halt to production."

Nobody could quite believe it. Shark got on the phone but Ben wouldn't take his call. In a rage Stark started for his Porsche.

I tried to stop him. "Look, why don't you come back and try and calm down? Ben does have his reasons—"

Shark knocked my hand from his shoulder and jumped into his car, screaming off down the highway toward L.A.

For a while I was actually relieved. At least *I* wasn't going to have to explain Ben's reasons for canceling the film to Shark. At the very least the explanation was awkward, but I didn't know the half of it—until I discussed the matter with Greg Spivey. "Oh my God, Bill," Greg said. "There's an awful lot you don't know. We've got to warn Ben."

I tried to reach Ben, but his secretary had been given strict orders to hold all calls.

## Kathy Petro

Eventually I told Beth all about Shark, though I left out the part about being turned on by him on Maui, because I knew she'd consider that sick. Well, needless to say she was completely outraged. "A man like that should be castrated," she said. "Or shot in the head the way you'd shoot a mad dog." She went on for hours and hours about how evil Shark was, how he'd violated me with his camera which was a "male instrument," how the whole history of cinema was a sexist attempt to dominate women and reduce them to visual objects. She was beside herself with fury and said if she ever saw Shark she would literally tear his testicles off with her bare hands.

Then one day she came back from a trip up to Los Angeles in a total blind rage. "This will be stopped!" she yelled and threw down a script, which I saw was *Scar*.

When I read it I became physically ill because you could tell—anyone could tell—that the lead character who was abducted by lesbians was me. She had the California Look, and even talked like me and everything. And the evil lesbian Scar was obviously based on Beth, because you know Beth had this big scar on her cheek where her ex-husband had cut her with a knife. I was completely freaked out, thinking: How did Shark know about us? Is he watching us? Is this place bugged? I mean, anything was possible. He was rich enough to hire detectives to spy on us round the clock.

Beth was ready to kill and kept saying, "This will be stopped, it will."

"How, Beth? How?" I said. "The movie is already shooting."

You see, I knew her only as Beth Womun, which was a feminist name she'd given herself cause she hated everything paternal. But finally she told me what her old name was.

## Mark Klieg

It was a moment of truth for my sister. Beth knew if she "came out" to our dad he'd disinherit her, and she hated to lose those millions. She had confided in me her desire to someday channel that money into an Orange County lesbian services center, which was a kind of ultimate treason because we both knew our dad had an especially virulent animosity towards lesbians since

248

the first woman he'd ever loved—before he met our mother—had dumped him for a WAC.

Beth called me at Stanford in a complete rage, telling me what she'd just learned about *Scar*. Even though I was thoroughly heterosexual—in desire if not yet in practice—I had long been ˜ympathetic to her and, as she well knew, definitely had my own reasons for hating our father. She said she just couldn't let Shark Trager get away with making *Scar*, which, the personal affront aside, was essentially to lesbians what *Birth of a Nation* had been to blacks. She said *Scar* was beyond being merely "politically incorrect," it was "tantamount to artistic genocide," and she had a moral obligation to stop it at any cost.

"Be careful, Beth," I told her. "You know what happens when you tangle with Dad."

She blew up and said, "Listen here, little brother. He may have beaten the courage out of you. But he hasn't molested it out of me."

## Kathy Petro

Beth and I marched into her dad's office, and he caught the drift before she even said a word. "No compromises" she'd said to me beforehand. "Can the femme act! *Cut the fluff!*" So we went in *butch*—in boots and dungarees and sloppy white tanktops showing our unshaven armpits, without the makeup or deodorant or other oppressive trappings of what Beth called "male-defined *beauty*."

"Hi, Dad," Beth said belligerently. "As you can see I'm a dyke—that's right, dyke, D-Y-K-E, dyke! And this here is Kat, my equally dyke lover. And we've come here to tell you that if you don't stop *Scar* right now, we're going to tell the whole story of your Mafia financing, *Dad*."

At the mention of the Mafia her father went kind of pale.

## Bill Kemmer

Of course, Hollywood financing is incredibly baroque and complicated but . . . Frankly, I prefer not to get into all this.

"Kill the film, you snake," Beth said to her father, indicating the phone. "Kill it now."

Ben nodded okay, but as soon as he reached Bill Kemmer at the location he swiveled around in his chair, speaking low into the phone so we wouldn't hear, though I picked out the words "Mafia," "a couple of lezes," and heard him mention my name.

"What are you doing?" Beth yelled, pulling his chair back around. "What kind of male trick is this? I'm not kidding you, *Dad*. I've got copies of your secret files going back to 1956—provided by Leona, your loyal private secretary, who just *happened* to be the *lesbian* who brought me out!"

That pretty much knocked his breath out.

"That's not possible," he said weakly. "Leona and I—"

"That word's *rape*, Dad. You sexually harrassed her for a decade, and then *raped* her, you goddamn male rapist molester."

He got this really stunned look.

"Kill it," Beth said. "Kill *Scar*."

For a second Ben couldn't even speak. He looked so bad I almost felt sorry for him. He was breathing kind of funny, which for some reason scared me a little. Finally, he just said, "Bill? Can't explain now. Tell Shark it's over." He banged down the phone, kind of missing the cradle.

I wanted to go then, but Beth was too wound up to stop. She just kept berating her father, attacking the whole nature of the film industry as male-dominated, making more and more demands. And Ben Klieg was so broken he kept agreeing to everything she said.

"You are going to do an epic version of Gertrude Stein's *The Making of Americans*," Beth yelled. "With an openly lesbian director and an all-lesbian crew!"

"All right, okay," Ben said, still breathing funny.

I knew Beth was stretching her luck because she didn't really have any proof of Mafia financing. It was just a guess on her part that at some point or other her father had probably had dealings with someone like that. I finally started pulling her toward the door.

"You are going to do a non-sexist, politically correct remake of *The Children's Hour* in which Audrey Hepburn and Shirley

MacLaine live happily ever after as proud lesbian lovers—*after James Garner hangs himself!''* Beth was still bellowing as I backed into Shark.

## Bill Kemmer

Greg Spivey and I arrived at Ben's office a few minutes behind Shark, having leased a chopper and flown into L.A., hoping to beat Shark there. We dashed in to find Shark and Beth grappling violently on the floor, Kathy Petro screaming, "Kill him, kill the son of a bitch," as she kicked Shark in the side.

## Kathy Petro

It was one of those rage things, I guess. I just lost control. 'Cause, you know, I did have all this repressed anger at Shark over everything he'd done to me.

## Greg Spivey

I pulled Kathy away from Shark, which wasn't easy. She was kicking and scratching and just possessed. Then Bill somehow managed to get a choke-hold on Beth. Shark was wasted, his face scratched and gouged, and in the aftermath everybody was completely winded, gasping for breath. Except Ben Klieg.

## Bill Kemmer

I knew Ben was dead the second I saw him, you could just tell. Sitting there in his seat of power, mouth open, eyes staring, the lights on his phone blinking with calls he would never return.

## Jean Klieg

I blamed Shark entirely for Ben's stroke. Certainly it was not Beth's finest moment, but once I understood the nature of her outrage over *Scar* I was not entirely unsympathetic.

Frankly, I never believed the story that she threatened to reveal a Mafia connection in her father's past. How utterly absurd, since no such connection existed.

Furthermore, nothing could ever convince me that my daugh-

251

ter's death was a "gangland execution." I still have my own theories about that.

## Mark Klieg

My mother was full of denial, trying to lay the blame for everything on Shark. I didn't think much of him myself, but I also saw the larger picture. "Mom, face reality," I said to her in the limousine on the way to Dad's funeral. "Dad was a monster. He's been beating me for years, and he molested Beth when she was still in her crib. He used to get drunk and poke his pud through the slates of her playpen. It wasn't quite 'Father Knows Best,' Mom—"

My mother became hysterical and ordered the driver to stop. "Get out of the car. You will not be welcome in my house again until you take back those pathological lies."

Well, it was all true, as my mother well knew. Our rift didn't last long however. We made up a few days later—in the wake of Beth's execution-style death.

## Woody Hazzard

Shark was totally demoralized after they shut down *Scar*, and when Ben Klieg checked out it threw everything into chaos.

More than anything though I think he was blown out by the way Kathy had acted when he was fighting with Beth.

"It's just like *Scar*," he'd say, sitting on the deck, looking really bad with all these scabs on his face. "Beth controls her now. She's turned Kathy into a man-hating dyke. Kathy's lost to me now, she really is."

Then—it could not have been more than a week after Ben Klieg's death—Shark got a call from Bill Kemmer saying, "Have you heard? Beth Klieg's been murdered."

## Greg Spivey

I'm sure it was the Mafia, regardless of what Jean Klieg may wish to think. Shark could be ruthless, but he wouldn't have jeopardized his own future by arranging a hit.

The confrontation between Beth and her father was loud. Many of the studio secretaries overheard. Beth's Mafia allegation had quickly became prime gossip, and clearly it reached someone who took lethal offense.

## Kathy Petro

I was really weirded-out after Ben Klieg's death, especially by Beth's attitude, 'cause she was saying, "Damn, we came so close. That old snake was going to give us everything! Millions of dollars for lesbian art! Now it's all lost. The studio is already being passed on to another pair of sweaty male hands."

She went on like that for days until I began to think, you know, sexual politics aside, maybe Beth was just really not a nice person.

Then one day I went to the market and as I came back I saw two big men in leisure suits leaving the house. I had a bad feeling as I watched them drive away in this baby blue Eldorado with Nevada license plates. I parked and got out and went up to the house, where a Holly Near record was playing way too loud.

"Beth?" I said. Then I stepped in and saw her lying on the carpet. They'd shot her in the back of the head. I just started screaming.

## Woody Hazzard

When we learned the details of Beth's murder I said to Shark at one point, "Poor Kathy. Finding Beth like that must've really fucked with her head."

"No more than she's fucked with mine," Shark said. Then he walked to the window and looked out at the ocean and announced in this momentous voice: "From this day forward, I forbid anyone to ever again mention Kathy Petro's name in my presence. As far as I'm concerned she no longer exists."

## Kathy Petro

All these cops came and everything and took pictures of Beth's body and asked me all these personal questions until I was just numb. Finally they stopped and I was sitting alone on the porch swing when I saw Daddy pull up in his Silver Cloud. He talked to the head detective for a minute, all the while glaring at me. Then he started up and I was really afraid. 'Cause he knew now

I'd been a lesbian and everything and I just thought he was going to kill me. He was just trembling with all this emotion as he suddenly grabbed me under the arms and lifted me way up in the air like he was going to throw me through the window or something. I was so scared!

Then very gently he put me down and said, "Kathy . . . let's go home." And I saw there were tears in his eyes, which I'd never seen before, 'cause he was just like John Wayne that way, he never wept. But the tears came now, and I wept too, just shaking and sobbing, hugging my daddy like a frightened little girl.

# 14 / **Carol**
## (1976)

### Greg Spivey

Shark knew it was time to leave Mastodon Pictures. Although Crane Hurter, the pragmatic Harvard-trained executive who replaced Ben Klieg, was eager to retain the studio's chief asset, Shark knew that at the very least the freedom he had enjoyed under Ben would be severely curtailed in the aftermath of the *Scar* fiasco. Then, too, he was well aware that Jean Klieg, who retained considerable influence within the parent company, blamed him for Ben's death and was pressing several members of the board for Shark's "total destruction." The possibility of hostile interference from the top, which would leave Shark "impotent and castrated as a filmmaker," compelled him to reach an amicable parting of the ways with Crane Hurter.

And so for a time Shark was without a studio—and he didn't even seem to care. Not that there weren't overtures from every studio in town. In spite of *Scar* everyone wanted him. *The Condoist* and *Hail!* were still among the ten top-grossing films of all time.

255

But Shark seemed to have lost interest in everything.

## Woody Hazzard

It was a strange time for Shark. Nothing seemed to get him off anymore. This beautiful young actress came by once, she and Shark went up to his room. Ten minutes later she comes down, and says, "He fell asleep in the middle of it."

"That's okay, honey," I told her, "I'm wide awake."

Shark would light a cigarette and look at it and say, "This tastes like shit," and punch it out.

One day I noticed a couple of grams of cocaine in the trash. "It bores me," he said.

This new Porsche he'd ordered came in—a blue Turbo, the first car I'd ever seen with a speaker phone, which of course became one of his trademarks later. That was the ultimate Shark Trager power call: that booming metallic speaker phone voice with the Porsche engine screaming in the background as he revved it and changed gears to punctuate what he was saying.

But even that bored him. He'd go for an aimless drive up the coast, Roxy Music blasting on the tape deck, and use the phone to order a pizza delivered, which would be cold by the time he got back to the house. "I've got everything money can buy," he said to me once. "And none of it means shit."

It got to be a drag to be around him. I was glad when he finally split for that Zen monastery in the mountains, and I threw a horrendous party while he was gone.

## Elliot Bernstein

Shark's experience with Zen Buddhism during the time he was seeing Judy Oshima in the mid-sixties had never completely left him. Indeed, in the years after Judy's death he had more than once wondered if that brief affair, and its tragic end, had not in fact been the true turning point of his life.

"If Judy had lived," he would say from the beatific vantage point of the mid-eighties, "I think the chances are good I might have eventually come to love her in a far more genuine way than I have ever loved anyone. And I might well have left the sorry peeping-Tom episode with Kathy where it belonged— among the discarded wreckage of my troubled adolescence."

256

He felt as well that a serious commitment to Zen practice would have altered his life course to an incalculable degree. "I believe I would have still pursued film," he said, "but I would have made a different *kind* of film, the result of a cleaner, purer vision. With a Zen clarity I cannot imagine that I would have ever felt compelled to imitate a discursively cerebral filmmaker like Jean-Claude Citroen—I would surely have been spared the emotional disfigurement which resulted from that excessively idolatrous act."

No doubt it was this train of thought which led him to the High Sierra Zen Monastery in '76, and accounted for what happened when he arrived.

## Woody Hazzard

Shark said when he pulled up to the Zen place the first thing he saw was this gray Vespa motor scooter parked by the gate. It was just like the one Judy Oshima had been riding the night she was hit by the Petro-Chem tank truck in 1966.

Even though he knew it had to be just a freaky coincidence he started breathing hard, feeling real weirded out.

## Elliot Bernstein

The Zen monks were expecting Shark, he had made a reservation to attend the week-long meditation *sesshin*. But he was a few minutes late, and the other attendees had already assumed their positions in the meditation hall as a monk led Shark in.

At the far end of the hall he saw a Japanese woman sitting in a lotus position, her back to him as she faced the wall. He could see little more than the line of her cheek, but his heart began pounding.

"It was completely insane, I see that now," he told me. "Of course, Judy was dead. There could be no doubt about that. Any conceivable scenario explaining how she might have actually survived would be hopelessly gothic and preposterous. But I made no attempt to devise a baroque rationale for what I felt. I simply knew it was her."

Shark pushed past the Zen monk, going straight to the woman. "Judy," he cried, touching her shoulder.

"Even when I saw that it was clearly not Judy, I still believed it was. She would have been thirty by then—in ten years her features might have changed, grown puffy."

He still thought it "might be" Judy, even after the Zen monks, unable to tolerate the disruption, had gently shown him out. "I stood there by the gate, by her Vespa, waiting for her to remember me and come out. It began raining and still I waited, my heart pounding. Then I noticed the light flashing on my car-phone. Somehow that mundane occurrence brought me back to earth."

It was a call from Brian Straight in New York.

## Greg Spivey

I'd stayed on with Shark in the wake of *Scar,* overseeing a few pointless development deals, but I'd begun exploring other career opportunities, thinking that Shark might be taking an early retirement. I was therefore heartened, indeed extremely excited, when Shark called to say he was flying back to New York to meet with Brian Straight, the president of Acropolis Pictures, and Harold Gay, chairman of the board of Sadcom, the parent company. Acropolis was really *the* happening studio then.

## Woody Hazzard

Shark told me later what happened in New York, in fact he told everyone. It became one of those classic Shark Trager stories, like something from a gross screwball comedy.

He'd got a suite at the Sherry-Netherland and it was the night before his big meeting at Sadcom and he had absolutely no idea what he was going to say. Here was this guy who was supposed to be the ultimate boy wonder bursting with energy and a jillion fantastic film ideas, and he said he felt "like the macho equivalent of Anne Bancroft in *The Pumpkin Eater*" after she'd had a hysterectomy or something. Like completely blank and depressed. He didn't know what his life was about or anything, and what had happened at the Zen monastery was still weighing heavily on his mind.

So he ordered a bottle of whiskey from room service and drank most of it down way too fast. Then he stepped out on the balcony to look at the Manhattan night skyline, and without warning threw up onto Fifth Avenue below.

Then two minutes later there's this violent knock on the door and he opens it, and it's Carol Van Der Hof and she's totally livid in a full-length mink coat that's wet and matted and stinking of whiskey.

## Carol Van Der Hof

You bet your breeches I was livid, and I gave Shark Trager quite a piece of my mind. "If you can't hold your drink, mister," I berated him, "I strongly suggest that you board the next plane back to California!"

At that he called me a spoiled socialite, though he was already grinning in that insidiously charming Errol Flynn manner of his.

"My dear sir," I said, "it may interest you to know that far from being a spoiled socialite, everything I own in this world is on my back. And just look what you've done to it!"

Then, furious at myself, I began to sniffle, for this indeed was the low point of my life.

His manner changed then as he noticed I suppose how truly ratty that pathetic mink was. "Say, you're not kidding. You are down on your luck." Then he attempted to remove the coat. "Come on now, that's a good girl, we'll have it dry-cleaned in a jif—"

But I swung free and proclaimed, "How dare *you* patronize *me*, sir? I'll have you know I come from one of the first ten Dutch families ever to set foot on this sliver of Indian marshland. If there were any justice in this world I should be a billionairess many times over." At that the dog-eared treatment for what eventually became *Mondo Jet Set* slipped from my mink coat pocket.

"What's this?" Shark said as he reached down and picked it up. I rather imagine it was then that he first became aware of my clubfoot.

## Brian Straight

Poor Carol—it had been a rough time for her. That truly horrendous business with her father. Really one of the first big society murder scandals, wasn't it?

## Carol Van Der Hof

I'd adored my father right up until that hideous Christmas morning in 1972 when he stepped into the parlor of our lovely

Connecticut manor house with an antique but operative Thompson submachine gun in each of his ruggedly masculine hands and opened fire, obliterating three generations of Van Der Hofs before turning one of the weapons on himself.

Fortunate me, I'd stepped into the kitchen to replenish Uncle Bill's toddy, but I *heard* it all. How could I ever forget Dad's last words, try though I might: "I've slept with you all, and if you really want to know . . . none of you was that hot."

Then the ghastly rat-tat-tat—the soundtrack of the Paul Muni *Scarface* superimposed with a deafening ferocity upon that quaint Currier and Ives tableau.

## Brian Straight

The sad thing for Carol, aside from the tragedy of losing her family, was the cruelty of her father's will. There were millions left to her in a trust, from which she was to receive only a minuscule fraction of the interest on a quarterly basis—little more than cigarette money—until she reached age sixty-five. If at that time, according to a stipulation of the will, she could undergo a medical examination which would verify that she had remained a life-long virgin, the principle would at last be disbursed to her. If she failed to "pass" the medical exam on her sixty-fifth birthday she would automatically forfeit her inheritance, and the Van Der Hof fortune would be used to establish an endowment fund for paroled murderers.

I know this because as a long-time friend Carol came to me with the will. We consulted the most powerful attorneys in New York, but the document was iron-clad, not a thing could be done.

"This is my father's revenge," Carol said. "Because unlike the others, I spurned him." Then she turned wryly philosophical. "It's a moot point anyway, Bri," she said. "I doubt I'd pass that exam even if I *were* to remain chaste for the next forty years. You see, I broke my hymen on Gogol when I was twelve." Gogol had been her horse.

"In that case, you may as well live it up, Carol," I told her.

But nothing was ever quite that simple for Carol.

## Tony Borgia

Carol—God, what a character! If she were in a movie no one would believe her, and she had the same problem in life, I can tell you. Of course, she was really the ultimate film buff, and as a result she knew everyone in the New York film scene. It's hard to recall a significant screening without seeing Carol somewhere in the crowd, chain-smoking those terrible unfiltered Camels—God, her stained little fingers, the nails bitten to the quick!—chattering loudly and fiercely in that Katherine Hepburn diction some assumed she affected, but was as natural to a Van Der Hof as polo and incest. And her hair, a Dutch bob parted on the side and plastered down, like Gloria Vanderbilt I suppose, though it was really more like Ayn Rand. She had a pretty face, though she took great if unconscious pains to obscure the fact, in an obvious attempt to discourage male overtures. Although she made light of it, I'm sure her clubfoot had a profound effect on her character.

## Brian Straight

She frequently made painful, feeble jokes about her deformity. "A Reuben for me, a club sandwich for my foot," that sort of thing.

As a result of her physical aberration—she wore a special shoe and walked with a slight limp—she had withdrawn at a very young age into a world of books and films. Then, too, I believe she'd known on some level what her father was up to with the other members of the family, and no doubt wished to escape from that.

Her feelings toward her father remained profoundly complex, and knowing Jack Van Der Hof, it was easy to see why. He cut quite a dashing figure. A sportsman, yachtsman, and finally an alcohol-deranged cocksman, he bore a strong resemblance to Errol Flynn.

But then so did Shark, didn't he?

## Tony Borgia

Her father was a truly evil man, in that he used his looks and charm as a means of exploring the outer limits of the demonic and forbidden. I think Carol felt her clubfoot had spared her from her father's incestuous advances—and yet subconsciously she'd taken his lack of interest in her as a devastating rejection.

I adored Carol though. My God, her mind! She was quite literally a genius. Her loft in SoHo was lined and piled with books, thousands of books. She just devoured them. I didn't doubt her when she told me that she'd once "slammed through" Dostoyevsky's *The Idiot* in its entirety while waiting for a date to join her at the Russian Tea Room—only realizing as she finished the book that she'd been stood up.

And when it came to film she had a literally photographic-memory. She could give you a detailed shot-for-shot analysis of anything she'd ever seen. No wonder her loft became a virtual non-stop salon.

But when it came to practical matters, like say putting out a cigarette or walking through a door . . . well, let me put it this way, we used to joke that Carol couldn't walk through the arch in Washington Square without managing to bang her shoulder, and she set her bed or a sofa or something on fire at least once a month.

God only knows how I ever thought she could function as a producer.

## Brian Straight

I had given Carol and Tony Borgia a development deal once, for a New York action picture which Carol was to produce, though I knew she was essentially incompetent. Not that she wasn't brilliant—in fact she was too brilliant. Her body was just something that hung from her mind, that was the feeling you got. Of course the deal fell apart as I knew it would. She had no budget, no sense of what a budget was, just astonishingly brilliant ideas and pockets full of illegibly scrawled notes. She really was committable, you know.

But I'd often think: If only someone could ground her!

## Carol Van Der Hof

I shall never forget that first night with Shark, for I quickly sensed it was the beginning of one of the most profound relationships of either of our lives. "My God, this is fantastic!" he cried, as he read the treatment of what eventually became *Mondo Jet Set*.

"Do you really think so? I'm rather fond of it," I said, and he exclaimed: "Yes, yes, *yes!*"

On a wave of euphoric rapport we soon found ourselves at Elaine's, neither of us able to contain our elation as our minds sparked and flashed together like the cascading fireworks behind Cary Grant and Grace Kelly as their lips met in *To Catch a Thief*.

"Yes, of course!" I cried, as he expressed his desire to someday produce a science fiction masterpiece in terms which quite accurately predicted *Blue Light*. "But it *should* allude heavily to classic fifties 'Red Scare metaphor' sci-fi, Shark! It *should* be a parodic hommage, even as it functions on a higher plane of genuine if pop religiosity!"

"My God, you're right!" he shot back. "It *could* work on both levels, couldn't it? I really *could* have my cake and eat it too!"

With what joyful abandon we laughed, Shark as taken with my filmic notions as I was with his. A nearly terminal giddiness seized us as I outlined a concept of mine called *Isabela, the Talking Andalusian Mare,* which I envisioned as a wickedly Buñuelian send-up of the Francis pictures with Donald O'Connor.

"Christ, I can't quit laughing," Shark cried, holding his stomach, oblivious to Capote's censoriously cocked eyebrow at the next table. "But wouldn't it be funnier still if instead of a mare it were a donkey . . . Yes, I've got it, a Mexican donkey in a sex show . . . and . . . and he loses his partner—let's call her Lupe—and becomes a detective, tracking her down."

I laughed so hard I nearly spit out a mouthful of tea. "Yes, yes, of course! My God, how utterly and deliciously outrageous, Shark! Of course, no studio will ever back such a picture." Needless to say, it was the germ of what eventually became *Looking for Lupe*.

Eventually we found ourselves back at my place in SoHo, gibbering like jaybirds on amphetamine till dawn—though neither of us had taken a thing, we didn't need to! He told me about his meeting that morning at Sadcom and I said, "Oh, don't worry about Bri. He puts on the tough act to compensate for everyone's unspoken knowledge of his homosexuality. But beneath that brutal businessman's facade beats the heart of a sentimental Heidi."

"You mean, Brian Straight is gay?" Shark said.

"Good Lord, you didn't know?"

"But he's been going with Margo Fray for years."

"Really, Shark, how naive you are. Margo owes her entire career to being photographed with powerful gay boys."

Shark was clearly shaken. "And Harold Gay, is he also . . . ?"

"No. Harold Gay is straight. That is, he's straight now. Dad knew him at Harvard and said he was gay for a time back then. And Brian Straight was straight as an arrow at Yale, only discovering his true bent after he moved to L.A. So Harold Gay was gay but went straight, and Brian Straight was straight but went gay. Though there *is* a rumor that Harold Gay may have never truly gone straight, but may still be quite guardedly gay, and that he and Brian Straight may in fact be secret lovers—although Brian may actually be straight and merely acceding to Harold's homosexual desires in order to advance his career."

Shark appeared confused. "I wish you were coming to this meeting with me, Carol. In fact, why don't you?" At that he focused on me with all his smoldering charm, punctuated with a rakish grin so like Flynn's in *The Sea Hawk*. "In fact," he said, "why don't you and I become partners, Carol?"

"Good God, Shark, it's almost seven A.M.," I said, my heart bursting with joy. "I thought you'd never ask."

## Brian Straight

Harold and I were both quite impressed with the projects Shark and Carol presented to us that morning, and their enthusiasm was indeed infectious. Privately, Harold expressed reservations about Carol, but my instincts told me to go the distance for them. "Harold, I smell success here, I foresee blockbusters and mega-bucks. Don't ask me to explain it, filmmaking isn't rational, but I sense a synergetic rapport between Shark and Carol that plunges deep into the heart of what movies are all about. Carol as the holy lunatic, Shark as the ruthless pragmatist. They need each other and we need them. If we pass on this opportunity, we'll be kicking ourselves for the rest of our lives."

"Okay, but it's your ass," Harold said. "And if you're wrong I'm going to personally carve a new hole in it, Brian."

## Greg Spivey

We were all elated by the Acropolis deal. The new offices on the Inglewood lot were even more posh than the ones we'd had at Mastodon. And everyone without exception was crazy about Carol.

## Cynthia Clive

She saved him, you know. Though I suppose he saved her as well from a lifetime of floundering. But what a change there was once Carol was about. Her diabolically infectious laughter, her incessant yet devastatingly brilliant talk! Shark was alive again, you could see it, living and breathing film as he was meant to. What years of joy those were!

## Woody Hazzard

Yeah, Carol was great if, you know, very East Coast. But she was definitely good for Shark, and she moved into the Santa Monica beach house right away. They practically lived in the basement screening room, watching everything you could imagine. They'd invite other people over in the evening, but long after everybody else had left, Shark and Carol would still be down there—Carol with her popcorn, Shark with his cream sodas—devouring movies till dawn.

After maybe a month I moved out and went to stay with this girl I'd been seeing up in Malibu. "I don't want to cramp your style," I told Shark, assuming he and Carol were getting it on. But he set me straight about that.

## Greg Spivey

It was fairly obvious, if you thought about it at all, that Carol was probably a virgin at age twenty-seven. Though you didn't think about it, that was the thing. She was just so cerebral, so asexual. Certainly I never thought for a second that Shark and Carol were involved romantically, though some people may have, since they were constantly together and soon developed the kind of shorthand you associate with lovers or, perhaps more to the point, a long-married couple. But Carol was really the antithesis of the sort of woman, the Kathy Petro sort of woman, Shark found most arousing.

In retrospect though, it's only too clear that Carol was in love with Shark from the start.

## Woody Hazzard

Not long after I moved to Malibu I got this idea for a screenplay about surfing and told it to Shark. Not a stupid beach picture like *Gidget* or something, but the real story of surfing as only a real surfer could tell it, about what it was like to surf in Orange County at places like Trestles and Huntington back in the sixties before everything got fucked up.

"I think it's a fantastic idea, Shark," Carol said, and convinced Shark who was dubious at first since I wasn't really a writer. Besides by then he had decided he wanted *Mondo Jet Set* to be his next movie and was working hard with the writer on that.

But I had this idea for a structure that even Shark liked too, since he was real big on structure. I said it would be the story of these surfers who go to Redondo Beach and then struggle to make their way back home to Laguna with various adventures along the way like in *Ulysses*, which I'd just seen on TV, with Kirk Douglas.

"Shark, we must say yes, we will, yes. Woody may well be the James Joyce of the South Bay," Carol said, in reference to the famous book on which they'd based the Kirk Douglas movie *[sic]*.

So I got a deal to write it and set off one afternoon on a research surfing trip to Orange County. That was when I ran into Kathy Petro.

## Kathy Petro

I was scared for a long time after Beth's death that the Mafia might try and rub me out too. Of course, it was never proven that it was in fact the Mafia, but in the mid-seventies hit men in leisure suits meant only one thing.

But after a while it kind of seemed to blow over, and I was seeing this shrink three times a week and everything, but I was getting bored so I'd go for these long drives down the coast in the 450SL Daddy had given me.

One afternoon I'd stopped at San Onofre, which was this really famous surfing spot with a nuclear reactor and everything, when who should pull up but Woody Hazzard.

At first I wasn't sure how I should feel about seeing him, because it did bring back memories of the acid days in the sixties and Jeff Stuben and the chainsaw. But then I thought: That wasn't really Woody's fault.

So we sat in my car and talked a long time. And then, as the sun went down and the lights on the nuclear reactor blinked on, Woody kissed me.

## Greg Spivey

Shark completely exhausted Tim Randolph, the original writer of *Mondo Jet Set,* and then dumped him and brought in a three-man/one-woman team and exhausted them as he distilled the script to its "superficial essence."

"This film must be all visual surfaces," he said, "with flat, one-dimensional characters who are nothing more than what they seem. I want glamour and chic iconography here. The music must carry the emotion, the people should be nothing more than sexy, appealing cartoons."

## Brian Straight

I read the script for *Mondo Jet Set* beside the pool in Palm Springs over the Labor Day weekend of 1976. "Harold," I said to our chairman who lay tanning beside me, "this is going to be our blockbuster for next summer."

He read it, then said, "Brian, it's all music."

"That's because it's a musical, Harold."

"All right," he said. "You're the movie mogul. But I doubt that I'm going out on a limb by telling you now, if this mindless mishmash so much as breaks even, I will personally give you the meanest blow job you've ever had."

"I'd just as soon take a cash bonus equivalent, Harold. How much would you say one of your blow jobs is worth?"

"One point five million," he said without hesitation.

"Uum. Mean, indeed. Could you put this in writing, Harold?"
He did. And we all know what happened.

# 15 / *Mondo Jet Set* (1976–1978)

## Carol Van Der Hof

What can you say about Rome in the fall? What a heady adventure our first filmic enterprise was. I believed that Joe Scalli was right for *Mondo Jet Set*, a youthful director with a bold style derived from Fellini and Welles and Nick Ray—an eye for the startling which I felt certain would assure Shark and me of the big commercial hit we so urgently needed.

I found the story quite charming, slight though it was, and thought Tom Reese most endearing as the fair-haired young Iowa Writer's Workshop novelist hurtled on a wave of sudden fame into *le monde jet set*. The spine of the tale—simplicity itself, as our young innocent moves through an increasingly bizarre and decadent Roman nightlife in pursuit of a blonde vision of equal purity. Shark insisted on the disco music—I'd been all for Nino Rota or perhaps Leonard Cohen—but he correctly foresaw that, however tedious it may have already become, the disco craze had yet to peak.

Shark convinced Joe Scalli to give Rita Flay what he called "the classic California girl look," though I argued vehemently against it, for it was all wrong, far too outdoorsy and natural. "Shark, Rita must be a rarefied ice princess, a haute couture madonna, remote and stylized, the antithesis of the tanned and vapidly grinning West Coast beach bunny."

We argued the matter quite passionately, until at last I simply surrendered, though Shark never did convince me he was right.

## Greg Spivey

As co-producer, in effect line producer, of *Mondo Jet Set* I was wired for sound on adrenaline, working far too speedily to watch everything I said. Once in a meeting with Shark and Carol, I made a passing reference, which Carol didn't even catch, to Rita Flay "sure looking like K.P. now," and Shark drew me aside afterwards and told me never to allude to Kathy Petro, by using her initials or by any other means, in his presence ever again. Then he asked me—he virtually pleaded with me—never to mention his past obsession with Kathy to Carol. "Carol is the best thing that's ever happened to me," he said, with a peculiar sort of fervor I found quite puzzling since I knew they weren't romantically involved. "And I won't have our relationship contaminated with the mistakes I've made in the past."

He went on to blame his fixation on Kathy on his cocaine use, which at this time had ceased. With the "childlike joy" Carol brought him, he said, he didn't need cocaine. It was only too clear he was merely using me as an acquiescent sounding board, trying to convince himself more than me that he was over Kathy—when it was obvious to anyone who watched the dailies of *Mondo Jet Set* that he wasn't.

## Carol Van Der Hof

One afternoon we'd all come up for air from the catacombs on the outskirts of Rome—where Joe was filming the extraordinary chase/dance sequence—when Shark saw a woman among a group of American tourists just beyond the trailers and absolutely froze. She was Japanese, perhaps fifty but quite youthful-looking, and she was just as startled to see him.

I followed as Shark approached her. I sensed correctly their history had been turbulent.

"Hello, Shark," she said guardedly.

"Carol, this is Miko Oshima," he said without taking his eyes off of her. "An old . . . I can't really say friend, can I? I'm not sure what we were."

"I don't think we were anything, Shark," she said. "My mind was closed to you because of my hatred for your father." She glanced about a bit nervously. "I sense that you haven't heard."

"Heard what?" Shark said.

At precisely that moment a man stepped around the trailer—I saw him a bit before Shark did. In his late fifties, he was stocky, with a steel-gray flattop, and bore a certain resemblance to the actor Glenn Ford.

"Come on, Miko," he said to the woman, before he noticed Shark. "Everything's closed 'cause of all this movie bullshit. Might as well mosey on back to Rome."

When Shark and his father saw one another they both froze in shock.

## Mac Trager

One afternoon in the fall of '75 I was leaving the Newport Beach post office when I saw Duke Wayne coming out of Gritt's Hardware store. I'd seen him around from time to time, but I hadn't spoken with the man since he quit coming into the station twenty-four years before. He was up in years by then, and something told me it might be my last chance to shake his hand and tell him how much I'd always admired him.

He was unlocking his Eldorado when I caught up to him.

"Hello, Mac," he said right off. And it kind of got to me that after all those years he still remembered my name.

We talked there for a minute, and then he said, "Say, I could use a drink. You in a hurry, Mac?"

Well, who would say no to a drink with John Wayne?

"This place all right?" he said when we came to the Yojimbo Steak House a couple doors down. It was some kind of Jap place I'd never been in. But if it was okay with the Duke, it was okay by me.

Then we stepped in the door and saw Miko Oshima. She was the hostess. "Howdy, Miko," the Duke said.

She glared at me. "I'm sorry, Mr. Wayne. But I cannot seat this man."

"Why the hell not?" the Duke said.

"I must ask this man to leave the restaurant," she said.

The Duke dug out a bill, and tried to slip it to her. "Let's just forget it, okay?"

She rebuffed him. "I don't want your money, Mr. Wayne. This is a question of moral principle."

"All right, that does it," the Duke said, losing his temper. "You don't know it yet, lady, but you just lost your job. Where's Yukio?"

The Duke started looking around for the owner, but I grabbed his arm. "Hold the phone, Duke," I said. "She's got a right to be sore."

But Miko was so sure she was going to be fired, she threw down her menus and took off back through the restaurant. I went after her.

When I caught up with her in the kitchen she was crying. "Look, I know you hate my guts," I said.

"Go to hell," she said.

Just then some waitress screamed, and a bunch of armed Japanese guys burst into the kitchen. "Hands up or you're dead," one of 'em yelled, and we all raised our hands, scared to death. Miko whispered under her breath: "Yakuza."

It was some kind of a shake-down deal, and the Duke had walked out right before they arrived. In a second two more of 'em pulled Yukio the owner into the kitchen and started forcing his face down over a pan of boiling water on the stove.

"You gonna pay? You gonna pay now?" they were yelling at Yukio, when I saw my chance and grabbed the one nearest me. I got his machine pistol away from him just as the others turned and I let 'em have it, spraying all four. They all dropped their weapons, wounded in their shoulders and arms, one guy with his trigger-finger shot off. Then another one came through the door and I threw that boiling water in his face—brother, did he howl! Then the one I'd disarmed grabbed Miko, and pressed a meat cleaver to her throat, but I shot him in the foot and he dropped it.

Luckily, the cops arrived then, since there were a half dozen more of those goddamn Yakuzas out in the dining room. When the cops stormed in they all gave up.

"Are you okay?" I said to Miko, who was shaking like a leaf, and she nodded.

"Look, I'm sorry about what happened in the past," I told her.

"I know," she said. "I'm sorry too."

We both smiled a little, and then I said, "Come on, I'll take you home."

## Carol Van Der Hof

Shark and his father stared at one another, as if the film crew activities about them did not even exist, until at last Mac Trager ventured a smile. "How ya doin', son?"

Shark appeared incapable of speech, his eyes now roving to-and-fro between Miko and his father. I too found the union difficult to comprehend, given what Shark had told me of his father's right-wing prejudices and especially virulent hatred of the Japanese.

But then love and hate are very close, aren't they?

## Mac Trager

Miko had had a tough life since her husband died, and as we got to talking I realized the war had cost her a lot too, what with being put in that relocation camp and all. I can't explain what happened really, except to say it was years of hatred giving way to the miracle of love.

## Carol Van Der Hof

"Look, son," Mac said to Shark. "I gotta tell you, I was real sore for a long time after I saw that *White Desert*, since it was plain that you based that couple that got gutted on Evelyn and me. But . . . I guess we probably had it coming."

Mac chuckled good-naturedly. But Shark's eyes were beginning to take on a lethal glint.

"Shark, I've changed," Mac said. "It's just that simple."

"He really has," Miko said, holding onto Mac's arm. "We both have."

"Son, I love Miko the same way you once loved her daughter Judy—"

"You *fuck*," Shark spat at his father, adding to no one in particular: "I want these people off the set." With that he stormed away.

272

Mac sighed, appearing sadly resigned, but Miko started after Shark.

Mac tried to stop her. "Honey, it's a lost cause." But she followed Shark into his trailer.

I simply couldn't resist stepping over to the trailer window so that I might overhear their conversation.

"Mac's forgiven you, why can't you forgive him?" Miko said.

"Do you want to know why your daughter's dead?" Shark said, ignoring her question.

Miko was silent a moment, then changed the subject. "Shark, I don't think you appreciate what it means that your father and I have come to love one another—the years of bitterness and hatred, the sense at least on my part that I was destined to live the rest of my days alone and never love another man. It's not a small thing that we've found each other before it's too late."

"Oh, that's beautiful," Shark said. "I'm really fucking moved. I'll tell you what killed Judy. My fear of that evil old scumbag out there, of his pathological bigotry."

"No, Shark," Miko said softly. "It's time to forgive your father, and yourself, as I've forgiven both of you. A Petro-Chem tank truck killed Judy, nothing more, nothing less."

"Look, I think we can end this meeting now," Shark said sarcastically. "I'm really not interested in doing a remake of *Cry for Happy* or *Teahouse of the August Moon.*"

"Then how about *Sayonara?* I'm dying," Miko said. "I've got cancer, a brain tumor, I'll be dead within four months.* That's why Mac married me, that's why he cashed in his life insurance policy so we could take this trip around the world. That's the kind of man your father is now, whatever he may have been in the past."

"Here, blow your nose," Shark said, and handed her a tissue. She was sniffling.

"Well, I'm sorry that you're dying," Shark said quietly. "But if that's the case, you'd really better get cracking. If you

---

*Worth mentioning here that this was a lie. Miko Oshima-Trager declined to be interviewed, but according to a close friend, Yuki Peterson: "Miko had always wanted to go around the world, but Mac was so cheap she felt that making up the brain tumor story was the only way." Mac and Miko were divorced in 1978.

catch the next bus back to Rome, you just might reach the Colosseum before the darkness descends.''

## Mac Trager

Miko was upset when she got back to me. "What did he say to you?" I asked her. "I want to know.''

"Let's just forget it, Mac," she said. "There isn't time.''

## Carol Van Der Hof

That night as we viewed the previous day's rushes, which were absolutely sensational—Tom and Rita darting about the catacombs in an intricate ballet set to a Donna Summer scratch-track—Shark sat there looking utterly glum.

"You're still upset about your father, aren't you?" I whispered.

Shark looked at me and for the first time ever said, "Carol, shut up.''

## Woody Hazzard

After I got it on with Kathy in her car at San Onofre I got real disturbed, knowing Shark would kill me if he knew, and swore I wouldn't see her anymore.

But since Shark was in Italy making *Mondo Jet Set,* one thing led to another, I broke up with this girl I'd been staying with in Malibu, and I ended up seeing Kathy again. By that time I was back at Shark's place in Santa Monica, house-sitting for him, and the first time Kathy came over it was a little freaky.

"So this is how Shark lives," she said, wandering around the house, touching things, both of us kind of scared in a way, half expecting Shark to walk in the door, even though we knew he was in Rome.

At first we'd just get it on in my room and then she'd drive back to Newport Beach so her folks wouldn't worry. Then she started making up stories and staying over, and we started sleeping in Shark's bed since it was bigger and more comfortable than the twin bed I had. Then she started staying the whole weekend, and it seemed cool at first. Since everyone knew Shark was in Europe, no one was coming around.

Then one afternoon Kathy and I were making love on the

living room floor when Neal Ridges came by and saw her through the window.

"You must be insane," he said to me. "Both of you must be insane."

"I can't help it, Neal," I told him. "I really fuckin' love her."

## Carol Van Der Hof

Joe Scalli was a genius, and a fast one, which is rare. He seldom exceeded three or four takes. We wrapped a full week ahead of schedule, which was virtually unheard of. Brian Straight was elated and dying to see Joe's rough cut, which was nearly completed since Joe—what a dynamo!—had been cutting as we shot.

We made plans to meet Brian in New York—Harold Gay was dying to see it too—but Shark said, "You and Joe take the film to New York, I'm flying straight back to L.A."

"Why?" I asked Shark, who seemed obscurely troubled. "Is there anything I should know?"

"I'm not sure why," he said. "I just have a feeling I should get back."

## Kathy Petro

I really loved Woody, I'm still not sure exactly why. He was really cute, I'm sure that was part of it, he had this really great surfer's body and was really gentle as a lover. I'd got so sick of guys always manhandling me, I think that's why I was so vulnerable when Beth came around, and in some ways Woody was very similar to her. So sweet and tender, just taking his time for hours, until we were almost living in this sensual daze.

It was strange being in Shark's house though, surrounded by his movie posters and everything, yet in another way it seemed so right. I don't know—I still don't understand this—but sometimes when Woody and I were making love in Shark's bed I would imagine that Shark was watching us—being forced to watch us, but bound and gagged and everything so he couldn't interfere. And I'd be thinking: See, Shark? *This* is what you've always wanted, isn't it? Only *you can't have it*. But I'm giving it to your *best friend* for free! Then I'd think: God, what a mean thought, what's happening to me?

So I finally said to Woody, "Look, I don't want to see you in this house anymore."

So about a week before Shark was due back from Europe Woody rented this little house a few miles up the coast in the surf colony at Topanga Beach, and I told my parents I was moving up to L.A. to be closer to my psychiatrist.

The afternoon Woody was moving out of Shark's we started kissing and ended up in Shark's bedroom making love when suddenly we heard Shark coming in the front door.

## Woody Hazzard

I almost shit. Kathy dived for the bathroom as Shark came up the stairs, calling my name, and he saw her! I'll swear to this day he saw her—but maybe his mind just wasn't willing to believe it was her, or maybe he just saw her bare ass and back.

"Hey, man," I said, adrenaline pounding through me.

"What's going on?" Shark said coldly. But I realized then he didn't know it was Kathy.

"What do you think?" I was just standing there with my dick all sticky, though my hard-on was rapidly wilting.

"It would really be cool," he said, "if you kept this action confined to your own room."

"Oh, yeah, I know. I'm sorry, man. But she's really wild, and I just have that small single bed."

Long pause. Then he said, "She's wild, huh?" And kind of smiled.

"Yeah," I said. "She's wearing me out."

"Oh yeah?" He definitely smiled. "You need some help?"

"I don't think she'd go for that. She's actually pretty strait-laced. Though I'm changing that." I tried to chuckle.

"Yeah, and rich too," Shark said, and I almost shit 'cause I realized he was referring to Kathy's 450SL parked out front. It even had these vanity plates that read: KATHY 76. But it must have been parked at an angle so that Shark hadn't seen the plates.

"Yeah, she's some Beverly Hills princess," I said. "I picked her up at Zuma."

He glanced at the bathroom door and spoke low so she wouldn't hear. "So why don't you get back to it, man?" He indicated the balcony that connected to the next room. "Part the drapes a little so I can come around and watch."

"She might see your shadow. If she did, man, she'd freak."

"Oh, bullshit," Shark said. "She must be super hot or you wouldn't be trying to keep her to yourself. Come on, man." He whipped out his dick. "Let's make a pussy sandwich."

He was laughing like it was a joke, even as he was ready to do it. So I laughed too and kind of shoved him back from the door, saying, "No, man, really. This is not that kind of scene."

When suddenly we heard a car start up and I knew it was Kathy's Mercedes. I got to the window just in time to see her pulling away below. The 450SL had its top off that day so I could look right down into it and see that Kathy was totally bare-assed naked, man! Like she'd climbed out the bathroom window and made it down to the car wrapped in this towel that fell off in the driveway or something. A couple of beachgoers were staring at her slack-jawed as she gunned off down PCH. By the time Shark got to the window the car was too far away for him to make out either Kathy or her plates.

"She must've heard you talking," I said to Shark. "You scared her away."

## Brian Straight

With *Mondo Jet Set* Shark most definitely delivered. I still believe it was the definitive disco musical, with *Saturday Night Fever* later that year a kind of cheesily home-grown imitation. Some people forget how phenomenally well we did, which I suppose is understandable, since '77 was also the summer of *Star Wars*.

## Julian Christopher, *Fire Island Review*, June 14, 1977

I'm in love with Tom Reese, the heart-breaking young star of *Mondo Jet Set*. He's a perfect blond doll and quick as a whip to boot. I'd lick his penny loafers if I were into that sort of thing. Who knows, maybe I am. If I were straight I'd be in love with Rita Flay too. What the hell, I am anyway— she's the loose, ecstatic soul of what's happening today. I'm wearing out the soundtrack album. I'm not kidding, I am. The Chumps, the Dill-Does, the B.J.s, Georgine Bazoom—*Mondo Jet Set* is a Who's Who of disco. I'm dancing as I write this—I'm serious, I am. I've seen this movie five times already, and used up all my poppers, and the summer's barely begun.

## Neal Ridges

Shark was riding high on the success of *Mondo Jet Set* when he gave me a deal to write and direct *Looking for Lupe*. Well, at first I was sure it was one of those ideas that would never be made, and took the deal strictly for the money, thinking: A talking sex donkey searching L.A. for his former "girlfriend"? I mean, come on. How low I had sunk since the high-art ambitions of *White Desert*.

Then as I worked on the story with Shark and Carol something extraordinary happened: I began to have fun. Of course, the concept was inane, the movie could never be more than trivial, vulgar entertainment. And yet we began laughing, holding our stomachs in convulsions of laughter, as we devised increasingly outrageous situations. "Shark, this will never be made," I'd say periodically. "We're going too far."

But it became more and more obvious, as *Mondo Jet Set* continued to rocket into the box office stratosphere with no ceiling in sight, that Acropolis was ready to do anything Shark wanted.

## Carol Van Der Hof

It was a golden time for us all. Has anyone ever laughed as hard as we did that summer developing *Looking for Lupe?* How I adored Neal from the very start, for I sensed he was an artist, and in his own way needed Shark as desperately as I did if he were to survive in the Hollywood jungle.

## Greg Spivey

Brian Straight was aghast when he saw the *Looking for Lupe* script. In a way, of course, it was *The Searchers* again, with Hector the Donkey in the John Wayne role. Naturally, those of us who were close to Shark knew the object of Hector's search was modeled on Lupe Sepulveda, Shark's former maid. The intrinsic raunchiness aside, Brian was concerned that Hector might be perceived as a kind of ethnic slur since he spoke with a Mexican accent. "Would you mind looking at thees peecture of my girlfriend Lupe?" he would say at the door of an Ozzie and Harriet house. "I understand she used to do thee housework for thee gringos in thees neighborhood."

Shark assured Brian we'd make it clear that Hector, whatever else he did, was a "supremely intelligent, sensitive individual, far wiser and more considerate than most human beings actually are." Needless to say, that wasn't good enough, and the script was eventually altered quite a bit.

## Brian Straight

I knew we had to drop the idea that Lupe and Hector had ever actually slept together.

"But it's not just crass sex," Shark argued. "They're genuinely in love."

"Shark, that's not the point," I told him. "Hector can express his longings in the most elevated poetic terms, but that doesn't change the fact that he's still *a donkey!*"

Neal Ridges finally came up with the perfect solution: "Okay, they're *just friends*. A sentimental Flicka/Black Beauty type friendship between a winsome Mexican girl and her beloved talking pet. In the Tijuana flashback, they pretend they're *about to* stage a live sex show. But once the thrill-hungry gringos have paid their money, Hector and Lupe split—without actually delivering."

## Greg Spivey

I was worried at first, fearing that Neal had fatally compromised the basic premise of the film, but it was a classic case of outsmarting the censors. Despite all the plot disclaimers to the contrary, the intimate tone Hector eventually took with Lupe left little doubt as to what was really going on between them. "Oh, *ba-by*, I just keep thinking about how *good* we were together," Hector tells her on the phone, which is not, you know, the sort of thing talking animals usually say to their platonic keepers.

## Neal Ridges

I had never mentioned catching Woody and Kathy Petro together to Shark, I just felt it wasn't my place.

Then one day Shark and I were out scouting locations for *Lupe* and stopped by Wood's place at Topanga Beach unannounced.

Woody was alone but seemed rattled to see us. I saw evidence of a woman in residence and put two and two together, and managed to move Shark toward the door as Woody became increasingly nervous.

Then on a pretext Woody drew me aside and said, "Don't ever let Shark come here again without calling. Kathy's staying here, man."

I told him I'd deduced that, and agreed to keep quiet, but I felt very uncomfortable about it. Here Woody was still working on his surfer screenplay, still taking money from Shark, and actually shacked up with Kathy Petro. It was just a double murder waiting to happen.

## Carol Van Der Hof

Woody finally showed us what he considered the finished screenplay and, well, to be frank, it was pretty bad. But Shark said, "I'm not sure how objective I can be since Woody is my best friend. Why don't we get Brian's opinion?"

I told him that was pointless, but he gave the script to Brian anyway. It seemed fairly inconsequential at the time. *Looking for Lupe* had begun filming, and all of our energies were focused on that.

## Brian Straight

It's funny how it happened. I think I'd seen the coverage of Woody's script, which of course advised a pass, when Woody called to find out my reaction, and for some reason I took the call. Something in his voice, that boyish sun-drenched surf vernacular, set off a spark of intuition. Maybe we shouldn't blow this project off just yet, I had a hunch. And so I set up a meeting.

Once I met Woody, this youthfully tanned and blond archetypal surfer in the flesh, I was even more convinced we might in fact have something here. And so I did something I never did in my capacity as president of the studio. I agreed to work on the screenplay personally with Woody on weekends at my place in the Colony. Together, I was sure we could yet shape his material into a workable script.

## Neal Ridges

When I heard that Woody was working closely with Brian Straight, I perceived yet another dimension to the disasters looming ahead—if the rumors of Brian's homosexuality were true. Woody was not the kind of guy who would graciously decline an advance of that sort. He'd probably knock Brian's teeth out or worse.

But then nobody seemed to really know the truth about Brian. It was true he was thirty-four and had never been married, but he didn't run with a gay crowd. In fact most of his "friends" were the much older A-party set, the sort of ancient farts you have to court if you want Brian's kind of power.

## Brian Straight

I was a very lonely man. I'd throw the Malibu bashes with all the right people. I'd wine and dine them all and appear to be oh-so-happy. But after all the couples had gone home, there I would be, alone—the great masturbator with his porno tapes and VCR.

In fact, I may as well tell you, as long as I'm telling you everything, that at age thirty-four I'd only had sex twice in my life, and both of those times with women.

## Kathy Petro

Woody started spending more and more time working on this script up at Brian Straight's place until I started getting a little jealous. 'Cause I really loved being with Woody and was really happy for the first time ever—with all these creamy sensations from Woody's love-making, and from this great new mood elevator my shrink was giving me.

Then one day Brian came by the Topanga beach house. It was a Saturday and he was dressed casually, driving this blue Ferrari, but I got a funny feeling about him right away. He looked at me and said to Woody, "So this is the woman you live with." The way he said it was weird and for some reason gave me a shiver.

Then Woody walked him out to his car, and I watched them through the curtains as they talked in the driveway. Right before Brian got into his Ferrari he gave Woody a quick kiss on the cheek.

## Woody Hazzard

I remember the afternoon I told Kathy I was gay. We'd just made love for what I knew was going to be the last time since Brian Straight had asked me to move in with him. So I told her as gently as I could where it was at as we lay there in bed watching this bitchin sunset.

She started to cry. "It's not fair. The first time I'm really happy and everything and then you go and . . . Woody, how *can* you be gay when you just made love to me the way you did?"

"I don't know," I said. "Life's weird, I guess. I never thought I was gay—"

"Is Brian paying you?" she said.

"No. I'm still living off the screenplay deal, you know that."

"Then what is it? He's certainly not that attractive."

"I don't know what it is, Kathy," I told her. "All I know is that I like the things he does to me, and the things I do to him. I like it when he sucks my cock till I come all over the place, and I like to chow down on his fat juicy knob. I like to punch my rod up his hot little bunghole, and I even kind of like it when he sticks his finger in mine and wriggles it around, though I haven't let him fuck me yet—"

At about that point Kathy covered her ears and started screaming.

But she calmed down eventually after she took another pill, and I said I still cared about her as a human being and everything, and we agreed we would continue to be friends.

## Neal Ridges

*Looking for Lupe* was a fairly smooth shoot, though we did have some problems with Hector the donkey. At first he kept springing a horrendous erection, usually during the middle of a take. His trainer began to feed him saltpeter, which took care of the hard-on problem, but seemed to make him generally more obstinate and testy. Then Shark became obsessed with the head movements and the braying in the close-ups which we planned to dub with Hector's dialogue. Shark wanted "absolute lip-sync perfection," which needless to say was a futile dream, so we shot a lot of useless film.

Then one night there was a fire in the stable where we were

keeping Hector. Not a serious fire really, it was quickly put out, but it panicked Hector enough that he kicked through the stall door and escaped to freedom. The next morning I noticed the red T-shirt Hector's trainer had been using to direct the donkey's attention as we filmed, and I couldn't help observing that it was soiled with hoof prints and a large quantity of dried donkey semen. The trainer explained that the T-shirt had been draped over the stall door and that Hector, panicked by the fire, had ejaculated in terror despite the saltpeter, thus drenching the T-shirt a moment before he kicked it as he broke through the stall door that was trapping him. As the trainer offered this rather odd explanation I noticed for the first time that the T-shirt in fact bore a likeness of Kathy Petro—the famous bathing suit shot from the early seventies posters. At the time it never occurred to me that her picture could have in any way "registered" in Hector's mind—though certainly what happened nearly a decade later in our nation's capital leads one inescapably to that conclusion.

Hector was even more temperamental after the fire, and soon began urinating and defecating on the set, which was funny in a way, though not to the guys who had to clean it up. There was one shot like that, of Hector defecating in the dining room of the suburban ranch house, which Shark fought to keep in the film right up to the answer print. He said it was a chance occurrence we could exploit as a gag. In the scene Hector had just read the riot act to this square gringo couple who had hired Lupe as a babysitter once, and Shark wanted to dub in a new line of Hector saying: "And another thing—" just before he took this humongous dump on the shag carpet.

I told Shark it was too much, but he wouldn't listen. Finally Brian demanded we take it out or he wouldn't release the picture.

## Carol Van Der Hof

Bri was right of course. The inclusion of that moment would have tipped the balance of the film. And what a tightrope Neal walked! With what finesse he negotiated that high wire of diabolically clever wit, greased ever so lightly with a soupçon of raunch, without ever once plummeting into the netless abyss of tastelessness and simpleminded crudity. We sensed it would be a massive hit with college audiences and the Westwood sneak proved us right.

## Neal Ridges

When Woody arrived at the Bruin sneak with Brian Straight my most errant speculations were confirmed. I knew Woody had moved in with Brian in the Colony, allegedly to work on that godawful script. And now here was Woody with hickies on his neck, wearing a tight LaCoste shirt and even tighter 501s, which seemed to be a kind of gay uniform in those days.

Shark was unbelievably dense about it though. "So you guys come stag?" Despite the rumors I don't think Shark could believe a guy as tough as Brian could be gay. And Woody . . . well, it seemed inconceivable.

I caught up with Woody in the men's room. "You'd better be careful," I told him. "I don't know which is going to enrage Shark more. Your going gay, or the fact that you were shacked up for four months with Kathy."

"The latter, I'm sure," he said with a new, fey edge to his voice.

"Is she back in Newport Beach?" I asked him.

"For the moment."

"What does that mean?"

"Haven't you heard?" We were at the urinals. He shook off and buttoned up. "Mr. Brian Straight plans to wed Miss Kathy Petro in June. Betcha can't guess who's gonna be the best man?"

# 16 / Tropics Redux (1978–1979)

### Carol Van Der Hof

How elated we were when *Looking for Lupe*'s first weekend broke nearly every record! And what legs the film had!

Of course the teens all adored it, and it was just "hip" enough for the young adult set. And even the critics who found the premise somewhat vulgar were compelled to acknowledge Neal Ridges's virtuoso stylistic flair. With what irresistible panache he'd cribbed both Eisenstein and Bertolucci!

### Cord Bucky, *Eastern Collegiate Review*, May 22, 1978

Had Vladimir Nabokov paused while writing *Lolita* to dash off a film script with the working title *Francis Goes to Suburbia,* and had Stanley Kubrick directed it on Spanish fly, the result might well have resembled *Looking for Lupe*. Visually astonishing

—not since *The Conformist* have I been put away like this—the film is at once a hilariously raunchy crowd-pleaser and, to anyone who cares to notice, a subtly profound critique of Ozzie-and-Harrietism grounded in a long-take/deep focus pictorialism which operates in seamless counterpoint to a blindingly brilliant neo-*Potemkin*-like use of montage. If the film has any flaw it is the casting of Diana Chadwick as Lupe, the runaway Mexican donkey-act star. The olive makeup has a faintly green tinge, you can see her blonde roots, and her Spanish accent wavers. Then again this could be intentional, a wry comment on Hollywood's notorious history of casting WASP actors in ethnic roles, for indeed *Looking for Lupe* is chock-full of just this sort of Buñuelian prank. Maybe that's why I've already seen it five times, and I'm on my way back for more right now—if my sore stomach muscles can take it. My girlfriend is threatening to leave me. The last time I said to her, "Come on, *ba-by*, let's go home," she gritted her teeth and walked away in disgust. What have you done to my love life, Neal Ridges, you diabolical genius?

## Greg Spivey

That Hector's last line in the movie became *the* pop-cultural cliché of the year certainly didn't do the film any harm. It seemed that everywhere you went someone was saying, "Come on, *ba-by*, let's go home" in a bad Spanish accent. It became the pickup line of the summer, parents were saying it to their children in supermarkets, employees were repeating it mindlessly in the workplace, you heard it from kids, teens, senior citizens, cops, TV talk show guests, President Carter worked it into a major foreign policy address*—until it did become a bit grating. But then that's our media-saturated culture, isn't it? I was happy for Neal.

## Neal Ridges

It was a great moment for me after years of anonymous struggle. But I held my breath, expecting murder and scandal to

*"And I say to Mr. Brezhnev, if he sincerely wants to meet with me in Geneva in an effort to halt the escalating nuclear terror which threatens both our great nations, then: 'Come on *ba-by*, let's go home.' " President Jimmy Carter, Princeton University, June 28, 1978.

poison our success at any moment, once Shark found out about Brian and Kathy's wedding plans. I wasn't going to be the messenger who brought him that news.

But June came and there'd still been no announcement. Were the wedding plans off? Had Woody been lying? I had no idea why Woody would invent such a dangerous rumor, knowing as well as anybody what it would do to Shark, but the more I thought about it, the more incomprehensible it seemed. How could Kathy Petro, still so beautiful and desirable, ever agree to such an intrinsically demeaning arrangement?

## Kathy Petro

I don't know, I guess I just kind of changed my mind about Brian after a while. I hated losing Woody to him and everything, and I talked to my psychiatrist about it, and he put me on a more powerful mood elevator and after that I just didn't care. I missed the sex with Woody for a while, but then I started eating all this ice cream—I just became addicted to Häagen Dazs vanilla—and I'd just get this giant sugar rush and think: Gee, you know, this is almost as good as when Woody used to make love to me, only I don't have to worry that this ice cream is going to go gay on me or anything. I mean, I know that sounds crazy, but that's what I thought.

And Woody and I were still friends. I moved back to my parents' in Newport, but it was so oppressive that I was really glad when Woody and Brian started inviting me to Malibu for dinner and everything. Brian was really nice to me, and even said nice things about my performance in *Manhattan Holiday,* which coming from him really made me think: Gee, maybe I wasn't that bad after all. He was charming and everything and one night he asked me if I'd like to go to an A-party with him, and I looked at Woody and said, "Do you mind?"

And Woody said, "No, of course not, why should I? We're all mature, sophisticated adults."

## Brian Straight

I went a little crazy with Woody, I suppose. I'd repressed my sexuality so long, spent so many years as a lonely, celibate workaholic—I was the J. Edgar Hoover of the film industry!

—that in the ecstatic joy of finding Woody I very nearly destroyed my career.

The Oscars in March of '78 were a typical example. Although I nominally escorted Dame Mildred Danvers, Woody was also at my side, his neck covered with my hickies, both of us reeking gay sex. It was all I could do to keep my hands off him when they lowered the lights to show the clips—in point of fact I couldn't resist giving his tuxedoed crotch a quick squeeze—and a part of me just didn't care anymore.

But word reached Harold Gay, who summoned me to New York and said, "Brian, the time has come for you to get married."

"That will never be, Harold," I told him. "For like you I am gay."

"I'm not gay," he told me. "I have been married to a woman I adore for twenty-three years and I am as straight as they come."

I was flabbergasted. "But Harold, I always thought that was merely a marriage of convenience."

"That story only started because of my association with you," he said. "As I'm sure you know, there have long been rumors, Brian, that you and I are having an affair."

"Yes, I've heard those rumors. The absurdity of it. I was a celibate masturbator until a few weeks ago. But that has all changed, Harold."

"Yes, I know. I know all about this young lad."

"I won't quit seeing him, Harold."

"I'm not asking you too, Brian. All I ask is that you be discreet. And that you take a wife."

"And live a lie?"

"Brian, we have a corporate image to protect. If you want to be a flaming queen, I suggest you go into interior design or hairdressing. But this . . ." He gestured to the Manhattan skyline. ". . . is American business."

## Woody Hazzard

Brian was real freaked out after his boss told him he had to get married. "I'm going to force the world to acknowledge us," he said one night as we lay in bed after sex.

"If you do, you might lose everything," I said.

288

"I don't care. I could live anywhere, even in some seedy Silver Lake bungalow, as long as I'm with you."

But I thought that house in the Colony was really bitchin, so I said, "Why don't you marry Kathy? She'd probably go for it. I know she's sick of being at her parents'."

At that Brian got real worried, 'cause by then I'd told him all about Shark's thing for Kathy. He knew that sooner or later Shark was going to find out I'd had a thing with Kathy, and he was going to find out about Brian and me.

"I like Kathy," Brian said. "But I couldn't do that to Shark."

What he really meant, of course, was that he didn't want to lose Shark, since his movies were raking in millions for Acropolis.

Then something came down that changed his mind about Shark.

## Brian Straight

One afternoon in the spring of '78, I met Shark for lunch at Celine's in Beverly Hills. Things were good. *Mondo Jet Set* was setting new records abroad, and we were gearing up for a wide release of *Lupe* which, our minor differences over a few scenes resolved, now smelled like a winner. As Shark and I schmoozed the subject of his early films for Sam Schlockmann came up, and we were laughing about that period of his life when I mentioned *Sex Kill à Go-Go,* the original, much-altered script of which he'd written with Tom Field.

"Really a shame about Tom," I said. "A true film genius. I knew him at Choate."

Shark laughed and said, "Tom was a pussy. Though I'll say one thing for him, he could sure suck cock. I let him blow me once, you know, though it was definitely one-way. That's why he killed himself. 'Cause I wouldn't let him cop my joint again."

Well, I virtually imploded right there in Celine's. For I had worshipped Tom Field. At Choate he had been the first, albeit secret and unrequited, love of my life. Tom was the reason I'd come to Hollywood, hoping that someday I might work with him. His suicide, while I was still an agent, had soured my heart forever.

I smiled as Shark went on to talk about all the "Malibu

snatch'' he was sure Woody and I were getting. But deep inside the sealed chamber of my heart I made a vow then to destroy Shark Trager.

## Kathy Petro

I couldn't believe it when Brian proposed to me, I thought he was joking at first. But then he explained how it would be in-name-only and everything, how I could live anywhere and do anything I wanted. All I had to do was go to a party or a premier with him once in a while and do some charity work and things like that. Otherwise I could spend as much money as I wanted, and see other men or even another woman if I wanted to, as long as I was discreet.

It seemed kind of phony in a way, but the more I thought about it, it sounded like a lot better deal than most guys had ever offered me. Plus, I was already thinking that someday I might like to try acting again, except this time do it right and take lessons and all that. And if I did decide to do that, being married to a studio president sure couldn't hurt. So I said yes. And we talked about this big June wedding, which was just the kind I'd always dreamed of someday having.

Then suddenly, right after *Looking for Lupe* opened and became this really huge hit, Brian said, ''Look, I want to postpone the wedding until next fall.''

I was really angry and disappointed at first, thinking Brian just didn't want to have the big falling out with Shark our wedding was bound to cause until after *Lupe* had pulled in all those millions of dollars.

Then Woody explained to me what Brian was really up to. ''For personal reasons he wants to really fuck Shark over, and a golden opportunity's come up.''

## Carol Van Der Hof

In the ecstatic rush of *Looking for Lupe*'s phenomenal success I persuaded Shark to do the one thing I'd long desired which he had always refused: to screen for me the work print of *Tropics*.

''I futzed around with it so long I can't tell if it's genius or shit,'' he said.

Of course by then the film was legendary, either as a lost masterpiece cruelly shelved by the ignorant business powers of

290

Hollywood, or as the worst film ever made—depending on whom you talked to.

In the screening room there at our Gold Coast haven I watched all four hours of it, reserving comment until the bitter end.

"Well?" Shark said.

"It's dreadful," I told him bluntly. "It's stilted and pretentious in the worst sort of way, it's an atrocious travesty of von Sternberg and yet . . . I believe it can be made to work."

"How?" he asked.

"In a word, it needs to be brutally recut," I said. "Tightened to ninety-five minutes. Then released as an American art film, on one level self-consciously kitsch, on another exceedingly profound."

"Of course!" Shark cried. "That's precisely how it might work! My God, you are a genius, Carol! Will you do it? Will *you* recut the picture?"

"We can do it together, Shark," I said, squeezing his wonderfully masculine hand on the red velvet arm of the screening room chair.

## Woody Hazzard

Brian saw *Tropics* as a chance to really humiliate the shit out of Shark. The film was so "inalterably, stupefyingly bad," Brian said, that no matter how Shark recut it, it would still be like "a bomb exploding in his hands."

"I'll give it a special press screening well in advance, inviting all the major critics," Brian said. "The reviews will be so savage no one will blame us for dumping it, and Shark's devastation will be intense."

By then Brian had told me about the Tom Field thing, which was one of the shittiest things I'd ever heard of Shark doing, so I agreed he deserved to take a tumble.

But I was worried about Carol. "I hear reviving *Tropics* was her idea," I told Brian. "How's she gonna feel?"

"I'll do what I can to warn Carol at the appropriate time," he said, "though it may already be too late. She's under his spell." He continued in the coldest voice I'd ever heard from him: "You've got to understand something, Woody. This is just the beginning. I'm going to fuck Shark Trager till he bleeds. And then I'm going to keep right on fucking. And anybody who tries to block my path is going to get fucked too, or at least splattered.''

## Cynthia Clive

Poor dear Carol. It was clear to us all that she was hopelessly in love with Shark, and therefore on a collision course with heartache. I was tempted to sit her down for a stern talking to, and I will always regret my lack of temerity. I might have pointed out how futile her longing was, for by then I knew well of Shark's obsession with Kathy Petro—not that he and I had ever discussed it. Far from it. No doubt the only reason I'd lasted as long as I had in his employ derived from my pretended ignorance of his personal affairs.

But the torture Carol endured!

## Carol Van Der Hof

It was during the intense and intimate recutting of *Topics* that my long-sublimated feelings for Shark drove my heart to the point of no return. The long hours of close physical proximity, as we sat side by side at the flatbed installed in the basement of the Gold Coast house, eroded my most elaborate mental defenses. How I longed for him to kiss me, I could no longer deny it, at least not to myself. And I knew he did love me on a plane far more profound than he could possibly love the others. And there were others. The blondes.

I'm quite sure *bimbo* is the word. Vacuous California airheads, Marina del Rey girls, all bonded teeth and perfect breasts and highlighted hair. An endless parade of one-night-stand Cindis and Debbis and Jodis—the "small *i* girls," I called them.

"Hi," one chirped to me once, padding down to the kitchen one morning in Shark's robe. "You must be Shark's sister. He mentioned that he lived with his sister." It was all I could do not to hurl scalding coffee in that vapid beach bunny's smug Barbie doll face.

## Neal Ridges

Shark and Carol invited me to a private screening of the recut version of *Tropics* at the beach in August of '78. I'd been in

Europe pushing *Lupe* and hadn't seen either of them in a couple of months and Carol looked bad. I thought it was just exhaustion at first. Then she drew me aside after the screening and said, "Neal, I can't take it much longer."

"Take what?"

"I love him so," Carol said, and began to cry.

"Oh Carol," I said, and hugged her. She'd sat beside me during the screening, whispering a remark at one point about the Amelia Earhart character looking too much like Kathy Petro. Amazingly, I realized, Carol was still unaware of Shark's past with Kathy. I was finally about to blurt out everything I knew—about Shark and Kathy, and Woody and Kathy and Brian and Woody. There'd still been no public announcement of Brian and Kathy's wedding plans, but there was just a sense that the time bomb had quit ticking and was about to explode, and I knew I had to warn Carol.

But Shark stepped up to us before I could speak. "Hey, what are you doing, Neal? Trying to steal my partner?" he joked, for I was still hugging Carol.

He saw her tears. "Jesus, you're crying. I guess that's a good sign, if as many times as you've seen it the ending still gets to you."

"Yes," Carol said, avoiding his eyes. "I'm a fool for sad endings. I still weep at *Now, Voyager*, you know that, Shark."

*Tropics*, despite the extensive re-editing, was still wretched by the way.

## Carol Van Der Hof

I suppose on some deeply buried level I always knew that, recut or not, *Tropics* remained by any objective standard something of a piece of shit. But the waves of rapture I felt toward Shark quite literally blinded me to that reality.

Still, I believe it may well have been a subconscious sense of what lay ahead which compelled me, the evening of the initial press screening, to at last show my hand.

I was dressing for the screening when Shark stepped into my bedroom. "Come on, we're running late," he said.

"Shark darling, would you be an angel and zip me up?" I said breezily.

As he complied I turned abruptly and took him in my arms. "Oh Shark," I sighed, and fool that I was, tried to kiss him.

He jumped back with a look of shock. "What on earth are you doing?" he said. "Have you lost your mind?"

"Shark, I love you," I said. "I love you and I know you love me."

"Carol," he said, recovering his composure, "I love many things about you. We've had more fun, you've brought me more joy, in these last few years than I've ever known. You mean more to me than all the women I've ever slept with combined. But I'm afraid I find you physically repulsive. Come on now, hop to it, we're late."

Well—if I'd had any pride or self-worth I would have walked out the door then and never come back. At the moment, I suppose, I was simply too devastated to take such a forthright action.

We drove in silence to the studio in his Porsche. As we mingled with the critics prior to the screening I felt disembodied. Shark was in his element, charming them all, even Sonya Heinz, who'd trashed everything he'd done since *White Desert*. Finally, as the lights came down I broke. Pushing my way to the aisle, much to Shark's irritation, I stumbled into the foyer, colliding with Brian Straight.

"Oh, Bri," I cried, and fell weeping into his arms.

"Get out, Carol," he said, after I told him what had happened. "Cut yourself free of Shark before it's too late."

"Why can't he love me, Bri?" I sobbed. "Is it my clubfoot?"

"It's not your clubfoot, Carol," he said. "It wouldn't matter if you were perfect in every possible way. Shark Trager is a man incapable of love. He worships a vision, a dream of love, a dream of blonde perfection no one could ever possibly fulfill. Not even Kathy Petro herself could live up to his masturbatory fantasy of her."

"What are you talking about?" I said, though on some unconscious level I'm sure I already suspected, for the images of Kathy proliferating through Shark's films could not all have been a simple generic similarity. I knew Shark and Kathy Petro had both grown up in Newport Beach. Once I had even asked Woody if Shark and Kathy had known one another. "You'd better ask Shark about that," he'd said, which was certainly a tip-off in itself. I suppose I hadn't wanted to know how impossible my love truly was.

Now Brian told me everything, all that Woody had shared

294

with him, of Shark's pathological fifteen-year obsession with this mindless blonde paper doll!

"And Kathy and I are going to be married," he added.

"But Bri, I thought you were gay."

"I am—now," he said, and told me about Woody.

I was speechless.

"Get out now, Carol. Don't be at ground zero when the bomb goes off."

I don't know how long we'd been talking in the foyer. But suddenly I became aware that people were laughing in the screening room—that hideous, snide laughter of critics who've discovered an "unintentional comedy."

Then Shark burst through the doors, scarlet with rage. As he did I heard Sonya Heinz' distinctive cackle, and she'd been sitting *next* to Shark—the reaction was that out of bounds.

"Let's go," Shark said to me. "Before I kill someone."

"Slough it off, Shark," Brian said with a venomous, insinuating sarcasm. "What do the critics know?"

The affront caught Shark utterly off guard. He could not then begin to imagine why Brian should so relish his mortification, let alone arrange it. Incredulous and enraged, as another gale of laughter erupted in the theater, Shark literally yanked me out the door.

"I think I know now why you don't care for me, Shark," I said as we approached his Porsche in the studio parking lot.

And then I let him have it, telling him everything Brian had just told me. I'm sure I wanted to hurt him as badly as he'd hurt me, which was why I concluded, "So you see? Your precious Kathy prefers sex with your gay best friend, and a fraudulent marriage to your gay best friend's lover, to even *once* going to bed with *you!*"

I'll never forget the way he looked at me then. If a dog were to look at you that way you'd know you had no choice but to have it put to sleep. For an endless moment I was certain he was going to physically attack me, and I was prepared to cry out for help. Instead, he got into his Porsche and screamed out of the lot with a stunning insane ferocity.

## Kathy Petro

I was staying at Brian's house, and had just taken a shower and put on my nightie when I heard the phone ring downstairs. It was one of those rare humid L.A. evenings, the air at the Colony all sultry and sensual so that we had the windows open, but you just felt all sticky and wearing much at all didn't really make sense. So I went downstairs, just wearing this sheer nightie, feeling kind of hot and crazy since I hadn't had sex in a real long time.

So there was Woody in the den watching *The Long, Hot Summer* on the big-screen TV as he talked on the phone, wearing these tight little swimtrunks Brian liked him to wear.

I could tell by the way Woody looked at me we were both getting the same idea, even though he was gay now and everything. So I stepped over to get a cigarette and my nightie kind of came open, and I was right next to where he was sitting and he slid his hand up between my legs and I started getting really excited.

I could tell after a while he was talking to Carol who was at the studio where they were screening *Tropics*. But Woody kept asking her what she was talking about, because he was getting more and more distracted, until finally he just put down the phone and buried his face in my you-know-what.

Very soon nothing else mattered except what Woody was doing to me, and I was only vaguely aware of Carol's voice still going, "Woody? Woody?" on the phone, when suddenly this whole big plate glass window just *shattered*, and at first I thought it was a bomb or an earthquake. But it was Shark.

## Woody Hazzard

Shark threw this deck chair through the window, which really shocked the shit out of us. Then the next thing I knew he was in the room, pulling Kathy off of me. He made out like he was going to slap her, but I caught his arm before he could, and then we both hit the floor. We struggled there for what seemed like forever, and at one point my face was real close to his and I wanted to say: Why are we doing this? This is so fucking stupid, I know we fuckin' love each other, man. But he was really trying to kill me, it was too late to stop, and my own adrenaline was going totally apeshit.

Then suddenly the gate guard was there pulling Shark off of me, and the security patrol guy was there with his weapon drawn—it seemed Shark had rammed through the gate barricade in his Porsche. We heard sirens in the distance, and then

Brian came dashing in. Kathy rushed to him and he put his arm around her, the way a husband would in a movie if he'd just rescued his wife. By that time Shark was just panting on the floor, and he wouldn't look at any of us, almost like he was embarrassed that he'd been taken alive.

## Brian Straight

The sheriff's deputies arrived and placed Shark in handcuffs in the back of their car. But I declined to press charges, and in fact did some pretty fast talking to stop the matter there, which seemed prudent at the time. I wasn't eager for a tabloid scandal to negate the entire point of my marrying Kathy.

## Kathy Petro

I think Brian paid everybody off. I watched from an upstairs window as the deputies let Shark go. He went to his Porsche, which was damaged in front, and right before he got in he looked up right at me, even though I was peeking very cautiously through the blinds in this completely dark room—there was no way he could've seen me. But somehow he knew I was there. It gave me this awful chill, the way you might feel if someone you hated was reading your mind.

Then, while the deputies watched him, he got in his car and roared away.

# 17 / **Red Surf**
## (1979–1981)

Sonya Heinz, *French Quarterly Review*
Winter 1979

FROM: "WHY MOVIES AREN'T ANY GOOD ANYMORE"

"Why are movies so dippy these days?" a transsexual friend asked me recently, and I couldn't help recalling how I'd felt after seeing Shark Trager's deliriously woozy, low-kitsch mock-von Sternberg movie *Tropics*.

"Because in Hollywood filmmaking has become a business, and all the films there are made by businessmen now," I told him/her. "The real artists have given up, leaving the businessmen in charge of everything."

*Tropics* shows us what happens when businessmen make what they think of as art in a place where all the businessmen are failed, bitter artists. They end up making vacant, jittery, turn-off movies, scuzzy, deadening camp movies filled with howlers, bad-art films that make us long for even the grungiest of the sick-joke counterculture movies of a few years ago.

*Tropics* is an angry, rejected artist's idea of raw, thick film sensuality. If David Selznick had been a frustrated lesbian he might have produced films like this. (And the comparison is apt, for though Dean Sutter nominally directed, this is a Shark Trager film. Does anyone even remember anymore who directed *Gone With the Wind?*) Trager, who began his career as a low-trash producer (*Redneck Scum, Tract House She-Devils*), before going on to mediocre big budget crowd-pleasers (*The Condoist, Hail!*), fey, bitchy "dance" movies (*Mondo Jet Set*) and gross-out/donkey act/teen raunch comedies (*Looking for Lupe*), originally wanted to be a director.

While at UCLA film school in the late sixties, Trager made a notorious sixteen-millimeter feature, *Pillow F\* \*k*, which earned him a reputation as "the next Orson Welles," though the plotless, experimental film probably owed a much greater debt to Jean-Claude Citroen, Trager's idol. When Citroen savaged the film, a tearful, petulant Trager destroyed the negative, and he's had it in for artists ever since. "God hath no fury like a woman scorned," the "Aviatrix" deadpans in *Tropics*. And the same is true of artists, who can also marry for money and become respectable whores. Whores don't kiss, according to custom, because they're saving their hearts for the time when they retire. But the sad thing about a whore like Trager is that he's been saving himself for nothing. From the sickly, gooey, spoiled fruit evidence of *Tropics*, it's depressingly apparent where his mouth has been.

## Cynthia Clive

Shark wept when he read that essay, the only time I ever saw him cry. Of course, you know he'd once adored Sonya Heinz, devouring each new review with joyful delight as far back as junior high. He credited her infectious love of film as a key inspiration, and even mentioned once in passing how uncannily she resembled his late mother Winnie. How desperately he longed for her nurturing approval.

## Brian Straight

At the risk of appearing somewhat unsympathetic, I must admit I snickered as I read the Sonya Heinz piece, knowing how deeply it would wound Shark. He was still on the lot, but I anticipated an imminent departure. Carol was staying in Laurel

Canyon with her old friend Tony Borgia, who in the wake of *Dogs of Saigon* was quite hot. I'd long been high on Tony's passionate brand of filmmaking, and looked toward a rewarding future with Tony and Carol—sans Shark.

## Tony Borgia

Sonya's essay was pretty rough. And I felt somewhat responsible since I was the one who'd told Sonya about Shark's UCLA experience, never suspecting she'd use it so viciously.

As Shark but few other people then knew, Sonya Heinz was actually my mother—though I'd been taken from her, and given to Federico and Ethel Borgia, shortly after birth. As she told it, my real father had been a "sexually magnetic Italian drifter," with whom she'd had an "ecstatic two-hour affair" in the grease pit of a Baton Rouge Flying A gas station one sticky summer night in 1949. As a struggling Southern intellectual barely supporting herself as a dancing snake lady in a French Quarter freak show, my mother had seen little choice but to give me up for adoption, in the process of which she'd been told only that I was to be placed with a "lovely out-of-state Italian couple." Free of the burden of raising me she'd been able to earn a Ph.D from Tulane, write eleven books, including *From Blanche to* Boom!, the definitive study of the films of Tennessee Williams, and eventually become the nation's foremost Cajun film critic. It was not until I was twenty-six that, as obsessed as James Dean in *East of Eden,* I finally tracked her down in New Orleans, by which time, ironically—never suspecting that I was in fact her son—she had already given my first two films ecstatic reviews. Though our mother-and-son reunion was mutually cathartic, we agreed to keep our true relationship under wraps so people wouldn't say, you know, "Well, of course she likes his films. She's his mother."

But Shark knew and that was why I braced myself when he called me at home one Sunday shortly after the piece appeared. "Shark, please don't take it personally," I told him. "Mom's on the rag, that's all. You're just an easy target. Actually, she liked *White Desert*—"

"Hey, it's no big deal," Shark said. "Your mother's a critic, that's what critics do. If you can't take the heat—" He laughed good-naturedly.

"I'm sorry *I* never got a chance to see *Tropics,*" I stammered.

"Hey, pal, not many people did. I think it played a couple of days in Pacoima before they ripped up the seats and threw 'em at the screen." Again, he laughed, as if to say: Win a few, lose a few, roll with the punches.

"Anyway, Tony, there *is* a reason I called."

I glanced at Carol, who'd been staying in my guest room since her fight with Shark. They hadn't spoken at all in the several weeks since that night, conducting their business affairs through third parties. But Shark knew she was staying with me.

"Carol doesn't want to talk to you, Shark," I told him bluntly.

"I know, I know," he said in a pained voice. "That's not why I called. But Tony, I do still love her. You might want to tell her that."

I wanted to ask him just what kind of love he meant, but couldn't very well with Carol standing there. "Sure, will do," I said.

"Tony," he said, abruptly shifting gears, "I've decided I want *Red Surf* to be my next picture. Has Carol shown you the script?"

I knew *Red Surf* was the most recent title of Woody Hazzard's screenplay, and I had looked at his original draft, which was so depressingly amateurish I'd only read a few pages before tossing it aside.

"Look, Shark, I'm from Michigan. I don't know shit about surfing. And frankly a beach picture modeled on the Ulysses myth strikes me as a bit—"

"Oh, no, no," he interrupted. "You must have seen an old draft. It's not like that anymore. The Ulysses plot's been completely junked. It's a crime thriller now. It's about a vicious serial killer who preys on surfers, both guys and girls."

*"Huh."* I felt a subconscious click.

"Tony, this script was made for you. It's like *Taxi Driver* and *In Cold Blood.*"

*"In Cold Blood* was a true story," I observed.

"So is this." And then he told me all about Brad "Pus" Jenkins, his tortured boyhood friend, whose eventual rash of homicides, the so-called Surf Killer murders of 1967, had terrorized Orange County and spoiled the Summer of Love for more than a few local teens.

"My God, this is extraordinary," I said. "And there's never been a book?"

301

"No, it's virgin territory, Tony. A virgin crime. Let me send you the script."

Well, the messenger delivered the script an hour later, and before I was twenty pages in I was trembling with excitement.

## Carol Van Der Hof

"Come on, Carol, forgive and forget," Tony said to me repeatedly, conveying Shark's wish that I join Tony and him in "the great adventure" *Red Surf* was undoubtedly going to be. By this point Shark had sent flowers, which I had returned with the accompanying apology note torn into little pieces.

But I had read *Red Surf*, and I had to admit it was pretty damn good. Brian's guidance had considerably improved Woody's writing, though the tone remained crude, primitivistic, visceral—precisely the raw material of a stunning Tony Borgia film. Still, I refused Shark's calls, even as he and Tony began meeting to discuss the project.

Then one morning I stepped out to get the paper and there in Tony's driveway was a car with a vanity license plate: CAROL. It was a bright red vintage MG sportscar restored to perfection, precisely the kind always driven so recklessly by jilted, spoiled debutantes in 1950s films—as Shark and I had amusedly noted more than once through the nights of our marathon screenings. For a moment I thought it was a cruel prank—for as Shark well knew, I had never learned to drive. Then I opened the envelope attached to the steering wheel, and found a gift certificate for driving lessons. At that point I began to weep.

Through my tears I saw Shark standing sheepishly at the foot of Tony's drive. Cathartically, we rushed to one another and embraced. As they never had before his lips pressed mine. It was not as one says a "soul kiss," though I was so blindly mad with love for him in that moment it might just as well have been.

I moved back into the Gold Coast beach house that same day.

## Kathy Petro

Shark sent Brian and me this really horrendous silver service as a wedding present—I mean, it must have cost thousands of dollars—with this note wishing us eternal bliss and everything. I showed Brian the note and said, "Is this a joke or what?"

"I'm not sure what it is," Brian said, and he seemed kind of nervous and scared and everything, because the wedding was only a few days away and we were all afraid Shark might still do something to spoil it.

Then suddenly Woody came in from surfing and said, "Guess what? Shark wants to do my screenplay."

## Woody Hazzard

I was surfing at Sunset, which Shark knew was one of my favorite spots, when I looked up and saw him getting out of his Porsche at the side of the highway. I was just coming up out of the water and I had this big rush of fear for a second, thinking, you know, maybe he's got a gun or something. Then as I got closer I saw there were tears in his eyes. And I got this big fuckin' lump in my throat, 'cause I mean we'd been through everything and I still loved the guy. We went into this big bearhug even though I was wet and got his vintage Hawaiian shirt all wet.

"You're still my brother, man," he said, patting my back.

"I'm sorry, man," I said. "About Kathy, I mean. I don't know, it just happened. It was crazy. I didn't want to hurt you, man. It's been such a weird fuckin' time for me . . . all this fuckin' sexual ambivalence—"

"It's okay, it's okay," he said. "Life's just a play, isn't it? We all switch partners and play many different roles."

"Yeah." The way he said it made it sound real profound. Like why do people fight anyway, when we all secretly know how fuckin' much we love each other?

Then he told how he wanted to do *Red Surf*. "Aside from making an astonishing film," he said, "my fondest hope is that the process will somehow bring us all together in laughter and joy."

## Brian Straight

"I don't want you to see Shark Trager," I told Woody.

"Look," he said, "I'm not your fuckin' wife, man. Don't tell me what to do. Shark's my best friend in the whole world."

"My God, have you forgotten what happened?" I shouted.

"He accepts us, Brian. Why can't you accept him?"

I refreshed his memory on the subject of Tom Field.

"I mentioned that to Shark," Woody said. "It didn't happen like that at all. He only told it that way 'cause at the time he thought you were straight. He said what actually came down with Tom and him was very beautiful. It was his only gay experience, and it was like something in a Walt Whitman poem."

"I'm not sure I believe that," I said.

But Woody kept after me, constantly nagging me to do *Red Surf*. "Brian, you helped me write it, man. Tony Borgia's a fuckin' genius. You know it'll be good."

I finally gave in against all my better judgment. The budget Shark submitted came to a little over nine million. The economics did make sense, unfortunately. And then when Tim Stroll agreed to play the lead for scale—well, he was getting two million a picture in 1979—it was a package I couldn't refuse.

Still, I made it clear I would only have dealings with Carol.

## Kathy Petro

We were on our honeymoon in Tahiti when Brian told me he'd approved *Red Surf*. "I don't believe it," I said. "You're actually going to work with this man again?"

"Kathy," Woody said. He and Brian were lolling in bed together and I had just come back from shopping. "Kathy, it's going to be a great picture. It'll be my first screen credit, plus Shark wants me to surf in it too."

"Oh, I see. We're one big happy family now. Is that it, Woody? Well, you can count me out."

"Settle down, Kathy," Brian said. "This is the nature of the film business. It's a small town. If you hold grudges—"

"All right, all right, mister gay baby mogul," I said. "But just don't you ever invite Shark Trager to our house. I'll do the charity work and smile on your arm at the Oscars. But don't you ever ask me to play polite hostess to that man who has ruined my life."

## Carol Van Der Hof

Once *Red Surf* received the go our imaginations shifted smoothly into fifth gear. Tony spoke messianically of "transforming the mundane,'' and it soon became apparent that what in mediocre hands might have been little more than a teen slasher film was to be instead an hallucinatory epic of the American suburban dream.

The extreme violence did bother me at first, especially after Tony researched the actual murders and found that Woody had really been a bit squeamish in the script. ''We've got to put in everything,'' Tony proclaimed. ''No matter how ostensibly 'disgusting' or 'deranged.' The film itself is *about* excess—the excess bred of stifling middle-class repression. The theme here is 'homeliness versus beauty.' The rage of the rejected against the vapid blonde icons of California perfection, for Pus Jenkins was the ultimate victim of an image-crazed culture that worships superficial appearance at the expense of more enduring values.''

I was easily won over, for I already shared Tony's view of art as catharsis. In this light I believed that with *Red Surf* Shark might well exorcise his obsessions once and for all—for it was difficult not to notice that many of the blonde surfer girl victims were generic Kathy Petros.

Through the alchemy of art Shark might still the past at last. His fetishistic longings vanquished he might see with clear eyes the love that stood before him, a love not blonde but genuine.

## Greg Spivey

You know, I'm not sure to this day why Shark drew Carol back into his life at the time of *Red Surf*. I think maybe he did really love her in a way, perhaps he even *wanted* to find her attractive, but simply could not do the necessary psychic rewiring.

He did play with her emotions though. ''You know, if you lost twenty pounds I just might do something crazy,'' he'd joke with her in the pre-production period.

But Carol took the remark seriously, enough to become a bulimic with a serious addiction to cocaine.

## Carol Van Der Hof

I had long eschewed cocaine since it tended to make me jittery. But now for some reason I reacted to it quite differently, indeed began to see what the fuss was all about.

I found it quelled my appetite so that I magically shed

pounds. I felt omnipotent, breathless, as I raced down the Pacific Coast Highway in my fire-red sportscar—for with *la cocaina* learning to drive had been a snap! How like a young and carefree Grace Kelly I felt the day I veered through the amusement park set, skidding giddily to a halt a few feet before Shark!

## Tony Borgia

The original amusement park in Long Beach where Brad Jenkins had worked the summer of the murders had since been torn down. But the setting was crucial as a sexual metaphor. The libidinous grunge of the moldering arcade, the seedy freak show and the urine-scented house of mirrors—the raunch of the id in opposition to the antiseptic superego of the Disneyland we would associate with Brad's vapid victims.

## Brian Straight

I was jolted when I saw the revised budget which, including the amusement park set and Tony's adjusted shooting schedule, upped the cost to twenty-one million.

But I approved it with a growing intuition that Shark might well be constructing his own doom. Which would be just fine since by this time I was secretly plotting a move to Mastodon Pictures. My "sudden departure" would be announced shortly after *Red Surf* commenced principal photography. Woody would never be able to say I hadn't supported the film. If—or more pointedly *when*—the film failed miserably I would be watching the flames at Acropolis from the safe vantage point of my new presidential chair at Mastodon, plausibly blaming the failure on the nervous new regime at Acropolis.

If on the other hand it grossed a hundred mil domestic—in this business anything could happen—I would be well within my rights to claim credit for having guided the development of a major hit.

## Woody Hazzard

I guess I first sensed that things might be getting weird the day we went down to Newport Beach to scout locations. It was Shark and Tony and the location manager and me, and we

306

drove all around the old neighborhoods until we came to the house where Pus Jenkins had killed Debbi Henderson, this ultra-wholesome girl who'd got me fired from the Taco Bell the night I'd first met Shark back in '66, for saying that I'd spit in her burrito. It was just this nondescript tract house on Abalone Drive, a few blocks from where Shark's dad still lived. Understandably bummed out, the Hendersons had sold the place shortly after the murder in 1967, so some other family was living there now.

We all went up to the door and said we were making a movie and everything, and the woman let us in to see what had been Debbi's bedroom, which was where the murder had taken place. Well, you could tell the woman didn't even know there'd been a murder there—I guess it's not the kind of thing real estate people point out—and we didn't tell her about it either. Shark just said he was making a "sixties nostalgia movie," and she signed the location release form and everything in exchange for a few thousand dollars.

Then we drove over to the Jenkins house, which was right across the street from Shark's dad's place on Mackerel Drive. I noticed Shark eyeing his boyhood home as we went up to the Jenkins' front door, but it didn't look like Mac was home.

Mr. and Mrs. Jenkins were real apprehensive at first, till they recognized Shark as Pus's boyhood friend. Then they smiled as if they hadn't smiled in about twenty years, and invited us in. Shark charmed them into letting us see Pus's old bedroom, and it was totally bizarre, because they'd kept it *exactly* as it had been the day the cops took Pus away in 1967. Tony was fuckin' awed. "This is better than any set could be," he said to me on the sly.

Finally Shark told the Jenkinses he was going to make a movie about the murders, and for a second they almost freaked out. But Shark was totally coked and did some real fast talking, saying how the film was going to make people understand how a basically good boy like Brad could become so confused and everything. But the capper was when he told them Tim Stroll was going to play Pus. "Yes, he does look something like Brad," Mrs. Jenkins said, even though he didn't at all because Tim was this total pretty boy, like just the opposite of Pus.

"So you don't mind if we shoot a few days here?" Shark finally said.

"Well, you should really ask Brad about that," Mr. Jenkins said.

Shark asked what Mr. Jenkins meant, and he said, "Well, we've tried to keep it quiet, but Brad was released from Vaccaville two months ago. He's been staying at a halfway house in Whittier and doing very well. And he's coming home next week."

## Brian Straight

*Red Surf* commenced principal photography on April 29, 1979, in the two-million-dollar amusement park set constructed on the site of the old amusement park in Long Beach.

Coincidentally, I learned that same afternoon that the Mastodon presidency was going to Bill Kemmer. My tenure at Acropolis suddenly extended, I was more than disturbed by the early reports from the set. I refer of course to the infamous first shot—though infamous is admittedly an entirely inadequate word.

## Carol Van Der Hof

Tony very simply wished to top Orson Welles's opening shot in *Touch of Evil*—though perhaps build on the master's precedent might be a truer way of characterizing his intent. Welles's four-minute tracking shot is a classic, inimitable bit of virtuoso filmmaking. But Tony was determined to "sustain the same level of seamless, unbroken cinematic elation" for a good twenty minutes not simply for the sake of showing off, but because he believed the overall complexity of that single shot was integral to the meaning of *Red Surf*. In terms of its sheer technical sweep, of course, the shot rendered Welles's accomplishment rather creakily rudimentary. If only dear Orson had had a Steadicam!

## Greg Spivey

The shot was insane. The camera had to track backwards through the arcade crowd, then track in on Tim Stroll and follow him into the house of mirrors where it was his job to clean the glass and mop the floors—all without the camera being reflected in any of the mirrors, of course. Then it follows Tim back out, lingering on several of his obnoxious future victims, before picking him up again in time for the snub from

the first victim couple; then it follows him back to the men's
room where an obviously homosexual man makes a furtive and
panic-inducing overture; then it follows him out to the beach
where he finds the couple making love and in spontaneous
confused rage stabs them repeatedly with his Boy Scout knife;
and then of course we track back for reasons of taste as he
alternately simulates sex with each of the bodies. I mean, it
was a monstrous shot, with literally thousands of things that
could go wrong, and I think every one of them did.

The camera showing in the mirrors—that must have ruined
twenty takes. Or the male arcade extra with an earring, which
guys didn't wear in '67. Once we got all the way to the murder
and Tim broke character when he had trouble opening the
knife.

Actually, you could say that Tony was very patient. After
twenty-seven days he was still saying calmly, "All right, people. One more time."

## Brian Straight

"He's been shooting for a month and he's still on the first
shot?" Harold Gay yelled over the phone from New York.
"It's unbelievable!"

"It's a complex shot, Harold. It's supposed to run twenty
minutes."

"One shot for twenty minutes? That's stupid. Boring and
stupid. Tell him to break it up or else."

"I've tried, Harold. He refuses. And Carol and Shark are on
his side."

"Then pull the plug," our chairman said.

## Carol Van Der Hof

We were up to take two hundred and seven and keeping our
fingers crossed, when Shark rushed into my trailer and said,
"We've got problems, Brian wants me at the studio."

Well, he hadn't seen Brian face-to-face since the trouble in
Malibu. "I'll go with you," I said.

"No. I'll handle this. But you can do me a favor and run
down to Newport Beach to pick up Pus."

"Pus? You don't mean *our* Pus?" I said.

"Oh Christ, I haven't told you, have I?" Well, he hadn't but he did now. It appeared that he and Tony and Tim Stroll had already met with Brad "Pus" Jenkins on several occasions since Brad's release from Vaccaville, as part of Tim's preparation for the role. "He's been at his parents for almost a month now and he's climbing the walls," Shark said. "Adjustment's been hard and he needs a job, so I offered him one, it's the least I could do."

"What sort of job?"

"Technical adviser. It's just a title."

It was really more than I could digest at the moment. "Shark, I can't leave now, we're about to try for another take. Surely you can send a driver—"

"Actually, Carol, he's expecting you. I've told him quite a bit about you, sort of paving the way, you might say. He's a big fan of *Looking for Lupe*, which he saw shortly after his release. When I told him the film was based on an idea of yours he flipped."

"Yes, I'll bet."

"I want you to look after him—"

"You're mad—"

"Carol, he's harmless. After fifteen years of powerful drugs and innumerable electroshock treatments and—this is privileged information—Brad was castrated in 1971."

"Good God."

"Yes, it was part of an experimental treatment program for criminal sex offenders, the theory being I suppose that without their testosterone the men's hyper-aggressive tendencies might be curtailed. And it worked apparently. Brad's a gentle, squishy lamb. You'll see."

Shark scribbled Brad's parents' address. "In any event, you're safe," he quipped as he climbed into his Porsche. "I think the gentleman preferred blondes."

"Ha-ha-ha," I called after him, and went into my trailer, expelled the enchiladas I'd recently consumed, and grabbed my car keys and a gram.

## Brian Straight

The gate alerted me when Shark arrived and I had several studio guards standing by in the next room in case there was trouble. I admit I was trembling as Shark was shown into my office—not with fear but excitement—for my time to obliterate Shark Trager had come.

"Don't sit down," I said, as he swaggered in. "You won't be here that long. You've done what I've always secretly hoped you'd do. You've gone too far. I'm shutting you down, and that's not all."

"No, you're not," he said, but I barely heard him. I'd waited too long for this moment to stop now.

"I'm going to destroy you," I said. "I've got a file on you, you son of a bitch, a dossier of sleaze ten inches thick. I know every shitty thing you've ever done, you evil little scumbag. I even know that Mike and Julie were really brother and sister—that you knowingly starred a pair of incestuous twins in *White Desert*—yes, I'm even going to level your one great film. You're finished in this town, you despicable piece of crud. By the time I'm through spreading the word on you, you'll be lucky to get a job producing hygiene films in Korea."

Shark remained virtually impassive throughout my harangue—only the mention of Mike and Julie caused a slight wince. He must have always known that would return to haunt him.

When he said nothing, merely staring with glazed, coked-out eyes at my framed photograph of Kathy, I added, "If there were anything more I could do to you I'd do it. If I could get away with it I'd strangle you right now with my own bare hands for what you did to Tom Field."

At last he looked at me, then sighed wearily and turned to the door. I thought I had won. This was Shark Trager beaten. But he stopped at the cabinet by the door, and the next thing I knew he was switching on my VCR, pulling a cassette from his pocket.

"What do you think you're doing?" I said. But a panic was already welling up inside me. I had anticipated that he might counter by threatening a public mention of my homosexuality, and I was prepared to tough that out—now that I was married to Kathy. But abstract allegations were one thing, graphic proof quite another. I recalled the several occasions on which Woody and I had fooled around on a seemingly deserted Tahiti beach. Was it possible Shark had dispatched video spies?

So I was quite relieved when I saw that his tape was in fact a vintage color film—until the crimson title seared the azure Spanish sky: *El Cristo Fugitivo*—directed by Rafael Avila. I knew of the supposedly lost surrealist film, I'd heard talk of its content, but since very few people had actually seen it, you always wondered how much to believe.*

Well, it was all true, I realized soon enough, as Shark fast-forwarded to a scene of the cowgirl Mary Magdalene having sex with the outlaw Cristo in the ruins of a church. Suffice it to

---

*El Cristo Fugitivo [The Fugitive Christ] was filmed in Spain in 1955 with an international, largely non-professional "bohemian" cast. Ostensibly the story of a western outlaw gang, the religious allegory isn't difficult to locate since "Cristo's boys" all bear the disciples' names. A rowdy fun-loving band, they ride through the surrealistic landscape, having sex with nuns, sheriffs' wives, schoolmarms, and each other, barely staying a jump ahead of a posse of enraged lawmen, husbands and priests. Along the way Cristo performs numerous surreal "miracles," including the resurrection of Mary Magdalene, a prostitute who had died of syphilis, by having sex with her apparently lifeless body. She subsequently joins the gang as a joyfully hard-riding cowgirl, but when she and Cristo pair off as lovers, the outlaw savior's chief sidekick Judas succumbs to the "true sin" of jealousy and, in league with the posse, lures Cristo into a trap.

As Edmund R. Frye stated in 1988 when El Cristo Fugitivo received its first belated public screening at the New York Film Institute: "The surreal crucifixion and subsequent resurrection, despite their considerable nudity, and some will say blasphemous sexual content, are among the most astonishing, authentically spiritual sequences ever placed on film. Rafael Avila, one of the original surrealist filmmakers, compelled to flee Spain after the Civil War and seek refuge in Hollywood, where, like his contemporary Buñuel, he toiled for over a decade dubbing insipid American films for export, came home in 1956 and made his masterpiece—indeed one of the greatest films of all time."

It was a film that was very nearly never seen. On the basis of a false script—a pious tale of nuns reforming roughnecks in old Arizona—the movie had been co-financed by the Catholic Film Consortium and the Spanish government; Avila found himself a fugitive in his homeland when, shortly after completion of photography, the true nature of the project became known. Although it was rumored that Avila had, at the time of his arrest, completed his editing of the film at a clandestine Barcelona facility, it was believed for many years that all the materials related to El Cristo Fugitivo had been confiscated and destroyed. According to legend, Generalissimo Francisco Franco was so incensed by the film's "sacrilegious obscenity"—a view still shared, incidentally, by numerous religious groups in 1988—that he ordered the surrealist's execution by "clutch-hook disembowelment," an event the Spanish dictator allegedly had filmed for subsequent home viewing.

Precisely how Shark Trager came into possession of a print of El Cristo Fugitivo remains unknown.

say, their intercourse was clearly not simulated, though in no sense could the sequence be termed pornographic. Indeed, the scene radiated an aura of almost embarrassing innocence, an utter lack of prurience, as if its maker were guilelessly unaware that there are those in this world who deem such things obscene. The glazed colors infused the activity with a dreamlike intensity. Visually, the film echoed and subtly parodied the glossy Hollywood western and its Biblical counterpart. And Cristo, with his flowing hair and beard, indeed evoked the classic 1950s Jesus seared into all our minds.

How finally to convey the ecstatic essence of the sequence? As the camera panned around the joined couple, it provided a passing view of the other randy outlaws, the apostles as it were, all but naked in the sun-drenched cemetery, laughing, several of them playfully fondling one another. Labels seemed beside the point. *El Cristo Fugitivo*, it was clear in even those few moments, was a rapturous ode to the polymorphous perverse, a transcendent joining of the sacred and profane, a joyous marriage of Heaven and Hell, indeed a rebirth of paradise in a landscape destroyed by stifled desire and its end product, war.

It was beyond all doubt the most astonishing film I had ever seen—the monitor seemed to open into another dimension. The amazing love in Cristo's eyes, the tenderness with which he made love to Magdalene amid the rays of sunlight, superimposed dissolves showing his coming crucifixion and Magdalene's imminent tears.

I was quite frankly so swept away I had virtually forgotten why Shark was showing me the film, until the picture dissolved to a closeup of the exquisitely soulful Magdalene—and my amazement gave way to shock.

I had no sense of how it could be, which was perhaps why I hadn't realized it sooner. But there was simply no denying that the luminously saintlike face was that, albeit twenty years younger, of our chairman's lovely wife, Arlene Gay.

Shark tossed a revised budget on my desk. "We're going to need another twenty million," he said and walked out, leaving the cassette running.

## Arlene Gay

"Is it true?" Harold asked me on our penthouse terrace after speaking to Brian in L.A.

"Well . . . yes," I replied, steadying myself against the rail.

"How could you do such a thing?"

"Harold, I was only twenty, a drama student with a headful of bohemian ideas on a Spanish holiday. Rafael was then an aging but still charismatic *enfant terrible* of surrealism, and we had a mad affair. He convinced me the film would be art, and it *is* art, I suppose—"

"I know what it is, it's filth," Harold said.

"It seemed very brave at the time." I began to cry. "I lost my head, I see that now, due in part to a near-constant use of Yenge, a powerful strain of Moroccan hashish. But you've got to understand, we all lived the film as we shot it, isolated as we were on Mallorca. We were all terribly in love with one another, or thought we were. Jan Delft, the Dutch actor who portrayed Cristo, was so truly—"

"You'll stop!" Harold roared, raising his hand as if to strike me, though he did not.

"Upon my return from Spain I discovered I was pregnant," I continued in a moment, sniffling. "I became hysterical and confessed everything to Dad [*aviation hero and Sadcom founder Rusty Diver, Ed.*]. I entered a private sanitarium, convinced by then I *had* gone mad. As I recovered my sanity and decency, eventually giving birth to twins which were put up for adoption, Dad spoke without my knowledge to his old pal the generalissimo." I sobbed anew, stung with a guilt I'd secretly carried for twenty-four years. "I can't imagine how a print survived."

Harold stared across Manhattan. "There are twelve of these . . . these apostles, as memory serves. How many of them do you do it with?"

"That's not a fair question."

"Answer me."

"No. You're trying to make the whole thing sound cheap. Harold, if you could only *see* the film—"

"That will never be," he said definitively. "I've heard enough to know that this . . . this *El Cristo Fugitivo* is undoubtedly the most offensive film ever made."

"I dispute that," I said shakily, averting my eyes from his judging gaze.

"Your lack of genuine remorse appalls me, Arlene. I shouldn't even care what happens to you now, knowing that you've done these vile things. And yet I do. And because I do . . ." With a terrible wounded tenderness he touched my cheek. ". . . I'm afraid we've no choice but to give Shark Trager everything he wants."

## Carol Van Der Hof

I drove to Newport Beach with considerable apprehension, but Brad proved to be precisely as Shark said. Gentle, docile, and poignantly overweight, that flabby, squishy marshmallow obesity one associates with eunuchs. He barely fit into my compact MG, his bulging thigh pressing the stickshift all the way back to the Long Beach location.

How terrible was that vacant stare, the lobotomized manner in which he spoke. Here was a being who had truly paid for his transgressions in spades.

"I really liked that *Looking for Lupe,* Carol," he said. "For a girl you sure got some sense of humor. That talking donkey was *so* funny."

For his sake I tried to steer the talk away from his criminal past, but he seemed compelled to allude to those events if only to set me at ease. "I don't really know for sure why I did those things," he said. "I guess I was jealous 'cause I have the kind of skin that doesn't tan. If you didn't have a tan in those days people said mean things."

"I've never cared for the beach myself," I told him. "Exposing myself to the sun, that is."

"Why? Because of your clubfoot?" he said, which startled me a bit. But really what refreshing childlike directness! What absurd circumlocutions most people negotiated in their efforts to avoid mentioning the obvious.

"Yes, I suppose my clubfoot is a factor. It's not very esthetically pleasing, I'm afraid."

"I've never cared much for beauty," he said. "Perfection is admirable, but it's not very lovable."

"No, I suppose it isn't, is it?"

He smiled so peacefully that I couldn't help thinking: My God, he truly has been cleansed. That a man who once committed such unspeakable crimes should be metamorphosized into such an innocent butterfly-like creature actually quite moved me. What a pity he had to lose his testicles in the bargain. If only life resembled mythic poetry more than it does a lurid tabloid collage, then Brad would surely have been reborn as a virile and muscular Byronic he-man instead of this heart-rendingly roly-poly glob.

## Brad Jenkins

I started getting funny feelings as soon as I saw that amusement park set. The way Carol and I came in it looked almost real except for these big movie lights overhead. But the people that were standing around on the arcade looked just like they had that night I killed the first couple. Only everybody was real quiet, all looking off toward the beach, which was all lit up, and then I saw what they were looking at. It was the murder, and something in me just snapped.

## Tony Borgia

It was take 209 and every nuance was perfect up to and including the stabbings, where exasperatingly most of our problems had occurred. There was nothing remaining but the backward tracking as Tim simulated sex with the corpses, and really there was little that could go wrong there. We were perhaps thirty crucial seconds from our first perfect take when I heard Brad scream. "No, no, no, stop!"

"Keep going! Don't look at him!" I shouted to Tim, for Brad was not in the frame yet—and we could easily dub the sound. But Brad was running out across the beach toward Tim.

"Stop that man!" I yelled.

Crew members converged on Brad as he screamed hysterically. "No, don't do it, stop, stop, stop!" They piled on Brad, throwing him to the sand a few critical feet outside the camera range.

But when I turned back to the scene I saw that Tim had stopped and was looking. "You're *looking!*" I screamed, for the take was ruined. "You stupid idiot, I told you not to look!

"Cut cut cut cut cut," I yelled as I charged over to Brad, really ready to kill.

Brad was sobbing plaintively as a grip helped him to his feet. "Tony, don't do this, don't make this movie," he wept. "I didn't know it would be like *this*."

"Do you have any idea what you've just done *now*, Brad?" I said, but he was so pathetic the rage was draining out of me.

He grabbed my shirt, tears running down his fat cheeks as he whimpered, "Tony, this movie will make other people kill. That's why I killed those people—because I saw *Psycho*. I thought Tony Perkins was *so cool* . . ."

I didn't believe that for a second. For starters, there'd been a seven-year lapse between *Psycho*'s release and the murders. Beyond that it was obviously a line some bleeding-heart psychologist had fed him, a specious pseudo-humanist, anti-art argument I found fascistic and despicable. I pried Brad's fingers from my shirt. "I want this man off my set," I told Carol. "You get him out of here now."

## Brad Jenkins

I cried like a baby all the way to Carol and Shark's house in Santa Monica. I just wanted to be free of the past!

## Carol Van Der Hof

Poor Brad. Once home I made a place for him on the sofa, and gave him a Valium and he finally calmed down. Then, just as I was climbing the stairs toward my room, he said, almost to himself, "I know the real reason I killed all those people. Shark made me do it."

I stopped and looked back down at him. "What do you mean, Brad?"

"Shark made me read books I should never have read. Books like Camus' *The Stranger*."

I was relieved. For a moment I'd suspected he meant something much more literal. "Perhaps you should stick to uplifting books, Brad."

I was nearly to my door when he spoke again. "Carol?"

"Yes, Brad."

"You won't tell Shark I had sex with Kathy Petro?"

I was stunned. Apparently in his confusion he believed he'd already revealed this to me. Needless to say, he had not. Until now.

"No. No, of course not, Brad," I said, concealing my utter astonishment. "I assure you, that bit of information stops here."

## Greg Spivey

Shark got back from the studio as we were setting up for take 210. "Brian's approved the jack-off dream sequence," he told Tony elatedly.

Tony was flabbergasted. "I don't believe it! I don't believe it!" He broke into a gleeful dance.

I could barely believe it myself. The very aptly named "jack-off dream sequence" was just that—a fantasy occurring in Brad Jenkins' mind as he masturbated, a truly deranged fantasy Tony had written near the end of a four-day stretch without sleep. Though this new sequence ran only five pages, it would easily cost an additional five million, for it required an untold number of hallucinatorily violent special effects as well as the outright destruction of an entire block of suburban homes.

## Tony Borgia

The word Shark used was "carte blanche."

"Brian feels the genius of this," he told me. "We're crossing a line, Tony, into a rarefied realm where money means absolutely nothing in the face of posterity. Hold your breath, my friend, for we have entered the sphere of pure art."

If I'd been gay I would have kissed Shark then. I felt omnipotent, both godlike and satanic—as I imagine Leni Riefenstahl must have felt when Goebbels told her, "Just make a masterpiece, *liebchen*. Don't worry your pretty little head about the bill."

The news spread quickly through the cast and crew. After a month of infuriating wheel spinning, how we needed that surge of speed in our veins! "Let's get it right this time, people," I shouted, and called "Action!" on take 210. And by God, sweet Jesus, we did! The cheers went up as Tim climbed off of Wendy's bloody corpse and I cried, "Cut! And . . . *print it!*"

## Brian Straight

After Long Beach the film moved to location in Orange County for some relatively inexpensive surfing sequences, though that dragged on for days as Tony waited for the right wave.

Woody was doing the surfing and from him I learned the details of the coming "jack-off dream sequence." Woody was delighted—like everyone else he was steam-shoveling cocaine—but I was appalled.

"Harold, they're insane. This is going to be another *Heaven's Gate*," I told our chairman. The Cimino film, shooting then in Montana, was already notorious, drawing the heat away from us. But that wouldn't last forever.

"Don't expect this to stop at thirty million," I told Harold, citing my rough projection of the final budget with the "jack-off dream sequence" added.

"Who knows?" Harold said philosophically. "The film might still be a hit. Another *Dogs of Saigon*." Tony's last film had come in at roughly eighteen million, and grossed nearly five times that, despite head-on competition in the stoned-futility-of-Vietnam genre from *Apocalypse Now*.

"I'm hearing bad things, Harold," I told him. "Bad, sick things. Excessive, sick things that make *Dawn of the Dead* sound like a Disney film."

"I've got the attorneys on it," Harold said. "In the meantime we're going to have to tough it out. I won't have Arlene's name dragged through the mud, that's all there is to it, Bri."

## Carol Van Der Hof

I spent several days calming Brad in Santa Monica, even as the film moved on to Laguna Beach.

"You think then that art can be cathartic?" Brad said as we strolled on the white sand beach.

"Yes, I'm sure of it. If it's art, that is, as opposed to prurient trash. And Tony Borgia is most definitely an artist."

"But what about those fatal stabbings that occurred during that gang picture?" Brad said, referring to several incidents which had abruptly squelched Hollywood's "gang-picture" cycle a year or so before.

"Brad, there've been fatal stabbings since civilization first began," I responded, "since long before cinema was even a twinkle in Lumière's eye. Besides, plenty of people have been stabbed at MGM musicals and Benji films. Why don't our self-appointed moral guardians ever mention that fact?"

"It's just that Tim Stroll is so handsome!" Brad said. "I'd hate to have anybody think if they killed a bunch of people they'd become as handsome as him."

"Tim's handsome in real life, Brad. But he hardly is in *Red Surf*. That's why he was so eager to play you, so that he might overcome his pretty-boy image. Perhaps you didn't notice but the makeup crew's done wonders, he's really quite a geek now. The sickening-looking plastered-down hair, the oozing acne—"

I stopped myself. Although Brad's acne was only scars now, his hair was still quite plastered down. "If anything, I believe the film will serve as a simultaneous release *and* deterrent to anyone toying with the idea of serial murder," I said.

"If so, the movie might actually be serving a very noble purpose," Brad observed.

"Indeed, it might," I replied, thinking more of Shark's personal catharsis, which I believed more than ever once the tides of *Red Surf* had receded would bring him at last to my arms.

## Brad Jenkins

One nice sunny day Carol and I drove down to Laguna Beach where they were shooting the surfing, even though Tony didn't want me around. We stood on a bluff above the camera and watched Woody Hazzard do these fancy show-off moves.

"I stalked him once," I said to Carol. "Once I saw him at the drive-in with some blonde girl. I followed them down to Crystal Cove and watched them sit in his car and smooch. And other things. Then another couple came and parked in their car. And I thought about doing all four. But I left."

I didn't even know why I'd told Carol this, except I liked her, maybe 'cause she wasn't blonde. Then she asked me about the time I had sex with Kathy Petro, and I said, I thought I told you. But she said no, so I told her then.

## Kathy Petro

It happened one summer afternoon in 1966, long before Pus committed any of the murders, when we were both sixteen and he was working at the Doolittle Camera Shop. I had just completely avoided that place since Shark's peeping-Tom movie thing, but I still felt raped just walking past the shop, knowing that Mr. Doolittle had seen that film.

Then one day I was home alone just relaxing on the patio in my bikini when the door bell rang. It was Pus. "I just thought I'd drop off these photos of your father's," he said.

I took them and said, "Gee, this is nice. You didn't have to drop them off."

And he got this funny look and said, "Oh, that's okay, I don't mind. By the way, I found this old movie film. I can't quite tell whose it is—"

When he took out this little reel of eight-millimeter film my heart just started pounding. "There's some girl in it though." He held the film up to the light. "And it looks like she's—"

"Let me see that." I grabbed the film from his hand and looked at it, and it was the peeping-Tom movie Shark had made of me.

Pus said it was a copy Mr. Doolittle had made for himself before turning the original over to the police.

I started to tear up the film and Brad grabbed it away from me. "Not so fast, Kathy."

"Let me have it," I said.

"That's what I'd like to do more than anything in the world," he said with a leer.

"If I let you do that, will you give me the film?"

He said yes. So we went into the den. When it was over—and it didn't take long—he gave me the film. I waited till he was outside, then I locked the door, and screamed at him through the grilled window. "You make me sick, you ugly dork. You're so stomach-turning no one's ever going to love you," on and on, all these horrible things, in revenge for what he'd just done to me.

I never told anyone about it. Then after he was arrested for the murders I just almost died, wondering if he was going to tell about me now. Or even if I'd wounded him so badly that I was partially responsible for, you know, what he'd done.

## Brad Jenkins

Carol and I were still standing on this bluff when Shark spotted us and came on up. I thought he was going to get mad but he didn't. Instead, he said, "Hey, Brad, I know you're not an actor, but how'd you like to play a small part in the film?"

## Tony Borgia

I was always against it, but Shark convinced me to let Brad assay the part of Debbi Henderson's father. It was a very small part, basically a matter of visual presence, with only one line, where he opens Debbi's bedroom door and finds her dismembered body. "Oh my God, no!" he cries, and I agreed to let Brad do it. If the line reading sucked we could always loop it. The thing was, Brad *was* physically right for the part. Mr.

Henderson had been quite obese himself, unlike the fellow we'd cast, so I said: All right, let's go for it.

## Greg Spivey

I didn't know about it until the day they were setting up the shot. We'd been at Debbi Henderson's old house for a couple of weeks filming the murder sequence, and we were already getting some heat from the neighbors, a number of whom had been living there since the time of the crimes and still knew the Hendersons, who were now living in San Diego. A lot of the complaints were the usual ones about how we were disrupting the neighborhood. Then somebody saw Brice, our special effects wizard, bringing in the dismembered body parts, which of necessity looked quite real. "You're sick!" one of the housewife neighbors called. "You Hollywood people are sick!"

Then Brad stepped out of one of the trailers in costume, a PetroChem work uniform like the one Mr. Henderson had worn. Some of the neighbors saw him. "My God, that's Pus Jenkins! That's *him!*"

The first shot of Brad had him pulling up to the house in his PetroChem truck, and one of the neighbors said, "My God, they've got Pus Jenkins playing George Henderson! They've got the actual killer playing the father of the girl he killed!"

And the crowd grew larger as more neighbors heard about it, until we had to call extra police to keep them at bay. Again and again, Tony filmed Brad getting out of the truck, every take disrupted by catcalls and abuse from the increasingly hostile crowd—though that wasn't what bothered Tony, he knew he could dub the sound later. But the crowd was making Brad nervous. He kept screwing up, dropping his lunchpail, or catching his shirttail in the truck door as he closed it, until Shark finally fed him so many Valium he just oozed across the lawn to the door.

## Brad Jenkins

I wanted to explain to those people what this thing was about, that we had to do this so it would stop someone else from killing other people. But Shark wouldn't let me go talk to them. Then he gave me Valium, which made everything seem like a dream.

When we got to Debbi's bedroom scene it did bring back memories. There was all that pretend blood everywhere, and the real-looking arms and legs, and the broken hacksaw blade. "Which window did Tim climb in?" I asked Shark, since they'd already done that part.

"That one," he said.

"Oh, that's wrong," I told him. "I crawled in this one over here."

"Don't tell Tony that," Shark said, looking around. "Or he'll want to reshoot the whole scene."

We did the scene a couple of times where I'd open the door and find Debbi's body. And on the third time something happened and I started to cry.

"What is it, what's wrong?" Tony said after he stopped the camera.

"I guess I'm just seeing this through Debbi's dad's eyes," I said. "And understanding for the first time what the sight must have done to him."

I was crying really hard and Carol put her arm around me. Then Tony called a lunch break, and as we went to the tables some guy in the crowd threw a rock at me.

## Mac Trager

The first I knew they were making a movie was when I came home one night and saw the trailers and what-not parked a few blocks up on Abalone Drive. The next day I found out that it was Shark's film based on the Pus Jenkins story. I figured Shark was over there, but I hadn't seen him since the deal in Rome and my attitude was: To hell with him.

Then the location guy came around one morning and said: We want to use your house. I said: You know where you can stick it, and he said: Look, we'll pay you money for it.

"How much?" I said.

And he said: "Two hundred thousand."

I said: "Man, you must be crazy. It's only worth one-fifty. What the hell do you want to do, blow up the place?"

And he said: "That's right. You must have been talking to your neighbors." Most of them had already signed.

I thought about it for a few minutes, then caught up with him at the Gruntleys' house. "All right," I said, "but you'd better make that a cashier's check."

## Paige Petro

Of course you know Jack had refused to attend Kathy's wedding, and had prevented my attending as well. I hadn't been too keen on the marriage myself—one had heard, shall we say, certain unappetizing rumors about Brian Straight—but I was willing to attend for Kathy's sake. Jack's chief objection was Woody Hazzard's presence as best man, and he and Kathy did have words about that.

"Have you forgotten that man's role in Jeff Stuben's tragic death?" Jack said to her.

Of course, at the time we had no idea Kathy had in fact been *living* with Woody up north. How dreadful this entire affair is!

When we first learned that *Red Surf* was planning to film in the bad part of town, Jack's initial attitude was one of benign disgust. At that point I believe we both thought it was some sort of nostalgia beach party film.

When we learned it was in fact the Brad Jenkins murder story Jack became incensed. "They're actually going to film poor little Debbi Henderson's murder in the very room where it occurred, if you can imagine *that*."

Jack made some inquiries with the city to see if all the permits were in order. Unfortunately, they were.

But the casting of Brad Jenkins himself as Debbi's father was the last straw.

"This is a moral atrocity," Jack said. "I think it's time I had a word with my son-in-law."

## Kathy Petro

I was sunning topless by the pool at Malibu when Consuela came out and said, "Your father, *Señora*." Before I could even pull on my top Daddy was there, and he was just fuming.

"I want to have a word with your husband," he said.

"He's upstairs," I said, rattled and everything, trying to pull on my top without him seeing my nipples.

So he started for the stairs, and then I said, "No, wait. Let me get him." But it was too late, he was already going up the stairs.

I finally got my top on and started up after him. Then I heard this terrible slap and Daddy yelled, "You goddamn queer!"

## Woody Hazzard

I was buttfucking the bejesus out of Brian when the bedroom door flew open and I almost shit, 'cause there was Jack Petro, towering above us like a red-faced Sunday school god in white Dacron slacks. Before I could even react he knocked me away from Brian, and started pummeling Brian with his fists, calling him a queer and stuff like that.

Then Kathy was there, pulling her dad off Brian, and as the two of them struggled Kathy's breasts slipped out of her top. This flustered her dad, and then I jumped him, and then Consuela the maid stepped into the room and stopped everything 'cause she had this shotgun trained on Jack Petro.

## Paige Petro

Jack returned from Malibu in a blind red fury. When he told me what he'd seen I dashed to the bathroom where I was physically ill.

"Our dear Kathy," I said upon my return.

"Kathy is dead," he said. "This is the limit. As of today, I have no daughter."

"Jack, you can't mean that. You're exhausted, that's all. You'll see it differently in the morning. We'll find a way to rescue our daughter."

"Not this time," he said, and poured himself a large bourbon. "I don't know, Paige. I just don't know anymore. I've tried to live a decent life. I started out as a paperboy and built a goddamn empire. There was a time where that meant something, but not anymore. Now the bleeding-heart environmentalists control everything, the fruits and the whale-lovers and the left-wing attorneys. Ever since the sixties . . . God, how I despise that decade."

"They're a pack of envious jackals," I said, referring to his proliferating enemies. "False accusers, the lot of them. There's always been cancer, Jack. Long before Petro-Chem was even a twinkle in your eye."

"Bless you, my darling love," he said. Which . . . I'm sorry . . . proved to be his final words.

He retired to his study, taking the bourbon bottle with him, as he frequently did when he wished to be alone with his thoughts. I went to bed, though sleep was impossible. A little before eleven I heard a single, obliterating shot.

## Greg Spivey

We wrapped at the Henderson house and then it was time for Mackerel Drive. Shark had secured the entire block for use in the "jack-off dream sequence." But first we had to shoot what was surely the most grisly of any of the murders where it had actually taken place—in the Jenkins' garage.

We had Mackerel Drive cordoned off, which kept the crowd of hostile neighbors some distance away down on Eel Road, but some of the people in that block of houses which we had in effect "bought" were still moving out, and the crowd on Eel Road was taunting them, as if they were union scabs: "Don't let 'em do it! Don't let 'em use your house!"

Of course, the people on Mackerel Drive could hardly refuse. This was essentially a middle- if not lower-middle-class neighborhood, remember, and the checks from Acropolis were more money in the hand than any of these people had ever thought they'd see.

## Carol Van Der Hof

I observed a touching moment between Brad and his parents as they were loading their personal possessions into a U-Haul trailer. Shark had insisted, and paid them handsomely, to leave their furniture and "set dressings" behind in the house, though naturally it was quite all right for them to take personal items such as clothing and old photographs, anything that couldn't be observed with the camera's eye.

They were almost ready to leave when Mrs. Jenkins noticed that in the process of laying camera tracks the crew had savagely trampled her tenderly nurtured flowerbed, and she began weeping. Brad, who was back at the garage acting out for Tony the double-murder he'd committed there, noticed his mother and rushed to her, hugging her as best he could considering his girth. "There, there, Mom," he said. "It's for the best. Once this house goes up in a big cathartic explosion, the past that took place in it will be gone too."

"I know," Mrs. Jenkins said. "Your father and I can buy a whole new life with three hundred thousand dollars. But I still hate to see people trample my pansy garden!"

On their way out, I understand, after fifteen years of compassionate acceptance, their Newport neighbors threw stones at the Jenkins, shattering the windows of their car.

## Mac Trager

As soon as I got that cashier's check I moved out lock, stock and barrel, leasing a beach-front Laguna Beach condo at four thousand dollars a month. I was out a good five days before that movie crew moved over to Mackerel Drive. Then while I was unpacking I realized with cold shock that one precious thing was missing.

So I went back to Mackerel Drive, hoping they hadn't blown up the house yet, and they hadn't. They were all across the street at the Jenkins' place as I ducked up the driveway into the garage and found my old wire recordings of Joe McCarthy right where I knew they'd be, stuck behind the workbench in a green fishing tackle box.

I was coming back up the driveway when I saw this girl all covered with blood being chased across the Jenkins' lawn by the actor who was playing Pus Jenkins. She started to scream but he covered her mouth and started dragging her toward the Jenkins' garage when all of a sudden the Borgia guy yelled, "Cut!" 'cause I had walked into the camera range.

Everything stopped and Borgia started over, cussing me out, when suddenly Shark stepped up and said, "Ease up, Tony. He's my dad."

Shark came over and said, "How you doin'?"

"I'm okay," I said.

"Your hair's white now," he said.

"Well, I'm sixty-one," I said.

"I heard you and Miko split up," he said.

"Yeah. I got pretty sore when I found out she wasn't really dying," I told him. "Took her all around the world for nothing."

"I guess I judged both of you kind of harshly in Rome," he said.

"Yeah, well—" I didn't like thinking about that.

"Are you all right?" he said. "You got a place to stay?"

I told him about the Laguna Beach condo.

He was wearing dark glasses but he took them off, and his eyes were crazy-looking and filled with tears.

"Dad," he said, and then he tried to hug me.

I jumped back, by instinct, and said, "All right now, none of that Hollywood queer shit."

Just then that old fishing tackle box snapped open, all those wire spools of Joe McCarthy's speeches spilling out everywhere. I remember seeing a funny look on Shark's face right before I went after one spool that was rolling back into the garage. As I bent down to pick it up Shark jumped me from behind. He was like a madman. The next thing I knew he had me pressed back across that old freezer, the same one we'd found Winnie in, and he was choking me, cutting off my wind. A couple of the movie guys finally pulled him off.

## Greg Spivey

"Shark, what happened?" I asked him in his trailer after we'd calmed him down.

"I'm not sure," he said, pouring himself a large whiskey. "When I tried to hug him, he rebuffed me—though I should have expected that. Then, when I saw those wire spools . . ." Shark winced and cupped his crotch, as if making some sort of subconscious sense-memory connection.* "I don't know . . . I just wanted to kill him."

Later that evening we heard about Jack Petro's suicide. At the time we knew nothing of the altercation in Malibu, pitting Brian and Woody and Kathy against her father; Petro's suicide seemed a distant, almost obscure event.

"That figures," Shark said when he heard Petro had done the shotgun-in-the-mouth routine. "He was definitely a Hemingway kind of guy. Tough on the outside, but underneath a pussy through and through."

## Woody Hazzard

I was having sex with Kathy at Malibu the day after Jack Petro paid his surprise visit—by this time I'd kind of decided I was pretty much bi for all practical purposes—we were making love slow-like to some Marvin Gaye song when the phone rang by the bed and Kathy reached for it, real irritated.

"Hello?" she said. Then: "Mom, please don't start—" Then she just listened for a minute and hung up without saying anything.

*See childhood snagged penis incident circa 1954, page 19.

"What is it?" I said, as we started moving again.

And she said, "I'll tell you later. Don't stop."

So we kept going, but pretty soon she started crying, like crying really hard, and I started to pull out, but she held me to her, saying, "No, don't stop."

But it was too weird, so I rolled back beside her, and by then she was really sobbing and said, "Daddy's dead."

I just held her for a long time after that, rocking her gently while she cried.

## Brad Jenkins

That scene in my garage made me feel real funny, 'cause by the time I finished showing Tony how the murders came down and they got ready to film it, it was almost like it was happening again. They had the guy who was playing Eddie tied up to the work bench, just like he'd been when I'd made him watch. And they had that actress Kit who was playing Becky Childers stripped right down to her panties, which were the exact shade of pink they'd been in real life. Then Tim would lift her up as she wriggled helplessly and start moving her wriggling body across the bench toward the power saw, the same saw I'd used in '67 to bisect Becky Childers right up the middle. And it all looked so real I began to get excited, even though I knew I shouldn't.

Then when that actress Kit lost her big toe I guess I kind of lost control.

## Tony Borgia

It was just one of those terrible accidents that sometimes occur no matter how careful you are. The power saw blade, I felt strongly, should be real. The audience can tell when something like that is fake—it's the first thing they look for. We had the shot carefully blocked out and rehearsed. There should not have been a problem.

Actually, Brad became excited first, that was why Tim moved slightly off his mark. The saw began humming, and Kit was writhing, mouth and wrists taped, breasts undulating sensuously as Tim moved her toward the blade—well, the scene *was* supposed to be horrifically arousing.

## Greg Spivey

Tim was moving Kit's feet toward the saw blade, which was to move up between her legs almost but not quite to her crotch—when suddenly out of nowhere Brad appeared, stepping right into the scene, his pants already down around his knees as he masturbated furiously. Well, it was a truly surrealistic moment: this crazed figure so grotesquely obese he could barely reach himself below his bulging abdomen—and no balls to boot!

Tim was so rattled by the sight he stepped back slightly, and in a bright splash of blood the blade took off Kit's big toe. A second later Brad spermlessly ejaculated in a paroxysm of pathological ecstasy.

For the first time I really began to wonder why I was involved with this film.

## Carol Van Der Hof

Poor Brad was in absolute torment afterwards. "I don't know what happened, Carol. I thought those feelings were all behind me."

He began banging his head against his parents' kitchen wall until Shark intervened. Then he fell whimpering into my arms, as I stroked his amply padded shoulders.

"Take him over to my house," Shark said. "Give him a Placidyl and put him to bed in my old bedroom."

I did as Shark said, as well as I could, for Shark's boyhood house on Mackerel Drive was all but empty, his father having taken all the furniture. In what appeared to have been Shark's old bedroom however there was a beaten twin mattress, surely thirty years old. On this I held poor Brad, his head in my lap. Rocking him I sang "Hush, Little Baby," and a slew of similar lullabies, until at last the sedative took effect.

## Tony Borgia

Kit was rushed to the hospital where they were able to sew her toe back on. But I had to let her go. Obviously, the scene wouldn't play with her foot bandaged. Then Jerry Spark, who'd been playing her boyfriend in the scene, physically attacked me, saying Kit's injury had been all my fault. So we had to let him go too.

"Don't worry," Shark said. "So much of art involves exploiting chance. I think I know just the pair to replace Kit and Jerry in this scene."

## Carol Van Der Hof

I was binging on Häagen Dazs in my trailer when Shark stepped in and said, "Call your friend Brian. Tell him I want Woody and Kathy on the set at six sharp tomorrow morning."

"You've gone mad," I said, realizing that he meant them to replace Kit and Jerry. And I wondered: Was it possible that he'd planned this all along? Could Shark have incited Brad to masturbation on the set at precisely that crucial moment, anticipating that it might cause a disruption and injury to Kit that would necessitate her replacement? My mind was racing crazily, for in the escalating dementia *Red Surf* was rapidly becoming, very little remained unthinkable.

"Shark, you can't be serious," I said, in response to this absurd casting whim. "Woody and Kathy are far too old. There's nothing as dispiriting as thirty-year-olds portraying teenagers."

"They're young at heart. We'll light them carefully. Make the call."

"Kathy will never do it," I said.

"Brian will convince her to," Shark said. And when I asked him why he thought so he told me for the first time of the print he'd found of *El Cristo Fugitivo,* featuring a graphically sexual Mrs. Harold Gay. Of course, I knew of Rafael Avila's suppressed surrealist masterpiece, rumored to have been perhaps the single greatest, albeit to some most offensive, film ever made. But the notion of Arlene Gay née Diver, unctuous star of the cloying Ginger film series,* portraying an incandescently obscene Mary Magdalene a scant two years before her brief time in the wholesome Hollywood sun, was not easily assimilated, though Shark assured me it was so.

---

*Ginger and the Clergyman* (1958), *Ginger Goes to Guam* (1959), *Ginger Goes Cuban* (1960). Acropolis Pictures' attempt to copy the successful Tammy formula, the first two films were hits, but the third entry bombed, a victim of changing attitudes towards Castro's Cuba, and ended the series. Arlene Diver made one more movie, *Isn't He a Dream?* (1961), before marrying Harold Gay and retiring from films.

"I see, then it's blackmail," I said, in my astonishment perhaps needlessly spelling out the obvious. "That's the reason Tony has carte blanche. It has nothing to do with art at all."

At that Shark fixed me with a look of weary contempt which I sensed had far less to do with what I'd just said than with his feelings, or lack of them, about me in general. For it was precisely the absence of any passionate emotion which made his gaze so devastating. Hatred, anger, even intense irritation, would have been preferable to that look of terminally bored disdain.

"You know, Carol, you really are a very stupid, silly woman," the man I adored said to me. "Once we finish this film I'm going to pack you and your ugly clubfoot right back to New York where you belong."

Well—I felt as if he'd killed me then, as if my life were over. I picked up the phone and wanted to throw it at him, but felt utterly drained of all strength. I dropped the phone on the floor. "Call Brian yourself," I said, and limped out into the night.

## Woody Hazzard

Around eight that night Kathy and I were watching TV in the Malibu den while Brian took a call in the other room. Kathy was still real grief-stricken about her dad's death, feeling like it was her fault, and I was saying, "Kathy, come on. It's an ego trip to think you're responsible for somebody else's suicide. Your dad was depressed about a lot of stuff."

"I know," she said. "But why wouldn't Mom let me go to the funeral? Why, why, why!" She began to cry again.

I was comforting her when Brian came back into the room, looking real drawn. He took a deep breath and said, "How would you kids like to do a bit in Shark's movie?"

Kathy looked at him like he was crazy, and then went through about nineteen changes, all of them bad, as Brian tried to calmly explain what the roles entailed. There were just a few lines of dialogue, and the partial nudity would be tasteful, but when he got to the part about the power saw that had cut off Kit's big toe, Kathy exploded.

"Brian, the answer is no! Do you not know that I would rather die first?"

"I don't think you understand," Brian said, and told us

about the surrealistic movie Shark had that showed this grinning cowboy Jesus cleaning out Arlene Gay's box.

"We've *got* to give Shark what he wants," Brian said to Kathy, "if only to finish *Red Surf* before it bankrupts the studio."

"And you want me to be in a Shark Trager film with a real power saw moving up between my legs? Well, *you are crazy!*"

"I'm telling you you're going to do it!" Brian yelled. "I've come too far to watch my entire career go down in flames because you—"

But suddenly Kathy was shaking violently. It was almost like that scene in *Alien*, where that thing burst out of the guy's stomach. She fell back on the sofa, her tongue lopping out, her eyes rolling back showing the whites—like this total balls-out fit.

"Oh my God, she's having a grand mal seizure," Brian said, and he and I tried to help her. "Christ, put something in her mouth before she bites off her tongue."

I grabbed the first thing I saw on the coffee table—this raunchy old leather cock ring. She nearly bit it in two, but it saved her tongue.


## Carol Van Der Hof

I returned alone to the Santa Monica beach house that night, more profoundly depressed than I had ever been. I was planning to pack my things and leave the City of Angels and the motion picture industry and Shark Trager forever. But I paused to binge on several Sara Lee cakes—those sticky sweet metaphors for all the erotic pleasures I had not, would never, share with Shark. I had barely finished throwing it all up when the phone jingled harshly. It was Brian.

"Kathy had a seizure," he said. "She was rushed to Saint John's. The doctors aren't sure yet but they think she might have lupus as well."

"You're telling the wrong person," I said.

He asked what I meant.

But suddenly I had a brainstorm, and quickly covered my tracks. "I mean, I'm mad at you, Bri. Why didn't you mention that Shark was blackmailing Harold Gay? No one tells me anything. It's sheer sexism."

I let Brian respond flusteredly to that, then steered the conversation back to the matter of Kathy's inability to appear in the film. "Don't worry, Bri. Not even Shark could blame an actress with lupus for missing a six A.M. call. Besides, I've got an excellent replacement in mind." Off the top of my head I named a young actress.

"Bless you, Carol," Brian said, adding, "Woody will be there though."

"Shark will be happy to hear that, I'm sure," I said. "And don't worry about *El Cristo Fugitivo*. I'll see that Shark comes to his senses on that score. Ciao, Bri."

## Greg Spivey

It was close to two A.M. and Shark and Tony and I were still going over the next day's schedule in Shark's trailer when Kathy called. At least I thought it was Kathy as I took the call. It just didn't occur to me at the time that it might be Carol doing the impression she'd occasionally employed for comic effect during the pre-production period, though never in Shark's presence. Kathy's voice isn't difficult to do, I suppose—it's more or less that classic Southern California beach girl speech pattern, which New Yorkers especially seemed to have just discovered in those days as an endless source of snide amusement—though Carol's mimicry had always contained a rather transparently envious and bitter edge.

## Tony Borgia

"It's for you," Greg Spivey said, offering Shark the receiver.

"Take a message, damn it," Shark snapped. By this time our nerves were shredded.

"It's Kathy Petro," Greg said.

Well, track in on Shark—it was that kind of moment. Shark took the phone from Greg. "Hello, Kathy," he said with the utmost tenderness as he irritably waved Greg and me out of the trailer so that he could speak to her in privacy.

Carol told me later what transpired.

"Hi, Shark," Carol said, imitating Kathy's voice. "I know it's late and everything. But I just wanted to talk to you, I guess. Can you talk now? Am I calling at a bad time?"

"No," Shark said gently. "No, no, not at all."

"Shark, listen," Carol said. "I know this is going to sound

really crazy. But I'm just really looking forward to being in *Red Surf* and everything, even if I only get to play a murder victim. Because, I don't know, this is going to sound really weird, but I can't get you out of my mind.''

Shark was silent for a moment, and Carol was afraid he'd detected the ruse. But he hadn't. ''Do you know that you are my life?'' he said, his voice trembling with emotion.

''Oh Shark,'' Carol replied with a provocative sigh. ''This is so crazy, but I really think that maybe we're meant to be together or something.''

Shark could barely speak. ''I have been waiting all my life to hear you say that,'' he finally said.

''Oh Shark,'' Carol sighed again. ''I wish I were with you right now. I just wish you had your arms around me and everything. I don't know, it's just really what I want. I think . . . this is so weird . . . but I think I really love you or something. You know?''

Again, Carol was afraid she might be laying it on too thick. But Shark fell for it hook, line and sinker. ''Are you in Malibu?'' he said.

''Yes. Shark, I wish my naked tan body were against yours right this second. Really, that's what I wish.''

''Come to me, my angel,'' Shark said. ''Come to me now. The freeways are empty. We're only an hour apart.''

''Oh Shark, oh yes,'' Carol sighed, pressing her luck. ''Oh. I'm already *wet*, oh I really am.''

Even before making the call, Carol said, she had found an old bottle of Clairol left behind by one of Shark's house guests and dyed her hair blonde.


## Carol Van Der Hof

I roared down the freeway, utterly blitzed on cocaine, my freshly blonde hair drying in the wind. I reached Mackerel Drive shortly after four in the morning and parked around the corner so Shark wouldn't see my car. A guard was posted, who recognized me, though he did a double-take, because of my hair no doubt. Then too as I passed him my trenchcoat flapped open in a sudden gust, revealing the scanty bikini I wore underneath—a bimbo souvenir that had long adorned Shark's bedpost.

Mackerel Drive was silent, most of the trailers dark, though a light was most definitely burning in Shark's.

I was trembling as I called his name in a stage whisper, fearful someone else might hear.

Shark appeared in the trailer door. "Kathy?"

I darted back toward the Jenkins' garage, through the maze of cables and lights awaiting the morning's shoot, knowing he would see me.

He came toward the driveway. "Kathy—"

I turned before the open garage, knowing the overhang would shield my features from the moonlight, and suggestively removed my coat. I was so thin by then Shark was easily deceived, seeing in the shadows what he wanted to see.

As he approached I waited until the last possible moment, then began lowering the garage door, blocking my face from his view. He stopped the door halfway down, crawled under it, and lowered it the rest of the way.

Then in the near-total darkness of that garage all of my rapturous dreams of love with Shark Trager came true, in a manner of speaking.

## Woody Hazzard

I reached Mackerel Drive around five-thirty that morning and went to Shark's trailer but he wasn't there. A lot of the crew people were already out, and Greg Spivey came over and said, "Did Kathy come with you?"

And I told him, "No, are you kidding? Don't you know what happened?"

So I told him and he said, "She can't be in intensive care. She called Shark at two in the morning."

So we're still trying to figure this out, and meanwhile other people are arriving, including the DP and the special effects guys and Tim Stroll, and I'm saying, "Shit, man. You mean you don't have a replacement for Kathy? Then how are we gonna do the scene?"

Then Tony Borgia comes out of his trailer and says, "What's the matter?"

And then I see Brad Jenkins coming out of Shark's old house, rubbing his eyes.

Then we hear this scream coming from Jenkins' garage, and everybody looks, but nobody can fuckin' believe it, because the garage door's open and the power saw's running, except it's been knocked over on its side. And Shark and Carol are standing there, Shark totally naked except for his socks, and Carol's naked except for this bikini top hanging from her shoulder and she's got her hair dyed this really phony-looking blonde. But the worst part is she's like totally cut off her foot.

## Tony Borgia

It was bad. There's something about real violence . . . I don't know . . . It kind of made me sick.

Apparently, a few of the crew guys had come up to the garage without Shark and Carol hearing them and abruptly raised the garage door. Well, in the sudden dawn light Shark saw instantly that he was having sex with Carol, rather than Kathy Petro, and his mind just stripped its gears.

He pushed Carol away so hard she fell back and knocked over the power saw, and the switch was hit as it fell on its side.

Shark stared at Carol, just completely destroyed. For something like two hours, after all, he'd thought that his ultimate dream had come true.

Carol was crazy by that time too, and she told me she could literally, viscerally, *feel* Shark's hatred as he glared at the body he'd been worshiping with his mouth only moments before in the dark. With a special disgust he glared at her clubfoot, Carol said.

"What is it, Shark?" she said to him. "Wasn't it good? As good as you ever thought *Kathy* would be? What is it that keeps you from loving me? Is it *this?* Is it my *foot?* Well, *that's* no problem, Shark."

At that Carol ran her ankle up against the spinning blade. It was over so quickly, a grip later said, there was barely time to wince, let alone intervene.

## Greg Spivey

It was madness. Carol, once the pain hit, screaming ceaselessly, her leg spewing blood. A script girl was throwing up, one of the caterers was hysterical, even the grips looked peaked and they were pretty tough guys. And then Brad Jenkins ran up to the garage, just completely crazed and driven, and started masturbating in a pathetic frenzy at the sight of all the blood, until I and several of the prop men grabbed him, pounding him to the ground.

## Woody Hazzard

The ambulance came. As they loaded Carol in she started laughing hysterically in pain and shock, and yelled at Shark, "Everyone's had Kathy, it's no big deal. Everyone but you! *Even Pus!*"

I'll never forget the look on Shark's face. He was just totally fuckin' devastated, man. Just completely wrecked.

He looked at Pus, who was laying on the lawn after Greg and a few other guys had creamed him. And Pus kind of gave Shark this sheepish smile, confirming what Carol had just said.

Then the ambulance was screaming away and Shark turned to me and his eyes were just totally insane.

The next thing I knew he was grabbing me, trying to pull me into the garage, screaming, "Get in there!" Then, to the crew: "Tie his arms and gag him. Let's shoot the scene."

He was so out of it I just knocked him away. Then he grabbed the Roto-Rooter snake, which had been the murder weapon used on the guy I was supposed to play, then he pushed me again. "Bend over the work bench. Pull down your pants. Move that fucking camera up here. Let's shoot the fucking scene!"

He was just cracking up, and Carol's blood was still everywhere, and everybody was like totally bummed. Tony finally came over and said, "Shark, that's enough."

Shark looked around and saw how everyone was staring at him and finally seemed to realize how bad he'd flipped out. He was breathing hard and sweating, just totally crazed. Then he dropped the Roto-Rooter snake and reeled off toward his trailer.

That was it for me, man. I split.


## Tony Borgia

I was shaken. I don't know . . . when real violence actually happens to someone you know, someone you care about, it's hard not to feel something, I guess.

But filmmaking is like war. There comes a time when you have to be ruthless, when you have to leave your wounded behind.

And so I hired two new actors, and Brice brought in the cow intestines and the split-woman dummy, which *was* rather extraordinary. And we shot the scene.

## Carol Van Der Hof

Luckily, the power saw cut was quite clean. As a result they were able to sew my foot back on. I'm quite glad they did now. What an act of madness on my part!

And yet it did serve a kind of purpose, for it made me see the light. Convalescing in the hospital, simultaneously detoxing from cocaine, I knew that I was over Shark, that my life with him had been a self-induced form of torture I would never subject myself to again.

I even felt a twinge of pity for Shark, knowing he was still down there in Newport Beach, in his own way as abjectly self destructive as I had been, hurtling toward the crazed *Götterdämmerung* of what would undoubtedly be his last film.

## Greg Spivey

Shark was absent from the set while Tony finished the Henderson garage scene—he was sleeping in Santa Monica, I guess.

Then as we began to set up for the "jack-off dream sequence," the production really reached a new pitch of madness. Tony was insane by then, coked out of his mind. It was harrowingly apparent that he'd crossed a line from irresponsible genius into sheer disembodied delusion. He began talking about junking the rest of the film, the "story" as it were, and just having a four-hour dream sequence of perpetual, unmotivated violence. "*This* is reality," he said as we began setting up for the slaughter. "The 'plot' is the dream."

By then we were keeping the TV crews at bay as well, because the story of Brad playing the part of Debbi's father had broken. There were headlines: KILLER PLAYS FATHER OF VICTIM IN FILM, that sort of thing. There was general outrage in all quarters, and quite a concerted effort to make the city shut down the film—but on that count I have reason to believe that some major money changed hands. Brad had been sent back to his parents, smuggled past the crowds on Eel Road in a catering van.

We were nearly ready to go on the dream sequence when Shark returned to the set.

## Tony Borgia

I know people want me to say I was crazy then, that I was on cocaine, that I went too far. But I will never say those things. I regret nothing. I expect to be hated the rest of my life. But I will die happily knowing that a thousand years from now when money no longer exists people will be astonished and swept away by *Red Surf*.

## Greg Spivey

The sequence was covered as no sequence had been covered since *Triumph of the Will*, with fifteen separate Steadicams. Tony wanted it to have a swirling hallucinatory feeling, or as Shark said, "Like an endless William Burroughs fantasy."

"Yes!" Tony would say. "Except with both girls and boys. We should have a boy hanging here in the Andersons' backyard, as a conscious Burroughs hommage. But I want fifteen Girl Scouts strung up here on the McPhersons' porch, their breasts lopped off in unison, so nobody think's I'm gay."

Essentially the scene called for Tim Stroll to work his way up the street, torturing and slaughtering the families in each house along the way. It was all shot at night, the lights tinged red. For at least two miles as you came up the coast highway you could see the hellish glow of that nightmare suburban inferno.

## Tim Stroll

Yes, I saw Hell then. For five solid months I lived in a preview of Hell. Satan controlled my mind and body with drugs, that is all I wish to say about it now. Today I live in the light of Jesus Christ, my Lord and Savior, whose infinite love has cleansed my soul of my Satan-ruled Hollywood past.

## Greg Spivey

Poor Tim. Hadn't he been raised as a Pentecostal or something? It was all too much for him. He was coking heavily and became, perhaps inevitably, unhinged.

Who wouldn't have? Who didn't? Brice's special effects were gruelingly real. The body parts flying, the gutters of Mackerel Drive literally clogged and overflowing with Karo syrup blood. The "Girl Scouts"—God, how many did we go through? The hysteria, the screaming stage mothers. Minds were being destroyed but nothing would stop Tony and Shark.

Then one night I came upon Tony looking at rushes on the Steenbeck set up in what had been Shark's boyhood house. He was alone, or so I thought at first. Then I saw the blonde woman's head between his legs. That was all—just her head, one of the very realistic dummy heads used in the decapitation sequence.

I stepped out to Mackerel Drive and threw up by a pile of latex surfer torsos. Then I walked off the set and did not come back.

## Tony Borgia

Charitably, I would say Greg imagined that. Perhaps he was thinking the sequence in the film where *Tim* has sex with the severed head. Admittedly, it was a time for all of us when the line between art and reality became smudged.

## Brian Straight

I was utterly sickened by what was going on and pleaded with Harold to let me stop it. The flak we were catching over Brad Jenkins playing his murder victim's father was unbelievable. What kind of studio would make a film like this?

Harold wouldn't budge. "Let's tough it out," he said from New York. "It can't go on much longer."

"Oh yes it can, Harold. This so-called dream sequence isn't even scripted. Tony and Shark are making it up as they go. They're both completely demented. Left on their own, they'll *never* stop!"

Harold sighed. "The board is meeting tomorrow. Perhaps . . ."

He never finished the sentence. A moment later Arlene came on the line. "Brian, would you please hang up so I can call the paramedics? I believe Harold's having a stroke."

## Tony Borgia

We were set up to shoot the final scene of the film when Brian Straight screamed past the barricades in his Ferrari, jumped out and ordered a halt to the production.

"You're finished," he yelled at Shark and me as he approached our command position on the top of the hill. "You are not exposing one more foot of film!'' As he reached us he glared at Shark and said, ''Harold's dead. And so are you.''

I looked at Shark with a sense of terrible desperation. I had been literally seconds from calling Action when Brian arrived. Every detail of the scene was ready, the houses wired with explosives, all of the cameras ready to roll. It was, to use a sexual metaphor, like being on the verge of an excruciating orgasm and being told to stop.

By the look in his eyes I saw that Shark felt the same way.

''Shoot the scene, Tony,'' he said.

''Tony—'' Brian whirled around to me.

''This is a take,'' I said into my walkie-talkie.

As the horn sounded Brian tried to grab the walkie-talkie from me, and Shark grabbed him. Each camera and soundman checked in as Shark and Brian struggled. Then, just as I called, ''Action!'' Brian saw something behind me and cried, ''Oh my God, no!''

I looked just in time to see the man coming at Shark, a fellow about fifty in a Petro-Chem work uniform, whom I recognized in the glare of the first explosion as Debbi Henderson's father. He had a large knife. ''Goddamn you to hell for what you've done to my little girl's memory,'' he screamed and drove the knife into Shark's stomach.

Shark reeled back, clutching his stomach, as Brian and I and a couple of grips subdued George Henderson, who was sobbing hysterically by then.

When I turned my attention back to Shark I saw that he was staggering down Mackerel Drive as, one after another, the houses began exploding around him.

There was no way to go after him, debris was flying everywhere. It was horrible to watch. He just staggered and staggered, trailing blood as he moved down the center of the street. At the time I was certain he was ruining the sequence, though we did save it later, cutting around him.

At last he reeled up his driveway and disappeared behind his old house. Then, in an especially large explosion, his old house blew up.

## Brian Straight

We were certain Shark was dead. The entire block had been leveled. In the aftermath there was just complete chaos and

342

Tony was nearly arrested—the local police and fire department had been deliberately kept in the dark as to the intended magnitude of the destruction. The debris had been scattered for blocks, in one case killing somebody's dog.

It was after midnight when the firemen finally found Shark. I ran to the spot as soon as I heard, ducking past the smoldering ruins of his boyhood home, back to where the firemen were gathered in the rubble of what had once been the garage. They were lifting Shark's blood-soaked body from an old freezer he'd climbed into, which was all that had saved him from being killed in the blast.

# 18/ **Buying It**
## (1981)

### Brian Straight

While Shark was in the hospital I surreptitiously borrowed Carol's keys—she was on the floor below his in the same hospital—and searched the Santa Monica beach house. I found a stack of rusty film cans containing a 35-millimeter print of *El Cristo Fugitivo* hidden in the wine cellar. Among Shark's extensive video tape collection I found a cassette labeled *The Eddy Duchin Story*—an unlikely movie for him to have saved—which proved to be another copy of the surrealist film. Fearing there might be still more cassette copies, similarly mislabeled, I took and destroyed his entire cassette collection—though I couldn't bring myself to destroy what I hoped was the last existing print of that scurrilous but astonishing film. I locked it away in my home vault, telling no one, least of all Arlene, when I reached her that night in Palm Beach, where she'd gone into seclusion following Harold's private funeral.

"I suppose there's a chance Shark ran off more cassette

copies," I told her. "And yet I somehow doubt it. Shark's a tough negotiator on the major points of a deal. But he bores quickly once he feels he's won, and tends to leave his ass in the air on the back end."

"I don't care if he does have another copy," Arlene said, her belated bravery inspired at least in part by the sedative which was also slurring her speech. "I should never have allowed Harold to give in to this blackmail in the first place. I should never have given in to my own shame. This film *is* art, after all. It's not as though I appeared in some sort of tawdry loop—"

"It's art, all right," I said. "But that won't stop millions of people from being enraged by it, Arlene."

"But in the proper setting, in the Museum of Modern Art, say, might it not be perceived in its true avant-garde light—"

"It's a moot point now."

I felt for her on one level, but on another I'd just about had it with her. Preserving her precious reputation had got us into this mess. The truth was I wanted Shark's blood so badly by that point I didn't much care if he'd already shipped cassettes of *El Cristo Fugitivo* to the *National Enquirer,* the Legion of Decency, "Sixty Minutes," and *Christian Life* magazine.

By then I knew Kathy had left me, you see. She'd disappeared from St. John's Hospital, where, I'd discovered, she hadn't had lupus at all. For days I'd heard nothing, had no idea where she was, or what she planned to do or say. I was frantic, so was Woody.

As for my career—sweet God. The way the press was ranting at Acropolis you'd have thought we'd bankrolled an epic kiddie-porn snuff film. The outraged response to the "unauthorized" Newport Beach detonations seemed to have no end, the lawsuits were already flying. The TV news kept showing the family who'd lost their collie in the blast, the kids crying over "Tippi"—again and again those crying kids. It was as if we'd deliberately disembowelled Lassie.

George Henderson, confined for observation to the psych unit of the Orange County Jail, was already being perceived as an all-American martyr, a decent dad driven over the edge by the soulless exploiters of Hollywood. Clearly, that was going to be his defense. God only knew how deeply his attorneys might dig in their attempt to shift the blame.

I flew back to New York for an emergency meeting with Clarke Tower, the new Sadcom chairman, and only then learned the *real* reason the board had allowed the madness of *Red Surf* to go on to the end.

"Harold told me privately about the *El Cristo Fugitivo* blackmail," Clarke explained in his office on the ninety-third floor of the Sadcom Building. "But I was certain the board would never acquiesce simply to preserve Arlene's reputation. And so . . . Harold and I told the board Shark had the goods on Sadcom's Nazi dealings."

"Nazi dealings?"

"Oil shipments via Spain during the war," Clarke said vaguely.

I was stunned. "Sadcom sold oil to Germany during World War II?"

"No, no, of course not. The shipments stopped with Pearl Harbor. But we had to tell the board something. Understand this, Brian. I would have gone to any length to spare Arlene," he said fervently of the woman he would marry six months later. "I've adored her from afar for over twenty years, since the moment I first beheld her fresh-scrubbed angel sweetness in *Ginger Goes to Guam* in 1959. I revered her then, and I revere her now—one lurid Spanish summer be damned."

I was touched. A secret love was something I could always relate to.

Clarke outlined our strategy. "We're going to blame the whole thing on Harold. We'll say he was charmed and tricked by Trager, the board in turn charmed and hoodwinked by Harold. If that doesn't play, we'll say Shark had proof of Harold's cannibalism."

"His *what?*"

"An incident in Arabia back in the thirties, not worth going into now." Clarke walked me to the door. "We're going to try and spare you, Brian. You've been our brightest light. God knows, this debacle was not your fault." He sighed. "Is any of it worth saving?"

"We should know soon enough," I said, expecting to view the damage upon my return to L.A.

Before I'd left I'd dispatched armed guards to seize the negative of *Red Surf*—though in fact it would take us another week to discover where Shark, on the phone from his hospital bed, had ordered it hidden.

## Tony Borgia

Somebody at the lab tipped me off that Brian was seizing the negative, but by the time I got there it was too late. I drove straight to the studio and entered Brian's office, more than prepared to beg.

"Brian, please, for God sake, let me have my film back."

"You're finished," he said.

"I swear I didn't know about *El Cristo Fugitivo*," I told him. "I was stunned when I found out. I thought you believed in me, in my art—"

"You fucking megalomaniac prick!" Brian yelled at me. "Do you know how much this piece of shit has cost so far?" He closed the door so the secretaries wouldn't hear. "Fifty-seven million dollars."

I was sobered but said, "All that means is that we've come too far to stop now. I'm the only one who can put the pieces together. Please, another ten million, that's all I ask."

He began yelling again, and I swallowed what was left of my pride and fell to my knees before his desk. "Please don't do this to me, Brian, I beg you, in the name of God and Mary, mother of Jesus. Don't nail me to the cross like Erich von Stroheim." An allusion, of course, to the silent film genius's martyrdom over his masterpiece *Greed*.

"The spikes are already driven through your hands," Brian said. "Get the fuck out. I don't want your blood on my carpet."


## Cynthia Clive

Rather like a war bride I had remained at Acropolis throughout the *Red Surf* production period, keeping the home fires burning. Naturally, tales of the battle atrocities did reach my ears, but that was war, wasn't it? Or in this case art. I refrained from passing judgment on the basis of Shark's enemies' propaganda and—tellingly, I see now—I refrained as well from viewing the rushes which might have led me to independently conclude that Shark and Tony Borgia had indeed lost their minds in that heart of darkness where one can only lament as Conrad had: "The horror, the horror."

How much of what I knew I suppressed in the name of compassion, playing nursemaid to Shark upon his release from

347

the hospital. He convalesced from his stab wound in the Santa Monica house, I moving into the garage apartment to be close by as he conducted his affairs from home. His wound was severe, the stitches quite ghastly. He took Percodan for the pain initially, and then despite my firmest admonitions, resumed use of cocaine. The stimulant as always made him cross—though he was considerably more than cross the day he learned Acropolis had seized his film.

## Tony Borgia

From my confrontation with Brian I went straight to Shark, roaring down the freeway in a blinding apocalyptic rage, my future vanishing before me. To be this close to my ultimate artistic achievement only to have it ripped away from me was more than unbearable. Certainly, I had growing doubts about Shark's character—what had happened with Carol had given me great pause—but nothing could be allowed to stand in my way now, not friendship nor sentiment nor human decency, so-called. We were in the suburbs of Moscow, the spires of the Kremlin in sight.

Shark had known for several hours that Acropolis had seized the film. By the time I arrived his initial fury was spent. "I'm afraid we've lost our leverage, Tony," he said, with a strange sort of preoccupied calm. He was convalescing by the pool, that horrendous scar exposed. In comparison, an older scar, the result of a steak knife poke from a hot-tempered maid, seemed little more than an ancient love scratch.

"Someone came into the house and found my 35-millimeter print of *El Cristo Fugitivo*," Shark explained, "as well as the single tape copy I'd made. In fact, they made off with all of my tapes, including my exhaustive film noir collection, a gratuitious act of cruelty that points a finger at Brian himself."

"Then it's hopeless," I said. "They've won and we've lost."

"It's not hopeless at all," Shark said and smiled. "I've always known it could come to this. There was always a chance they would tough out *El Cristo Fugitivo*. If they had, my friend, I was prepared to do then what I'm going to do now."

"What do you mean?"

"I'm going to buy the film."

"Dear God." I mentioned Brian's fifty-seven million dollar figure and cited what we both knew was a somewhat low postproduction figure.

"I'm worth that," Shark said mildly. "Tony, sit down. Have some blow or a drink. I'm expecting a call from the bank."

Well, the call came. And easily, too easily, Shark got what he wanted, though he had to put up literally everything he had.

I broke down and wept.

"Don't cry," Shark said. "Only high-strung little ballerinas cry. Get up, Tony, and go to work. This is going to have to be the best goddamn movie ever made or we're both going down the toilet."

## Brian Straight

I actually experienced a kind of physical seizure of glee when I learned Shark wanted to buy *Red Surf*. It was only too perfect. "What do you think? Should we let him have it?" I asked Clarke Tower.

You could have hung up the phone and still heard him laughing in New York.

The timing couldn't have been better. The transaction was barely complete, our separation from that deranged cinematic monstrosity had just been officially announced, when the whole matter surged into the headlines again in the wake of George Henderson's freakish death.

## Greg Spivey

Somehow, he was electrocuted while watching "The 700 Club" on an Orange County Jail TV. They'd just scrubbed the floor or something, it was still wet, and the TV was bolted into a metal frame, which he touched. Tragically, his release on bail was imminent, a George Henderson Defense Fund having been established with that as its first objective.

Of course, the media and the public blamed Shark and Tony, their exploitation of Debbi's murder having driven her father so far over the edge that his death seemed somehow tragically inevitable. No one seemed to blame George for having tried to kill Shark. On the contrary, nearly everyone asked in a random street sampling said they would have done the same thing.

## Brian Straight

The guy's death was sad, there's no getting around it. But it did spare us all a big messy "Hollywood made me do it" sort of trial.

## Woody Hazzard

Brian made it a condition of the sale of *Red Surf* that Shark use a pseudonym for my screenplay credit.

"But what if the film turns out to be a hit?" I said.

"That's not going to happen," Brian said. Then he showed me a tape dub of some of the footage from the so-called dream sequence and all I could say was, "I see what you mean."

I was driving by Shark's place one day when I saw a lot of activity out front, guys moving in Steenbecks and stuff like that. And I wondered, you know, if maybe I was wrong, if Brian was wrong. I mean, what could you tell from raw footage? Maybe Shark would pull it off yet, weirder things had happened.

Just then I caught a glimpse of Shark and some babe he was with. But there was no way I was gonna stop and talk to him or anything. I still really hated his guts for what he'd done to everyone in the name of art or whatever the fuck it was.

I was on my way to visit Kathy that day actually. She'd filed for divorce through her attorneys and everything, and made me promise not to tell Brian where she was.

## Kathy Petro

Gray was the doctor on duty in the St. John's emergency room that night I was brought there after my seizure. He was so handsome and kindly and said, "Look, you don't have any history of epilepsy, I strongly suspect this attack was psychosomatic in origin. Are you under any pressure? Why don't you tell me about it, Mrs. Straight?"

Well, the dam just burst, I began sobbing and told him

350

everything. About Brian wanting me to be in this film with the power saw, and about Brian being gay and my marriage being a sham. I just sobbed and sobbed and Gray held my hand—but it wasn't sexual or anything, just comforting.

"I don't want to go back there," I said.

"You don't have to," he said.

I guess in a way I fell in love with him right there in that hospital that very first night. He was so young and sandy-haired and innocent and everything. He was smart, the ways doctors are, and yet so gentle and kind. I just looked into his blue eyes and felt really safe for the first time in years.

## Tony Borgia

The post-production on *Red Surf* was difficult because of all the assholes we had to work with. Initially, we hired one of the top editors in town, a woman whose work I'd long admired. So you can imagine how I felt when she turned to me at the Steenbeck one day and said out of the blue: "This film is sexist garbage, and you're a very sick man."

I was hurt for a second before I said, "Then take a hike, ballbuster, before I edit your nipples with this splicer."

A lot of people quit, mostly because of Shark. I controlled my temper for the most part, but he didn't. I don't think I'm being paranoid when I say a lot of people wanted me to fail. That was certainly the feeling in the industry at large, and it extended to the people who were supposedly on our team. There were many instances of unconscious sabotage disguised as incompetence or "mistakes brought on by fatigue." But my worse enemy of all proved to be Shark.

## Ray Boil

I was the fourth editor to work on *Red Surf,* and I have to say I only did it for the money, the film really kind of made me sick. Not the violence so much as the waste. You could've made twenty good films for what they'd spent. I steeled myself and gave them what they wanted, though looking back I don't think what I made was worth the grief.

It was a real bad environment, everybody coked out of their skulls, which I don't object to per se. But Shark and Tony were way beyond being jacked up—they were both fried right out of their minds, constantly screeching at each other like monkeys in a cage. It got physical too, but they always made up more or less. Shark was obligated to give Tony his director's cut, but if the preview didn't go well Shark could dump Tony and recut the picture himself, and Tony thought Shark was deliberately trying to fuck him up so that would happen.

"I'm gonna kill him," Tony told me once when we'd stepped out for some air. "I'm really gonna fucking kill him. I'm gonna shove his face into the flatbed screen and grind off his head on the broken glass."

The only sane one around there was Shark's secretary, the English gal. And I'm not so sure about her.

## Cynthia Clive

I did try to be a rock of stability for Shark, for of course, however I might feel toward him in my secret heart of hearts, I had long realized that he regarded me as a surrogate Lorna figure, after his beloved aunt by that name, whom he had spoken of on any number of occasions as the only "good woman" in his life.

And I suppose however tinged with a latent romanticism my emotions may have been, they were also heavily laced with an auntly, nay maternal, concern. For the talk about Shark was exceedingly cruel. People did so want him to fail—out of envy, I never doubted. He had been a winner for *too* long, you see. The boy-wonder was thirty, a boy no more. There were schools of vicious younger sharks circling and watching for the first drop of blood so that they might attack and devour him and assume his place.

It was a nightmarish ordeal for him whenever he ventured out to one of the "in" spots, a never-ending gauntlet of malevolent glares and snide grins. The cocaine and lack of sleep made him even more sensitive to it, I suppose. Needless to say, the worst example of that sort of thing was the incident at Breton's.

## Tony Borgia

Breton's was a trendy new restaurant in Beverly Hills that year, *the* place to be seen for lunch. Shark and I were at a table with a distribution honcho and a couple of his underlings, and the

352

lunch had not gone well, so Shark was already testy when he saw Jean-Claude Citroen come in. Jean-Claude was with a group of people, including Philippe Villon, who was being pushed as the new Gerard Départdieu in Europe that year, and was that kind of guy, very macho and tough.

Shark smirked cockily as he watched Jean-Claude cross the room, as if clinging in this moment of colossal insecurity to the threadbare ego-thrill of recalling how thoroughly he'd wasted the French auteur on a Riviera beach eight years before.

He waited for Jean-Claude to spot him, and he wasn't disappointed. Even though they were a number of tables away, Jean-Claude involuntarily flinched when he finally noticed Shark, and fearfully averted his eyes from Shark's stare.

"Cower, you fucking frog," Shark said under his breath. "That's right, cringe." Then he laughed in a very sick and bitter way that disturbed the distribution honcho and his underlings, and bothered me too.

Presently, we got up to leave and Shark glared at Jean-Claude once again. Jean-Claude was ignoring him now, but Philippe Villon was glaring hatefully at Shark, though I don't think Shark noticed.

In the foyer Shark said something rude and dismissive to the distribution honcho, and he and his underlings left in a huff.

"I've got to use the men's room," I said, wanting to do a couple of lines as a way of bracing myself for Shark's inevitable tirade in the car on the way back. As I ducked up the hall Shark stepped out to have the valet bring around his Porsche.

When I came out a minute later, I expected to find Shark waiting in the car. Instead, I found Philippe Villon holding Shark's arms behind his back in the parking lot as Jean-Claude slugged him repeatedly in the stomach and the face.

"Stop it," I yelled, and pulled Jean-Claude away.

Philippe released Shark and gave me a few shoves, as Shark sort of rolled along the hood of a white Rolls Royce, his face bleeding severely. Finally, Shark crumpled to the pavement, and by then more people were coming out, a number of very big-name Hollywood people, and they just stepped around Shark, a few of them swallowing laughs, a few snickering quite openly.

Shark was disoriented, trying to get up but unable to. It reminded me of a James Dean scene, like the title sequence in *Rebel*, I guess. Or perhaps more pointedly, Jett Rink's reeling last scene in *Giant*.

I finally managed to get Shark to the car. I drove, and he bled all the way home in his Porsche.

## Carol Van Der Hof

I received a formal invitation to the Westwood preview—if you can imagine that! By then I was beyond either laughter or tears when it came to Shark Trager, though the vindictive side of me did relish the notion of witnessing what could only be his penultimate humiliation. But I let go of all that, preferring to spend a quiet evening at home with Joel, a sensitive young UCLA film student I'd met at a campus screening of Cocteau's *The Blood of a Poet*. Sweet Joel, who loved me for being just who I was, clubfoot and all!

## Greg Spivey

Shark invited a number of people from the production, as if he were really unaware that most of us considered *Red Surf* the worst experience of our lives. In the same heedless spirit, the preview audience was packed with openly hostile industry people, executives, other producers, agents, actors—all of the most influential people in town, not to mention the key critics. Either Shark had a profound death wish, an unconscious desire for catastrophic public humiliation or—what is probably closer to the truth—he was so deluded by that time that he really thought *Red Surf* was going to blow everyone away.

I attended even though I hadn't spoken to Shark since I'd walked off the set. But it was just one of those nights that for better or worse you couldn't miss.

I approached Shark in the Bruin lobby, where people were milling around him, gleaming with phony smiles, but secretly drooling for the kill. I could hear bits of conversation in the crowd, "It runs four hours? I'm leaving." "It destroyed Tim Stroll. *Imagine*, that handsome young man smashing his head through a mirrored-glass window!" "I understand it's even more incoherent and lumbering than *Heaven's Gate*." On and on, just trashing the shit out of the film before they'd even seen it. There was no way Shark could win that night.

He looked bad. He was thin and pale and wearing dark glasses, his face still bruised from the beating he'd received from Jean-Claude at Breton's, which of course everyone had heard about.

But when he saw me he opened his arms and we hugged. He was coked, of course, and hugged me so intensely I half-expected a Michael Corleone-style kiss and a "Greg, you broke my heart." But it was precisely as he was hugging me that he saw something outside and broke away, dashing out the door.

I stepped out after him to see what was going on. It was summer and still light out, and there were Kathy Petro and Gray Skinner, the young doctor she eventually married, cutting across the street.

## Kathy Petro

I remember that evening well. Gray and I had walked down to a little Italian restaurant for dinner and were strolling through Westwood Village, where in those days it was really nice to stroll. I hadn't a care in the world until I saw the klieg lights and limos and all that up ahead at the Bruin. Then I saw *Red Surf* on the marquee and said, "Gray, I think I'm going to have an anxiety attack."

"There, there, love," he said. "We'll cross the street. None of that has anything to do with you now."

So we crossed the street, but I felt an icky, creepy feeling all the rest of the way home.

## Greg Spivey

Shark told me later he followed Gray and Kathy through the crowded Westwood Village streets until they reached their apartment in the adjacent residential neighborhood. He watched as a light went on—it was dusk by this time and back at the Bruin *Red Surf* had started without him—then he sneaked up through the bushes and looked in the window.

He saw Gray and Kathy kissing in the living room, and then Gray began unbuttoning Kathy's blouse. He said Gray had his back to the window at first, and he hadn't really got a good look at him yet, but finally he did and he was shocked. Because Gray bore a very strong resemblance to Shark—a few years younger, but it's not stretching it much to say that given slight adjustments they could have almost passed for twins.

As a result, Shark was galvanized. He said it was like watching himself with Kathy in a pornographic movie, for that was what happened: Gray and Kathy made love right there on the living room floor.

Shark said he watched for quite a long time, until Gray came and then tenderly held Kathy. At that point, Shark said, he suddenly felt "dirty," because it was no longer like pornography; he could tell they were really in love. So he crept away from the window, feeling very strange and guilty. Just as he reached the sidewalk the porch light snapped on and he was afraid they had heard him in the bushes, so he took off running. He ran all the way back to the Bruin.

## Tony Borgia

It was unbearable. People hissed the titles, and the boos began within the first minute of the opening tracking shot, increasing as that infinitely delicate visual dance moved inexorably toward the first murders. When the murders did take place, there were cries of disapproval and perhaps three dozen walkouts. Then the comments started, the talking to the screen. We'd laid in a voice-over in postproduction—Tim talking to himself—and people began answering that. "I don't know why I do these things," Tim would say. "Neither do we," somebody would shout and the audience would guffaw. When the second murder came there were more walkouts. "This is sick, Tony Borgia is sick!" yelled a fellow director I had long revered. Then more gales of laughter. I felt ill and ran to the john.

## Greg Spivey

Shark said the Bruin lobby was empty when he returned from Kathy and Gray's, but he heard the audience laughing and knew it was all over. To brace himself he went upstairs to the john to do some cocaine. As he approached the men's room door he heard retching, and entered to find Tony clutching the sink where he'd been sick, as Sonya Heinz tried to comfort him. Well, at the time Shark knew the critic was really Tony's mother, as few other people did.

"Tony," she was saying, "what do these Hollywood people know? An artist has to have the right to fail."

*"Fail?"* Tony said spacily, by this point in a kind of stupor.

Then Sonya saw Shark. As you know, there was no love lost between them.

"I'd better go back," Sonya said to Tony. "It wouldn't look good if I were seen comforting you."

"Like a *mother*, huh?" Shark said, letting her know that he knew her true relation to Tony. And she was jolted, for Tony had supposedly told no one.

Shark followed Sonya out of the men's room, stopping her at the top of the stairs. "You *are* going to give your son's movie a good review—"

Well, Sonya was nearly sixty by then, but still one tough little Cajun crocodile. "I'm going to say what I think really happened," she said to Shark. "That Tony Borgia is one of the few authentic cinematic geniuses of the 1980s, and this might have been his greatest film. But you ruined it. You distorted the true story into a lurid, wigged-out personal psychodrama, which is always the failed, frustrated artist's woozy notion of what art is. Because that is what you are, a florid, tawdry hack and a crummy, mediocre whore, a bitter, rejected artist turned Hollywood businessman, who in his impotent rage and envy has deliberately destroyed the truly gifted artist he himself could never be, much as Salieri destroyed Mozart in *Amadeus,* which probably won't make a very good Milos Forman film, if his stumpy, wrongheaded *Ragtime* is any indication, but which does provide a useful analogy here."

"You twat," Shark said. "You dirty old twat."

Shark admitted he was "very aware" that Sonya was standing at the top of a steep flight of stairs, and was fighting back the impulse to "give her a shove," when Tony stepped from the men's room, having overheard Shark's crude remark to his mother. In a wordless rage Tony grabbed Shark by the lapels, "his face as red as a blood clot, his eyes like a poisoned rat's"—when suddenly a new group of walkouts burst into the lobby below, their vicious comments distracting Tony to the extent that Shark was able to pull free of his grasp. Shark

357

smoothed down his jacket, snorted at Tony and Sonya with cocky contempt, and went back down the stairs.

## Tony Borgia

It was just after Shark insulted my mother that the shit really hit the fan. He had just reached the bottom of the stairs when people began *pouring* into the lobby, and I could tell by the soundtrack that the dream sequence had begun. People were groaning with disgust, which seemed odd, because nothing truly horrific had even happened yet. "I don't believe it," I heard a Paramount executive say. "This is really the limit."

"I'm not going to stay and watch that man jerk off," I heard a top female agent say, and I assumed she was talking about Tim's simulated masturbation in the film . . . or, figuratively speaking, about me as an artist. I had no idea at that point that she actually meant Brad Jenkins.

## Greg Spivey

It wasn't surprising that Brad got an invitation too—in a way it was perfect. He had come in after the lights had gone down— later I recalled seeing an obese man taking a seat on the side down in front. But nobody recognized him until he stood up as the dream sequence started and began masturbating furiously, his penis momentarily brushing the blonde hair of an actress in the seat before his. She let out a little cry of revulsion when she saw what had touched her, and her burly date stood, about to punch Brad out, I think, but decided it wasn't worth it. Everyone's attention was on Brad by then, and word spread quickly as to who he was, and it was just too much for nearly everyone.

I was leaving myself when Shark pushed in past me, confused at first until he saw Brad, who was still masturbating away. In a rage Shark went for his boyhood friend.

## Tony Borgia

People screamed as Shark pulled Brad out into the lobby. Brad's pants were still down around his ankles as Shark pulled him through the crowd and shoved him out the door onto the Westwood sidewalk.

358

It was then that *I* lost control.

## Greg Spivey

No sooner had Shark booted Brad into the street—where the usual well-heeled date-night couples were gasping at the sight of the pathetic, exposed castrate lying in the gutter—than Tony pulled a knife from behind the concession counter. I still don't know what that knife was doing there, an enormous, shiny kitchen knife—maybe they used it to split open those big sacks of pre-popped popcorn or something. Whatever, it was there, and before anyone could stop him Tony raised the gleaming knife in a blinding flash of murderous rage. *"You don't call my mother a twat!"* he roared at Shark.

Of course, we know where the blade came down.

## Tony Borgia

I blame Shark for my mother's death. I was trying to kill *him*, that was obvious to everyone who saw what happened. Shark had driven me to that diminished state of temporary insanity, and then my mother simply stumbled into the space between us. When that knife sank into her back right up to the handle I swear to you I died as well.

## Greg Spivey

It was a stunning, terrible tragedy. Sonya died instantly, which is something, I suppose. At least she didn't suffer, though you couldn't say the same for Tony.

Inevitably, there were those who suggested he subconsciously *wanted* to stab his mother out of some sort of Oedipal, or even Hitchcockian, bent of mind. I always felt that was rubbish, dimestore psychology, drive-through Freud.

Less easily dismissed was the sense of karmic retribution pervading the incident. Tony had celebrated a painless, estheticized violence for so long it seemed almost horrifyingly logical that he should have to spend the rest of his life bearing the guilt of having killed in reality the only person he'd ever truly loved without reservation.

The last time I visited him at Porterville State Hospital, he was fine, quite cordial and witty, until I inadvertently touched upon the subject of Sonya's death. Then he began to sob uncontrollably, even though it had been well over six years since that awful night.


## Kathy Petro

Gray and I were watching the TV news in bed that night when the story came on about Tony killing Sonya Heinz at the preview. They showed the theater and Sonya's body under a sheet, and there was blood all over the concession stand and—I'll never forget—this one close-up of all the popcorn just soaked in blood.

"Oh God, I can't look at this," I said.

So Gray changed the channel.


## Brian Straight

It was a sad thing. I'd never been a big fan of Sonya's, but still.

It was a pity in several ways. I can't help but believe that when it came right down to it, Sonya might have given *Red Surf* its only forgiving review. In the wake of her death the reviews were uniformly obliterating—"vile," "despicable," and "insane" seemed to be the favored adjectives—though I imagine they would have been nearly as lacerating even without such a literal assault on an esteemed member of the critical community. When the mother/son relationship was eventually revealed it did add a poignant dimension to the matter though.

Somehow as a result of that final cruel occurrence my desire for revenge on Shark Trager was spent. It was with no great relish that I noted his subsequent professional demise. Shark was a dead horse—or to use the more obvious metaphor, a once sleek and vicious Great White now gutted and stinking on the beach.


## Greg Spivey

Shark had been on the verge of closing what was, all things considered, a reasonably fair distribution deal with Tramcorp. But after the preview they backed out, and the few other offers

Shark received were so bad you couldn't really blame him for refusing them.

In the end he lost the film, of course, just as he lost everything else. When the dust finally settled, the film had gone to Sword Communications, whose standard fare was crap like *Panty Beach Massacre* and *This Film No Star BRUCE LEE*, and they didn't even bother with a theatrical release. *Red Surf*, all sixty-six million dollars of it, went directly to videocassette.

## Cynthia Clive

Shark was ruined financially, so it came as no surprise when he summoned me into the house one afternoon to inform me he had no choice but to let me go. I could tell he'd been drinking in addition to his usual quota of cocaine—what little cash he had hidden away all seemed to be going for that. They'd found poor Gramps dismembered in the brushy hills of Calabasas, so a new drug man had been coming around, a horrid reptilian fellow with long stringy blond hair, though I confess my occasional attempts to confuse him away were perfunctory at best. How could I censure Shark's desire for escape now, knowing what emotional agony he endured? To have risen so high, to have had so much, only to be dropped into the abyss.

He presented me with my severance pay in cash plus a bonus which, knowing his circumstances, caused me to weep. Then he hugged me, as he never had before, for he had always respected my reserve and was not, as one usually thinks of the term, a demonstrative man. I sensed something odd in the air just before he said, "You know, Mrs. Clive, I believe you're the only woman who's passed through my Hollywood life whom I've never fucked. Why don't we rectify that now?"

At that he began to maul me, not forcefully as if he meant to overpower me, but rather as if he were sure I would readily give in. But it was pathetic, you know. All of the starlets who'd been so willing when he'd been on top had abandoned ship like rats. There was no one left to validate him, and I was not about to. Which was why I raised my knee quite abruptly between his legs.

As he buckled to the floor, I said, "Do you realize what you've just done? I was the last person in this world who still

361

cared about you. And now you've alienated even me. You've got no one now.''

He said nothing, merely groaning as he rocked on the floor, holding himself between the legs. That would prove to be my last image of Shark Trager.

## Woody Hazzard

One day I was driving up PCH through Santa Monica and noticed a For Sale sign on Shark's house. I stopped, just out of some weird sense of nostalgia, I guess, since I could tell the house was empty. I peered in the windows at the rooms where Shark and I had once had some pretty bitchin times. My hatred for him was cooling out, 1 guess, and even though I still thought he was a pig who'd got what he deserved, I knew a part of me would always remember the good days too.

As I was leaving I saw this cream soda bottle by the chair on the patio, the same kind of cream soda Kathy always drank. The bottle had a bunch of cigarette butts in it, and I imagined Shark sitting there alone his last night at the house, drinking the soda, then smoking all those cigarettes one after another as he listened to the waves crash and stared at the stars.

# 19/ **Maya**
## (1981–1982)

## Todd Jarrett

I met Shark Trager in the spring of 1981 at the Ray-Mar Theater the night our projectionist became rabid. I was still at UCLA film school then, working nights at the concession counter. The Ray-Mar is gone now, demolished a few years ago, which was really a crime—it should have been restored. It was Art Deco like you wouldn't believe, opulent and cavernous, musty and decadent, with scuffed red velvet seats and the poignant reek of fifty years of spilled buttered popcorn and Coca-Cola and tears. There's a Ross Dress-For-Less discount clothing store there now.

Even in '81 we knew our days were numbered. The Ray-Mar was a revival house and the so-called video revolution was already eating into our business. It was sad and infuriating really. You could rent some piece of shit starring Chuck Norris for a buck a night at Music Plus, but soon there'd be no place left to show a crisp 35-millimeter print of *Shanghai Express*—

which was playing, billed with *Blonde Venus*, the night Shark struck up a conversation at intermission.

It was raining that night, there were only maybe a dozen patrons, so there was plenty of time to talk. Shark had a thick blond beard at that point and was rather seedily dressed; I certainly didn't recognize him as the notorious producer of *Red Surf*. We were lamenting the state of things and he had just got around to mentioning his own UCLA film school background, when Ernie the projectionist reeled down the curving staircase in the midst of a fit. I thought it was a joke at first—he did things like that—until he fell on the Art Deco carpet actually foaming at the mouth. Fred the manager came running and I remembered that Ernie had recently been bitten by a dog. "Christ, it's rabies," I said and we called an ambulance. While we waited for it to arrive Shark took off his belt and stuck it in Ernie's mouth so he wouldn't bite off his tongue, and then restrained Ernie's thrashing arms despite considerable danger to himself.

As the paramedics took Ernie out Fred shook his head and said, "That's it for tonight. We can give them half their money back."

And Shark said, "Look, I can do it."

Fred was leery, we'd had some projectionists' union problems a while back. When he mentioned this, Shark dug out a projectionists' union card. Fred and I were both jolted when we saw Shark's name on the card.

"I got this a while back so I could operate my own projector," Shark explained, seeing by our reaction that we knew who he was. "It cost me a lot of money to get it, but it's completely legitimate."

Some people were already complaining about the delay, so Fred said all right. And Shark went up and ran *Blonde Venus* without a hitch.


## Fred Thal

It was hard for me to reconcile my image of Shark Trager the producer with the man I met that night at the Ray-Mar. In my mind Shark Trager stood for everything I loathed about Hollywood—that greedy materialistic powerfreak schlockmeister attitude that was really destroying movies. He *had* produced

*White Desert*, he had that to his credit. But everything since . . .

Yet here was a man who was paying for his transgressions, you could see that at a glance. Not just in the material sense, though for a man who was used to having everything that must have been humiliating enough. He was staying in some flophouse on Sawtelle—you know, where the illegal aliens stand on the corners to be hired for shit work—and he didn't even have a car. This guy who'd paid sixty thousand cash for his last car was now taking the bus. Do you know what that can do to a man's self-esteem in L.A.?

But the real pain was in his eyes. It was a psychic or even spiritual pain he just carried with him every minute he was awake, though you could see he was fighting hard not to give in to it. To do so, I suppose, would have meant committing suicide.

He came back the second night since Ernie was still in the hospital and Shark definitely needed the money. We talked quite a bit and I began to have compassion for him. I began to see why his life had gone the way it had. We drank some wine in the lobby after the last show and he told me about his days at UCLA, and the rejection from Jean-Claude Citroen that must have been so devastating, though he tried to make light of it. I just couldn't help but feel for him.

Finally I got up to leave, and he did too, mentioning that he was concerned about returning to the Sawtelle flophouse, since he owed a week's back rent. "Look, why don't you sleep in the loft tonight?" I said, and he did.

Not long after that Ernie told me he was going back to Arizona as soon as he was well enough to travel, so Shark became our permanent projectionist and moved into the loft, though he didn't have much to move.

## Todd Jarrett

The loft was a room that adjoined the projection booth. It was something like a press box, with a huge picture window that provided a view of the screen. The glass was a one-way mirror on the auditorium side, so you could look out at the screen but the audience below couldn't see in. The story was that Norman Mar, the guy who'd built the theater in the thirties, had these hideously deformed twin daughters, and built the room so they could watch the movies without disturbing the experience of the other patrons. That may be apocryphal, but the fact remained it was a very strange room. It had a Murphy bed and a kitchenette and its own bathroom with a shower and a bidet; it was like a little apartment with a celluloid view. Shark would stretch out on the bed and watch the movies, enjoying all the comforts and privacy of home video with the esthetic superiority of a true silver screen.

I became quite good friends with Shark and I have to say that despite what you might expect I think he was happy for quite a while. We talked about films from an esthetic or critical perspective for the most part, though of course he would sometimes refer to his own practical experience. But he didn't seem angry or bitter about what had happened to him. On the contrary, he seemed serene, as if it was finally a relief not to have to fight in that jungle anymore.

If he'd done a lot of cocaine before, he certainly wasn't now. He couldn't afford it. Alcohol was his drug of choice, cheap California wine, not rotgut exactly, but whatever was on special at Boy's Market in the gallon jugs.

I think he drank himself to sleep most every night, but earlier in the evening while he was working he would pace himself. There were never any problems with his competence on the job until the night of the Fritz Lang double-bill—a night that sabotaged his serenity and opened a series of doors that no doubt should have remained shut and locked forever.

## Maya Dietrichson

I had come to the Ray-Mar with Billy Freeze, our new drummer in Spione, the group I was singing with then, so Billy could see the Fritz Lang film *Spione,* from which I had taken our name. It means spies in German. At first I had wanted us to call ourselves Spies in the House of Love from the book by Anaïs Nin, but we knew that was too long for the club marquees, so then I thought of the Fritz Lang film.

It was a silent film and this made Billy angry since I hadn't told him in advance. There was music, you know, but he was getting jumpy and I was getting angry with him. "Can't you just watch the pictures and read the occasional title? What's wrong with you? Can't you get along without mindless chatter?'' I said and he became quite miffed. I was not then aware that he couldn't read.

Then the reel changed and the picture was badly out of focus and stayed that way even though people started calling out. So I became furious and went out to complain.

## Todd Jarrett

Maya was just extraordinarily, stunningly beautiful in this ethereal, dreamlike way. In my mind's eye I always see Maya in black and white, a luminous close-up on nitrate film. I swear she always looked like that, as if Lee Garmes [*von Sternberg's cinematographer, Ed.*] were following her around, lighting her every move. I saw her in a Seven-Eleven once and even there she looked like that—like Marlene Dietrich paying for a microwave hamburger. A lot of it was cultivated, of course, the result of her makeup and attire, that New Wave Neo-Expressionist thing she was into. Then too there was the German accent, a sultry, insinuating Lola Lola impression, which by the time I met her had become a constant pathological affectation. For as everyone knew she'd been born and raised in Granada Hills in the San Fernando Valley.

## Maya Dietrichson

I complained to Todd Jarrett and together he and I went up to the projection room to see what the hell was going on. There we found Shark passed out on the Murphy bed in that little room with the view of the screen. I shook him awake, seeing that he was drunk, and he staggered to the projector. He tried to focus the picture but was too drunk to see when it was right, so I said, "Here, let me do it. You're pathetic, you're a mess.''

Todd was embarrassed and said, "I'll make him some coffee.'' But he fumbled with that so I said, "Look, I'll do it.'' So I put on the coffee and Todd left, and once he did I gave Shark some cocaine. I didn't know who he was then, he had a terrible beard. But we talked and I said, "You know, I'll bet under that beard you're quite a good-looking fellow. Why don't you let me shave it?''

So I did, using a scissors, then several Bic razors. He *was* very handsome and I became excited, and he became excited too.

"What about this?" I said, brushing his chest hair. "Shall I shave this too?"

He pulled my hand away and his strength further excited me.

"What about *this?*" I said, and put my hand on his crotch, where he was already hard. "Why don't I shave this?"

At that he threw me on the Murphy bed and we made violent love.

## Billy Freeze

It was a big sex thing at first, I think. Maya and I were just friends, on account of working together and everything. Plus I'd heard too many stories about guys she'd fucked over, or who got obsessed with her or something and ended up killing themselves, which was something you could tell she would get off on. She wanted guys to worship her and die at her feet and that sort of thing.

## Fred Thal

It was total sex, Last Tango at the Ray-Mar. Shark told me later it was something like two weeks before he even realized Maya wasn't really German. And she didn't know who he was for a long time either, and Shark was really elated about that. "She's hot for *me,* man," he said. "Just for me and my hot bod. Not because she wants something from me."

That made sense, I suppose, since most of the women Shark had known in his Hollywood days had been actresses on the make and that sort of thing, though it was difficult to imagine Maya, or anyone, being so deluded as to think Shark could help them now.

I had no prior knowledge of Maya since I wasn't into the local music scene like Todd was. When he began telling me about her reputation as a maneater I was tempted to say something to Shark, but I didn't, deciding to mind my own business.

## Maya Dietrichson

I knew that people said I was cruel because I would let no man possess me. It's not easy to be beautiful, for people always want you and when you don't let them have you their rage and frustration know no bounds. But with Shark I initially believed I had at last found my equal in beauty. I didn't care who he was—when I found out it didn't matter. Our pasts were unimportant. I only cared about the immediate physical presence of his body.

I see now it was the high point of my erotic life, those exquisite days and nights through which we fed upon one another. Though inevitably, I suppose, when you have gorged yourself on simple fare, you begin to develop an appetite for the truly forbidden fruit.

## Todd Jarrett

Maya introduced Shark to opium, which was her drug of choice. She received money from a trust fund, I think, not a lot but enough to pay for that apartment on Windward Avenue in Venice and sustain her opium habit. I smelled the sweet aroma of it wafting down from the projection room one night and went up to tell them to cool it. There they were, virtually naked on the Murphy bed, the room lit with a single amber bulb, lolling sinuously in their opium den with a view. *Morocco* was on the screen. It was all Shark could do to float to the projector in time to change the reel. I glanced back on my way to the stairs and caught a glimpse of Maya woozily going down on Shark in the flickering projector light.

## Fred Thal

It was obvious things had taken a dark turn when Shark began wearing the dog collar.

## Maya Dietrichson

He worshipped me, that's all, and I sensed his inner needs.

One night we were in the loft, a sentimental movie on the screen—*Somewhere in Time,* as I recall—and I began to yawn even as his fingers made me wet.

"Tell me about yourself," Shark said. "The truth about yourself."

"Why?" I said. "So we can bore one other like a normal couple?"

"Tell me about Granada Hills," he said, and I became furious.

"I don't know anything about it," I said. "I didn't grow up there, some other girl did. A bland and boring girl who dreamed dull dreams of one day owning a bikini boutique. A vacuous creature who squealed with unctuous glee when she won a Kathy Petro look-alike contest at age fifteen. Do you want to hear more?"

"No," he said. And for some reason unknown to me then he got a shell-shocked look, like a handsome sweaty-faced soldier in a war. This excited me.

"Go down on me," I ordered him with aristocratic contempt. "You talk too much and I'm tired of it. Do something worthwhile with your mouth."

He became quite excited and obeyed my command with great zeal.

"That's right," I said. "Yes. Eat me. Eat me like a dog."

## Todd Jarret

Shark never mentioned Kathy Petro to me. I knew nothing about his obsession with her. But it's funny, I do remember once noticing that Maya did bear a certain basic resemblance to Kathy Petro, and idly thinking that if Maya had remained sane and true to her Valley beginnings she would probably have become just another vacuously wholesome Kathy Petro California blonde.

Nobody ever accused Maya of being wholesome, but when she started leading Shark around on that leash I felt things were going too far. Granted, it did seem like something of a joke at first, a deliberately outrageous put-on, but still.

## Maya Dietrichson

I said, "You're a dog and you love to lick me, don't you?"

And he nodded obediently yes.

So I put on the dog collar, I put it on tight, till his tongue lapped out like a dog's, which excited me. Then I loosened it a bit so he wouldn't choke. "You're my sex slave now," I said, and put the chain through the collar. "You're Maya's sex slave, that's all you're going to be."

370

We were in my apartment on Windward in Venice and he was naked and aroused and panting at my feet. I wanted to take him for a walk like that out along the boardwalk, but I knew if I did we'd be arrested. So instead I made him eat me while I imagined that we were on the boardwalk and everyone was watching as I made this handsome man do my bidding.

## Billy Freeze

Maya lived next door to me at the Charleton Arms, this raunchy old apartment building a block up from the boardwalk at Windward and Speedway. Windward is the street with the arches where they'd shot that Orson Welles movie *Touch of Evil*, though I guess there were a lot more arches back then. The street was pretty grungy in '81, all these closed-up rollerskate shops and sun-burnt winos staggering around. Maya's third story window overlooked Windward and you could hear the weird shit she was into with Shark going on up there. Like you'd hear a slap, then a cry of pain or maybe pleasure. For a long time I thought it was just her dominating him.

Then one night we had a gig and I went to get Maya and Shark opened the door. The room reeked of opium and Shark was naked and his poor overworked crank was red as a beet. "Okay," he said, "but I want her back here by two at the latest." And there was Maya in this black corset, gagged and tied spread-eagled to the posts of the brass bed.

## Maya Dietrichson

We began switching off because I got tired of doing all the work. I said, "All right, you can dominate me if you think you're man enough to do it. But I warn you, I'm going to fight you every inch of the way."

So we had our battles. But he enjoyed the idea of having to rape me. Several times I really scratched him, so he had to tie me down. I'd had him sniveling for so long, he really relished getting even.

## Neal Ridges

Shark had vanished so completely from the Hollywood scene a

number of people really thought he was dead. As much of a disaster as *Red Surf* had been, he could have continued on some level if he'd wanted to. I mean, look at Mike Cimino; even after *Heaven's Gate* he got deals and came back. Granted, Shark's situation was far worse, it wasn't just the failure of the film, it was everything that had surrounded it. The insanity on the location, the capper of Sonya Heinz's death. Still, Shark could have got some sort of deal somewhere. His exile was definitely self-imposed.

Then—well over a year after *Red Surf*—I ran into Sue Schlockmann on the Mastodon lot and she said, "You'll never guess who I saw last night."

## Sue Schlockmann

Elliot and I had a production deal at Mastodon for a teen drama with music—the one-line concept that got us the deal was "MTV Gidget goes to South Africa"—and one night I went with a girl friend to check out Spione at Blue Angel, a music club on Olympic in West L.A. I liked their single, a New Wave remake of "River Deep/Mountain High," and thought the German girl singer had a look that was right for a Pretoria club sequence in the film.

The place was packed, and Shelia and I had tried to dress punk, but we still felt out of place, and were kind of hunkering in the back when Spione came on.

Well, the girl was everything I'd expected: cool, blonde and Teutonic. She had a long chain looped over her wrist, rather like a dog leash, though I didn't give it much thought at first since she and the guys in the group were all kind of into that leathery, chainy, punk S&M look. She sang this astonishingly affectless rendition of "Gloria" as if she were a statue, moving nothing but her lips, even as everyone else in the club was gyrating maniacally. Then they began another song, but she stopped it, distracted by something off stage.

"Hold it, hold it. This really pisses me off, you know. I bring my pet along with me and he makes a mess backstage."

So she pulled the leash, reeling this shirtless skin-headed punk out to her, the other end of the leash attached to the dog collar around his neck. I nearly dropped my drink when I realized it was Shark.

You could tell he was ripped on something, he had this glassy-eyed, fixated look. She ordered him down on his knees and rolled up a newspaper. "Bad boy," she scolded. "Bad boy." And began swatting his black Levi'ed behind with the paper.

I thought it was an act at first, which in a way I guess it was. I told myself it was okay, he was doing it because he wanted to, and a lot of people were laughing. But I didn't think it was funny.

She began ordering him to do dog tricks, like stand on his haunches, which he did, panting happily. Then she made him roll over. Then fetch—she took a bite from an apple, nonchalantly tossed it across the dirty floor, and ordered him to retrieve it. He did, picking up the dirty apple with his teeth. I'd seen enough at that point and so had Shelia. We were trying to push through the crowd when Maya Dietrichson ordered him to beg, and he did, and then—in a way you could tell wasn't planned—abruptly buried his face in her crotch. She lifted her short skirt—you could see that the gasps of genuine shock excited her—and she was wearing crotchless panties. Shark began going down on her in an extremely exhibitionistic, pornographic way. The audience was going crazy, yowling and cheering wildly, but the guys in Spione were unplugging their guitars and leaving the stage in disgust.

I supposed he eventually humped her on the stage, but Shelia and I didn't stick around to find out. I'd already seen him do that.

## Maya Dietrichson

Shark wanted to take his thing out, but I wouldn't let him. Finally, I shot him in the face with a seltzer bottle, getting his handsome face all wet.

## Billy Freeze

That was almost the end of Spione that night. We were all furious, though I can't say I was totally surprised. I knew Maya got very turned on on stage and had a strong exhibitionistic streak, and I guess Shark did too.

## Maya Dietrichson

He told me all his fantasies, and I told him all of mine. Then we lived them. Every one. Until there was only one fantasy left.

## Todd Jarrett

Shark told me later how it all came about. He said he and Maya had collapsed exhausted on the bed at her place one night after a two-day session involving bondage and discipline and copious quantities of opium and intravenous cocaine, and Maya said, "If you could die in a sexual manner how would you do it?"

And Shark said, "I would like to come and explode at the same time. What about you?"

"I would like to die violently in the midst of an orgasm in a speeding out-of-control car."

Shark said this wasn't a surprise to him since J.G. Ballard was Maya's favorite writer, and she became very aroused reading aloud grisly passages from the Ballard novel *Crash*. So they devised a way in which they could join their fantasies into one.

## Maya Dietrichson

I had a Volkswagen beetle, but that wouldn't do. Shark however had been saving up his money toward purchasing a car, so I chipped in and we bought a powerful 1970 Chrysler 300 for eight hundred dollars. It was huge and made a terrible roar and began to shimmy at fifty miles an hour. The tires were bald, but that was okay. We weren't going far.

For two hundred dollars Mouse, an old friend of mine, built a powerful car bomb. He was a retired Hell's Angel who knew of such things. I told him I wished to blow up an old rival in love, and he showed me how to attach the bomb so it would go off when the car reached eighty miles an hour—using the Chrysler, he thought, merely for demonstration purposes.

"Are you sure this bitch will *go* eighty?" Mouse asked, in reference to my fictitious rival.

"Yes, she's a speeder," I told him.

"But what if she's on the freeway, trying to pass a busload

of innocent children?'' he said. ''Why not set it to go off when she fires the ignition?''

''Because I want her to die with the wind in her stupid hair,'' I told him. ''Don't worry, she only speeds down empty, moonlit roads.''


## Fred Thal

I watched Shark and Maya pull into the Ray-Mar parking lot in that Chrysler one evening and I sensed that something bad was about to happen. It was not a car anyone in their right mind would buy. Just a total piece of shit, belching exhaust, muffler dragging, a joke. Shark and Maya floated out of the car, utterly blitzed, and she went on upstairs—it was nearly showtime—as I drew Shark aside.

''Are you all right?'' I said, knowing he wasn't, that he hadn't been for months.

He was so high he could barely talk. ''This dream is almost over,'' he finally replied in a tortured Christopher Walken whisper.

''You're blowing it,'' I said, because lately his drug use had begun to affect his job performance. Several times he'd mixed up the order of the reels. A few nights before he'd stuck a reel of *Mean Streets* into *Taxi Driver*, though sadly only one person had complained.

''Nothing can hurt me anymore,'' he said spacily. ''I feel good now, I feel at peace, knowing I won't have to die alone.''

''What are you talking about?''

''It's almost seven,'' he said, focusing with some difficulty on the clock. ''I want to really enjoy these movies tonight. I want to really enjoy them.''

I watched him float up the stairs. Then I went to Todd and said, ''I think we may have a problem tonight.''


## Maya Dietrichson

The bill that night was two Ava Gardner films, *The Barefoot Contessa* and *Pandora and the Flying Dutchman*, both old wide-screen prints which had really turned to shit. We smoked opium on the bed during *Pandora*, which I found really stupid and boring, so I shot some cocaine into one of Shark's magnificent veins, then hit myself up.

"I'm climbing the walls," I said around nine o'clock. "Both of these movies are so tedious and stultifying, I don't want them to be the last films I ever see. Maybe we should wait until something good is playing and choose that night to die."

Shark saw my point and said, "Yes, maybe we should wait till Saturday when we're showing two of my favorite films."

That was only two days away and the films were already there, I saw, as he tapped the cans which were labeled *The Magnificent Ambersons* and *Touch of Evil.*

"I don't know if the car will last that long," I said. "Why not show one of them right now? What can they do to you? Fire you? So what? Which of the two is your favorite?"

## Kathy Petro

I was kind of out of it that night because my shoulder was acting up again and I'd been taking these codeine tablets that Gray had prescribed for me. Gray had been working really hard but had the night off, so when he said, "Why don't we go to a movie?" I said okay, even though I didn't really feel like it.

None of the current movies in Westwood sounded that exciting, so when he finally said, "Here are two old Ava Gardner movies in Mar Vista," and the titles sounded romantic, I said: Sure, that's fine.

So we went to the Ray-Mar, this grungy old theater which smelled really bad and had awful broken seats. We sat down and the movie started, but I just kept wishing we'd rented a cassette or something so I could be home in bed cuddled up with Gray. And then suddenly without warning the picture changed. I mean, one minute Ava Gardner was talking to James Mason in this faded pink color, then suddenly it was black and white and I saw the title *Touch of Evil,* and I got this funny feeling because I'd always heard it was one of Shark's favorite films.

People started getting angry and shouting up at the projector, and then the sound got painfully loud, and I started to feel sick. "I have to get out of here," I said to Gray. "I'm having an anxiety attack."

So we went into the lobby, where the manager was trying to

reassure people that the problem was being taken care of. But I still felt anxious and just wanted to go. Then suddenly I felt faint from the codeine or something and had to sit down on this old couch in the lobby while Gray went to get me a cup of water.

## Todd Jarrett

I raced up the stairs to find out what the fuck was going on, and the projection booth door was locked. I pounded on it, really steamed, and Shark finally opened it.

"Are you crazy?" I said.

"What's the problem?" he said affectlessly, opium smoke wafting out the door, Maya lolling on the bed back in the loft.

"The problem is people paid to see two fucking Ava Gardner films, not *Touch of Evil.*"

"Maybe," he said. "But *Touch of Evil* is by far a better film."

"It's overrated," I said, then blew up, angry at myself for even dignifying his argument. "Goddamn it, Shark, put the other film back on!"

At that point Maya drifted up to the door, her breasts exposed, which didn't especially embarrass me—but I heard someone else coming up the stairs. "For Christ sake," I said to Maya, who didn't seem to care. I looked back, expecting to see an angry patron coming up to complain.

It was Kathy Petro—heading for the ladies room directly opposite the top of the stairs. She seemed disoriented or even sick, and didn't bother to look at us.

But Shark most definitely saw her. He appeared stunned.

## Fred Thal

I was about to go up to Shark myself when I saw through the open doors that *Pandora* was back on the screen. "See, folks? It's all straightened out," I said, as cheerfully as I could, and people did start going back in.

At that point I went up to the booth, passing Kathy Petro on her way down the stairs.

## Kathy Petro

When I came down from using the ladies room Gray said the movie was back on the screen and everything. I didn't really want to go back in, but he said, "Oh, come on, Kat, they've got it straightened out now. Hurry, before we miss something." So we went back in.

## Fred Thal

"This is too much," I told Shark. "I really can't tolerate this. This is your last night. I'm letting you go."

"That's cool, Fred. That's all right," he said.

Maya was eying me disdainfully as she tucked in her blouse. I noticed a syringe on the floor by the bed.

"I hope you know you're destroying yourself," I said to Shark.

"Why don't you leave him alone?" Maya said. "What do you know about anything? It's mediocre people like you who've driven artists like Shark to the point of seeing what a dull joke life is."

"I take it back," I said to Shark. "You're letting this psycho Valley girl destroy you."

Shark wouldn't look at me. He was looking down at the screen as if he hadn't even heard me. Or perhaps he was trying to locate Kathy Petro in the audience.

## Maya Dietrichson

"Fuck all of this, Shark," I said. "Let's just go. Everything's ready. The bomb is in place. All I need to do is attach one more wire."

But he ignored me, and began rummaging through all the junk piled up in the loft.

"What are you doing?" I said. "What are you looking for? Didn't you hear me!

Finally he pulled out a rusty old film can. Sixteen millimeter. He took out the reel and began threading it through the sixteen-millimeter projector.

"What is this film? What is it?" I said, but he wouldn't answer me.

## Kathy Petro

The Ava Gardner movie was almost over, the music was coming up and everything, when suddenly the picture changed again, getting a lot smaller.

"Oh, no, not again," Gray said.

And then it came into focus and I couldn't believe it. For a long time I couldn't even move. I just couldn't accept what I was seeing.

It was a film of Jeff Stuben and me lying on the sun porch at my parents' house in Newport Beach. I saw, as Jeff began to kiss me, that it was the afternoon we'd made love there back in 1967! And I realized that *Shark* must have shot the film with a high-power lens from Woody's house down the block. Which meant that somehow *Shark,* right now, was . . . My mind couldn't handle it.

"What's this?" Gray was saying. "My God, is that *you?*"

Suddenly a voice boomed out over the speakers, which I recognized instantly as Shark's voice. "Kathy," he said in this deep, creepy voice. "This is all I've ever had of you. Just these few moments of vicarious bliss. How many times I've masturbated to this movie, Kathy, projecting myself into this scene, imagining it was me you were loving like this. Oh, Kathy, this is truly the end."

"What's going on, what's going on?" Gray said, and he was really panicked, too.

Shark just kept saying all these weird creepy things. And then on the screen Jeff climbed on top of me, and I covered my ears and started screaming, "Stop it, stop it, stop it, stop it!"

## Maya Dietrichson

"What are you doing?" I said to Shark as he spoke into the microphone. "Who are you talking to? Who is *Kathy?* What is this film?"

Then I realized that the girl in the film was a very young Kathy Petro getting it on with a bulky jock. But I still didn't understand.

## Todd Jarrett

It was crazy. People were going nuts again, and then Kathy Petro started screaming, and the next thing I knew her boyfriend was pulling her into the lobby. And she kind of hurtled into me, still screaming, as he charged up the stairs to the projection booth.

## Fred Thal

I ran up right behind Kathy Petro's boyfriend, reaching the projection booth a second after he did. It was empty, the film running out into a pile on the floor.

"Where is he?" her boyfriend said. "Where is Shark Trager?"

I saw that the fire door was open. We reached it in time to see Shark and Maya pulling out of the parking lot below in that lumbering death machine.

Kathy Petro was still screaming hysterically down in the lobby as her boyfriend tore the film of her from the projector and ripped it to shreds.

## Maya Dietrichson

We stopped at Sav-On to pick up a new syringe on the prescription I had, and then hit each other up with cocaine and Dilaudid as we sat in the car with the engine running. Then I got out and popped the hood and placed the final wire on the bomb which was taped to the manifold.

"We're ready," I said, and unzipped Shark's pants as we got on the San Diego Freeway.

"The Sepulveda Pass," I said. "We can gain great speed there, going down the grade into the Valley."

So we roared up the freeway, a Spione cassette on the deck, so I could die listening to my own coldly beautiful voice.

As we hurtled past Sunset I straddled Shark, my back against the steering wheel.

"Move the seat back," I said. "The wheel is gouging my kidneys."

He tried but the seat was stuck.

The Sepulveda Pass was coming up fast. "It's time," I said. "Enter me."

But his tool wasn't hard.

"Oh Christ, not now," I said. "What a time you've picked to be impotent."

"I can't help it," he said. "I feel rotten."

"I don't believe this," I said. "We are blistering right into the penultimate moment of existential will and you are going to start whimpering like some kind of pantywaist. I don't want to hear it."

"I don't know why I did what I did back there," he said, ignoring my anger. "I only succeeded in injuring Kathy yet again. Why, why do I always injure her, when all I've ever really wanted to do was love her?"

"Who cares?" I said. "Goddamn you anyway, you'd better start fucking me and you'd better start soon. Look, we're already pushing seventy."

But he still couldn't get it up. I tried yanking him, that sometimes worked, but not this time. We were soaring down the Sepulveda grade, the wheels shimmying violently, which excited me terribly.

"Why do people hurt each other?" Shark said. "What is love, anyway? Is all romantic love really just obsession? Is there another kind of love that's more genuine, but which by its very nature precludes sex? Is there a love that's genuine that *includes* sex and yet is not obsessional? If so, it's a kind of love I've never known."

"Look, you get that cock up right now or I'm going to scratch your face off," I said. Glancing over my shoulder I saw that the speedometer was at seventy-nine!

"I can't do this," he said.

"You asshole!" I yelled. "You coward, you yellow-bellied killjoy, you've ruined it now. We're going to die and we're not even fucking!"

But I could feel that we were slowing and heard the squeak of the brakes.

"You make me sick," I said, and climbed off of him and lit a cigarette.

"I'm sorry, Maya," he said. "Maybe I had to come this close to death to see how much more there is still to know and do and feel in this life."

"Oh, shut up," I said. "Just shut up and take me home."


## Billy Freeze

I was talking with some friends in front of the Charleton Arms when Shark and Maya pulled up in the Chrysler. It was a warm summer night and there were lots of people out and everybody turned to look as that noisy piece of shit lumbered up Windward Avenue. Shark pulled over but kept the engine running and Maya got out. Then Shark jumped out and went after her, grabbing her arm as she tried to cross the street. She started yelling, "Fuck you, go to hell." And he said, "Maya, goddamn it, disarm the fucking bomb." And she said, "Do it yourself. You're so smart, you can figure it out."

He tried to pull her back to the car, but she scratched his face and broke free. Then he chased her into the Charleton Arms.

I went in after them and saw them fighting, just scratching and whacking the shit out of each other on the stairs, when suddenly there was this horrendous blast out in the street.

They stopped fighting, and we all went to see what it was. The Chrysler was engulfed in flames and you could see the burning silhouette of a man at the wheel.

## Maya Dietrichson

Some asshole tried to steal the car and the bomb short-circuited. It took the cops a while to find out who he was, his wallet was burned beyond recognition. At one point they thought he might be a young husband whose wife had gone into labor in the next block. His car was in the shop and he'd run out, desperately in search of a car with which to rush his wife to the hospital. Or so the woman believed. In reality he had simply chosen that moment to desert her.

The dead man was finally identified as a sociopathic criminal who had been raping old ladies in the Venice area for months. Shark convinced the police the bomb must have already been in the car when we bought it that afternoon, and the used car dealer caught hell before the investigation eventually petered out.

I saw Shark in the flesh for the last time as we stepped from the police station that morning at dawn. By then I had cooled off, and wished to resume our relationship, but he left me standing there in the rain-slick parking lot.

Perhaps a week later I spoke to him on the phone. "You're playing difficult," I said. "Giving me a dose of my own medicine. You want me to beg for it, don't you?"

"I don't want you to do anything, Maya," he told me. "It's over."

"I've heard that before," I replied. "You're a Sunday school boy now, but that won't last. The next time that big tool of yours gets good and hard, you'll think about Maya. Face it, you're addicted to me. You'll be coming back for more. It's just a matter of time."

He hung up on me.

Many months would pass before I quit thinking whenever the phone rang that it might be him.

## Fred Thal

Shark apologized for what had happened in a very sober, genuine way, explaining in an almost jaunty manner what it was all about. "This gal I've got a thing for," was how he described his sad fixation on Kathy Petro.

Though I felt for him I just couldn't trust him anymore. I had no choice but to send him on his way.

## Todd Jarrett

"I guess you can do what you want with my stuff," Shark said, indicating the junk in the loft. "I don't have any place to put it."

"You don't have a place to stay yet?" I said, feeling a little guilty for not offering to let him sleep on my sofa. But my girlfriend had just moved in. And I was still quite disturbed by what he'd done.

"No, but it's summer," he said. "And this is Southern California. There are a lot worse things than sleeping on the beach."

# 20/ **Beached**
(1983)

## Letter from Shark Trager to
## Kathy Petro, June 23, 1983

Dear Kathy:

I hope it doesn't frighten you that I've memorized your
address. Don't worry, I won't bother you—not now or
ever again. This letter will be the last you ever hear of
me, and I just want you to know finally and clearly how
truly sorry I am for everything.

I have no excuse for what I did at the Ray-Mar except
that I was truly insane that night, my mind utterly distorted with opium and cocaine. I was involved in a sick
relationship then, which I knew in my heart was sick, and
I think what I did was a cry for help, an attempt to reach
out to the goodness I have always associated with you,
Kathy, though I see now that my method was wrong and
could only have caused you great pain.

I am glad Gray destroyed that old film—I should have

done it myself years ago. Needless to say, I should never have filmed you with Jeff Stuben like that in the first place. Of course, you know how in love with you I was then, I suppose I just couldn't help myself.

But love is the wrong word, I see that now. I was obsessed with you, Kathy. You were always on my mind. I was like a jealous lover who had never even been your lover. God, how many times I've wished I'd never kissed you.

I'm just sorry for everything. I see now how unforgivably selfish I was. How I never really thought of your feelings, what you wanted or didn't want. I was in love with my dream of you, with my fantasies of what we might have been like together, all of which had nothing to do with the real you. I'm so sorry for the trouble I've caused. If I could go back to 1965 I would cut off my own hands for what I did to you with that camera then.

Films are like dreams, it's been said. And I've always thought that dreams are a place for us to live out the things we can't, or dare not, do in real life. In that light I ask your forgiveness for all the instances in my films in which I have vented my frustrated longings for you. Remember *Tropics* if you remember any of my films at all—and if you choose not to, I will understand. *Tropics* was my dream of what might have been.

It's so easy for me to recall that movie now, it's easy for me to get in that mood. I'm on the beach, Kathy, your and my beloved beach, under a faded lifeguard station with a jug of Bali Hai. Sweet tropical wine, sweet tropical sunset. As always when I stare far out to sea I imagine the sputter of Earhart's Electra and see that silver plane going down against the sun.

I know there is an island where there is sweet music, where lovers eat guavas by the light of the moon. For three ninety-five plus tax I can go there, my love, and drown in my dream of your kisses for the rest of my life.

My dream. Perhaps this is what I've always really wanted. To live and die in my dream of you.

But you are a creature of reality. Gray seems like a super guy. Are you happy at last? I hope so, I really do. You deserve it, kid.

The sun's below the water now, it's time for me to go. Bless you, my darling love. Go on ahead with your everyday life, and forget this craven dreamer who once tried to love you but didn't quite know how. Be free and cheerful for the world is not necessarily a bad place. Love Gray, as I know you do, for he is one lucky fella to have landed a gal like you.

Respectfully yours,
Shark

## Kathy Petro

I knew the letter was from Shark before I even opened it. My name and address were scrawled on this dirty envelope with no return address but it had a Venice postmark. I got very upset when I read it because I was just starting to get over what had happened at the Ray-Mar, and the letter just brought it all back.

Then I heard Gray coming in the door and hid the letter before he saw it. He'd been so mad at Shark he couldn't see straight, and I just didn't want to get him going again. Gray hugged me and I thought: Yes, it's true, I am happy now, and the past is finally behind me.

But I couldn't get to sleep that night, not even after Gray and I had made slow, beautiful love for hours. I got up and took a few more pain killers for my shoulder, which always seemed to act up whenever I thought about Shark. The codeine wasn't strong enough so I had borrowed one of Gray's triplicate prescription pads, which—not wanting to bother him about every ache and pain—I simply filled out with his name and got myself the somewhat stronger analgesics, Dilaulid and Percodan. I tossed back two of each with a glass of Wild Turkey, and smoked a cigarette in the dark living room, staring out the window at the full moon, wondering how Shark had discovered my address.

## "Wet Brain"

Shark liked that Bali Hai, but the dye in it made me sick. I stuck to short dogs. At first he had money and he loaned me some. He had some gal's bank card and knew her code. We'd go to Wells Fargo and get a hundred dollars. Then one night the machine took the card.

We slept in the Venice pavilion till the night Scooter got stabbed. Then we moved up the beach to Rose Avenue where it was safer.

He said he used to make movies and I said yeah, I was Ava Gardner's boyfriend once in Puerto Vallarta, which was true. I spent the night with her, then I became a hippie, but the peyote split my mind into forty thousand separate worlds. I had to keep my thumb and finger taped together all the time, so the universe wouldn't fly apart.

## Woody Hazzard

I liked to surf Venice sometimes, and one Sunday morning I was going down to the water with my board when I almost stepped on this wino who was sleeping by the sewage drain wall. I hadn't even seen him at first underneath this cruddy blanket, and when I realized it was Shark I almost shit. He had a long dirty blond beard and was sunburnt the way the derelicts in Venice always are, and he had scabs or wine sores on his hands. He was snoring and right by his head was his empty half-gallon jug of Bali Hai.

I thought about waking him up but I didn't know what I'd say. I wasn't pissed off at him anymore but I guess seeing him like that just kind of freaked me out. So I started to split. Then I felt guilty so I went back and stuck two twenties in his pocket, and then I drove on up to Sunset and surfed there.

## Lupe Sepulveda

One Sunday afternoon I was roller-skating with my husband along the bike trail in Venice when I almost collided with Shark. I didn't recognize him at first, thinking only that a derelict had staggered into my path. But I stopped and looked back and could hardly believe it.

The sight of him really touched me. I'd been so angry when *Looking for Lupe* came out since the lead character was so clearly modeled on me, though needless to say I had never slept with a donkey. But seeing Shark now in this awful state I felt no more anger. I couldn't feel anything but pity—even

387

when he looked at me without recognizing me, and blaming me for the near collision, mumbled: *"Whore."*

Victor, my husband, skated back around. *"What* did he say to you?"

"Nothing," I said. "He's just a drunken bum, forget it."

So we went on. If Victor had known it was the man who had used me as a sex toy and then made *Looking for Lupe* I don't think he would have shared my compassion.


## Todd Jarrett

Shark became something of a fixture on the boardwalk, hanging out at the gazebo near Horizon where all the derelicts liked to gather. He seemed to have one buddy, the aptly named "Wet Brain," a lumbering schizophrenic who was even grungier than Shark. They seemed to fight a lot—that is, have verbal arguments. And Shark would respond to Wet Brain's delusional gibberish—"You are wrong, Karen Valentine is the *sister* not the *mother* of God!"—to the extent that I feared for his mind as well.

I gave him a few bucks once in a while, knowing full well that it would go for more wine, not the food he said he wanted it for. He would try to prolong the encounter, but it was really painful to see him like that, so I'd try and slip off as quickly as I could.

Then one afternoon I was coming out of an office on that chic first block of Market Street where I'd just had a screenplay ripped to shreds by an independent producer, when Shark called to me from the doorway where he was urinating on Speedway. I was in a foul, dejected mood, wondering if I wasn't wasting my time playing these stupid Hollywood games, and against my better judgement I told Shark what had just happened.

When I mentioned the producer's name, Shark said, "He's a turd. Let me read it. I'll tell you if it's any good or not."

And before I could stop him he took the script from my hand. He was obviously too drunk to read it at the moment. "Give me the weekend," he said. "We can have lunch and discuss it on Monday."

## "Wet Brain"

One night Shark read a typewritten message from God. He started bawling like a baby.

## Todd Jarrett

I approached Shark out by the sewage drain wall that Monday with some sandwiches for lunch—he was too grungy to take into any restaurant—but what I really wanted was just to get my screenplay back. I'd realized later it was my only clean copy, so my heart sank when I saw it beside him, torn and dog-eared and stained with Bali Hai. It was ten in the morning and he was already ripped.

"It was mag-nificent!" he said, and there were tears in his eyes. "Man, do you know this reminds me so much of the first film I ever made! Back when I was twelve years old! Before sex! *Innocent!* My very first movie with an old Bell & Howell."

"That's great," I said.

"Your story *moved* me, man!" he said, a sob in his throat. "It really fuckin' *got* to me."

Obviously it had, but in the wrong way. The script was essentially a dark and biting satire, a vicious parody of so-called heart-warming films, a merciless explication of the unctuous rot behind the sickly sweet facade of sentimental manipulators like Capra and Spielberg. All of which was lost on Shark.

"That sweet little girl," he said of the deliberately cloying little cretin known as Debbi in the script. "Not since Dorothy in *The Wizard of Oz* . . ." A tear rolled down his cheek.

He was right about the reference though. That was definitely one of the stale fantasies I meant to trash.

"Shark, can I have the script back now?" I said.

He began thumbing through the pages. "Saucers!" he cried. "Real honest-to-God flying saucers! None of that lighting fixture shit like *Close Encounters.*"

I tried to take the script from him, but he obviously held on to it. "And my God, the ending! All the missiles launched. The Reds and us both shitting! Then, at the very last moment, *Jesus* stops 'em midair! My God, my God!"

"It's a nice moment, isn't it?" I said. It was meant to be absurd, crypto-religious kitsch. "Can I please have the script?"

"I want to option it," he said.

I wanted to laugh but couldn't. It was too sad.

"It's being considered elsewhere," I said, which wasn't true. It *had* been everywhere, but in Hollywood true originality invariably terrifies people.

"Here." Shark dug out a quarter and put it in my hand. "This is all I've got right now, man. But I'll let you have it for a six-month option against a purchase price of two hundred thousand. We gotta shake on it now. I don't want you trying to fuck me later if we land Sean Penn for the lead."

"It's tempting," I said. I'd given options for less. "But I think I should talk to my agent first." At the time I didn't even have an agent.

"Okay, I can dig that," he said. "But Todd, I have a feeling about this. I saw the saucers in my dreams last night, more clearly than I've seen anything in years. I *know* that this movie can save both our lives."

"I'm sure you're right." I finally got the script away from him. "Keep me posted," I said, and started back across the sand. But I was really thinking: I'm going to have to make sure I don't run into him again.

## Sue Schlockmann

One afternoon in the fall of 1983, Elliot and I met Neal Ridges and Carol Van Der Hof for lunch at 9 Ocean Front, a rather expensive but good new restaurant on the boardwalk in Venice. It was in one of the old arched buildings used so famously in *Touch of Evil*, though it had been extensively renovated, very clean and spare inside, the space between the arches filled in with treated plate glass. From the dining room you had an unobstructed view of the colorful boardwalk and the beach and sea beyond. But on the boardwalk side the glass was blue and opaque, shielding the chic and frequently famous diners from the stray invasive eye.

We were there to discuss a script Carol had written which Neal wanted to direct, a semi-autobiographical story of a club-footed New York socialite who marries a charming but abusive cad who leads her into drug addiction before she finally breaks free of him and discovers genuine love with a sensitive younger man. I was quite high on the concept, and we were all sparking to one another, so carried away we hadn't even ordered yet, when Carol glanced out the window and said, "I feel ill."

## Neal Ridges

It was Shark, arguing with another drunk on the boardwalk directly opposite the window. Of course, he couldn't see us because of the treated glass, and we couldn't really hear him. But it was definitely Shark and he looked really bad—deeply tanned, but emaciated in a creepy checked sportcoat and filthy cords.

"Just ignore him," Sue said. "He's where he wants to be."

## Elliot Bernstein

We tried to continue talking, but it was impossible to forget that Shark was there. He wasn't moving either. He and this other guy were really getting into it, a protracted, animated argument. Sue would say to Carol, "Elliot and I were both extremely impressed by your mastery of dialogue. Weren't we, Elliot?"

"Right, great dialogue," I'd say. But I was spacing out. In spite of everything Shark had done, I couldn't help thinking: That guy out there was once my best friend.

## Carol Van Der Hof

I somehow thought that I'd forgiven Shark until that afternoon. Pity is so much easier at a distance. Actually seeing him in the flesh I felt rage, disgust and panic. "Let's go!" I wanted to say. "It was a mistake to come here. Why did we choose this restaurant, knowing full well this is his stomping ground now?"

## Neal Ridges

Carol was getting jumpy, her eyes darting to Shark. Then she closed her eyes and said, "Oh Christ, he's coming over."

Well, sure enough he was reeling right up to the window.

"Carol, it's all right. He can't see in. The glass is treated," I said.

It was hard to believe that though, since to us it was just like window glass. And then Shark unzipped his fly.


## Elliot Bernstein

I really don't think he knew there were people inside watching him. It was just a sheet of mirrored glass back in an alcove to him.

People gasped as he fished out his tool and proceeded to take a leisurely piss against the glass right next to our table. He was closest to Sue, who glanced at his member and feigned nonchalance. "I wasn't impressed then," she said, "I'm not impressed now."

Carol however was livid and jumped up, calling for someone to make Shark stop. The French maître d' pounded on the glass, which only caused Shark to scowl in puzzlement. The maître d' made a helpless gesture to Carol. "I'm sorry. These bums, they think this alcove is a pissoir."

Neal was covering his brow and trying not to laugh. I thought it was wrenchingly sad.


## Neal Ridges

I thought it was both funny and sad at the same time. But I was glad when Shark finally shook off, stuffed his dick back in his pants and moved on. We were trying to calm Carol down when she said, "Here he comes again."


## Carol Van Der Hof

He'd begun talking with a group of black men he appeared to know. A very rough-looking bunch, one of whom had what I believe is called a boom box. Suddenly, Shark began adjusting the knobs and we heard a loud throbbing burst of Roxy Music's "The Thrill of It All."

## Elliot Bernstein

Shark took the boom box from the black guy and began dancing around with it, this awful drunken staggering dance to Roxy Music's "The Thrill of It All." He was in a kind of mesmerized trance, and refused to return the boom box. So the black guys started pushing him around, and finally got the radio back. Then he must have said something inflammatory, because the next thing we knew the black guys were attacking him, just beating him mercilessly as he stumbled back into the alcove by our table.

## Neal Ridges

These guys were just pounding the shit out of Shark, and Elliot and I jumped up at the same time.

"Elliot!" Sue said, but he ignored her.

Elliot and I raced out to the boardwalk.

## Elliot Bernstein

"That's enough," I yelled as Neal and I reached the scene. It could have been very bad for us, there were maybe six or seven of these black guys, but they were pretty much finished with Shark, their anger spent by the time we got there. There was some grumbling and then they moved on.

Neal lifted Shark's head from the pavement where he'd fallen in his own urine.

## Neal Ridges

His face was a mess. He could only open one eye but he recognized me. "Neal?" he said. "Is that really you, man?"

"It's all right, Shark. It's all right now," I said, and felt tears in my eyes. "We'll take care of you now."

I looked up at Elliot and there were tears in his eyes too.

## Elliot Bernstein

We helped Shark into the back seat of Sue's Mercedes and she bitched that he was going to get his blood and smell on the leather upholstery. He did smell pretty awful. Carol limped off in a huff because we were helping Shark, and she tore out of the lot in that red fifties' MG he had given her.

# 21 / **Flash Flood**
## (1983)

### Bill Kemmer

In the fall of 1983, at the age of thirty-two, I ascended to the presidency of Mastodon Pictures, thereby becoming one of the three or four most powerful executives in Hollywood. In the years following Ben Klieg's death the struggle for control of the company had been fierce, but through sheer tenacity and will I had at last emerged victorious.

But at what a cost. For my brutal workaholism had been fueled by increasingly horrendous amounts of cocaine, and now that I had achieved the ultimate success . . . I was coming apart. Fearfully—and not being able to distinguish real from false fear was a crucial problem—I took a three-week medical leave, supposedly to undergo a hemorrhoid operation. In fact I admitted myself to the Kolon Clinic in Palm Springs.

## Neal Ridges

The Kolon Clinic was considered *the* substance abuse treatment center of choice at the time. This was several years before the beating death scandal which forced its closure, and to those in the know Ernst Kolon was most definitely *the* recovery guru of the hour. Of course, the Betty Ford Center was still getting all the publicity, which was part of what made the Kolon Clinic so attractive to the ultra-rich and ultra-famous and ultra-strung-out. If you really wanted to kick in total privacy the Kolon Clinic was the only place to go.

From the Venice boardwalk, we took Shark to UCLA Emergency where his superficial lacerations were treated. By then he was on the verge of DTs, and when the doctors told us the UCLA detox unit was full, the Kolon Clinic immediately came to mind. At five thousand a day it wasn't cheap, but Elliot and I both felt we owed it to Shark. We split the expense, which we could easily afford—thanks to the breaks Shark had once given us.

He was choppered from UCLA to Burbank airport and flown to the desert. I don't think he understood where he was going, though we tried to explain. He was strapped to a stretcher and babbling incoherently as we saw him off on the UCLA roof.

## Bill Kemmer

I was in the lodge chatting with Narges Pahlavi-Bardahl when the chopper set down. We watched through the plate glass windows as they unloaded the patient, an astonishingly grungy, sunburnt wino type—a complete aberration at the Kolon Clinic. Though most of us you could say were "dying inside," on the face of it we still looked pretty good. I watched in disgust as they brought the man up on the stretcher, telling myself he had to be *somebody* or he wouldn't be here, mindful of what a mess Howard Hughes had become.

"My God, I don't believe it," I said to Narges when I finally recognized Shark. "I thought I heard he was dead."

## Ernst Kolon

Shark was a sickening mess at first. I put him in the detox unit for several days so he could go through the worst of the physical withdrawal. I knew who he was of course, and from his movies I knew what a sick guy he was—though I did like *Hail!*, which was good entertainment. It so happened they had been showing that movie on the plane when I flew in from Zurich in 1975 on my mission to save the élite of America from their own weakness of mind.

## Bill Kemmer

Ernst was this gruff, no-bullshit "tough love" kind of guy, about sixty then but built like a goddamn Panzer tank—an accurate allusion since he'd been a medic with the Africa Korps. He claimed not to have been a Nazi per se, just a "male Wehrmacht nurse," and of course Rommel and the whole North African thing were sort of the "pure" part of World War II, weren't they? Ernst had albino-white hair, a deep leathery tan, and wore khaki shorts and shirt that only lacked the eagle-and-swastika insignia.

But the guy knew how to deal with addictive personalities. There was just no way you could con him; he knew every game. He'd been there himself, having been a benzedrine addict in North Africa, an alcoholic in post-war Munich and a heroin addict in West Berlin. And he had no respect for money or fame or inflated star egos. No matter who you thought you were, he treated you like shit.

## Ernst Kolon

The first night in detox Shark tried to get pills, a Valium or something to ease his withdrawal. "Shut up, you stupid piece of garbage!" I shouted in his face. "Suffer, you goddamn weakling! I have no sympathy for you, you make me sick. Suffer and pay for all the cowardly escaping you've bought with the bottle. And just maybe if you're lucky you will hurt for the last time."

So he was cussing me out as the boys strapped him down to the bed. He was naked and I could see he was in bad shape. Thin from not eating, and his muscles atrophied. He would be oozing the poisons for days, but he'd ooze them much quicker if he began working out. So I sent in Drake.

I couldn't fuckin' believe it when I saw Shark's name on the chart. Christ, it had been fifteen years. I told Ernst that Shark and I had a history and told him what it was—Ernst knew all about my past—and he said, "Good. He can work out his repressed hatred for you."

So I went into Shark's room and said, "All right, get that skinny wino ass in gear. I'm gonna make a man out of you yet."

And Shark almost shit when he recognized me. "Drake? Is that really you? Jesus Christ."

I thought he might still be mad, but he wasn't at all. He broke into a grin and then we hugged with me squeezing the shit out of him. "Christ, you're as thin as a delicate little girl," I said. "We gotta put some meat on you."

He couldn't get over seeing me again. "I thought you'd be in prison by now," he said, "considering all the raping you used to do."

"I did six years in Soledad," I told him, "from '69 to '75. But it wasn't till after I got out that I paid the ultimate price. See, while I was in the joint I ran an ad and started up a pen-pal relationship with a girl named Judy who lived in Tennessee. She helped me work through my anger at women—which went back to my mother who'd been alternately abusive and smothering—and predictably enough as Judy and I wrote back and forth over the years we fell deeply in love. When I got my release date she agreed to come and get me. I'd never seen her in the flesh but for five long years I'd jacked off to her beautiful photo. Then the big day came and she was nowhere to be seen. Then suddenly this stumpy broad came up and tried to hug me and I almost crapped. It was Judy all right—see, I'd received a number of replies from different lonely women and somehow mixed up the photos. I was so upset, and she was too, that on the highway back to L.A. she crashed the car. She died in my arms, and I've been kicking myself ever since. So what if she was stumpy—inside she was the girl I loved."

As always I fought back tears at that point.

"That's a sad story, Drake," Shark said. "But that was eight years ago. Why do I sense that you're still single?"

"Because I am," I told him. "I turned to weights with a vengeance after that, and now it's too late." I explained how the steroids had atrophied my nuts and dick. "It's probably for the best," I told him. "Sex was a hassle anyway. Now all my energy is self-contained right here in the world's bitchinest bod." I pounded on one of my chrome-hard pecs. I had a body by then that made Schwartzenegger look like a slob.

We talked some more and then Shark said, "Drake, listen, I feel like shit. How about rustling me up a drink, for old times' sake?"

I slapped him hard across the face—the approved Kolon response to that kind of shit. "Get up, you sniveling pussy!" I yelled. "You don't know it yet, but you've had your last goddamn drink ever. Put on your jock and your workout shorts. We're going on a grueling desert hike."

## Bill Kemmer

I was in the lodge, with Narges again, and a number of other patients—actors, singers, a jet set princess and a literary lion or two, who for obvious reasons I don't feel I should name— when we saw Drake Brewster leading Shark in a jog across the desert. Shark was sweating profusely—it was maybe a hundred degrees that day, though we were protected by the air-conditioning. And Narges was already beginning to shift her attention to Shark, which was a great relief to me. As soon as she'd learned I was president of Mastodon she'd been unshakable. A distant relative of the Shah who'd escaped Iran in '79 to be near her ninety million in American assets, she was indeed beautiful, with long black hair, almond eyes, olive skin and a svelte little body that just didn't quit. Under different circumstances I might have enjoyed a casual sexual relationship with her, but she had been admitted to the Kolon Clinic against her will and clearly had no desire to achieve a state of permanent freedom from drugs. On the contrary, she was defiant and only biding her time. "I can't wait to base again," she said repeatedly. "Bill, you must come to my palace in Rancho Mirage once we are free of this concentration camp. We can have a big sex and drug blow-out to celebrate."

Well, my life and career were at stake, so when she expressed curiosity about Shark I deliberately colored the truth just to get her off my back. She was impressed by his credits, especially *Mondo Jet Set*. "He made that movie? How I adored that! I associate that film with the last great days in Teheran!"

To explain Shark's derelict state upon admission I used the Howard Hughes model. "He's eccentric."

"Yes," she said. "I can sympathize with that. A man who cares nothing for outward appearances, who sees the stupidity of fashionplate *Gentleman's Quarterly* clothes. I too have come to see the emptiness of mere material wealth."

She was especially impressed watching Shark jog across the desert, for by then he had received a haircut and had shaved off his ratty beard. "My God, he is handsome," Narges said. "I sensed that he would be." Then she confessed, "How I would like to sit upon that handsome face and free-base at the same time."

Our attention was suddenly drawn to a British film star who was making a scene with Ernst across the room. "I've changed my mind," he was booming. "My father died at Tobruk. If I'd had any idea you fought with Rommel . . . Open the door. I demand that you let me leave."

"I don't care if your mother was fried in a tank at El Alamein!" Ernst yelled in the actor's face. "It would only be a pretext. Your addiction is like a demon that wants you to chicken out. That's why you're not going anywhere." He slapped the British star hard across the face. "Sit down and shut up, you whimpering limey sniveler!"

No one could leave, that was part of the admission policy. Once you came in you were there for three weeks unless you simply died.

I was comforting the British actor, who was extremely chagrined, when I glanced out the window and saw a new patient being led through the courtyard back toward the detox unit. I recognized the woman with a jolt.

## Kathy Petro

Finally one day this pharmacist called Gray and said, "There's a woman in here trying to get three hundred Percodan with an obviously forged prescription." And I was still waiting when Gray came into the drug store and I just broke down and started sobbing. "It's all right, Kathy," he said. "It's not your fault. You're not a bad person. You're just an addict, that's all." So he sent me to the Kolon Clinic, which was expensive, but by

400

then I had my settlement from Brian and we'd moved into this big house on Stone Canyon and everything.

I was having cold sweats by the time Gray dropped me off, and the attendants were leading me to the detox unit when I saw these two men jogging toward me. One was real muscle-bound like Arnold Schwartzenegger or somebody and the other one was skinny and drenched with sweat. I went into a kind of shock I guess when I realized the skinny man was Shark.

He was winded and everything but managed to say, "Hello, Kathy."

This horrible panic just welled up inside me and I ran for the gate. I got there but it was locked. I could still see Gray's new BMW going off up the desert road, and I called, but he was too far away to see or hear me. I started screaming and shaking the gate, and Ernst Kolon came out.

## Ernst Kolon

She was hysterical. "Let me out, let me out, I can't do this, I can't be here with that man." Then she told me she had a history with Shark that stretched back twenty years. I didn't catch all the details but it was clear she was angry.

"You have resentments towards him then?" I said.

"Resentments? *Resentments?*" she yelled. "Do you know what he's done to me? *Shark Trager has ruined my life!*"

"Then good," I told her. "You are lucky that he's here. You have a golden opportunity to break up a major chunk of rage."

She began pounding on my chest with her fists, so I slapped her across the face, then put her into detox.

## Drake Brewster

It was clear that seeing Kathy Petro had shocked the shit out of Shark. "What is it?" I said as I watched him take his shower. "She one of your ex-fucks?"

"You watch your goddamn mouth, Drake," he said, and I grinned. It was the first real spunk he'd showed.

"Oh, I see, it was serious then," I said.

Then he looked real sad. "It was never really anything.

Except in my mind.'' Then a minute later he said, ''Why does she have to be here now? Is it possible that after all the crap and madness . . . it really is meant to be?''

## Kathy Petro

Ernst came to see me in detox. They had me on some kind of mellowing drug 'cause if I'd just stopped everything cold turkey I would have gone into convulsions. So I had this real calm feeling, like a cow in a sunny field or something, and Ernst was really gentle this time and held my hand and everything.

''How would you like to be free forever of the need to hide your feelings with drugs?'' he said.

I said that sounded okay.

''How would you like to get even with Shark Trager once and for all?''

I said that sounded good too, but I didn't want to go to prison for murder. He said that wouldn't be necessary, and gave me a copy of his *43 Steps of Recovery,* and said I could do anything I wanted to Shark, starting first thing tomorrow.

## Bill Kemmer

Ernst had developed his own forty-three-step recovery program, which he characterized as an ''improved version'' of A.A.'s twelve steps, though in fact there was little more than a structural resemblance. Ernst was extremely eclectic, borrowing from a variety of New Age therapies, both au courant and passé, as well as from oldline German philosophy—the key word in his program was ''will'' in the Nietzschean sense. ''The forty-third step marks the *triumph* of the will,'' he would say, unaware I think of the allusion to the Leni Riefenstahl film.

The first fourteen steps, and the first week of the program, were devoted to getting in touch with and giving vent to our rage.

## Ernst Kolon

The addict is an angry person but too cowardly to show these feelings. So we have them make a list of everyone they've ever

402

hated, beginning with their parents, then we put them with the dolls.

## Bill Kemmer

The dolls were life-size and made of spongy rubber. They were predominantly flesh-colored, though he kept black ones in stock for the occasional black singer or comedian, and they could be dressed up a variety of ways as an aid to the imagination. The rage therapy took place in a large empty room with a padded floor, rather like a gymnastics room, with ropes hanging down so that if the patients desired it the dolls could be suspended from the ceiling. There was a choice of weapons for use on the dolls—clubs, knives, even a sledgehammer, though the machetes tended to be the most popular.

The rage therapy sessions were private, but one afternoon I arrived for my session as Shark was still in the midst of his. Ernst was facilitating as Shark clobbered a doll in a gas station uniform with the sledgehammer.

"Tell him!" Ernst was yelling. "Tell him what he did!"

"You killed my mother, you son of a bitch!" Shark screamed, as the sledgehammer broke the rubber head apart.

## Ernst Kolon

First I had Shark take it out on his parents: his father, a confused, lonely anal type with a homosexual panic complex, and his mother, a classic weakling who dressed him as a girl, then abandoned him. He destroyed both those dolls, which was good, you know. He really got it out of his system. The next time I brought in a new doll in a bikini and blonde wig and said, "You know who this is, don't you?"

At first he wouldn't act. "That wound is healed," he said. "I wrote Kathy a letter."

"Bullshit," I yelled at him. "What are you, a saint now?"

"Hardly," he said. "But I did all the damage to her. She has every right to be angry at me, but I have no right to be mad at her."

*"Rights?"* I shouted in his face. "The human psyche doesn't know about *rights*. You're furious with her, it's all too apparent. Look at you. You're trembling like a cowardly little

scaredy-cat. She teased you, didn't she? She promised you everything, the way women do, but didn't put out. Isn't that the truth of it?''

He tried to hide in confusion. So I pushed the doll at him, aping Kathy's voice: "Come on, Shark, don't you want it? Don't you want my blonde pussy? Well, *you can't have it*. I'm too good for you, Shark—''

At that he exploded and picked up the machete. If I hadn't jumped back quickly he might have hacked off my hand.

## Kathy Petro

I see now that Ernst deliberately kept Shark and me separated the first week. He put us in different discussion groups and made sure we were never in the lodge or the dining room at the same time, which was really smart, I guess. I still knew Shark was around though—in fact I thought of little else. I saw him a few times going out across the desert with Drake, and I just got madder and madder. Part of it was the withdrawal—my nerves were just raw. And what a convenient focus for all my irritability he was!

Still, I almost laughed when Ernst showed me this rubber doll wearing the exact same kind of workout shorts Shark was always wearing. "Normally, we start with the parents," Ernst said. "But in this case I think your hatred of Shark is by far more immediate and compelling.''

I almost couldn't do it at first, it seemed so stupid and everything. So I just picked up this billy club.

"What is the first bad thing he ever did to you?" Ernst said.

"He took advantage of me when I was on antihistamines at the drive-in," I said.

"Then pretend you are there now and respond to that," Ernst said.

So I said, "Don't do that, keep your hand out of there," and hit the doll on the arm with the club, but the club just bounced off.

"Oh Christ, he didn't even feel it!" Ernst yelled. "Come on, don't be such a nice girl! He's going to fingerbang you, then tell all the guys about it. He's going to spoil your reputation. Stop him!''

404

So I hit the doll really hard, and Ernst yelled, "Right!" So I did it again, and felt this big rush of adrenaline, and it felt really good.

"What's the next thing he did?" Ernst yelled.

"He made a peeping-Tom movie of me," I said, and just snapped. I just went crazy and the club wasn't good enough, so I grabbed the machete.

## Ernst Kolon

The boiling fury inside the girl! She literally hacked the Shark doll into small rubber pieces, one of the most thorough ventings I have ever facilitated. In the end she was spent and wrung out . . . and free. She had exorcised Shark Trager from her emotions forever. As is always the case once the mind is emptied of the anger, the actual person seems reduced and insignificant if encountered in the flesh.

To make sure this was the case, I deliberately placed Kathy and Shark together.

## Narges Pahlavi-Bardahl

We had all gone through our rage therapy, which I had enjoyed, repeatedly stabbing my brother for sending me to this place, and hacking up my late husband, Steve Bardahl the race car driver, who had died in a fiery crash, for taking his hot body from me.

At dinner I had begun sitting with Shark, for I had decided I wanted him. I knew by then he didn't have any money left, but that didn't matter, I had enough for both of us. I had a crush on him and really wanted him to fuck me, and didn't think that I could wait until we got out. Then one night we were locked in conversation at the table when Kathy Petro came in, and right away from the looks they exchanged I sensed competition.

## Bill Kemmer

I remember well the night Kathy first encountered Shark in the dining room. I saw a flicker of fear in her eyes, an instant when she wanted to take flight, but she held his gaze and nodded tentatively before taking her tray to another table.

Shark was with Narges, who by that point was glued to him, and she was clearly put out when Shark excused himself and approached Kathy's table.

## Kathy Petro

Shark came over and said, "Do you mind if I join you for a moment?"

I was unloading my tray and said, "I guess not. If it's just for a moment."

He sat down opposite me. His whole manner had this strangely peaceful and gentle quality to it, unlike anything I'd ever experienced from him before. It's hard to explain, but I really got the feeling that, as hard as it was to believe, he really didn't want anything from me anymore. Which is not to say I wasn't still guarded.

"You got my letter?" he said.

"Yeah, I got it."

"I was very drunk when I wrote it—"

"Yeah, I could tell."

"So some of what I said was pretty fucked-up. About living in a Bali Hai dream and all that—"

"So what's your point?" I said.

"Look, I don't want to lay anything on you—"

"Then don't."

"I just want you to know that I meant the apology part of the letter. That still goes. I'm sorry for everything, I really am. That's all."

And at that he got up and went back to Narges, whom I'd heard was a distant relative of the Shah of Iran or something.

## Drake Brewster

I whipped Shark into shape, got him back on the free weights till he was sweatin' like a pig. One day afterwards he was sore as hell, so I said, "Shower off, then stretch out in here. I give rubdowns now too."

I was giving him one of my powerhouse massages, breaking up the tense knots in his back, when I said, "Boy, I see you still got lots of hair on your butt. Had all mine taken off a few years back. Electrolysis. Too much of a bitch, trying to shave your own butt."

"Yeah?" Shark said. "Well, do me a favor, Drake, and just keep your eyes off mine."

When he said that it brought back what had happened that day in Santa Barbara when I'd tried to nail that hippie gal he married eventually, then almost cornholed him. Thinking about it made me feel bad.

"Look, Shark," I said. "I know we've avoided talking about this, and I don't want to open old wounds. But I am sorry for what happened back in '68."

"I know, Drake," he said, and sat up. "You couldn't help how you were back then, I see that now. I guess I wasn't the best roommate in the world. And for that I'm sorry too."

We hugged, even though he was naked, but there was nothing funny about it.

Forgiveness was the happening thing then, I guess, since that was the big theme of Week Two.


## Bill Kemmer

It was one of the apparent inconsistencies of Ernst's program that Week Two was devoted to forgiving the very people we had vented our rage on in Week One. As a result, I found myself apologizing to Shark—whose surrogate rubber doll I had bludgeoned mercilessly—though I must say I was never entirely convinced I had done anything to him that required a plea of forgiveness.


## Narges Pahlavi-Bardahl

I was sunning by the pool with Shark when Bill Kemmer came up and said, "You know, Shark, I'm really sorry about the way I handled *Scar*. I hope there are no hard feelings."

Shark got up and the two of them hugged and Shark said, "No, *I'm* sorry, Bill. I was out of control then. I'm sorry I put you through that difficult time."

After Bill left I said, "This is good, Shark. Now maybe he will make our film."

## Todd Jarrett

Shark called me at the Ray-Mar Theater one night and asked if my script was still available. It was—I'd gotten nowhere with it—but I said, "Well, Spielberg's reading it this weekend," which to me was an obvious joke.

"I'll pay you cash for it," Shark said. "Two hundred thousand. Is it a deal?"

I had a funny feeling. I hadn't seen him since the pathetic option discussion on the beach several months before, and had no reason to believe anything had changed. But he didn't sound drunk. "Where are you?" I said.

And he told me he was at the Kolon Clinic in Palm Springs, putting together a deal with Bill Kemmer.

## Bill Kemmer

We were supposed to be incommunicado but somehow Shark got the script smuggled in. He slipped it to me one night when the attendants weren't looking, after having given me a riveting pitch.

Reading the script in bed I saw immediately how grossly he'd misinterpreted it. Far from being a "cathartic tale of spiritual rebirth," it was a vicious, cynical, sacrilegious parody that no one in their right mind would produce.

Narges had apparently missed the satire too—perhaps due to the language problem—for she shared Shark's enthusiastic belief in its potential as another *E.T.*

## Narges Pahlavi-Bardahl

*Blue Light* really swept my heart up. It had everything: flying saucers, children, a nuclear war, even Jesus Christ! How could it not be a very huge blockbuster! It was so beautiful, like a vision you would see while basing. You know, when a drug high becomes almost religious? It was like that.

I knew also it was a metaphor for our sudden love. I knew I was in love with Shark the first night we had sex in his cabin and it came to pass that I did sit upon his face and it was almost as good as basing. And I knew the love was mutual because he told me so.

408

## Bill Kemmer

I tried to let Shark and Narges down easy. I knew they'd begun a discreet affair, and suspected their enthusiasm for the script was woven heavily into the fabric of their new feelings for one another, as well as their recovery in general—and I certainly didn't want to unravel *that*.

"The script needs work," I told Shark.

"You won't take a chance on me, will you?" Shark said. "That's the truth of it, isn't it, Bill?"

"It might be tough," I confessed. "Jean Klieg still carries weight with the board. I may have forgiven you, Shark. But she hasn't."

"Then let's end the conversation here," Shark said. "I don't want to take advantage of you, Bill. I shouldn't have even mentioned it, I see that now. Not in this setting."

"That's all right, Shark. I'm glad to see that you're thinking about doing something again." I nervously cleared my throat.

"I took quite a fall," he said. "I suppose I'm going to have to prove myself again. Win back people's trust."

"That's not going to be easy, Shark. Once bitten—"

He smiled, and squeezed my arm, though he wasn't looking at me. I followed his line of vision to the swimming pool in the distance where Kathy Petro was executing a dive.

## Kathy Petro

After Shark apologized in the dining room he really did just leave me alone. We were in different discussion groups and everything and whenever I did see him he was always with Narges and just completely ignored me. I mean completely. Like I'd glance at him on the sly to see if he was glancing at me on the sly, you know what I mean? You can tell if someone's pretending to ignore you. But he wasn't pretending, he really was.

And the weird thing was, in spite of everything I found myself resenting it. Thinking, you know, what's wrong with me? Have I changed, have I gotten old? I was only thirty-three and my body looked twenty-six, though I did have these laugh lines. Was that it? Was I too old?

It kind of pissed me off in a way, if that was it. Like he's all obsessed with me for twenty years, then suddenly I'm too old? He was not exactly some twenty-year-old blond surfer himself.

I don't know, it just really began to get to me, this number he was doing with Narges. Lovey-dovey by the pool and all that. She was pretty for an Arab, but it was bullshit, she wasn't his type. I was his type. I decided he was deliberately trying to play with my mind and thought, you know: Two can play that game.

So I thought, maybe I'll come onto *Bill,* that will really frost him. We'll see if I start rubbing my bare legs up against Bill's by the pool if Shark can ignore *that*—when suddenly I thought: What am I thinking, am I crazy? I love *Gray!* Gray is the only man who's ever treated me like a real human being. Am I ready to throw that away just to play some weird mind game with Shark?


## Ernst Kolon

Kathy came to me and said she was still having some problems in her own mind about Shark. I found it hard to believe she was still angry at him, but she said it wasn't anger exactly.

"Love and hate are very close," I told her.

And she said, "Look, I don't want to hear that."

"Why don't you start going for long walks by yourself in the desert?" I said. "In the evening when it's cool. You can walk off this residue of negative emotion."


## Narges Pahlavi-Bardahl

One evening Shark and I were leaving a Thirty-third-Step discussion group meeting in the lodge when we paused to hug and watch the orange sunset and discuss the coming film.

"I don't think you should assume all the risk," Shark said to me. "We'll set up a limited partnership—"

"No, really, why bother?" I told him. "I want to be your patron. Twenty million to me, Shark—it's not that big a deal."

"It could be more like thirty, Narges."

"Then kiss me," I said.

He did but I saw that his eyes were looking off beyond me. So I turned and saw Kathy Petro walking down into the dry gulch that ran like a path through the desert toward the distant purple mountains. A breeze blew her blonde hair.

"I used to think she was really something back when she was young," I told Shark. "I was in the French *Vogue* once, and you know what they said of me? They said I was the Kathy Petro of Iran."

"There's really no resemblance," Shark said with a sudden coldness that startled me. And then, as if heavily distracted, he simply walked away.

## Bill Kemmer

We had a "free period" that night after dinner, and Shark and Narges appeared to be having a tiff, so Shark and I played a game of chess in the lodge. Around eight it began to rain, one of those sudden and ferocious desert storms. I got up once to get another Perrier and heard a flash flood bulletin on the TV in the next room. I mentioned it to Shark as I sat down again. "I hope we're safe here."

"Yeah, I think we are," he said. "It's just the dry riverbeds and gulches where the shit really hits the fan."

A minute later Ernst came into the room and asked if anyone had seen Kathy. She wasn't in her room and had missed a therapy session at six.

"We saw her around five, didn't we, Shark?" Narges said, leaning in the door.

Shark looked very pale. Without saying a word he dashed out into the rain.

## Drake Brewster

Shark told me later he almost shit when he reached the gulch because it was like a fucking rapids. He was really afraid Kathy had been caught in the flash flood and washed away and drowned. But he ran on down the edge of the gulch anyway, the rain thundering down as he called her name.

He went on and on for a mile or more, getting more and more freaked out, like certain she was done for, but still calling her name. He said he was so drenched he couldn't even tell if he was crying. And it was like totally dark everywhere, just this rain coming down, there was nothing but desert and then suddenly he saw this shape up ahead, a big square in the sky,

411

which he realized a second later was a drive-in movie screen. It was this old shut-down drive-in, completely dark and abandoned, and it really bummed him out for some reason, and he cried out at the top of his lungs like a wounded animal, "Kathy!" like totally certain she was dead.

Then he heard her through the rain, calling back, "Over here!"

So he slogged up through the sand to the drive-in where the whole parking lot was like this sea from all the rain. But right in the middle of it, there was this one old wreck of a car, an old Chevy, and that was where Kathy had taken shelter from the storm.

## Kathy Petro

I was sopping wet by the time I reached this old car and the rain was coming down so hard I couldn't even tell which way the clinic was. So I just climbed in the car, even though the upholstery was all torn up and everything and for all I knew there were rattlesnakes inside. But there was no place else to take cover from the rain.

My blouse was soaked so I took it off and wrung it out. My bra was all wet so I took that off too. When I heard the voice call my name I didn't realize at first it was Shark. I just thought it was a rescue party so I responded. I tried to pull on my blouse but it got caught on the door handle and ripped. I was going: "Oh darn," when I saw Shark bounding through this huge puddle toward the car.

I thought about locking the car door before he reached it, but it would have been pointless since the window was broken. He climbed in on the driver's side.

He was winded and soaked, water running down his face as he looked at me, and I could see how worried about me he'd been. I just saw everything in his eyes, that he'd been looking for me and thought I might be dead, I just saw it all—he didn't have to say a thing. And he didn't.

I was holding my torn, wet blouse in front of my breasts, and I sensed what was going to happen. And I wanted it to happen. I couldn't, didn't want to, take my eyes off of his.

For a second I thought he was going to do something really crude, like yank my blouse away. But he didn't do that, he

412

didn't do that at all. He reached out, his hand trembling, and very gently touched my cheek. Then, very slowly, he leaned over to me and kissed me more tenderly than anyone ever has. Then he pulled back a little and I saw there were tears in his eyes. I touched his hand and he kissed me again. Then we kissed long and deep and I couldn't believe all the sweetness I felt. It was crazy, but suddenly I just knew how much he'd always loved me, that all the weird things he'd done were just expressions of stifled love. All he'd ever really wanted was to love me like this. And crazier still, I realized that as much as I'd hated him I'd always really loved him too, even though it wasn't what I thought love was supposed to be. Ernst was right. Love and hate are very close. You don't spend twenty years hating someone you're indifferent to.

His mouth moved to my breasts, and then one thing led to another. It was one of those big type of Chevrolets with a roomy front seat and we made love there with my head on the armrest. Once he was inside me it felt so right I thought: Why didn't we do this back when we were young? Not that thirty-three was that old, but we had wasted a lot of time. It was just so clear that our bodies were right for each other. Maybe *that* was what it was all about. Our bodies had just instantly wanted each other even though there were all these mental reasons why we shouldn't be together. I saw that was what had happened the very first time we had kissed at the Flying Wing Drive-In. I had wanted him then, but my mind said he wasn't appropriate. I had wanted him on Maui, but Daddy got in the way that time. So here we finally were, almost twenty years after that very first kiss, picking up where we'd left off because our bodies just wouldn't take no for an answer.

We made love all night, just lost in each other. We stopped a few times and smoked cigarettes, but were just drawn back into each other. In a way time stopped, I wasn't even aware of the passing of the hours until I noticed that it was getting light.

At first it was just this cold gray light. Then suddenly the sun cracked through the gray clouds, and like you'd turn off a tap the rain just stopped. We watched the hot yellow sun coming up over the clean rain-fresh mountains.

Shark lit our final cigarette, which we shared. Suddenly I was frightened, not sure what this really meant.

"We'd better get back," he said, the first words he'd

spoken in hours. "They're probably going to be out looking for us."

"They probably think we went off to get loaded or drunk," I said, a little giddy from the lack of sleep and from what we'd been doing.

"Yeah," Shark said. But he seemed distant, as if there were still some loneliness in his soul that even this night had not touched.

"You know, this was really—" I began in what I guess was a romantic tone of voice, and he stopped me.

"Let's not reduce it with words," he said, which reassured me in a way. At least he felt there was something to reduce.

He opened that rusty old car door, and we both laughed a little as it squeaked. He really did have a nice smile.

"We'd better go back separately," he said. "So people don't think things."

Suddenly the real world came back in a rush. I thought about Gray, whom I really, really did love, and for a second I felt really awful. But guilt was stupid, I told myself quickly. Besides, what we'd just done had no effect on my love for Gray. This was something else, on some other kind of level.

The sun was burning brightly, hurting my eyes as I climbed out of the car and squinted back at Shark. Already, the night was beginning to seem like an unreal dream.

"You're in love with Narges, aren't you?" I said impulsively, both hoping he would say yes and afraid he was going to.

"It's not love, it's business," he said. He was trying to act tough and wouldn't look at me. He reached for a cigarette, forgetting he was out.

Again, I wanted to say something endearing but he'd blocked that path. So I just said, "Well, see you around," even though it seemed like a dumb thing to say after what had just happened.

## Narges Pahlavi-Bardahl

Shark returned that morning maybe an hour after Kathy with a hickie on his neck. So I knew what had happened and called him on it.

"This is not a subject we will ever discuss," he said to me in a calm tone of voice but with a look in his eyes that frightened and silenced me.

But I observed that he was staying away from Kathy just as he had before. So naturally I assumed that their sex had not worked out.

## Bill Kemmer

I was sure, as we all were despite their stories, that Shark and Kathy had spent the night together. In the days that followed Shark appeared strangely subdued and preoccupied. I tried my best to be supportive in a general sense, but didn't feel it was my place to pry into what had happened.

## Drake Brewster

"You finally fucked her, didn't you?" I said to Shark in the weight room, and he set down his dumbbells and pinned me back to the wall.

"You fucking moron. I should rip your brain right out of your skull," he said.

"Ease up, Jack," I told him. "Sorry I mentioned it."

He cooled off later and apologized. Then he said: "Drake, how'd you like to come to work for me? As a combination bodyguard/trainer?"

I said, "You're full of shit, man. I know for a fact you don't have a dime."

He said that had been the case, but he now had a ninety-million-dollar line of credit.

## Narges Pahlavi-Bardahl

Shark and I made up in the final week of the program, where the theme was "taking responsibility." We both saw that was precisely what we were doing with *Blue Light*, which we were going to push on with despite every obstacle. We began talking excitedly about it all the time, and having wild sex every night. I kept my mouth shut about Kathy Petro, since that was so clearly over.

Then two days before the program was to end I did something which today I regret. I had an appointment with Ernst, and as I waited for him in his office I noticed Shark's rage therapy folder on his desk, and I could not resist taking a peek.

I only managed to read a single item—quite a juicy one—before I heard Ernst coming and quickly put the folder down.

## Kathy Petro

I was really confused that final week. Shark was just ignoring me, which seemed prudent in one way, but it also kind of hurt me. He was still lovey-dovey with Narges all the time and I knew I had no right to be jealous, since I was still committed to Gray. I didn't want to leave Gray or anything but . . . I didn't know, I just felt really confused.

## Bill Kemmer

The program ended on a Saturday with a group singing of "Kum Ba Yah" in the lodge. I couldn't help noticing the looks Shark and Kathy were giving one another as we all joined arms and sang and swayed in unison. When the song was finished there was an orgy of hugging, and people growing tearful with Ernst—this bastard we'd hated for three weeks but who had turned our lives around. I noticed that Kathy ducked out of the room before it got to be her turn to hug Shark.

Around noon the cars began arriving. I was watching for my girlfriend's Jaguar from the foyer when I heard Shark and Kathy in the adjoining room. I knew I was being a snoop, but I couldn't resist stepping closer so I could hear what they were saying and discreetly observe them through the crack of the door.

"I just want you to know I'm never going to forget what happened," Shark said to Kathy.

"I never will either," she replied, avoiding his eyes in an effort to suppress her emotions.

"I've always loved you, Kathy. And I always will."

"I know," she said softly.

"But you're happy with Gray, aren't you?"

She looked at him forthrightly. "Yes, I am. I love him very much."

At just that point I saw an anthracite BMW pulling up—with the license plate: GRAY. A good-looking, if somewhat haggard, young man got out—a man who bore, it was hard not to notice, a rather eerie resemblance to Shark.

"Then go about your happy life with him," Shark said to

Kathy, neither of them aware of Gray's arrival. "I set you free, my darling love."

Very gently, Shark kissed Kathy . . . just as Gray stepped into the foyer.

I felt obliged to warn them, so I called Shark's name.

## Kathy Petro

Shark was kissing me good-bye when suddenly Bill Kemmer called his name from the foyer, and then a second later Gray stepped through the door. He just missed seeing us kissing, but he still caught the vibes, I guess. My eyes were misty.

He recognized Shark and went through about nineteen changes in three seconds flat.

"Gray, it's all right. We've forgiven each other. It was part of the therapy."

Gray was trembling with anger, and shot a dagger look at me. "Let's go."

Shark didn't say anything, thank God. If he'd tried to be friendly I'm sure Gray would have punched him out. So we just left, but I looked back at Shark one last time. He had this sweet, tender smile like you'd see on a wounded saint, even though he wasn't looking at me, or at anything in particular.

# 22 / **Blue Light**
## (1983–1984)

### Todd Jarrett

Shark invited me up to that place in Bel-Air a week or so after he got out of the Kolon Clinic. It was a huge Italianate mansion with an electric gate and all that, one of Narges' many homes around the world. He'd mentioned that she was his "co-producer," and that she was a distant relative of the Shah or something, but I didn't really get the gist of the relationship till I met her. She was hanging all over him like some sort of femme fatale in a sex stupor. Shark had her completely . . . What's the opposite of pussy-whipped? Prick-whipped, I guess.

### Narges Pahlavi-Bardahl

With Shark I lost all my desire to free-base, which is saying quite a lot, for it was a powerful addiction. Very psychological, you know? But he fucked it out of me. Quite literally.

Or so it seemed in those first fevered weeks.

## Todd Jarrett

Shark and Narges raved about my script, Shark calling it "Capraesque," Narges hailing it as "truly Spielbergian in the best possible sense," both of them still completely missing the point. Shark was especially wild about the title, which he found "evocatively spiritual without giving too much away," not even catching the sledgehammer Nazi reference.*

But I kept my mouth shut and signed the contracts. And Shark handed me a cashier's check for two hundred thousand dollars. Of course, I felt like a whore and swore I'd get even with them both someday.

"It *is* going to need some revision," Shark said. "And I don't know if you're up to it, Todd. It might be too painful. I think I know what this script means to you."

It meant a lot to me actually, but not in the way he thought. I knew it was the best, the most bitterly brilliant writing I'd ever done. And now in his cloying, sickeningly sweet, born-again cokehead pseudo-humanism, Shark was going to hack off its balls. I didn't even want to hear what he had to say. But he steered me out to the veranda, his arm over my shoulder, the carpet of city lights twinkling insipidly behind him, as he raptly described his desert vision.


## Greg Spivey

Shark told me about his Palm Springs "vision" during our intoxicated conversation on Christmas Eve in Beirut. He spoke of what had immediately preceded the hallucination: his night with Kathy in the abandoned Chevrolet. He said it was by far the best sex he'd ever had, though of course it was impossible to speak of it merely as sex since it involved so much more. Indeed, it was the culmination of a twenty-year desire which he realized finally was as much spiritual as sexual. It was so good, he said, that he sensed nothing else could ever come close to that night. He felt as if, through the act of making love to Kathy, he had achieved a kind of ultimate life goal. As a result he was frightened afterward, with a terrible sense that he'd just passed through the peak moment of his existence, and really

---

*He no doubt means *Das Blaue Licht*, Leni Riefenstahl's mytho-fascist 1932 German "mountain film."

wondered if there were any point in "toughing out another thirty or forty years of tedium, tepid thrills and low-level pain."

He said a brute, compulsive part of him still wanted Kathy, wanted to possess her in a very literal sense—that is, make her his sex slave, keep her chained to a bed in a room somewhere, and continue having sex with her "until one or the other of us died." He said he knew that was where it would lead, because she would be like a drug to him, there would never be enough, he would never be "satisfied." And so, with all the effort he had, he released her. Because he said he knew, a higher part of him had glimpsed, that Kathy was finally only a symbol of a great spiritual longing that, if the Hindus were right, might well have endured through many lifetimes. And he knew as well that she was a person, "a divine manifestation of the timeless Atman, or universal soul, in her own right," on her own spiritual path and he could not simply use her as a means to his own ends.

He said he watched her heading back to the clinic that morning and knew he had reached the outer limits of what sex was. He waited a few minutes, then started back across the desert himself. The day was already hot, the sun pounding down, and he soon realized he had lost his way. There was nothing in any direction but desert, so he picked a direction and plodded on, sweating by that time, lightheaded from lack of sleep and the night's dissipation.

Suddenly a flash of reflected light in the sky caught his attention. At first he thought it was a plane, a silver plane. Then he saw what it was, and for a moment he thought he was actually going to crap.

It was a spacecraft, not a saucer exactly, but a silver craft that greatly resembled a 1955 Porsche Spyder without wheels. It was humming, hovering. And then it descended before him.

At first, he said, Jesus Christ was at the wheel. The classic Jesus we all know: shoulder-length brown hair and beard, white robes, compassionate brown eyes. He said Christ placed a finger to his lips and adjusted the craft-radio, which was playing "How Much Is That Doggie in the Window?"

Then, before Shark's astonished eyes, Christ "transmuted" —something as a werewolf might in a film, only in reverse. His beard drew back into his face, his hair grew short and light, his eyes changed to blue as his features remolded themselves, and his robes reformed into a white T-shirt and red windbreaker jacket. As Patti Page gave way to Bo Diddley on the radio, so Jesus Christ had become James Dean.

But only for a moment. For as Shark watched, on the verge of peeing now, Dean turned into an alien from outer space. A Deanoid alien however, a stylized "silver-skinned" version of the flesh-and-blood Dean, the face and hair now hard and metallic, but still identifiable as the iconographic Dean.

In this final metamorphosis, the music changed to a post-New Wave futurist sound, and the Spyder craft ascended. It paused momentarily as the Dean-oid alien—or as he would be called in *Blue Light*, "Deem"—beckoned to Shark, indicating the way back to the clinic. Then, in a blinding flash of blue light, the craft simply vanished as if it had slipped through an invisible crack in the sky into another dimension.

## Todd Jarrett

I wanted to laugh as Shark told me about his "vision." I wanted him to laugh, but he didn't. Then I just wanted to get out of there. I was sure he was crazy.

## Greg Spivey

Shark said he continued having sex with Narges, even though his heart wasn't really in it, only because she was able and willing to finance *Blue Light*, which he now saw as a "delivered vision" which must be shared with the world at any cost.

But finally he reached a point where the sex with Narges became so "painful," he just couldn't do it anymore. "I sensed that the only true road for me was celibacy," he told me months later in Beirut. "I suppose I'd known that in my heart ever since the night with Kathy, and I could simply no longer use my body as a female prostitute might use hers. If Narges couldn't find a way to love me on a spiritual plane, then . . . maybe it wasn't really love."

## Narges Pahlavi-Bardahl

He spoke of Yogic principles, the need to conserve his energies and channel them into the film. I did not take it well.

"If I had blonde hair and a toothy smile I'll bet you would feel differently," I said, alluding to Kathy Petro.

He became quite steamed. "I told you, that is a subject we will never discuss."

I stalked off through the house, slamming many doors. I was still furious later that evening when we went to the Bernsteins for dinner.

## Elliot Bernstein

Sue was not at all keen on the idea of having Shark to dinner, remaining quite cynical about his alleged transformation. She was curt and brittle when Shark and Narges arrived. Neal arrived moments later, and he and Shark stepped into the solarium for a private discussion, during which Neal passed on directing *Blue Light*.

## Neal Ridges

Shark had sent me a heavily revised screenplay, which I had read over the weekend. The new writer on the script was Drake Brewster, Shark's bodyguard/trainer, who had remained behind the night of the Bernsteins' dinner—understandably, since he had once tried to rape Sue. Clearly, although Drake may have written in the changes, the ideas were all Shark's.

On one level the story was about an abused teenage girl in an Orange County suburb who fantasizes a romantic affair with an extraterrestrial who resembles James Dean. In Todd Jarrett's original draft—you could still detect—those opening scenes had been unrelievedly harsh: the sadistic redneck father savagely spanking his panties-clad teenage daughter Patti—a parody of the prurient have-it-both-ways TV-movie approach, both titillating and moralizing at the same time. Shark had toned that down—the father was now merely "overly strict" and given to "occasional caustic remarks," the cretinous alcoholic mother now newly sober and "struggling to become a wise and loving mother at last." "There are no real villains in this piece," Shark had told me. "Only hurting, misguided people."

The affair between Patti and Deem, the alien, struck me as highly insipid. He may have resembled James Dean but he talked more like Robby Benson. He and Patti cruise over the suburbs in his Porschelike spacecraft and eventually make love, but when she gets pregnant things veer into vintage Sandra Dee. She wants to marry Deem and have his baby, society and her parents be damned. But when Patti's father discovers she's pregnant—"knocked up by a nerd," he believes—and repeatedly slaps her, Deem comes to her rescue, and the two of them take off. This part wasn't bad—going back to *White Desert*, I'd always liked lovers on the run. And when the Porschecraft breaks down over Beirut, and the couple is pursued through the labyrinthine streets by heavily armed Shiites, you had all the makings of a neat little action film.

## Drake Brewster

My favorite part was where that Air Force guy goes ahead and nukes Beirut. I got off on that, when all those A-rab bastards got vaporized. I liked writing that part, Shark telling me what to put down. "All right!" I yowled. "Let's get down in it! It's about time America started fucking again!"

## Neal Ridges

Of course Patti's escape from Beirut was completely implausible. But you could see the visual possibilities as the warhead spins down through the sky directly at Deem and explodes.

The ending was too much though—and not to say expensive. The Moscow stuff as the Russians, believing the U.S. has started World War III with the strike on Beirut, launch a full-scale counterattack. The Oval Office scenes, as we respond. The thousands of missiles midair . . . when, only seconds from oblivion, Deem "rematerializes" from the ashes of Beirut and projects a "beam of love" from his heart that blankets the globe and melts every warhead before it can explode. Saved from the brink of obliteration the entire world convulses in a paroxysm of cathartic enlightenment. But the Soviet premier sobbing, "Thank you, Jesus," on his knees in the Kremlin . . . I mean, come on!

"Not Jesus," his general tells him. "Deem!" And the cry goes up all around the world, from Calcutta to Capetown, from Beijing to Boston: "Deem! Deem! Deem!" as Deem and Patti flash away through a space-and-time warp to dwell for eternity in the distant and infinite blue light.

"It's kitsch," I told Shark. "It'll be laughed off the screen." I hated being so blunt, but I felt an obligation to save him from his own . . . what? Neo-naiveté?

"I'm sorry you feel that way, Neal," he said, seeming more sad than angry. "I suppose when you've been knocking around this town as long as you have it's hard not to be cynical."

That angered me. But I sensed that Shark was someone who really needed handling with kid gloves now.

"You may be right, Shark," I said. "I'll probably kick myself later." At that we joined the others.

## Narges Pahlavi-Bardahl

I was furious at Shark all through the dinner. The Bernstein woman kept glaring at me. She drank too much wine and turned nasty.

## Elliot Bernstein

I knew there was going to be trouble. Shark was expounding on his new philosophy of art, the need for a "core of compassion" within all his film characters, the moral obligation of the artist to show "the redemptive power of love." And Sue kept muttering, "Bullshit, no sale."

"I believe that people are basically good," Shark said over dessert. "People basically want to love one another—"

And Sue blurted out, "Oh sure. You made that point real well with *Red Surf.*"

"I intend to make amends to the world for that, Sue," Shark said evenly. "That's what *Blue Light* is all about."

"Right," Sue shot back. "You're going to make this piece of kitsch dreck with your Iranian scumbag money—"

At that Narges threw down her spoon. "How dare you insult me! You should speak of dreck. I know what kind of shit films your father used to make—"

"At least my father didn't build an empire on torture and bleed a whole country dry like the goddamn Shah—"

Narges lunged across the table, trying to jab Sue with a butter knife. "How *dare* you speak ill of my late relative the Shah, you Zionist bitch—"

## Neal Ridges

Shark and I restrained Narges as Elliot calmed Sue. But that was it for the evening. Nobody finished their desserts.

424

## Greg Spivey

I had just finished line-producing a depressing teen computer comedy when Shark approached me about *Blue Light*. I still don't know why I took the job exactly. I didn't think much of the script I read, the one he'd revised with Drake Brewster. But I did believe that Shark had genuinely changed. He apologized at great length for the "weirdness" he'd put me through with *Red Surf*. "I've been through the fire, Greg," he said. "And I know I am not the only one who got burned. Join me in this great adventure, my friend, so that we may all be healed in a sea of genuine love and compassion."

Well, what could I say?

Several directors had already passed on the project—understandably given the script, given Shark's last film. "I wish there were someone young and gifted," Shark said. "A virginal genius who hasn't been battered and scarred yet."

I suppose I must accept the responsibility for suggesting Gary Schnell.

## Gary Schnell

I was still asleep in this little Bel-Air cottage my parents had got for me when Shark showed up one morning with the script. He said he'd seen my student film which he thought was astonishing, and he wanted me to direct *Blue Light*.

I read the script that morning and I was weeping by the end. I called him with tears still in my eyes and said, "This is going to be my *E.T.*"

I mentioned that of course I'd have to talk to the high-powered agent I'd just signed with, and Shark got nervous for a second. Then he said, "Okay, but be sure and mention that we're prepared to pay you a fee of two million dollars."

## Greg Spivey

I had seen Gary's short at a USC screening. It was a twenty-minute science-fiction story about a shy, chubby teenage boy—no doubt an alter-ego for Gary—who, faced with sexual rejection from a coarse high school girl, regresses back through a time-warp into a sexless Disney-ized Mark Twain world. It was extremely vapid but extremely well-made, with a number of stunning, and expensive, visual effects. It was obvious he'd out-spent the other students by a wide margin. Gary's father was Earl Schnell of Schnell Petroleum in Houston.

## Drake Brewster

Gary was a fat-ass so I started whipping him into shape. He and Shark worked on that script long and hard. Shark tried to include Narges but she wasn't interested. She was still pissed off because Shark wouldn't fuck her any more.

## Narges Pahlavi-Bardahl

It made me so angry I even thought about stopping the film. I could do it just like that with one phone call to the bank. But I knew if I did Shark truly would never have sex with me again. I kept telling myself: this can't last forever. He's a virile man. Sooner or later he's going to be in a sexy mood again. So I waited. But I grew restless. So I began to base again.

## Gary Schnell

I kept getting more and more excited as Shark and I worked on the pre-production. My agent had been negative at first because of Shark's past, but I convinced him that Shark had really changed. He did insist that I get my entire fee up front though, minus his two hundred thousand dollar commission.

We dropped the pregnancy angle from the script. "It makes it cheap and dirty if they actually have sex," I told Shark. "They should just kiss and be in love. It's more touching that way."

Shark saw my point and went along. "Yes, the era of frivolous premarital sex appears to be drawing to a close," he said. "As a filmmaker I'm beginning to feel a strong moral imperative not to glorify promiscuity anymore."

## Greg Spivey

Gary was twenty-four and, I'm sure, still a virgin. He was not bad-looking, but one of these kids who'd spent his adolescence holed up in a movie theater, who had, for whatever complex of reasons, been terrified of sex long before there was anything to especially fear.

426

We had an open call for the part of Patti, during which I made a joking remark to Gary about all the hordes of "young Hollywood snatch" we were seeing. Gary turned red as a beet and said, "Greg, please don't talk about women like that. I don't want anything to vulgarize the atmosphere of this film."

## Drake Brewster

About a week before we left for Beirut Shark and Gary went to lunch at Breton's. I went along since that was where Jean-Claude Citroen and his frog actor buddy had wasted Shark. Even though the chances of running into them again were remote, there were still a whole lot of people around who hated Shark.

Narges came too, but she kept going to the bathroom. We knew she was coking again but Shark felt helpless. "I've tried to talk to her, but she denies it hysterically," he'd told me. By then they were sleeping in different wings of the house.

People were discreetly checking Shark out, but everything was fine till Bill Kemmer and Carol Van Der Hof came in.

## Bill Kemmer

I saw Carol tense, and felt her anger, as Shark approached our table. "Give him a break, Carol," I said, anticipating what Shark was going to say.

"Carol, I don't blame you for hating me," Shark began.

"Good," she said, refusing to meet his eyes.

"I never wanted to hurt you, Carol. I think you know how much you meant to me. I was crazy, that's all, quite literally out of my mind."

Completely ignoring Shark, Carol said to me, "I smell something *dead* in here, don't you, Bill?"

"I just want you to know that I'm sorry," Shark said gently. "I can't compel, or even expect, you to forgive me."

"I know what I smell," Carol said loudly. "A dead fish! A dead rotting fish all doused with a sickly sweet cologne. But it still has that rotting fish stench!"

Everyone was looking by then and Shark was embarrassed. He maintained his saintly expression, but under his breath he said to Carol, "You cunt."

Just then all hell broke loose in the ladies room.

## Narges Pahlavi-Bardahl

I was trying to base when some fake blonde bitch made a scene, saying I shouldn't do it there. "Why not?" I said, "I could buy this stupid restaurant." At that she nearly set my hair on fire, so I began to pull on hers, and soon we fell into the dining room.

## Drake Brewster

Narges was rolling on the floor with some TV actress, and when I pulled her up she bit my hand, and spilled coke on the carpet. It was a real bad scene.

## Gary Schnell

I felt bad for Shark. He was trying so hard to be a truly decent man. You could tell that the other industry people in the restaurant were only too eager to think cynical thoughts.

## Bill Kemmer

Narges was still spitting like a viper as Drake, his hand bleeding, shoved her into the Rolls in the parking lot.

Carol and I were climbing into my Ferrari when Shark came bounding over. "Carol, look," he said. "I'm sorry I called you a cunt."

"Oh, go drown," Carol said, rolling up her window.

## Gary Schnell

Shark was driving as we pulled up to the gate of the Bel-Air house and saw a grungy old man yelling into the intercom.

"A friend of yours?" I said to Shark as a joke, certain the old guy was a bum, one of the sad homeless people you saw in increasing numbers during those years.

"He's not a friend," Shark said, as he stopped the car. "He's my father."

## Mac Trager

It ripped me up inside to come to him but I had no place else to go. "I'm in bad shape, son," I told him there by the gate. "I went to Vegas and lost every dime. One of those showgirls got me drunk and kept me gambling. I hadn't slept with a woman in over five years, not since Miko cleared out, and I just lost control."

"What about the condo in Laguna Beach?" he said.

"That's gone too," I said, the tears stinging my eyes.

"Look, son, I've changed," I told him. "It's the eighties now, and I've left *all* my bigotry behind. It's a process that started with Miko, who raised my consciousness about the plight of Asian-Americans. But now I extend that same tolerance to everyone, of whatever religion or race or minority life-style. Different strokes, son. If you're a member of the gay and lesbian community, it's fine with me, as long as it makes you happy and you're being true to yourself."

"I'm not gay, Dad," Shark said, and then he hugged me. I wanted to jump back but I forced myself not to.

"It's all right," he said real gentle-like. "This is a time of healing. Father, come inside."

## Greg Spivey

I was against Shark bringing his father along to Beirut. Mac Trager was a hard drinker with a big mouth and things were touchy enough as it was—Beirut being Beirut. I wanted to use Tel Aviv or Athens but Shark insisted on authenticity.

It was frightening. The first day we were setting up a chase scene on a rubble-filled street in East Beirut when a fire fight broke out less than two blocks away in the Western sector.

Gary was furious. "Somebody go over there and tell them to cool it. We're trying to make a movie here and they're ruining our sound."

"Gary," I said, "why don't you go tell them yourself? It might mean more if they hear it directly from you."

He started over but Shark stopped him.

## Gary Schnell

I'll never forget Beirut. Until you've seen a real war you just don't know what it's like.

"I thought I told you to keep these bodies in the background," I said to a prop man one day before a set-up that involved some dummy corpses. He lifted the dummy I was referring to, but it wasn't a dummy at all, and real intestines covered with maggots slipped out. I threw up and then became more convinced than ever that *Blue Light* might be the film that stopped the madness of human violence once and for all.

## Joey Joel

Playing Deem was a very physically demanding role. Once Luis had glued that silver latex Deem head in place over my own, it was on for the day, and my only nourishment came from sipping drinks through a straw inserted in my nostril. Snort, then swallow—not a fun way to drink a milkshake, believe me.

Beirut was really terrifying—especially after a group of midwestern lady Sunday school teachers who'd been staying at our hotel "disappeared." That was very freaky. They went out on a sight-seeing tour and then their bus was found, shot-up and abandoned. The rumor was they'd been kidnapped, though it was being kept out of the news because of allegedly "delicate negotiations." Whatever, it certainly didn't contribute to an atmosphere of security.

There was always so much gunfire going on in the background, not to mention the rocket attacks and bombardments, that we just gave up on the sound. Then on the last day of filming Luis came up to me after a take and said, "What's this? How did you do this?" There was a bullet hole through the top of my latex Deem head. It had missed my skull by a millimeter.

I was so shaken I went straight to Sharon's dressing room where, without even trying to remove my head, the two of us had sex. In the heat of the moment we neglected to close the blinds.

## Greg Spivey

It was obvious that Gary had a crush on Sharon—that was why he'd cast her as Patti. But he idealized her, you know, confusing her with the role. So when he walked by Sharon's trailer on the last day of the Beirut shoot and saw her having sex with Joey he was very disturbed.

## Gary Schnell

It did bother me, I guess. Because Sharon was really the picture of everything Patti was about: sweet and pure, a kind of

fresh-scrubbed angel really. But when I saw her with Joey—
they were doing it "dogstyle"—I realized she was just another
Hollywood slut like my dad had always warned me about.

## Drake Brewster

Gary came to me that night in the Beirut hotel and said he was
upset 'cause he'd seen Joey giving it to Sharon.

"It's a natural thing," I told him. "A real man has urges. I
used to myself till the steroids shrunk up my nuts and dick."

Then I started to tell him about my rapist days of yore, but
he stopped me and said, "I don't think I want to hear this,
Drake. I don't want to stop being fond of you."

Then he went upstairs and caught Narges with Mac.

## Mac Trager

From the point where Shark and I hugged by the gate in
Bel-Air it was all downhill. We tried talking once but had
nothing to say, so we watched a Raiders game, but Shark kept
talking on the phone. Then he said, "Come on to Beirut, Dad."

So I went, thinking things might pick up there, but they
didn't. I stayed at the hotel drinking in my room, bored as hell,
nothing but A-rabs and dubbed Elke Sommer movies on the TV.

Then one night Narges invited me into her room. She wasn't
bad for an A-rab. Real high-fashion type, none of that veil shit.

"You know, you're very attractive for a somewhat older
man," she said, sidling up beside me on the sofa. The Israelis
were bombing some ridge in the distance.

"You're okay too," I told her, knocking back a glass of
Jack D. "But aren't you fuckin' my son?"

"No," she said. "For some time now, Shark has been
opting for celibacy."

"Opting for it, huh?" I grinned at the notion. "Well, no
wonder you're smokin'."

I ran my hand up her skirt, and she spread her legs and
moaned. We were going at it like gangbusters right there on the
sofa when Gary walked in.

## Greg Spivey

Shark and I were going over the L.A. shooting schedule when
Gary stuck his head in the door. "I thought you might like to

know that I just came upon your father and Narges having sexual intercourse."

Shark looked stunned for a moment, then said, "Thank you for telling me, Gary. It takes a great deal of courage and moral authority to be the bearer of such news."

## Narges Pahlavi-Bardahl

Gary was due in my room for a meeting, that was why I had sex with Mac. I knew Gary was a prude and would report it immediately. I only did it to make Shark jealous.

## Mac Trager

Narges and I had just wrapped it up, and she was in the bathroom, when Shark barged in. I pulled up my pants and grinned at him. "Not bad," I said. "You oughta try her sometime."

"Where is she?" he said, then opened the bathroom door.

She was smoking cocaine with a torch deal and he knocked it out of her hands. "You're a mess and I'm sick of it," he said. "You haven't done shit since we got here except base your stupid brains out. I want you to go back to L.A."

"All right, Shark," she said, picking up her bra. "But let's see how you finish this film without my money, huh?"

He grabbed her arm. For the first time since I'd come around he looked really mad. "If you try and fuck me, Narges—"

"I've been trying to do that for weeks," she said. "Obviously, your father is much better equipped to do that job than you. I'll bet if *he* had made love to Kathy Petro she would still be with *him*—"

## Narges Pahlavi-Bardahl

Shark got a funny, squinty-eyed look at the mention of Kathy Petro. Had I not been so high I would have realized the danger I was putting myself in.

"How dare you mention her name in that context?" Shark said. "How dare you conjure up that sort of mental image?"

"Oh, there's a lot I could conjure up, Shark," I said with foolish abandon. "I could even conjure up what happened to you in the Orange County Jail when you were fourteen years old."

## Mac Trager

I got a sick feeling. It was a door that should've stayed shut.

## Narges Pahlavi-Bardahl

Shark appeared shaken, which pleased me. I went in for the kill. "I saw your rage therapy folder in Ernst Kolon's office, Shark. I know all about the time you got *buttfucked by Negroes!*"

## Mac Trager

Shark flipped his lid and tried to strangle Narges. I felt it my duty to come to her aid, and was doing so when Drake came in with a gun.

## Drake Brewster

I'd been packing a .357 since we arrived—everybody was armed in Beirut. I aimed it at Mac, and he backed off from Shark, then Shark let go of Narges and said, "Give me the gun." So I did, seeing a second too late that he was crazy.

"I'm gonna blow your Iranian pig brains all over this wall," he said, trying to jam the gun into Narges' mouth as she screamed.

"Don't do it, Shark, not here!" I said, thinking of his future. But I was turned on. I mean, this scene was *hot*.

## Narges Pahlavi-Bardahl

Shark was insane. When I saw *Blue Velvet* a few years later it was like a terrifying flashback. Because Dennis Hopper had the same look in his eyes as Shark in Beirut!

## Drake Brewster

Mac tried to say something and Shark turned on him with an unhinged fury, whacking him back and forth across the face. "You shut your fucking hole, you goddamn fuck! I should have squashed you like a bug years ago for what you did to me!"

I was getting *real* turned on! Shark was like a fuckin'

animal, man, flipped out on the natch. I could see in his eyes that his mind was running to wild, crazy places way beyond right and wrong and all that phony fuckin' Sunday school shit. Man, I was *aroused!*

"I just don't know what to do with this pair," Shark said, in a low, scary Clint Eastwood voice. "You got any ideas, Drake?"

"You bet I do," I said, feeling my dick jerk. "Let's fuck 'em both, then kill 'em."

He grinned and said, "You know? That sounds like a plan."

## Mac Trager

I was starting to get unnerved. Shark and Drake took us down the express elevator to the Mercedes in the hotel garage, Shark saying he'd blow our brains out on the spot if we tried anything. He was beyond reason, and Drake was egging him on. I could believe they were gonna fuck Narges, but not me, you know? But as we drove up an alley past a bullet-riddled sign that warned we were entering West Beirut I began to get a real bad feeling that anything was possible.

## Narges Pahlavi-Bardahl

By the time Drake pulled to a stop on an empty rubble-strewn street in West Beirut, he and Shark were like a couple of psychopathic killers—like the pair in *In Cold Blood* perhaps, only far sicker. They had entered that realm where reason and morality no longer exist as we know them.

"Do you want to fuck your father?" Drake said to Shark. "Or should I?"

Shark considered the matter, then said, "You do it," and laughed like a fiend. "You do it and I'll watch. I'll watch while you buttfuck my dear old Dad, just like he let those black prisoners buttfuck the innocence out of a terrified teenage boy. I'll watch and relish his agony, and force Narges to watch. And blow off her head at the exact moment you come."

## Mac Trager

I started hyperventilating in the back seat of the car.

## Drake Brewster

Shark ordered Narges and Mac to get out of the car. By then he was talking in a Southern redneck voice, why I don't know, telling Mac again and again how I was gonna make him *"squeal* like a pig!"

I didn't much want to assfuck Mac—in fact I wasn't sure if I was up to fuckin' at all. To be blunt my dick had shrunk up almost to nothing, man. I'd been kind of hoping Shark would do all the fuckin', and I could just watch and then blow 'em away.

## Narges Pahlavi-Bardahl

Shark ordered Mac to lower his trousers and lean over the hood of the Mercedes and told Drake to make Mac "squeal like a pig."

But Mac refused to do it, so Shark placed the gun to my temple, and I said, "For God sake, Mac, do as he says."

## Mac Trager

I asked myself, "What would John Wayne do in a mess like this?" And I knew the answer: He'd slug his way out of it. So I came at Drake with a right hook to the jaw. I see now it was the wrong thing to do. The blow barely phased him, but it did set him off, and the next thing I knew he threw me over the hood and yanked down my pants. I saw his pecker, but it wasn't like no pecker I'd ever seen before.

Then just as the worst was about to happen, Shark said in a strangely calm tone of voice, "All right, Drake. That's enough."

And I looked back at Shark and he had the gun trained on Drake.

"What's the problem?" Drake said.

"No problem," Shark said. "This is wrong, that's all. It's wrong and it's sick, and it's really no fun. It's not joyous and loving, and that's what I'm trying to be now. Thank God I've come to my senses in time."

"Aw shit, man," Drake said. "Are you gonna puss out now? This takes the cake."

Narges was trembling, as confused as I was.

"Put your penis away, Drake," Shark said. "Dad, it's okay, pull up your pants. No one's going to harm you."

So I pulled my pants up quick and then I heard a pop and saw blood on Drake's thigh. For a second I thought Shark had shot him, but a magnum don't make a pop, you know? Then we seen a bunch of A-rabs with automatic rifles coming up the street.

## Narges Pahlavi-Bardahl

Suddenly there was shooting and Drake was struck in the thigh and nearly fell. Shark pulled him into an alley, firing at the Lebanese who were armed with automatic weapons.

Mac and I ducked into the alley also. "Come quickly," I said to Mac, and we ran on ahead of Shark who was helping Drake.

"Get help!" Shark called after us.

## Mac Trager

Narges and I cut between two buildings as we heard more shooting. Then we heard the A-rabs coming up the alley after us.

"In here," she said, when she found an open door. And we ducked right into a room full of Shiites who were armed to the teeth.

## Drake Brewster

Shark pulled me back into a bombed-out building as the Arabs ran past us. Luckily it was so dark they didn't see my trail of blood.

"You'd better leave me, man," I told Shark. "Save yourself."

He hesitated, then said, "No, I can't do that, Drake. I realize now that you're an evil influence on me. You represent an old part of me I have to let go of. Beyond that, however, you are still a human being. So you sit tight. I'll be back with help, possibly the Marines."

## Narges Pahlavi-Bardahl

As Mac and I stumbled into the room all the Shiites grabbed their weapons. I knew they were the most extreme splinter group of Shiites because of the framed portrait of Khomeini on the wall, and because all of them were ugly with evil, dirty grins and rotting teeth.

"So . . . an American," one of them said, his face an inch from Mac's.

Stupidly, I was carrying my passport. When they saw the name Pahlavi they virtually convulsed with glee, several of the more disgusting ones literally drooling.

"Put them with the others," the apparent leader ordered.

And they pulled back a long sliding door to reveal the twelve kidnapped American lady Sunday School teachers cowering fearfully in a filthy room where flies buzzed.

## Mac Trager

I saw red when I saw all those Sunday School teachers. Good, decent Kansas women, both wives and spinsters, young and fresh, and old and sweet like dear old grandmothers. It just tore my heart out to see 'em in that state, slop holes in the floor, bowls of that couscous or whatever that A-rab shit is. Yet you could see the brave dignity in those broads' eyes.

## Drake Brewster

Shark told me later that right after he left me the Arabs almost caught him. They were all over the place and he ducked into another gutted building. As he watched them pass, he said, he smelled something foul in the room and saw it was a corpse that had been there for days and was rotting real bad. Fighting back nausea, he looked closer at the body and saw it was that of a boy no older than six, though he was wearing combat boots, his stiff fingers gripping an AK-47. It was then, Shark said, that he truly understood for the first time the graphic futility of war.

But knowing he was in a jungle—not of his making, but one in which it was his duty to many others to survive—he picked up the AK-47, checked the clip, which was full, and moved on. Then as he ducked between a couple of buildings he heard a bunch of American women singing "Onward Christian Soldiers."

## Mac Trager

Those broads had balls, I'll say that. In what was clearly a preplanned act of defiance, they started singing "Onward Christian Soldiers'' in unison, knowing it would drive those A-rabs nuts, and it did. They kept screaming like animals at the women to shut up, then started poking 'em with their rifles, which made me think: Okay, ladies, you've made your point, don't press your luck. But those broads were real wound up.

## Narges Pahlavi-Bardahi

It was an act of sheerest stupidity. In the Islamic world the woman does as the man tells her. The song itself was bad enough, but when they wouldn't stop as they were told the Shiite men really blew their tops. I believe they were only one second away from slaughtering the whole choir when Shark burst through the door with the AK-47.

## Mac Trager

It was my son's finest moment, bar none. If it had been me, I'd have blown the shit clean out of that whole A-rab crew. But Shark sensed—correctly I see now—that once the shooting started they'd have nailed him and me and Narges and all those broads too.

So he bluffed 'em. "I don't just have this rifle," he yelled. "I'm wired with twenty pounds of plastic explosives. If anybody fires the whole block's going up."

The thing was, he was wearing a T-shirt and khaki pants. The pants were baggy, but what the hell did they think? That he had the explosives taped to his ankles? It was nothing but pure . . . what's that Jewish word? Chutzpah. That's what it was. And those dumb A-rabs bought it hook, line and sinker.

## Narges Pahlavi-Bardahi

It was an astonishing display of bravery on Shark's part, there is no denying it. What élan! He reminded me of the young Errol Flynn in that moment, and in spite of the terribleness of some minutes before, I fell in love with him all over again.

What a magnetically bold figure he cut, ordering those Shiites to drop their weapons, which they did in a heap on the floor. With that accomplished Rambo would have annihilated them, don't you think? But Shark was not like that—he had far too much grace and panache under pressure to ever play the macho buffoon.

438

As Shark covered the Shiites Mac and I steered the Sunday school teachers out the door, several of them whimpering by then, their eyes filled with tears of gratitude, more than one as she passed Shark saying a heartfelt, "God bless you."

## Mac Trager

Shark ordered the A-rabs into the room where the broads had been and told me to pull the door shut and lock it. But I said to him on the sly, "Come on, the broads are out of here. Why don't you grease 'em now?"

And he looked at me like *I* was sick or something. "That's really what you'd do, isn't it, Dad? You think violence is the answer to everything—you and your generation who glorified slaughter in World War II, who got us into Vietnam in the name of your rancid Duke Wayne heroics, and last but not least invented the bomb."

"Lookie here, bud," I said. "A half hour ago you were fixin' to let that muscle-bound Rambo poke his steroid-shriveled pole up my wrinkled old bunghole till I squealed like a pig. So don't come on now like Mahatma Gandhi."

Shark got a pained look like some kind of saint, which I thought was fake till I saw the tears welling up in his eyes. "Father, forgive me," he said real gentle-like. "I knew not what I was about to do."

"Let's just forget it, okay?" I said, and locked those A-rabs up in that room so we could get the hell out of there.

## Greg Spivey

The jubilation when Shark returned to the hotel with the Sunday school teachers was brief. Soon the place was swarming with embassy officials and/or CIA men, the women were sequestered, and Shark was told in no uncertain terms not to speak to anyone about what had happened. "The women are safe, that's the important thing," the ambassador told Shark when he arrived. The political situation was "just too precarious," he explained, "to rock the boat with something like this now."

Shark was confused, demoralized even, and Narges was angry. "But Shark was a hero," she said. "It's not right that he shouldn't get credit for his bravery."

Mac felt the same way, we all did.

Shark finally went to bed around dawn—by then we knew Drake was safe. The following evening, which was Christmas Eve, the call came from President Reagan.

Shark took the call in the bar, where Mac was drinking heavily. I don't really know precisely what the president said. "Yes, sir, I understand, sir," Shark said into the phone, with a final, rather sad, "You're more than welcome, Mr. President. Merry Christmas to you and Nancy too."

Shark said nothing for a moment after he hung up. Then he ordered a double bourbon. I knew it was his first drink since the Kolon Clinic and should have objected. But I joined him instead. So began our Christmas Eve soul-baring. By then it was just Shark and me—and Mac a few stools away, passed out with his head on the bar.

## Drake Brewster

A bunch of Marines came and got me just like Shark said they would. On the way to the hospital one of them said, "What the hell were you doing in West Beirut?"

"Aw hell," I said. "We just went for a joyride. You know how that is."

## Gary Schnell

Some of us exchanged gifts in my suite on Christmas Day. My mom had sent a tree with ornaments and tinsel and presents from Neiman-Marcus for me to give everyone. Shark seemed out of it that morning, as if he hadn't slept much, and he didn't have a present for me, but that was all right, I understood. I really thought he'd done a courageous thing and I was so glad he hadn't killed anyone. "I don't think I could live with myself if I ever killed another human being," I said to him. "Could you?" He said he couldn't.

I gave Shark an original framed gel of Bambi, which had cost quite a bit but it was worth it to see the smile of joy that came to his face. With some difficulty I had collected the complete films of Rossano Brazzi on thirty-seven leather-bound videocassettes for Narges, since I knew she had a deep affection for the actor. But she didn't come to the gift-opening party. When I asked Shark where she was he drew me aside.

"Gary, I'm concerned about the future of our film," he said very soberly.

I was shaken. "Why? What do you mean?"

"Something happened with Narges the night of the rescue—"

"What?"

"I don't want to go into it. It's too sick. And you see, that's the thing. You're part of my new, decent life, Gary. Narges, I'm afraid, is part of the old. Her cocaine usage—" Shark shook his head.

"Yes, I know. I've suspected that she uses it." I'd tried coke, but hadn't liked it. "It's sad."

"It's worse than sad, Gary. Narges is a very sick woman, if not genuinely evil. She's a selfish, promiscuous slut and I simply will not play her game anymore. I won't use drugs with her or be her sexual toy. As a result, I believe that as soon as we get back to L.A. she's going to pull the plug on the film."

In a way I wasn't surprised. With a woman as unstable as Narges it had crossed my mind before that something like this could happen. So I was not unprepared. "We don't need her, Shark," I said. "I talked to my dad in Houston just a little while ago. He'd heard some bad things about you, you know, and was never too keen on my making this film with you. But today—the State Department blackout be damned—when I told him what you'd done, he said: 'You tell Shark Trager he is my kind of American.'"

## Narges Pahlavi-Bardahl

A production assistant—acting on Shark's orders, I discovered later—had given me a powerful Lebanese sleeping tablet as I went to bed on Christmas Eve. I did not awaken till the following evening. When I did Shark was sitting on the edge of the bed. "Merry Christmas," he said, and for the first time in months kissed me full on the lips. Then he showed me Gary's gift and I clapped my hands. "But I adore Rossano Brazzi! How did he know?"

"Listen, kiddo," he said, "I want you to know how rotten I feel about sticking that gun in your mouth—"

"Let's not talk about it now, Shark, it's Christmas," I said, and placed *South Pacific* in the VCR.

As the tape began Shark caressed my shoulder, and continued: "But when you mentioned that Orange County Jail episode—"

"I was mad from basing, and from stifled desire for you. Still, there is no excuse. I had no right to examine your rage therapy file."

Shark stared blankly at the TV. "The thing is," he said, "I lied to Ernst. That's not even what happened. What actually happened was far worse. I wasn't raped by black men—"

"Oh, look at the South Seas photography, isn't it stunning?" I said, trying to change the subject. But there was no stopping his confession.

"There was *another* boy in the county jail that day," he said, as if staring into his memory. "Eighteen, I guess, though he looked much younger. Fair, blond, you'd even have to say beautiful—a kind of Orange County suburban Billy Budd." Shark continued with difficulty as the memory became painful. "It quickly became apparent that a number of older prisoners, hardened criminals most of whom happened to be dark-skinned, were going to have their way with this young blond Christ figure. And I had to decide. Do you understand what I'm saying?"

"No," I told him.

"I had to choose. Two large black prisoners held his pale body spread-eagle against the iron bars as their fellows repeatedly impaled him. My choice was to join his crucifiers . . . or to join him on the cross. I picked the former, and proved myself according to their brute animal law."

"It was a long time ago, Shark," I said to him. "It sounds to me like you really had no choice."

"He died that night," Shark said, staring out the window at the cobalt sky. "He and I shared a cell. He'd been injured internally but bore it in silence. 'I'm sorry,' I whispered to him, as he lay on the bunk above mine. 'Please . . . can you forgive me?' He said nothing. And in the empty silence I realized I couldn't hear his breath."

Shark caressed me mechanically, lost in his own pain.

"It sounds like *Sophie's Choice*," I told him. "Perhaps the stakes were not quite as grueling but the principle remains the same. Whichever way you had gone, it was still going to be very bad."

"Yes." He stared absently at the TV as Rossano began to sing "Some Enchanted Evening."

In a moment he said, "Are you in love with my father?"

442

The question startled me. "No, no. I was only trying to make you jealous, that's all it was."

"Then you prefer me." He slid his hand between my legs.

"You know I do. There's no comparison."

Soon we made love. "Oh Shark, I've missed this so," I cried as he moved into me.

That night he loved me more tenderly yet thoroughly than he ever had before. For a while I really felt that after all the weeks of strain and tension, capped by a momentary lapse into madness, we were at last back together where we should be once again.

Of course, I see now he was only giving me something to remember him by.

# 23/Redeemed
## (1984–1985)

### Drake Brewster

Shark and Greg came to get me at the Beirut hospital for the flight home. But Shark seemed funny, distant and all, and wouldn't be alone with me, which pissed me off, 'cause I felt we needed to talk.

On the plane I caught him by the toilets and said, "Hey, look, man. Don't try and lay the whole thing off on me. You were ready to fuck and kill 'em too."

And he said, "We'll talk about it later, Drake," and went and sat back down beside that simp Gary.

Then I saw him talking to Mac, and when he finished he and Mac shook hands, but Mac looked pale.

### Mac Trager

Shark sat down beside me and said, "Look, Dad, I'm still sorry about what happened with Drake and me. It was an aberration, there's no doubt about it, a kind of flashback to my old psychotic behavior. But the fact remains that you are dogshit disguised as a human being, and I never want to see you again. So here's the deal. I'll give you fifty thousand a year for the rest of your life to keep your mouth shut about what happened. All right?''

## Narges Pahlavi-Bardahl

Shark began acting strange on the flight home. I still felt so delicious from our lovemaking that I wanted to cuddle. But when I touched him he cringed.

Then as we set down in Los Angeles he said, "Narges, Gary's father is going to buy you out of the picture. You are dog vomit disguised as a human being, and I never want to see you again. As you may know, Earl Schnell is an extremely wealthy and powerful man with heavy Washington connections. I know what your immigration status is, dear heart. If you try and make waves I will see that you are deported back to Teheran.''

I was too stunned to speak.

## Drake Brewster

I was trying to find Shark after I went through Customs when Greg Spivey came up and handed me an envelope. ''Shark wants you to have this,'' he said.

It was a thousand bucks in cash along with a note. ''You are out of my life, you sick fuck,'' the note said. ''And lest you think for a minute that you can fuck with me in any way, Drake, you should know that I have the number of a secret international feminist revenge organization. One phone call, in which I explain to them how many rapes you actually committed and how lightly you got off, and these women will stop at nothing until you are castrated and dead. Nuf said?''

I was angry and hurt. I went over to Mac and Narges and said, "Hey look, I admit I got a little rowdy but—" And they both cut me dead and went out to a limo that was waiting and drove off. I had to take the fuckin' bus, then walk up into Bel-Air. When I reached the house all my shit was piled by the gate.

## Gary Schnell

''It's for the best,'' I told Shark when he told me he'd bid adieu to Narges and Drake and his father. "It's too bad about your dad though. There's nothing sadder than watching the love go out of a family."

"My father abused me," Shark said out of the blue, as we watched *Fantasia* at my place in Bel-Air that night. "He used to whip my bare ass in the garage . . . right by the freezer where my mother died."

"It's okay, Shark," I said and we hugged. "We'll be your family now."

Then we got in our twin beds and watched the rest of *Fantasia*, and lay there talking about the special effects for hours in the dark.


## Kathy Petro

I remember when *Blue Light* was filming in Fountain Valley because they did this segment on "Hollywood Tonight" about how it was Shark's first film since *Red Surf* and everything. I was kind of half-watching the TV and half-trying to come up with a title for my book.

Gray had encouraged me to write about my battle with drugs since I'd been a role model for so many American women and everything, but it was scary at first because I wasn't really a writer. I thought about working with someone but then I decided: No, I should tell what happened in my own words. So I sat down at the typewriter and it just poured out, all of it: my grass and acid days including Jeff Stuben's tragic death, which certainly was a warning to the teenagers of today. Then my abusive heroin-fogged relationship with Derek Horus—I could use his name since he was dead. I told about the cocaine and mood medications I'd used when I was married to Brian—though I had to tread softly there since Brian was still very powerful. I ended on a note of hope and new beginnings, my pain killers left behind forever, thanks to Ernst Kolon and the infinite love and patience of Gray, the world's most handsome, understanding man.

I was jotting down titles: *Smiling on the Outside, Dying on the Inside; First You Smile; I'm Smiling as Hard as I Can;* finally just settling on *Behind the Smile,* though I didn't really like it that much, when the TV showed Sharon Shay being interviewed on the set in Fountain Valley. And I mean I couldn't help noticing that she did kind of look like me at sixteen. And I was kind of thinking: Well, Shark's up to his old tricks again, but at least this time it's flattering, he's not trying to "get" me or something. And just then Gray came in, looking very pale and even thinner than usual, though he'd lost a lot of weight lately—from working so hard, he said.

"Kathy, I've got cancer," he said just like that. "I just got the test results. It's inoperable. I'm going to die."

I thought he was joking at first. When I realized he wasn't I just came unglued.


## Joey Joel

After Beirut the filming in Orange County was fairly uneventful. But the crisis atmosphere of the Lebanese adventure had actually served to bring us all together. Something magical happened on *Blue Light* once we were back in the States. We just appreciated America and each other in a whole new way, and we really became a kind of family. We were always hugging—everybody, the cast, the crew, even the Teamsters. The entire production was bathed in a warm glow—Gary's jealousy over Sharon and me just completely vanished. Of course, what had begun as brute tension-relieving sex had became something else entirely as Sharon and I fell deeply and genuinely in love. "I'm just glad you kids are happy," Gary said, like a benevolent father.

If Gary was our father, then Shark had come to exist for us on an even higher level. Of course, we all knew about his heroism in Beirut, though it hadn't been revealed in the media yet. I don't know how to put it—he just exuded this wondrous joy and love. I'm reluctant to use religious terminology because Shark would be the first to insist he was "just another guy from the neighborhood." But in our hearts, I think, he became something like our fondest hopes of what God might be. Knowing all that he'd been through especially, there was just no way you couldn't love the man.


## Sharon Shay

I don't think there was a dry eye at the wrap party. By then we all knew from the dailies how good the film was going to be. If it failed we were all prepared to turn our backs on Hollywood forever.

447

## Greg Spivey

There was a kind of rapturous aura about those final weeks of filming. Though I pride myself on being a bit cynical, I have to say that *Blue Light* remains the ecstatic high point of my career. On occasion I would reflect on Shark's seething dementia during the final days of *Red Surf*. But that seemed a lifetime away, the madness of another man. Shark Trager truly had been reborn.

I will never forget the afternoon Gary and Shark and I drove down to Costa Mesa. It was a few days before the end of filming and Shark wanted to have the wrap party in the drive-in where he had been born. But when we got there, just as the sun was setting, we found that the drive-in was gone.

## Gary Schnell

It was an indescribably poignant moment. Shark had rhapsodized about the Flying Wing Drive-In all the way down—the neon, the fading mural, an early romantic experience he'd had there during a Doris Day film, his charming contention that he recalled *Gun Crazy* on the screen the night he was born. But when we reached the site there was nothing but a plowed-up field and a sign announcing the imminent construction of the Caligari Mall.

"Video," Shark said. "In a few years there won't be any theaters left anywhere, except small ones in museums. Everything will be rented on cassette, watched on a small, stupid box. We're a dying breed, gentlemen. The makers of the last true mythic iconography. Soon everything will be reduced to the level of a 'Hazel' rerun."

Saddened, we drove back to Fountain Valley, where we held the wrap party at a drive-in church.

## Greg Spivey

The post-production period was long because of all the special effects, and Shark worked closely with Gary and the editors. Gary really is a gifted, intuitive filmmaker, but at that point anyway he was still insecure and always deferred to Shark's judgment. "He's like my big brother," Gary would say. They were always hugging and going around with their arms over each other's shoulders, the way a couple of kids might. There was absolutely nothing gay about it—it was a totally pure kind of Mark Twain buddy thing—though it was clear that Gary really idolized Shark.

We had a rough cut by May of '85 and it was just the best thing that any of us had ever seen. So Shark showed it to Bill Kemmer.

## Bill Kemmer

Well, I was blown away. That screening was beyond all doubt the most affecting moment of my Hollywood life. I was really not prepared. I don't know what I expected . . . but when Deem rose from the ashes of Beirut and melted the missiles midair . . . Well, it touched something deep inside me, some primal wish which I guess we all have, which goes back to childhood, the wish of: Please, God, make it all right.

I hugged Shark afterwards. "I love you," I said, which to be frank I hadn't said to anyone for quite some time, including, sadly, my wife. But I was saying it a lot, and meaning it, after *Blue Light*. That's the kind of movie it is.

## Greg Spivey

Bill was so swept away by the film it almost seemed crass to discuss money at all. It was just understood the film was going to be huge and Shark made a very good distribution deal.

## Gary Schnell

My parents flew out to see the film and my mom just sobbed at the ending. Even my dad was misty-eyed and said, "Son, I'm proud of you."

Then he shook my hand real hard, but I said, "Oh heck, Dad, let's hug." And we did, even though my dad was a real tough guy, kind of a cross between Lyndon Johnson and Robert Duvall.

Then he and Shark hugged. "You steered my boy right," Dad said to him.

My mom was just wild about Shark. She had invented the first polyester pantsuit back in 1964, which had brought in a fortune, though the pantsuit business had waned in recent years. Shark kept telling her, "They'll come back, Sue Bee. Everything comes back."

"Well, you certainly know about movies," Mom would say. "Maybe you know about fashion too."

Mom hadn't been to L.A. for years so we all went out sight-seeing. We went to Disneyland, and to the Chinese Theater, and then one day we drove up the coast because Mom wanted to see Malibu. I was driving the Corniche convertible past the Colony when suddenly Shark said, "Hold it, pull over." And he got out and went up to a blond-haired surfer who was gassing up his Corvette at the Mobil station.

## Woody Hazzard

I crapped for a second when I saw it was Shark. I almost didn't recognize him at first, and it wasn't because he'd changed that much physically. He looked good, healthier than during *Red Surf* by a long shot, but more than that he'd changed in his eyes, in his vibes, in his soul. That was really what I felt as he opened his arms like he wanted to hug me. It wasn't like the time at Sunset beach where he'd just been manipulating me. I sensed it was real now—he didn't want anything.

We hugged a long time. "Woody," he said. "I'm so sorry, man. I'm so fuckin' sorry. I still love you so much, man. I really fuckin' do."

"I know you do," I said. "And I love you too. Shit, you were my best fuckin' friend for years."

We talked for a while and he invited me to the premier of *Blue Light*. Then he asked about Brian, if Brian still hated his guts, and I said I was pretty sure he did, and we both laughed about that. Then he asked about Kathy, mentioning that he'd kind of resolved things with her at the Kolon Clinic, and I said, "Yeah, that's what I heard."

"Then you're still in touch her?"

"Oh yeah."

"How's she doing?"

"As well as can be expected, I guess," I told him.

"What do you mean?" he asked.

And I said, "Oh, Jeez, I guess you don't know. Gray died."

## Kathy Petro

I remember the day that Shark's card arrived by messenger. I was walking aimlessly around that suddenly enormous and empty Stone Canyon house in a numb stupor as I had been for weeks. The answering machine was clogged with messages from my New York publisher about how well the book was doing, and how they knew it was a difficult time for me and everything, but couldn't I try and pull myself together enough to do Merv this Thursday night?

Well, no. There was no way I could do Merv this Thursday or any Thursday ever. How could I laugh effusively at Merv's stupid jokes when the only man I'd ever truly loved was dead?

"Dear Kathy," the card read. "I just found out. I won't devalue the profundity of your grief by facilely trying to cheer you up. Know simply that you are now and forever, with no strings attached, in my heart. You are sunshine itself, Kathy. I know that warm days will come once again to your life." It was signed: "Your friend, Shark," with a P.S.: "If there's anything ever I can do, no matter how trivial, please don't hesitate to call." And then there was a number, which I recognized as a Bel-Air exchange.

I thought it was sweet, but for some reason I didn't understand I tore up the card.

## Greg Spivey

The premiere of course is history now. At the Village in Westwood, klieg lights, the works—Mastodon pulled out the stops. The Village, of course, is right across from the Bruin, the site of Shark's *Götterdämmerung*. But the only reference I heard him make to that debacle was a jaunty remark to Gary: "Just don't stab any critics in the lobby, Gary. That's how Tony Borgia lost his mother and his one good review."

"I'd never stab my mother, Shark," Gary said. "I love her. In fact, I don't intend to marry until I find a gal at least half as good as her."

As it turned out Shark didn't need to worry. The critical praise was virtually unanimous. *Blue Light* was one of those rare cinematic experiences that literally pleased everybody. It was above all a *film* film, accessible and emotionally involving to the average man or woman in the street, yet so well made, so chock-full of *purposeful* filmic allusions, such an astonishing tour de force of cinematic high art, that even the most erudite and élitist of the critics were completely overwhelmed.

The single bad review, as I recall, was the unconscionable hatchet job by Edmund Himmler in the *New York Review of Reviews*. But then he's always been the quintessentially vicious critic—a sour, repressed and loveless male spinster with a bitter ax to grind.

## Edmund Himmler, *New York Review of Reviews*, July 16, 1985

FROM "BLUE KITSCH"

If the mothership in *Close Encounters* resembles a lighting fixture in a Las Vegas casino, if E.T. resembles a repulsive bug anyone in his right mind would squash with his shoe, then surely "Deem," the cloying alien protagonist in Shark Trager's latest cinematic production *Blue Light,* resembles nothing so much as a chrome-plated stool sample with a fruitily pouting mouth and a pair of simpering girl's blue eyes.

Are American audiences so starved for reassurance in the face of imminent nuclear catastrophe that they will embrace this nauseating swirl of demented treacle? Yes, apparently. For the film has become this year's cheap catharsis, a tearjerking resolution of the East/West conflict for scared, stupid people everywhere.

## Gary Schnell

Shark shook his head and sighed when he finished reading the Edmund Himmler review. "This was written by a very sick man. You can feel the pain between the lines. I have nothing but pity and genuine compassion for him."

But Shark wouldn't let me read it. "Gary, it would be like letting you pet a mad, snarling dog."

Of course, by then one bad review didn't mean much anyway. What had started at the premiere just continued on and on: the audiences crying and applauding afterwards, carrying the sense of joy and hope out of the theater and into their lives, just as I'd always prayed they would.

In a strange way the figures just didn't seem to matter. I mean, *of course* it was breaking every house record. *Of course* it had the top grossing opening weekend in the history of film. *Of course* it was going to pass *E.T.* as the top grossing film of all time. But *so what?* To use the obvious religious analogy, you might as well try and put a monetary value on the second coming of Jesus.

## Bill Kemmer

I knew it was going to be a monster hit, but not even I was prepared for what happened. And the merchandising—Jesus God! How many Deem dolls were sold the first month? They couldn't keep them in stock.

It was just a phenomenon, and I must say my heart was full for Shark. To say it was a comeback wouldn't quite describe it. As much as people had despised him after *Red Surf*, the entire industry worshiped him now. Thank God we'd closed a first-look production deal with Shark on the basis of the screening, a very generous deal, because once the picture passed the hundred million mark in a record twenty-one days he could have written his own ticket at any studio in town. Of course, the media was clamoring for interviews with Shark and Gary, all of which they refused—Gary out of shyness, I think. As for Shark, well, I can't say why.

## Greg Spivey

It all got to be too much for Shark. He was happy, of course, though he would always insist it was Gary's picture. "I'm just a businessman. Gary's the artist." Which was both true and not true, because *Blue Light* in its look and texture and overall production design was as much a Shark Trager film as *White Desert*, or for that matter *Red Surf*.

I think Shark found the sheer velocity of the success disorienting. He'd had his blockbusters in the seventies, God knows, but what was happening with *Blue Light* was really on a whole other level. "I don't want to lose my balance," he said. "I can't let that happen this time."

So he checked into a Zen monastery up near Big Sur for a week of brutal, no-frills meditation. It was while he was there, incommunicado, that the inevitable happened. Despite all the government attempts to suppress it, the story of Shark's Beirut rescue finally exploded through the media.

At just the point where *Blue Light* was beginning to taper off ever so slightly, Shark Trager became a national hero.

# 24 / American Hero
## (1985)

## Kathy Petro

I was in bed one morning watching the *Today Show*, and Juanita was bringing me my breakfast, when the story came on about how Shark had rescued those Sunday school teachers in Beirut. And it was so thrilling I found myself saying to Juanita, "I know him. He's an old friend."

I guess that was when I knew Shark had really and truly changed. The old Shark would just never have done anything that heroic—he would have been too concerned with saving his own skin. So it really made me think: Was I being selfish myself by grieving over Gray so long? Whatever happened to my vows to help others and everything? Wasn't that why I'd written the book in the first place, so that maybe I could save at least just one other person from having to go through what I'd gone through? Maybe I should be out on the lecture circuit or something instead of just moping around all the time.

Yet I still found myself in a deep, numb depression every time I thought about Gray. So that afternoon I walked into Westwood, mainly just to get out of the house, and ended up seeing *Blue Light*.

Well, the film just did something to me. It was exciting and suspenseful—especially when they fired off all the nuclear missiles and you were thinking: My God, what can save us now? But there was also just so much love in it. It was just filled up with human compassion for everyone, even the Russians, who like everyone else were just longing for love.

But the ending especially really broke my heart. When Deem and Patti go out through space and vanish into the endless blue light it just reminded me of heaven. I don't know if Shark and Gary meant it that way, but that's how I took it. And it seemed to be saying: Yes, there is a place where people go when they die, where lovers can be together forever. I know it sounds corny, but it really made me see that yes, I would see Gray again, that once you've loved someone that love will always be, since life really has no beginning or end.

I stepped into the Westwood sunshine feeling calm and healed.

## Greg Spivey

As the story began breaking the White House called, and they were referred to the Zen monastery, which refused to summon Shark to the phone. When Shark found out several days later that the president had been trying to reach him, and he hadn't been informed, he became quite upset.

## Roshi Guy Yokomoto

"Why didn't you tell me Ronald Reagan was calling?" Shark said to me.

"Because it was merely another distraction," I told him. "Why add one more to your monkey mind?"

"But it was the president," he said.

"That's neither here nor there," I told him. "If it wasn't the president it would be something else, which you would judge either good or bad. You are trapped in duality. Go back and sit!"

But he left. He was in love with his delusions.

## Greg Spivey

Shark told me later the Zen roshi tried to "put a hex" on him. I said, "Come on, Shark, Zen Buddhists don't do things like that," but he insisted it was true.

"He told me there was no such thing as success and failure, but that since I obviously thought there was, I was doomed."

"He said that? Doomed?"

"Words to that effect."

"It's envy," I told Shark. "He's probably got an unsold screenplay in a drawer somewhere."

"You know," Shark said, "in his case I don't think so."

He went on to tell me about his meditation experience: "The oddest thing, Greg, was that as my mind began to empty, one of the last things to go was that ancient image of Kathy as she looked in the car the night we kissed at the Flying Wing Drive-In in 1964."

I was reacting to this with appropriate solemnity when the phone rang. As we expected, it was President Reagan.

## Bill Kemmer

Shark told me later it was a classic bit of Reagan backtracking. The president contended that his previous request that Shark understand the need "not to rock the boat" in Lebanon had been based on a "bad briefing from George [Schultz]." With a clearer understanding of the full situation, the president said, he would be honored to present Shark with a Davy Crockett Medal of Bravery in a special Oval Office ceremony. Naturally everyone who'd been involved would be invited to attend: the Sunday school teachers . . . and Narges and Drake and Mac.

## Mac Trager

I was in my new condo in Marina Del Rey when Shark's secretary called about going to Washington. She was that gal who later wrote *Teamster Secretary* before she was killed,* and I'll tell you she did sound tough on the phone. She said if I "behaved" there was a bonus in it for me. And if I didn't I might find my legs crushed by a truck.

---

*Stacy Joy Decker, who stepped into an empty elevator shaft after a 1986 "Nightline" appearance in which she defended her best-selling account of

## Drake Brewster

I was mopping floors at a downtown gym when his secretary called me. She said I'd get a thousand bucks if I stayed in line at the White House. But I'd been thinking about Shark's threat to have me offed by some feminist hit squad and realized it was bullshit. So I said, "Yeah, I'll be there, no problem." But I was thinking, what with Shark making millions off *Blue Light*, and me not even getting a shared screenplay credit for all the work I'd done, the time had definitely come to put on the squeeze.

## Narges Pahlavi-Bardahl

I was basing with a famous actor when Shark's secretary called me. She threatened me with deportation if I didn't "smile and act like a lady" as I met President Reagan.

I said, "We'll see about that," and she asked me how I would like to hobble off the plane in Teheran with both of my legs in casts.

I hung up on her and thought to myself: What a scene it would be if right in the middle of the ceremony, in front of the cameras and the president and everyone, I blurted out: "Shark Trager is a madman. He was going to blow my head off, and his henchman Drake Brewster was going to sodomize Shark's father—I'll tell you what really happened." I amused myself with this scenario as I went back to basing with the famous actor.

## Gary Schnell

Shark told me he read Kathy Petro's book *Behind the Smile* on the plane to Washington. He said he was deeply moved by her candid recital of her struggle with various drugs, and at the same time profoundly grateful for her discretion. Reading between the lines, he said, he knew that when she spoke of a "long-time admirer," or "a man from my teenage years who

Teamster violence and corruption, including the sensational allegation that her one-time boss, labor leader Jimmy Hoffa, had "bragged during sex" of having arranged the "mob execution" of John F. Kennedy. Shark Trager, for whom Decker worked for less than a month, perhaps best characterized the visually kittenish but hard secretary-turned-author as "a cross between Joey Heatherton and Lee J. Cobb."

still had a crush on me," that of course she was alluding to him.

At one point she wrote of "a man who did something really awful to me once which filled me with resentment for decades to come. But I see now that I *chose* to be resentful. He was only trying to love me, but like so many of us, did not know how to show love." I asked Shark if that was about him too, and he said it was, but he wouldn't tell me what it was he'd done to her.

### Narges Pahlavi-Bardahl

I began drinking heavily at the hotel bar in Washington because I hadn't slept for several days and my nerves were shot. Then the Secret Service came to get me and the sidewalk was wet and I slipped and skinned both of my knees.

### Mac Trager

I met Shark in the waiting room outside the Oval Office. He was polite but distant, you know. Then the hens he'd saved started showing up, gushing all over him. And he was smiling away like some kind of goodie-two-shoes, which kind of made me sick. Then Drake arrived in a cheap-looking suit, and Shark barely said hello to him. Then the White House staffers started telling us how the thing was going to go, and then we heard some commotion and there came Narges, drunk as a skunk and all riled up.

### Drake Brewster

Narges was real fucked up. These Secret Service guys were trying to calm her down as they led her in. But she was saying, "Get your hands off of me. What are you trying to do, cop a feel?" So Shark went over to her and said something, and she piped right down.

### Narges Pahlavi-Bardahl

Shark was deliberately playing with my mind, I see that now. He said, "You know, Narges, I've been thinking a lot lately of how great it was when you sat on my face in Palm Springs. I was thinking how it might be fun to try that again back at your hotel after this ceremony. Of course, if you're in a foul mood . . ."

So I pulled myself together, for he was turning me on. The way he was looking into my eyes, it was just like the old days.

## Mac Trager

The door finally opened and there was Ronald Reagan. Shark shook hands with the president and the two of them talked while the staffers showed everybody where to stand. Then Drake went up and interrupted Shark and the president.

## Drake Brewster

I went up and squeezed the back of Shark's neck, like we were buddies, except I did it real hard. I could tell Shark was in pain but he kept smiling at Reagan. "He's a good man, sir," I said to the president. "You should send him in commando-style to take care of Khadafi once and for all. Send us both in, sir." I grinned at Shark. "We could do to Khadafi what we were fixin' to do that night in Beirut before those Shiites came along." I laughed and winked at Shark, knowing he'd get it, but the Gipper wouldn't.

"Well, I'm certainly open to any suggestions you fellas might have," the Gipper said, and kind of chuckled.

"Drake's a sociopath, Mr. President," Shark said, and slid his hand down my back. "I'm afraid you'd find his suggestions demented at best." Then, without Reagan being able to see it, Shark jammed his hand down the back of my pants and for a second I thought he was gonna dig his finger right up my butthole. So I quit squeezing his neck real fast.

"Well, I've got nothing against a sociopath per se," the Gipper said, "as long as he's on our team."

Suddenly we heard something rip and Narges let out a yelp.

## Mac Trager

I thought it was funny myself. The staffers were trying to move Narges back by the Sunday school teachers, but she kind of stumbled and caught her dress on the wing of an eagle statuette on the president's desk. Then she whirled around real fast and her skirt tore clean off. She wasn't wearing any panties.

## Drake Brewster

There were already a bunch of photographers there, but some staff guy rushed up, waving his arms, saying, "No pictures. Come on, fellas. Give us a break on this one."

Narges was freaked out, trying to pick up her skirt. But one of the Sunday school teachers was standing on it, and when Narges picked it up, it ripped again. Finally she got it and the Secret Service guys hustled her out.

Shark was saying something to Reagan about what a pathetic case Narges was, I guess. 'Cause Reagan was shaking his head with this look of understanding pity.

## Narges Pahlavi-Bardahl

I was so humiliated I had to go and base. They gave me a maid's dress to put on and I went straight to the nearest bathroom, and dug out my torch and stash.

Within moments I took what I truly believe was my very last hit of cocaine. For no sooner had I done so than I noticed a *small human mouth* growing in the palm of my hand! A mouth I recognized at once as that of my adored Rossano Brazzi. "Narges," the little mouth instructed me gently but firmly in the only voice I was still capable of hearing. "Narges, flush that cocaine down the toilet."

So I did.

## Drake Brewster

After Narges split, everything went okay. The Gipper said a few words about Shark being an example of what made this country great. Then he handed Shark that bronze medal with a picture of Duke Wayne in a coonskin cap at the Alamo on it, and the cameras clicked away. Shark had to stand there for a long time posing with the president. But at a certain point he started staring out the window real hard. There was something else going on outside, a bunch of broads on the White House lawn.

## Mac Trager

I saw what Shark was looking at. There were a bunch of gals out there with Nancy Reagan. And one of 'em was Kathy Petro.

It was a gathering of women from all over the world who shared the First Lady's concern with the problem of drug abuse. I'd been really honored by the invitation, and by the kind things Mrs. Reagan had to say about my book. I had heard that Shark was going to receive the Davy Crockett medal, but I didn't really know it would be the exact day and hour that I was there on the grounds. The speechmaking part of the gathering was going on a lot longer than I'd expected, so I finally slipped away to go find a phone since I had a bookstore appearance scheduled for later that day and could tell I was going to be late. As I crossed the portico I heard the president of Mexico's wife saying into the microphone that she had brought "a gift from the people of Mexico," which might "come in handy" on the Reagans' Santa Barbara ranch, but I didn't really pay much attention because suddenly right there ahead of me was Shark.

I was so stunned I just stopped in my tracks. He was looking at me and I couldn't take my eyes off of his.

In the background I kind of heard Mrs. Reagan saying, "Well, I'm sure Ronnie and I can find something for him to do."

And the First Lady of Mexico said, "Well, you know, he used to be a movie star too, Mrs. Reagan."

And Nancy said, "Oh my. I'd better not tell Ronnie that. He's still trying to live down *Bedtime for Bonzo*."

Then there was polite laughter, but it was like the sound in a distant dream, for the only reality was the man who stood before me.

The air was crisp and I didn't have a wrap. Maybe that's why my nipples were getting hard, I don't know. Or maybe it was the way Shark was looking at me as he stepped toward me. He looked so handsome that afternoon. So youthful and just . . . really so good. And his eyes were clear and filled with a kind of pure hunger.

I was trembling as he reached me, and he didn't say a word. I thought he was just going to kiss me, but instead he took my hand. Waves of raw euphoria washed through me as his fingertips touched mine.

He lead me into the White House, along an empty corridor, my heart buzzing like a hummingbird's wings. Then he thrust open a door and we entered a room with a huge old bed and an ancient portrait of Abraham Lincoln.

There he kissed me and I kissed him. And soon we couldn't get enough of each other.

## Elliot Bernstein

Shark told me that as he made love with Kathy in the Lincoln bedroom he had a *"Vertigo* experience." He said they were both so fevered with desire they did not bother to remove their clothes. Rather, he held Kathy from behind against the high bed as she hiked her skirt, and he pulled his erect member from his fly. Though the scene might have appeared raunchily pornographic from a "cinematic" point of view, subjectively it was anything but, Shark emphasized. As he and Kathy connected there, he felt a swirling sensation, he said. And although they remained fixed in place against the bed, moving only in a rhythmic, locomotive manner, the walls began to move around them as if they were in a diorama composed of rear-projection screens, the room giving way, Shark said, to other times and other places. As Kathy turned her head so he could kiss her, they would be back in the car at the Flying Wing Drive-In in 1964. Then, as he thrust still deeper inside her, he would see the windswept grassy hill on Maui where her bare breasts had pressed his chest and he'd longed to take her ten years before. Then, as she gasped, they were there in her bathroom in Newport Beach—his teenage fantasy of climbing in the window and making love to her there made real at last. Then that bathroom gave way to the one in Derek Horus's house on the French Riviera as it was the night he'd come to "rescue" her in 1973. Then they were other places: in the James Dean A-frame in Sherman Oaks, in the Gold Coast bedroom, in the loft of the Ray-Mar Theater—places Kathy had never been, but where Shark had poignantly, fervently masturbated to his mental image of her. All of these seemingly futile lost moments were now redeemed.

## Kathy Petro

Something really beautiful and extraordinary happened as Shark and I made love there in that quaint old bedroom. But I still feel a little crazy even talking about it. All I know is that I got so far out that I guess I began to hallucinate, the whole Lincoln bedroom and everything just dissolving away. Suddenly we'd be in that car at the drive-in when we were fourteen years old! Then we'd be on this hill on Maui doing all the things we might have done if Daddy hadn't been there. Then we'd be in my bathroom in Newport Beach the night he made the peeping-Tom movie of me. We'd be making ravenous love and I'd look over his shoulder and see his Bell and Howell movie camera all glistening and masculine on the pink tile, and I'd feel this terrible welling-up of ancient terror and excitement and a million other emotions all at once.

Then we'd be in some weird A-frame kind of place I'd never seen before, and suddenly for some reason he would look like James Dean. And, I don't know, it just began to occur to me that Shark *was* every man I'd ever really wanted. He was James Dean and Errol Flynn and Harvey Keitel and everybody else you could ever think of all rolled into one virile ball. And he was blowing those emotional floodgates—which I'd kept so tightly shut when Gray was still alive—right off their hinges! There was no reason why we shouldn't be together now just like this forever! Shark knew it and I knew it—that's why we were devouring each other.

Then suddenly we heard this braying sound—you know, this donkey going: *Hee-haw!* And for some reason my heart just stopped.

## Drake Brewster

I'd watched Shark turn from the Oval Office window and ask the Gipper where the men's room was. The Gipper'd pointed to a door and when Shark ducked out I'd followed, thinking it might be my only chance to get him alone.

But instead of going to the men's room Shark cut out across the White House lawn and I soon saw why. Up there on the walkway he intercepted Kathy Petro. I hung back and watched as he took her hand and led her inside. Even at thirty paces you could feel the sex vibes, so I knew what they were up to. I was about to go in after them when the thing with the broads on the lawn broke up. I hid behind a pillar as they all trooped back into the White House, the Gipper's wife among 'em.

When the coast was finally clear I went in to look for Shark. It was eerie in a way, this long empty hallway. You could hear the broads yakking in some distant room somewhere, but there was no one in the immediate area, no Secret Service or nothing. I started up the hall and then I heard Shark and Kathy getting it on. You know, gasps from her and that slippedy-sloppedy sound. Why the broads hadn't heard 'em as they passed that room I don't know—I guess 'cause they were yakking so much.

So I went up and opened the door real quiet-like and there they were, doing it dog-style against this big old bed. It was pretty hot and I was getting turned on—they hadn't seen me yet—but I was just about to say something when I heard this fuckin' donkey bray! I looked back and saw this donkey—which I found out later was a gift to the Reagans from the president of Mexico's wife—just standing there in the door, like he was looking around for something. Some guy was running up from the lawn, yelling, "Come here, you stupid donkey."

Then I looked back when I heard the braying and saw this donkey and saw Kathy Petro. At just that moment she was looking back at me over her shoulder so that donkey got a real good look at her face.

## Kathy Petro

I looked back when I heard the braying and saw Drake Brewster standing in the door. Before I could even react to his presence I saw the donkey behind him, and the next thing I knew the donkey was charging just the way a bull might.

## Drake Brewster

It was crazy. That donkey just made a bee-line straight for Kathy Petro. I barely stepped out of the way. Shark saw it coming too, and pulled away from Kathy just as that donkey barreled into the Lincoln bedroom. For a second or two Kathy was still there braced against the bed with her butt exposed and I thought sure as shit that donkey was gonna nail her. 'Cause you couldn't help but notice it had a hardon about two feet long. It brayed again. And Kathy screamed.

464

## Kathy Petro

Right at the very last second Shark pushed me up across the bed. It was the only thing he could do. That donkey was coming too fast to stop it. I screamed as the donkey put his front feet on the bed, almost stepping on my hands, like he was trying to mount me. I shivered with revulsion as I felt his bulbous you-know-what touch my calf.

Shark lunged across the bed as best he could with his pants still down, so he could pull me to safety. And Drake, bless his heart, grabbed that beast by the tail.

## Drake Brewster

It was just instinct, I guess. I knew that thing would kill her. But grabbing the tail was a mistake. The son of a bitch kicked me back into the bureau, where I cracked the mirror with the back of my skull.

Then he turned on me, and for a second I thought he was gonna try and mount *me* or some weird deal like that. But he brayed again—and it was worse than any sound in a horror movie. And then he started kicking that big old bed apart.

## Kathy Petro

Shark was still pulling me across the bed as the donkey began kicking the frame. I screamed as the mattress and box springs fell to the floor. For a second I was trapped there in this big hollow as the donkey kicked the frame again. But at last Shark pulled me to safety and we ducked through a door that led to the next room.

Shark leaned against the door, both our hearts pounding, and said, "Go get help. I'm going back for Drake."

"No," I pleaded. "Don't go in there again, not by yourself. I'll be right back."

Suddenly the kicking in the Lincoln bedroom stopped, which was somehow more unnerving than anything. What was that donkey doing to Drake?

"Run," Shark said. "Hurry!"

So I ducked out to the hall, smoothing down my skirt, trying to collect myself. I couldn't understand why someone hadn't heard the racket and already come, but that part of the White House just seemed completely deserted.

I hurried up the hallway and went around a corner and saw all the women I'd been with having lunch in this large sunny room at the end of the hall. As I entered the room everyone stopped eating and stared, since I was quite a mess, I guess, all freaked out and everything plus probably reeking of sex. Mrs. Reagan approached me and said, "Kathy, what on earth—"

But before I could say a word I heard another *hee-haw* and looked back and saw that donkey charging into the room.

## Drake Brewster

I was picking myself up, my head bleeding from the mirror, when Shark burst back into the Lincoln bedroom.

"Where's Hector?" he said. By then I guess he'd put it together that it was Hector the donkey they'd used in *Looking for Lupe*, which he explained later had been negatively conditioned to Kathy's picture on a T-shirt the donkey had been looking at during a fire in a stable.

"I guess he split," I told Shark. "Must've gone out that way into the hall."

"Oh shit," Shark said, and he and I ducked out to the hall.

Then we heard the broads scream and tore off around the corner. We reached this ballroom where all the broads were just in time to see Hector kick a Secret Service man back across the floor. Then Hector charged Kathy, the Gipper's wife jumping back with a horrified look.

Kathy tripped on the carpet as Hector closed in. But when the Secret Service man fell his gun had slipped out and clattered across the floor. So Shark picked up the gun while all these broads were going apeshit and drew a bead on Hector as he said to the broads through gritted teeth: "*Get down.*"

As the broads ducked down behind the tables Shark squeezed the trigger, plugging poor old Hector in the head. The donkey lurched just short of Kathy Petro, then kind of reeled like he was stunned, blood shooting out of his head like it was coming from a hose, throwing arcs all over the white tablecloths.

Then Hector staggered over toward this grand piano, blood still going everywhere, and then he shot off. I mean that big old dick of his just fired off about a quart of donkey jiz, big old long streaks of it going every which way. The broads kind of keened. The Gipper's wife jumped back, but she still got a big old streak of donkey jiz on her orange dress.

Then Hector lurched into the piano, knocking the support out, so that the top banged down on his head. Then he croaked, just going limp, kind of hanging there, with his head caught in the grand piano.

## Kathy Petro

Shark helped me up from the floor and held me, and I just wanted him to hold me forever. Most of the women were whimpering by that time from the horror of it all. Then the Secret Service just arrived en masse, and we were told that we would be adjourning to another room for coffee. But I just wanted to leave.

I was numb in a way, but I felt safe with Shark. He left me for a minute to speak privately with the Secret Service men, and when he came back he put his arms around me and said everything was going to be all right, and I said, "Please just don't ever let me go."

I kept holding onto him, just wishing I could literally hide under his jacket, as we waited for the limousine to come around. At that point Mrs. Reagan came out in a fresh dress. She told Shark that what he'd done was very brave, but she seemed troubled, and Shark read her mind.

"Mrs. Reagan, I just want you to know that as far as I'm concerned this tasteless and horrifying episode never occurred. I did what I felt I had to, but it is not something I will ever speak of to anyone. When I recall this date in my memoirs it will be only to say that you were a consummately gracious hostess as I made an impromptu stop at your utterly decorous luncheon to briefly say hello."

At that Mrs. Reagan gave Shark a hug and said, "God bless you." She smiled at me. "Both of you." Then she added, with a twinkle in her eye: "I sense a great love in the making here."

"You sense correctly," Shark told her. "Odd as this may sound to Kathy, I feel as if we've only just begun."

I felt myself blushing as Mrs. Reagan said, "I just know you're going to be very happy. Kathy, with a man like Shark you can't go wrong."

As insane as it may seem now, on that crisp afternoon, which had been both so rapturous and so revolting, I had no doubt that she was right.

## Drake Brewster

The Secret Service guys took me to a hospital there in Washington to get my head stitched, and all the time the doctor was working they kept trying to get me to promise not to talk about what happened. But I kept saying, "Well, I might keep my mouth shut if there's something in it for me." And they were getting real steamed when Shark came in.

As soon as we were alone Shark said, "Drake, you surprised me this afternoon. Grabbing Hector's tail was a very courageous act and no doubt prevented an occurrence too grisly to contemplate. I am therefore going to give you one point in *Blue Light* as a token of my appreciation."

Then he went on to say he still thought I was dogshit and that as part of the deal I would have to sign a paper saying that if I ever talked to anyone about what had happened at the White House or about any of my associations with Shark in the past I would forfeit my profit participation and, he hinted, there were forces in the government that might punish me much more severely than that.

Well, I had some idea how much a point of *Blue Light* was worth, so for the last time I shook Shark Trager's hand.

## Mac Trager

Narges and I got back together again there in D.C. She became abject at the White House after the Secret Service found her muttering to herself in the john. *"You* take her back to the hotel," they told me, and she sobbed in the back seat of the limousine.

"I feel so terrible," she said. "I can't go on like this."

"There, there, it's okay," I said, and put my arm around her. "Old Mac'll take care of you, you sweet Iranian thing, you. We'll get you off that cocaine one way or another."

As it turned out we were on the same flight back to L.A. as Shark and Kathy. They sat up ahead of us all lovey-dovey, but no more so than Narges and me. We got us a couple of blankets, and I finger-banged her crazy little Persian box from sea to shining sea. "Don't stop, Mac," she said over Kansas. "When you make me feel this good I have no desire for drugs."

## Kathy Petro

I felt so dreamy flying home with Shark. It just seemed so right to be with him at last. We whispered sweet nothings and spoke of the future. He said he was going to buy the old VistaVision Ranch.

"I don't care where I am," I told him. "A hovel in La Puente, a tract house in Torrance, it wouldn't matter how grungy it was. As long as it had a bedroom where we could pull down the shades and stay in bed all day making love, love, love."

Then he kissed me and we melted into one another as we descended through the smog into the endless brown expanses of L.A.

# 25 / **VistaVision**
## (1985–1986)

### Greg Spivey

Amazingly, the White House donkey incident did not make the news, although there were several female reporters present at the luncheon. Out of respect for the First Lady, I suppose, and probably because there was really no way to tastefully describe what had happened, there was a kind of tacit consensus among the Washington press corps that the incident should simply be quietly forgotten.

Out of curiosity however Shark did trace the route Hector had taken from *Looking for Lupe* to the president of Mexico, and every owner told the same tale of initial elation—Hector having become more or less the "Francis" of the seventies—followed by disgust as Hector's penchant for untimely defecation and general rowdiness became apparent. It was therefore obvious that the gift to the Reagans was in fact a malicious prank, but Shark never passed this information on. Nor did he tell Kathy Petro why Hector had specifically attacked her since to do so, he told me, would only evoke the "negative obsessional energies of the past." So as far as Kathy knew, the donkey had simply gone mad.

It was obvious however that Shark's "obsessional energies" were not all in the past. As soon as they got back to L.A. Shark and Kathy moved into an unctuously picturesque Bel-Air cottage—a temporary home while the VistaVision Ranch was being renovated—and spent the last four months of 1985 doing little more than fucking their brains out.

## Kathy Petro

We called it our Enchanted Cottage because that's what it was. It was just this adorable little house like something in a fairy tale with all this Hansel and Gretel Bavarian gingerbread everywhere. And the flowers! The whole lot, the whole house, was just covered with flowers, it seemed like every kind of flower you could think of. And a florist came in several times a week and put cut flowers in every room, so the whole place was just laced with natural fragrances. Flowers and sunshine and bees and hummingbirds—that's my main memory of that wondrous autumn. The flowers and the sunshine and the sweetness of Shark's love.

The dreamy days melted into one another as we made love day and night, only pausing it sometimes seemed to eat and sleep. I don't know what it was, it was sex yet somehow beyond sex at the same time. It was as if we'd been held apart all our lives by fear and complications and now that we were finally together we just wanted to merge and become one, and since we had bodies we used our bodies to do that.

## Bill Kemmer

I understood how much Kathy meant to Shark—and thought I understood why he had opted for seclusion with her at a time when the media interest in his Beirut heroism was most ravenous*

---

*Shark deflected all interview requests, and book and commercial endorsement offers, in the wake of the Beirut rescue story with a high-toned prepared statement in which he spoke of "a moral obligation not to exploit myself for doing nothing more (or less) than any other patriotic American would have done under similar circumstances."

—but I began to grow irritated nonetheless. He had projects in development but nothing all that promising and for weeks on end he seemed to have forgotten entirely that he was in a position to make virtually any film he wished. So I was relieved when after the first of the year he began driving up to the VistaVision Ranch to check on the progress, though I understand he and Kathy made something of a lewd spectacle of themselves on several visits.

## Greg Spivey

The VistaVision Ranch was essentially a gift to Shark from Jake Skyler, the chairman of Montanacom International, which had acquired Mastodon Pictures in late 1984. Jake was a tough old western tycoon, a kind of real-life John Wayne character, who took an instant liking to Shark and, significantly, an instant disliking to Gary Schnell, whom Jake referred to behind Gary's back as "No Nuts," which described only too well Gary's cloyingly "nice" and sexless personality. As a result Jake gave Shark the ranch and told him to "bill Mastodon" for the renovation expenses, which came to millions. And Gary got the Pangborn Building, a cramped Streamline Moderne one-story structure on the Mastodon lot, which was extremely rundown and pervaded with a subtle but disgusting smell—the result of decaying rats in the walls, it was said.

Gary was miffed and began obsessively comparing his seedy facilities to Spielberg's headquarters at Universal. "Steven's got a game room, a projection room. All I've got is this rusty Art Deco water cooler, and even that was plugged up with something that looked like Xavier Cugat's toupée."

"*Blue Light* was only your first film, Gary," I'd tell him. "Give it a little time."

But of course it was a question of ego. And Gary was green with envy the first time he saw the VistaVision Ranch, which Shark was developing into a major base of operations, a kind of Skywalker Ranch South, set in the dry Malibu brush of Kelp Canyon.

## Gary Schnell

It did bother me the first time I saw that place, because it had everything I wanted. There was a huge swimming pool and stables and posh state-of-the-art editing suites and guesthouses for dozens of people. There was a special effects facility and a helicopter pad and tennis and racquet ball courts and an astonishing view of the ocean several miles below. And the ranch house itself had been redone in this 1930s Will Rogers lodge style with deep leather sofas and antlers and all that and it had every amenity you could think of. The screening room had been expensively upgraded so that it could show anything, including old nitrate prints, and it could accommodate almost two hundred people in luxurious deep oxblood leather overstuffed chairs. There was even an abandoned church by the front gate which Shark said he was going to turn into an office for me since he knew how much I hated the Pangborn Building. But I told him I didn't think it would be right to do that to a church. In reality though, I was so stirred up inside with different conflicting emotions I didn't know if I could ever work with Shark again.

Besides, he was so busy having compulsive sex with Kathy Petro it remained to be seen if he'd ever even make another movie. It was clear to me that she was sapping his energy and pulling him down into a kind of erotic insanity. The day he showed me around the ranch I went to use the bathroom and when I came back I caught them doing something unbelievably crude.

## Greg Spivey

Shark told me Gary caught a glimpse of Kathy going down on him in the ranch house den. Embarrassed, Gary quickly ducked away before Kathy saw him. But Shark saw Gary and confessed that for some reason he found the idea of Gary watching a turn-on—his old exhibitionistic streak, I guess. Of course, Shark was aware that he'd been neglecting his friendship with Gary since Kathy entered the picture, and knew Gary was feeling hurt and a little jealous, though not in any gay sense. Shark reflected on the entire matter and realized that the only way to provide Gary with a true perspective on the difference between platonic friendship and erotic love was to see that Gary finally got laid.

## Tina Veer

I guess you could say I had been one of Shark's one-night-stands in the late 1970s. We got it on in that beach house in

Santa Monica. It was the usual horseshit, him saying I was just right for some part and how much I reminded him of Gloria Grahame because of the way my mouth was—I'd heard that before, I guess we did have similar mouths, which along with a buck would buy me a cup of coffee. I knew he was full of shit but I fucked him anyway, 'cause in a town like Hollywood you never know. But the next film he made was *Red Surf*. That happened a lot. For some strange mystical reason I always seemed to fuck the wrong guy.

By '86 I was twenty-eight and bitter, having done a bunch of episodic TV shit and flashed my tits in a couple of raunchy teen pics. So when Shark called me out to the VistaVision Ranch—he was still in the process of moving in—and asked me how I'd like to pop Gary Schnell's cherry I laughed and said, "Well, that just all depends. What's in it for me?"

He said there might be a part in a movie and I guffawed, thinking: Yeah, sure, *riiight*.

Then he said, "Look, Tina, try and be sweet. You still *look* sweet for some reason, that's why I thought of you. Just try and pretend you're not a hard little barracuda and you just might land a hell of a real-life part too."

So what the fuck, I thought. Gary Schnell *was* a very hot director and not *that* bad to look at, his millions of dollars creating, shall we say, a certain charisma. "All right, how's this?" I said, and pursed my lips like some prim and prissy little virgin. "Is this what he wants? Is it this?"

## Kathy Petro

Shark and I moved to the VistaVision Ranch in early 1986, and I really hated to see the Enchanted Cottage go. Those months had been like a timeless idyll in paradise—and I still believe that sunny autumn is destined to remain one of the peak experiences of my life. But nothing lasts forever. We both knew it was time for us to return to the world of everyday reality, Shark to make movies, me to promote my book which had just come out in paperback and to use my fame to speak out in the fight against drug abuse.

And so our period of isolation ended. For though we could still be alone in the ranch house and make glorious love for hours on end, we could frequently hear the voices of the many others on the grounds. We began inviting people in for huge breakfasts and barbecues and the sounds of joyful laughter echoed through those scrubby hills. Yet Shark seemed restless. He spent his time pouring over technical details as they completed the work on what was almost a self-contained ministudio. But now that he had everything any moviemaker could ever want, it was like he didn't know what to do with it.

## Greg Spivey

At first I thought it was just the *81/2* syndrome. How could Shark top himself after *Blue Light?* We had some scripts in development that weren't all that bad, but it was clear none of them really excited Shark.

Then one afternoon I was talking with Shark on the ranch house porch when it came time for Kathy to leave for the airport. She was going back east for a week of public appearances. Shark put her luggage in that specially built aquamarine Ferrari Clarapetacci he'd recently given her, and then they passionately and protractedly kissed good-bye. I couldn't help noticing however that Kathy was by far the more passionate of the two of them. You could just see, and feel, how crazy she was about him. And it wasn't just sexual, though it obviously included that. But you could see that she really loved *him,* if you know what I mean. Which made what followed all the more heart-rending.

For as Shark stepped back to me he appeared profoundly, indeed numbingly depressed. As we watched Kathy rumble throatily down the driveway toward the gate Shark said, "You know, Greg, it's a scary thing when you really get everything you've ever wanted."

"Yes, I know," I said, trying to sound sardonic. "The terrible cost of success."

But Shark didn't smile. "Take Kathy, for example," he said. And as I had so many times before, I sensed that he was about to tell me things that were none of my business, but which I suppose he had to tell someone.

"For over twenty years I longed for that woman with every fiber of my being. And now that I've got her, do you know what, Greg? You're going to love this."

"What, Shark?"

"She bores the shit out of me."

I was momentarily at a loss for words. For I saw that Shark

was simply telling the truth. And it struck me as somehow so terribly, so desolately sad.

"I suppose we can dream of someone so long that when we're finally with them they inevitably fall short of our dreams," I said.

"She's a dim bulb," Shark said. "She's got the IQ of a stuffed toy. If she says more than two words I start to yawn."

"She's got a good heart, Shark."

"She has an unerring instinct for the trite observation and the vapid remark."

"She's an extraordinarily beautiful woman, you can't deny that."

"Yes, and she's good sex too. But do you know something, Greg? I never thought I'd say this, but I'm even bored with that."

"Perhaps you should try some new things in bed—"

"Greg." The emptiness in his eyes made me look away. "We've done it all."

"I don't know what to tell you, Shark."

"I'm scared, Greg," he said with an intensity that startled me. "I don't want to feel this way about Kathy, but I do. I knew the sex wouldn't last forever. We were burning too brightly, but . . . I must find a way to rekindle my feeling for her, or . . ." He didn't finish.

"It's too bad she can't act," I said, perhaps a bit tactlessly. By the way he stared at me I thought sure he'd taken offense.

"What makes you think she can't act?" Shark said.

"Well, *Manhattan Holiday*. I hate to even mention it, but . . ."

"But that film was a piece of shit," Shark said. "The problem was Andreji's nauseating script and inept direction. Even Meryl Streep would have stunk in that."

I didn't agree but held my tongue. It was clear that Shark's wheels were already turning, so I suppose I must take credit for planting the seed that grew into *Home to the Heart*.

## Elliot Bernstein

I always felt that *Home to the Heart* was a fairly calculated attempt to woo the Academy after what happened in 1986.

## Bill Kemmer

We were all disappointed but not really surprised when *Blue Light* was only nominated for technical awards, for as is so frequently the case when a film does that well, a rather severe backlash had set in. It was a terribly cruel phenomenon to witness though, a number of the critics in effect reversing their opinions, confessing they'd been "taken in" by the film's "manipulative sentimentality," many of them, I suppose, shamed and sobered by Edmund Himmler's merciless review. By the time the Academy balloting took place I think the members were skittish of voting for a "flashy special effects cartoon movie," a big slick "cheaply cathartic, crypto-religious" fantasy blockbuster, especially in a year that was heavy with small, "relevant" human dramas featuring a number of virtuoso Oscar-fodder acting turns. Of course, James Dustin's semi-autobiographical *A Farm to Come Back To* went on to sweep the awards, stealing the recognition that Shark no doubt felt should have been his.

As it happened, I was with Gary Schnell when the nominations were announced, and he became extremely dejected. I tried to call Shark at the ranch, only to be told he was "incommunicado."

Later we learned that he was actually writing—or to be specific, dictating—the script of what I still believe will go down in history as his most shatteringly poignant film.

## Woody Hazzard

I had seen Shark a few times since we made up but we were not in any sense hanging out together. Part of the reason for that was Brian, since he still hated Shark's guts, and I still cared a lot about Brian, so I hadn't even mentioned the one time I'd gone up to the VistaVision Ranch. I'd been real impressed by the place and Shark had said something about how I should try writing another screenplay some day, but I just kind of winced and said, "No, I think *Red Surf* was it for me."

Then one afternoon he called and said, "Woody, this is it. You've got to come up here immediately. Something astounding is happening inside me and only you can help me bring it out."

I didn't know what he was talking about and it sounded weird—*he* sounded weird—but I drove up anyway, partly out of curiosity, I guess. Besides, Kelp Canyon wasn't that far from the Colony. It was spooky driving up there though. Kelp Canyon was basically this one-lane road with lots of blind turns running through the middle of nowhere, just empty chaparral hills, and that winter was super-dry, there hadn't been a drop of rain yet, and there was a bad Santa Ana blowing, which always made everybody real jumpy.

It was a Sunday and when I got there the place seemed deserted. Shark buzzed me through the gate and I drove up to the ranch house and Shark was waiting there, shirtless and sweaty, with this funny look in his eyes, and I just knew instantly he was on something.

Then I stepped into the house and there on the table were these two mounds of powder—one was white and clearly cocaine, but the other one was brown. And I said, "Oh shit, is this what I think it is?"

"Don't lay a guilt trip on me, okay?" Shark said. "I need it for inspiration. To break through the mental blocks. I'm using it very scientifically."

"This is smack, isn't it, you dodo?" I said. "You're snorting speedballs. Didn't you learn anything from Belushi's death?"

"Don't lecture me," Shark said. "There isn't time. I've got a movie in my head, I can see the entire thing, and you've got to write it down."

"You're nuts, man," I said. "Is this what you asked me up here for? I'm not going to be a party to this. Fuck this."

I started for the door, but he blocked my path.

"Woody, please, I'm not kidding, I need you."

"Why don't you write it yourself, Shark, if it's such a great idea?" By then I was totally pissed because of the drugs. I just saw all the weird shit from the past starting up all over again.

"I can't write it," Shark said. "I just can't do that."

"Yeah, I know," I said. "And you know why you can't? 'Cause you're chickenshit. You want somebody else to take the heat in case it goes down the tubes like *Red Surf*. That's the story of your life, you know that, Shark? You could have been a great director if you hadn't pussed out. You could've been another Orson Welles—"

"Yes, exactly, in every sense, you moron!" he yelled at me. "I would've ended up beaten and broken. What do you know about anything, you asshole? Sit down and shut up and turn on that computer."

"Fuck you," I said and went out the door. I was crossing the porch when I heard a gun click. I couldn't believe it at first, it was like something in a movie. But I looked back and he had

478

this big fucking Colt .45 in his hand, one of those Old West models with a foot-long barrel.

"Come back in here, Woody," he said.

"You're nuts, man," I said, but I went back in.

"Sit down at the word processor," he said.

"I don't know how to use one of these things," I told him.

"It's easy," he said, and switched it on, still keeping me covered. "It's ready now. You just type the way you would on a typewriter."

So I started to sit down and he said, "Wait. Take off your clothes."

"What?"

"I want to make sure you don't try and make a run for it."

"Where am I gonna go?" I said. "The whole fucking property's fenced and the gate's a quarter mile away."

"Peel off your duds, Woody. Just do it," he said almost gently.

"This is too weird, man," I said, but I took off my clothes.

## Kathy Petro

I had sensed for a while that something wasn't quite right with Shark, but I thought it was just that he hadn't decided what movie to make next. I didn't see, or didn't want to see, that he was already growing tired of me. I was just not prepared to accept that, not at a time when I had finally come to love and appreciate him in a way that really scared me at times, since my heart was right out there on the line. I had always known the early sexual intensity wouldn't last forever, I knew enough about relationships to know that. I therefore sensed that we were passing through a critical period where, if we were to last and my heart was not to be broken, we would really have to come up with something to hold us together besides sex.

This train of thought was reinforced by a conversation I had with a noted psychologist backstage before the "Donahue" Show. "Don't tell *me* these things," she said. "You should be expressing these feelings directly to Shark." She also suggested that Shark and I make separate lists of our likes and dislikes and then compare them. "You're bound to locate areas of mutual interest that way, as well as discovering the things you should never do together."

I thought about that a long time and it seemed like such a

good idea I decided to cut my trip short by two days and started making my own list on the flight back to L.A. Then as we came into LAX I noticed all this black smoke up the coast in the Malibu area.

## Woody Hazzard

I smelled the smoke around three that afternoon. By then I was up to about page eighty of the screenplay. Shark wasn't kidding, it was all in his head, he hardly changed a line and kept going as fast as I could type, only pausing to lean over the table and snort more smack and cocaine.

I didn't pay much attention to what I was typing at the time, I was too blown out to really visualize it as I went. All I could see in my mind was Shark sitting behind me with that gun. But I was kind of aware it was at least partly autobiographical, since his mom and dad were the main characters. Mac and Winnie. Except they weren't like any Mac and Winnie I'd ever known or heard of. His mom had checked out before Shark and I were ever friends, you know, but I'd heard she was pathologically withdrawn and probably crazy. But the Winnie in the script I was being forced to write was like some character Sally Field would play, you know? This real stand-up-and-be-counted dynamo type.

"You know, I think there's a fire over there in Tuna Canyon," I said to Shark, when I saw all these clouds of smoke to the west.

"Damn it, you made me lose it," he said, and I looked back and saw how hard he was concentrating. The gun was resting on the arm of the chair and I considered making a lunge for it. In a way I couldn't really believe he would shoot me. But on the other hand the dope was clearly affecting his mind. A lot of the story seemed ultra-sentimental as well as basically a lie, like some real boorish junkie getting all nostalgic about how great his parents were or something, you know?

"Okay, I've got it," he said, and looked up before I could go for the gun. "Interior, J. Edgar Hoover's Office, FBI Building, Day. Hoover stands before a portrait of President Eisenhower as Winnie storms in. She shakes her finger in Hoover's startled face, tears welling in her eyes. Winnie: 'Now you listen to me, Mr. Director. My husband Mac is a loyal American . . .' " It went on like that.

But the smoke kept getting worse until it turned the sun this weird cherry-red color and so much ash was drifting through the window I had to keep blowing it off the computer keys.

"Shark, I'm worried about this fire," I said. "It looks like it's just on the other side of that ridge."

"Don't be a pussy," he said. "Just keep typing. Interior, Hospital Room, Day. Winnie appears nauseated from the cobalt treatment . . ."

Then I looked out the window and saw these huge fucking flames coming down our side of the ridge.

## Kathy Petro

I tried calling Shark from the airport, but the service said he'd left word not to be disturbed. "Look, this is me, Kathy," I said, and they said, "Sorry, Miss Petro, but he gave specific orders."

So I was irked, but I also had a funny feeling that Shark might be in grave danger because of the fire. I hurried out to my Ferrari and drove toward Malibu as fast as I could. When I reached PCH I saw how bad the fire really was, these huge clouds of smoke billowing out over the sea. Fire trucks were screaming past me and when I reached the Kelp Canyon turn-off it was closed off with a barricade. There was nobody there though, so I got out and moved the barricade and drove on up. By the time the ranch came into view the smoke was so bad my eyes were smarting. I opened the gate and drove up to the house where I saw that sure enough Shark's Porsche was still there. And Woody's Corvette was parked beside it. Then I saw that the fire was burning right behind the house, right up to the line where they'd cleared the brush! I dashed into the house, yelling, "Shark!" and found him wrestling with Woody, who was nude, on the floor.

## Woody Hazzard

I'd finally stood up and said, "Go ahead and shoot me, man. 'Cause if we stay here we're gonna burn."

And Shark looked at me and said, "I can't shoot you, man. This old gun isn't even loaded."

But instead of being relieved I flipped. "You son of a bitch," I said and laid into him.

The next thing I knew we were grappling on the floor. It was weird, but for some reason I started to get turned on. At one point our faces were real close and I knew that on some level what I really wanted to do was kiss him, you know, just ferociously start making out. But to Shark it was just a fight and nothing more and he was determined to win, so I fought back and eventually got him in a scissor hold, you know, with my dick squashed up right in his face. And it was at that point that Kathy came in.

## Kathy Petro

I reeled when I saw them like that, not really sure what was going on. At first it looked like a fight, but then I thought: Why is Woody nude? What in fact is going on here? Is this really a fight, or some sort of homosexual wrestling match? And then I saw the cocaine and heroin on the table and I just freaked.

I ran out to the Ferrari, but I was so upset I drove off the driveway and got stuck in the dirt. The wheels just spun and the car wouldn't budge, so I got out and ran down to the gate.

## Woody Hazzard

Seeing Kathy jolted Shark more than it did me. He quit fighting and said, "Let me up, man. Let me up."

So I did and Shark and I were both winded, and he seemed suddenly sobered. He was holding his head like he was finally seeing how badly he'd flipped out, and saying, "Oh my God, what have I done? What am I doing? What must she think?"

Then he ran out to the porch and called, "Kathy?" But she didn't answer and the smoke was so bad you couldn't even see down to the gate. I was pulling on my pants as he dashed back in. "My God, she's taken off on foot," he said. "Come on, we've got to find her. It looks like the fire's about to burn across the road."

"Fuck you," I said. "You're crazy, man. I knew I should never have come up here."

"You're right, I've been a bad boy, you can spank me later if you want," he said. "But right now all that matters is finding Kathy. I know you still love her on some level, just as you love me, and I love you and Kathy."

"You're nuts," I said, and grabbed my shoes and ran out to my car.

482

He ran out after me, calling Kathy's name again. The fire was burning right up behind the house, a couple of the umbrellas around the pool igniting. I got in my Corvette and started the engine. "You better get the fuck out of here," I yelled at him, but he seemed dazed, looking off through the smoke for some sign of Kathy. "Did you hear me, Shark?" I said, and he didn't respond. So I said: "Fuck him" to myself and peeled out.

I caught up with Kathy a quarter mile down the road. "Come on, get in," I yelled as I pulled up beside her.

"Homo," she said.

"Kathy, that's not nice. Come on, get the fuck in. The fire's coming close."

"Is Shark gay now too?"

"No, no, no. It's not what you think. He was literally holding a gun to my head. Kathy, for fuck's sake, get in."

The fire was ripping right down to the road, so she finally got in. Just as I pulled out we heard this massive explosion and I saw a fireball back up the road in my rearview mirror. Then it was out of sight as we went around a bend, but it came back into view again and Kathy was looking back and said, "Oh my God, it's the Porsche! He's burning up in his Porsche! Go back, go back!"

"I can't," I said. And I couldn't, the fire had cut us off. We had to get out of there fast to save our own butts.

"Oh my God," Kathy kept saying, "Oh my God." By the time we reached PCH she was hysterical.

## Brian Straight

We gave Kathy a sedative at the Colony house. I had not seen her since the divorce. "Well," I said eventually, "I suppose it's the end of an era."

"Yes, and you're glad, aren't you, Brian?" she said. "You're glad Shark's dead."

"Don't be silly, Kathy," I replied. "Shark Trager did more for the Hollywood film industry this year than any other single man."

"You're being sardonic as always," she said. "And it's not appropriate, Brian. There's a time for everything and the time for that is not now."

"At least he died trying to save you, Kathy," Woody said, with his arm around her on the couch.

"He did?" Kathy said, and Woody nodded. And she began sobbing against his chest.

## Woody Hazzard

It was a very weird night. I kept making calls, trying to find out what the fuck was going on, and finally talked to Greg Spivey around midnight and learned that the VistaVision Ranch had been spared.

"I guess the brush clearing paid off," I said to Kathy, who was watching the fire reports on the TV in a numb, sedated stupor.

Then she got up and said, "I'm going for a walk on the beach."

"Are you all right?" I said, scenes from different movies where people walked in the Malibu surf flashing through my mind.

"Yes," she said. "I just want some air."

## Kathy Petro

I walked along the shoreline and smoked my last cigarette. I did think about suicide. I mean, who wouldn't under the circumstances? Mostly, I was just numb though. Numb and oddly grateful that at least Shark and I had had a few wondrous months. For that was what I saw, how truly precious that time in the Enchanted Cottage had been. That ultimate pinnacle of romance and sex, instead of just one or the other. How many people in this world ever really have a time like that?

The waves crashed, the icy water getting into my shoes. The pungent smell of the fire still laced the night air, and I wiped my cheeks where soot was stuck to my tears. What a crazy roller coaster ride it had been! How could I even imagine my life without Shark Trager? As irritant, pest, pathological obsessive and finally mind-shattering lover. Sweet God, what a time we had had!

And then, you know, I saw him. As I turned back to the house I saw him coming out across the sand. His bare torso, still so hard and muscular at thirty-seven, was smeared with soot. So was his face, that boyishly handsome face, resembling in the moonlight that of a battle-weary Errol Flynn with a touch of Kevin Costner. As he came closer I saw that his dirty blond hair was singed in several places. And then I could barely see anything at all, I was crying so heavily. Then he held me and I held him.

## Woody Hazzard

I'd answered the door and needless to say it shocked the shit out of me to see Shark standing there. "Fuck, man. You're *alive*."

"Yeah, I jumped out of the Porsche just as the flames began to engulf it," he said, looking past me. "Did you get Kathy?"

I told him she was on the beach, and he went right out to her. I watched them hug and kiss. Then as they came back toward the house Shark broke away from her and came up to me.

"You can tell me to fuck off, I won't blame you," he said. "But I really am sorry, Woody. It was the drugs, and it's not going to happen again. Lesson learned, I swear."

So I went ahead and hugged him, glad he was alive and everything. But to tell you the truth it was never the same, not after the other weird shit that had come down that day.

# 26 / Home to the Heart (1986–1987)

## Gary Schnell

I was in bed with a woman I thought I loved when Shark called me to say he wanted me to read a new script Woody Hazzard had written. "You're too late, Shark," I told him. "Brian Straight just gave me a green light on my Houston project at Acropolis."

"You've got to be kidding," Shark said. "You can't work for him. You know how I feel about Brian."

"That's your problem, Shark," I said, as Tina kissed her way down my stomach. "You may have old enemies in this town but I don't."

"But Gary, no one else can possibly make this picture. It's a warm, tender elegy to a bygone era, but one that's coming back as people see that there were many virtues intrinsic to the 1950s that are well worth reclaiming. And it's extremely autobiographical."

"Then why don't you direct it yourself, Shark?" I said.

There was a pause and I sensed he was suppressing his anger.

"At least read it, Gary."

"Shark, I'm busy at the moment—"

"I'm coming by," he said and hung up.

"Damn it," I said, not wanting to get out of bed, not that day or ever. What a world of physical delight I had denied myself out of shyness! And the way it happened with Tina was so spontaneous and therefore so right.

## Tina Veer

It was a pretty simple ploy. I just parked my old Pinto on Sunset, then walked up to Gary's gate in Bel-Air and buzzed. "Look, my car broke down and a couple of sinister guys offered me a lift. I told them to leave me alone and now they're out cruising around looking for me. Please help." It was almost midnight and I was dressed square like Marie Osmond on her way home from a church function.

He buzzed me in. In the living room I grew faint and he offered me a glass of mineral water. Belatedly, I pretended to recognize him. I gushed over *Blue Light*. He said, "You're an actress, aren't you?" He actually remembered me from a bit I'd done on "Quincy" years ago.

And then a strange thing happened. Even though it was part of the plan that I was gonna break down and cry about how badly my career was going, I began to cry for real. I mean, I really got into it, and it wasn't an act.

And he became very tender, treating me like no guy had in I don't know how long. And when we made love, I don't know . . . I don't even want to talk about it. It would make it cheap if I talked about it. He touched something inside me that hadn't been touched in years. And if you think that's funny or dirty, fuck you.

## Gary Schnell

Tina was in the kitchen when Shark arrived, and in retrospect I see there was something funny going on as I introduced them. Tina seemed frightened, even though she was acting like she and Shark had never met before.

Shark and I went out to the patio and he gave me the script of *Home to The Heart,* insisting that I read it right then. I did, while he went in the house to use the phone. And even though I was prepared to dislike it, I had to admit it was pretty good. The last twenty pages where Winnie was dying of cancer really got to me. It was even more wrenching than the last half hour of *Terms of Endearment.* I didn't actually cry, but I knew I would if I saw it on film, and I knew audiences would.

"Well?" Shark said, as I put the script down.

"You were right," I said. "It's warm and sweet and tender. And it's a human story about real, ordinary people, a story of heroism in everyday life, uplifting and yet heartbreaking without being a downer in any way. I've only met Woody briefly, I had no idea he was this sensitive. This script is as delicately structured as a Mozart concerto."

"Then let's make a movie," Shark said.

But I told him about my Houston project, an epic *Giant* for the eighties, telling the story of my parents and their parents before them, a sprawling saga of the oil and petroleum by-products industry, with a subplot exploring the tempestuous courtship of our close family friends, former Governor John Connally and his vivacious wife Nellie. But as I outlined the story Shark yawned.

"Texas," he said. "People are sick of all that rich Texan shit, it's been done to death. Besides, just in terms of entertainment value, your parents are basically a drag, Gary. Who gives a shit who invented the pantsuit?"

"I do," I said. "And you'd better watch what you say about my mom."

"Gary, I love your mother, you know that," he said. "She's a sensational woman in real life. But *this—*" he tapped his script "—is art, and that's a different bird. Sleep on it, Gary. Without being preachy, this film will make an important statement about traditional American values that needs to be made. And it's a small, intimate character piece with zero special effects. You need this film as much as I do, Gary, if you're to be a truly class director and not just a kid cranking out expensive cartoons. I think you already sense there's an Oscar in this for you, lots of Oscars, enough for everyone involved."

With that he left. I met him the next afternoon in Bill Kemmer's office at Mastodon. At the end of the meeting, Bill said to us, "You're on."

## Woody Hazzard

Against my better judgment I helped Shark finish the screenplay of *Home to the Heart*. Part of the reason, to be honest, was the two hundred thousand dollar fee. I knew that my days with Brian were numbered. I still cared about him but wouldn't sleep with him anymore, since I'd found out that he'd had sex with a couple of other guys and I was real scared of getting AIDS. With the screenwriting fee I planned to move to the South Bay, open a surfboard shop, and hopefully meet a young gay surfer who had never actually had sex with a man before.

Shark was real pleasant as we finished the script, making a big point of letting me know the ranch hand who'd scored the cocaine and heroin for him had been fired. "If alcoholism and drug addiction are a disease," he said, "then what I had was a minor relapse, and I'm not going to beat myself up about it now. The important thing is I'm back to my true decent and loving self." And as far as you could tell that seemed to be the case.

One morning I went with him to a dealership in the Valley to pick up this new Porsche he'd ordered. It was spooky in a way—or at least it seems so now—but as we drove down Ventura Boulevard he told me the dealership was the same one James Dean had gone to to pick up his silver Spyder the day he died. It was called Competition Motors then, but it had a different name now. Shark got into this whole trip about it as we pulled up to the dealership garage. "That's where James Dean had 'em paint 'Little Bastard' on his car, right there. He stood *right there* thirty-one years ago."

And then we saw Shark's Porsche, and it's no exaggeration to say it was the ultimate Porsche, beyond any doubt the bitchinest Porsche ever made. It was one of a kind, specially built for Shark: the Porsche 997, with a five-hundred-horsepower twin-turbo engine and a top speed of two-hundred-twenty miles-per-hour. I think it set him back almost three hundred grand, but if you cared anything at all about cars it was worth every cent. When you fired that ignition, man, it made your nuts start to rumble and it was all you could do not to come all over the dash.

## Kathy Petro

The first time Shark took me out in that silver monster it scared me to death. He did this big Grand Prix number on the Kelp Canyon road while I clutched the dash. "Don't worry, this fucker can stop on a dime!" he yelled. And then he proved it and I nearly peed!

Then he tore out again so fast that the gravity socked me back into the seat. I was terrified yet excited when he finally pulled to a halt at the very crest of Kelp Mountain, the ocean and Catalina stretched out far below.

"I want you to star in *Home to the Heart*," he said. "I want you to portray my mother Winnie."

"What?" I said. "Are you talking to me?" I was completely incredulous.

"I know you can do it, Kathy. You're mature now. Forget about *Manhattan Holiday* and that Yugoslavian drip—that never happened."

"But Shark," I said. "I'm not an actress. I'm an aging model with laugh lines."

"That's what I mean. You're no longer vapidly pretty."

"I'm not?" I said, feeling vaguely insulted.

"You're still pretty, but not vapidly pretty. In fact, pretty isn't the right word. You're beautiful, Kathy, you will always be beautiful. But you have a kind of inner beauty now that you didn't used to have. You've been around the block a few times and it shows, but in a positive way. You're developing a kind of earthy, wise sensuality, the sort of aura one associates with certain soulful French actresses."

"Gee, really?" I said, feeling kind of flattered, and strangely comforted. Because getting old did worry me. Especially in California you're just really aware of how much everybody worships youth and everything.

"It would be nice if I could become a serious actress," I said. "It has occurred to me that I can't go on talking about drug abuse forever. I really do need something else to do with my time."

## Greg Spivey

*Home to the Heart* was really a fantasy, wasn't it? Shark took real characters but completely revised reality, though I guess the affair between Mac and Gladys was based roughly on actual events. The politics were so incredibly odd though—I still don't have an exact fix on that. In one sense it was a kind of liberal-humanist tract—I mean, the subplot about the black family being driven out of the white Orange County suburb.

But the business of Mac's defense contractor boss being a Communist spy was nothing less than vintage McCarthyite paranoia, and a deliberate pandering to the neo-patriotic jingoism of the mid-1980s.

The roles of Mac and Winnie were essentially reversed, for as I'd always understood it in real life Winnie was the pathological weakling. Her "lifting disease" and all that. And of course she'd committed suicide, climbing into the freezer, rather than waging the valiant battle against cancer depicted in the film. The cinematic Winnie was clearly the mother Shark wished he had had, a powerhouse who forced her ninny husband to stand up for America. "I can't tell the FBI about my boss," Mac protests in the movie. "If he's arrested for selling secrets to the Russians, the company will go under, I'll lose my job and we'll lose this house."

"Come to your senses, Mac," Winnie reprimands him. "If the Reds take over this country we're going to lose a lot more than our house. You've got to do what's right!"

The real Gladys I understand was just a wayward fifties tramp with a Gloria Grahame mouth who for a time shacked up with Mac on Mackerel Drive, even as Winnie withdrew to her bedroom, becoming more and more disassociated from reality. Gladys's status as FBI undercover agent in the film did make her more "sympathetic," which of course was part of Shark's overall "humanity-affirming" slant that there were "no truly evil people"—not even the boss, who was only committing treason to finance an orphanage in Italy where, during the war, he'd accidently machine-gunned a pregnant woman. And in the film Mac and Gladys' furtive and guilt-ridden if "understandable" affair took place in a seedy motel far from the wholesome goodness and warmth of the home.

I once asked Shark why he'd excluded himself from the story, giving his cinematic parents a pair of twins instead, the five-year-olds Gene and Jan, described in the script as "perfect, angelic mirror reflections of one other, in every way except their clothes." Shark waved the question away with a smile. "Let's leave that one to my biographer, Greg."

I knew when I read the scene where the twins drown in the swimming pool that whoever played Winnie would win an Academy Award. It was just one of those scenes. Winnie alone in the house, deserted by her cad of a husband, and by that time confined to a wheelchair with cancer of the spine. She's knitting matching sweaters when she happens to glance up through the plate glass window in time to see the twins thrashing in the pool as they begin to drown. She wheels to the patio and cries out for help as the twins gurgle under—but the next-door neighbors, seen in a cutaway, are watching Lawrence Welk on TV and don't hear. Frantically, Winnie wheels to the phone in the hall. Just as her hand touches the receiver her wheels lock up suddenly in a snarl of yarn, the abrupt stop throwing her out across the floor. As she falls, still holding the phone, the cord is torn from the wall, and . . . well, you could tell the scene was going to play for at least three minutes: as she pulls the heavy weight of her body inch by inch across the carpet toward the sliding glass door, excruciatingly, helplessly watching the twins drown . . . It just had Best Actress stamped all over it.

When Shark said Kathy was going to play the part I nearly laughed.

## Gary Schnell

I did laugh. I was sure he was kidding, then I saw that he wasn't. By that time we had cast Tina as Gladys and I saw what Shark was up to all right.

"Did you even really *show* the script to Meryl Streep?" I said.

"Yeah, I told you, she's booked up until 1990."

"I don't believe you. I'm going to call her."

Shark stopped my hand on the phone. "Look, forget that it's Kathy. Just let her read, that's all I ask, Gary. If after that you don't think she's right for the part I'll never mention it again. Forget that I love her. Pretend that she means nothing at all to either of us."

So I let Kathy read. And the strange thing was, even if she hadn't been Shark's girlfriend, even if Shark Trager had not existed, I would have cast her to play Winnie after the first few minutes of that reading. She was that good.

## Kathy Petro

Shark had me prepare for the reading with a method acting teacher, and luckily for me I was a quick study. I had this really big breakthrough the very first session and saw how phony I'd been during *Manhattan Holiday*. I'd been pretending to be an "actress" back then, doing what I thought actresses did or something. But Maurice kept yelling at me: "Don't act!" And once when I did something really fake he actually slapped my face! I ran off in tears but came back and delivered a scene from *Who's Afraid of Virginia Woolf* that terrified everyone in the class.

## Greg Spivey

*Home to the Heart* rolled in Torrance, California, in late August 1986, as we grabbed the Mac and Gladys tryst scenes and the black family scenes first. Torrance, a South Bay suburb, had a lot of fifties motel and coffee shop architecture that hadn't been filmed before, and whatever else might be said of the film, Ernesto Fonseca's delicately gold-tinged cinematography imbued each shot with a preternatural poignance.

Kathy's scenes began when we moved to the Palos Verdes location, a glass-walled Richard Neutra-designed residence considerably more stylish than Shark's boyhood home in Newport Beach, where perhaps eighty percent of the film took place. And from the very first day Kathy was astonishing. Somehow, I'm still not sure how, she had tapped into something inside her, some depth of being, that I for one never suspected was there.

As usual, Shark was constantly on the set. While he seemed at first to be leaving all the essential directorial decisions to Gary, offering even fewer suggestions than usual, it eventually became apparent that between takes Shark was privately coaching Kathy on her performances. This began to irritate Gary quite a bit.

## Gary Schnell

To be honest I never really liked Kathy that much as a person. I tried to keep my moral views to myself because in the beginning especially she was delivering quite a good performance. But in the back of my mind I could never forget that she'd once been a pig. Of course most women her age had been, because of the so-called sexual revolution. On that score I was glad to have found Tina, who at the time I believed had only slept with one other man before me. Believing that, it seemed ironic that

Tina was playing such a loose character while Kathy Petro, one of the world's biggest retired sluts, was portraying this pure and noble American mom.

That's why what Shark began doing infuriated me so. Because I would spend all this time getting a quiet, restrained performance from Kathy and then Shark would whisper something in her ear and she'd come back and start playing it big and raw and sometimes downright crude—to be frank, almost as if she were in heat. Well, the idea of trying to imply that there was some sort of sexual undercurrent in Winnie's maternal character just offended me to the very core of my being.

## Greg Spivey

With only a few key pages left to shoot in Palos Verdes we were rained-out for a week in late September, and so returned to Mastodon's fabled soundstage one to pick the Washington interiors. That was where Gary finally lost it, when Kathy tried to play the scene with J. Edgar Hoover without a bra.

"Cut!" he yelled. "What the hell is going on? We can see your nipples, Miss Petro. Who told you to take off your bra?"

Kathy looked at Shark.

Gary went over to Shark, trembling with anger. "It's 1957. No decent woman would walk into FBI headquarters in a tight semi-diaphanous blouse without a bra."

"I want a sexual subtext to the scene," Shark said. "I think Hoover should notice her nipples and appear flustered."

"That's not what the scene is about!" Gary screamed. "And I am directing this goddamn picture!"

"You are because I asked you to, Gary," Shark said evenly. "You exist because I gave you a break, you spoiled-rotten little prig. And I can replace you so fast it'll make your head spin."

Gary was livid. "We'll see about that, Shark."

## Gary Schnell

I was enraged. I came close to walking off the picture that morning. But we had less than two weeks left to shoot, including the crucial swimming pool sequence, and I knew that despite Shark's interference I had the coverage I needed to make my best film. So I decided to fight back and called Dad.

## Kathy Petro

The night before we were to shoot the swimming pool scene Shark got a call from Bill Kemmer and found out that Earl Schnell was trying to buy Mastodon Pictures. Shark got right on the phone to Jake Skyler, who assured him that Montanacom would never let that happen, but the idea that Gary would go to such lengths to gain total control of the film just infuriated Shark.

"That evil little prima donna," Shark said. "When this is over I'm going to destroy him."

"Shark, let's just finish the picture. We've only got a few days left. I don't want anything bad to happen now."

"We'll finish the picture all right," he said. "But as soon as we wrap, that double-crossing schmuck is dead."

Well, I barely slept at all that night. I was already keyed-up anyway anticipating my most difficult scene—I just didn't need all the extra tension. The next morning the vibes on the Palos Verdes set were just awful.

## Greg Spivey

"You've fucked up bad, pal," I told Gary that morning. "Shark knows your dad's trying to take over the studio."

"If you're smart you'll side with me, Greg," Gary said. "Because it's going to happen."

## Tina Veer

I was on the set even though my scenes were finished. But if I'd known what was coming I would have gone far away. Shark and Gary weren't speaking. And from the very first take, Gary treated Kathy viciously.

## Kathy Petro

I was really trying hard to forget about the tension and get into the scene. But every time I fell out of the wheelchair Gary would call, "Cut!" and say mean things. "No, no, no! That's horrible, you're pathetic. Your twins are drowning, for Christ sake! You're acting like you just smelled the roast burning."

Again and again we'd start the scene, and he'd stop it. Finally, he said, "Boy, you stink, you know that? You just plain stink!" And I started to cry and Shark, who'd been simmering, started toward Gary with violence in his eyes.

I stopped him. "No, please, Shark. Let me try it one more time."

So I did, and Gary stopped it again and said, "Phony, phony, phony!" And I ran to my dressing room in tears.

Shark came in after me and held me and said, "Look, I've got an idea."

## Greg Spivey

Without Gary being aware of it, Shark had Kathy fitted with a wireless earphone so that he could speak to her during the take, in effect directing her through it. He also instructed the camera and sound men to keep rolling no matter what Gary said, and since by that time nearly everybody thought Gary was an asshole, they went along.

## Kathy Petro

It was always supposed to be this really long take of my crawling across the floor, basically this close-up of my face as I went through all these emotions, and Shark just said he would "cue" me. I was never really sure exactly what he meant, but by that time I just wanted to get the scene over with. My hip was all bruised from falling out of the wheelchair so many times.

So finally we were ready and Gary called, "Action!" As soon as I fell from the wheelchair, Shark started talking to me through the earphone. "Oh my God, *Jeff Stuben!*" he said. "He loved you but you gave him acid and he cut off his head! He picked up that chainsaw and went *bzzzzzzz!* Right before your eyes!"

I started crying and screaming, "No, no!"

"Derek Horus died too. A heart attack! He fell back through a window—there he goes now!"

And I saw it and just came unglued.

"And what about *Beth!* In a pool of blood on the floor! Is *that* what happens to everyone who loves you!"

"No, no, no!" I sobbed, as the Panaflex camera swooped in on my face. I think I kind of heard Gary call, "Cut," but I was too wrecked by then to stop.

"And your dear old dad. *You killed him!*" Shark yelled in my ear. "He blew his brains out because you knowingly married a homo. You drove him to suicide!"

By then I was crawling across the carpet, tears coursing down my cheeks. "No, no, somebody stop it!" I cried.

"And Gray," Shark said in my ear. "Let's talk about your dear, precious Gray."

"Oh no, *please*," I pleaded.

"How did you feel when you knew Gray had cancer? When you watched the sweetest love of your life die! He's dead! Gray's dead! He's gone!"

I just became totally hysterical, pounding the floor. I kind of blacked out, I guess. I don't even remember tearing off the earphone, but I understand I did.

### Greg Spivey

By the time Kathy tore off the earphone Gary was beside himself. He'd called cut about thirty seconds into the take, and now it was up to nearly three minutes. For a long time he was too wiped to react with more than incredulity. "What's going on? Why are you still running?" he said to the camera and sound men. "Is everybody crazy?" Kathy was miked in such a way that Gary's comments didn't spoil the sound.

### Gary Schnell

I was stunned. I've never heard of anything like that happening on a movie set before or since, a crew openly defying a director's authority. I finally just stood back and watched Kathy's breakdown—because that's what it was. In my book that wasn't acting. And I realized what was going on the second I saw that earphone.

### Greg Spivey

Gary picked up the earphone and heard Shark talking through it. "Where is he?" Gary yelled and tore out to the trailers.

### Gary Schnell

I found Shark in his trailer still talking into the mike, unaware that the scene was finally over. "Gray is wasting away now, taking his last breath. His death rattle, Kathy . . ."

"You monster," I said, as I grabbed him. We grappled out onto the pavement where a couple of the grips pulled us apart.

"How did it play?" Shark said, out of breath, as the grips finally let him go. As he spoke we saw Kathy being helped to her trailer in a state of abject hysteria. And Shark looked pleased. Pleased!

"You're beneath contempt, you evil bastard," I said to Shark. "I hope you realize you've just destroyed what was left of that aging slut's mind."

## Tina Veer

"Ohhhh, Gary," Shark said lethally, glancing at me. "You should watch what you say about the woman I love. You're in no position to talk, my ignorant little friend."

"Shark, no," I said, sensing what was coming. "Please don't do this."

"Tina's a whore," he said. "I paid her a thousand bucks to pop your cherry. She's the biggest pig in tinsel town, pal. She's literally fucked every guy in the industry."

"Gary?" I touched his arm. I wanted so much for him to say he loved me anyway, and to explain that however it had started I genuinely loved him.

"Is it true?" Gary said to me.

"Well, not literally every guy."

"Then it's true," he said coldly, and walked away from me.

I walked up to Shark Trager and spit in his face. A year would pass before I had to look at that face again, the night I picked up my Best Supporting Actress award.

# 27/The Last Time (1987–1988)

## Greg Spivey

Kathy was admitted to Saint John's Hospital for nervous exhaustion, and from there she left Shark. He was furious and tried to locate her, but she'd covered her tracks. Or to be more precise, a number of us knew where she was but were not about to tell Shark. When it was understood what he'd done to her on the set everyone was on Kathy's side, and as the story of the incident spread through the industry Shark's reputation began sinking to a new low. How quickly people were ready to cite Shark's cruelty to Kathy as evidence that despite *Blue Light,* despite what some were even calling his ''Beirut grandstanding,'' he hadn't *really* changed.

The awful thing was, the scene worked. Shark had a rough cut by July, and in context you believed totally that Kathy was watching her twins drown and the scene was just lacerating. But Shark kept fiddling with the film, pushing back the release

499

date, and a lot of the reason was that he'd begun coking heavily again.

## Elliot Bernstein

"I hear he's coking again," I told Kathy in late summer. After spending a few days with Woody, who was living in the South Bay after his breakup with Brian, Kathy had come to stay with Sue and me in Bel-Air.

"Maybe I should go back to him," Kathy said. "He's like John Lennon now, the time Yoko left him. Without me, he's lost."

"Don't be a sap," Sue said. "He doesn't love you, Kathy. For Christ sake, don't you understand that even yet? It was always just his fantasy of you he loved, not the real you."

"What's the real me?" Kathy said, with a terrible lost look.

## Greg Spivey

"You know where Kathy is, don't you, Greg?" Shark said to me one night at the VistaVision Ranch as we watched a new cut of one of the Mac and Gladys infidelity scenes.

"No, I don't know where she is. I'm on your side, Shark. Though sometimes I wonder why."

"I'll tell you why," Shark said, as he dabbed cocaine up his nose. "Because I'm a fucking genius, and your time with me has been the most exciting time of your life."

"Your egotism is not one of your more endearing traits, Shark."

"I'm not egotistical," he said. "I just happen to be the next best thing to God, that's all. Look at this movie! Look at the stupid twat up there." He indicated Tina. "And that washed-up oaf." He meant Ben Killard as Mac, of course. "I've given those fucks new careers. And where are they now? They're off bad-mouthing me somewhere, just like everybody else in this town."

"Not everybody, Shark. It's basically just your director. It's a shame you and Gary can't patch things up before this comes out."

And I really meant that, because in spite of all the bullshit, the film was really good.

## Gary Schnell

I was furious and so was Dad. It was humiliating to be kicked off the picture, even though most people knew that I hadn't done anything wrong, that it was basically because Shark was crazy. There were times where I thought: I'll just kill it. Dad could have his lawyers tie the film up for years. By then we knew his buying Mastodon Pictures was out, for some baroque financial reasons—and that pissed me off too.

Then Bill Kemmer, who was sympathetic to me, got ahold of a cassette of Shark's rough cut. Security was tight at the VistaVision Ranch, but the studio had a spy there. When I saw the rough cut I flipped. "This isn't my picture, Bill. Almost without exception Shark has chosen the very worst takes. And Kathy's swimming pool scene! It's camp now! It's *Mommie Dearest*, it'll be guffawed off the screen."

## Bill Kemmer

"You're right, it's not your vision," I told Gary. "But the fact is it's a very good film. And it's the one we're going to release."

"Then I want my name taken off of it."

"I'm not sure that's possible, Gary. You did direct it."

"I don't care. I hate it now. I hate the film, I hate Shark, I hate Tina, and most of all I hate what this town has done to me. I never knew hatred before I came here. This town has taught me how to hate."

"I hear the new Robert Benton film is a dog," I told Gary. "The Pollack picture's been pushed back to '88. As for Francis, well . . . I'm glad it's not our money . . ."

"What are you saying?" Gary said.

"The same thing I've been saying all along. How old are you now, Gary?"

"Twenty-seven."

"Then you'll be the youngest winner in the history of the Academy. A certified boy wonder."

"Yeah?" Gary laughed nastily and flashed a disturbingly carnivorous grin as he warmed to the notion. *"Yeah*, maybe so. Unless some old fuck who's about to croak comes out with some stupid little masterpiece that steals all my thunder."

## Brian Straight

We revived Gary's Houston project shortly after he was fired from *Home to the Heart*, but he was not the same Gary I had worked with before. To be blunt, I think the breakup with Tina Veer shattered him. He became hard and animalistic and began to drink and coke heavily. It was not a pretty transition to witness, but I didn't feel it was my place to intervene. I was going through a difficult period myself since Woody's departure, kicking myself for having been unfaithful when I'd known how strongly Woody felt that monogamy was essential in the terrifying sexual atmosphere of the mid-1980s.

Gary began running with a succession of mean, brutal women, and there were several embarrassing scenes in restaurants about town. A fistfight in Breton's, and an obscenity-shouting and vomiting incident that got him eighty-sixed, I think, from Spago. The odd thing was that no matter how belligerent and obnoxious Gary became, people seemed to have an endless supply of compassion and pity for him. I suppose because of his youth and talent and terrible naiveté Gary represented to many their own lost innocence. And as Gary viciously put down his former producer everywhere he went it was unsettling how readily people began to question the legitimacy of Shark's "new" post-Kolon Clinic persona. Of course, the story was out that Shark was coking again and rapidly reverting to his old paranoid behavior.

## Greg Spivey

Shark was getting paranoid and not without reason. He knew that Gary was trashing him mercilessly all over town, and he was fearful that especially after the colossal success of *Blue Light,* his mean-spirited industry peers would be only too eager to see him fail disastrously with *Home to the Heart.* So he kept tinkering with the film, obsessively adjusting it as the months passed, even though it was perfectly fine. I'd tell him that and he'd say, "No, it's not there yet. Do you want me to embarrass myself?"

Sometimes I felt like saying, "Fear of embarrassment has never stopped you in the past, Shark."

But he was far past the point of being able to take good-natured sarcasm. By the fall of '87 we'd been through a number of editors and Shark announced one night, "I've lost my way. I can't finish this picture unless Kathy comes back. Will you tell her that, Greg?"

"I have no idea how to get in touch with her, Shark."

"You're a fucking liar, Greg. You've been talking to her for months. She's at the Bernsteins, I know that."

## Kathy Petro

I guess I did put Greg Spivey in a difficult situation, because I knew he was Shark's main confidant and everything. But I really liked Greg, and in spite of what had happened I had never quit caring about Shark, and so I would check with Greg every so often to find out how he was doing. I got more and more upset, just certain Shark was spinning out of control again because I'd left him.

Sue kept bad-mouthing Shark all the time, until I finally asked her to stop. "You're just bitter, Sue," I said. "Because you loved Shark at a time when he was hopelessly obsessed with me."

"You really are stupid," she said and I became upset.

Elliot came to me later and apologized on Sue's behalf, but said I should maybe start thinking of finding another place to stay.

Then when Greg called and said Shark couldn't finish the film without me I became very confused.

"What do *you* think I should do, Greg?" I said.

"I don't know, Kathy. What Shark did to you was an unconscionable act of blatant cruelty in the name of art. But the fact is he misses you terribly, and if you don't come back I believe he'll eventually destroy himself."

"Greg, tell me one thing," I said. "Do you think Shark really loves me? I mean, *me* as opposed to his fantasy of me?"

Greg paused for a moment. "That's a tough one, Kathy," he said finally. "But if you want to know what I think, I think Shark loves you more than he himself knows. But then what do I know about love? I've never stayed with any single woman longer than a year."

"Greg, where is he now?"

"He's with the editors. He hasn't slept in two days."

"Greg," I said, "I'm leaving right now."

## Greg Spivey

I didn't tell Shark Kathy was coming. But I will never forget the look on his face when he saw her there in the editing room door. He was so exhausted he nearly collapsed in her arms. And he wept. It was the only time I ever saw Shark cry. I think if I'd ever had any doubt that he really loved Kathy it was erased then. He could play intellectual games with himself forever about what love was or wasn't, what was genuine love as opposed to obsession or fantasy, and all that sort of thing.

Who wouldn't become confused trying to figure all that out? But he did love her. And I know she loved him.

And he finished the film.

## Bill Kemmer

I wept when I saw the finished film. *Home to the Heart* did not of course elicit the kind of joyfully tearful catharsis you experienced with *Blue Light*. On the contrary it was an ending of genuine and poignant sorrow. As devastating as Kathy's swimming pool scene was, it was her deathbed scene which literally tore out my heart. I was still teary as I got Gary Schnell on the phone. "You mustn't be an asshole about this," I told him. "It's a masterpiece and it's going to gross a hundred mil easy. We're pulling out the stops so we can have it in theaters in time to qualify for the Awards."

## Gary Schnell

I finally saw the finished film at Mastodon about a week before the New York premiere, and it kind of made me sick. This little coked-out airhead I took—I can't even remember her name now—cried during the deathbed scene, and I said, "Come on, get serious. It's fucked! Shark ruined it!" Then we got into a fight in the parking lot afterwards and I said, "Walk, twat," and dumped her. I just wanted to disappear. I was sure the critics were going to murder me for a crime I hadn't even committed.

## Kathy Petro

Things were beautiful for quite a while after I came back to Shark. He apologized so profusely for what he'd done to me that I was embarrassed. "I don't expect you to believe this," he said, "but I took that heinous shortcut for you. You were shutting down more and more as the scene progressed—understandably, given Gary's assaultive behavior. I saw that if I didn't do something radical, amoral even, your big screen moment was going to be blown."

"I know, baby. I know," I said, just so glad to be back in his arms.

He stopped the cocaine at my insistence, saying, "I don't need it as long as you're with me. You're all I've ever really needed."

And we made love in the big western bedroom and it was far sweeter than it had ever been, even sweeter than the time in the Enchanted Cottage, for that lovemaking, if the truth be told, did have a certain frantic edge to it. We had been making up for so much lost time. But now in those golden months of late 1987 we were somehow like an old married couple who had remained fervently in love despite the passage of years. Really, that's what it was, I see now. We had our old age compressed into a few months.

## Greg Spivey

Filmmaking is an odd thing. No matter what sort of ugly crap happens during production, once a movie comes out, if it's good and a hit, everything is forgotten. At least that's usually the case. And it was certainly my sense of what was happening with *Home to the Heart* as Mastodon geared up for a wide Christmas release.

You could feel the excitement in the air. People were smiling again at the VistaVision Ranch, including Shark. There was a press screening in L.A. and as the first rave reviews began appearing our elation grew. It fell to me to try to convince Gary to attend the gala New York premiere, but he was nowhere to be found. The story was that fearing disaster he'd pulled a male version of Geraldine Page's stunt in *Sweet Bird of Youth*, roaring off across America in a restored '58 Cadillac convertible with a pound of cocaine, a case of Jack Daniels and a mean little porno actress with mainstream dreams running her hand up his leg.

## Bill Kemmer

I suppose that while the applause lasted the New York premiere was one of the peak moments of Shark's life. Who could have predicted that on the very heels of that vindication an interrelated series of wrenching events would occur which would irrevocably mark the beginning of Shark Trager's end.

## Kathy Petro

I sat there in this awful dress I was wearing just going out of my skin as the lights went down, wanting a Valium so bad I could taste it. Even though the early reviews had lavishly praised my performance I just didn't believe it. This was the real moment of truth, a tough New York audience, and I just couldn't take it. While the titles were still on I bolted to the lobby, Shark following me.

"Kathy, it's all right. Come on back in."

"No, I can't. I can't watch myself, it's too weird."

And so I didn't go back in. You know, I've never seen the whole film, just little bits and pieces. Once they showed a clip of the swimming pool scene on TV, but I couldn't even watch it. So Shark just held me in the empty lobby, rocking me in his arms. The picture had been playing for maybe twenty minutes when Edmund Himmler, the powerful New York film critic, arrived with his aged wheelchair-ridden mother.

## Greg Spivey

Shark told me later that he felt his blood boil when he saw Edmund Himmler wheeling his mother into the lobby, recalling the critic's vicious review of *Blue Light*. He said Himmler saw him and grinned and whispered something to his mother, an ancient woman with silvery-blonde Teutonic braids, who reminded Shark of Claude Rains's evil Nazi mother in *Notorious*. She grinned too, Shark said, and his first impulse was to stomp them both.

But for Kathy's sake he quelled his anger. "This man is spiritually sick," he observed in tones only Kathy could hear. "He's a very sad man, who has probably never had sex with another human being, not even her."

But Shark said his heart was still pounding with adrenaline as he watched Himmler wheel his mother into the theater, knowing all too well that a critic of Himmler's temperament was incapable of giving *Home to the Heart* anything but a ferociously negative review.

## Kathy Petro

Shark was still rocking me in the lobby when we heard the applause. "You see?" he said. "You see?" And he tried to pull me back into the theater just as the doors opened and people flooded out like some kind of ecstatic throng or something, and the next thing I knew they were all over us! People hugging me with tears on their cheeks, saying I was better than

Meryl Streep and Sally Field and Debra Winger and everybody! And they were hugging Shark too, and he had tears in *his* eyes! It was like the ending of a Rocky movie or something: people were practically lifting Shark up on their shoulders. I half-expected an American flag to drop down from the ceiling and drape over him at any moment.

## Woody Hazzard

Shark paid my way to New York to attend the premiere, which was the first time I saw the movie. I have to say, I think Gary saved the picture. The shit about the Communists especially— that could've been real bad, but Gary had this knack for having everybody play low-key. A lot of the lines were really pretty bad, but somehow it all came out believable.

The scene in the lobby afterwards was like total jubilation— you really expected everybody to break into some big song or something like the end of a fifties musical—and all kinds of people were coming on to me, other producers and executives and so forth, when they learned I was the writer. Let's do lunch, that kind of thing. You should direct your next script. I didn't know what to say.

I kept trying to get over to Shark, but people were crowded in around him like sardines. Then, in one of those fluke shifts, the crowd parted right in front of him so that he had a clear view of Carol Van Der Hof as she limped from the theater into the lobby.

She was with that rock video director guy Joel she'd had an on-again/off-again thing with for years. *He* got the premiere invitation, but Shark must have known the chances were good he'd bring Carol if he came. She totally froze when she saw Shark, and they just stared at each other for a long time without saying a word. Then Shark opened his arms like he wanted to hug her, and you could see all the love and longing for recon-ciliation in his eyes.

And Carol just cut him totally dead, like he didn't even exist. She limped past him and went up to Kathy and said, "My dear, I just want to tell you how much I enjoyed your performance." And Kathy smiled and said thank you, looking kind of dazed by then from all the compliments. And then Carol added in a voice loud enough for Shark to hear, "You know, Kathy, I portrayed *you* once. Did Shark ever tell you about *that?*"

Kathy looked confused, picking up this weird lethal vibe from Carol. And Shark pushed up to Carol, saying, "You shut your cunt mouth," and people gasped.

"I portrayed you in a pitch-black garage," Carol continued to Kathy. "And Shark made love to me as I seriously doubt he ever has to the actual you—"

"You fuck-twat," Shark said, and smacked Carol across the face hard enough to knock off her glasses. It was gasp city, man.

Joel laid into Shark, and they grappled a little, Joel clipping Shark's nose pretty good, till several guys, myself included, pulled them apart. Shark's nose was bleeding, getting blood all over his suit.

## Kathy Petro

I was aghast. I had no idea at the time what Carol was referring to. I had been spared a full recitation of the events leading up to Carol's well-known power saw accident during *Red Surf*. All I knew was that this evil New York woman, who had obviously once had a crush on Shark, was marring what was otherwise a flawless night of jubilation.

I watched as Woody gave Shark a handkerchief to staunch his bleeding nose and helped him toward the basement men's room. And when I saw Edmund Himmler bringing his mother up the basement stairs in her wheelchair I just sensed that something even more horrible was about to happen.

## Woody Hazzard

Himmler was pulling his mom up the stairs backwards, one step at a time, as Shark and I started down on the way to the men's room. When Himmler saw the blood on Shark's face he grinned and said in that snide George Sanders voice he had, "Well, Shark, I see you're already bleeding. But let me tell you, you're going to have to tie a tourniquet around your *neck* once you've read my scathing review of that nauseating piece of kitsch treacle."

At that Shark made a move *toward* Himmler, but I swear he never touched him. Himmler flinched though, and threw up his arms to cover his face. And his mom's wheelchair just started rolling down the stairs.

"Eddie! Eddie! Ahhhh!" the old lady cried, but there was no

way to stop her plunge. The wheelchair just bounced down step after step, until it reached the bottom and she went sprawling out across the marble floor.

"Mother!" Himmler cried. And as he started down after her he tripped on his own feet and plunged down the stairs. I will swear on my own mom's grave that Shark never touched him, in spite of what people said later.

## Bill Kemmer

I was sick when I saw Edmund Himmler and his mother at the bottom of the stairs, sensing even before I received an explanation that it was going to cast a negative pall over the film. The evening ended horribly with ambulances arriving—at that point Edmund Himmler was unconscious and his mother was too dazed to speak. The police questioned Woody and Shark and, lacking any testimony to the contrary, tentatively accepted their *accident* version of what had happened and let them leave. We learned soon enough that Himmler's mother had sustained little more than bruises. But the critic had struck his head hard against the marble floor and remained in a coma as Shark and Kathy returned to L.A.

## Kathy Petro

Shark was extremely upset about what had happened. As much as he disliked Edmund Himmler he said he didn't wish for him to be in a coma, though inevitably at one point he did quip, "At least we don't have to worry about his review."

Almost all the other reviews were glowing, except for a few that were clearly written in the days after the Himmler incident, since they fired a few shots at Shark personally even as they praised my performance and Gary's direction of the film.

By then we knew the story was going around that Shark had pushed both the Himmlers down those steps. But Shark and I both figured those kinds of shots were just an inevitable by-product of success, especially after *Home to the Heart* had the biggest opening weekend in the history of motion pictures, breaking Shark's own previous record with *Blue Light*.

## Bill Kemmer

It was a stunning victory for everyone involved. The audiences were transported from coast to coast, and the critics, with a few late exceptions, were rhapsodic in their praise. But those late exceptions bothered me, as did the persistent rumors that Shark had deliberately pushed both Himmlers down the stairs. The critic remained in a coma. Working in Shark's favor was the fact that Himmler, far more so than any other film critic, was almost universally despised. His name worked against him for one thing, with its unavoidable Nazi connotation. And since the last film he'd praised unqualifiedly had been *The Night Porter*, there were many who felt Shark had finally given him what he deserved. If only his crippled mother hadn't gone down those stairs as well.

## Kathy Petro

Shark and I flew to Maui a few days before the Oscar nominations were due to be announced. I don't think either of us had ever been higher without taking a thing. We were just riding this super-big wave of self-perpetuating success, which I guess is what America at its best is all about. The film just kept going and going, and I was just inundated with scripts and offers. The Meryl Streep comparisons really pleased me the most though, because she had always been my idea of a really serious actress. I remember telling Shark on the flight over to Hana, "I want to do something with an unusual accent next time."

We had a rustic little house just up the road from the Lindbergh place, not far from the house Daddy had owned back in '75. But we never went by that house. We had no need for nostalgia. The present was plenty for us.

We had both brought along scripts to read but we ended up just baking in the sun all day and making love way into the night. We unplugged the phones, and went around nude, and just couldn't keep our hands off each other. I see now that those days were truly our last good time.

Monday night Shark switched on the TV news while I was in the shower, and when I stepped out he said I'd just missed the Awards nominations story, so I asked him how many we got.

"Eleven in all," he said. "Including Best Picture, Best Director, Best Screenplay, which will certainly get a laugh and a smirk out of Woody! Best Actor for Ben, Best Supporting Actress for Miss Veer. And the music and cinematography and a few other things."

"Is that all?" I said.

"Yes, I think so. Oh, wait. Kathy what's-her-name . . . Oh Christ, I can't think of it now. You know who I mean. Used to be a model. Made a real turkey about thirteen years ago. She got a Best Actress nomination, if you can figure that . . ."

"Oh, Shark!" I squealed with joy as he lifted me up off my feet and kind of swung me around. In a way I still think that moment was our peak. I just didn't see how things could get any better.

## Bill Kemmer

Of course we were elated by the nominations. But we had one small problem: We couldn't find Gary. He'd been "missing" for weeks by that point, and his parents were extremely distraught. He had established a reputation for shyness during *Blue Light,* which we used to keep the press at bay for a while. But the stories of his unruly behavior had begun appearing in the tabloids, along with photos of Gary and some of his more unsavory companions, and we began to fear that something horrible might have happened to him.

As if to confirm our most dire projections, his American Express bill came in in late February, the charges tracing a chaotic trail across the continent, terminating in New Orleans where a number of horrendous bills had been run up at sleazy French Quarter dives, the last stubs clearly forged. I spoke to Earl Schnell and he dispatched private detectives.

Then a Beverly Hills bank called Gary's business manager about a two hundred thousand dollar check made out to the Carl Grubb Ministries in Shreveport.

## Gary Schnell

I had sunk so low. I remember little of New Orleans, save one horrific flash image of Jan, my partner in Hell, injecting cocaine into a vein in my penis. I vaguely recall a seedy room with a stained mattress on the floor and an old black and white TV, on which a fuzzy picture of Carl Grubb appeared, and through which I felt the healing power of Jesus.

## Bill Kemmer

"My boy's been born again," Earl Schnell told me over the phone from Houston, "and he will be attending the Awards."

I was relieved, yet in some way I couldn't quite put my finger on, apprehensive. I passed the word on to Shark, who was quite amused. It was the fateful Sunday eight days before the Academy Awards.

## Kathy Petro

Shark shook his head when he heard that Gary had gone sexually and narcotically berserk and then ended up in the clutches of Carl Grubb, this really awful redneck evangelist. "It's only too predictable," he said in the living room at the VistaVision Ranch. "You take a guy like Gary who's basically a sheltered pussy—if you'll pardon the randy expression, my love—and of course he goes too far once he discovers pleasure, and inevitably feels guilty, and turns back to being a self-righteous prude."

"Well, at least he's not dead," I said. "Maybe someday he'll get tired of being a fundamentalist Christian and find some kind of balance between denial and excess."

"Perhaps," Shark said.

Later that evening we were cuddled up on the sofa getting ready to watch "Sunday Evening," which Shark liked better than "Sixty Minutes," which he thought had "gone soft." As Shark nuzzled me he mused, "You know, tomorrow is the balloting deadline. I'll bet any number of Academy members are sweating out their final decisions right now."

"I'm thinking positive thoughts," I said.

"You've got a very good chance, my love," Shark said. "Your only serious competition is Irene Greerson for her feisty grandmother shtick in *Sunset Lake,* since the word is out that she's got terminal cancer."

"It's ironic, isn't it?" I said to Shark. "That I might win for playing a cancer victim, but Irene might win for actually having it."

"I suppose it's too late to spread any rumors," Shark said, and kissed my forehead as the "Sunday Evening" intro came on.

Well, needless to say, he almost died when he saw they were doing a story on him called: SHARK TRAGER: HERO OR "SCUMBAG"?

## Bill Kemmer

It was a hatchet job, plain and simple. Hank Dye was the most vicious of any of the "Sunday Evening" reporters for starters, and his lead was a blatantly inflammatory reference to Trudl Himmler's persistent allegations that Shark had actually attacked Edmund and her at the New York premiere. "What kind of man would allegedly push an eighty-year-old wheelchair-ridden woman down a flight of stairs? Is this something an 'American hero' would do? But *is* Shark Trager an American hero? We asked a few people who should know."

## Kathy Petro

Shark moaned when, after recapping the Sunday School teacher rescue in Beirut, the picture cut to a closeup of Narges.

"Shark got me severely addicted to free-basing, encouraging me to resume it even after the Kolon Clinic treatments," she said. "When I finally refused to take any more drugs with him, he and his bodyguard Drake Brewster, a convicted rapist, took Mac Trager and me into West Beirut, where they were about to have sex with both of us, then kill us, when the Shiites disrupted their sick plan at the very last second. Yes, I'm telling you, it's true. Shark was about to [bleep] and kill me and [bleep] and kill his own father. That's the kind of man they gave the Davy Crockett Medal to."

Shark covered his brow and shook his head.

## Mac Trager

I tried to talk Narges out of going on TV, but she wouldn't listen. By the time Hank Dye and his crew came up to the Bel-Air house she knew that Shark and Gary had had a falling out, so she figured Shark couldn't press Earl Schnell anymore to use his Washington connections to get her deported. I went for a walk around the grounds that day though. I didn't want to tell Hank Dye nothing. I didn't know for sure what *she'd* told him till I saw it myself on TV.

"Hell, that's not what happened, Narges," I said, as we watched her tell her version of Beirut. "Shark had a change of heart."

"I don't care," she said. "He played with my mind once too often. This is my revenge. And you'd better just accept it, Mac, if you want to go on humping me."

## Kathy Petro

"Is that true?" I asked Shark about what Narges had said.

513

"No, no, of course not. The woman's insane with jealousy. She knew I wanted only you."

I squeezed Shark's hand. But he winced and I groaned as the TV picture cut to a clip of Hector the Donkey in *Looking for Lupe*.

## Greg Spivey

I was watching "Sunday Evening" at my girlfriend's house. Since Shark had described to me in convincing detail what had happened at the White House after the Oval Office ceremony, I was aghast at the distorted version Hank Dye presented.

"Yet, according to informed sources," Dye said in a shocked, incredulous voice, "Trager chased the terrified animal through the *Lincoln bedroom*, virtually destroying this national shrine! Like something in a debased Marx Brothers comedy? Maybe. But what happened next was like an outtake from Trager's own dementedly violent *Red Surf*. For as a number of visiting dignitaries—including, we are told, the First Lady herself!—watched in horror, Trager 'borrowed' a Secret Service revolver and gratuitously *shot* the beloved animal point-blank in the head."

## Kathy Petro

It just went on and on. They were just out to murder him. The only good thing was that at least they didn't say anything about Shark and me having sex in the White House. Drake was conspicuously absent. Thank God Shark had made a deal with him.

They interviewed Carol Van Der Hof, who said Shark had destroyed everyone who'd ever loved him and blamed him for her own drug addiction and even said it was Shark's fault that Tony Borgia had flipped out and accidentally stabbed his mother. "Shark drove Tony to it by creating the atmosphere of pornographic violence that permeated *Red Surf*, which also led to my own 'accident.' The man quite frankly is a monster. I for one never bought his 'new' Shark Trager act for a moment. He may be handsome and successful, and imbued with a certain rancid charm, but in my book Shark Trager is, was, and always will be an evil, sleazy scumbag, debasing what remains of the American dream."

## Greg Spivey

I felt Hank Dye's final remarks were pandering in the extreme. "One fortunate postscript: Gary Schnell, the talented young director of *Blue Light* and Trager's current mega-hit *Home to the Heart*, seems to have narrowly avoided the grueling fate of so many others who naively trusted this man. After a near-terminal bout of drug abuse and sexual frenzy, Schnell is now on the road to full recovery thanks to the loving support of his family and a new but profound faith in Jesus Christ.''

## Kathy Petro

By then the lights were flashing on the telephone, but Shark was too wiped out to answer.

## Bill Kemmer

It was just a nightmare. Monday we heard that the Academy was being besieged by members requesting new ballots, so they could change their votes before the five P.M. deadline. As the week progressed the reaction grew increasingly severe. The editorials demanding that Shark be stripped of the Davy Crockett Medal of Bravery. The statement of censure from the SPCA and the enraged demands of animal rights groups that Shark be prosecuted for ''murdering'' Hector. Of course, the White House was stonewalling that matter with a vengeance. It was deemed to be ''under investigation,'' but the ''Sunday Evening'' report had obviously broken the tacit agreement of silence among the White House press corps. It was just a matter of time until the true story came out, which—as I understood it from Greg—would reveal that Kathy's salacious behavior with Shark in the Lincoln bedroom had precipitated the sex-maddened donkey's destruction of that room.

## Kathy Petro

It was strange in a way. Shark didn't get angry or anything, he just withdrew. He became very quiet and just went into the den where he started working on the screenplay for the sequel to *Blue Light*. It was kind of telling, I see now, since the sequel was all set way out in space in the sphere of blue light, which I had always thought was supposed to be heaven.

He wouldn't take any calls or watch TV or anything. But I did, until I couldn't stand what they were doing to him anymore.

''I'm going to hold a press conference,'' I said one night when he finally came to bed.

"Like hell you are."

"I am. I'm going to tell what really happened at the White House—I can do that much at least. You *had* to shoot that donkey. It was an act of consummate bravery."

He took my hand on the sheet. We hadn't made love since the report aired. "You'll do nothing of the kind," he said. "So far, you've been spared. I won't have your name dragged through the dirt . . ."

"I don't care," I said. "I'm not ashamed of what we did."

"You will be," Shark said. "When you see how it's depicted in the media."

I felt a rush of anxiety. "You think it *will* come out?"

He squeezed my hand. "You might give some thought to cutting yourself free of me, Kathy." His voice was flat and tired. I guess I already knew he was coking again, but I didn't want to deal with it.

"Don't be absurd," I told him. "I love you. Shark, your whole life has been one long series of ups and downs. This too shall pass."

"I have loved you, Kathy," he said. "If it weren't for you I would have gone belly-up a long time ago." He leaned over and kissed me.

And then we made love for what turned out to be the last time.

# 28 / **Hollywood Ending**
## (1988)

### Kathy Petro

Bill Kemmer called Friday and said, "You'd better brace yourself," and explained that he understood the Saturday edition of "Hollywood Tonight" was going to do a story about what had happened at the White House.

"Let them," I said. "To quote Edith Piaf, 'I regret nothing.' "

"I don't think you understand," Bill said. "It may not be an entirely accurate version of what happened. If it were," he added cryptically, "I seriously doubt that you would still be alive to take this call."

Well, I found out what he meant soon enough. That Saturday proved to be the second most emotionally lacerating night of my life—the first being still to come.

### Greg Spivey

I was with Kathy in the ranch house living room when the report came on and she quickly became hysterical. Shark was in the den with the door closed, working determinedly on the sequel to *Blue Light* as he had been all week, as if it was only through that effort that he held onto his sanity.

Kathy was sobbing. "No! No! No! It's not true!" And even though the den was well within earshot Shark did not come out. Finally, I left Kathy in the care of several of the secretaries and bolted into the den.

Shark had his back to me as I entered and did not look up from the word processor. He was wearing a Walkman and hadn't heard me enter, any more than he had heard Kathy's sobs in the next room. I could hear the faint murmur of a Roxy Music song as I pulled the headphones from his ears.

"You just might like to know that they're saying that Kathy actually and willingly had sex with Hector in the Lincoln bedroom."

He looked stunned for a moment, as if he were having trouble coming out his imaginary world. There was a mound of cocaine on the desk next to the keyboard. *"What?"* he said finally, completely incredulous, and heard Kathy sobbing in the other room.

Belatedly, he went to her.

## Kathy Petro

I just couldn't believe it. The "Hollywood Tonight" reporter had spoken to Drake, even though he'd signed this paper promising he'd never talk about Shark. Well, maybe that was the loophole, because he didn't talk about Shark—he just talked about *me!*

## Drake Brewster

For one thing I wasn't getting my one percent of *Blue Light* like Shark had promised. It turned out it was a net point, not a gross point, and Mastodon kept giving me the runaround. So I was still broke and living in this crummy apartment near Gold's Gym in Venice, and didn't really have much to lose.

I was angry at Shark, and knew the best way to get him was to dump on Kathy—though now I wish I hadn't said what I said.

## Bill Kemmer

Of course, the story was preposterous. And it was the height of journalistic irresponsibility to repeat Drake's clearly insane allegations at all. But once the image of Kathy having sex with the donkey in the Lincoln bedroom was planted in the American mind, it stuck. Factual refutation, even physiological common sense, were beside the point. It was the classic dilemma of the smeared. BEST ACTRESS NOMINEE DENIES HAVING SEX WITH DONKEY, the headlines might well scream—but the denial itself would only elicit yet another replay of the lurid images already seething in the shock-hungry popular mind.

I felt for Kathy, certain the scandal spelled the end of her career as a serious Hollywood actress. But wouldn't it be a poignant capstone to the whole ghastly affair, I couldn't help thinking, if come Monday night she nevertheless walked off with an Academy Award?

## Greg Spivey

Kathy remained in seclusion all day Sunday, resting in a numb stupor in the master bedroom. Shark stayed with her for a while, comforting her, I noticed, in an oddly affectless way. Rather disconcertingly, he had yet to show any signs of anger, even when he replayed the tape of the "Hollywood Tonight" report. All he'd said as he'd watched it was, "This is silly. Hector had a gargantuan dick, at least two feet long." He indicated the female reporter who was doing the piece. "I wonder if *she'd* still be smiling if she'd straddled that."

Late Sunday afternoon I heard him mention something about his tuxedo to one of the secretaries. "Good God, Shark, you're not still going to the Awards," I said.

"Of course, I'm going," he replied in a dry, exhausted voice that frightened me. "For Kathy's sake. She's going to win, you know."

## Kathy Petro

Shark never came to bed Sunday night. I woke up Monday morning and then went right back to sleep again, I just didn't even want to get out of bed, ever. I just wanted to leave Hollywood and never come back. Or maybe just regress—I even thought about that. Maybe just go insane and become a little girl again so I wouldn't have to deal with anything ever again.

Then sometime in the early afternoon Shark came in and said, "Come on, Kathy, it's time to start getting ready for the Awards."

I couldn't even speak at first. The thought of all those people made me start to hyperventilate. Finally, I managed to say, "I can't."

"Come on, kitten," Shark said, kissing my shoulder. "I know you're a fighter. This is one of those times when you've got to show the world what you're made of. I'll be beside you all the way."

"I can't, Shark," I said. "Don't make me go. I can't face all those people, knowing that when they look at me they'll be thinking just one thing."

"We can't be quitters, Kathy," he said. "Not when we're this close to victory. I'm going to go. Rambo couldn't stop me. But to be frank, I'm nervous too. I could sure use the gal I love by my side."

Suddenly, I realized how selfish I'd been. Of course, he needed me, more now than he ever had before. We needed each other. "All right, you win," I said, and sat up. "Where's that stupid gown?"

## Greg Spivey

The limo pulled up to the ranch house a little after five, and Shark and Kathy emerged looking as sensational in a way as either had ever looked, Shark in a sharply cut black tuxedo, Kathy in a sensuously slinky black gown with a plunging neckline she seemed a bit self-conscious about. Both of them wore shades.

They were almost to the limo, where the chauffeur waited by the open door, when Shark said impulsively, "Let's take the Porsche."

With that apparent whim, I've always felt, Shark Trager connected with his fate.

## Kathy Petro

I will never forget that drive into town. It was sunset, one of those painfully beautiful sunsets when the sky seems to stay orange forever, and you feel that you somehow understand what California is all about. We drove in silence and for once I was not afraid of the horrendous power of that car. Even when I noticed he was pushing it past ninety I still felt safe. I realized then that whatever did or didn't happen, none of it mattered as long as I was with Shark. Even if we went broke somehow and ended up in some grungy little tract house in Azusa, so what?

As we reached downtown Los Angeles, the sky turning azure blue before us, he switched on the tape player, saying, "You know, this has always been my favorite song."

It was that old Roxy Music song, "The Thrill of It All," which I'd never much cared for because it sounded like several songs playing all at once. But I realized the title was the same as the Doris Day movie that had been playing at the Flying Wing Drive-In the night Shark and I first kissed so many years before. As we got off the freeway—how Shark did love the Los Angeles freeways—the song came to an end.

And so, as the Music Center loomed up ahead and Shark pulled over, parking arrogantly in a red zone, I kissed the man who was responsible for both the best and the worst moments of my life for the last time.

"Whatever happens tonight, know that you have been my life," he said as we drew apart.

"Don't be so final-sounding," I said, and tried to smile. "We'll get through this. You know that."

And he smiled too, a thin, sad smile I will never forget. Then we got out of the Porsche.

The Music Center was up at the end of the next block. You could see the limos pulling up and the bleachers where the fans were. We were just about to cross the street when Shark said, "Wait here, I forgot something," and went back to the car.

I had a good idea what he was going to do, so I went back after him, and caught him bending down to the glove compartment, tooting up a really huge amount of cocaine. He stopped when he saw me. "I thought I told you to wait," he said softly.

"Give me the straw," I said. "I need some of that too."

"No," he said. "You've been clean since the Kolon Clinic. I won't let you . . ."

"I can handle it," I said. "Give me the straw. You're not the only one who needs some artificial courage tonight."

Reluctantly, he handed me the straw. As I sniffed several thick lines he was already feeling the effects of the drug, and not liking it at all. "This stuff is shit," he said with a scowl. "I used up my own supply and scored this from the pool man just before we left. It's been heavily cut with speed."

He was right. I could feel the harsh amphetamine high as we started up the sidewalk again. My heart was pounding furiously as Goldie Hawn came into view, stepping from her limo to the applause of the fans. I felt breathless and vaguely paranoid as the klieg lights momentarily blinded me.

"Oh Christ," Shark said under his breath. "Oh Christ."

He was grinding his teeth, his hands forming red fists, as if he were going into a state of violent rage. He'd told me that he couldn't handle speed, that it did bad things to him, as it had in his teens when a doctor had prescribed it for weight control. He'd even admitted that in his early obsessive feelings toward me the drug had been a major factor, that he would never have made that peeping-Tom movie of me if he'd hadn't been high on speed.

"Goddamn it," he kept saying under his breath, as we approached the red carpet. And by that time his face was turning red too.

"Shark, please don't cause any trouble," I said. "I just want to get through this. Whatever happens tonight, won't you at least try and be gracious?"

## Elliot Bernstein

Sue and I were up near the door, where we'd paused to exchange gushy inanities with a few people, when we saw Shark and Kathy arrive. I had to give them both credit for having the guts to show up. But that feeling quickly gave way to apprehension when I caught the aura of anger emanating from Shark.

## Sue Schlockmann

You couldn't help but feel badly for Kathy. Exuberantly idolatrous toward Goldie Hawn a moment before, the fans fell deadeningly silent as Kathy passed. Shark led her quickly along that gauntlet of accusing stares. It was so very sad. You know the sort of overzealous, possessive fans who crowd those bleachers every year for a glimpse of their favorite stars. Well, only days before they had cherished Kathy. But now it was as if she had committed an act of personal betrayal against each of them. They looked upon her with a scorn they might have shown their real-life mother, were she to be accused of a similar act of depravity and raunch.

## Elliot Bernstein

I sensed trouble when I saw Shark drawing Kathy toward the

522

TV reporters—Doug and Cindi from Channel 8—who were grabbing the arriving stars for a few quick words. The trouble was that after a word and a smile from Goldie Hawn, both Doug and Cindi were turning their attention to Bette Midler, whose limo was just pulling up, looking beyond Kathy and Shark as if they were not even there.

## Kathy Petro

It was so terrible. Cindi got this look of shock when she saw us coming and said something to Doug, and then they just ignored us. It was like we were invisible, but Shark was pulling me over, and I said, "No, let's skip it. Let's just go in."

And Doug was looking beyond us, saying, "Well, here comes Bette Midler . . ." And Shark was steering me up to Doug and Cindi, saying, "Goddamn it, they are going to acknowledge you."

## Elliot Bernstein

Ignoring Sue's admonition that I not get involved, I started over to Shark as he spoke to Doug. "Hi, Doug," he said, knowing they were on the air. "Don't you think Kathy looks lovely tonight?"

Doug stared right through Shark, saying into his mike, "And I see Steven Spielberg pulling up now too . . ."

And Shark grabbed Doug by the lapels, saying, "I asked you a question, fuckface."

And Doug said, "Oh my God," knowing the obscenity had gone out live, since the pre-Awards broadcast was live, to millions of people.

"I want an answer, you smiling puke, or I'm going to cram that microphone down your throat," Shark said, as I reached him.

"She looks lovely tonight," Doug said, extremely rattled. "She looks lovely, doesn't she, Cindi?"

"Someone stop this," Cindi said through her smile, as several TV crew guys started toward Shark.

I took his arm. "Shark, for God sake—"

"Agree with Doug," Shark said to Cindi, covering her microphone with his hand—which didn't stop millions of viewers from hearing him spit: "Agree with him, you cocksucking Barbie doll."

"Yes, Kathy Petro has never looked lovelier," Cindi cried,

and dropped the microphone, as several of the TV crew guys pulled Shark away.

## Kathy Petro

I was humiliated. Thank God for Elliot. And then Neal Ridges came to the rescue too.

## Neal Ridges

I was inside when I saw the commotion and dashed out to help. It was essentially over by then, Elliot and a couple of the TV crew guys restraining Shark out of camera range as Doug and Cindi tried to regain their composure. Kathy looked like she just wanted to disappear. The TV director was furious and had called the security guards. I did some fast talking to assure everybody that it was all okay now, and hustled Shark and Kathy inside.

Shark was still angry as we moved through the crowded lobby, and every eye was on him. "What are *you* looking at, you simple shit?" he said to one of the Best Director nominees.

"Shark, get a grip on yourself," I said.

## Kathy Petro

I felt panicky and claustrophobic in the lobby, my heart pounding frantically after what had happened outside. I still expected someone to come up at any moment and ask Shark to leave. As far as I was concerned the evening was already ruined, even though it had barely begun.

Everybody was staring at us, *everybody*. Neal and Elliot were trying to calm Shark, and then Sue, the last person I expected to do such a thing, offered me the support of a friend.

## Sue Schlockmann

I saw that Kathy was jacked up on something, literally trembling like a terrified bird, and appeared on the verge of tears. I couldn't help feeling for her. "Come on, hon'," I said. "Let's go to the ladies room."

Shark glared at me as I began to lead Kathy away.

"Where do you think *you're* going?" he said to her.

Elliot calmed him. "Simmer down, Shark, it's all right."

## Elliot Bernstein

Shark was just flipped out, there's no other way to describe it. Completely stuck in this pugnacious, paranoid, cocky mind-set—like an extremely depressing parody of a James Cagney gangster. He stood there, sort of bouncing on his heels, punching his fist in his palm, confronting as many staring eyes as he could.

"You're a twat," he said to a three-time Oscar winning actress. "You've always made me sick, you know that?"

"Shark, cut it out," I said.

"Up your asshole," he said to a young actor, giving him the finger. The fellow started over, but his girlfriend restrained him.

## Neal Ridges

I realized that Shark was looking around for someone and I feared it was Gary Schnell. Since I knew Gary and his parents had already gone to their seats, if we could keep Shark in the lobby until the show started I thought we might be all right.

So I was actually relieved when Shark said he had to use the men's room.

## Elliot Bernstein

I accompanied Shark to the men's room, and I was quite angry with him by then, though I tried not to show it. But I was thinking: This man is a mental case, he should be in Camarillo [State Hospital] not the Dorothy Chandler Pavilion, because I am not a goddamn psychiatric nurse.

"Do you want to hold it for me?" Shark said with a smirk as he stepped to the urinal.

"I don't know why I even care what happens to you, Shark," I said as I turned to the mirror to check my hair while he took a leak.

I was stunned a second later to see in the mirror that Shark had actually grabbed, and appeared to be trying to yank off, the dick of the man at the urinal next to his.

## Sue Schlockmann

Kathy began sniffling in the ladies room as I dug a couple of Valiums from my purse. "Here, take these. And blot your eyes before the mascara runs."

"Sue, I don't know how to thank you," Kathy said.

As Kathy tossed back the Valiums I heard a loud, familiar voice: "Don't you *smell* something, Jane? *I* certainly do. An extremely rank and raunchy *barnyard* smell?"

Kathy whirled around with a frightened, wounded look and saw Carol Van Der Hof gloating at her in the mirror.

## Neal Ridges

I was waiting for Elliot and Shark to return when I felt a soft hand on mine. "Neal," Simone Gatane sighed, and kissed me on the cheek. "It's been years."

We hugged and she asked, "What happened? I understand there was some trouble with Shark."

"Everything's okay now, I think," I told her. "He's in the men's room with Elliot."

Simone gasped. "But Neal! I am back with Jean-Claude. And he has gone to use the men's room, too."

## Elliot Bernstein

"I'm going to rip this thing off and flush it down the toilet, you fucking frog," Shark yelled as he pulled Jean-Claude Citroen's penis. *"I worshiped you! And you destroyed my life!"*

Jean-Claude keened in agony, helplessly waving his arms in the air, as I and two other men grabbed Shark and finally forced him to let go. Jean-Claude crumpled to the floor, cupping his penis as he tried to catch his breath.

## Sue Schlockmann

"Frankly, I'm surprised she's still standing," Carol said of Kathy to the actress next to her at the mirror, who seemed terribly embarrassed. "Though she does walk a bit strangely, doesn't she? Precisely as if she'd once squatted upon a truly gargantuan—"

At that, Kathy pulled Carol around. "If you have something to say, Carol, why don't you say it to my face."

I couldn't help but admire Kathy's courage, a forthright bravery that in fact echoed several of her finer moments in *Home to the Heart.*

"I find *that* prospect exceedingly revolting," Carol said to Kathy. "For really now, who knows where *that face* has been."

Kathy slapped Carol, and I didn't blame her a bit.

"Why, you've knocked out my contacts, you pea-brained blonde pig!" Carol yelled.

And before any of us there could stop it, the two women were on one another, pulling each other's hair.

## Neal Ridges

Simone and I heard the commotion in the men's room and dashed in to find Elliot and several other men restraining Shark. Simone ducked down to Jean-Claude, who was rocking on the floor, teeth chattering, as he cupped his genitals.

"My God, are you all right?" Simone said to Jean-Claude. Then she glared up at Shark. "You're a madman!"

"French whore," Shark said, and tried to kick Simone in the face.

Elliot and I pulled Shark back out to the lobby, guiding him back into a more or less private alcove. "Shark, you get it together right now or we will have security remove you," I told him.

"You know something, Neal? You owe me everything," he said. "There are thousands of guys with more talent than you in their little fingers who will never do shit. But you had the luck to know me. It's just too bad I never made you suck my cock."

"You're sick," I said. "You're pathetic." I let go of him, feeling more contempt for him at that moment than I'd ever felt for anyone. "He's all yours," I said to Elliot, and went to find my girlfriend.

Inside, the orchestra had begun to play.

## Sue Schlockmann

A number of us managed to separate Carol and Kathy, but not before Carol tore one of the thin straps of Kathy's gown, and ravaged her hair. I pulled Kathy to the ladies room foyer, where I tied the strap back in place even though it looked like hell, and did what I could to smooth down her hair. Carol was still carrying on loudly back in the ladies room, and Kathy was still quite worked up, so I said, "Come on, let's go in, I hear the music starting."

## Kathy Petro

I could barely believe I had lost it so badly since I am really not a violent person. But I was just not ready to take what Carol said.

As we found Shark and Elliot in the lobby, Shark said, "What's wrong? What happened to your dress?"

"It's nothing," I said. "Let's just go in."

## Elliot Bernstein

Nearly everyone was seated by the time we entered, the orchestra playing a medley of movie themes, and Shark and Kathy's seats were in the middle of the row about half way down. I saw a little flareup as they moved down the row, Shark apparently stepping on a woman's feet. He said something to her, and her husband stood up threateningly. But Kathy pulled Shark on to their seats. Sue and I were mercifully on the far side of the aisle.

## Woody Hazzard

Brian and I took our seats late too, since we had been in this men's room stall all during the thing between Shark and Jean-Claude Citroen, and we had to wait till everybody left before we could come out.

I'd come with this girl Margo who lived next door to me in Hermosa Beach, and Brian was there with some eccentric actress friend of his.

When we saw each other in the lobby something just happened. We just started looking in each others' eyes, and it was like nobody else was even there. I knew we still really loved each other, and he knew it too. "You know what I'd like?" he said in this totally intimate voice, and I really wanted to fuckin' kiss him right there. "What I'd really like is for you to give it to me right now."

And it was crazy—I mean, at the Academy Awards, man! But my dick started doing its number.

Brian glanced toward the men's room. But I said, "Wait, I don't know, man. I'm real freaked out about this AIDS thing."

And he said, "Woody, the few others guys I saw—we only had safe sex, I swear. Do you think I'm stupid?"

"I don't know."

"Woody, if you come back to me, I promise you I'll never step out again. It's not worth it. I love you too much." There were tears in his eyes.

"Oh man." I choked up.

"Look, I've got a rubber in my wallet," he said.

So the next thing I knew we were in this stall, like completely into this passionate if Trojanized scene, when suddenly we heard the commotion with Shark and Jean-Claude and like totally froze. We didn't move or make a sound till everybody'd gone. Disengaging and pulling ourselves together real fast I guess we weren't too careful.

I noticed people looking at me funny as I made my way to my seat. But I had no idea till later that I had this used rubber stuck to my right shoulder. Margo didn't see it either since she was seated on my left.

## Brian Straight

I nearly died when, taking my seat, I saw Woody several rows below with the condom on his shoulder. But there was no way to alert him, save passing a note. Surely, I thought, someone else would bring it to his attention, but the minutes crept along and no one did.

At least as disturbing however was the presence of Shark four rows below me. And three rows below him sat Gary Schnell with his parents. You could actually feel the moment when Shark spotted Gary. And Gary felt it too, touching the back of his head as if Shark's stare were a death ray.

## Gary Schnell

I did feel Shark's presence, but I did not turn around. There was nothing to be gained by making eye contact with Satan, for by then I had little doubt about which force of the universe Shark was serving. And so I closed my eyes and prayed that Jesus might protect me and that He might through a miracle enter Shark Trager's heart.

## Greg Spivey

I watched the Awards on TV at my girlfriend's. Hecton Preck, the master of ceremonies, seemed nervous from the start, flubbing his lines as he introduced the guy from Price-Waterhouse and all that.

## Hecton Preck

We had a crisis meeting moments before we went on the air, and I was all for having Shark Trager arrested. The sort of language he'd used in the pre-show interview was completely unconscionable, though mercifully that had been a local telecast. But now we were going out to two hundred million people all around the globe. The man was a foul-mouthed sociopath. And if by chance *Home to the Heart* won . . .

But the word was he'd taken his seat, and the next thing we knew it was thirty seconds to airtime. If we removed him now, the first thing those millions of viewers would see . . . Well, there seemed little choice but to tough it out and hope the worst was over. How I regret that decision now.

## Bill Kemmer

I arrived late with Tina Veer. I'd rushed to UCLA Emergency after her roommate had called to inform me that Tina had dressed for the Awards and then, still despondent over Gary's rejection, slit her wrists. By the time I reached the hospital her wrists had been bandaged and she was pumped full of Thorazine and eager to continue on to the Music Center.

"Tina, are you sure you're up to it?" I said.

"Yes, I see now how foolish I was," she said in a numb affectless voice. "Besides, these bandages match my dress."

In fact, she was wearing a rather gauzy white gown.

We found our seats as Twain Roberts won the Best Supporting Actor award for his portrayal of "Catfish" Rivers, the poor but patriotic black janitor in *Home to the Heart*. And in more ways than one it was an indication of how the evening was going to go.

## Sue Schlockmann

What Shark did during Twain's acceptance speech was unforgivable, conclusive evidence if it were needed that Shark had gone completely out of his mind. Twain was surely one of the finest and most distinguished black actors in America, and it seemed doubly ironic that Shark chose to echo the contention of one or two critics that the part he himself had created for Twain was a regressive racial stereotype.

## Kathy Petro

When Shark started singing "Zip-A-Dee-Doo-Dah" in a darkie voice I just wanted to die. It was just so stupid and unfunny, it was almost beyond belief. Poor Twain!

## Brian Straight

I cringed. Sad to say, a number of people, while offended by the interruption, seemed almost equally baffled, failing to comprehend why comparing Twain to the beloved Uncle Remus should even *be* an insult.

A lot of us got it though. Several of the people closest to Shark were furious, and words were exchanged.

## Kathy Petro

A distinguished old producer sitting directly in front of Shark turned around and said, *"You,* sir, are an idiot." And Shark mashed the man's face back, saying, "Siddown, fuckface."

Several other men stood up, and I grabbed Shark's arm. "Please, for God sake," I said.

Then everybody started applauding Twain Roberts, practically a standing ovation to show their admiration for his dignity in the face of Shark's insult. And the other men sat down again, but the producer and his wife left. So Shark put his feet up over the empty seat.

"Actually, I like Twain," Shark said. "I've got nothing against black people, as long as they don't go around raping teenage boys in prison."

## Elliot Bernstein

Shark fell quiet for some time after the Twain Roberts incident, scrunched down in his seat, legs over the chair in front of him, occasionally rubbing his crotch. As the Best Costume Design winner—for *Star Cop IV*—thanked the Academy at length, Shark began to loudly snore.

## Bill Kemmer

By the time the Best Supporting Actress Award came up, the fellow next to me had filled me in on what had occurred earlier during the pre-Awards broadcast. After what had happened with Twain Roberts I feared an even greater embarrassment—if Tina won.

## Tina Veer

It was both the best and the worst night of my life. It didn't even register at first. But suddenly Bill was nudging me, saying, "You won."

## Sue Schlockmann

I sensed that something was terribly wrong when I saw the strangely mechanical way Tina was moving to the stage. I noticed what appeared to be bandages on both of her wrists. Though they might have been part of her costume for the evening—they did match her gown, which was eccentric—I sensed they were not.

She seemed to stand there forever clutching her Oscar before she finally said, "This is a miracle. You know, I . . . I tried to kill myself tonight."

There was no one in the Dorothy Chandler Pavilion who didn't gasp—except possibly Shark.

After a lengthy, wavering pause, Tina concluded with a fervent: "I love you, Gary."

And a split second before the tumultuous applause, Shark very distinctly made an *oinking* sound, and Gary Schnell shot up from his seat like a ramrod.

## Gary Schnell

For a moment I did want to kill him. For I had come to realize how harshly I'd judged Tina. I had prayed that she would win and that I might have a chance to speak to her that night, for I knew then, having passed through the fire myself, that Jesus Christ could wash away any amount of sin. When I saw how she had mortified her own flesh I longed to embrace her in Christ's forgiveness. And when Shark made that sound I was ready to rip out his heart with my bare hands. But my father restrained me. "Gary," he said, "don't spoil the best night of your life. It's not worth it. Shark Trager is finished in this town."

## Kathy Petro

When Shark saw Gary stand up and glare at him, he began to unzip his fly as if he were going to pull out his you-know-what and wave it at Gary. I stopped his hand. "Oh please," I said. "Please, just stop."

"He's a punk," Shark said. "Look at him. He's a pussy. He doesn't have the balls to come back here."

Thank God Gary sat back down.

I just kept thinking: God, I wish I could climb into a time machine and zip ahead an hour to when this will all be over. Needless to say, if I'd known what was going to be happening in an hour, I might have wished to go back in time to some nice, safe place, like 1955, instead.

## Woody Hazzard

I never really thought I had much chance of winning the Best Screenplay award. I was up against some real heavyweights, especially that English guy who wrote *Schweitzer*. He was sitting down the aisle with his wife, and it seemed like they were both glaring at me. I really expected him to win, so it took me a second to realize they'd actually said my name.

Margo squealed in my ear, and the next thing I knew I was floating down to the stage. It was like totally unreal.

## Greg Spivey

"What's that on his shoulder?" my girlfriend said as the camera followed Woody to the stage.

"I don't know," I said. "If I didn't know better, I'd say it was a used rubber."

## Brian Straight

I couldn't look.

## Greg Spivey

"My God. It *is* a used rubber," I said as they cut to a close shot of Woody accepting his Oscar.

## Woody Hazzard

"This is really weird," I said at the microphone, and there was this strange rumble going on in the audience, like they knew something I didn't, which was definitely the case. I almost felt like looking down to see if my fly was open or something. "I really feel like I don't deserve this," I said, and several people clapped.

"I wouldn't even be here," I continued, "if Shark Trager hadn't held a gun to my head."

533

## Neal Ridges

There were a few scattered boos when Woody mentioned Shark's name. There was something on Woody's shoulder, but from where I was sitting you couldn't tell what it was. The people in the first rows could though, and the word quickly spread on a wave of astonished disgust.

## Kathy Petro

"What's that on his shoulder?" I said to Shark. And then we heard somebody say, "A condom? Oh my God, I don't believe it. What's happening tonight?"

And Woody was kind of rattling on nervously, saying, "Yeah, this is really only my second screenplay. I guess you know what the first one was." When suddenly Shark called out, "Hey, Woody. You've got a rubber on your shoulder."

## Woody Hazzard

I looked and saw it and almost fuckin' shit.

## Neal Ridges

I have to say, I think Woody handled the situation with considerable élan. He simply peeled the condom from his tuxedo shoulder as if it were a wet leaf, nonchalantly looking around for someplace to dispose of it. Hecton Preck, clearly livid, ducked out and gingerly took it from him.

"Thanks," Woody said sheepishly, and then picked up his Oscar, saying into the mike, "Thanks for this too."

## Hecton Preck

The incident was a low point in bad taste. That's really all I care to say about it.

## Bill Kemmer

After Woody's award Debbie Swann sang the final nominated Best Song, Paul Vichy's poignantly nostalgic "Home to the Heart," and it appeared for a time as if the music had soothed the savage Shark. He fell quiet, making a waving motion in the air with his hand. But it was a stealthy, menacing sentimentality, and for some reason it suddenly occurred to me: My God, he's Jett Rink in the last scenes of *Giant*.

## Elliot Bernstein

When "Home to the Heart" won as Best Song, Shark jumped to his feet, clapping violently and yowling as one might at an especially rowdy rock concert. As Paul Vichy, an extremely gifted and sensitive man, accepted the award, you could see he was shaken by what had happened so far.

As Paul said, "And most of all I want to thank my loving and infinitely patient wife Fran . . ." Shark yowled raunchily, casting a horrendously inappropriate sexual pall over the remark. Pressing the point he yelled: *"Ow! Get down in it!"*

Hurt and angry, Paul quickly concluded his remarks.

## Simone Gatane

I remained with Jean-Claude in the lobby where he rested, still shaken from Shark's physical assault, though he claimed the pain in his genitals had begun to subside.

"I wonder," Jean-Claude said as I lit his cigarette, "if there is anything to what Shark said about my ruining his life."

"Your criticism was merciless," I replied. "Even though it has been twenty years I can still see that terrible scene as if it were only last night."

"The truth is," Jean-Claude said in an admission of frailty less rare than it once was, for with his advancing age he had mellowed. "The truth is—I was jealous of Shark Trager. I was envious—and frightened of his genius. For with his very first film, his maiden student effort, he had taken all of my ideas as far as they could go. This intuitive boy wonder had, in effect, already made the ultimate Jean-Claude Citroen film—thus rendering my life's work meaningless. I had no choice but to attack him with all the force I had."

"Yes, I know," I said, unable to hold Jean-Claude's gaze. "I know what you're saying is true. I've always known."

Jean-Claude sighed. "He might have been the Rimbaud of the cinema, the greatest director of all time. He had that kind of passion and fire and audacity. But with a few cruel words I broke him. If there were a God, He would punish me for what I have done, Simone."

There was nothing more to say. I knew these things were so.

From inside we heard polite applause as they announced the Cinematography award.

## Kathy Petro

Shark had been glum through several song and dance numbers and awards—for Best Editing and a few other things that went to other pictures. When Ernesto Fonseca won Best Cinematography for *Home to the Heart,* Shark shrugged. "The camera work was pedestrian," he said, as if the award only showed how dimwitted the voters were.

Then, as they started to read the Best Actor nominations, Shark pulled out the bag of speed and started dabbing more of it up his nose.

"My God, are you crazy?" I said, as the couple on the other side of him got up to leave.

"I'm getting bored," he said. "If they have one more lame production number I'm going to personally go down there and take a giant *shit* on the *stage!"*

At that I saw another couple seated behind us getting up to leave.

Then Shark was just flabbergasted when Ben Killard didn't win as Best Actor.

## Bill Kemmer

When they announced that Reginald Wheaton had won for *Schweitzer,* Shark sat up and did this big antic shocked shtick, like a coach on the sidelines reacting to a bad call. "That wasn't *acting,"* Shark said, in reference to Wheaton's quietly powerful portrayal of the great humanitarian. "That was *makeup."*

## Kathy Petro

Shark kept making these scoffing sounds all during Reginald's acceptance speech. I knew what was coming next so I finally said, "Shark, if you love me at all, please just stop."

And then, strangely, he did. As they applauded Reginald I felt a sudden wave of love coming from Shark, a warm glow of intense affection I'd thought I'd never feel again. As Hecton Preck introduced the Best Actresses presenters, Shark took my hand. Astonishingly, after all that had just happened, he was

536

gentle again, and it was almost as if we were alone. In fact, there was space all around us because of all the people who had left.

He kept holding my hand as Mary Trish Beth, the previous year's winner, read the nominations. It occurred to me as she read my name that the TV cameras were showing a picture of me in a little square on the screen, that eight hundred million people all over the world were examining me with a microscope. But I kept my attention focused on Shark. What a painful tenderness I felt as we looked at one another, and at ourselves, reflected in one another's dark glasses.

"I love you," Shark said, as Mary Trish opened the envelope.

## Greg Spivey

Mary Trish should have won an Oscar herself for her performance when she saw the name of the winner. At least twenty seconds passed as she ran the gamut of facial reactions from giddy shock to bleak disgust before finally saying, "I suppose I may as well tell you . . . the winner is Kathy Petro."

## Sue Schlockmann

Well, there were the gasps, then that terrible rumble of incredulous murmuring, and finally worst of all that feeble smattering of applause. My heart just went out to Kathy, though I must confess I was too stunned to applaud myself.

## Bill Kemmer

I was not that surprised, since I'd always felt it would be either Kathy or Irene Greerson. Once the donkey story broke I had actually prayed that Kathy would lose, if only so she wouldn't have to face that condemning crowd. I must say she did prove what she was made of that night.

## Kathy Petro

How can I possibly describe the mix of emotions I felt as Mary Trish read my name? The utter terror and elation. The joy that my peers had once wished to so honor me, stained with the knowledge that if they could recast their votes now I would surely be stripped of the award and ostracized forever.

Shark held my hand fiercely, a tear shooting down his cheek

from beneath his dark glasses. "Shark, I've got to go down there," I said, and he finally released my hand.

## Neal Ridges

Kathy was still wearing her dark glasses as Mary Trish, snide Vassar bitch that she is, handed Kathy the statuette with an air of haughty distaste.

I'll never forget the way people gasped as Kathy stepped to the microphone and, with impeccable dramatic timing, tore off her shades. For the look in her eyes was absolutely stunning. Brilliant, hard, defiant. You could tell she was about to kick ass. And she did.

## Bill Kemmer

Her gaze was withering, and so was her voice. "I know what some of you are thinking tonight," she said. "You're wishing there were some way to take this away from me."

There was scattered applause, but Kathy cut into it like a knife: "Well, let me tell you something! I worked hard for this! I put everything I had into this role . . ."

Then she added, in what I think was a really stunningly brave tactic: "I don't believe in doing *anything*—anything at all—half-assed!"

## Neal Ridges

That remark showed real courage and style. It would have been so easy for Kathy to use her time to deny the donkey story, to try and appear victimized by the media, to beg her peers, and the world, to believe she was innocent. Instead, she was saying in effect: Even if it *were* true, it wouldn't change the fact that I damn well earned this award!

## Sue Schlockmann

"There are many people I could thank for this," Kathy said, and I braced myself. "But there are only two I will thank. It's a shame they're at odds tonight. Because I know deep down they love each other as much as two men can without actually being gay."

## Gary Schnell

That remark disturbed me. Though Kathy's voice was trembling with seemingly heartfelt emotion, I sensed demonic forces lurking about her. I wished she'd just sit down and shut up.

## Sue Schlockmann

"I want to thank Gary Schnell," Kathy said. There was a burst of applause, and then I really braced myself. "But first and foremost I want to thank the man without whom *Home to the Heart* would have never been made, the man I love, the man I know that deep in your secret hearts many of you love too. I want to thank Shark Trager.

Predictably enough there were boos. I saw that Shark had his fingers pressed together at his lips, as if he meant to seal them with prayer.

## Bill Kemmer

The boos angered Kathy. "Shark Trager is exactly what you've made him, nothing more and nothing less," she cried defiantly.

And in the silence following that remark someone let loose with a piercing imitation of Hector the donkey's rowdy bray.

Well, everyone gasped in shock. And I saw that it was Carol Van Der Hof, her hands cupped to her mouth as she brayed again with an astonishing force and malevolence.

Kathy glared at her heckler. *"That* says much more about you than it does me, Carol. You're an extremely bitter woman, and I think we all know why . . ."

At that point someone cued the orchestra, which began playing "Home to the Heart." Then Hecton Preck stepped up, leading the applause to get Kathy off the stage.

"I'm not finished," Kathy said.

The mike picked up Hecton saying, "Oh yes you are, my dear."

Hecton took her by the elbow to steer her away, and as she twisted free of him the strap of her gown came undone, revealing her bare breast to the millions.

## Greg Spivey

"My God, I don't believe this," my girlfriend said as the TV picture cut from a flash of Kathy's breast to a wide shot of the audience. You could see Shark making his way toward the aisle as Elliot Bernstein ducked down to intervene.

## Elliot Bernstein

I grabbed Shark just as he reached the aisle. I had truly had it with him by then. "Shark, you sit down and shut up or I am going to personally knock out your lights," I said.

Shark was incensed, glaring at Carol, who looked back at him and smirked. But I'd stopped him long enough for Kathy, who was hastily retying her broken gown strap, to make her way back up the aisle. As she reached us, Shark helped her retie the strap and then, still shooting murderous looks at Carol, guided Kathy back to her seat. I took the empty seat beside Shark to keep watch.

## Kathy Petro

At the time I was too angry to care that millions of strangers had just seen my breast. That really seemed the least of it.

## Woody Hazzard

The next award was for Best Director, and when the guy said, "And the winner is . . . Gary Schnell for *Home to the Heart*," the whole place just went wild. Practically everybody was on their feet. I stood up too, mainly so I could see how Shark was taking it.

He had sunk back down in his seat, his legs up over the empty seat in front of him, and he was yawning like he was bored. Beside him Kathy was sulking, her shades back on, as if the awfulness of how people had treated her was belatedly hitting her real hard.

## Bill Kemmer

The applause for Gary seemed to go on forever. You could see tears glistening in his eyes by the time people sat back down.

"To me," he said, holding up his statuette, "this award is about love. And the miracle of love that can come shining through even the darkest night. You can't stop love, no one can!"

## Woody Hazzard

A lot of people started to cry during Gary's love speech.

## Greg Spivey

I found Gary's remarks extremely unctuous and manipulative, but my girlfriend began to sniffle.

## Neal Ridges

"Love," Gary cried. "That's what this movie is all about. Some of us seem to have forgotten that! The love of a husband and wife for one another, the love of parents for their children, and children for their moms and dads. The love of a white family for a less fortunate black family!"

## Elliot Bernstein

At that point Shark said, as an aside to me, "The love of Mac for Gladys's hot little snatch." He sniggered nastily.

## Bill Kemmer

"There was so much love packed into this film that nothing or no one could dim its glow!" Gary said. "Even if Satan himself had been given final cut I believe that the pure light of love in this film would still have come shining through!"

There was applause.

"I did not make this movie by myself," he said, and went on to list a number of cast and crew members—with the notable exception of Kathy. "But more than anyone," he concluded, "I want to thank one man without whom this film would never have been possible."

There was a rumble of apprehension.

"A man who has suffered and given more than any of the rest of us can ever possibly comprehend."

## Kathy Petro

I was touched by Gary's apparent generosity. But Shark said, "He's gonna shit on me, wait and see. He'll kill me with the capper."

## Bill Kemmer

"A man so far ahead of his time that the rest of us forced him to pay the ultimate price," Gary said. "A man who is finally not a man at all, though he bore his lonely agony like a man!"

## Elliot Bernstein

"My God, he loves me," Shark said.

## Bill Kemmer

"I want to thank Jesus Christ, my Lord and Savior," Gary cried. "God bless you all and good night."

## Elliot Bernstein

As the applause erupted again Shark appeared stunned—he'd really thought Gary was talking about him. "What? Jesus Christ?" he said sarcastically. "There was nobody with that name on the picture. I've seen the payroll."

"Settle down, Shark," I said. But in fact he wasn't angry. On the contrary, his mood had turned cocky and arrogant. There was only one award left, the big one. And despite the flurry of activity in the last twenty-four hours before the balloting closed, Shark clearly believed, on the basis of what had happened so far, that *Home to the Heart* was going to win.

The lights came down as they showed clips from the nominated films, and I noticed several security men watching Shark from either aisle, ready to move in if he made any more trouble.

Shark looked bored during the first three clips. When they showed Kathy's swimming pool scene from *Home to the Heart,* he yowled and clapped wildly, though the response from the audience was noticeably ambivalent, indeed confused. On the one hand they wanted to acknowledge Gary's direction again. On the other, they knew who was going to pick up the award if the picture won.

## Bill Kemmer

The clips concluded with the epidemic scene from *Schweitzer,* and at precisely the most affecting moment Shark loudly snored. In fact, at three and a half hours the film was extremely lumbering and tedious. But it was just the sort of uplifting prestige picture that so frequently wins the top award.

How can I describe the tension, the visceral excitement and dread, that permeated the Dorothy Chandler Pavilion as the lights came back up? What was going to happen? What exactly did the last-minute change of votes mean? Had there been a rush to vote for *Home to the Heart* because of Gary? Or against it because of Shark? I think we all literally held our breath. The tension proved too much for Harold Hawkor, whose job it was to present the award.

## Neal Ridges

Hawkor was eighty-nine, and he clearly didn't have much time left. Really one of the last great Hollywood directors, the sole remaining member of the club which had once included Hitchcock and Ford. Well, he'd been trembly, like Kate Hepburn, for years, so that was nothing new. But I had a bad premonition as he fumbled with the envelope.

## Elliot Bernstein

It was excruciating. "And the winner is . . ." Then he dropped the envelope and couldn't bend over to get it. So Hecton Preck rushed out and picked it up for him.

"And the winner is . . ." But his hands were shaking so severely he couldn't break the seal. So Hecton Preck came out and did that too.

"The winner is . . ." But he couldn't read it. So he fumbled for at least half a minute, pulling his glasses from their case, nearly dropping them, putting them on, adjusting them. "For best picture, the winner is . . ." Then he dropped the envelope again.

## Woody Hazzard

That guy was driving everybody crazy.

## Elliot Bernstein

"Come on, goddamn it!" Shark said through gritted teeth, as Hecton Preck picked up the envelope for Harold Hawkor a second time, and stood by to make sure he read it.

"And the best picture is . . ." Hawkor gasped. And the rest is history, I suppose.

## Greg Spivey

Hawkor dropped the envelope again, clutched his heart, and collapsed in Hecton Preck's arms. The way his eyes rolled back in his head you just knew it was a case of sudden massive coronary thrombosis. People were running out to the podium, the audience gasping with horrified incredulity, as Hecton Preck cried into the microphone, "The winner is *Simple Folks.*"

## Bill Kemmer

I was stunned. *Simple Folks* was the ultimate dark horse of any of the nominated films, a truly dim little Southwestern character story about a tight-lipped widower and a plain, laconic waitress.

Fortuitously, the producers of *Simple Folks* were the only ones of any of the nominated films not in attendance that night. Therefore, Hecton Preck was able to say, "On behalf of Rex and Betty Rogers, the Academy accepts the award," as Harold Hawkor's lifeless body was removed from the stage.

## Kathy Petro

I couldn't believe it. I started crying. I guess a lot of other people did too. But Shark was angry. *"Simple Folks?* This is ridiculous! That film is dogshit! *Schweitzer*—I could see losing to *Schweitzer!* The movie was a yawn, but at least Schweitzer the guy was okay. But *Simple Folks?* That film was a zero, ninety minutes of dobro music and people saying, 'Pass the ketchup.' A boring film about boring people. A stultifying little naturalistic fart in the desert breeze!"

"For God sake, Shark," I said. "Harold Hawkor just dropped dead. Doesn't that mean anything to you at all?"

"He was eighty-nine," Shark said. "What do you want me to do, sob? He made more films than I ever will."

## Elliot Bernstein

Hecton Preck said, "Good night," to the cameras and that was it. People got up to leave, most in a state of numb shock, though quite a number of the women were still crying.

Shark remained slouched in his seat as people moved up the aisles. "This is fucked up," he said to me. "Something stinks about this whole thing. I can't believe that stupid film won."

"Go home, Shark," I said.

"I'm not going anywhere," he said, "until I get what's mine."

I got a sinking feeling when I saw that he was looking at Gary Schnell.

## Kathy Petro

"Shark, let's just go," I said. "I can't take anymore, I really can't."

Then I saw that he was staring at Gary Schnell, who was moving up the aisle with his parents. The security men were still watching Shark, but by then the crowd was too thick for them to intervene.

## Gary Schnell

I saw Shark coming up the row to intercept me and I began to pray. He had a bad look in his eyes. "I want that, I earned it," he said, indicating my Oscar. "Give it here."

"You're crazy," I said, and he came at me.

## Woody Hazzard

It looked like Shark tried to grab Gary's Oscar, but Earl Schnell and a couple other guys stopped him from doing it. Then Shark pulled free of them and lunged for Gary again, and Gary pushed his way frantically through the crowd trying to get away from Shark.

## Brian Straight

I was in the hallway that led to the press room when Gary pushed past me, and I looked back and saw Shark slamming through the crowd after him.

## Tina Veer

I was in the press room when Gary burst through the door, Shark right behind him. Shark tackled Gary and they fell amid the TV cameras as the astonished reporters jumped back.

"This is mine!" Shark yelled as he got the Oscar away from Gary.

Everyone was horrified as Shark got to his feet, clutching the Oscar like some kind of crazed fiend. Gary was angry by then too—at least as angry as he was scared—and got up ready for a fight. Reporters jammed the doorway, photographers clicking away, as Shark and Gary stood each other off.

"You're a very troubled man, Shark," Gary said. "That is not yours, you did not win it. Give it to me."

"I earned it," Shark said, his insane eyes flitting over the crowd, surely realizing on some level that it was all over. "It *should* be mine," he said, his voice cracking painfully. "It was my movie. Winnie was *my mother!*"

## Elliot Bernstein

It was a sad, terrible moment, everyone staring at Shark, at the tortured pathetic spectacle he'd become. "Give Gary his Oscar," I said to him evenly.

Kathy held out her Oscar and said, "Shark, we have this one."

"Let me have it," Gary said, his voice trembling.

"All right," Shark said finally with a weary, defeated sigh. "I'll let you have it, Gary."

And then, before anyone could stop him, Shark jumped on Gary, threw him face down on the floor and tore down Gary's tuxedo trousers. "I'll let you have it just the way you've always wanted it!"

Some of the women present screamed.

## Woody Hazzard

Basically I guess Shark tried to shove the Oscar up Gary's ass, though he didn't actually do it, people stopped him before he could. But I'll never forget the glimpse I got through the crowd—it was like a one-second shot in a movie—of Shark digging that statuette into the crack of Gary's hairy little butt while Gary went: "Oh. Oh. Jesus, oh no."

## Neal Ridges

It was just insanity. It took maybe five or six of us to restrain Shark. Hecton Preck was there by then, a towering paragon of Biblical rage: "Sir, you are a disgrace to the motion picture industry!"

Gary was shaken, needless to say, and when Earl Schnell arrived and heard what Shark had done, he had to be physically restrained as well. The security men hustled Shark to an adjoining room.

## Bill Kemmer

God knows I wish now I had not intervened in Shark's behalf, but I did, convincing the security chief not to turn Shark over to the police. "Just go," I said to Shark, and by then he was relieved that he wasn't going to be arrested.

"Okay, okay, no problem," he said cockily, looking around for Kathy.

He spotted her in the adjoining corridor, where Sue was offering her support.

"Kathy!" he called sharply. "Let's go!"

## Sue Schlockmann

"You don't have to go with him," I whispered to Kathy.

"Yes, I do," she said quietly.

And I see now that she meant that their fates were joined.

## Kathy Petro

"Oh my God," I said more than once as we walked to the car. "What have you done tonight? What have you done?"

"Oh, shut up," Shark said. "You won your fucking Oscar. What are you moaning about?"

"How could you do that to Gary?"

"It was easy. I only wish I'd had some Vaseline. Maybe next year."

"There isn't going to be any next year, Shark. Not for either of us after this."

"Oh, you never know, my love. They said I was finished after *Red Surf.*"

When we got into the Porsche he opened the glove compartment and took out another baggie of speed.

"For God sake, Shark, no more," I said. "That was half your problem tonight."

"And what was the other half, my darling love?" he said sarcastically.

So he snorted up some more of it and said, in this rowdy rock-and-roll manner, "Oh yeah! Okay! It's all right now!"

As he started the engine I said, "You make me sick."

"Well, the feeling is quite mutual, I'm sure." He peeled out so brutally the force threw me back against the seat. "You know, Kathy, you haven't turned out to be quite what I used to dream about."

"That's right, destroy me too," I said. "You've destroyed everything else tonight."

"That can be arranged, my sugary sweet," he said, veering dangerously around a sharp corner.

"Slow down, for Christ sake," I said. *"You* obviously have a death wish, but I don't."

"Shut your hole," he said, and switched on the tape deck. That Roxy Music song came on loud.

The downtown streets were virtually empty, all these big, silent buildings everywhere, as he roared over a bridge toward, the freeway entrance. He must have been doing sixty or seventy. I clutched the dash and pressed my foot to the floorboard. "You really are an asshole, you know that?" I said.

Then I saw her. I had no idea what a woman with a baby carriage was doing on that empty downtown street at that time of night—but there she was in the crosswalk right in front of the freeway entrance!

"Oh my God, look out!" I yelled as we hit her.

I screamed as the baby hit the windshield and bounced off. There was a *clump-clump* sensation under the wheels as we dragged the mother. I looked back as Shark floored it and we shot onto the freeway, finally releasing the woman's body at the end of a long red smear.

"Oh my God, oh my God!" I screamed.

"Shut up!" Shark yelled. "Shut your goddamn hole!"

"Oh God! Go back! Go back!"

"We're on the freeway, baby! There *is* no going back!"

He turned the tape deck up past the threshold of pain, snapping his fingers to the beat like a fiend.

I became hysterical. "You're insane! Stop the car! Let me out! Let me out!"

"Can't stop, baby! *We're on the freeway!*" he yelled above the music, the speedometer passing a hundred. "But if you want out, then get out!" He reached across me and opened my door.

"So long," he said, and pushed me out of the Porsche.

# 29 / Movies Till Dawn
## (1988)

## Greg Spivey

I think it's safe to say that Shark Trager's last twelve hours must have been the most tortured and lonely of his life.

I arrived at the VistaVision Ranch shortly after eight Tuesday morning and entered the ranch house. The coffee in the mug beside Shark's bed was still warm. I couldn't have missed him by more than a few minutes.

The bedroom TV was showing snow and you could see how he'd spent the night by the cassettes scattered on the floor before the VCR. *Touch of Evil*, *Rebel Without a Cause*, *Vertigo*, *The Searchers*, his own *White Desert*, and absurdly, poignantly, as a kind of frothy dessert, *The Thrill of It All*. Indeed, I remember thinking: Yes, these are the remnants of Shark Trager's last cinematic meal.

I cleaned up the cocaine residue just moments before the sheriff's deputies arrived—even then protecting him by rote, as I see now I had done far too frequently before.

## Woody Hazzard

I'll always think that Shark died believing he'd killed Kathy. What else could he think? It was nothing short of a miracle that she survived. He might have heard about it on the Porsche radio, I guess. But my hunch is that Shark was too far gone by then to be listening to the news.

He had to believe he'd run down an innocent mother and her baby, too, since it wasn't till the next day that the truth about that began to come out: that the woman he hit was actually a fugitive homeless psychotic lady wanted by the cops for letting her pit bull terrier severely maul a couple of Salvadoran refugee kids in a park in downtown L.A. The woman was totally flipped out, just wandering around the downtown streets with this baby carriage. Kathy was certain Shark shared her impression that an actual baby had bounced off the windshield. It all happened so fast they had no way of knowing it was really the woman's pit bull wrapped up in a dirty blue baby blanket, and that the dog was already stiff as a bat, having starved to death at least a week before.

## Ellen Weir

I'd seen the story on the morning news where they said that Shark Trager had mowed down a woman with a dead pit bull in a baby carriage and then pushed Kathy Petro from the car. They said the car was a silver Porsche, and I understood that our house on Mackerel Drive was built on the spot where Shark Trager's boyhood house had been before he blew it up in that movie. So when I saw a silver Porsche with blood on the hood cruising slow past our house I put two and two together and called the police.

## Woody Hazzard

I think Shark took a sentimental journey, like he did a lot when things in Hollywood got too strange. I think he probably just drove all around the old neighborhood, thinking about how things used to be. Maybe he was thinking of killing himself, or of trying to get away, and was trying to make up his mind which to do.

I don't know why he pushed Kathy out of that car. I know he loved her. I guess he just went crazy after he ran down that woman he thought was an innocent mother with her baby. In fact, it was the crazy woman's fault. According to Kathy, she was crossing even though the sign said: Don't Walk.

I think when Shark fully realized what he'd done to Kathy it must have really killed him. Even though she irritated the shit out of him at times, she was his fuckin' life, man. Everybody knows that.

## Gus Cord

Yeah, I remember that day all right. It was hot, hot for March, one of them Santa Anas blowing. I was the clerk there at U-Lock-It Storage, which was right alongside the Newport Freeway, and I did a double take when Shark pulled up in that big silver Porsche. I didn't know who he was or about nothing that had happened, since I hadn't watched the Awards show the night before. But you could see something real bad had happened to the Porsche.

"Yeah, I hit a dog," he said when I asked him where the blood came from. "He was a mean dog too. Tried to bite my nose off."

I sensed something bad about him, but let it go at that. He signed in for unit fifty-four and drove on down to it.

He was still down there maybe ten, fifteen minutes later when a sheriff's car coming down the highway spotted his car and made a hard U-turn and lunged into the lot with his siren yelping.

## Elliot Bernstein

The storage unit had apparently been rented during *Red Surf*, so that Shark could store the things from the Mackerel Drive house he didn't wanted destroyed in the film, namely, his bedroom furniture and a number of mementos—including his original Bell and Howell eight-millimeter movie camera, which I understand Kathy now has.

## Kathy Petro

I went down to that storage place with Mac about six months after Shark died. It was difficult physically—I was still in a lot of pain then—*and* emotionally. Mac and I stood there and looked at Shark's things. When I saw the camera I felt a chill but said, "Do you mind if I keep this, Mac? It has a certain sentimental value."

Mac said, no, he didn't mind, but he wouldn't look at me.

When I saw that old, fire-blackened freezer I asked Mac why Shark had kept something like that. But Mac wouldn't tell me.

## Gus Cord

Shark jumped back in his Porsche when he heard the cops coming and tore out of there like you wouldn't believe. I mean, that car was fast!

## Orange County Sheriff's Deputy Glenn Smegg

We pursued the suspect up the Ramona Highway, which runs parallel to, then under, the Newport Freeway into Costa Mesa. At the intersection of Ramona and Don Diego Road, three more Sheriff's units joined the pursuit. Four Costa Mesa Police Department units converged on the suspect's vehicle from a northerly and southerly direction on Loretta Drive as he crossed that thoroughfare at a speed of approximately ninety miles an hour. The suspect's vehicle then jumped a curb and careened through the parking lot surrounding the Caligari Mall.

## Woody Hazzard

There was some restaurant under construction alongside the main mall building, some franchise place—the Norman Rockwell Pancake House or something like that. But it was basically just a framework then and Shark plowed right through it. In the back, where it was flush against the mall building, there was just a bunch of plywood. And on the other side of the plywood was the Caligari Cineplex, one of those places with eighteen separate movie screens.

## Neal Ridges

We figured out later that the Caligari Cineplex was actually built on the exact spot where the Flying Wing Drive-In had once stood. And so Shark died where he had first kissed Kathy

Petro and where he had actually been born—taking fourteen innocent children with him.

## George Harl

*Home to the Heart* was playing in theater five, our largest, with a capacity of three hundred, and the first show that day was packed. The little retarded children from a nearby special school had arrived just as the movie was beginning, so they were occupying the less desirable remaining seats down in front. There had been some disturbance from them during the movie, gibbering and so forth—the protracted swimming pool drowning scene seemed to especially agitate the children. So as manager I was standing in the back as the film entered its final few minutes, planning to guide the retarded children and their teachers toward one of the lower exit doors.

Kathy Petro was dying on the screen and a number of patrons were crying. By then, I believe, most everyone had heard that she'd been pushed out on the freeway after the Awards the night before and was in critical condition and not expected to live. And I think everyone who had judged her on the basis of that donkey business was feeling more than a little contrite. Her personal life aside, it really was a heart-rending screen performance. She was in her death bed, saying good-bye to her friends and family—and you couldn't help thinking: My God, life is imitating art, the poor woman is dying for real in the hospital right now, though not even able to say good-bye. And as many times as I'd seen the film I too was beginning to weep when I heard a crash and a screaming engine as Shark Trager's silver Porsche came through Kathy Petro's face on the screen.

## Kippi Morgan

It was my idea to take the kids to see *Home to the Heart*, which at least was a decent, all-American film. If I'd only known! That car came right through the screen and didn't stop till it plowed through the first three rows! Those kids never had a chance!

## Orange County Sheriff's Deputy Glenn Smegg

As we entered on foot through the large opening the vehicle had made in the movie screen, the suspect was climbing out of his Porsche. I suppose when we saw the maimed children all about, some of us in a sense lost control. As the suspect staggered towards us with a shiny metallic object in his raised hand a number of the law enforcement personnel on the scene opened fire.

## Woody Hazzard

They obliterated him. It was never proved, but I'm pretty sure at least some of those kids died from stray police bullets. 'Cause I saw Shark's body at the morgue and it was just ripped to shit.

## Alfredo Barabbas Dillinger

It was something else. We were sitting halfway back, but my girlfriend still caught a round in the shoulder, though we didn't know till later since she didn't feel nothing and the blood matched her dress. Man, those cops kicked out the jams, I'm talking *serious* rock-and-roll! *Bam! Bam! Bam! Bam! Bam!* Blood flying everywhere, big fuckin' squirts of it arcing through the air like wet scarlet flares, big splashes going every which way like bursting red roses, while Trager jerked and shook in a mean hucklebuck like a man having ten thousand orgasms at once. He *yowled* like Warren Oates at the tail end of *The Wild Bunch* as his body blew apart and the girls and women keened, and those heavy-duty cop guns kept on belching rounds like nickel-plated hard-ons packed with cherry bombs: *Bam! Bam! Bam! Bam!*

## Sister Mary Madelyn

"Please, in the name of Jesus, *stop*," I prayed through my tears, clutching my rosary beside Sister Teresa perhaps ten rows back from the screen on the side.

And then, for a moment, they did stop. And in that moment there was a kind of silence, even the whimpering of the injured seemed to taper off, there was only the dim whir of the projector.

Shark Trager turned, his face in the beam of bright movie light. It seemed to blind him and he dropped a small object and held up his hands, both of which were pierced through with bullet holes.

I will never forget the look in his eyes then, as the beam projected Kathy Petro's tear-streaked face onto his. Or perhaps the tears were his, I don't know. He reached up to the light and spoke her name, "Kathy," as if he believed she were already up there somewhere beyond the light and he was now to join her.

Sister Teresa and I crossed ourselves as the police opened fire again.

## George Harl

The police response was perhaps excessive, though at the time I didn't think so. I was so shocked and enraged by what had happened I wished I'd had a gun myself.

I have to say, however, contrary to the police version, that while Trager did have something in his hand initially, his hand was not raised in a threatening gesture, and it would have been very difficult to mistake what he was holding for any sort of weapon.

## Greg Spivey

To my mind, what happened at the Caligari Mall was nothing more, or less, than a tragic accident. I believe Shark meant to escape the country, and when the cops pursued him he simply lost control of that horrendous car. The fact that he died on virtually the exact spot where he'd been born creates precisely the sort of vacuous symmetry Shark himself had such an unfortunate weakness for in his films. It's just the sort of fluke irony that lends itself to facile overinterpretation, and there's certainly been no lack of that.

## Neal Ridges

It was obviously his fate. And his karma that he would die in an orgy of wanton self-destruction complete with the taking of the most innocent lives. Though Shark Trager had at times brought joy to millions it was intrinsic to his megalomania that he would eventually bring agony as well.

## Elliot Bernstein

The question of just how innocent Shark's victims really were presented itself, to my mind, as soon as it was learned that their supposed retardation was in fact a cynical hoax employed by their teachers to save a few dollars on a group handicapped admission—a hoax which of course required the children to convincingly "act like a bunch of spastics," as one of the survivors put it. By then it was apparent that they weren't, technically speaking, *children* at all, but rather in their early teens, and a disturbingly nasty, mean-spirited adolescent crew at that.

I sensed there was going to be more to the story. But I don't think anyone was prepared for the bombshell revelation that the teenagers' so-called private school was in fact a heavily guarded neo-Nazi training facility.

Those of us who initially condemned Shark have been compelled to reconsider our judgment in recent weeks as we've watched the TV investigation reports showing the hateful parents and defiant, unabashedly right-wing extremist "school" officials, as we've seen the displays, following the FBI raid, of the weapons caches and textbooks espousing racism and bigotry of the most demented sort, all of it paid for with hundreds of thousands of dollars of fraudulently obtained state and federal aid. Far from being "innocent," the smirking little California Reich *Jungen* killed at the Caligari Mall were as close to an embodiment of pure evil as we in America are ever likely to know. It's entirely conceivable that Shark, in one of the stunning paradoxes that punctuated his life, may have in the seemingly wanton slaughter of his death scene actually saved the world from a grassroots American Hitler.

## Sue Schlockmann

That's crap, and Elliot knows it. There is absolutely no way to prove such a flagrantly outlandish contention. The crucial point is that Shark didn't *know* those kids were neo-Nazis when he mowed them down. Anyway, they were still human beings, for God sake, and I for one don't believe that anyone is unsavable. Had they lived, any number of them might have eventually escaped their parents' influence and come to see the light. In fact, several of them were actually gifted—geniuses really. Who's to say one of them might not have gone on to discover a cure for cancer or AIDS or a means of eliminating nuclear

556

weapons, or at the very least become an accomplished, life-affirming painter or musician or poet?

Shark was an egomaniacal, life-denying, narcissistic pig who never gave a damn about anybody but himself, that's the truth of it. Anyone who got in his way, whether it was a talented director or a chairman of a parent company or a pitiful schizophrenic woman with a dead pet in a baby carriage—they met the same fate. Not even his most passionate apologists can begin to excuse what he did to Kathy—the woman he supposedly *loved?* He didn't know the meaning of the word. To the various strained attempts to resurrect Shark Trager I say: Pass. *No sale.*

## Elliot Bernstein

Certainly, there's no excuse for what Shark did to Kathy, other than to say he was clearly out of his mind. I believe he had come to genuinely love Kathy though, despite the early years of mental obsession, despite his final lapse into madness, and I think Sue knows that as well. It isn't difficult to understand why so many of the women who passed through Shark's life remain so irredeemably bitter.

## Carol Van Der Hof

*"Arrivederci,* scumbag," I sing.

## Narges Pahlavi-Bardahl

I think of him now as merely the worst side effect of my cocaine addiction.

## Maya Dietrichson

He had a great body, that's the main thing I choose to remember. So did I in those days.

I'm not bitter though. We had our fun.

## Greg Spivey

"I'd like that to be my epitaph," Shark said to me once at the end of *Touch of Evil.* Of course, he was referring to Marlene

Dietrich's pronouncement following Orson Welles's collapse into the garbage-clogged Venice canal: "He was some kind of man." To which she adds poignantly: "What does it matter what you say about people?"

## Woody Hazzard

There was no funeral service. Everybody hated Shark's guts at that point because they still thought he'd killed a bunch of innocent retarded kids instead of a bunch of evil neo-Nazis.

According to Shark's will his body was supposed to be dumped into the ocean at a certain spot off Catalina in a burial at sea. Greg Spivey made the arrangements, but he said he wasn't up to going out on the boat.

I went down to the boat in San Pedro, and I kind of figured somebody else would show up, maybe Elliot or Neal, somebody who still had some good memories of Shark. But there was nobody. I was the only one.

Then, just as they were about to raise the gangplank, Simone Gatane pulled up.

## Simone Gatane

It was an astonishingly beautiful day, so clear and cloudless, the sky such a brilliant blue—the kind of day Shark would have loved. As the ship coursed toward its destination Woody and I shared a chilled bottle of wine, and despite the nightmarish events of less than one week before, we found ourselves reminiscing about the good early times we had both known with Shark so long ago.

"I can still recall the first time we met," I told Woody, "how Shark spilled hot chocolate down the front of my blouse as I watched *The Nutty Professor* on the flatbed at UCLA. How incensed I was. How sweetly we made love that night in the James Dean house in Sherman Oaks."

"I remember the night Shark and I got busted in Newport Beach," Woody said, "and Shark swallowed the evidence—ten thousand micrograms of acid. And I held him in the drunk tank as he shook and quaked like there were bombs going off inside him. I held him like that all night."

I saw a tear in Woody's eye.

## Woody Hazzard

It was sadder than shit, especially when they finally dumped his body. It was just wrapped in this old canvas sack, and you could see where the blood was kind of starting to soak through, which I guess was the whole idea. I don't think it was even legal, but Shark had paid a lot of money up front to make sure they did it the way he wanted.

They tossed him overboard, and the sack wasn't even weighted, but it was at this real specific spot off Catalina, so I guess Shark knew what was going to happen.

The sack disappeared under the water. There was a lot of glare on the surface, but I saw the dark shape of a fin. Then suddenly it was like thrash city, man, with fins and tails flying, and the water was red with Shark's blood.

## Simone Gatane

I couldn't watch. I knew it was what he had wanted, but it was too horrible. I poured myself another glass of wine as the thrashing continued. But it didn't last long.

## Woody Hazzard

A seagull came screaming across the sky, and then it was over. The blood dispersed, and the sea was blue and sparkling again, the waves rolling on just like they had for thousands of years.

## Elliot Bernstein

The police eventually revealed that the object in Shark's hand when he died was a small reel of eight-millimeter film—that was what he had gone to the storage facility to retrieve. As I understand it, the film is now in Kathy Petro's possession.

## Kathy Petro

The police said it was an old film of me, that's all they told Mac before he gave it to me. I ignored it for a long time. The little reel was rusty and then I saw that some of the rust was actually dried blood. But finally one day I drew out the film and held it up to the light. I was fearing the worst, thinking that it might be a copy of the peeping-Tom movie, but I saw soon enough that it wasn't. So I found an old eight-millimeter projector and ran the reel, and there I was at age fourteen sitting on the beach with several girl friends. Shark must have been a short ways up the beach, I had certainly not been aware of him, and could not remember the day, it was so like so many other days. I was snapping my fingers to a song on the radio, and as he zoomed in on my face, I could read my own lips. I was singing "Hold Me Tight," that early Beatles song. I laughed at something one of my girl friends said, and then a man with big tan shoulders passed through the frame. Probably Jeff Stuben because I was blushing. Shark's camera held my face as my expression turned sad, as if I were a girl who thought she'd never find real love. I had a crush on Jeff then, I guess, and probably thought he didn't know I existed. The way Shark's camera held my face—there was this terrible kind of tenderness to it. It was as if he was *really* holding my face, gently, in his hands. I don't know . . . The film ran out.

As I switched off the projector I thought for a moment that I might cry. Then I looked down at the scars on my legs and I didn't.

ABOUT THE AUTHOR

JAMES ROBERT BAKER is a novelist and screenwriter who has received the prestigious Samuel Goldwyn Writing Award at UCLA film school. His novel *Fuel-Injected Dreams* has been optioned for the movies, with Baker writing the screenplay. He lives in Pacific Palisades, California.